Cases and Mater...

Law in Context

Editors: William Twining (University College, London) and
Christopher McCrudden (Lincoln College, Oxford)

Ashworth: *Sentencing and Justice*
Barton and Douglas: *Parents and Parentage*
Bercusson: *European Labour Law*
Birkinshaw: *Freedom of Information: The Law, the Practice and the Ideal*
Cane: *Atiyah's Accidents, Compensation and the Law*
Collins: *The Law of Contract*
Cranston: *Legal Foundations of the Welfare State*
Davies and Freeland: *Labour Law Text and Materials*
Detmold: *Courts and Administrators: A Study of Jurisprudence*
Doggett: *Marriage, Wife-Beating and the Law in Victorian England*
Dummett and Nicol: *Subjects, Citizens, Aliens and Others: Nationality and Immigration Law*
Goodrich: *Languages of Law*
Hadden: *Company Law and Capitalism*
Harlow and Rawlings: *Law and Administration Text and Materials*
Harris: *An Introduction to Law*
Harris: *Remedies in Contract and Tort*
Lacey, Wells and Meure: *Reconstructing Criminal Law–Text and Materials*
Lewis: *Choice and the Legal Order: Rising above Politics*
Moffat: *Trusts law–Text and Materials*
Norrie: *Crime, Reason and History*
Page and Fergusson: *Investor Protection*
Picciotto: *International Business Taxation*
Ramsay: *Consumer Protection: Text and Materials*
Richardson: *Law, Process and Custody*
Snyder: *New Directions in European Community Law*
Stapleton: *Product Liability*
Turpin: *British Government and the Constitution–Text, Cases and Materials*
Twining and Anderson: *Analysis of Evidence*
Twining and Miers: *How to do Things with Rules*
Ward: *A Critical Introduction to European Law*
Zander: *Cases and Materials on the English Legal System*
Zander: *The Law-Making Process*

Cases and Materials on the English Legal System

Seventh edition

Michael Zander

Professor of Law,
London School of Economics

Butterworths
London, Dublin, Edinburgh
1996

United Kingdom	Butterworths, a Division of Reed Elsevier (UK) Ltd, Halsbury House, 35 Chancery Lane, LONDON WC2A 1EL and 4 Hill Street, EDINBURGH EH2 3JZ
Australia	Butterworths, SYDNEY, MELBOURNE, BRISBANE, ADELAIDE, PERTH, CANBERRA and HOBART
Canada	Butterworths Canada Ltd, TORONTO and VANCOUVER
Ireland	Butterworth (Ireland) Ltd, DUBLIN
Malaysia	Malayan Law Journal Sdn Bhd, KUALA LUMPUR
New Zealand	Butterworths of New Zealand Ltd, WELLINGTON and AUCKLAND
Singapore	Reed Elsevier (Singapore) Ptd Ltd, SINGAPORE
South Africa	Butterworths Publishers (Pty) Ltd, DURBAN
USA	Northwestern University Press, 625 Colfax Street, Evanston, Illinois 60208-4210

A CIP Catalogue record for this book is available from the British Library.

ISBN 0 406 08176 X

Printed by Mackays of Chatham Plc, Chatham, Kent

Preface to the seventh edition

It is now getting on for a quarter of a century since the first edition of this work was published. The seventh edition builds on the structure established by the previous editions. The main purpose has again been to reflect the enormous number of both major and minor changes and developments that have taken place in the four years since the last edition.

Major developments in the years 1992 to 1996 included the Report of the Runciman Royal Commission on Criminal Justice, the dramatic changes outlined for legal aid in the Lord Chancellor's Green Paper of May 1995 and Lord Woolf's Interim Report on Access to Justice in civil cases of June 1995. Each receives extensive treatment in the new edition.

The Runciman Report has already resulted in many legislative changes, not least in the provisions of the Criminal Justice and Public Order Act 1994 which abolished the 'right to silence' and the provisions of the Criminal Appeal Act 1995 establishing the Criminal Cases Review Commission.

The Runciman Report was accompanied by 22 research reports and these, and a variety of other new research studies are covered in the book, as is a mass of new case-law.

The one structural change in this edition is that the short chapter on Enforcement of Judgment Debts has been dropped. The chapter was in a sense always anomalous in that the book did not cover sentencing in criminal cases and therefore, logically, should not have covered enforcement in civil cases. Another reason for dropping the chapter was perhaps that it was the one topic covered in the book that seemed to be largely static with few developments of note over the years.

For the main text of the book the latest date taken into account, unless otherwise indicated, was 31 May 1996. But the Government's radical and very important Legal Aid White paper was published just in time to be included in a special Appendix to the book. (It was however not possible to include the Appendix in the index.)

May 1996   Michael Zander
London

Preface to the first edition

This book is concerned with dispute settlement in courts and tribunals in England and Wales. The aim is to make available a selection of materials which reveal the actual workings of the system, its problems and difficulties, and which suggest ways in which it might be improved. The emphasis is contemporary and critical. The materials selected come from a wide variety of sources. Some, of course, are drawn from conventional legal sources–statutes and judicial decisions. But many more are taken from articles, official reports, books and surveys. Wherever possible they draw on empirical work, though there are still far too many areas of concern where no empirical investigation has yet been undertaken. The work is intended mainly as a source-book for those taking courses on the English legal system for a law degree or an equivalent course for a degree in some other subject. My intention is not merely to make a collection of scattered sources conveniently accessible, but also to stimulate constructively critical thought about the subject. I also hope that anyone who wishes to learn about the actual operation of the legal system or who is interested in its reform will find it useful.

The book does not attempt to cover all topics that are sometimes included in legal system courses, such as the sources of law, the legal profession, the machinery of law reform and sentencing. Excellent works on each of these topics are readily available, and it would not have been possible to do justice to these subjects within short compass. Nor does this book attempt to replace standard descriptive texts. Rather it attempts to supplement them by focusing through the basic texts on points where the legal system is under stress or is the subject of controversy. The aim is to give a better understanding of the reality of the law in action.

July 1972   Michael Zander
London

Acknowledgments

All the materials in the book appear here with the permission of those who hold the copyright. I wish to express my sincere gratitude to all the individuals and institutions who have so kindly and generously allowed the material to be reprinted in this form. In particular I wish to thank the Controller of Her Majesty's Stationery Office for permission to include extracts from official publications; to the Incorporated Council of Law Reporting for England and Wales for extracts from the *Law Reports* and the *Weekly Law Reports* and Butterworths for extracts from the *All England Law Reports*. I am indebted to the following publishers and journals for permission to use extracts: Basil Blackwell for permission to use material from the *Journal of Law and Society*, Sweet and Maxwell Ltd for extracts from *Civil Justice Quarterly,* the *Criminal Law Review and the Criminal Appeal Reports;* to the *Law Quarterly Review*, *Legal Action*, the *Magistrate*, the *Modern Law Review*, the *Solicitor's Journal*, the *Law Guardian*, the *New Law Journal*, the *Law Society's Gazette*, the *International* and *Comparative Law Quarterly*, *New Society*, *The Times* and *The Guardian*. The Social Administration Research Trust gave permission for use of an extract from Susanne Dell's book *Silent in Court*. The Law Society gave permission for use to be made of articles in the *Law Society's Gazette*. The BBC and Sir Robert Mark gave permission for use of an extract from Sir Robert's Dimbleby lecture on BBC television. The *New Statesman* and CR Rolph allowed me to use the extract from Mr Rolph's 1969 article on police discretion.

Command papers, Hansard, House of Commons papers and other official publications excerpted

(in chronological order)

Books, pamphlets, memoranda and articles excerpted

Contents

Table of statutes

References in this Table of Statutes are to Halsbury's Statutes of England (Fourth Edition) showing the volume and page at which the annotated text of an Act may be found.

Table of cases

Page numbers in bold type indicate case extracts

CHAPTER 1

The organisation of trial courts

The first chapter considers the organisation of trial courts, the work they do, the allocation of cases between them, their similarities and differences. The structure and the problems of the appeal system are considered separately in the penultimate chapter.

The structure and organisation of the courts has been the subject of various official inquiries. Until the 1990s, the two most significant in modern times were the Beeching Royal Commission on Assizes and Quarter Sessions, 1969, which looked at the conduct of civil and criminal business outside London at the higher level, (its report was largely implemented in the Courts Act 1971–see pp 10–11 below); and the Civil Justice Review, instituted by the then Lord Chancellor, Lord Hailsham, in February 1985. The purpose of the Civil Justice Review was to improve the machinery of civil justice by means of reforms in jurisdiction, procedure and court administration and, in particular, to attempt to find ways of reducing delays, cost and complexity.[1]

In March 1987, on the basis of the five consultation papers produced by the Civil Justice Review, the Lord Chancellor's Department issued a *General Issues Paper* in which problems common to civil justice as a whole were identified and discussed. The Final Report, *Report of the Review Body on Civil Justice* (Cm 394), was published in June 1988. Many of the proposals in this Final Report were implemented in the Courts and Legal Services Act 1990 and by delegated legislation that became operative as from July 1991.

In July 1992 the Bar Council and the Law Society set up an independent committee (the Heilbron-Hodge Committee, named for its joint chairman Miss Hilary Heilbron QC and Mr Henry Hodge) to 'undertake a radical review of the business of the civil courts and to make recommendations for the more efficient disposal of civil cases in keeping with public needs and expectations'. The committee produced its report *Civil Justice on Trial–The Case for Change* in June 1993

In March 1994 the Lord Chancellor, Lord Mackay initiated an important new development in regard to civil justice. He asked Lord Woolf, a law lord, to review the current rules and procedures of the civil courts in England and Wales. The aims of the review were stated to be: to improve access to justice and reduce the cost of litigation; to reduce the complexity of the rules and modernise terminology; and to remove

---

1 The Civil Justice Review, in short order, produced five consultation papers: *Personal Injuries* (February 1986); *Small Claims* (September 1986); *Commercial Court* (November 1986); *Enforcement of Debt* (January 1987); and *Housing Cases* (January 1987). In each case the consultation paper set out the basic data produced by an empirical study, together with analysis and options, with preferred solutions. (Each paper was produced and published by the Lord Chancellor's Department.)

unnecessary distinctions of practice and procedure. Lord Woolf worked with a small team of civil servants from the Lord Chancellor's Department, with five assessors and an academic consultant. He did not ask for written or oral evidence but he received submissions from many relevant bodies and persons. He also held a number of seminars in different parts of the country. Lord Woolf published his Interim Report entitled *Access to Justice* in June 1995. For a book of essays commenting on the Interim Report see *The Reform of Civil Procedure–Essays on Access to Justice* (ed Zuckerman and Cranston, OUP, 1995, More detail about the Woolf proposals emerged in a series of six Consultation Issues Papers circulated in January 1996. (The final report was due in Summer 1996.)

The recommendations of the Civil Justice Review, the Report of the Heilbron-Hodge Committee and Lord Woolf's Interim Report are relevant both in this chapter and the next.

The objectives of the system

The *General Issues Paper* of the Civil Justice Review suggested that the primary aim in all branches of civil justice was the pursuit of high-quality justice, which included fairness of procedures and methods of adjudication such as to ensure to each party an opportunity to present his case and to have it impartially considered, and quality, fairness and consistency of judicial decisions (para 55).

But the primary aim was not sovereign. It had to be balanced against a second aim, namely that of limiting to a level proportionate to the subject-matter, the incidence of delay, cost to the parties and cost to the court service. This aim (of efficiency) included the following elements: time targets for the handling of cases; effective deployment of judges, court staff and court facilities; the appropriate matching of judges to cases; the adoption of streamlined procedures for simple cases; and limiting costs to the parties and to the court service (para 56).

There was also the aim that the system should be effective–responsive to the variety of types of business; adaptable to changing economic and social circumstances; with court locations and court hours that were convenient; providing simple rules regarding jurisdiction, venue and procedure; and securing to litigants the assistance they needed with their cases.

One difference between civil and criminal business was that, while crime was relatively homogeneous, civil matters involved an enormous variety of matters. A whole variety of specialist jurisdictions had developed. This had both good and bad aspects. The advantages included the fact that specialist skills and familiarity with the business might speed up the despatch of business. But the danger was that specialist jurisdictions blocked mobility of transfer of judicial and court personnel, quasi-monopolies grew up amongst practitioners, traditions of separateness ossified and became difficult to reform and the different jurisdictions might not produce a rational allocation of resources.

See generally IR Scott, 'Problems in Court Structure and Processes', 44 *Current Legal Problems*, 1991, pp 15–38.

Before looking at these issues more closely, the next sections describe the existing structure as it has developed.

1. THE WORK HANDLED BY THE COURTS

(a) The civil courts

There are three different levels of trial courts for civil cases: the High Court, the county court and the magistrates' court.

(1) The High Court

(i) History[2]

The High Court is divided into three Divisions–the Queen's Bench Division, the Chancery Division and the Family Division. The High Court came into existence in the Judicature Acts of 1873–5, in replacement for the ancient Queen's Bench Court, Court of Common Pleas, Court of Exchequer, Chancery Court, and the Probate, Divorce and Admiralty Court. Under the 1873–5 legislation these five separate courts became the five Divisions of the High Court; but in 1888 the three common-law courts (Queen's Bench, Common Pleas and Exchequer) were merged into a single Division, the Queen's Bench Division (QBD). The Probate, Divorce and Admiralty Division was broken up in the Administration of Justice Act 1970 which allocated its functions between the QBD, the Chancery Division and the new Family Division.[3]

(ii) The High Court today

The jurisdiction of the High Court is now to be found in the provisions of the Supreme Court Act 1981.

The Queen's Bench Division   This consists of the Lord Chief Justice and some 60 High Court judges. It deals primarily with claims for contract and tort. The largest single category of work is for goods sold and delivered, work done, materials supplied or professional work done. (In 1994, this category accounted for 70% of all the claims brought in the QBD in London. The comparable figure for claims started outside London was not available.) The next largest categories typically are: claims for damages for negligence, the great majority of which arise from road and factory accidents; claims for other forms of debt; claims by banks and finance houses in respect of loans; breach of contract cases; and actions for recovery of land. Some four-fifths of claims are for a specific, 'liquidated', sum. The number of cases dealt with by the QBD has been declining sharply in recent years, at least in part because of the planned transfer of cases from the QBD to the county court (see below pp 24–25). In 1990 the number of proceedings started in the QBD was over 350,000; in 1994 it had sunk to some 150,000.

The overwhelming majority of the claims are always disposed of without a trial (see further p 34-38 below).

The Queen's Bench Division additionally has two special types of jurisdiction. One is the Admiralty Court, previously part of the Probate, Divorce and Admiralty Division

---

2   For an outstanding historical account see B Abel-Smith and R Stevens, *Lawyers and the Courts* (Heinemann, 1967).
3   For the Lord Chancellor's explanation see 306 House of Lords, *Hansard*, 4 December 1969, cols 197–9.

which was abolished by the Administration of Justice Act 1970. Admiralty cases typically concern collisions at sea, damage to cargo and personal injuries suffered at sea. (In 1994 there were 623 writs and summonses issued in admiralty cases but only two cases were actually tried!) The second category is the Commercial Court, which consists of judges specially chosen for their experience to try heavy commercial cases.

It should also be noted that the Divisional Court of the Queen's Bench Division sitting with two or three judges sits to exercise a very important first instance jurisdiction by way of review of the acts of bureaucrats and officials, Ministers and local councillors. Traditionally this was by way of the ancient prerogative writs (certiorari, mandamus, prohibition and habeas corpus). Today it is normally by an application for judicial review under Order 53 of the Rules of the Supreme Court. Leave is required and applications for leave are heard normally by a single judge. In 1994 there were 2,887 applications for leave to apply for judicial review in civil matters (a third of which concerned immigration) and 321 in regard to criminal cases. (There were no applications for habeas corpus.) As a result of recent changes, specialist judges with knowledge of administrative law have been appointed to handle these cases and as a result there is now virtually an administrative law division of the Queen's Bench Division. (On the introduction of this new system see Louis Blom-Cooper, 'The New Face of Judicial Review: Administrative Changes in Order 53', *Public Law*, 1982, p 250.)

The Chancery Division   As has been seen, this is the successor to the ancient Chancery Court. It consists of the Vice Chancellor and some 17 High Court judges. They deal with corporate and personal insolvency disputes, business, trade and industry disputes, the enforcement of mortgages, professional negligence, intellectual property matters, copyright and patents, trusts, wills and probate matters. The Chancery Division also includes a specialist Companies Court and Patents Court. In 1994, the total number of proceedings was just under 39,000, of which some 17,000 were Companies Court matters and 11,500 were bankruptcy petitions.

The Family Division   As has been seen, this was created in 1970 when the Probate, Divorce and Admiralty Division was split up. It consists of the President and some 15 High Court judges. It hears defended divorce cases and ancillary disputes over children and property. It also deals with wardship, guardianship of infants, adoption and legitimacy cases. The Family Division nominally also deals with non-contentious probate work but in practice this work is handled by administrative or bureaucratic rather than by judicial proceedings.

There are three other special jurisdictions which may be mentioned.

The Restrictive Practices Court   This is independent of the High Court but is a superior court of record, dealing with applications under the Restrictive Trade Practices Act 1976 and the Fair Trading Act 1973. It has three High Court judges plus up to ten lay members. The court sits with a judge and two or more lay members. But in practice it has few cases. (In 1994 it sat for a total of only nine court days.)

The Official Referees   These take difficult or technical issues of fact on reference from the Queen's Bench Division or the Chancery Division after an application made by either party. Usually the cases involve building and construction disputes. Circuit judges are nominated to conduct Official Referee business.

The Court of Protection   This is responsible for the management and administration of the property and affairs of people suffering from mental disorder. Most of the work is done by masters and deputy masters (see below) rather than by judges. But judges of the Chancery Division do exercise some of the powers. There are normally some 30,000 estates under administration.

(iii) Interlocutory work in the High Court

Most actual trials are handled by judges. But the pre-trial ('interlocutory') work is conducted in London by masters in the Queen's Bench and Chancery Divisions and by registrars in the Family Division. Outside London there are no masters. High Court interlocutory business outside London is handled in District Registries by district judges (formerly called registrars) who are normally also the district judges for the county court. District Registries are physically located in county courts. There are over a hundred District Registries. All the District Registries deal with Queen's Bench, Chancery and Family Division work. Most, though not all, are authorized to take undefended divorce cases.

Judges in High Court cases

The judges who sit in High Court cases are: High Court judges (who in 1994 sat on 47% of High Court judge days); circuit judges (18%); district judges and part-time deputy district judges (19%); Deputy High Court judges–who are sometimes practitioners and sometimes retired judges (12%); Lords Justices of Appeal (2%) and recorders and assistant recorders–who are practitioners (2%).

Sittings outside London

The Queen's Bench Division and the Family Division sit in London and over twenty locations throughout the country; the Chancery Division sits in London and eight other cities. The Divisional Court, like the Court of Appeal and the House of Lords, sit only in London–save that the Court of Appeal Criminal Division very occasionally sits outside London.

Allocation of judges and separate High Court Divisions

The judges of the High Court on appointment are allocated by the Lord Chancellor to one or other division and usually then remain in that Division.

The Civil Justice Review General Issues Consultation Paper (para 68) said that there was no comprehensive planning or forecasting procedure available for the purpose of reviewing the total workload of the High Court and its Divisions. Each Division manages its affairs virtually independently of the others and this 'stands in the way of overall management of civil business'. One of the country's leading experts on courts' management, Professor Ian Scott (who was also a member of the Civil Justice Review), has added: 'It may be argued that the present three-fold Division structure stands in the way of development of a range of procedures suited to the many varieties of business arising in the High Court and that what is required nowadays is not three divisions but multiple, "substance-sensitive" procedural and administrative arrangements reflecting the wide jurisdiction of the Court' (*Civil Justice Quarterly*, January 1989, p 5).

In 1988 a Committee on the Deployment of the High Court Bench under the chairmanship of Sir Stephen Brown recommended, amongst other things, that in principle every High Court judge should be available to deal with the whole range of High Court work–although there would always remain a need for judicial specialisation.

The Committee also recommended that the High Court in London should have a single listing office but that there should be a number of lists each under the direction of its own listing officer. The process of listing should be subject to judicial oversight. The listing office should be responsible for the deployment of all High Court judges. The full benefit of a single listing office could be achieved only in a unified High Court. The report, which was not published, has not been implemented.

The Heilbron-Hodge Report in 1992 suggested that the present arrangements resulted in the inflexible and inefficient use of judge power and wasted time and expense in transferring cases from one Division to another. It recommended that the QBD and the Chancery Divisions be amalgamated into one and that cases should be allocated by way of two general lists and a number of specialist lists. Thus, there might be a General List to include personal injury, medical negligence and tort cases, excluding professional negligence; and a General Business List to include much of the caseload of the Chancery Division together with other general business litigation. There should also be Specialist Lists viz: the Commercial Court; the Admiralty Court; the Jury List; the Company and Insolvency List; the Patent List; the Intellectual Property List etc.

Lord Woolf's Interim Report in 1995 said that it could in addition be argued that separate practices and a separate culture between the Chancery and the Queen's Bench Divisions might cause difficulties for outsiders. On the other hand, the Chancery Division provided a convenient umbrella for a number of specialist jurisdictions which were serviced by specialist judges and specialist members of the bar. These jurisdictions, which included companies, bankruptcy and the administration of estates and trusts, were of a quasi-administrative nature and required a different approach from other litigation. The sense of team spirit among the Chancery judges and their special relationship with the Chancery Bar resulted in a more effective and efficient disposal of work. Moreover, if the 17 Chancery judges were amalgamated with the 63 judges of the QBD they might just be absorbed to meet the needs of the QBD. Lord Woolf's conclusion (p 77, para 23) was that it was not desirable, at least at this stage, to merge the two Divisions. Implementing his other recommendations would involve other changes of a very substantial nature and it was preferable not to add to those changes the upheaval that a merger of the two Divisions would involve.

He would, however, follow the Heilbron-Hodge Report to the extent of nominating judges to lists according to their expertise, regardless of which Division to which the lists belonged. So a judge could be attached not only to lists in the Chancery Division but also to the Commercial Court in the Queen's Bench Division. If however, the retention of the Chancery Division proved inimical to the uniform and flexible approach which he considered essential the question of a merger could be reconsidered.

(2) The county court

The county court was established in 1846 with a jurisdiction limited to £20 for actions in contract and tort. During the next hundred years the jurisdiction was increased very slowly–to £50 in 1850, £100 in 1903 and £200 in 1938. In 1955 the jurisdiction of the county courts was raised to £400. In 1966 it went up to £500, in 1969 to £750 and in 1974 to £1,000. It next jumped to £2,000 in 1977 and in 1981 it was more than doubled to £5,000–and in equity matters £30,000. In 1990 the limit was abolished. As from 1 July 1991 county courts have been able to deal with all contract and tort claims and recovery of land actions, regardless of value plus equity matters where the value of the trust fund or estate does not exceed £30,000.

There are some 260 county courts in England and Wales. The county courts handle a vast amount of business. In 1994 there were 2.4 million money plaints started in the county court plus 171,000 plaints for the recovery of land. (The numbers have declined in each year since 1991 In that year there were 3.4 million money plaints and 306,000 actions for the recovery of land.) But the ordinary claim brought in the county court is consistently low. In 1989 (the last year for which this figure was available) about one-fifth of all money claims for fixed amounts were for sums of £100 or less, and 60 per cent were for sums of £500 or less.

By far the largest proportion of cases brought in the county court are money claims, which represent over 90 per cent of the total. As in the QBD, actions of this kind are mainly for goods sold and delivered, work done, materials supplied and professional fees. The other largest categories of work done by the county court are undefended divorce and ancillary relief in regard to children and matrimonial property and actions for the recovery of land and premises. The county court has an admiralty and equity jurisdiction, can hear contested probate actions, and deals with bankruptcy and companies winding up. It also hears cases under the Race Relations 1976. One hundred and seventy of the 260 county courts are authorized to deal with undefended divorce work.

In terms of cases and the variety of its work, the county court could be said to be the chief civil court in the country. A better sense of the nature of its case-load may be gained from a study conducted by the Consumer Council (*Justice Out of Reach*, 1970). The report was based on a sample of cases drawn from six courts. (It did not include possession actions nor undefended divorces.) Nearly 90 per cent of the summonses in the sample had been taken out by firms or utility boards (nearly always a gas or electricity board). An individual was the plaintiff in only nine per cent of summonses. (However, undefended divorces were added to the court's jurisdiction subsequently and they account for nearly 10 per cent of the actions started.)

The Consumer Council's 1970 study showing that individuals hardly ever used the county courts as plaintiffs was influential in helping to promote concern about this fact. It led in due course to various changes in county court procedure designed to make them more attractive to ordinary citizens pursuing small claims–see, in regard to pre-trial procedure, p 80 below, in regard to less formal trial methods, p 303 below, and in regard to costs, p 435 below. Originally the limit for small claims cases was £75. By 1979 this figure had been increased to £200. In 1979 it went up to £500 and in 1991 to £1,000. Lord Woolf's Interim Report in June 1995, proposed that it be increased to £3,000–save for personal injury cases. This was implemented in January 1996.

The advantages of 'repeat players'

The fact that most county court plaintiffs are institutions of one sort or another is hardly surprising. Litigation is not something that the ordinary citizen is likely to want to undertake. He will be nervous about the likely costs, both in terms of time and money. He will worry whether he may at the end have to appear in court–not knowing that most cases settle out of court. He will be unfamiliar with the procedures of the legal system and will not know how to 'use the system'. He will not normally be in regular contact with lawyers who can take up his case. He will not know how to calculate the pros and cons of taking up the cudgels in terms of the likely outcome as against the costs of the case.

None of these factors inhibit the large institution or, if at all, not nearly to the same extent. Marc Galanter, a noted American scholar in the field of the sociology of law, has analysed the differences between parties who have only occasional recourse to the law ('one-shotters') as against those who take part in litigation repeatedly ('repeat players'). The repeat players' advantages include the following:

(1) Having done it before, they can structure the next transaction and thus gain over the one-shotter. It is the repeat player who writes the standard-form contract and who can adjust it if a particular clause has been interpreted unhelpfully in a previous case.

(2) Repeat players develop expertise, can employ specialists, enjoy economies of scale and have low start-up costs for any new case.

(3) Repeat players have developed informal relations with those who work the legal system, such as lawyers and court officials.

(4) Repeat players can play the odds. Because they have large numbers of cases they can afford to take risks with particular cases providing they come out ahead overall. The one-shotter by comparison cannot afford to lose his one case and therefore cannot take the risks involved in going for the maximum result.

(5) Repeat players can play to alter the rules through test-case litigation or even by lobbying for legislative or administrative changes. Repeat players can select from among their cases the most favourable ones to fight into the courts and up the appellate levels in order to achieve the best results. This gives them advantages in the area of law-making through litigation.

(See M Galanter, 'Why the "Haves" Come out Ahead', 9 *Law and Society Review*, 1974, p 95 and 'Explaining Litigation', *ibid,* p 347.)

A paper produced by the Lord Chancellor's Department in July 1987 stated that in 1986 over 60 per cent of the two million debt cases started in the county court were brought by 'bulk plaintiffs' such as water authorities suing for rates, gas and electricity boards for services relating to fuel supplied, finance houses, banks and mail-order companies. They issued anything between 1,000 and 100,000 summonses a year. (For computerization of bulk issue, see pp 42 and 44 below.)

Note also the fact that, although both in the QBD and in the county court by far the majority of actions commenced are money claims, they are only a tiny fraction of those tried. This is because so high a proportion of debt cases are concluded by some means other than trial. Of the actions *tried* in the QBD, personal injury claims used to represent about three-quarters of the total case-load. (Today it would be less, due to the recent moves to transfer personal injury cases from the High Court to the county court on which see p 24 below.) In Galanter's sense, personal injury plaintiffs are one-shotters. The fact that they can bring actions against institutions (employers and insurance companies) is due to the levelling effect of legal aid and the support of trades unions and insurance companies. But the repeat player still has many advantages including above all the fact that it is a matter of little overall consequence whether he wins or loses any particular case. This tells–especially in such matters as payment into court (p 55 below), credibility in bargaining (so that the threat to go the whole way by taking it to the court has to be seen as a real threat), and the fact that the repeat player can select the most advantageous cases to press. On the other hand, the existence of the legal aid system and financial support of trades unions with their own specialists and lawyers does to an extent equalize the position.

County court judges

Each county court is assigned at least one circuit judge and one district judge. Circuit judges generally hear the bigger claims and matters of greater importance and complexity. District judges generally deal with uncontested matters and hear claims of under £5,000 including small claims cases called 'arbitrations'.

(3) Magistrates' courts

Magistrates' courts have always had a significant jurisdiction in the civil field. Most of it was in the field of domestic relations–especially maintenance for deserted wives and children, custody disputes, adoption, guardianship, and protection of battered wives. A different kind of civil jurisdiction is the collection of various statutory debts such as income tax, national insurance, social security, rates and legal aid contributions.

In the field of domestic relations there was a great deal of overlap between the jurisdiction of the magistrates and that of the county court. As will be seen, the issue of what to do about this jurisdiction culminated in the Children Act 1989 which led to a significant re-casting both of the relevant law and of the responsibilities of the different levels of civil courts. The magistrates' courts functions in this field have been renamed 'family proceedings courts'.

For a wide-ranging consideration of the role of the civil courts, see Ross Cranston, What Do Courts Do?', *Civil Justice Quarterly*, April 1986, p 123.

(b) The criminal courts

There are two trial courts for criminal cases: the crown court and the magistrates' court.

(1) The crown court

The crown court dates from 1 January 1972, the day on which the Courts Act 1971 came into force. The Courts Act was the result of the *Report of the Royal Commission on Assizes and Quarter Sessions* (the Beeching Report, 1969, Cmnd 4153). The Beeching Royal Commission was set up in 1966 in order to investigate and propose reforms to the system of assize and quarter sessions courts that had remained substantially unchanged for centuries.

The Royal Commission found that the then existing system was seriously defective. The ancient assize towns were no longer necessarily main centres of population; the fact that the same judge did both civil and criminal work meant that the civil cases always had to wait for the more urgent criminal cases to be finished first; the sittings of the assize courts were fixed long before anyone had an idea as to the likely case-load; when the allotted time was up the judge had to go to the next assize town, rather than finish the list; the judges spent too much of their time on the road travelling between assize towns and whilst he and the court staff were all travelling, the entire courts system was inaccessible.

The solutions recommended by the Beeching Commission to the ills it had diagnosed were clear cut:

(1) The abolition of Assizes and Quarter Sessions and their replacement by a new higher criminal court to be called the crown court. This court would sit as and where needed. The siting of crown courts would be based on the principle 'that virtually the whole population will be within reasonable daily travelling distance of at least one such site, and that no regard shall be paid to civic boundaries established for other purposes'.

(2) The division of the criminal from the civil business of the higher courts so that civil litigants would no longer have to wait for the completion of criminal cases.

(3) Instead of the judges processing from town to town, they should to a much greater extent sit in courts' centres in permanent or more or less permanent session. In addition, there should be mini-circuits to handle the criminal work that could not be dealt with in the main court centres.

(4) Cases should be divided into different categories and allocated to judges by reference to their gravity and the level of seniority of judge required.

(5) The judges should all be able to sit in any crown court anywhere in the country.

(6) County court judges should be restyled Circuit judges, who should sit both in crown courts to conduct criminal cases and in county courts to conduct civil business.

(7) There should be a new title of Recorder for part-time judges eligible to sit in any crown court, who could be solicitors as well as barristers.

(8) The country should be divided into six, as compared with the previous seven, circuits. Each circuit should be run by two Presiding judges and a Circuit administrator.

(9) There should be a unified court administrative service, appointed and paid by the Lord Chancellor.

(10) The Lord Chancellor should be the minister responsible for all the higher courts and the county court.

The Royal Commission was set up by a Labour Government but the report was implemented by the incoming Conservative Government. It accepted every one of the recommendations listed above. The Courts Act 1971 provided for the establishment of the crown court, whose business was to be handled by High Court judges, circuit judges and recorders. (The crown court for the City of London was, however, allowed to keep its hallowed name 'the Central Criminal Court', otherwise known as the Old Bailey.)

The crown court sits at some 90 locations throughout the country. The court centres are of three kinds. First-tier centres (of which there are twenty-five) are those visited by High Court judges, circuit judges and recorders for the full range of crown court work–as well as by High Court judges of the Queen's Bench Division and Family Division for civil work. Second-tier centres (of which there are seventeen) are those at which crown court work (but not civil business) is dealt with by High Court judges, circuit judges and recorders. Third-tier centres (of which there are some forty) are those visited only by circuit judges and recorders or deputy circuit judges and assistant recorders.

The distribution of business in the crown court is governed by directions given by the Lord Chief Justice with the concurrence of the Lord Chancellor. (For the latest *Practice Note* see [1995] 2 All ER 90).) These divide offences, for the purposes of trial, into four classes. The most serious (Class 1) are generally to be tried by a High Court judge. They include treason, murder and espionage. Offences in Class 2 must be tried by a High Court judge unless released by, or on the authority of, a Presiding judge for trial by a circuit judge or recorder. The offences include manslaughter, rape and abortion. Offences in Class 3 may be listed for trial by a High Court judge or by a circuit judge or recorder; in normal circumstances they are listed for trial by a High Court judge unless the listing officer, acting under the directions of a judge, decides that a particular case should be listed for trial by a circuit judge, recorder or assistant recorder. The offences include all offences triable only in the crown court unless they are specifically assigned to classes 1, 2 or 4. Cases in Class 4 are normally listed for trial by a circuit judge or recorder, though they may be tried by a High Court judge. They include grievous bodily harm with intent, robbery and conspiracy and all 'either way' offences (see p 18 below). Most other proceedings in the crown court, including appeals, committals for sentence and proceedings under the court's limited civil jurisdiction (derived from the civil jurisdiction of Quarter Sessions), are listed for trial by a circuit judge or recorder. Lay magistrates sit with a professional judge for the appellate work of the court and deal with cases committed for sentence only.

Class 1 offences constitute some one per cent of those dealt with by the crown court. Class 2 cases represent between one and two per cent of the case-load. Class 3 cases are around three or four per cent of the total. Well over 90 per cent, therefore, are Class 4 offences.

Discretion in listing

The dry recital of the basic principles on which allocation of cases is done conceals a fascinating and little-studied aspect of judicial administration, namely how cases are allocated to individual judges. That this is a subject well worthy of some inquiry emerged from a pilot study of sentencing which showed that court clerks who actually do the listing can be influenced by personal views as to what they think should be the outcome of the case. Thus, the study suggested that if they thought the defendant deserved a severe sentence they have the power, and sometimes exercised it, of making sure that he did not appear before someone they considered to be a lenient judge, or even of ensuring that he was dealt with by someone they think would be suitably severe! (See A Ashworth *et al, Sentencing in the Crown Court*, Centre for Criminological Research, Occasional Paper No 10, 1984, pp 60–64.) See also A Lovegrove, 'The Listing of Cases in the Crown Court as an Administrative Discretion' (1984) *Criminal Law Review*, p 738.

Crown court judicial manpower

The Beeching Royal Commission in its 1969 report estimated that there would be a need for some 150 full-time circuit judges and 120 part-time recorders. This proved to be a considerable underestimate. In 1972 there were 69 High Court judges, 205 circuit judges and 287 recorders. By 1994 there were 95 High Court judges, 504 circuit judges and 856 part-time recorders most of whom are barristers but some of whom are solicitors. In addition, in 1994 there were 398 assistant recorders.[4]

The extraordinary growth in the business of the higher criminal courts may be judged from the number of crown court days sat annually:

1958	6,966
1967	17,930
1977	55,529
1987	71,209
1994	87,894

In 1994, circuit judges handled 64 per cent of crown court work, recorders 19 per cent, assistant recorders 11 per cent, and High Court judges 5 per cent.

(2) Magistrates' courts

Magistrates' courts, which are manned mainly by lay justices, handle some 97 per cent of all criminal cases. In 1994 there were 1.95 million cases tried in magistrates' courts. Of these, 0.86 million were minor motoring charges, 0.59 million were other cases that could only be tried in the magistrates' courts, and 0.5 million were cases that could have been tried in the crown court but the defendant chose instead to have the case dealt with summarily before the magistrates. (On this last category see further below, pp 17–22.)

There are some 600 or so magistrates' courts, some of which sit every day, some of which sit only occasionally. They are manned by some 30,000 lay (and unpaid) magistrates and by some 85 or so professional, full-time and paid 'stipendiary' magistrates. The lay justices typically sit once every two weeks.

The magistracy is older even than the Justices of the Peace Act 1361, which in effect gave statutory recognition to the institution and made magistrates into a form of local government. They still have some essentially administrative tasks such as liquor licensing, but for at least the past century justices have been mainly concerned with judicial functions. The organisation of magistrates' courts was historically outside the national scheme under the Lord Chancellor which covered the civil courts and the crown courts. The magistrates' courts service was a local service locally administered. From 1949 the Home Office assumed the burden of financing 80 per cent of the cost of the magistrates' courts. (The Home Secretary had a discretion to withhold grant but it seems that this power was only exercised on one occasion.) The actual level of funding was set by the local Magistrates' Courts Committee in consultation with the paying local authority. These committees consisted of magistrates elected by their fellow magistrates in the area. Subject to the approval of the Home Secretary, the Committee appointed the Justices' Clerk who was both the chief administrator of the

---

4   Recorders and assistant recorders sit as judges for 20 days, or one working month, per year.

court and its chief clerk. (On recent changes made by the Police and Magistrates' Courts Act 1994, see pp 16–17 below.)

2. MANAGING THE COURTS

In April 1979 the Court Service was launched as an executive agency of the Lord Chancellor's Department. The Service took over responsibility for administrative and operational functions of the Supreme Court of England and Wales (comprising the Court of Appeal, the High Court–including the probate service–and the crown court), county courts and seven tribunals.[5] (It does not cover administrative support for the magistrates' courts–as regards which see pp 16–17 below.

At the launch press conference Lord Mackay, the Lord Chancellor, said the change in status was 'an integral part of the Government's Next Steps programme' and that it reinforced 'our commitment to improving both management and quality of public services under the umbrella of the Citizen's Charter'. Although a fundamental principle underlying the creation of Next Steps agencies was to free Ministers from day to day involvement in purely operational matters, thereby allowing them more time for policy development, he would 'continue to take a keen interest in the overall approach of the Court Service'. The establishment of the agency would not alter the relationship with the judiciary.

The first chief executive of the Court Service, Mr Michael Huebner, said at the same launch event: 'Agency status is all about giving managers the freedom to manage. Instead of being told how to manage, we will be told what end-product we must produce, using the resources allocated to us'. The Lord Chancellor would decide on the ends to be achieved. These would be translated into specific objectives and targets which could be measured. The Court Service would be free to decide for itself where to spend money, where to deploy staff and so on, in order to achieve its targets.

The launch was accompanied by three documents: a Framework Document, a Corporate Plan, and a Business Plan.

The Framework Document set out the overall structure of accountability with the Lord Chancellor as the Minister answerable to Parliament. He appoints a Chief Executive and delegates to him responsibility for the exercise of the functions of the Service. His principal adviser is the Permanent Secretary. The Permanent Secretary is also the Principal Accounting Officer for the Department responsible for standards of financial management. Both the Permanent Secretary and the Chief Executive can be summoned to appear before the Public Accounts Committee and the House of Commons Home Affairs Select Committee. MPs and peers would be encouraged to write to the Chief Executive rather than the Lord Chancellor on matters concerning the day to day operation of the Court Service. The Lord Chancellor would continue to deal with complaints about members of the judiciary.

When an MP or peer tabled a Parliamentary Question on the day to day operation of the Court Service, he or she would normally be informed that the Chief Executive

5   The Immigration Appellate Authorities, the Lands Tribunal, the Pensions Appeals Tribunal, the Social Security and Child Support Commissioners, the Value Added Tax and Duties Tribunals (including both the General and Special Commissioners of Income Tax) and the Transport Tribunal, the Banking Tribunal, and the Building Societies Tribunal.

would reply direct to the Member or peer concerned. Such replies would be published in the Official Report.

The administrative work of the Court Service is subject to the jurisdiction of the Parliamentary Commissioner for Administration (Parliamentary Ombudsman). Under the Courts and Legal Services Act 1990, s 110(2) work done by the Court Service at the direction or on the authority of a judge is however not subject to the Parliamentary Commissioner's jurisdiction.

The Corporate Plan identified two major challenges for the new Service. One was improving the quality of service provided to the public in the courts, in particular reducing waiting time for trial or hearing. The other was countering the increasing gap between expenditure on civil business and income derived from court fees. Fee revenue met most of the administrative costs of running the civil courts. In 1992 the Lord Chancellor had decided that court fees should in principle also meet the costs of the judiciary.

The Business Plan identified eight key performance indicators against which the Lord Chancellor had set targets. These were:

(1) the percentage of courts and offices meeting all of the standards set out in the Courts Charter (target: 95%);

(2) the percentage of the costs of civil courts recovered (target: 75%);

(3) the percentage of Supreme Court administrative process dealt with within target time (target: 93%);

(4) the percentage of Crown Court defendants committed for trial waiting target time of 16 weeks or less (target: 70%);

(5) the unit cost of a productive courtroom hour in the Crown Court (target: £462.40);

(6) the percentage of administrative processes in the county court dealt with within target time (target: 90%);

(7) the number of county court warrants paid as a percentage of the number of correctly directed warrants (target: 65%);

(8) the unit cost of an hour of administrative work (target: £53.39).

The Court Service periodically publishes a Charter for Court Users in which it sets out its current objectives: eg to answer telephone calls within thirty seconds, to give jurors not less than four weeks' notice of jury service, to provide separate waiting rooms for witnesses, to start crown court cases within sixteen weeks of their transfer from magistrates' courts, to issue civil proceedings within five to ten days from receipt of all the documentation and the fee etc.

The Court Service publishes an annual report. (There is also an annual report entitled the *Judicial Statistics* published by the Lord Chancellor's Department and the annual *Criminal Statistics* published by the Home Office.)

It has to be said that relations between the judges and the Lord Chancellor's Department have not always been harmonious. Ever since the early 1970s with the implementation of the Beeching Royal Commission Report there has been a degree of tension as to the running of the system between the judiciary and the executive. For expression of some of the concerns felt by the judiciary see for instance Sir Nicolas Browne-Wilkinson, 'The Independence of the Judiciary in the 1980s', *Public Law*, Spring 1988, pp 44–57; Sir Francis Purchas, 'The Constitution in the Market Place',

New Law Journal, 12 November 1993, pp 1604–09; Judge Harold Wilson, 'The County Court Judge in Limbo', *New Law Journal*, 21 October 1994, p 1453.

Note–Lord Chancellor's Department takes over magistrates' courts

From the early 1970s the question was raised in a variety of official reports whether the management of magistrates' courts should be centralised. (For the details of these reports and discussions see the sixth edition of this work, pp 20–24.) The culmination of these reports was the 1979 Home Office Scrutiny Report (the Le Vay Report) which stated: 'There is no coherent management structure for the service. At the national level, the role of the Home Office is so uncertain, and its powers so limited, that it might be truer to say that there are 105 local services, each run by a committee of magistrates. But the local structure is just as confused, with 285 justices' clerks enjoying a semi-autonomous status, under committees which are fundamentally ill-suited to the task of management. It is impossible to locate clear management responsibility or accountability anywhere in the structure.' The Scrutiny proposed a radical solution, that the service be restructured as a single national service, operated as an executive agency.

In December 1991 it was announced that as from 1 April 1992 ministerial responsibility for the magistrates' courts would be transferred from the Home Office to the Lord Chancellor's Department (LCD). On that day, the LCD took over responsibility for their finance, organisation and management. But the Government rejected the proposal that had been canvassed by the Le Vay Scrutiny Report of a national executive agency to run the courts. The December 1991 announcement stated that magistrates' courts would continue to be a locally based service. There would however be a new national inspectorate to improve efficiency. Also a local chief executive would take over the administrative responsibilities of the clerk to the justices. The announcement also said that a new Junior Minister from the House of Commons would be established within his Department. The Home Secretary would retain responsibility for criminal law and procedure.

The details of the Government's plans for the magistrates' courts were presented in February 1992 in a White Paper ('A New Framework for Local Justice', Cm 1829, 1992). The White Paper stated, inter alia, that the number of magistrates' courts committees would be reduced from 105 to 50 or 60, that the committees would have a maximum of 12 members supported by a corporate management team of senior staff, that non-magistrates could be co-opted and that the pay of court clerks would be related to performance. (See further *Law Society's Gazette*, 4 March 1992, p 4.)

From 1992/93 magistrates' courts have had to work on cash-limited budgets on the basis of a formula: 60 per cent based on completed caseload, 25 per cent based on effectiveness of fine enforcement, 10 per cent based on the throughput of cases, 5 per cent based on the quality of service (as measured by such things as numbers of chairs or telephones).

The scheme was announced by the Home Office in October 1991. It was severely criticised by the Magistrates' Association, the Justices' Clerks Society, the Law Society and the Bar. See, for instance, *Law Society's Gazette*, 23 October 1991, p 7.

The Magistrates' Courts Service Inspectorate was established on a non-statutory basis in autumn 1993 The chief function of the inspectorate is to carry out a rolling programme of efficiency and effectiveness inspections of the administration and management of all services provided by magistrates' courts committees.

In December 1993 the Government introduced in the House of Lords the Police and Magistrates' Courts Bill to implement the White Paper of February 1992. For months prior to the introduction of the Bill there had been skirmishing between the LCD on the one hand, and opponents of the threatened legislation led by the Magistrates' Association and the Justices' Clerks Society. When the Bill was published the criticism became even fiercer. Opposition was focussed in particular on the provisions that appointment of chairmen of magistrates' courts committees and renewal of contracts for justices' clerks would require the approval of the Lord Chancellor; fixed term contracts and performance related pay for clerks; the introduction of the new management tier of chief justices' clerks as line managers for justices' clerks; and the fear that concern about budgets would affect the advice given by clerks in regard to judicial decision making.

On the Second Reading debate in the House of Lords the opponents of these provisions in the Bill included Lord Taylor, the Lord Chief Justice. He took particular exception to the threat to the independence of court clerks both in the advice they gave magistrates and in the exercise of judicial functions in their own right. They already had power to grant adjournments, to renew bail, to extend the time allowed to pay fines and to grant or refuse legal aid. They had important responsibilities under the Children Act 1989–see below p 27. New powers were to be devolved on them. 'It is absolutely fundamental', he said, 'that nobody providing legal directions or advice to a tribunal of fact, or who is taking decisions which affect the rights or liabilities of parties to proceedings, should be or appear to be susceptible to outside influences of any kind.' (House of Lords, *Hansard*, 18 January 1994, col 476.) The Bill, he thought, infringed this principle. The Lord Chancellor was to have power to specify the terms of the contract between the clerk and his employing committee. The White Paper foreshadowed the hidden agenda which included fixed term contracts and performance related pay. They might be useful tools in a purely managerial context 'but in a judicial context, or where there exists a judicial element, they can have no place' (*ibid*).

The Lord Chief Justice also took exception to the provision that each area committee should appoint their chief justices' clerk from a list approved by the Lord Chancellor. This new official who would manage the justices' clerks in his area was to be capable of exercising any of the functions of a clerk and to have the duty to 'promote discussions relating to the law, practice and procedure' among the clerks for whom he was responsible. Lord Taylor said he found that 'a chilling phrase'. Asserting that this was not a threat to judicial independence was not good enough. How could litigants have confidence, for instance, that applications for adjournments or applications for legal aid would be dealt with on their merits rather than in the light of the economic considerations of through-put of cases or overall budgetting?

In the face of the formidable weight of criticism, the Government had to amend the Bill. The effect of the amendments was that chairmen of magistrates' courts committees continue to be appointed by members of the committee without requiring the approval of the Lord Chancellor, the terms of contract between the chief justices' clerk or justices' clerks and their committee is left to local discretion and the Lord Chancellor therefore has no power to require that they be for fixed terms or that remuneration be related to performance, and the renewal of appointments of chief justices' clerks and justices' clerks does not require the approval of the Lord Chancellor.

(However, their initial appointment does require his approval.) The title 'chief justices' clerk' was changed to 'justices' chief executive'. The chief executive must be legally qualified but he only has power to act as a justices' clerk if so appointed by the magistrates' courts committee. He reports to, and is employed by, the committee.

The Act received the Royal Assent in July 1994 Under the provisions of the Act and the regulations, amalgamations of magistrates' courts committees (MCCs) can be required by the Lord Chancellor providing he has gone through a required procedure of consultation (s 69); MCCs have a membership of up to twelve magistrates plus two members co-opted by the committee or appointed by the Lord Chancellor (s 70); MCCs appoint their own chairman (s 72); MCCs are 'responsible for the efficient and effective administration of the magistrates' courts for their area' (s 73); the Lord Chancellor can give directions to MCCs requiring them to meet specified standards of performance (s 73)–for instance in regard to provision made for the disabled or relating to probity in the handling of public money. The Act also states that when exercising legal functions a justices' clerk 'shall not be subject to the direction of the magistrates' courts committee, the justices' chief executive or any other person' and a member of the staff of a magistrates' courts committee shall likewise not be subject to direction by the committee or of the justices' chief executive (s 78). The inspectorate was placed on a statutory basis (ss 86–87). The Audit Committee can undertake efficiency studies at the request of a MCC (s 89).

3. PROBLEMS OF TRIAL COURTS' ORGANISATION

(a) The allocation of cases between higher and lower trial courts–criminal cases

Historically there were three criminal courts: assize courts, quarter sessions courts and magistrates' courts. The judges began to go out on assize to hear criminal cases from the early part of the 12th century. In 1361 a statute provided that justices of the peace were required to keep the peace and to arrest and punish offenders. The following year a further statute required them to meet four times a year–from which the origin of Quarter Sessions Courts is derived. In times of crisis such as the Wars of the Roses in the 15th century and the Civil War in the 17th century, when it was not possible to assemble the justices at Quarter Sessions, they started to sit to hear cases out of sessions without a jury. At first this was done without authority, but by the end of the 16th century powers of summary jurisdiction were conferred on these meetings, which came to be called Petty Sessions.

Until the middle of the 19th century there were only two categories of offence: those triable on indictment at either assizes or quarter sessions, and those triable only summarily by magistrates. From 1847 onwards, however, the legislature gradually gave magistrates power also to deal with various categories of indictable offence. In 1847 their powers of sentence were three months' imprisonment or a fine of £3. Today the maximum is six months' imprisonment or a fine of £5,000. The Criminal Justice Act 1982, Part III, established a system of grading of offences which had five scale levels. Under the 1991 Criminal Justice Act the actual figures were altered: Level 5 up to £5,000; Level 4 to £2,500; Level 3 to £1,000; Level 2 to £500; Level 1 to £200.

The right to have trial by jury

It is widely believed that the defendant's right to claim trial by jury in more serious cases dates back to Magna Carta. This is a misconception. In fact the defendant was first given a right to claim trial by jury in the higher court by the 1879 Summary Jurisdiction Act. It applied to all offences carrying a maximum sentence of more than three months' imprisonment. Today, as will be seen, the right exists in relation to all 'either-way' offences which make up some 80 per cent of all cases sent to trial in crown courts. But if the defendant opts for summary trial (as most do), the court retains the right to send the case for trial. (For detailed guidance to magistrates as to how to exercise their discretion see *Practice Note* [1990] 3 All ER 979, also printed in *New Law Journal*, 2 November 1990, p 1534.)

Where several defendants are charged with either-way offences, each defendant has an individual right of election. If one elects for trial at the crown court, this does not mean that the others can be forced to have a crown court trial. (*Nicholls v Brentwood Justices* [1991] 3 All ER 359, HL.)

The question of the allocation of cases between the higher and the lower criminal court has now been on the political agenda for many years. From the perspective of government it has been fuelled mainly by a wish to reduce the cost of criminal proceedings. In 1993 the Runciman Royal Commission on Criminal Justice stated that the Home Office estimated that the average cost of a contested case in the crown court was some £13,500 as against £1,500 in the magistrates' court and the cost of a guilty plea case was £2,500 as against £500 in the magistrates' court–see Report, 1993, Cm 2263, p 5, para 18

The James Committee   In 1979 the issue was explored by the James Committee, whose report (*The Distribution of Criminal Business between the Crown Court and Magistrates' Courts*, 1975, Cmnd 6323) recommended the transfer of substantial categories of work to the lower court. The Committee was not asked to consider whether the division between higher and lower courts should be continued and it therefore assumed that it would. It did, however, consider the criteria which should determine whether an offence ought to be tried at one or the other level. The primary, though not the only criterion, it thought, was its seriousness in the eyes of the community. It would be impracticable to categorize offences by reference to their gravity in the mind of the defendant since that would vary from person to person. The Committee said there should continue to be offences which were so serious that they should be triable only on indictment 'because the offences are so serious that trial on indictment is necessary in order to signify the gravity with which society regards them' (para 43). At the other end of the scale there were many offences for which the elaborate procedures and expense of trial on indictment would not be justified. But between these two categories it thought there should be an intermediate category of offences triable either way.

The Committee considered a variety of ways for determining the level of court for a trial of offences triable either way. It thought the defendant's right to elect for trial by jury should be retained. It was only used in about a tenth of the cases in which it could be exercised, but it was widely regarded as important both by defendants and by those who represented them.

If the defendant opted for trial summarily, the magistrates should, however, have the right to send the case for trial at the higher level– having first heard representations from the prosecution. These proposals were implemented in the Criminal Law Act 1977.

The James Committee also made proposals for the reallocation of cases. Some of them carrying no right of summary trial should, it thought, be put into the intermediate category of offences triable either way. This should apply, for instance, to burglary in a dwelling where force or deception was used to gain entry, unlawful sexual intercourse with a girl under 16, bigamy, causing death by reckless or dangerous driving and forgery and perjury other than in judicial proceedings. These recommendations also were implemented in the Criminal Law Act 1977.

The Committee proposed, further, that some offences previously triable either summarily or on indictment should become summary-only offences. This it said should apply, for instance, to all drink-driving offences, using threatening or insulting words or behaviour under s 5 of the Public Order Act, homosexual soliciting, and theft of amounts under £20 or criminal damage where the value of the damage did not exceed £100. The Government accepted all these recommendations and they were included in the Bill. But the proposals to make small theft and small criminal damage cases triable only summarily provoked great opposition, and the Government eventually dropped the proposal from the Bill. The Committee's other recommendations for making offences triable only summarily were implemented in the 1977 Act and in 1980 (in the Magistrates' Courts Act, s 22 and Sch 2) criminal damage cases involving amounts under £200 became triable only summarily.

The process of transferring cases to the summary-only category continued. In the Criminal Justice Act 1988, criminal damage cases became summary-only if they involved sums of under £2,000 and driving while disqualified, taking a motor vehicle without authority, and common assault and battery were all reduced to this category. The £2,000 limit for summary-only criminal damage cases was raised to £5,000 by the Criminal Justice and Public Order Act 1994.

A Consultation Paper produced by the Home Office in 1986 again raised for consideration the controversial question of whether small theft cases should be transferred to the summary-only category. A survey had shown that cases of theft and handling of goods worth less than £50 constituted 10 per cent of the crown court's case load and 8.8 per cent of court time ('The Distribution of Business between the Crown Court and Magistrates' Courts', Home Office, 1986, para 21). The proposal floated in the Consultation Paper was that there should be a statutory presumption that indictable offences should be tried summarily but trial on indictment would be available 'where special circumstances made the offence one of exceptional gravity' (*ibid*, para 27). It would be for the magistrates to decide this question. There might also be a case for allowing a person with no prior conviction for dishonesty to elect for trial on indictment for an offence of that character.

The proposal again ran into considerable opposition and in the end the Government decided not to pursue it. (See House of Lords, *Hansard*, 19 November 1987, col 309.) But the Home Office returned to the issue in 1991 in its evidence to the Runciman Royal Commission on Criminal Justice and suggested that small theft cases should become summary only.

In 1990 the Lord Chief Justice issued *Practice Note (offences triable either way: mode of trial)* [1990] 3 All ER 979 to assist magistrates in making the mode of trial decision. The court should never make its decision on grounds of convenience or expedition. The accused's prior record was irrelevant. 'In general, except where otherwise stated, either way offences should be tried summarily unless the court considers that the particular case has one of the features set out in the following pages [relating to named offences] *and* that its sentencing powers are insufficient.' This was intended to increase the proportion of cases dealt with summarily but it did not have a great impact.

The Runciman Royal Commission on Criminal Justice (1993, Cm 2263, pp 85–89) recommended a radical change by proposing that the defendant should no longer have a right to demand trial by jury in either way offences. Instead, he should have a right only to *ask* for crown court trial. If the prosecution agreed that would be sufficient. If the prosecution disagreed, the matter would be decided by the magistrates after hearing representations from both sides. The magistrates' decision should be guided by statutory indications as to what factors should be taken into account. These should include the gravity of the offence, the defendant's prior record, if any, the complexity of the case, and the effect of conviction and the likely sentence on the defendant.

The main reasons that led the Commission to this unanimous recommendation were:

(1) The decision as to whether a case properly belongs in the higher or the lower court is one that should be made by the system not by the defendant. In regard to indictable only and summary only offences the decision was made by the legislature. In regard to either way offences it would be more rational that the decision be made by the court than by the defendant.

(2) Many defendants chose crown court trial because statistically juries acquitted more often than magistrates. But the defendant should no more have the right to choose the court that gave him a better chance of an acquittal than to choose a lenient judge.

(3) The great majority of those who asked for crown court trial in either way offences in fact eventually pleaded guilty. (The proportion was nearly 75% not 83% as wrongly stated in the Commission's Report, p 86, para 7.)

(4) These cases of last minute guilty pleas in the crown court clogged up the system, caused additional cost in preparation of cases that in the event were wasted, resulted in witnesses being brought needlessly to court, and added to the numbers in prison.

(5) According to Home Office research,[6] half of those who elected for trial by crown court did so in the mistaken belief that if convicted the sentence would be lighter. In fact when samples were matched judges were three times as likely to impose immediate custody and sentences were on average two and a half times as long. Overall, judges imposed seven times as much custody as on comparable cases in the magistrates' courts.

(6) The same research showed that one third of the defendants in the sample who elected crown court trial would, in retrospect, have preferred to have been dealt with at a magistrates' court.

(7) The research also showed that in over 60 per cent of cases in which the magistrates declined jurisdiction, the crown court imposed a sentence that would have been within the power of the magistrates' to impose.

6   C Hedderman and D Moxon, *Magistrates' Court or Crown Court? Mode of Trial Decisions*, HMSO, 1992, Home Office Research Study, No 125.

(8) The objection that justice in the magistrates' courts was inferior to that in the crown court was not a reason to preserve the defendant's right to insist on jury trial. Magistrates handled over 90 per cent of all criminal cases and 'should be trusted to handle cases fairly' (*ibid*, p 88, para 18).

This proved to be the most controversial of all the 352 recommendations made by the Runciman Royal Commission. Defence of the accused's right to trial by jury aroused strong emotion. Critics of the Commission's proposal included the Bar, the Law Society and the Lord Chief Justice. The Lord Chief Justice's objection was principally that the Commission's recommendation would lead to 'two-tier' justice: that is jury trial for those with no record and the most reputation to lose, but magistrates' trial for recidivists.

For two years the Government gave no indication of its view regarding the Royal Commission's proposal. Then, in July 1995, it published a Consultation Document *Mode of Trial*.

The Consultation Document first set out the statistical background. The proportion of cases triable either way which were sent to the crown court for trial had fluctuated. (It went from 15% in 1980 to 23% in 1987 but then dropped to 17% in 1992.) The actual numbers had also fluctuated. (59,600 in 1980, 93,100 in 1987, 73,800 in 1992.) The proportion which went to the crown court because the magistrates declined jurisdiction had risen significantly. (In 1987 these cases were 47% of either way offences that went to the crown court. In 1991 they were 64%, in 1992, 63% and in 1993, 65%.) The document stated (para 2): 'This increase in the number of committals to the crown court has contributed to an increase in the remand and the sentenced population and has had substantial resource implications for the police, the Crown Prosecution Service, other prosecutors, the courts and the legal aid fund.'

The Consultation Document then canvassed three options. One was the recommendation made by the Runciman Royal Commission considered above. The second was statutory reclassification of either way offences to summary-only. Thus reclassification to summary-only status of thefts of under £100 could divert about 9,000 cases from the crown court each year. But there were powerful arguments for permitting a defendant who faced loss of reputation on conviction for theft to retain the right to trial by jury. An appendix set out ten other offences that could be candidates for reclassification. In aggregate the ten offences accounted for about one per cent of the total number of offenders sentenced at the crown court in 1992 for indictable and either way non-motoring offences. The one involving most cases by far (444 convictions in 1992) was possession of an offensive weapon. In 1992, 89 per cent of crown court sentences for that offence were within magistrates' court limits and 83 per cent of those sentences were non-custodial. The crown court imposed sentences of more than six months' custody in only 47 instances, and of more than one year in only nine. But, the Consultation Document suggested, it might be thought to be inappropriate for the maximum sentence for the offence to be reduced from two years to six months' imprisonment which was the maximum that could be imposed by magistrates.

The third option canvassed was a new procedural device of requiring defendants to enter a plea *before* the mode of trial decision. A plea could not be entered when magistrates decided to commit for trial. If this rule were changed and the defendant pleaded guilty, the magistrates would deal with sentencing unless they considered their sentencing powers were insufficient, in which case they would transfer the case for sentence only.

The research by Hedderman and Moxon (see above) had found that nearly three-quarters (73%) of defendants who had been dealt with at the crown court because magistrates' declined jurisdiction, would, if they had had a choice, have chosen to be dealt with by the magistrates. A further 4 per cent had no preference as between crown court and magistrates' court.

Hedderman and Moxon had also found that about two-thirds of defendants committed by magistrates reported that they were ready to plead guilty at the first opportunity available to them. This suggested that, if the defendant in such cases could enter a plea at the magistrates' court, some 25,000 defendants now dealt with at the crown court might have been willing to plead guilty at the magistrates' courts and be sentenced there or have their case transferred to the crown court for sentence only.

Early guilty pleas in the magistrates' court would also be encouraged by sentence reduction for an early guilty plea first recognised in statute by the Criminal Justice and Public Order Act 1994, s 48–see p 259 below. The most recent Magistrates' Association Sentencing Guidelines issued in September 1993 advised magistrates that a timely plea of guilty might be regarded as a mitigating factor for which a sentencing discount of about one third might be given.

The Consultation Document ended by drawing attention to the fact that retaining more cases in magistrates' courts would produce significant savings for the police, the Crown Prosecution Service, courts administration and the legal aid budget. But it would also benefit the quality of justice–cases in the magistrates' courts were usually heard sooner, the trial was usually shorter and the process was less daunting. 'Consequently, victims, witnesses (both civilian and police) and defendants would be put to less inconvenience and stress.' (para 28).

Views were sought by October 1995, but in November the Government introduced in the House of Lords its Criminal Procedure and Investigations Bill. Section 49(1) of the Act, adding a new s 17A to the Magistrates' Courts Act 1980 adopted a modified version of the last of the three options. But rather than the defendant being required to enter a plea before the mode of trial decision, he was to be *invited* to indicate his plea. (See pp 259–60 below.) There was nothing in the Bill to implement the Royal Commission's recommendation to take the decision of mode of trial in either way offences away from the defendant.

(b) The allocation of cases between higher and lower trial courts– civil cases

The problem of the proper relationship between the higher and lower level of civil court has been a topic of debate for many years. It raises the preliminary question whether it is actually necessary to have two levels of trial court or whether it would not be better to amalgamate the High Court and the county court. Assuming the two levels of court are retained, the second question is by what criteria is work allocated to each level.

The question of a possible merger between the High Court and the county court was considered as long ago as 1969 in the Report of the Beeching Royal Commission on Assizes and Quarter Sessions. The Royal Commission also considered a proposal from the Law Society that all civil proceedings should begin in common form and that at an appropriate stage an officer of the court would decide whether it should be heard by the High Court or the county court. It concluded that it could not give effect to either proposal because to have done so would have required a fusion of the rules of procedure and the study of this question would seriously have delayed the report (*Report of the Royal Commission on Assizes and Quarter Sessions*, Cm 4153, 1969, para 205). Although the Beeching Commission did not recommend a merger of the two levels of civil court, it did propose a more flexible use of judge power.

1969–1988

After the Beeching Commission's report, the following changes altered the position somewhat:

(1) Judges were flexibly deployed throughout the system. High Court judges, circuit judges and recorders were made judges of the crown court–even Lords Justices of Appeal may sit there if requested so to do by the Lord Chancellor. Civil cases in the county court are tried by circuit judges but they can be asked by the Lord Chancellor to sit as judges of the High Court for civil business. Recorders sit mainly in the crown court but they can be asked to sit in the county court and occasionally even in the High Court.

(2) The jurisdiction of the county courts was extended in rapid stages from £500 to £5,000, which covered the great bulk of cases tried in the Queen's Bench Division. Up to the level of £5,000 the High Court and the county court had concurrent jurisdiction. In 1991 the £5,000 limit was abolished.

(3) The Supreme Court Act 1981 provided that cases could be transferred from the High Court to the county court or from the county court to the High Court not simply as before by consent of the parties, but on the court's own motion. (The Act said (Sch 3, s 75A(1)) that a High Court judge could order a transfer if he considered that the claim was within the jurisdiction of the county court, the proceedings 'are not likely to raise an important question of law or fact and are suitable for determination by a county court'. A considerable proportion of personal injury cases set down for trial in the High Court were so transferred.) Conversely, a county court judge could order a transfer to the High Court where the claim was outside the county court's jurisdiction or the court considered that some important question of law or fact was likely to arise–Sch 3, s 75C(1). (In such a case, the court could award damages in excess of the maximum jurisdiction of the county court.)

(4) The County Court Rules (CCR) which came into force in 1981 reduced the differences in procedure between county courts and the High Court. (The chief draftsman of the new Rules wrote in 1983 that it was hoped that this major revision would 'take the courts well into the twenty-first century and perhaps pave the way for the eventual amalgamation of the county courts and the High Court' (RCL Gregory, *Civil Justice Quarterly*, January 1983, p 6).)

The Bar has always in the past objected strenuously to every increase in the jurisdiction of the county court–no doubt because in the county court it shared the right to appear as an advocate (called the 'right of audience') with solicitors whereas in the High Court until the 1990s it enjoyed a monopoly over the right of audience. (On this sustained campaign, see B Abel-Smith and R Stevens, *Lawyers and the Courts* (Heinemann, 1963), pp 33, 34, 36, 48, 83, 84, 92, 233–4. On the present position regarding the right of audience in the higher courts see below, pp 564–69)

Civil Justice Review

The *Final Report of the Civil Justice Review* was published in June 1988 (Cm 394).[7]
Its conclusions were:

(1) The High Court and the county court should remain separate (para 116).

(2) There should be no upper limit for the jurisdiction of the county court (para 125).

(3) There should be a lower limit of £25,000 for cases in the High Court. All cases below that should be heard in the county court unless they involved public law or specialist problems, or were cases of unusual complexity (para 124).

(4) Cases involving amounts between £25,000 and £50,000 should be heard in either the High Court or the county court (para 124).

(5) All personal injury cases should start in the county court (para 155).

(6) Registrars should be given the title of district judge and have their jurisdiction increased to £5,000.

Courts and Legal Services Act 1990

The Lord Chancellor announced his broad acceptance of these proposals in April 1989 and they were in fact implemented by the Courts and Legal Services Act 1990 and the High Court and County Courts Jurisdiction Order 1991 (SI 1991/724)[8] which came into force on 1 July 1991.

The effect of the changes was that cases are allocated for trial according to substance, importance and complexity. Generally, cases involving amounts below £25,000 are tried in the county court; those involving amounts above £50,000 in the High Court; and amounts in between in either court depending on the criteria and judicial availability.

The 1991 Order abolished the financial limits on county court jurisdiction over many actions including ordinary actions in contract and tort (art 2). Cases which include a claim for damages in respect of personal injuries must now be started in the county court unless the claim is worth more than £50,000 (art 5). If the High Court thinks that the person bringing the proceedings knew or ought to have known that the action should have been brought in the county court, the court can order that the proceedings be struck out. (The 1990 Act, s 40–for exploration of this provision see D Brethwick, 'Court in a Trap? *Law Society's Gazette*, 13 April 1994, p 34.)

An action involving an amount under £25,000 should be tried in the county court unless:

(1) The court considers that under the new criteria it should be transferred to the High Court. The criteria (set out in art 7(5)) are:

   (a) the financial substance of the action, including any counter-claim;

   (b) whether the action is otherwise important and, in particular, whether it raises questions of importance to persons who are not parties or questions of general public interest;

   (c) the complexity of the facts, legal issues, remedies or procedures involved;

7 For an account of the Civil Justice Review Body's *General Issues* Consultation Paper 1987 see 6th edition of this work, pp 34–37.

8 See also the County Court (Amendment No 2) Rules 1991, SI 1991/1126 and (Amendment No 3) Rules 1991, SI 1991/1328 and the Rules of the Supreme Court (Amendment No 2) 1991, SI 1991/1329.

(d) whether the transfer is likely to result in a more speedy trial of the action–but no action should be transferred on the grounds of speedy trial alone.

(2) It having started in the High Court, it considers that under the new criteria it should stay there.

Actions with a value that falls into the middle range or which have no quantifiable value can be tried in either jurisdiction.

The 'value of an action' is defined by art 9 as the amount which the plaintiff reasonably expects to recover.

For further details see *Law Society's Gazette*, 26 June 1991, p 18; *Civil Justice Quarterly*, October 1991, p 282. For the transfer rules see *Practice Direction* [1991] 3 All ER 349.

The jurisdiction of registrars which was formerly limited to £1,000, was increased by the 1990 Act to £5,000 and their title was changed to district judge. But important or difficult cases are listed for hearing by a circuit judge rather than a district judge. (See *Practice Direction* [1991] 3 All ER 722.)

For a sharply critical and pessimistic assessment of the reform seven months on, see Anne Grosskurth, 'Can the County Courts Cope' *Legal Action*, March 1992, p 7.

The Woolf Report

The origin of the Woolf Inquiry on civil justice (see p 1 above) was the Lord Chancellor's request to Lord Woolf to remove unnecessary differences between the procedural rules of the High Court and the county court. Lord Woolf got the Lord Chancellor's approval for expansion of this original remit to a much wider brief.

In his Interim Report in June 1995 Lord Woolf proposed that the rules of the High Court and the county court should basically be the same (and that he would produce a draft of a single code of rules for High Court and county court cases), that an action could be commenced at any court and that the court rather the parties should have the responsibility for allocating the case to the appropriate track. He suggested (p 73, para 4), that these recommendations, together with others he made as to case management, 'will mean that the question of whether a case is a High Court or a county court case will be of reduced significance'. (On the distinction between Lord Woolf's fast track and multi track cases see pp 31, 41 below.)

The distinction between High court and county court would be of continuing importance then in relation to different rights of audience as between barristers and solicitors (on which see pp 565–69 below), judicial review, the grant of remedies such as Mareva and Anton Piller injunctions (see pp 65–66 below), and defamation actions. There are also differences in the methods of enforcement of judgments in the two courts.

He had considered whether to recommend the unification or amalgamation of the two courts:

Interim Report of the Woolf *Inquiry into Civil Justice, Access to Justice*, 1995, pp 73–75

6. I have therefore considered whether to recommend the unification of the two courts. This would be an additional step in reducing the complexity of the system. It would be an advance since it would produce a single, vertically integrated court. However, very much the same result could be achieved if the movement towards aligning the jurisdiction of the county courts

and the High Court was continued and the powers of Circuit judges were to be extended. This would make it generally unnecessary to identify the criteria which mark the boundary between the jurisdiction.

7. Nothing I have said so far is intended to suggest that the two tiers of the judiciary should be assimilated. On the contrary, my recommendations are intended to reaffirm the principle that High Court judges, and only High Court judges, should deal with the most demanding cases in the system.

8. I accept that for constitutional reasons it is essential that the separate status of the High Court judge is maintained and not undermined in any way. Although it is not impossible to preserve distinct judicial tiers in a single court (as, for example, in the Crown Court), this would become more difficult if the High Court itself were merged in a single court.

9. However, the further alignment of the jurisdictions of the High Court and the county courts should continue, both as to subject matter (the obvious example is defamation) and as to powers. For example, the restrictions on Circuit judges granting Mareva and Anton Piller injunctions should be removed.

10. I should make it clear that I am not proposing total alignment. There would be no point, for example, in extending the power to hear small claims to High Court judges or to confer on the High Court the various statutory jurisdictions of the county courts. Conversely, it would not be appropriate to give county courts general jurisdiction over judicial reviews (except for certain categories which I will consider further in my final report).

11. It is more appropriate and more effective for cases to be allocated to the correct level for trial as a result of a judicial examination of all the circumstances of the particular case, taking into account any general guidance which has been issued as part of the management of the case, than for the case to be allocated as a result of some technical rule as to jurisdiction.

12. There are difficulties in amalgamating the High Court and the county courts which go beyond my remit. In particular, there is the problem of rights of audience, which is the subject of a separate statutory regime. I therefore do not suggest that the two courts should be unified. Instead, I seek to achieve the same benefits that would flow from the courts being unified by the recommendations elsewhere in this report.

13. The new unified rules will provide a common procedure for the conduct of civil business. A new, common approach to the handling of cases centred on the concept of judicial control and case management will introduce a strong unifying element into the way in which cases are handled by all the civil courts. This will be crucially reinforced by the appointment of the Head of Civil Justice, who will have overall responsibility for the management and organisation of civil business throughout England and Wales at every level in the system. The approach will be reinforced by a partnership between judges and administrators at key levels throughout the civil courts system.

14. The new multi-track will itself straddle the High Court and the county courts. Within it cases will be handled by High Court judges, Circuit judges, Masters and district judges. The courts, through the procedural judges, will have responsibility for ensuring that cases are dealt with at the appropriate level.

15. Out of London, the divide between the two courts has in any event become indistinct. The increasing use of the Chancery and Mercantile jurisdiction of the High Court in key centres means that heavy cases are often heard locally by Circuit judges. There will no longer be any reason to distinguish physically between the High Court and county courts outside London. Already outside London, the High Court and the county courts at the larger centres share the same buildings. There is at present, however, a separation of the administration which will become unnecessary when the new unified rules introduce a common procedure. I recommend that they should share the same administration, although there are many county courts where High Court business is most unlikely to be heard.

16. In London the situation is different. The Royal Courts of Justice are the permanent seat of the most complex and specialised litigation and of the two divisions of the Court of Appeal. They are administered separately from the Central London County Court, where the heaviest

county court litigation is dealt with. I see no reason for any change in these arrangements. Nonetheless, the relationship between the Central London County Court and the Royal Courts of Justice should be as close as possible.

(c) The distribution of family law work

Jurisdiction over family law matters is shared between the High Court, the county court and the magistrates' courts. For many years these arrangements were the subject of serious criticism. An example was the Finer Report over twenty years ago (*One Parent Families*, Cmnd 5629, 1974, pp 193–5).

Between 1974 and 1989 there were a variety of further initiatives, including two Consultation Papers issued by the Lord Chancellor's Department in 1983 and 1986 respectively. (For details see the 6th edition of this book, at pp 40–43.)

The Children Act 1989

In December 1988 Lord Mackay, Lord Chancellor, introduced the Children's Bill, which he said would make significant reforms to the handling of cases involving children and effectively usher in family courts. The Government had decided against the introduction of a separate family court. It was not 'practical or desirable to throw over existing machinery wholesale'. Instead the problem would be dealt with 'in ordered stages', linking reform of the courts' jurisdiction and procedures with reform of the law. The Bill became law in 1989 and the Children Act 1989 was implemented in October 1991.

The Act did not provide for a single point of entry for all family-law cases. But it did provide for concurrent jurisdiction between the magistrates' courts, the county courts and the High Court. Child care cases all start in the magistrates' courts and most are determined there. But criteria relating to the weight, complexity and urgency guide magistrates in selecting the most appropriate court.

There is a specialist cadre of some 50 circuit judges for family work in the county courts who are specially trained. The Judicial Studies Board undertook a series of 17 one-day seminars throughout the country to educate more than 1,000 judges at all levels. They were encouraged to abandon traditional attitudes–including traditional dress by not wearing their wigs.

There are 94 'family hearing centres' to handle, for instance, most of the 2,800 cases previously dealt with in the High Court as wardship proceedings. Fifty of the 94 family hearing centres are also designated as 'care centres', which hear the child care cases transferred to those centres from the magistrates' courts.

All courts with divorce jurisdiction continued to deal with such cases, but work requiring the attention of a circuit judge was concentrated on the network of family hearing centres.

Family court service committees and family court business committees were set up to promote smooth implementation of the Act. Their task was to facilitate full liaison between the various courts and agencies involved in working with children.

The allocation of cases is dealt with in the Children (Allocation of Proceedings) Order 1991 (SI 1991/1677). For the rules regarding transfer of proceedings between High Court and county court see *Practice Direction* [1992] 3 All ER 151. The Children

Act rules distinguish between 'public law' and 'private law' proceedings. (Public-law applications are those made under Parts IV, V and s 25 of the Act; private-law applications are those made under Parts I and II.)

The Allocation of Proceedings Order specifies that, in general, public-law cases start in the magistrates' courts and sets out criteria by reference to which cases can be transferred either horizontally or vertically. In private-law cases the applicant has a choice of court, but such cases too can be transferred.

There are three criteria for transfer of public-law proceedings from magistrates' courts to higher courts:

(1) exceptional gravity, importance or complexity;
(2) consolidation with pending proceedings; and
(3) if the transfer is likely significantly to accelerate the decision, where delay would seriously prejudice the interests of the child.

For an article on the case law on this difficult issue see Paul Tain, 'Allocating Family Law Cases', *Solicitors' Journal*, 3 March 1995, p 192. The article comments on the gradual loss by magistrates to professional judges of the most interesting cases such that the resources of the 7,000 plus justices on the Family Panels are becoming an under-used resource.

If transfer is refused, any party can appeal to a nominated care district judge. If transfer is ordered, the complete file is sent to a 'care centre' county court. Each magistrates' court is linked to a particular 'care centre'. The district judge must consider whether the case should be further transferred to the High Court. Cases should be transferred to the High Court where this is appropriate and transfer would be in the interests of the child.

Private-law applications can be transferred up to county courts by magistrates' courts if the proceedings could be dealt with there more appropriately. County courts cannot transfer such cases down to magistrates' courts but can send them up to the High Court.

See further, *New Law Journal*, 6 September 1991, p 1194 and 11 October 1991, p 1368; and the special supplement to the *Solicitors' Journal*, 20 September 1991, p xiv.

4. THE TRIBUNAL SYSTEM

The work of the courts is supplemented by the large number of administrative tribunals in different fields. Tribunals alone sit for more days than the High Court and the county courts together. Indeed tribunals hear six times the number of contested cases tried by those courts. Tribunals cover a wide variety of issues, such as the allocation of school places for children, immigration, unfair dismissal, the discharge of patients detained under the Mental Health Act, social security, rents, rates and taxation.

There are sixty different types of administrative tribunal. To deal with some subjects there is only one actual tribunal, which, following the practice of the regular courts, is based in London. This is the case with the Air Transport Licensing Board, the Transport Tribunal, the Betting Levy Tribunal and the Performing Rights Tribunal. The Lands Tribunal, the Pensions Appeals Tribunal and the Social Commissioners of Income Tax sit in different parts of the country, the Lands Tribunal sitting as required and the special Commissioners making circuits. At the other extreme there are over 400 general commissioners of income tax, some 400 service committees dealing with complaints under the national Health Service, 163 local tribunals dealing with disputes under the national insurance scheme and appeals under the industrial injuries scheme. Some of these tribunals sit in the office of the department concerned, although the practice is discouraged. Others sit in separate offices acquired for the purpose or in rooms in the county court building.

The tribunals with the largest case-loads are: rent assessment committees; immigration adjudicators; industrial tribunals (dealing with unfair dismissal, equal pay, sex and race discrimination claims); valuation tribunals dealing with council tax and social security appeal tribunals. (See the Annual Report of the Council on Tribunals.)

An excellent early book on tribunals is Harry Street's *Justice in the Welfare State* (Stevens, 1968), which is easy to read and short. In the 1970s there were a number of significant works in this field. See especially JA Farmer, *Tribunals and Government* (Weidenfeld and Nicolson, 1974); G Ganz, *Administrative Procedures* (Sweet and Maxwell, 1974); RE Wraith and PG Hutchesson, *Administrative Tribunals* (Allen and Unwin, 1973); and Kathleen Bell *et al*, 'National Insurance Local Tribunals'. 3 *Journal of Social policy*, p 289, and 4 *Journal of Social Policy*, p I. See also Kathleen Bell, *Research Study on Supplementary Benefit Appeal Tribunals, Main Findings* (HMSO, 1975).

For a detailed and highly critical review of the performance of the Industrial Tribunals in sex discrimination and equal pay cases, see Alice M Leonard, *Judging Inequality* (Cobden Trust, 1987). For a brief description of the industrial tribunal system, see AA McFadyen, 'No Legal Aid for Representation before Industrial Tribunals', *Law Society's Gazette*, 21 March 1984, p 795. This makes the point that 'the industrial tribunal now has many similarities with civil court procedure, which include orders for further and better particulars, discovery, interlocutory hearings and cost rules and it has become complex'.

See also JUSTICE, *Industrial Tribunals* (1987). For an excellent study of representation in tribunals see Hazel and Yvette Genn, 'The Effectiveness of Representation at Tribunals', Lord Chancellor's Department, July 1989. See also WA Bogart, 'Courts and Tribunals', *Civil Justice Quarterly*, January 1989, p 7; DGT Williams, 'The Tribunal System–Its Future Control and Supervision', *Civil Justice Quarterly*, January 1990, p 27 and M Sayers and A Webb, 'Franks Revisited: A Model of the Ideal Tribunal', *ibid*, p 36.

CHAPTER 2

Pre-trial civil proceedings

This chapter deals with the problems of the pre-trial stages of a civil action which set the stage for the trial if there is one. There are two main reasons why the pre-trial stage of litigation is vital. One is that in the great majority of cases the proceedings never reach trial. Secondly, in the rare cases that go to trial, the outcome is usually determined by what has been achieved by way of collection and preparation of evidence in the pre-trial stage.

The subject of pre-trial process has been a subject of intense controversy for many years. In 1968 there was the report of the Winn Committee (Committee on Personal Injuries Litigation, 1968, Cmnd 369), which led to certain reforms. In the period 1985–88 there was the Civil Justice Review set in hand by the then Lord Chancellor, Lord Hailsham which again led to reforms.[1] In June 1995, publication of the Interim Report of Lord Woolf's Inquiry Access to Justice brought forward for discussion a whole raft of radical new proposals implementation of which would transform pre-trial civil process. (For a detailed account of the proposals in Lord Woolf's Interim Report see *Civil Justice Quarterly*, October 1995, pp 231–49.)

Lord Woolf's proposals contemplated dividing civil cases into three tracks–*small claims* dealt with under the existing procedure (see pp 303–06 below) but with a jurisdiction increased from £1,000 to £3,000, heard mainly by district judges; *fast track* cases where the amount in dispute is between £3,000 and £10,000 which would have a set pre-trial timetable of 20 to 30 weeks with a notification of the week of trial fixed at the outset, limited pre-trial procedure, a trial confined to no more than three hours, no oral evidence from experts and standard fixed costs, heard mainly by district judges but in some cases by circuit judges; and *multi track* cases, where there would be appropriate case management by the court usually including two pre-trial hearings. They would be heard by High Court judges or circuit judges.

In January 1996 Lord Woolf issued six Consultation Issues Papers on *fast track* cases, housing cases, multi-party actions, medical negligence cases, expert evidence and costs. Each, except that on costs, was prepared by a separate working group including practitioners and other relevant experts. That on costs consisted of a paper from Dr AAS Zuckerman of University College, Oxford. For the most part the

1 For a full account of its recommendations, see the thirty-page note in the *Civil Justice Quarterly*, 1988, pp 281–312. See also the reflections of a member of the Civil Justice Review formerly with the National Consumer Council: Richard Thomas,'Civil Justice Review–Treating Litigants as Consumers', *Civil Justice Quarterly*, January 1990, p 51.

Consultation Papers identified questions on which views were sought. Responses were requested by March.

Lord Woolf was due to publish the final part of his report on 26 July 1996. (For details see the weekly legal journals for the following week.) By then the only part of the Woolf proposals that had been implemented was the increase in jurisdiction in small claims cases to £3,000 which took place in January 1996. On 27 March 1996, before Lord Woolf published his final report, the Lord Chancellor said in a speech (to the Kent Law Society) that he intended to implement the Woolf proposals. (The writer is one of the critics of Lord Woolf's proposals.) For details of reaction to the Woolf proposals, see pp 96–98, below.

For basic reading on the subject of this chapter, see especially the 1986 Hamlyn Lectures given by Sir Jack Jacob QC published under the title: *The Fabric of English Civil Justice* (Sweet & Maxwell, 1987). For reference see N Andrews, *Principles of Civil Procedure* (Sweet & Maxwell, 1994).

1. TO WHAT EXTENT CAN ONE FIND OUT WHAT HAPPENED BEFORE THE ISSUE OF PROCEEDINGS?

One of the difficulties prior to the issue of proceedings is that it is often difficult to discover whether there is the basis for a provable claim unless one can speak to a vital witness, visit the site of the accident or study a report made, say, by a police officer or factory inspector.

The first question addressed here is whether one side can 'own' a potential witness in the sense of preventing or inhibiting the other side from speaking to the witness. Can someone who wishes to inquire of a witness be told the witness has already given a statement to 'the other side' and that he cannot speak to the inquirer?

(a) Is there any property in a witness?

The Law Society, *A Guide to the Professional Conduct of Solicitors*, 6th edn, 1993, pp 393–4

22.05 Interviewing witnesses

Principle
It is permissible for a solicitor acting for any party to interview and take statements from any witness or prospective witness at any stage in the proceedings, whether or not that witness has been interviewed or called as a witness by another party.

Commentary
1. This Principle stems from the fact that there is no property in a witness and applies both before and after the witness has given evidence at the hearing.

2. A solicitor must not, of course, tamper with the evidence of a witness or attempt to suborn the witness into changing evidence. Once a witness has given evidence, the case must be very unusual in which a solicitor acting for the other side needs to interview that witness without seeking to persuade the witness to change evidence.

3. A solicitor should be aware that in seeking to exercise the right to interview a witness who has already been called by the other side or who to the solicitor's knowledge is likely to be called by them, the solicitor may well be exposed to the suggestion that he or she has improperly tampered with the evidence. This may be so particularly where the witness subsequently changes his or her evidence. It is wise in these circumstances for such solicitor to offer to interview the witness in the presence of a representative of the other side.

4. In interviewing an expert witness or professional agent instructed by the other side there should be no attempt to induce the witness to disclose privileged information. In these circumstances also it would be wise to offer to interview the witness in the presence of the other solicitor or representative.

5. As a general rule, it is not improper for a solicitor to advise a witness from whom a statement is being sought that he or she need not make such statement. The advice that the solicitor should give must depend upon the client's interests and the circumstances of the case.

6. A solicitor must not, without leave of the court, or without the consent of counsel or solicitor for the other party, discuss the case with a witness whether or not the witness is the client, whilst the witness is in the course of giving evidence. This prohibition covers the whole of the relevant time including adjournments and weekends.

In practice, in civil cases solicitors are very chary about even approaching a witness associated with the other side for fear of running foul of the prohibition on tampering with the evidence. This is very different from the position for instance in the United States where, as will be seen, (p 70 below) there is a formal pre-trial procedure for taking statements from possibly adverse witnesses.

By contrast in criminal cases, both the prosecution and the defence may find it necessary to interview the same witnesses. It was recently held to have been contempt of court for the police deliberately to impede inquiries by a private investigator working for the defence who was trying to find potential alibi witnesses in a murder case. The accused's alibi was that he stayed overnight at a hostel with three 'travellers' known to him only by their first names. The police had asked the hostel management to ensure that the hostel staff not talk to the investigator. (*Connolly v Dale* [1996] QB 120.)

The rule that there is no property in a witness applies also to expert witnesses. This was established by the Court of Appeal in *Harmony Shipping Co SA v Davis* [1979] 3 All ER 177. The plaintiffs in an action approached a handwriting expert to advise on the authenticity of a document the genuineness of which was crucial to their case. The expert advised that the document was not genuine. Subsequently he was approached for advice by the other side. Not realizing that he had already advised the plaintiffs in the same case, he advised the defendants that the document was not genuine. Later he realized what had happened and told the defendants that he could not accept any further instructions in the matter from them. The defendants, who wanted him to testify as to the genuineness of the document, issued a subpoena requiring him to attend to give evidence. The plaintiffs tried to have the subpoena set aside on the ground that there was an express or implied contract that the expert would not advise both sides and that the defendants were therefore not able to call him.

The Court of Appeal unanimously rejected this contention. The court held that the rule that there was no property in a witness applied to experts as much as to witnesses of fact. The only difference was that an expert could not be required to give evidence about matters that were covered by legal professional privilege. Insofar as he had been told things in confidence by the solicitors, such information was privileged and could not be made the subject of testimony. But anything not covered by legal professional privilege was available to the defendants in the case as much as to the plaintiffs.

(b) Can the injured person inspect the premises or machinery where the accident occurred?

There is no *right* to inspect premises under someone else's control. Employers sometimes refuse permission to an injured employee or his legal representatives or an engineer or other expert to inspect the site to take photographs or to make investigations.

The Winn Committee in 1968 recommended that access should be obtainable on order of the court–subject to the proviso that in asking for such access the injured person should have to indicate in an open letter his own knowledge, however vague, of how the accident happened or that he had none if that was the case. This would avoid the danger that he would use the occasion of his visit to 'work up a case' (*Report of the Committee on Personal Injuries Litigation*, 1968, Cmnd 369, paras 179, 182–3).

Mr Robin Thompson (a prominent plaintiff's solicitor) in a strong Minority Report disagreed with the Committee's recommendation that the plaintiff be required to state his own knowledge in an open letter:

I am afraid that in my view such feelings show a completely wrong approach to this topic. On the one hand there is the defendant occupying premises or owning highly complicated machinery to which he has unlimited access. He is fully aware of any previous accidents and can have as many inspections by as many engineers as he sees fit, and he has all the advantages of management and technical expertise. The claimant on the other hand is not even to be allowed to arrange for his advisers to inspect where his accident occurred or the piece of machinery involved without disclosing in advance his case or the fact that he has no knowledge as to how this accident occurred. Why should he be required to do this? [*Minority Report*, para 64, pp 169–70.]

The Winn Committee's proposal was implemented in the Administration of Justice Act 1969, s 21. The relevant provision is now in the Supreme Court Act 1981, s 33(1), which provides that: 'On the application of any person in accordance with rules of court, the High Court shall, in such circumstances as may be specified in the rules, have the power to make an order providing for any one or more of the following matters, that is to say (a) the inspection . . . of property which appears to the court to be property which may become the subject matter of subsequent proceedings in the High Court or as to which any question may arise in any such proceedings'. The relevant rule is Rules of the Supreme Court (here 'RSC') Ord 29, r 2. This permits the court to make an order granting the right to inspect and for that purpose to enter any land or building in the possession of any party to the action.

The courts have had to pronounce in a few cases on whether, if the plaintiff wants such a right to inspect before issuing his statement of claim, he can be required to give an indication of his theory of what happened. In such cases the view taken is that this is appropriate. For a summary of the cases, see RL Denyer, 'Pre-Trial Inspection of Plant and Premises in Personal Injury Cases', *Law Society's Gazette*, 3 July 1985, p 1945.

See also Bernard C Cairns, 'Discovery and Preservation of Evidence under Inherent Jurisdiction', *Civil Justice Quarterly*, October 1985, pp 309, 311–19.

2. MOST CASES DO NOT REACH COURT

The majority of claims brought to solicitors are settled without proceedings ever being started. In cases where proceedings are started, the majority of cases are disposed of by settlement without any court judgment. There are no regular national statistics regarding this phenomenon but all the studies done confirm it.

The Coal Board told the Winn Committee that about 17 per cent of claims reached the stage of a writ, of which just under a quarter went to judgment (*Report of the Committee on Personal Injuries Litigation*, 1968, Cmnd 369, para 118). The London Passenger Transport Board told the Winn Committee that of about 5,000 claims a year, some 4,900 (98 per cent) were disposed of without proceedings. Of the 100 or so in which proceedings were started, only about a quarter went to judgment (*ibid*, para 116). Ten years later the Pearson Royal Commission stated that about 86 per cent of personal injury claims were settled without the issue of a writ, 11 per cent were disposed of after a writ was issued but before being set down for trial, 2 per cent between setting down and trial and a mere 1 per cent reached the courts. (*Report of the Royal Commission on Civil Liability and Compensation for Personal Injury*, 1978, Cmnd 7054-II, p 20.) The Cantley Committee in their report in 1979 stated: 'In round figures, for every 9,000 personal injury writs issued in London there are no more than about 300 judgments. Outside the personal injuries field, for every 100,000 writs issued in London there are fewer than 300 judgments after trial. The figures for District Registries are not dissimilar.' (*Report of the Personal Injuries Litigation Procedure Working Party*, 1979, Cmnd 7476, para 9.)

A court hearing is rare even in cases that result in a taxed bill (on taxation of bills see below pp 424–25). In a study of 664 personal injury cases based on bills taxed in 1973–4, it was found that there was no court hearing at all in 69 per cent. In a further 11 per cent the hearing was a pure formality, lasting only a few minutes, to tell the court about a settlement arrived at outside the door of the court. There was a real contest in only 19 per cent. (M Zander, 'The Costs of Litigation', *Guardian Gazette*, 25 June 1975, p 679).

But perhaps the fullest empirical evidence regarding the progress of claims came from the massive study of personal injury cases conducted by the Oxford Socio-Legal Centre (Don Harris et al, *Compensation and Support for Illness and Injury*, Clarendon Press, Oxford, 1984). The study was based on a huge national household survey which produced a random sample of 1,711 accident victims all of whom had suffered some impairment for at least two weeks. Of these, only 26 per cent had even considered claiming damages, 14 per cent had actually consulted a solicitor most of whom (12 per cent) actually got damages (Fig 2.1, p 26).

Where damages were obtained, the plaintiff negotiated his own settlement in nearly 8 per cent (14 out of 198 cases). Most of these settlements were for small sums (from £30 to £200), but a few were larger (£600, £700 and £940 in three road-accident cases and £2,000 for pneumoconiosis contracted by a miner). The authors commented that 'in comparison with our data on claimants who use solicitors, this group appears under-compensated' (p 82). In most of such cases the person had had no adequate advice.

A writ was issued in just under 40 per cent of the cases in which damages were obtained (p 112). There were only five cases which ended with a court hearing. This represented 2.7 per cent of the 182 cases in which damages were obtained; but only 0.2 per cent of the 1,711 accident cases in the sample.

There were 169 cases in which the amount of damages was known. In 104 the plaintiff accepted the first offer made, in 32 the second offer, in 23 the third offer. In six cases the plaintiff accepted the fourth or fifth offer (p 95). There was no evidence to support the hypothesis that the bigger the claim, the more negotiations, nor that the rejection of offers was explained by the seriousness of the case (pp 95–7).

The pressures on the plaintiff to settle are many. First, he faces the uncertainty as to whether he can prove the case–will his witnesses and other evidence establish the defendant's negligence? Secondly, can he establish the necessary causal relationship between the defendant's negligence and his injuries? Can he prove the full extent of his injuries or losses? What is the medical prognosis? How will a judge evaluate such imponderables as 'pain and suffering', the 'loss of ability to lead a normal life', loss of expectancy of life? To what extent, if any, will the defence be able to show contributory negligence on his part? How long will the matter drag on?

If the claimant is on legal aid, the lawyers' fees will be paid by the legal aid fund or the defendant. But if he is not, the lawyer may influence the plaintiff to accept an offer of damages plus legal costs rather than risk an action which may fail, in which case the lawyer will have to ask the plaintiff to pay his fees. There is, in other words, a potential conflict of interest between the lawyer and his client. (And see now conditional fees, pp 469–76 below.)

Those who delayed in consulting a solicitor for more than six months had decidedly less success in getting damages (p 105). The mean delay between the date of the accident and receipt of damages was a little over 19 months and the median was 16 months. Three-quarters of the settlements were reached within two years and 90 per cent within three years.

There were eighty cases in the sample in which a claim was made and then abandoned. The reasons given by claimants and the proportion of cases in which the reason was advanced were:

	%
Problems over obtaining evidence	45
Victim's own fault caused accident	18
Fear of legal expenses	16
Denial of liability by defendant	15
Problems with trade union over case	15
Problems with solicitors over case (incompetence)	8
Delay	6
The bother or trouble of pursuing claim	6
Fear of affecting continuing relationship	6
Problems with insurance	5
Injuries not serious enough	5
No one was at fault	4
No loss of income	3
Satisfied with industrial injury benefits	3

(Table 3.12, p 114)

On the process of negotiating a settlement, see further J Phillips and K Hawkins, 'Some Economic Aspects of the Settlement Process: A Study of Personal Injury Claims', *Modern Law Review*, 1976, p 497; and Hazel Genn, *Hard Bargaining: A Study of the Process of Out of Court Settlement In Personal Injury Actions 1987* (OUP, 1988).

For a powerful argument that settlement is not necessarily a good thing, see Owen Fiss, 'Against Settlement', *Yale LJ*, 1984, p 1073.

Legal privileges that promote settlement

Negotiations designed to explore the possibility of settlement are assisted by legal privileges. These were described over thirty years ago in a report of the Law Reform Committee.

Law Reform Committee, *Privilege in Civil Proceedings*, 1967, Cmnd 3472

Privileges in aid of settlement and conciliation

34. It has always been regarded as being in the public interest that persons should settle their private differences without recourse to litigation and, if litigation is started, that it should be brought to an end by compromise as soon as possible so that time and expense to the parties may be saved. Now that a high proportion of civil litigation is conducted under 'Legal Aid', the public has a direct financial interest in the saving of expense. Potential litigants may be inhibited from embarking on negotiations for a settlement which normally calls for mutual concessions on each side unless they can be assured that what they say or offer in the course of the negotiations will not be used against them in the subsequent litigation if the negotiations fail. This is so whether the negotiations are conducted directly between the parties or their legal advisers, or through the good offices of some third person.

Negotiations 'without prejudice'

35. Before any privilege in respect of negotiations can arise there must exist between the parties to the negotiations a dispute which is the subject of pending or contemplated litigation between them–a requirement which is sometimes overlooked when a letter is headed 'Without Prejudice', Even when the requirement is fulfilled, negotiations for a compromise can be and often are conducted without any privilege. Each party may wish the court to know the terms upon which he was prepared to compromise the suit. But any party is entitled to make an offer to compromise for which he can claim privilege if the negotiations initiated by his offer ultimately fail. This he normally does by stating that his offer is 'without prejudice'. The other party need not accept the invitation to negotiate 'without prejudice', in which case the privilege extends to the original offer alone and can be waived by the offeror. But if the offeree does accept the invitation (and, if he does not expressly reject it, he will normally be taken to have accepted) the privilege extends to all communications made by each party to the negotiations; the privilege for all such communications is the joint privilege of all the parties to the negotiations and the consent of all is required to give a waiver of the privilege. The purpose of the privilege is to prevent statements made in the course of such negotiations from being relied upon as admissions in the litigation to which they relate. If the negotiations result in an agreement for compromise, the need for the privilege lapses and the agreement can be proved like any other contract. The privilege is well understood and works well in practice and, since it relates to communications *inter partes*, there is no difficulty in ascertaining whether or not it can be claimed.

For an illustration of the rule see *Rush & Tomkins Ltd v Greater London Council* [1988] 3 All ER 737, HL and for comment GR Hickin 'Without Prejudice Clarified', *Law Society's Gazette* 31 August 1988 p 18.

Note that the immunity from disclosure does not necessarily apply at the point when the court has to consider costs *after* the action. As will be seen below (pp 55–56), the question of costs can be affected by whether the defendant has made a payment into court or has made a reasonable offer without a payment-in. In *Cutts v Head* [1984] Ch 290, the Court of Appeal held that for this purpose the court could look at an offer even though it had been made 'without prejudice'. See for comment R Bernstein, 'Without Prejudice Offers and Costs–the Defendant's Trump Card, *Law Society' s Gazette*, 8

May 1985, p 1340; AN Khan, 'Without Prejudice Communications', *Solicitors' Journal*, 26 September 1985, p 703. See also DW Williams, 'Without Prejudice Explained', *Law Society's Gazette*, 28 January 1987, p 244; and J McEwan, 'Without Prejudice-Negotiating the Minefield', *Civil Justice Quarterly*, April 1994, pp 133–55.

The report of the Law Reform Committee continued:

Conciliation
36. Negotiations 'without prejudice' between parties to civil actions other than matrimonial causes are generally conducted through professional legal advisers or trade unions or insurance companies. They are familiar with the rules governing the privilege and with the need for making it clear that the negotiations are to be subject to it. But in matrimonial disputes matters may be dealt with much more informally and the good offices of mediators such as probation officers, marriage guidance counsellors, clergymen, doctors or family friends, are frequently used. These may be unfamiliar with the formula 'without prejudice' and, in any event, where differences arise between husband and wife it may be difficult to identify the stage at which the spouses first contemplate recourse to the courts. It is now settled law that such a mediator cannot, without the consent of both the spouses, disclose any communications with either of them if made while he was acting as conciliator between them in connection with pending or contemplated matrimonial proceedings. They are made upon the tacit understanding that attempts at conciliation are meant to be 'without prejudice' even though this formula is not expressly used: see *Mole v Mole* [1951] P 21, *Pool v Pool [1951]* P 470 and cf *Bostock v Bostock* [1950] P 154; this principle has recently been extended to cover direct negotiations between the spouses themselves where no third party intervenes: *Theodoropoulas v Theodoropoulas* [1964] P 311. As respects the requirement that matrimonial proceedings must be in contemplation in order that the privilege may attach, it is, we think, a reasonable inference from the fact that a third party has been called in by one or other of the spouses to act as mediator that such proceedings are sufficiently in contemplation to give rise to the privilege, and the courts today readily draw such inference. Where the negotiations take place directly between the spouses it may be more difficult for the court to decide whether such inference should be drawn; we do not, however, see any distinction of principle between the two situations.

See further A Bowhill, 'Without Prejudice Negotiations' *Law Society's Gazette*, 1968, p 1049.

Note–compulsory meetings of experts

A new rule which came into force in October 1986 provided that in cases other than those for personal injuries, the court can direct that the experts on both sides should meet in advance to see whether 'without prejudice' they can agree their report. Any agreed report is then put forward. Any remaining disagreement is carried forward to the trial and, because the meeting was 'without prejudice' no details of the discussion can be revealed or used by either side (Rules of the Supreme Court (Amendment No 2) 1986, SI 1987/1187). (On Lord Woolf's recommendations for expert evidence see pp 74–77 below.)

See also payment into court (pp 55–56 below)–a device that helps to promote settlement by concentrating the mind of the plaintiff on the desirability of accepting an offer made by the defendant.

3. INITIATION OF PROCEEDINGS

(a) Who has the right to initiate legal proceedings for others?

At some point the solicitor to the claimant may advise his client that he will need to start legal proceedings if he is to get his legal rights. Anyone can commerce legal proceedings on their own behalf, but apart from this right only solicitors have had a right to start an action.

The Benson Royal Commission on Legal Services in 1979 recommended no change in the solicitor's existing monopoly. Litigation involved knowledge and integrity of the practitioner. It was for the solicitor, for instance, to draw up lists of documents and to specify which were available for inspection and which were privileged. He had to decide which were relevant and which were not. This could involve difficult and technical questions. He might have to disclose documents even though it was against his clients' interest to do so: 'A person who was not subject to the same direct duty to the court and to professional discipline could not be expected to exercise responsibilities of this sort, and the courts as now constituted have no means of exercising direct supervision over work of this character' (Cmnd 7648, 1979, para 19.17, p 227). It did not recommend any relaxation of the present restrictions on the right to conduct litigation in courts of law in favour of those without legal qualifications, or any special group (claims assessors, debt collectors or any others) whether acting for reward or not. In November 1983 the Government stated that it accepted the Royal Commission's view (*The Government's Response to the Report of the Royal Commission on Legal Services*, Cmnd 9077, 1983, p 20).

The position has, however, been changed now as a result of the Courts and Legal Services Act 1990. As will be seen below (pp 563–86), the 1990 Act followed the Thatcher Government's onslaught on the whole array of restrictive practices affecting the operation of the legal profession. One monopoly affected is that of solicitors to initiate legal proceedings.

Under the 1990 Act (s 28 and Sch 4) it is now possible for other professional (or other) bodies to seek the right to conduct litigation for their members. The process for seeking such rights is complex (see pp 564–66). By 1996 the only such application was one from the Institute of Commercial Litigators representing quantity surveyors who asked the Advisory Committee to approve its application to be allowed to conduct litigation from start to finish in the field of housing cases. However the Advisory Committee was not impressed and rejected the request.

(b) Should proceedings be started in the High Court or the county court?

The question of choice of venue between county court and High Court has recently been affected by the changes made under the Courts and Legal Services Act 1990 (pp 24–26 above). It will be even more drastically affected if the proposals in Lord Woolf's Interim Report are implemented.

Until 1990 the county court's jurisdiction was restricted to claims (in contract and tort) of up to £5,000. That meant that in claims up to that amount the High Court and the county court had concurrent jurisdiction. Most cases within the jurisdiction of the county court of course were (and are) brought there.

The main reason is cost. The cost of initiating proceedings is lower, lawyers' costs are lower and the costs of enforcement of a judgment debt are lower. Also there is a considerable cost disincentive to bringing actions in the High Court that could have been brought in the county court. Previously, if the plaintiff recovered less than £3,000 he recovered costs from the loser not on the High Court scale but instead only on the county court scale (under ss 19, 20 of the County Courts Act 1984). If he recovered less than £600 he got no costs at all. Now that the £5,000 ceiling on county court cases has gone the costs sanction has been altered. The High Court can reduce the costs recoverable by the winner by up to 25 per cent if it thinks that the action should have been brought in the county court (see Courts and Legal Services Act 1990, s 4, amending s 51 of the Supreme Court Act 1981).

As has been seen (p 23 above), the 1981 Supreme Court Act gave both the High Court and the county court the power to transfer cases up or down and that power remains (see *Practice Direction* [1991] 3 All ER 349).

Despite the various reasons for bringing one's case in the county court, a surprising number of cases that could have been brought there were in fact brought in the High Court. There are a variety of reasons for preferring the High Court. One is the lawyers' sense that the High Court is a more effective system for the plaintiff. The damages obtainable from the High Court are felt to be higher, the enforcement process is thought to be more efficient, the High Court generally is better at coping with a case that is likely to last more than a day, costs recoverable from the loser in the county court are lower. Plaintiffs' lawyers feel more in control of the process in the High Court since the court (as yet) interferes less with the conduct of the case. Service of process by the court in the county court is not always as convenient as organising service oneself to suit one's own timing. Also if the plaintiff is a 'repeat player' (see p 8 above) wishing to establish a precedent, it will be necessary to have the issue decided by the High Court, since county court decisions have no weight as precedents.

As has been seen, the basic thrust of the 1990–1 reforms was that that there should be a significant shift of business from the High Court to the county court notably in personal injury cases which formed such a large part of the contested cases in the Queen's Bench Division. Lord Mackay the Lord Chancellor said the reason was: 'Too many cases of relatively low importance, substance and complexity were being handled and tried at an inappropriately high level. This was wasteful of High Court resources, inflated the cost of smaller cases and clogged up the courts, exacerbating delay'. ('Litigation in the 1990s' ((1991) *Modern Law Review* p 171).

Personal injury cases must now all start in the county court unless the amount claimed is in excess of £50,000. But for other actions there is a considerable area of choice as between the two levels of civil court.

Not long after the 1991 reforms took effect Anne Grosskurth, then of the Legal Action Group, wrote a powerful critique of the new system: 'Some seven months after the transfer order took effect, the fears of many lawyers specialising in personal injury (PI) litigation have been realised. Procedural problems in county courts are rife: papers lost, letters and phone calls unanswered, inconsistent or inadequate procedures, irrational listing systems, too few administrators and a shortage of experienced, informed judges . . . complaints about delay are widespread' ('Can the county courts cope?' (Legal *Action*, March 1992, p 7).

The High Court has since 1984 had a power actually to strike out an action if it thinks that it should have been brought in the county court. The power was originally under the County Courts Act 1984, s 40 and is now under the Courts and Legal Services Act 1990, s 2(1). It arises 'if the court is satisfied that the person bringing the proceedings knew, or ought to have known, of that requirement [that certain actions should be brought in the county court], order that they be struck out'. In *Groom v Norman Motors (Wallisdown) Ltd* [1993] PIQR P 125 it was held that the court had no discretion–that the word 'shall' was mandatory. But the Court of Appeal has now held that the court does have a discretion and that this draconian power is to be used only in exceptional circumstances, for instance, where the failure to start the action in the county court was an attempt to harass a defendant or a deliberate attempt to run up unnecessary costs–*Restick v Crickmore* [1994] 2 All ER 112. (The Court of Appeal in that instance applied the discretion to five separate appeals being heard together and in each case found that there were extenuating circumstances permitting it to transfer the case to the county court rather than strike it out.)

Lord Woolf's fast track and multi track cases

As has been seen, Lord Woolf's Interim Report proposed the division of cases between small claims cases, fast track cases, and multi track cases with the allocation of cases made essentially either by rule or decision of the procedural judge. If the plaintiff had a choice he could exercise it to choose his forum but the court would then allocate the case to the appropriate level court–as well as the appropriate venue (see p 43 below).

As from 1996, with a few exceptions, small claims cases are those where the amount in dispute is under £3,000. The exceptions are personal injury cases where the amount claimed is more than £1,000; claims for possession of land, and cases excluded by the district judge because of their complexity.

Fast track cases would be most of those where the amount in dispute is between £3,000 and £10,000. Exceptions would be medical negligence cases, jury trials, fixed date possession actions, actions for the return of goods and cases meeting the criteria for transfer to the multi-track. The criteria for transfer to the multi-track cases would be cases raising issues of public importance, test cases, cases involving several experts and cases requiring significant oral evidence. (See Fast Track Issues Paper, January 1996, pp 4–5)

Multi-track cases would be those that were not either small claims or fast track cases.

(c) What kind of proceedings should be started?

There are four ordinary ways of starting proceedings in the High Court: writ of summons, originating summons, originating motion and petition. Motions and petitions may be used only if specially required or authorized by some Act or by the Rules of Court. Generally the choice is between writ and originating summons.

Some types of action *must* be started by writ. These include claims for tort other than trespass to land, claims based on an allegation of fraud, claims for damages for breach of duty including damages for death or personal injury or damage to property. Proceedings by way of an application to the court under the provisions of a statute must be started by originating summons–for instance, an application for the approval by the court of a variation of the terms of a trust under the Variation of Trusts Act 1958. The two categories of case that are particularly suitable to be begun by originating summons are those in which there is not likely to be any substantial dispute as to fact and those in which the sole or main question is the construction of a statute, deed, will, contract or some other document, or a question of law.

The procedure by way of originating summons is simpler, cheaper and does not involve pleadings. Most actions in the Queen's Bench Division are started by writ, many proceedings in the Chancery Division are started by originating summons.

In the county court, proceedings involving a dispute between two or more parties are always commenced by summons (or plaint). (Proceedings asking the court to construe a statute or a document are commenced by application or petition.) The summons (formerly known as a *praecipe*) is a less imposing version of the High Court writ.

Formerly summonses were divided into default or ordinary summonses, but from 1981 the distinction has been between default and fixed-date summonses. All claims for a money remedy only are by default summons; those that claim some other remedy, such as possession of land or an injunction, are called fixed-date summonses (County Court Rules, ('CCR.') Ord 3, r 2).

The chief difference between the two forms of summons is that a default summons has no return date on which the next stage should take place, whereas a fixed-date summons bears a date either for the hearing or for a pre-trial review. In a default summons, as will be seen below, summary judgment can be entered against the defendant unless he takes appropriate steps within fourteen days. If such steps are taken, the court decides on a return date then. (For the text of both forms of summons see *New Law Journal*, 1982, pp 511, 536.) Notice of the proceedings must, however be served in the proper way. Service can be either personally on the defendant or by post.

Lord Woolf's Interim Report stated that his new code of procedure would have provision for a single method of starting all types of claim (*op cit* p 209, para 11).

Cost of issue   As from October 1995 issue of a High Court writ went up from £100 to £120. The fee on issue of a divorce petition was doubled from £40 to £80. Issue of a county court summons went from 10p per £1 to graduated flat fees. Up to £600 the fee remained 10 per cent. Above that figure the cost went down slightly. For money claims in the county court of over £5,000 the fee was set at £80 regardless of the amount (or £75 if made through the computerised County Court Bulk Summons Production Centre, see pp 42,44 below). The signs were that further, swingeing fee increases were under consideration on the basis of a new attitude taken by the Conservative Government that litigants should fund the full court costs of civil litigation. For a different approach see the Australian Report to the Attorney General entitled *Access to Justice: an Action Plan*, 1994:

We consider that there should be some court fees, even if simply in recognition of the need to fund an expensive social service. . .However, we strongly believe that even though it is only particular individuals who are engaged in litigation, the whole community may be classified as 'users' of the court system. This is because everyone benefits from having disputes resolved in an orderly manner and legal rights clarified. We adopt the view expressed by Sir Anthony Mason, the Chief Justice of Australia, that ready availability and equality of access to the courts is vital to a democracy that takes pride in its system of justice and in the ordered settlement of disputes [pp 38–82].

Court fees can be waived or reduced if the applicant can demonstrate that paying the fee would involve undue hardship.

(d) Venue

High Court cases can be started in the Royal Courts of Justice in the Strand or in any District Registry, as the plaintiff chooses, subject to provision for transfer to another District Registry or the Royal Courts as the case may be. Divorce proceedings can be started in any divorce county court. In the county court, by contrast, the rule was that the proceedings should be in the defendant's local court or the court with which the case is most closely connected. The Civil Justice Review's *General Issues Paper* proposed that the more flexible High Court rule should be adopted throughout the system. Cases would start in the county court most convenient to the plaintiff, subject to transfer to a court more convenient to the defendant in the event of a hearing or other requirement to attend court (paras 143–4). Insofar as most debt cases would in future be handled by post (or computer), the court should have power to direct it to be transferred to a court to suit managerial interests as well as the interests of the parties (para 145).

This proposal was adopted in the 1990–1 reforms in respect of default summonses (see CCR, Ords 1, 4 and 16). Venue restrictions for other types of proceeding continue. But to protect defendants, where a substantive defence is filed in a claim for a liquidated (fixed) sum of money, the case is automatically transferred to the defendant's home court if it differs from the issue court. In other words, the plaintiff is entitled to choose the most convenient court for the commencement of the proceedings, but if it is contested the matter is transferred to the defendant's local court.

Lord Woolf's Interim Report proposed that, irrespective of the nature of the proceedings, the plaintiff should be able to apply to *any* court and it would be for the court to allocate the case to the appropriate track and the appropriate court (*op cit*, p 36, para 14).

(e) Issue and service of proceedings

Service by post has been permitted since 1980. In High Court proceedings, service has always been handled by the plaintiff or some kind of process server on his behalf. In the county court, by contrast, service was undertaken by the bailiff. But in 1983 the Lord Chancellor's Office abolished this, as an economy measure, for all but exceptional cases.

A company may be served by leaving the document at, or sending it by post to, the company's registered office. If ordinary service is not possible because the defendant's whereabouts are not known, the court can be asked for permission to allow 'substituted service', for example by putting an advertisement in a local newspaper. Where a property owner is trying to get back possession of premises occupied by squatters, service on those on the premises (whose names would normally not be known) is allowed to be made by posting up a notice of the proceedings on the door or some other appropriate place. (In *Hastie and Jenkerson v McMahon* [1991] 1 All ER 255 the Court of Appeal held that documents that do not have to be served personally or that do not initiate proceedings can be served validly by fax. But by definition this does not apply to writs.)

There can be and often is a considerable delay between issue and service of a writ. The rules used to allow 12 months from issue of the writ for its service. The Civil Justice Review's *Personal Injuries Consultation Paper* recommended that, in the interests of speeding up the process, this period should be cut from 12 months to 2 months. The Review's *General Issues Paper* proposed that this should apply across the board to all cases, subject to a right to apply for additional time where this was justice. The Final Report of the Civil Justice Review recommended that the period from issue to service of the writ should be a maximum of four months– and this was implemented in 1989 (see Rules of the Supreme Court (Amendment No 4) 1989, SI 1989/2427).

Computerised bulk issue in the county court

Since 1990 there has been a special issuing of process service available to bulk issuers such as banks, finance houses, public utilities, mail order firms, store card firms and firms that specialise in handling bad debts. The Summons Production Centre (SPC) guarantees that summonses will be issued and served within 24 to 48 hours. In 1994–95 it issued 114 million summonses on behalf of 128 plaintiffs.

(f) Representative, class and group or multi-party actions

English law has not in the past given much scope for what are called representative or class actions but in recent years there has been a considerable development of something similar, the group action. What is in issue here is an action involving several and often many persons either as plaintiff or defendant. Sometimes such an action arises out of a sudden disaster–a plane crash is an obvious example. Sometimes it arises out of the sale to many persons over a period of time of some consumer product such as a drug.

In the United States, class actions are used on a significant scale under the terms of Rule 23 of the Federal Rules of Civil Procedure which permits such actions where:

(1) the class is so numerous that joinder of all members is impracticable;
(2) there are questions of law or fact common to the class;
(3) the claims or defences of the representative are typical of the claims or defences of the class; and
(4) the representative parties will fairly and adequately protect the interests of the class.

The equivalent English rule is Rules of the Supreme Court Ord 15, r 12, which states that 'Where numerous persons have the same interest in any proceedings–the proceedings may be begun and, unless the court otherwise orders, continued, by or against any one or more of them as representing all or as representing all except any one or more.'

The English rule would appear about as hospitable as the American to a liberal view of the representative action, but in practice it was viewed much more restrictively. Notably in *Markt & Co Ltd v Knight SS Co Ltd* [1910] 2 KB 1021, it was held that damages could not be awarded to a representative plaintiff on behalf of a whole class. ('Damages are personal only. To my mind no representative action can lie where the sole relief is damages because they have to be proved separately in the case of each plaintiff and therefore the possibility of representation ceases', p 1040.)

The courts have also ruled that the members of the class must all have the same interest and the same grievance (*Duke of Bedford v Ellis* [1901] AC 1).

But the restrictive aspects of the English approach appear to be giving way to a new and more open interpretation–see the decision of Vinelott J in *Prudential Assurance Co Ltd v Newman Industries Ltd* [1981] Ch 229; [1979] 3 All ER 507. The judge upheld representative proceedings brought by minority shareholders in Newman claiming a declaration and damages on behalf of themselves and all other shareholders. The defendants sought to persuade the judge to apply the statement in the *Supreme Court Practice* (the 'White Book'), that 'No representative action will lie to establish the right of numerous persons to recover damages each in his own several right where the only relief claimed is damages'. The judge held that the White Book was wrong. A representative action could be employed even when each plaintiff had a separate cause of action, subject to certain conditions. First, the court could not make an order which would give a member of the class a right which he could not have claimed in a separate action. Secondly, there must be a common element in the claim of all members of the class. Thirdly, the action must be for a declaration and for damages, and the individual members of the class would then have to come separately and prove their own individual damages. (For comments on the case and assessment of the case-law, see K Uff, 'Class, Representative and Shareholders–Derivative Actions in English Law', *Civil Justice Quarterly*, January 1986, p 50; and 'Recent Developments in Representative Actions', *Civil Justice Quarterly*, January 1987, p 15.)

The *Prudential* case was followed in *EMI Records Ltd v Riley* [1981] 1 WLR 923 where an injunction was granted to a representative plaintiff on behalf of an association of record manufacturers. The concept was also endorsed in *M Michuels (Furriers) Ltd v Askew* (1983) 127 Sol Jo 597, CA where an injunction was granted against a representative defendant, thus binding members of the class he represented without their being parties to the litigation. But in 1986 it was held that three members of a branch of the union SOGAT could not be sued on behalf of or as representatives of all members of that branch.

The first massive group action for damages along American lines in the English courts was the claim of some 1,500 plaintiffs against Eli Lilly, the manufacturers of the drug Opren. The actions were coordinated by a consortium of a small number of solicitors' firms. Instead of separate statements of claim, plaintiffs were using two-page schedules which referred to a master statement of the claim running to over a hundred pages. (See *New Law Journal*, 19 September 1986, p 883.) In July 1986 Hirst J ruled that a number of 'lead cases' should be chosen to be litigated on the different issues of liability. The remaining actions would then be stayed pending the result in these cases.

Technically, the position is different from that in an American class action. Under the American procedure, the result binds all members of the class. In the English system this is not so. Any Opren litigant could in theory have continued to fight his own case after the conclusion of the 'test cases'. But this is pure theory. In reality, the members of the class in the English situation are just as much bound by the result. Those on legal aid would not be allowed to continue the case and those not on legal aid would not be able to afford to do so. Various preliminary matters in this litigation reached the courts. In one, the Master of the Rolls Sir John Donaldson said that the whole question whether our system should adopt the American-style class action should be considered by the 'appropriate authorities'. Meanwhile the court should, he said, be 'as flexible and adaptable as possible in the application of existing procedures with a view to reaching decisions quickly and economically' (*Davies v Eli Lilly & Co* [1987] 3 All ER 94, 96).

(See further R Campbell and W Morrison, 'Class Actions', *Law Society's Gazette*, 16 September 1987, p 2585.)

In an article in 1989 Andrew Lockley, Director of Legal Practice at the Law Society, pointed to the recent proliferation of group legal actions arising out of major disasters: the Zeebrugge ferry disaster, the King's Cross fire, the Clapham and Purley rail crashes, the Lockerbie air crash, the Hillsborough football stadium tragedy and lawsuits against the makers of the Dalkon Shield contraceptive device and Benzodiazepene-based tranquillizers.[2]

It had been thought that the procedural problems posed by the English rules for representative actions could be circumvented by the 'lead case' device where one strong case was selected as a test case. Typically, a plaintiff on legal aid poor enough to be on a nil contribution would be selected. The other plaintiffs would issue their proceedings but their claims would be stayed until the test case was determined. It was thought that the costs of the litigation could be thrown on to the state through this use of the legal aid fund. But this approach was prevented by the decision of the Master of the Rolls in the Opren litigation (see p 433 below) holding that, if the action failed, the costs would then have to be met by all the plaintiffs. A new way to handle such actions had to be found.

There were several difficult policy issues. One was who should certify whether an action should proceed as a class action? Another was the criteria to identify the group. A third was what happened to those with similar claims who were not in the group. A fourth was the whole issue of how such actions should be funded. (See on these issues National Consumer Council 'Group Action, Learning from Opren', January 1989 summarised in *Law Society's Gazette*, 25 January 1989, p 7.)

In May 1991 the Supreme Court Procedure Committee issued a *Guide for Use in Group Actions*. It suggested that the plaintiffs should consider forming a Solicitors' group and a group to represent the lay litigants. The Law Society is available to assist in the formation of these groups through its Multi-Party Action Coordination Service. It places a notice in the *Gazette* notifying the profession that a register has been opened of solicitors already involved and inviting others to register. The Law Society may convene a meeting of solicitors. At such a meeting a Coordinating Committee of firms to conduct the litigation can be elected. Typically the Coordinating Committee nominates one of its members to be the lead firm and solicitor on the record. The lead firm is then the channel of communication between the Coordinating Committee and the other firms.

The *Guide* discusses the different kinds of action that can be used. Representative actions (under Ord 15, r 12) had not on the whole found favour with practitioners conducting disaster litigation. A second possibility was that the plaintiffs would be joined in one writ (under Ord 15, r 4), which had the advantage of saving money on court fees. This could be followed by a common Statement of Claim with a separate schedule showing allegations peculiar to each plaintiff. But in practice it might be

2   'Regulating Group Actions' *New Law Journal*, 9 June 1989, p 798.

difficult to organise. The third possibility was to consolidate a number of different actions (Ord 4, r 9). Ord 4, r 9 permitted the court to select a 'lead action' and to stay others 'so that typical issues can be litigated . . . for the benefit of other litigants in other cases in the group'. In such cases it is appropriate for a judge to be nominated to handle the case from the earliest possible time throughout the interlocutory stage and then the trial.

In September 1995 the Law Society's Civil Litigation Committee issued a substantial new report entitled 'Group Actions Made Easier'. This proposed that a new rule of court should be made for such cases. The rule should provide for judicial control and case management from an early stage. The court should define the role of the lead solicitors. In the interests of economy and efficiency there could be some restriction on the client's freedom of choice of lawyers. Generally there should be a lead firm of solicitors or a coordinating group of solicitors. Individual claimants should not have to issue separate writs but should join the action by a notice/register system. The court should set cut-off dates for joining the action. Lead cases should only be settled or discontinued with leave of the court. With the approval of the court the defendant should be able to make global offers to settle the entire case. All settlements should require a court hearing. Questions of costs should be in the discretion of the court. (See 'Class Action', *Law Society's Gazette*, 22 November 1995, p 16.)

On the crucial question of the financing of group litigation see pp 433–34 below.

For an argument that the English system should adopt the broader American approach to class actions, see Gerry Bates, 'A Case for the Introduction of Class Actions into English Law', *New Law Journal*, 3 July 1980, p 560; and Geraldine van Bueren, 'Statutory Class Action', *LAG Bulletin*, August 1983, p 7. See also Robin Widdison, 'Class Actions: A Survey', *New Law Journal*, 2 September 1983, p 778; and J A Jolowicz, 'Protection of Diffuse, Fragmented and Collective Interests in Civil Litigation: English Law', *Camb LJ* 1983, p 222. Professor Jolowicz canvassed in his article not only class actions but a variety of other techniques for representing 'diffuse interests', including proceedings by the Attorney-General; relator actions; litigation by a private litigant who claims that he has suffered a private wrong over and above a wrong done to members of the public; and applications for judicial review.

On the American system see further A Miller, 'Of Frankenstein Monsters and Shining Knights: Myth, Reality and 'The Class of Action Problem', *Harvard Law Review*, 1979, p 664; and Larry S Bush, 'My Brother's Keeper–Some Observations on Federal Rule 23 and Mass Tort Class Action in the United States', *Civil Justice Quarterly*, April 1986, p 109; *ibid*, July 1986, p 201.

4. INTERLOCUTORY PROCEEDINGS

(a) Acknowledgement of service and judgment in default

The High Court writ calls on the defendant to return an acknowledgement of service within 14 days stating, among other things, whether he intends to defend (see *New Law Journal*, 20 March 1980, p 287). In the county court, the defendant to a default or fixed date action has 14 days within which to file with the court a defence or counterclaim.

Failure by the defendant within 14 days in the High Court to acknowledge service or to indicate an intention to defend entitles the plaintiff to obtain summary judgment in default (RSC, Ord 13). If the claim is for a definite amount (liquidated damages), such judgment is final. If the claim is for an unspecified sum, judgment is interlocutory and the amount of damages is referred to a master for assessment. Before getting judgment in default of appearance, the plaintiff must file an affidavit proving that the writ (or county court summons) was properly served on the defendant or his solicitor. If it later appears that there was some valid excuse for the non-appearance or there was some irregularity, or the defendant does have a defence, he may be able to persuade the court to set the judgment aside to permit him to make his defence.

In the county court likewise, a plaintiff can obtain judgment in default when the defendant fails to state that he intends to defend (CCR 1981, Ord 9, r 6). If the action is a default action (see p 42 above), the plaintiff can also obtain summary judgment in default if the defendant pays into court the amount claimed or admits the claim but asks for time to pay.

(b) Summary judgment after no defence or bogus defence

If, after the defendant has acknowledged service, the plaintiff considers that there is no defence to the claim, he can ask for summary judgment to be entered in the High Court under RSC Ord 14 and in the county court under CCR Ord 9, r 14, The procedure can be used in virtually any High Court action begun by writ in the Queen's Bench Division or Chancery Division. The application is by summons to the pre-trial judge in London called 'master', or outside London called district judge, accompanied by an affidavit asserting the facts on which the claim is based and stating that in the plaintiff's belief there is no defence to the claim or no defence except as to the amount of damages. The summons has to be served on the defendant not less than ten days before the hearing. At the hearing the master or district judge has power to give judgment for the plaintiff or he can give the defendant leave to defend, on the ground that there is the basis of an issue which needs to be tried. (For the procedure for obtaining summary judgment, see *New Law Journal*, 1981, p 905.) Summary judgment can be set aside or varied on such terms as the court thinks fit, as under Ord 13.

In 1990 a new procedure was introduced to permit summary judgment where the only issue between the parties is one of law or construction of a document–Ord 14A inserted by Rules of the Supreme Court (Amendment No 3) 1990, SI 1990/2599– see Gordon Exall, 'Summary Judgment on a Question of Law: The New Ord 14A', *Solicitors' Journal*, 19 April 1991, p 475. But normally Ord 14 is not supposed to be used for lengthy cases–see *British and Commonwealth Holdings plc v Quadrex* [1989] 3 All ER 492; *RG Carter v Clarke* [1990] 2 All ER 209; and *Home and Overseas Insurance Co Ltd v Mentor Insurance Co UK Ltd* [1990] 1 WLR 153.

Note also the procedure under RSC Ord 27, r 3, by which the plaintiff can get judgment if he can persuade the court that the defendant has admitted the claim in the pleadings 'or otherwise'. (For the implications of this and its relationship to the Ord 14 procedure, see Gordon Exall, 'Pure Genius? Judgment on Admissions after Guinness', *Solicitors' Journal*, 14 December 1990, p 1470.)

In February 1996 the Lord Chancellor introduced his Defamation Bill clause 8 of which provided for a new device for summary disposal of defamation claims where there is no realistic defence, there is no reason why it should be brought to trial and damages of up to £10,000 awarded by the judge would adequately compensate the plaintiff.

Infrequency of judgment after trial

Judgment after a trial is in fact exceedingly rare. In 1994, in the Queen's Bench Division in London there were 17,456 cases in which judgment was given. In 93 per cent judgment was by default, in 7 per cent it was given under Ord 14 and a mere 3 per cent (570) were cases where judgment was given after a trial. (*Judicial Statistics*, 1994, Cm 2891, Tables 3.3 and 3.4. The *Judicial Statistics* no longer give these figures for District Registries outside London but in former years when the figures were given, the ratios outside London were more or less the same as in London).

In the county court the position is broadly the same. The only significant difference is that the number of trials is greater if one counts small-claim 'arbitrations' (p 303 below). Thus in 1994 there were 1,545,933 judgments entered of which 6 per cent (87,885) were arbitration decisions, 1.6 per cent (24,219) were proceedings disposed of by trial—and the remaining 92.4 per cent were judgments in default. (*ibid*, Tables 4.7, 4.8 and 4.11).

One troublesome question is whether a significant number of cases occur where defendants who actually have good grounds of defence (or counter-claim) allow judgment to be entered against them without seeking or getting legal or other competent advice.

This question received some sort of answer in the study done by Touche Ross for the Civil Justice Review on the Enforcement of Debt. The survey of county court debtors showed that as many as nearly one-third said they disputed the claim but did not file a defence (1986, para 180, p 47). This does not of course prove that they had valid grounds of defence, but the fact that so many claimed to have a defence is worrying.

(c) Pleadings

The pleadings are the formal documents exchanged between the parties after the service of the writ or plaint. Their function is to define the issues in the case so as to enable each party to prepare its evidence for the trial. Strictly, parties are limited at the trial to matters which have been pleaded[3]–though the court has a discretion to admit by amendment issues that were not pleaded. For a case in which the pleadings determined the outcome of the case with disastrous results for the plaintiff, see *Esso Petroleum Co Ltd v Southport Corpn* [1956] AC 218.

It is possible to have trial without pleadings on application to the master–where, for instance, the parties are agreed on all the facts. This is, however, rare.

The pleadings start with the 'statement of claim'. The defendant answers with a 'defence' and at the same time he may himself make a 'counter-claim'. As has been seen, if the defendant fails to enter a defence, judgment can be entered against him in default of pleadings. In the county court the defendant who wishes to contest the claim puts in an answer.

3　Pleadings can, however, be amended pre-trial.

If the plaintiff wishes to answer the defence, he will put in a 'reply'. But failure to put in a reply does not mean that the plaintiff accepts what is said in the defence. Failure to reply puts all the material facts in the defence 'in issue'. Pleadings after a reply need the consent of the court. With consent there can be a 'rejoinder' by the defendant; 'surrejoinder' by the plaintiff; 'rebutter' by the defendant; and 'surrebutter' by the plaintiff.

The pleadings are closed if no reply is served fourteen days after the service of the defence. If there is a reply, the pleadings are closed fourteen days after this.

Pleadings in High Court cases are normally drafted by barristers. The basic rule is that:

Every pleading must contain, and contain only, a statement in a summary form of the material facts on which the party pleading relies for his claim or defence, as the case may be, but not the evidence by which those facts are to be proved, and the statement must be as brief as the nature of the case admits [RSC Ord 18, r 7(1)].

The significance of pleadings was explained by the greatest British civil proceduralist Sir Jack Jacob:

Master IH Jacob, 'The Present Importance of Pleadings', *Current Legal Problems* (1960), p 171

. . . pleadings do not only define the issues between the parties for the final decision of the court at the trial; they manifest and exert their importance throughout the whole process of the litigation. They contain the particulars of the allegations of which further and better particulars may be requested or ordered, which help still further to narrow the issues or reveal more clearly what case each party is making. They limit the ambit and range of the discovery of documents and the interrogatories that may be ordered. They show on their face whether a reasonable cause of action or defence is disclosed. They provide a guide for the proper mode of trial and particularly for the trial of preliminary issues of law or fact. They demonstrate upon which party the burden of proof lies, and who has the right to open the case. They act as a measure for comparing the evidence of a party with the case which he has pleaded. They determine the range of the admissible evidence which the parties should be prepared to adduce at the trial. They delimit the relief which the court can award. They provide the cases for the defence of *res judicata* in subsequent proceedings by reference to the record in the earlier proceedings.

But although pleadings are supposed to reveal to each side what the other side's case will be, they frequently do not achieve this aim. The Winn Committee made some acid comments on the state of modern pleadings:

Report of the (Winn) *Committee on Personal Injuries Litigation, 1968,* Cmnd 369

Pleadings are supposed to set out all facts necessary to success, though not the evidence to prove them.

237. A perusal of the RSC Ord 18 from end to end, with all notes and quotations, constitutes a fascinating experience, for a practitioner, in the nature of a trip through territory unknown to him and in a climate which he has not experienced in his daily life. No set of rules could have been more carefully devised, no judicial comment could be more cogently expressed; practice all too regrettably often reveals little relationship to the Rules; the judicial comments pass unregarded.[4]

252. Sometimes at least it might be efficient to isolate and so emphasize specifically, the several statutory duties together with the relevant alleged breach in factual terms. It is all-important to make clear in the pleading the causal connection between the facts alleged and the

breach of duty which is alleged to flow from them. Thus it happens that a statement of claim pleads that the plaintiff sustained a fall at work (without saying how or why) and adds that this was 'caused' by the negligence and/or breach of statutory duty of the defendants. There follows an assortment of complaints, such as failing to fence a stock-bar, failing to maintain the floor, failing to provide protective clothing, etc. This may conceal a perfectly coherent case, eg that the plaintiff tripped in a cavity in the floor, caught his sleeve in an unfenced stock-bar, and was whirled across the room, falling and breaking his ankle, which would not have occurred had he been provided with boots instead of plimsolls. Yet the pleading discloses nothing.. . .

254. In road traffic cases, the statement of claim seldom requires any great intellectual effort and, perhaps for this reason, tends to be a shoddy product. Far too many such pleadings follow a stock form of which the dominant characteristic is that no cause of collision known to practitioners is omitted. In this type of litigation superfluity and irrelevance are rampant vices.. . .

266. We have no hesitation in saying it is in defence that the current practice of pleading calls for the harshest criticism. One of the most experienced Queen's Bench Masters told us that at present 'The defence is a blot on our procedure' and he regrets that trial Judges seem to be unwilling to penalize unsuccessful formal denials by an order for costs (which is not easy to frame). 'The chief defect of our system,' he avers, 'is that a defendant is permitted to make wide denials.'

The position in the mid 1990s was much the same as that described in 1968 by the Winn Report.

The leading practitioner's work is J Jacob and IS Goldrein, *Pleadings: Principles and Practice* (Sweet and Maxwell, 1990). See also Gareth Watkins, 'Particulars of pleadings', *Law Society's Gazette*, 27 November 1985, p 3437; and IS Goldrein, 'Personal Injury Litigation–How to Keep the Plaintiff in the Saddle', I, *New Law Journal*, 31 January 1986, p 85; II, *ibid*, 7 February 1986, p 110; III, *ibid*, 14 February 1986, p 147; IV, *ibid*, 21 February 1986, p 171.

Note–more informative pleadings?

A rule change in 1990 required that in both the High Court and the county court a plaintiff in a personal injuries case must serve with his statement of claim a medical report and a statement of special damages claimed. ('Special' damages are those which can be quantified.) This means that the plaintiff now has to disclose his medical evidence from the outset. The statement as to special damages also requires an estimate of future expenses and losses including loss of earnings and pension rights. (See RSC Ord 18, r 12(1) and CCR Ord 6, r 1 (5).)

Note also a rule change in 1994 for defamation actions to enable either party to ask for a ruling from a judge as to whether the words complained of are capable of bearing a meaning attributed to them in the pleadings. (RSC Ord 82, r 3A). It has been suggested that this new rule will result in changes of practice in pleading–see P Milmo, 'Changes to Procedure in Defamation Actions', *New Law Journal*, 16, September 1994, p 1247.

---

4   Cf the words of Lord Justice May in *Morrell v International Thomson Publishing Ltd* [1989] 3 All ER 733: 'In defamation I am forced to conclude that the purpose [of pleadings] is to put forward a defence which gives away as little of the case which it is intended to advance at trial as possible without running the risk of being struck out. The rules regarding the plaintiff's pleadings are not much better. The result of compelling parties to engage in this archaic saraband– to call it a minuet as had previously been done was to give it too delicate and attractive a description . . . was that defamation litigation was too complicated, too lengthy and too costly'(ed).

Another new 1994 rule in defamation actions requires the plaintiff who seeks to prove the truth of the libel specifically to reply to any statement from the defendant admitting or denying the truth of the libel (RSC Ord 82, r 3(2A)). A further new sub-rule (RSC Ord 82, r 3(3A)) requires the plaintiff to give full particulars in his statement of claim of the facts and matters on which he relies in support of his claim for damages, including details of any conduct by the defendant which it is alleged has increased the loss suffered and of any loss which is peculiar to the plaintiff's own circumstances. Previously the plaintiff could make general sweeping statements that he had been 'gravely damaged in his credit and reputation and had been brought into hatred, ridicule and contempt' which enabled all sorts of evidence to be introduced on general damages. Now any such matter has to be specifically pleaded. These changes resulted from the Report of Lord Justice Neill's Working Group on Defamation, 1991.

Woolf on pleadings

Lord Woolf in the Interim Report of his Inquiry said (p 153) that among the main purposes of pleadings were (a) to define the area of dispute and eliminate matters which turn out not to be in dispute; (b) to focus on what the parties will really need to prove at trial; and (c) to illuminate the nature of disputed matters, so that the most suitable method of disposal can be chosen. In the context of his inquiry, pleadings could enable the court to direct summary trial of specific issues and to limit the matters to be tried, they could also help the court to make decisions about appropriate case management.

Lord Woolf (p 153) said that pleadings often failed to set out facts clearly and so impeded identification of the issues. They concentrated too much on causes of action and defences, rather than on facts, which in turn contributed to over-use of alternative positions. Defences in particular were deliberately framed to keep all options open for as long as possible.

There was a widespread failure of courts to apply meaningful sanctions. 'There is no routine scrutiny, and incomplete, obscure, evasive or longwinded pleadings are therefore not subject to criticism as a matter of course' (p 154, para 5). If a penalty was imposed in the form of an award of costs it had little, if any, effect on behaviour.

Lord Woolf said that the time had come for 'a completely new approach and a change of culture' (p 154, para 6). The answer lay in his recommended switch to a 'managed system of litigation' which must extend to the way in which parties set out their claims and defences. (For an account of Lord Woolf's proposed system of managed litigation see p 95 below.) Mere exhortation would achieve little. It was time to return to the basic functions of pleadings–to state the facts of the case.

He therefore proposed (p 155, para 9):

(1) The claimant and defendant should each set out 'all the material matters on which they rely'.
(2) The claim and defence are considered by the procedural judge after the defence is filed.
(3) The procedural judge gives directions which could include directions to clarify points in the claim or defence. If the factual allegations are so unclear that the matters in dispute cannot be identified, he would hold a case management conference. If the case was on the proposed 'fast track' (most cases involving

amounts between £3,000 and £10,000) the conference would normally be on the telephone.

A major aim of the case management conference would be to produce an agreed statement of the issues in dispute. This would take over from the pleadings.

There were bound to be practical difficulties initially in obtaining a reliable record of any resulting changes in the pleadings but it was essential to make this approach work.

As a consequence, the need for further exchanges between the parties (requests for further and better particulars, notices to admit, interrogatories) should largely be eliminated.

The new rules of procedure for both High Court and county court should simplify the rules regarding pleadings. One aim would be to avoid technicality. There should be non-prescribed forms of claim for common types of proceedings–possibly in questionnaire format. Statement of claim and defence might face each other in the same document. Eventually this could be computerised.

The claim should contain (a) a succinct statement of the facts entitling the claimant to a remedy; (b) the remedy or remedies claimed; (c) any matters of law which entitled the claimant to a remedy; and (d) the legal nature of the claim–breach of contract, patent infringement etc (p 159, para 21).

The defence should state (a) the parts of the claim admitted and not admitted; (b) the defendant's version of the facts so far as different from those stated in the statement of claim; (c) specific defences–voluntary assumption of risk, failure to mitigate loss etc and any grounds for denying the claim arising out of facts stated by the defendant or for disputing its value; and (d) where no facts or legal grounds are relied upon, a statement that the defendant does not know whether the facts stated by the claimant are true and requiring the claimant to prove them.

All pleadings would have to conclude with a declaration, by or on behalf the litigant, of belief in the accuracy and truth of the matters put forward.

Lord Woolf said (p 161, para 31) that although requiring the parties to bring forward their evidence at that stage would have certain advantages, it was important to avoid incurring costs by front-loading simpler cases which might settle anyway. He would therefore permit a party who wished to identify his likely witnesses, or even what they would say, to do so. In the light of experience it might be made mandatory.

Parties should be required to identify the principal documents on which they relied and would be permitted though not required to attach them to the pleading.

In order to signal a change of culture the word 'pleading' which was synonymous with obfuscation should be replaced by 'statement of case' (p 162, para 33).

The Consultation Paper on fast track cases issued in January 1996 proposed that standard statements of case for claimants and defendants might be developed for common types of defended actions. There might even be a booklet format where claim and defence were set alongside each other in response to proforma questions. To assist practitioners best practice guides should be developed for the taking of instructions from the client.

If implemented and made to work, Lord Woolf's proposals would be revolutionary. There must be a serious question however whether even if the rules were changed, practitioners and judges would conform to the new pleading culture.

(d) Payment into court

If the defendant believes he will lose on liability, he assesses what damages are likely to be awarded by the court and can offer the plaintiff something less, which he pays into the court. The plaintiff then has a choice. Either he takes the sum offered (usually plus costs) in full and final settlement of his claim, or he rejects the offer and continues to trial. (If the payment is made before the hearing, the plaintiff may within 21 days of receiving notice of the fact accept the money offered. But where the payment-in is made or increased after the hearing has already begun, the plaintiff must accept it, if at all, before the judge has started his judgment (or summing up to the jury).) If at the trial he is awarded more than the amount offered, he gets his costs in the ordinary way. But if he gets less (or the same amount), the defendant only has to pay his costs up to the date of the payment-in and gets his costs from that date.[5] Since most of the costs of a case are usually incurred in the final stages of the trial, the effect of this can be disastrous on the plaintiff. Most of his damages may be swallowed in paying costs. Payment-in is therefore a gamble–with the advantage decidedly with the defendant, usually an insurance company. In the event of a trial, the fact that payment into court has been made or its amount is not communicated to the court lest it be influenced by such knowledge. (But on an appeal the Court of Appeal does sometimes know.)

The rules are set out in RSC Ord 22 and CCR Ord 11. (Payment into court does not apply however to small claims cases.) Usually the rules are adhered to strictly. If the plaintiff and his lawyers are wrong in their evaluation of the likely damages by so much as £1, the penalty of having to pay the costs from the date of payment-in is exacted. That this is not absolutely invariably so, however, was shown in December 1985. Mr Patrick Wilson, a Rastafarian in a wheelchair, won damages of £1,750 against the Metropolitan Police for assault. But the newspaper accounts of his victory the next day revealed that the police had paid into court the sum of £2,505 and as a result Mr Wilson would not get a penny of his damages, all of which were swallowed up by the costs. The judge thereupon reconvened and, most unusually, announced that he had changed his mind. He ordered the police to pay all Mr Wilson's costs. His reason, he said, was that he had not taken into account the police's disgraceful conduct. See *The Guardian*, 11 December 1985.

Payment-in technically applies only where the case concerns a damages claim. But the same principle has been adapted for use in other cases. If the defendant makes an offer of settlement 'without prejudice save as to costs', this is treated by the courts in virtually the same way as if it were a payment into court. (The technique has come to be known as a Calderbank letter–after the case of *Calderbank v Calderbank* [1975] 3 All ER 333.) The Calderbank offer has been recognised by the rules of court–see RSC Ord 22, r 14 and CCR Ord 11, r 10.

Payment into court cannot be used in respect of specific issues, only in regard to the entire action. The Calderbank offer by contrast can relate to a specific issue.

The Court of Appeal held in *Cutts v Head* [1984] Ch 290 that the court could look at a letter marked 'without prejudice' but expressly reserving the issue of costs. In a case where a payment into court was not practicable, this would suffice. Where payment-in was practicable, however, it would still be required to achieve the effect.

---

5   For the position where one of several co-defendants makes a payment-in, see *Hodgson v Guardall* [1991] 3 All ER 823.

An insurance company therefore cannot get the benefit of the rule in a personal injury case without backing its offer by actual money.

In a study of 664 personal injury cases based on bills taxed in 1973–4 there proved to be 272 cases (41 per cent) in which payment into court had been made. In 61 per cent of these cases the payment-in was accepted. In 39 per cent it was not. But in 77 of the 105 cases (71 per cent) in which the first offer was not accepted, the offer was improved and the case was settled without a hearing. If these cases are added to those where the first offer was accepted, then payment-in was accepted in 244 cases out of 272, or 90 per cent. Out of the 124 cases that went for trial, payment-in had been made in only 28 (or 22 per cent). Of the 18 contested cases that involved damages of over £10,000, payment-in had been made in only 3 cases (or 16 per cent).

Most of the plaintiffs who refused the payment-in and pursued the case to judgment proved markedly successful. But there were 4 cases out of the 28 in which the margin between the amount paid in and the amount awarded was very small. In another 2 cases the amount paid in was accepted only after the trial had started and the costs had to be paid by the plaintiff up to that point. In only 2 cases the amount awarded was less than the amount paid in. (See M Zander, 'Payment into Court', *New Law Journal*, 3 July 1975, p 638.)

Proposals for reform of the rule

The Winn Committee thought that there were two main problems about the system of payment into court. One was that the sum awarded might be only very slightly below the sum paid in but the plaintiff would be seriously penalized as to the costs. (See *Wagman v Vale Motors Ltd* [1959] 1 WLR 853.) The other was that many trials consisted of contests of both liability and quantum of damages. The issues of liability might take up most of the trial and the plaintiff might win on that point. The issue of damages could be disposed of very quickly, but if the amount awarded was less than that paid into court the plaintiff would have to pay his own and his opponent's costs even on the liability issue where he won.

One way to deal with the question would be to give the court a discretion in dealing with the issue of costs. The Cantley Committee on *Personal Injuries Litigation Procedure* (1979, Cmnd 7476) thought that this would be to create too wide a discretion for the courts with too few guidelines and would produce lack of uniformity and uncertainty 'so that such a change would create as many problems as it set out to solve' (para 93, p 32).

A solution proposed by the Winn Committee (paras 520–25) was to replace the present system in personal injury cases with one in which the defendant would make one offer in regard to liability and another on quantum. At the trial the court would make separate orders in regard to costs, taking into account the outcome on each issue.

The Cantley Committee said (para 99) it was attracted by this proposal but further modification in the procedural rules would be required to give the plaintiff access to the defendant's documents and the premises where the accident occurred. This would promote earlier discovery but it would not reduce costs. On balance the Cantley Committee thought that, although it had faults, the existing system should remain.

In 1981 a committee of JUSTICE issued a fresh report on the subject of payment into court. It said it was not impressed by the Cantley Committee's criticisms of the

Winn Committee's proposal. The problem of a lack of information for the plaintiff when he decided whether to accept the sum paid in existed under the present system.

The JUSTICE Committee said that it was vital for the judge to exercise a real discretion on costs, taking into account the offers and counter-offers that had been made and their timing. The judge should make up his mind on the basis of an assessment of the reasonableness of the parties in the negotiating process.

The only change that has been made, however, was to give the court power to make an order for a split trial–with liability and quantum being taken separately. In such a case the defendant is permitted to make a written offer to accept liability up to a stated amount (RSC Ord 33, r 5A). The rule does not provide for the effect of such an offer. It simply says that it shall be brought to the attention of the judge after the issue of liability has been decided. But the rules still require that the award of costs be determined by the outcome–regardless of the extent of the over or under assessment of the level of damages.

The Civil Justice Review's *General Issues Paper* considered the problem of payment-in briefly (paras 195–98). It did not propose any solutions, but asked a number of questions. These included:

(1)   Should it continue to be necessary actually to pay money into court?
(2)   Should the proposals of the Winn Committee be adopted either for personal injuries cases or generally?
(3)   Should the system encourage the making of counter-offers–offers by each party so as to equalize the costs sanction and promote more settlements?
(4)   Should the payment-in and written-offer system be abolished?

The Final Report of the Civil Justice Review said that this was not an issue on which action seemed to be required at present (para 273).

Reform in the English system has been nonexistent so far. By contrast in Canada and Australia the movement to reform the payment-in principle has gone further–in the direction of permitting the plaintiff too to initiate a settlement by indicating what sum of damages or other settlement he will accept. In Ontario for instance, a new rule was introduced as from January 1985 with application to monetary and other claims (see *New Law Journal*, 4 January 1985, p 3). Under this rule, if the plaintiff makes an offer and obtains judgment at least as favourable as the terms of the offer, he is entitled to 'standard' costs to the date of payment-in, and to the more generous 'indemnity' costs from that date. (For the meaning of these terms, see p 422 below.) For a similar proposal see M Tiplady, 'Payments into Court for Plaintiffs' , *Law Society's Gazette*, 28 August 1991, p 17.

In England, as will be seen (p 422 below), these categories of costs have now been changed and the winning plaintiff should now expect to get a higher proportion of his costs than under the old 'party and party' formula. This would reduce the impact of a rule such as that introduced in Ontario. Moreover in litigation against insurance companies it must be doubtful whether the threat of the costs sanction would work anyway. The Law Reform Commission of British Columbia proposed that the court could be given a power to order that the defendant pay up to double the plaintiff's costs where it failed to accept his reasonable offer. But this proposal proved unpopular and was later modified to require the defendant to pay the plaintiff's 'actual costs'. (See *Civil Justice Quarterly*, April 1986, pp 99–102.)

For an analysis of payment into court and other economic aspects of the settlement process, see Jenny Phillips and Keith Hawkins, 'Some Economic Aspects of the Settlement Process: A Study of Personal Injury Claims', 39 *Modern Law Review*, September 1976, p 497.

Woolf on payment into court

Lord Woolf in his Interim Report in June 1995 made a number of proposals regarding payment into court:

(1) That the actual payment-in of money should stop and that instead a Calderbank letter would suffice in all cases (p 194, para 5).

(2) An offer should be capable of being made either in respect of the whole case or of specific issues (p 194, para 5).

(3) The plaintiff should be able to make an offer to settle–as was already permitted in a number of Australian and Canadian jurisdictions. If the plaintiff's offer was refused and he then was awarded as much or more, he should be entitled to 'additional costs' in the form of costs on the indemnity basis (see p 422 below) plus interest at an enhanced rate. But the scope of this recommendation was qualified by the caveat that it should only apply to what Lord Woolf calls the 'multi track cases' (normally over £10,000 in amount) and therefore not to the much larger number of 'fast track cases' because 'it would detract from the pre-determined costs regime which is an integral feature of that track' (p 196, para 9).

If the plaintiff beat the defendant's offer but not his own, Lord Woolf proposed that he should only be entitled to normal costs (as now).

An offer by either side should be capable of dealing either with the whole case or with one or more issues and should be capable of being made even before the start of proceedings (p 197, para 17).

Courts should have (and should exercise) a discretion to modify the normal cost rule in the light of the way in which offers are made–to take account for instance of sham offers, or last minute offers or withdrawals of offers (pp 197–8, paras 18–20).

(e) Discovery of documents and 'cards on the table'

After pleadings are closed, each party in a High Court case must 'make discovery'. This means that each side must make available to the other any relevant documents they have regarding the case. Under RSC Ord 24 (and CCR Ord 14) each must inform the other whether he has (or had) in his possession, custody or power, documents relating to matters at issue in the case. (On what is meant by 'power' in this context, see *Lonrho v Shell* [1980] 1 WLR 627 but cf *B v B* [1979] 1 All ER 801.) (In proceedings for judicial review under RSC Ord 53 general discovery is not available but an application for discovery can be made which will be refused if discovery is not necessary to dispose of the case fairly–see *R v Secretary of State for Foreign Affairs, ex p World Development Movement Ltd* [1995] 1 All ER 611,620 (Div Ct).)

Discovery has two stages–first, making lists of documents which are supposed to be exchanged within 14 days of the close of pleadings, and second, production or giving an opportunity for inspection.

By virtue of a recent change in the rules a party may request that copies of any documents he wishes to inspect should be supplied, at his cost (see RSC Ord 24, r 11A; CCR Ord 14, r 5A).

One of the most vexing problems of modern civil litigation is the proliferation of documents through the use of photocopiers. For an exploration of the courts' approach to the problem see C Hodges, 'Taming the Juggernaut', *New Law Journal*, 25 October 1991, p 1457.

The duty to make full disclosure as required by the rules lies on both parties and their lawyers. In *Rockwell v Barrus* [1968] 2 All ER 98, Megarry J pointed out that many litigants have little appreciation of the scope of discovery and the duty of making full disclosure: 'Accordingly it seems to me necessary for solicitors to take positive steps to ensure that the client appreciates at an early stage of the litigation, promptly after writ issued, not only the duty of discovery and its width but also the duty of not destroying documents which have to be disclosed.' In a company, this means that such knowledge must be passed to whoever in the company may be affected by it.

There are various sanctions that can be used if the rules are broken. The action can be dismissed, a defence may be struck out, a party may be ordered to pay costs; in extreme cases it may even result in an order for committal of the person responsible to prison. In *Infabrics v Jaytex* [1985] FSR 75, 79, inadvertent destruction of documents that should have been disclosed led to the court making assumptions in favour of the other side in regard to matters in dispute.

Discovery usually takes place without any order to that effect from the court, as an automatic procedure under RSC Ord 24(2). If a party is recalcitrant, the other can ask for an order from the master or, outside London, from a district judge. The rules require that a list of documents be produced in two categories. One is of documents which will be produced without objection; the other is of those documents discovery of which is opposed, because it is claimed they are covered by privilege or public interest immunity (see below).

Heilbron-Hodge on discovery

The Report of the Bar and Law Society Heilbron-Hodge Committee in 1993 said 'At present, the cost of litigation makes it uneconomic to go to court unless the amounts at stake are very large. Our system of justice is in practice available only to the very rich or the very poor. *Much of the expense is caused by discovery.*' (Civil Justice on Trial-the Case for Change, 1993, p 44, para 5.1, emphasis supplied). In the majority of cases the system worked reasonably well because there were few documents but in document-heavy cases and where the parties did not cooperate, serious problems arose. It was becoming increasingly common for parties to approach discovery in an adversarial and obstructive manner.

Heilbron-Hodge proposed a new system:

(1) After close of pleadings–and before preparing their lists of documents–the parties should be required to confer with a view to agreeing on the scope of discovery. Such a conference could be dispensed with if the parties agree, possibly over the telephone, that general discovery is appropriate.

(2) If parties cannot agree, they should seek directions from the court. The court would decide on the scope of discovery, applying a 'necessity' test.

(3) In the absence of directions there would be automatic general discovery but subject to a more restrictive test requiring of a party discovery of documents upon which he intends to rely or disclosure of which may have a significant effect on the course or outcome of the action or disclosure of which is otherwise necessary for fairly disposing of the action or for saving costs.

(4) Every list of documents should be accompanied by an affidavit that the list contains nothing except relevant documents.

(5) The list should be accompanied by a core bundle containing only the most important documents.

The Committee accepted that its proposals involved added cost. It said:

However, such front-end loading of costs is in our view desirable to promote earlier settlements, narrow issues and reduce trial length. We would therefore expect the additional costs incurred at an earlier stage in the litigation process to result in an overall economy in the long run. Fewer and shorter trials would result which would release judicial resources to other cases and speed up the overall process of justice. Furthermore, in the majority of cases which would involve few documents the additional cost burden will be insignificant. It will only bite in the document-heavy cases which are proving most problematic.

Woolf on discovery

In his Interim Report in June 1995 Lord Woolf stated that he had received many submissions that in a minority of complex cases discovery created a significant problem in terms of a burden of resources and cost. In his view discovery (which he wants to rename 'disclosure'), should be retained but curbed. He differentiated four categories of documents: (1) the documents relied on by the parties; (2) adverse documents, which could help the other side; (3) other relevant documents; (4) documents which could lead to a train of inquiry that might produce relevant documents. The category that generated most of the problem, he suggested, was the third.

Lord Woolf categorised (1) and (2) as suitable for 'standard discovery' and (3) and (4) as 'extra discovery'.

In regard to his fast track category of case only standard discovery should normally be permitted. But extra discovery could be ordered if a case could be made out. In fast track cases this would be very rare.

The Fast Track Consultation Paper issued by the Woolf Inquiry in January 1996 suggested that guidelines or protocols should be drawn up for the conduct of a legal case 'pre-issue' ie before the start of legal proceedings. They should be agreed between representatives of both claimants and defendants in common areas of business and would cover such matters as 'exchange of documents from agreed lists, such as in an employer's liability case, accident book records and wage slips and experts' evidence' (p 8, para 25). This would aid the process of disclosure post-issue.

The parties would have to certify that they had disclosed all documents required under standard discovery.

In what he called multi track cases Lord Woolf suggested that the approach would have to be adjusted to the needs of the case. The procedural judge would decide on the scope and extent of discovery at the case management conference–on which see p 95 below. Discovery might be ordered on the basis of a rolling programme.

The core of the problem was how to avoid lawyers having to trawl through all category (3) documents in order to eliminate the possibility of overlooking category (2) documents. The Bar suggested that initial disclosure should be confined to documents which are 'capable of being located without undue difficulty and expense'. Lord Woolf said that he supported this approach but he formulated the test slightly differently–'initial disclosure should apply to documents of which a party is aware at the time when the obligation to disclose arises' (p 171, para 34). It was for consideration whether this formula should be enlarged to include potentially adverse documents of which a party would have been aware if he had not deliberately closed his mind to their existence.

In making an order for extra discovery the procedural judge would have in mind the circumstances of the parties and of the case.

Note also the Lord Chief Justice's Practice Direction of January 1995, (p 92 below) which states that in the interests of the paramount importance of reducing the cost of civil litigation the court would exercise its discretion to limit, *inter alia*, discovery. On the exercise of this discretion see C Passmore, 'Controlling a Juggernaut', *Law Society's Gazette*, 25 October 1995, p 20.

No discovery if legal professional privilege applies

It is important that clients should be able to communicate fully with their legal advisers without fear that these communications will become known to the other side. Legal professional privilege is therefore an exception to the principle of discovery. (The same doctrine applies equally to restrict police searches for, and seizure of evidence in criminal proceedings, see p 174–75 below.)

Privilege applies to documents prepared for the purposes of getting or giving legal advice and to documents prepared with a view to litigation and opinions of counsel. In *Ventouris v Mountain , The Italia Express* [1991] 3 All ER 472 the Court of Appeal, reversing the trial judge, applied the principle when it held that privilege did not apply to documents obtained by solicitors for the purposes of preparing for litigation if the documents did not come into existence for the purposes of the litigation.

Normally, if an original document does not have privilege, a photocopy likewise does not have privilege even if the photocopy came into existence for the purpose of seeking legal advice–*Dubai Bank Ltd v Galadari* [1989] 3 All ER 769. But if a solicitor has exercised skill and judgment in selecting the document for consideration it may attract privilege–the Court of Appeal in *Dubai Bank* interpreting *R v Board of Inland Revenue, ex p Goldberg* [1988] 3 All ER 248 (Div Ct); *Barclay's Bank plc v Eustice* [1995] 4 All ER 511, CA. Definition of the exception is fraught with practical difficulties–see N Andrews, *Principles of Civil Procedure* (Sweet & Maxwell, 1994, pp 343–46).

In *Alfred Crompton Amusement Machines Ltd v Customs and Excise Comrs (No 2)* ([1973] 2 All ER 1169, the House of Lords held that privilege does not attach to a communication passing between a party and his non-professional agent or a third party, unless the communication was made after a decision which would lead to solicitors being instructed to start or defend legal proceedings.

Where a document is prepared for a dual purpose, the test of whether it is privileged is what was the dominant purpose. In *Waugh v British Railways Board* [1979] 2 All ER 1169, HL privilege was denied to a British Railways internal inquiry as to the circumstances of a fatal accident. The report had two purposes–the prevention of accidents for the future and assistance in dealing with the particular claim. The House of Lords held that its dominant purpose was the prevention of accidents and it therefore was not privileged. See similarly *Peach v Metropolitan Comr* [1986] 2 All ER 129. (See further G McFarlane, 'Professional Privilege: The Dominant Purpose', *New Law Journal*, 1 February 1985, p 111.)

The privilege is that of the client, and only the client can waive it. If, however, a copy of the document has somehow (even through improper means) come into the possession of the other side, evidence of its contents can be given unless the court can be persuaded to grant an injunction against such use on the ground that it would involve breach of confidence. (See *Calcraft v Guest* [1898] 1 QB 759, *Goddard v Nationwide Building Society* [1986] 3 All ER 264; *Guinness Peat Properties Ltd v Fitzroy Robinson Partnership* [1987] 2 All ER 716; and *British Coal Corpn v Dennis Rye Ltd (No 2)* [1988] 3 All ER 816.)

See generally C Tapper, 'Privilege and Confidence', *Modern Law Review*, 1972, p 83; JD Heydon, 'Legal Professional Privilege and Third Parties, *Modern Law Review*, 1974, p 601; Neil J Williams, 'Four Questions of Privilege: the Litigation Aspect of Legal Professional Privilege', *Civil Justice Quarterly*, April 1990, p 139; C Hodges and G Hickinbottom, 'Evidence Collection or Evidence Suppression', *New Law Journal*, 1 June 1990, p 778; C Grazin, 'Recent Changes in the Law of Discovery', *Solicitors' Journal*, 8 February 1991, pp 149, 150–1.

Public interest immunity (formerly called Crown Privilege)

The second main ground of immunity from disclosure is where disclosure is contrary to the public interest. Such immunity may arise because of the contents of the document or because the document belongs to a class or category which has immunity regardless of its contents.

It is for the courts and not for the executive to determine whether a document has immunity (*Conway v Rimmer* [1968] AC 910).

Before deciding on a claim for public interest immunity the court can call for the actual documents in question and can look at them without showing them to the party applying for access to them. But in *Air Canada v Secretary of State for Trade (No 2)* [1983] 1 All ER 910, the House of Lords held that the court should only do this if the party applying for discovery had shown that the information in the documents was likely to assist his case, in the sense that there was a reasonable probability that it would and not just a mere speculative belief that it would do so. See also *Balfour v Foreign and Commonwealth Office* [1994] 2 All ER 588 where the Court of Appeal held that once there was an actual or potential risk to national security demonstrated by an appropriate certificate by a minister the court should not exercise its right to inspect the documents. The Court of Appeal applied the decision of the House of Lords in *Council of Civil Service Unions v Minister for the Civil Service* [1985] AC 374, [1984] 3 All ER 935, arising out of the banning of trades union at GCHQ. See generally N Zaltsman, 'Public Interest Immunity in Civil Proceedings: Protecting the Supply of Information to the Public Authority', *Public Law*, 1984, p 423.

There have been many examples over the years of public interest immunity. In *Alfred Crompton Amusement Machines v Customs and Excise Comrs* [1974] AC 405, the House of Lords gave protection to information obtained confidentially by the

Crown for the purposes of valuing goods for tax purposes; in *Gaming Board for Great Britain v Rogers* [1973] AC 388, the House of Lords protected confidential inquiries by the Gaming Board from the police as to applicants; in *D v National Society for the Prevention of Cruelty to Children* [1978] AC 171, the House of Lords upheld a claim to avoid disclosure by NSPCC of the name of an informant about child cruelty where the mother wanted to sue the informant or the NSPCC. See also: *Burmah Oil Co Ltd v Bank of England* [1979] 3 All ER 700, HL in which immunity was granted in relation to documents exchanged between government ministers and the Bank of England regarding the price to be paid by the Treasury for the purchase of Burmah Oil shares. In *Neilson v Laugharne* [1981] 1 All ER 829 and *Makanjuola v Metropolitan Police Comr* [1992] 3 All ER 617, immunity was allowed for statements given to the police in connection with an inquiry into a complaint against the police. But these decisions were overturned by the House of Lords in *R v Chief Constable of the West Midlands Police, ex p Wiley* [1994] 3 All ER 420. The House of Lords held there that a class claim to immunity in such cases was unjustified since it tended to defeat the object it was designed to achieve. By contrast, see *Taylor v Anderton* [1995] 2 All ER 420, CA.

In *Williams v Home Office* [1981] 1 All ER 1151, immunity was refused to hundreds of pages of internal Home Office documents relating to the establishment of 'control units' in prisons. In *Evans v Chief Constable of Surrey* [1989] 2 All ER 594 the Divisional Court said there could be no disclosure of reports from the police to the DPP about a murder in which the applicant was implicated. In *Re HIV Haemophiliacs, Litigation* [1990] NLJR 1349, the Department of Health was ordered by the Court of Appeal to hand over documents for which public interest immunity had been claimed regarding the plaintiffs' infection with AIDS. The 900 or so plaintiffs had shown a *prima facie* case against the department in negligence and the claim to immunity was overridden by the public interest in the full and fair trial of the plaintiffs' claim. (This decision led to an out-of-court aggregate settlement of £42m for the plaintiffs.)

The doctrine applies also to criminal cases. A spectacular illustration was the so-called Matrix Churchill case in which the trial judge, Judge Smedley, quashed public interest immunity certificates served by the prosecution, designed to suppress evidence about intelligence sources, about information held by the Security Service (MI5) and the Secret Intelligence Service (MI6), and high level inter-departmental and ministerial contact over a licence application to export material for a super-gun to Iraq. The judge's decision led to the collapse of the prosecution against the executives in the machine tool company who had been charged with deception in obtaining export licences. (See A Tomkins, 'Public Interest Immunity after Matrix Churchill', *Public Law*, Winter 1993, pp 650–68. For a detailed account of the case see D Leigh *Betrayed: The Real Story of the Matrix Churchill Trial* (London, 1993).) It led also to the establishment of the 'arms for Iraq' inquiry by Lord Justice Scott.

Discovery is subject to undertakings

Discovery is made subject to an undertaking that the documents disclosed should not be used for any 'improper, collateral or ulterior purpose'.

In the above mentioned case of *Williams v Home Office*, the plaintiff's solicitor was prosecuted for contempt of court because she showed the documents disclosed to a journalist who wrote about them in *The Guardian*. The documents she showed to the journalist had all been read in open court. She was nevertheless held to have been in contempt of court by the House of Lords–see *Home Office v Harman* [1982] 1 All ER 532.

The solicitor, Miss Harriet Harman, then took the case to Strasbourg under the European Convention on Human Rights. The case ended with a 'friendly settlement' when the Government agreed to change the Rules of the Supreme Court. The new rule came into force in 1987. It provides that once a document is read or referred to in open court, any implicit or explicit undertaking that the parties and their lawyers will not use it for purposes other than the case, ceases to apply. If a party wants to stop the other party from using the document in such a way it will, however, have the right to apply to the court for an order that the undertaking should continue to apply (Rules of the Supreme Court (Amendment) 1987, SI 1987/1423).

Discovery against someone who is not (or is not yet) a party

Discovery is traditionally only available against the person who is the object of the proceedings. Information or documents in the possession of third parties can normally only be obtained by issuing a *subpoena duces tecum* requiring them to come to the trial with the documents.

This fundamental rule of English procedure has recently been somewhat subverted by a new procedural manoeuvre of issuing a *subpoena duces tecum* to a non-party but making the operative date some time before the trial. In *Khanna v Lovell White Durrant* [1994] 4 All ER 267 the Vice Chancellor gave this his blessing. It avoided the adjournment of the trial for reading of the documents. It enabled witness statements to be prepared and payment into court to be considered and it was in line with the modern 'cards on the table' approach to litigation, avoiding surprises at trial. But for a critical reaction to this development see P Matthews, 'Truth, Justice and the American Way', *New Law Journal*, 30 September 1994, p 1317–emphasising its potentially serious effect in greatly expanding pre-trial discovery and the resulting cost of the trial. Moreover the other side had no standing to object either to the *subpoena* or to its terms. The non-party could object but often he would have no reason to do so. The easiest thing for him might simply be to hand over the documents.

The objection that discovery only applied if proceedings had actually started and only applied to parties was considered by the Winn Committee in 1968. It recommended that discovery by order of the court should be available where a claim in respect of personal injuries or in respect of someone's death was 'likely to be made'. The Administration of Justice Act 1970, s 31, implemented this recommendation, which only applies, however, to actions arising out of personal injuries or death. The power is now to be found in s 33 of the Supreme Court Act 1981 (see also RSC Ord 24, r 7A). Lord Woolf in his Interim Report in 1995 (p 173, para 41) recommended that in order to promote early settlement offers, the restriction of this power to personal injuries cases should be removed.

Section 31 of the 1970 Act was applied in *Dunning v United Liverpool Hospital's Board of Governors* [1973] 2 All ER 454, in which the Court of Appeal ordered a hospital to disclose medical records prior to the issue of any writ. The injured person wanted to see the records in order to see whether to bring action against the hospital. See also *Shaw v Vauxhall Motors Ltd* [1974] 2 All ER 1185, CA in which the Court of Appeal held that the words 'likely to be sued', should be construed liberally to include the case where the bringing of an action may be dependent on the outcome of the discovery.

The Winn Committee proposed a second exception to the general rule in regard to claims for damages arising out of personal injuries or death. This was to allow a party to seek an order for discovery against a third party who was holding relevant documents. This recommendation was implemented in s 32 of the Administration of Justice Act 1970 and is now to be found in s 34 of the Supreme Court Act 1981, and Ord 24, r 7A.

The power was utilized in *Paterson v Chadwick* [1974] 2 All ER 772, in which the court ordered discovery against a hospital in the course of proceedings brought against a solicitor. The solicitor was being sued for negligence in allowing the plaintiff's personal injuries claim against the hospital to become statute barred by lapse of time. The hospital argued that the claim against the solicitor was not a personal injuries action and therefore fell outside the ambit of s 32, but the court held that for the purposes of the section the action arose out of a personal injuries case. (See generally Richard Bragg, 'Pre-trial inspection' *Solicitors' Journal*, 21 August 1992, p 836.)

See also the Access to Health Records Act 1990 which established a right for a patient, or someone authorised to apply on his behalf, to get medical records created after November 1990. Note also the Data Protection Act 1984 which gave a person a right of access to information about him which is held in computerised form. But the right to get data on computer is qualified by secondary legislation which states that there is no right to inspect a health record if access would be likely to cause serious harm to the physical or mental health of the applicant or would be likely to disclose another person's identity. (Data Protection (Subject Access Modification) (Health) Order 1987, SI 1987/1903.)

(On a new protocol for getting access to medical records see R Vallance, 'Medical Records', *Law Society's Gazette*, 31 August 1995, p 24.)

The courts have developed a further exception to the general rule under which discovery can be ordered against a third party who for some reason has information which is needed to deal with wrongdoing and who in some sense is implicated in the wrongdoing. Thus in *Norwich Pharmacal Co v Customs and Excise Comrs* [1974] AC 133, the House of Lords held that the Customs authorities had to disclose the names of persons importing materials allegedly in breach of the plaintiff's patent because dishonest traders did not deserve protection. Lord Reid said (at p 175) that 'if through no fault of his own a person gets mixed up in the tortious acts of others so as to facilitate their wrongdoing he may incur no personal liability but he comes under a duty to assist the person who has been wronged by giving him full information and disclosing the identity of the wrongdoer'. This same principle was applied by the House of Lords in *British Steel Corpn v Granada Television Ltd* [1981] AC 1096, to order Granada to hand over to British Steel the name of the 'mole' who had passed it confidential documents relating to the company's handling of the steel strike. Granada, like the Customs in *Norwich Pharmacal*, was an innocent third party, but the courts ordered discovery in order to permit the plaintiff to get a remedy in regard to wrongdoing.

The same doctrine was applied in *Bankers Trust Co v Shapira* [1980] 3 All ER 353, when the court ordered a bank to reveal the details of a customer's account in order to give effect to a defrauded plaintiff's equitable right to trace his money. (By contrast, see *X v Y* [1988] 2 All ER 648 and *Arab Monetary Fund v Hashim (No 5)* [1992] 2 All ER 911.)

But the person against whom the order is made must somehow be involved. It would not be possible under this doctrine, for instance, to order a passer-by who saw a road accident to reveal the name prior to the hearing of the action. He would be a 'mere witness'.

This principle was prayed in aid in *Harrington v North London Polytechnic* [1984] 3 All ER 666, by lecturers at the polytechnic who had been ordered by the court to disclose the names of picketing students. The action was brought by Patrick Harrington, a member of the National Front, after he had been prevented from pursuing his studies by other students who objected to his presence. He obtained an injunction against the polytechnic, but when the injunction was ignored by picketing students, Harrington asked for a further order requiring certain teachers to identify persons in photographs taken of the picketing. The lecturers claimed they were not parties to the action and that they should be protected from the order by the 'mere witness' rule. They also said that such an order would be contrary to public policy since it would damage the special relationship between staff and students. The Court of Appeal held that they were not 'mere witnesses'. In fact they were not witnesses at all since they had not been present at the time of the picketing. They could be made subject to such an order as employees of the polytechnic. But since they had not been given a chance to put their argument, the case should be sent back to the High Court for proper argument on the public-policy aspects.

On the related but separate question of whether it is possible compulsorily to take oral statements from potential witnesses at the pre-trial stage see p 70 below.

Mareva injunctions

In a case in 1992 Mr Justice Hoffmann (as he then was) said 'The last 20 years have seen a judge-made revolution in English civil procedure. Under pressure from the increase in commercial fraud, the courts have provided plaintiffs with remedies and investigative powers which previously, if they existed at all, were available only to the police'. (*Arab Monetary Fund v Hashim (No 5)* [1992] 2 All ER 911, 913.) He was referring in particular to Mareva injunctions and Anton Piller orders (below). (The Mareva injunction and the Anton Piller Order have been described as 'the two nuclear weapons of the law'.)

A Mareva injunction prevents the other party from transferring his assets abroad or disposing of them so as to defeat the plaintiff's hope of satisfying any judgment he may ultimately win. The power derives from a 1975 case, *Mareva Cia Naviera SA v International Bulkcarriers SA* [1980] 1 All ER 213n, [1975] 2 Lloyd's Rep 509, CA. The Court of Appeal held that an injunction to prevent assets from being removed could be granted in any case in which the court thought it to be just or convenient. (See especially, *Third Chandris Shipping Corpn v Unimarine SA* [1979] QB 645, 668–9; *The Siskina* [1979] AC 210, 261; *Barclay-Johnson v Yuill* [1980] 1 WLR 1259.) The new jurisdiction was recognized in the Supreme Court Act 1981, s 37, which makes it clear that such orders can be made regardless of whether the subject of the order is domiciled, resident or even merely present within the jurisdiction. (See MA Grant, 'The Mareva Injunction Four Years On', *New Law Journal*, 1980, p 985.)

Section 37(1) of the 1981 Act empowers the High Court to grant an injunction in all cases in which it appears to the court to be just and convenient to do so. Section 37(3) extends that power to restraining a party to any proceedings from 'dealing with' assets within the jurisdiction. 'Dealing with' includes disposing of, selling, pledging or charging an asset. When a Mareva injunction is sought in a county court case the application must normally be heard by a High Court judge.

The order in effect freezes the assets pending the outcome of the proceedings. It has been held that such an order can apply to assets worldwide: *Derby & Co Ltd v Weldon (No 2)* [1989] 1 All ER 1002, CA, but that such worldwide Marevas should be granted only in exceptional circumstances: *Republic of Haiti v Duvalier* [1990]1 QB 202, CA.

Usually the order only relates to the amount of the claim–leaving the defendant free to use the rest of his assets. The defendant must be left enough to meet his reasonable living expenses and to meet certain debts (*PCW (Underwriting Agencies) Ltd v Dixon* [1983] 2 All ER 697n). The defendant must also normally be allowed to make payments in the ordinary course of business conducted in good faith (*Iraqi Ministry of Defence v Arcepey Shipping Co SA* [1981] QB 65).

See further R Ough, 'The Mareva Injunction: a Practical Guide', *New Law Journal*, 1 May 1987, p 413 and M Bundock, 'The Onward March of the Mareva', *New Law Journal*, 14 April 1989, p 496.

Mareva injunctions have become vastly popular. In a case in 1986, Bingham J. said that such applications had become 'commonplace, hundreds being made each year and relatively few refused' (*Siporex Trade SA v Comdel Commodities* [1986] 2 Lloyd's Rep 428 at 539).

The procedure for obtaining a Mareva injunction is now laid down in a lengthy Practice Direction–see *Practice Direction* (Mareva and Anton Piller orders: new forms) [1994] 4 All ER 52, [1994] 1 WLR 1233. Annex 2 of the Practice Direction deals with worldwide Marevas; annex 3 deals with Marevas limited to assets within the jurisdiction. The text was published in full in *New Law Journal*, 12 August 1994, p 1134.

Anton Piller orders

The other draconian order developed recently by the courts is the Anton Piller order, which permits the plaintiff to enter the defendant's premises to search for evidence. For a (somewhat unconvincing) explanation of the judicial basis for such an order, see *Bhimji v Chatwani* [1991] 1 All ER 705, 708 (per Scott J).

The order is made *ex parte*, that is to say, in the absence of the defendant. The name derives from the decision which initiated this development–*Anton Piller KG v Manufacturing Processes Ltd* [1976] 1 All ER 779, CA. The plaintiffs there wanted to restrain a breach of copyright by a rival firm. They feared that if the defendants knew, they would destroy the documents showing their guilt. They therefore applied for an *ex parte* order, which was granted. The Court of Appeal held that such an order should, however, only be made in an extreme case where there was grave danger of property being smuggled away or vital evidence destroyed.

Since that decision the courts have developed the concept of Anton Piller orders. The application is heard *in camera* so as not to alert the other side to the application and thus risk that the material may be destroyed.

The plaintiff must satisfy the court that he has a very strong *prima facie* case on the merits, that he is likely to suffer very serious actual or potential damage from the defendant's actions, and that there is clear evidence that the defendant has incriminating material on his premises which he would be likely to destroy if no order were made. If the court is satisfied that the effect of such an order would not be excessive or out of proportion, it may order the defendant to permit the plaintiff to enter his premises, to search for goods or documents which are relevant to his claim and to remove, inspect, photograph or make copies of such material. The plaintiff has to give an undertaking that he will pay the defendant damages if a judge should later hold that damages ought to be paid because of the way the order was executed. The order must be precise. It should be enforced with circumspection and the plaintiff's solicitor being an officer of the court should be present. The defendant must be allowed to contact his solicitor and, unlike the police with a search warrant, if the defendant refuses entry, the plaintiff is not entitled to use force. But the defendant may find himself liable to proceedings, including committal to prison, for contempt of court. (See especially *Rank Film Distributors Ltd v Video Information Centre* [1982] AC 380; *Vapormatic Co Ltd v Sparex Ltd* [1976] 1 WLR 939; *Yousif v Salama* [1980] 1 WLR 1540.

The whole subject of Anton Piller orders was exhaustively considered by Scott J in *Columbia Picture Industries Inc v Robinson* [1986] 3 All ER 338. He held that the order had been carried out in an oppressive manner by the plaintiff's solicitors and ordered them to pay the defendant, Robinson, damages of £7,500, plus £2,500 for his company. For discussion and comment, see *Civil Justice Quarterly*, January 1987, p 10. See generally Anne Staines, 'The Protection of Intellectual Property Rights: Anton Piller Orders', 46 *Modern Law Review*, 1983, p 274 and M Dockray and H Laddie, 'Piller Problems' (1990) *Law Quarterly Review* 601.

See especially also the strong decision of the Vice Chancellor in *Universal Thermosensors Ltd v Hibben* [1992] 3 All ER 257 and for comment G Exall, 'Anton Pillers after *Hibben', Solicitors' Journal*, 6 March 1992, p 218 and S Lovick, 'Pillers of Justice', *New Law Journal*, 6 March 1992, p 323. In *Hibben* the Vice Chancellor said (pp 275–6) that in suitable and strictly limited cases, especially in blatant cases of fraud, Anton Piller orders were very valuable. But they should not be allowed to fall into disrepute. The execution of Anton Piller orders should be subject to the following safeguards: (1) execution should be on working days in office hours so that the defendant can get legal advice if he wishes to have it; (2) if execution is at a private house where a woman may be at home alone, the solicitor serving the order must be, or must be accompanied by a woman; (3) unless it is wholly impracticable, the order should normally require that a detailed list of what is taken away should be prepared on the premises and that the defendant should have an opportunity of checking the list; (4) it should not be executed at business premises save in the presence of a responsible officer of the business; (5) means should be found, if possible, to prevent execution at a competitor's premises from including a search of all the competitor's documents. Serious consideration should also be given to requiring that a solicitor experienced in dealing with Anton Piller orders from another firm be there to supervise and that the independent solicitor make a report on the execution for the court.

In the *Rank Film* case (above) the House of Lords held that the defendant retained his privilege against self-incrimination and the court therefore should not make an order compelling disclosure of documents where the evidence showed that this would put the defendant in danger of self-incrimination. But the effect of this decision was negatived by the Supreme Court Act 1981, s 72, in regard to proceedings in the High Court for infringement of intellectual property (patents, trade marks, copyright, etc) or for passing off. (See Neil Garnham, 'Section 72 of the Supreme Court Act 1981: Its Effect on the Making of Anton Piller Orders', *New Law Journal*, 1982, p 983.) Section 72 removes the privilege but provides that answers given or documents handed over cannot be used in subsequent criminal proceedings. Section 31 of the Theft Act 1968 is to like effect. But in two major cases in 1990 it was held that the privilege against self-incrimination could be claimed to prevent Mareva and Anton Piller orders against individuals in connection with conspiracy to defraud: *Sociedade Nacional de Combustiveis de Angola UEE (Sonangol) v Lundqvist* [1990] 3 All ER 283 and *Tate Access Floors Inc v Boswell* [1990] 3 All ER 303. Giving judgment in the first of these two cases Sir Nicolas Browne-Wilkinson, as he then was, said he was greatly concerned about the implications of the Court of Appeal's ruling. Parliament should act urgently to close this gap by provisions similar to those in s 31 of the Theft Act or s 72 of the Supreme Court Act.

A Consultation Paper issued by the Lord Chancellor's Department in 1992 entitled *The Privilege against Self-incrimination in Civil Proceedings* recommended that the privilege should no longer apply in civil proceedings but to date this recommendation has not been implemented.

The Anton Piller order and the Mareva injunction have been developed primarily in intellectual property, passing off and other commercial matters. Anton Piller orders are often sought by employers against ex-employees to prevent them using confidential information such as customers' lists, price lists etc. They can be used equally in matrimonial proceedings. Thus in *Emanuel v Emanuel* (1982) 12 Fam Law 62 an Anton Piller order was granted to enable a wife to search at her former husband's home for documents which he had unreasonably refused to produce in regard to his income. (See Gordon Exall, 'Using the Anton Piller Order in Matrimonial Proceedings', *Legal Action*, May 1990, p 20.)

In November 1992 the Lord Chancellor's Department issued a Consultation Paper on Anton Piller orders prepared by a Committee of Judges appointed by the Judges' Council. They made a number of serious criticisms of the basic concept. One was that the courts had no inherent power to authorise plaintiffs, or anyone else, to enter the premises of other persons. Statute had given the courts the power to do so in the form of search warrants or entry by customs officers. But there was no such power in civil proceedings. Anton Piller orders attempted to circumvent the lack of power by ordering the respondent to permit the entry and search. The right to search arose not from the court's order but from the consent given by the defendant. Such consent, being demanded under threat of imprisonment, could hardly be regarded as voluntary. ('It is questionable whether a consent procured by a threat of imprisonment is a sound basis for the acquisition by the plaintiff of a right of entry that he would not otherwise have' (para 2.12).) Also it was customary for such orders to be made to the respondent and his 'agents or employees or other persons appearing to be in control of' the premises. But it could not be supposed that such persons were authorised to give consent for entry and search in such circumstances. In other words, the execution of Anton Piller orders was at best based 'upon a spurious consent, and in cases where the requisite authority is lacking, on no effective consent at all' (*ibid*, para 2.15).

The Consultation Paper recommended that in view of the draconian nature of Anton Piller orders there should be a statutory regime. Despite its correct analysis of the unreality of consent, the Consultation Paper recommended that entry should only be with the consent of the defendant or someone acting on his behalf. The statute should require an automatic 'return date' when the plaintiff would have to return to the court issuing the order to explain and justify himself and when the defendant would be able to ask for the order to be lifted and damages paid.

The 1994 Practice Direction dealing with Marevas (p 92 above) dealt also with Anton Piller orders. The specimen order adopts the proposal in *Universal Thermosensors* for execution of the order to be supervised by an experienced, independent solicitor. Annex 1 of the Practice Direction sets out a Notice to the Defendant. This states, inter alia, 'You are entitled to refuse to permit entry before 9.30 am or after 5.30 pm or at all on Saturday and Sunday'. But it also states that during proper hours the defendant must allow entry to the named supervising solicitor together with a named partner in the firm of solicitors acting for the plaintiff and up to a specified number of other persons. The order must be complied with by the defendant or by a responsible employee or by the person appearing to be in control of the premises. See M Davies, 'Anton Piller Orders after the Practice Direction', *Civil Justice Quarterly*, January 1996, pp 13–17.

Ancillary relief, stopping the defendant leaving the country

In *Bayer AG v Winter* [1986] 1 All ER 733, the Court of Appeal held that in support of a Mareva injunction and Anton Piller order the court could also give further relief in the form of a requirement that the defendant hand in his passport and an order that he not leave the country. For a comment, see Lesley J Anderson, 'Anton Piller Orders– Cause for Concern?', *Law Society's Gazette*, 1 October 1986, p 2897.

Other techniques for identifying the other party's case

Written questions called *interrogatories* can be put to the opponent. Such questions used to require the consent of the master and they had to be restricted to questions that were 'necessary or useful', concepts that were interpreted narrowly by the masters. Now they must be necessary either for disposing fairly of the cause or for saving costs. But they must not be used for a 'fishing expedition'–to discover unknown things in order to bring a different kind of case . The requirement of leave was abolished in 1990 (RSC Ord 26, r 1(1)), (See *Hall v Selvaco Ltd* (1996) Times, 27 March.)

Interrogatories are not much used. They are not supposed to be used until other methods have been tried. Thus the litigant should first ask for *further and better particulars* or send his opponent a *notice to admit facts*. But in his Interim Report Lord Woolf said that submissions to his Inquiry indicated that the new rule allowing one interrogatory to be administered without the leave of the court was being abused. It was 'all too easy with the assistance of word processors to produce standard interrogatories which result in unjustified expense' (p 173, para 42). On this see A Kleanthus, 'The Use and Abuse of Interrogatories', *Solicitors' Journal*, 9 September 1994, p 906.

Since the contents of pleadings would under his proposals need to be verified, Lord Woolf said he could see no role for interrogatories in proceedings on the fast track. They might have some use in multi track proceedings but that should be a matter to be raised at the case management conference–see pp 82–83 below.

Obtaining advance notice of one's opponent's witnesses and of their evidence

Traditionally there was no procedure to enable one party to obtain the names of his opponent's witnesses, let alone their statements, and there was equally no procedure for oral examination of the other side's witnesses in advance of the trial. But in this area there have recently been some dramatic changes which have transformed English pre-trial procedure.

The changes began with the Report of the Winn Committee in 1968. The Committee considered but rejected the proposal for compulsory exchange of witness statements (called 'proofs') and for pre-trial examination of the other side's witnesses. In regard to the suggestion that proofs of witnesses should be exchanged the Committee said simply: 'We do not think the time has yet come, if it ever will, when this fundamental change should be recommended'.[6] There was no further treatment of the subject nor any discussion of what made the suggestion inappropriate.

In regard to the suggestion that names of witnesses should be exchanged together with their addresses, the Committee said: 'we equally think that this should not take place. Foreign jurisdictions seem to be equally divided in relation to the exchanging of names of witnesses. Except in some American States the strong tendency of countries operating in a common-law atmosphere is against exchange' (para 370). Again there was no further argument. In relation to the suggestion that the other side's witnesses should be examinable by some form of pre-trial examination, the Committee said this would so complicate, delay and increase the cost of litigation that it should be rejected (para 355).

In the United States, by contrast, each party can require not only the other party but also anyone with knowledge of relevant facts to answer questions in an oral examination called 'taking a deposition' in regard to those facts and to produce any relevant documents. Any party may take the testimony of such a person either by way of oral examination or written interrogatories. Under the Federal Rules of Civil Procedure a witness, including a party, must give names, addresses and other details of all witnesses known to him. If the pre-trial examination of a witness is oral, his testimony can be used to impeach the witness (for example, to challenge the evidence that he gives at trial). For an evaluation of the pros and cons of this procedure see Geoffrey Bindman, 'Another Kind of Discovery', *Law Guardian*, May 1965.

For a graphic illustration of the American system in action, see Richard Rashke, *The Killing of Karen Silkwood* (Sphere Books, 1983). The book, which was the basis of a film starring Meryl Streep, describes the case brought by Miss Silkwood's estate against her employers, alleging that her death was due to its negligence in regard to contamination by plutonium. Most of the inquiries made by the lawyers were pursued through the means of pre-trial depositions. In the end there were over 6,000 pages of such depositions. The case ended with a verdict awarding damages of $10 million. It is difficult to imagine that the case could have had a successful outcome in England, where there is no equivalent procedure permitting a party to require a potential witness of fact to answer questions pre-trial. See *Bayer AG v Winter* [1986] 1 All ER 733.

But although the Winn Committee in 1968 was against a general principle of exchange of witness statements it did favour *some* exchange. It described the traditional approach to litigation as one of 'trial by ambush':

Our present procedures . . . adopt the adversary system as 'trial by ambush'. The courtroom resembles an arena. It is regarded as good tactics to keep the other side in the dark so far as it is possible, and if one party can spring a surprise upon the other, then an advantage has been obtained by which such party may profit [para 131].

---

6   *Report of the Committee on Personal Injuries Litigation*, 1968, Cmnd 369, para 368.

Rules for the exchange of evidence

The Winn Committee recommended that medical evidence be subject to a rule of exchange, and that where such exchange had been ordered, no medical evidence should be admitted at the trial unless its substance had been exchanged in advance. This recommendation became the basis of the rapid change in English procedure which resulted in new rules requiring each side save in exceptional circumstances to give to the other pre-trial the statements of *any* witness they intend to call. Failure to comply normally results in not being permitted to call that witness at the trial. (For a detailed account of the successive stages of this reform process see the 6th edition of this work pp 97–104 and a note in *Civil Justice Quarterly*, January 1993, pp 5–8. See also the note in *Civil Justice Quarterly*, October 1995, pp 228–30.)

Pre-trial disclosure of non-expert (RSC Ord 38, r 2A) and expert witness statements (Ord 38, rr 36, 37) is now mandatory in every Division of the High Court. RSC Ord 38, r 2A states:

At the summons for directions in an action commenced by writ the Court shall direct every party to serve on the other parties, within 14 weeks (or such other period as the Court may specify) of the hearing of the summons and on such terms as the Court may specify, written statements of the oral evidence which the party intends to adduce on any issues of fact to be decided at the trial.

The equivalent rule in the county court is CCR Ord 20, r 12A which is identical except that the period normally prescribed is 10 instead of 14 weeks.

Indeed, the matter has gone further still in that the witness statement is now normally used not merely pre-trial, but stands as the witness' evidence at the trial itself. In January 1995 the Lord Chief Justice and the Vice Chancellor issued a *Practice Note* ([1995] 1 All ER 385) stating: 'Unless otherwise ordered, every witness statement shall stand as the evidence in chief of the witness concerned'.

In a matter of ten years or so therefore the English system has gone from the position where witness statements were never available before trial to a position where they are virtually always available–and indeed normally constitute that party's evidence-in-chief at trial.

There are however situations where exchange will not be ordered. In *Richard Saunders & Partners v Eastglen Ltd* [1990] 3 All ER 946 it was held that an order would not be made under Ord 38, r 2A, where fraud was alleged and it might be necessary to preserve an element of surprise, or where exchange would be oppressive because there would be great difficulty or expense in obtaining a statement, or where the application is made too late and the preparation of witness statements at that stage would add to rather than save costs.

In *McGuinness v Kellogg Co of Great Britain Ltd* [1988] 2 All ER 902 the Court of Appeal approved a decision to allow the defendants to show a video of the plaintiff made by the insurance company's inquiry agent in a personal injuries case–without first disclosing it pre-trial to the plaintiff or his advisers. But the Court of Appeal took the opposite view in a later similar case *Khan v Armaguard Ltd* [1994] 3 All ER 545 on the ground that it was precisely in cases where video evidence exposed the plaintiff's fraud that pre-trial disclosure was appropriate.

Parties cannot be *compelled* to disclose documents or information under Ord 38, r 2A, but if they decline to do so they can be prevented from calling evidence as to that issue. The privilege not to disclose matters covered by legal professional privilege remains–see *Comfort Hotels Ltd v Wembley Stadium Ltd* [1988] 3 All ER 53. But once a witness statement has been disclosed following a direction under Ord 38, r 2A, the statement is no longer privileged as having been obtained for the purpose of litigation. See *Black & Decker Inc v Flymo Ltd* [1991] 3 All ER 158. If, on the other hand, the privileged evidence is disclosed in error, the mistake can be corrected by an application for an injunction to prevent the use of the information–see cases discussed in D Tribe and G Korgaonkar, 'Mistaken Disclosure of Medical Evidence', *Solicitors' Journal*, 26 March 1993, p 268.

Has the exchange of witness statements proved beneficial?

The exchange of witness statements was introduced as a way of improving the process of civil litigation but to some critics it has made matters worse. A county court judge Judge Nicholas Brandt published a letter to Lord Woolf in March 1995 in which he said: 'Exchange of witness statements was thought to promote settlements, and, in default, to speed up trials, thereby reducing expense. Experience has demonstrated the futility of these aspirations. The overwhelming majority of cases (about 97 per cent) settle anyway and there is no evidence that this device has increased the percentage. There is overwhelming evidence that the preparation of these statements has turned into a cottage industry. I have talked to members of the bar who cheerfully confess to spending hours drafting these documents. *Cui bono?*–not the litigant. incidentally, some are badly drafted, containing much irrelevance and hearsay, leading to applications to strike out and more expense.' ('Some serious thoughts from Essex on civil justice', *New Law Journal*, 10 March 1995, p 350.) For a wide-ranging critique of the cost and delays inherent in the modern insistence on 'cards on the table'– discovery, witness statements, interrogatories, pleadings etc–see A Jack, 'Radical Surgery for Civil Procedure', *New Law Journal*, 18 June 1993, p 891. For similar views, expressed by a member of the Bar, see Anthony Speaight, 'A Bonfire of the Paper Mountain', *Counsel*, November/December 1994, p 4.)

Speaight suggested that witness statements gave a significant advantage to the wealthier litigant. If they stand as the witness' evidence-in-chief, the ascertainment of the truth becomes more difficult because the judge no longer has the opportunity of seeing the witness telling his story in his own words. The cost of trials had been considerably increased.

In the same issue of the Bar's journal *Counsel*, Fiona Bawdon said that witness statements had taken on a significance undreamed of hitherto–'witness statements are getting longer and longer, and lawyers are spending hours and hours working on them with their clients'. In many cases they became not so much witness statements as lawyers' statements. She quoted a leading commercial QC: 'The lawyer knows what has to be proved. It is lawyers' language which is used.' As a result of statements currently being so finely crafted, the potential for injustice increased. 'You are effectively manufacturing evidence.'

On abuse of witness statements see also *ZYX Music GmbH v King* [1995] 3 All ER 1, per Lightman J and the note on the case in *Civil Justice Quarterly*, October 1995, p 228.

Woolf on exchange of witness statements

Lord Woolf, in his Interim Report, said that his Inquiry had received 'a considerable volume of information indicating that the exchange of statements is not proving as beneficial as had been intended' (p 176, para 6). 'At a meeting of the Commercial Court Users' Committee on 1 February 1995, there was general agreement that it was having a devastating effect on costs. This was because statements were being treated by the parties as documents which had to be as precise as pleadings and which went through many drafts' (*ibid*). A Commercial judge said that 'an enormous amount of time is now spent by lawyers ironing and massaging witness statements; that is extremely expensive for clients, and the statements can bear very little relation to what a witness of fact would say' (op *cit* para 7). A leading QC said that in a case of his, £100,000 had been expended in preparing witness statements.

Lord Woolf concluded (p 176, para 9): 'There is justification for the concerns which are being expressed about the results of requiring witness statements to be exchanged. The problem is primarily in relation to the heavier litigation. Nonetheless, it does spread to more modest litigation and it needs to be addressed.'

He firmly endorsed the practice of requiring the exchange of witness statements as a way of ensuring that the parties are aware before the trial of the strengths and weaknesses of the case they have to meet. 'The sooner a party is aware of this, the more likely it is that the outcome of the dispute will be a just one, whether it is settled or tried' (p 177, para 10). But the excesses should be eliminated.

The new industry devoted to the creation of witness statements would be more likely to wither if the courts adopted a more relaxed attitude to the statements: 'If it is generally understood that a witness will be allowed to develop points already referred to in a witness statement, most of the benefits which are to be derived from the exchange of witness statements should still be achieved, but without the need for exhaustive drafting intended to achieve pedantic accuracy' (p 178, para 13).

In his fast track cases the witness statement should be no more than a succinct summary of the evidence which the witness can give. Where practicable, they should be exchanged at the latest within 28 days of the delivery of the defence. Within a period of a further eight weeks, each party should indicate the witnesses he wants to have called by the other side and the issues with which the witness will be required to deal. The decision as to which witnesses should be called would be taken by the court. It was important that the issues should be identified as this would assist the judge in reaching his decision. Any witness statements not challenged would be deemed to be admitted (p 178, para 14).

In multi track cases, the parties could adopt a two-stage approach. For the initial case management conference the obligation would be to provide no more than a summary identifying the witnesses the party proposed to rely on and the principal topics the witness would deal with. This would avoid the expense of preparing witness statements before the issues had been defined. The witnesses from whom statements would be required would be identified at the case management conference. Those statements would then be delivered sufficiently long before the second stage pre-trial review for the other party to indicate the witnesses he would like called. and again, the issues on which the evidence was challenged. At the pre-trial review, a decision would be taken as to which witnesses should be called, and the issues in relation to which they would be required to give evidence would be identified. This would then enable the programme for the trial to be constructed. The judge would decide which witnesses were to be called taking into account the views of the parties.

On both the fast track and the multitrack, 'the parties should be prepared to disclose at an early stage the identities of witnesses and the issues with which they deal' (p 179, para 16).

The parties would however be entitled to supplement what was in the summary in the case of the fast track, and in the statements in the case of the multi-track, so long as that evidence was confined to amplifying what was in the summary and the statements. New points would only be allowed with the leave of the judge.

A remarkable further proposal in Lord Woolf's Interim Report was that cross-examination on the contents of witness statements should only be allowed with the leave of the judge. 'Such leave should not be given for cross-examination in detail. Nor should it usually be necessary even when a more significant feature is relied upon. The advocate's comment will be all that the judge will usually require'! (p 179, para 18.)

If the judge thought that the witness statements were too long or detailed he should order that the costs of their preparation should not be recoverable.

Lord Woolf concluded this section with a hope repeated several times in his Interim Report (p 179, para 21):

In the case of witness statements . . ., the solution to the present problem will depend on practitioners behaving in a sensible and co-operative way. If the court is prepared to adopt a more flexible attitude, the parties and their advisers will need to respond by adopting a more sensible approach to the preparation of witness statements. If they do not, the court must make it clear that they will bear the cost.

One asks how likely it is that lawyers acting for litigants will be brought to behave in a 'sensible and co-operative way' and, if they do not, how likely it is that the courts will in fact penalise them in costs sufficiently and sufficiently often to affect their conduct?

(f) Woolf on the expert witness in the pre-trial process

As has been seen, for some years already the rules have required the parties to exchange the reports and statements of the experts on whom they intend to rely at the trial. In his Interim Report Lord Woolf said that the subject of expert evidence had caused his Inquiry much concern. Concern had been expressed in particular that the need to engage experts was 'a source of excessive expense, delay and in some cases, increased complexity through the excessive or inappropriate use of experts' (p 181, para 1). Concern had also been expressed regarding a lack of independence of experts. Neither the Civil Justice Review nor the Heilbron-Hodge Report had referred to the issue.

Most of the problems with expert evidence arose because the expert was initially recruited as part of the team and then had to change roles and seek to provide the independent expert evidence which the court was entitled to expect. The judges often exercised their power to ask the experts to meet to try to agree. But this did not seem to deal with the problem of the partisan approach of the respective experts. Before such meetings, the experts were quite often instructed by their respective parties not to agree to anything. Alternatively they were told that anything agreed between the experts had to be referred back to the lawyers for ratification.

Lord Woolf cited an editorial in the Bar's journal *Counsel* in November/December 1994 which said that expert witnesses today were 'hired guns'. There was, it suggested, a 'new breed of litigation hangers on, whose main expertise is to craft reports which will conceal anything that might be to the disadvantage of their clients'. The disclosure of expert reports 'which originally seemed eminently sensible, has degenerated into a costly second tier of written advocacy'. This 'deplorable development' had been unwittingly encouraged by a generation of judges who wanted to read experts' reports before coming into court, and by practice directions stipulating that the reports be lodged in court to enable them to do so.

Waiting for experts' reports, Lord Woolf said, was also a cause of much delay. It was not uncommon for six to nine months to elapse between a request for a report and its delivery (p 184, para 12).

This unhappy situation had become institutionalised. Lawyers repeatedly instructed a limited class of consultants for reports. There was a serious shortage of suitable experts. The best doctors tended also to be the busiest.

Lord Woolf proposed various changes that would address these issues:

(1) In multi track cases the judge at the initial case management conference would distil the issues from the parties' statements of case and, if necessary, would decide what expert evidence was needed on each issue. The key issues should then be narrowed through exchange of experts' reports and through meetings of experts, so that only areas of disagreement would have to be decided by the court (p 185, para 18).

(2) In some cases the court should appoint an independent expert. There was already power to do so under RSC Ord 40 on application by either party–a power that was hardly ever used. Parties did not like it because the cost was in addition to their own experts and they did not trust the court expert. Lord Woolf said these were real concerns, but 'as long as they are borne in mind, there will be cases where it will be the best course to appoint an independent expert' (p 186, para 22). The court 'is perfectly capable of deciding which cases would be appropriate for a court expert and then of appointing an expert with the necessary qualifications and ensuring that he is used effectively' (p 187, para 23). If the parties could not agree on the appropriate independent expert, the relevant professional body could be asked to make the appointment.

(3) Rules of court should permit the court to appoint an independent expert of its own motion and to limit the parties' power to call any expert save under the direction of the court (p 187, para 23). This would not however prevent the parties from having their own expert to guide them, especially in regard to cross-examination of any other expert who gave evidence. The additional cost of the neutral expert would usually be justified 'by helping to achieve a settlement, or in the assistance he will provide to the judge' (*ibid*).

In complex litigation the court could sometimes be assisted by the appointment of an assessor, as already happened in the Admiralty Court (p 187, para 24).

There should be a wide power for the court of its own motion to refer issues to experts either for determination or report. If the power was used, Lord Woolf suggested hopefully, 'the court will soon acquire the knowledge necessary to determine when this course is appropriate' (p 187, para 25).

When the court appointed an independent expert his costs should be the re-sponsibility of the parties–though the court itself should have the power to meet the expert's fees in the first instance (pp 187–8, para 26).

(4) All experts should address their reports to the court. Any instructions they received from the party employing them should be disclosed in the report. The report should end by a declaration that it includes everything the expert regards as relevant (p 188, para 27).

(5) If experts meet at the direction of the court it should be understood that they are under a duty if possible to reach any agreement that is appropriate. If they cannot do so they should specify the reasons. It should be unprofessional conduct for an expert to accept instructions not to reach agreement at such a meeting. Once an expert has been instructed to prepare a report for use of the court, any communications between the expert and the client or his advisers should no longer be privileged (p 188, para 28).

(6) No *subpoena* for attendance of a medical expert should be issued without leave of the procedural judge (p 189, para 29).

(7) In fast track cases, because the time-table was very tight and trial would be limited to three hours, it would be necessary for the court to be able to resolve expert issues without oral evidence. In order to achieve that the court should choose from among the following options–(a) the joint appointment of an expert at the outset, chosen, if possible by the parties, if not by the court; failing that no more than one expert per side; (b) separate reports from the experts with the court deciding the issue on the basis of the reports plus argument by counsel; or (c) the reference of the issue to an expert to determine or report when the expert would communicate with experts appointed by the parties before coming to his conclusion (pp 189–90, para 32).

(8) In personal injury cases involving claims of under £3,000, the court should use the report of the treating doctor. Insurers had told Lord Woolf that in small cases they would not challenge such reports. Plaintiffs' lawyers did not like the suggestion because treating doctors tended to be over-optimistic about the treatment they prescribed and might also lack forensic experience. But the advantage of using the doctor who had been treating the plaintiff outweighed any disadvantages (p 190, para 33).

(9) In cases on the fast track, the defendant should be able to comment on the plaintiff's decision to instruct his own expert. Where possible the parties should agree on whom to appoint. In any event the defendant should have the right to give whatever instructions he wished to the plaintiff's doctor. If the defendant wished also to instruct his own doctor, both doctors would be required to communicate with eachother with a view to producing a joint report if possible. The plaintiff would have the opportunity to put any instructions he wished before the defendant's doctor (pp 190–91, para 34).

The January 1996 Consultation Papers issued by Lord Woolf dealt with the problem of experts in two ways–there was a separate Consultation Paper on the subject, and the subject was dealt with in the Consultation Paper on fast track cases. In the Consultation Paper on fast track cases it was proposed that in order to facilitate the appointment of an agreed expert, local and national lists of approved experts would be drawn up. Also, district judges should have the discretion to call for oral evidence from experts–though this would be rare.

The Consultation Paper said that the new approach would be necessary to avoid 'excessive inappropriate and over long reports' and best practice guides should cover standard report presentation (p 13, para 55). The Law Society and the British Orthopaedic Association had drawn up a code of practice for instructing medical experts which included a standard format both for the instruction and for the expert's report–and an agreed time frame for producing reports. This could be a model for other areas of expertise. Another proposal was that standard reports should list the research literature on which they were based. Experts should not accept instructions unless they were able to deliver in the time frame of the case. The timetable required that expert evidence should be exchanged within 56 days of the directions order.

(g) Pre-trial hearings: summons for directions, pre-trial reviews/ hearings/conferences

There has for many years been an active debate as to how far it is useful to have some form of pre-trial hearing and what should be the purpose of such a procedure. One form of such hearing is a procedural device simply to deal with certain preliminary matters; another is to sift and sort out the issues that are likely to come up in the trial in order to reduce the area of conflict; a third is to attempt to arrive at a pre-trial settlement.

(1) The summons for directions

The summons for directions has been the first type of pre-trial hearing. In High Court litigation it is the occasion at which the master reviews the situation and gives directions as to where the trial should take place, whether it should be by judge or by jury, how many expert witnesses are to be called, and the like.

The Evershed Committee which reported in 1953, after six years of deliberation, on how to simplify civil procedure considered that its best hope for reducing delays and costs lay in a 'robust' summons for directions. But this proposal was never implemented. The normal summons for directions continued to be a perfunctory affair lasting only a few minutes conducted by clerks in front of the master. (See Master Diamond, 'The Summons for Directions', 75 *Law Quarterly Review*, 1959, p 43.) In a paper prepared for a Workshop on Civil Procedure in London in 1970, Sir Jack Jacob wrote, 'in most personal injury actions the Summons for Directions is a very mild affair and cannot possibly be called robust, since the only order that is made is the limitation of medical and perhaps other experts, plans and photographs, and place and mode of trial, and setting down'.

Because the summons for directions had become a formality, the Winn Committee (para 352) recommended that this should be recognized by making the process automatic. Provision, it said, should be made for automatic directions without a summons and without an order. This proposal was not, however, implemented then. The report of the Cantley Working Party urged that it be implemented. The report said that 'in practice competent solicitors know what they want and agree it in advance or in chambers and a two minute hearing suffices in nearly all personal injury cases . . . In fact the two minute hearing to obtain the Master's order on an agreed summons is in most cases quite unnecessary' (*Report of the Personal Injuries Litigation Procedure Working Party* (the Cantley Report), 1979, Cmnd 7476, para 33). Moreover, the Cantley Committee said, the order was normally in standard form–the plaintiff to give discovery of special damage; the defendant to give discovery other than in road accident cases;

inspection; one or two medical reports to be disclosed; expert evidence to be disclosed in factory accident (but not in road accident) cases; directions for trial. The Cantley Committee said that an automatic rule for directions would be similar to that which applied in discovery. If a party wanted any unusual directions it would still be able to apply to the master.

The Cantley Committee also said that there might be a case for another committee to look at devices to reduce surprise at the trial, and to improve the quality of settlements such as pre-trial examination of parties and witnesses, disclosure of proofs of evidence and pre-trial settlement conferences, all of which were known to the North American system. There was a good deal to be said in favour of some of these proposals although their introduction here would 'certainly prolong both the settlement and the trial process and make both more expensive' (para 84, p 31).

The proposal that there should be automatic directions unless the parties asked for something different was implemented for High Court cases in 1980 in Ord 25, r 8, in regard to personal injury actions. This provided that at the close of pleadings the following directions take place automatically:

(1) there shall be discovery of documents within 14 days and inspection 7 days later;
(2) parties intending to rely on expert evidence at the trial should disclose the substance of that evidence within 10 weeks in the form of a written report which should be agreed if possible;
(3) unless the evidence is agreed, the parties shall only be able to call as experts the witnesses whose evidence has been disclosed, but the maximum number of medical experts shall be two and not more than one in the case of non-medical experts;
(4) photographs, a sketch plan and the contents of any police accident report book shall be receivable in evidence at the trial and shall be agreed if possible;
(5) the action shall be tried in London if it is proceeding in London but if it is proceeding at a District Registry it shall be tried at the trial centre designated for that District Registry;
(6) the trial shall be by judge alone; and
(7) the court shall be notified, on being set down for trial, of the estimated length of the trial. However, either party can apply for a variation of any of these directions.

A similar change was made in Chancery cases in 1982.

The Civil Justice Review Body in its Final Report in 1988 recommended (para 254) that standard directions should be devised for all cases where such directions were appropriate. The parties should be free to apply to the court for additional or different directions or for a general stock-taking. The court should be entitled to initiate a general stock-taking on any hearing whether or not it was applied for by either of the parties.

In cases where there were no automatic directions it should continue to be possible to have a summons for directions or, in the county courts, a pre-trial hearing.

Automatic directions were introduced for almost all cases in the county court in October 1990–see CCR Ord 17, r 11; *Legal Action*, April 1991, p 20 and John O'Hare, 'Civil Litigation–Automatic Directions in the County Court' and 'Varying the Automatic Directions in County Court Cases', *New Law Journal*, 4 September 1992, p 1200 and 18 September 1992, p 1272.

Summonses by telephone

A new procedural development took place in November 1995 when Mr Justice Jacob (son of the renowned Sir Jack Jacob) issued a *Practice Statement* as judge in charge of the patents list. In future Patent Court judges would be willing to hear summonses by telephone conference for short matters unless it concerned a matter of general public importance. The party issuing the summons was responsible for setting up the conference call by contacting British Telecom on a prescribed 0800 number. (See [1996]1 All ER 63.)

Lord Woolf's proposals

Lord Woolf's Interim Report and January 1996 Consultation Issues Paper for fast track cases envisage a 'directions hearings'. The January 1996 Consultation Paper stated that there would be 'suitably tailored standard directions' linked to the timetable for the case. District judges would thus: see all defences when filed, decide venue, allocate cases to the appropriate track, give the necessary directions, set a timetable, and allocate a hearing week (p 14, para 59). Other options at the directions hearing would be an application for summary disposal, striking out of the claim if it had no realistic chance of success, or because no valid defence was shown (the present Order 13 and Order 14.) The Woolf 'directions hearing' sounds remarkably like the 'robust summons for directions' envisaged in 1953 by the Evershed Committee!

Standard timetable   The timetable for fast track cases would normally be the standard timetable but it could be varied. As envisaged in the January 1996 Consultation Paper, the standard timetable would allow 28 days for discovery, and another 28 days for exchange of witness statements and experts' reports. The court would send out a listing questionnaire 70 days from the start of the timetable. It would have to be returned within 84 days of the start date. If it was not returned, the court would call the parties in for a hearing. A warned week would be given at the start for the trial and the trial would be fixed within that week. Notice of that date would be given at least six weeks before the hearing.

Sanctions   Woolf's Consultation Paper said that 'No timetable can be effective unless it is backed by effective sanctions for non-compliance'. The sanctions had to be fair, proportionate, simple to apply and not create delay. The onus should be on the wrongdoer to ask for relief. Also sanctions should not lead to more litigation. Possible sanctions for fast track cases would include costs sanctions against a party, the striking out of the case or debarring particular evidence or issues, specific sanctions related to the actual 'offence' or fines on practitioners.

(2) Pre-trial review in the county court and the High Court

In county court actions there had never previously been anything like a summons for directions. From 1972, however, all actions that appeared to be likely to go for trial had to come before the registrar for a pre-trial review. If the defendant did not turn up, or if his defence was clearly no defence in law, the plaintiff could obtain judgment immediately. In these cases the pre-trial review hearing was like summary judgment. Otherwise the occasion was used for the giving of directions–for instance, as to further and better particulars, discovery, admission of facts or interrogatories. The rules provided that at the pre-trial review the registrar should endeavour to get the parties to make all such admissions and agreements as 'ought reasonably to be made' (CCR Ord 21). However that has now changed.

An early study concluded that the pre-trial review was a very useful change in county court procedure in this field. It helped to achieve settlements, helped solicitors to prepare their cases and was of value to the more intelligent litigant in person. But it did not appear to have helped as much for the average litigant in person. There was also some comment that the two-tier stage requiring at least two visits to the court caused delay and extra expense. (See G Appleby, *Small Claims in England and Wales*, Institute of Judicial Administration, Birmingham University, 1978, pp 8–18.)

But when the same issue was studied as part of the Civil Justice Review, it was found that the pre-trial review was not after all so useful. The study by management consultants found that preliminary hearings were held in most cases. In some it was viewed as an occasion to try to resolve the case either by encouraging the parties to settle or by making an award at that stage. If it was not resolved, the registrar would tell the parties what evidence they required. The alternative approach was to use it as a genuine preliminary hearing. In some courts the tendency was to avoid having a preliminary hearing.

Sixty per cent of litigants interviewed said that the preliminary hearing had not helped them to prepare their case for the main hearing; 32 per cent said that it had. The preliminary hearing appeared to delay matters. The Small Claims Consultation Paper therefore proposed that courts should aim to dispose of small claims at a single hearing even though it might mean that there would be less information available. This would be a small price for the advantage of avoiding the necessity of two visits to the court. If an essential piece of information was not available on the first date, the case could be adjourned (paras 94–5).

The Final Report of the Civil Justice Review Body agreed with this recommendation (para 521). But it thought that preliminary hearings might still be needed in small claims cases involving personal injuries where one or other party was not legally represented. There might also be a need for such a hearing in other cases which were especially complex (paras 523–4).

CCR Ord 17, r 11 now provides for automatic directions in regard to discovery (to take place within 28 days of close of pleadings); numbers of expert witnesses (maximum of two, or in personal injury cases, two medical and one other expert); exchange of witness statements within ten weeks; a date to be fixed for the hearing within six months. Automatic directions apply unless the parties want specific directions in which case there will be a pre-trial review. A pre-trial review also takes place in certain other cases, notably, possession and rent actions, consumer credit cases and actions for the delivery up of goods.

The preliminary-hearing concept also had a somewhat unsuccessful test in the Family Division. In 1979 it was announced that the 'pre-trial review' concept would in future be applied to contested matrimonial causes in the Family Division. The *Practice Direction* [1979] 1 All ER 112 stated that 'the prime objective behind the pre-trial review procedure is to enable the registrar to ascertain the true state of the case and to give such directions as are necessary for its just, expeditious and economic disposal'. In practice, where it had been tried experimentally it had been found that 'under the registrar's guidance the parties are often able to compose their differences, or to drop insubstantial charges and defences, and to concentrate on the main issues in dispute'.

This scheme did not, however, prove successful. It ran as an experiment for fourteen months before being cancelled by a further Practice Direction in June 1981. (See *New Law Journal*, 1981, p 623). Research revealed that the reason for the failure of the scheme was that it did not sufficiently achieve the objectives of securing more settlements or even of clarifying issues for the trial.

Only about 3 per cent of the cases that came for pre-trial review were settled at that stage. Many were settled at a later stage but it was not necessarily because of the pre-trial review. The mediation of the registrar had apparently failed to galvanize the parties into an agreement at a significantly earlier stage than before. One reason was that often both sides did not turn up or only solicitors were there rather than the parties or their barristers. There did not appear to have been a campaign by the Principal Registry to inform practitioners of the object of the exercise to try to get their full cooperation. What finally got the parties to settle their differences was the pressure of being at the door of the court. Also the pre-trial work involved in getting ready for the pre-trial review was not as well paid as the trial itself. There was therefore no incentive on the practitioners to utilize the procedure. (See G Davis and K Bader, 'An Experiment that Failed', *Law Society's Gazette*, 1983, pp 627, 679; *LAG Bulletin*, January 1983, p 4.)

For reports on conciliation schemes in matrimonial cases as part of the court procedure, see G Davis and K Bader, 'Can In-Court Mediation Work?' *LAG Bulletin*, July 1983, p 10 and, by the same authors, 'In-Court Mediation Observed', *New Law Journal*, 1983, pp 355, 403. In July 1983 an inter-departmental committee on conciliation published its report. Officials from the various government departments concerned had reviewed current arrangements for assisting parties to actual or potential matrimonial proceedings to bring about a settlement or to reduce the area or intensity of conflicts between them. The report was not overly impressed by out-of-court conciliation schemes. It found that overall they did not save money and they appeared to be less cost-effective than in-court schemes. The committee did not think it worth the central government funding such schemes. Conciliation was best provided, the committee thought, as an adjunct to the court system but further study was needed to determine the best model for such schemes.

Out-of-court schemes are run by volunteers and are designed to see couples early in their dispute to see whether agreement can be reached. In-court schemes are organized through district judges with Divorce Court Welfare Officers. The district judge sees the parties and their lawyers before preparations for trial are too advanced to see if agreement is possible.

The committee estimated the cost of a national out-of-court service at £8.8m and said the expense would not be warranted.

(3) The pre-trial settlement conference

In the United States the courts have gone in for pre-trial settlement conferences at which *the judge* actively explores the prospects for a settlement.

The Winn Committee considered but rejected the idea. The Committee's reason for rejecting the pre-trial conference were: first that the evidence from the USA did not show clearly that it did result in a higher level of settlements; second, that it would 'complicate, delay and increase the cost of litigation' (para 355); third, that it would result in undesirable pressure from the judge that the case should be settled even though he had not seen the witnesses.

Master Jacob entered a Note of Reservation on the point, urging that this was an appropriate role for the court to play. In America it was done by the trial judge, which created an obvious danger of pressure and prejudice if the case then went to trial. In England, he suggested, it could be done by the masters and registrars under the protection of 'without prejudice' negotiations and without the trial judge knowing anything about it (p 153).

The Civil Justice Review did not address the issue of settlement conferences directly. However, the Final Report said that some of the evidence received had referred to the need for such settlement conferences. But it expressed the opinion that 'in view of the proposals for early exchange of witness statements it is thought that opportunities for settlement will be increased and that pre-trial intervention by judges should be reserved to a pre-trial hearing in the more substantial cases' (para 259).

It also thought that the value of pre-trial hearings should be evaluated by empirical research.

(For evaluation of the role of German judges in settling cases, see Klaus F Rohl, 'The Judge as Mediator', *Civil Justice Quarterly*, July 1985, p 235.)

Woolf on pre-trial hearings

As has already been seen, pre-trial hearings play a crucial role in Lord Woolf's scheme for civil litigation as outlined in his Interim Report. The exception was for small claims cases:

I regard the part-hearing of small claims as particularly undesirable. The present more restrictive rule on preliminary hearings was introduced to encourage the disposal of small claims at a single, substantive hearing and that is an objective which I support. If, after his initial examination of the papers, the district judge needs to seek clarification from the parties, that should, wherever possible, be done by correspondence or telephone. That approach would minimise the need for either a preliminary hearing or an adjournment of the substantive hearing (p 109, para 29).

But for Lord Woolf's fast track and multi track cases pre-trial processing by the court would be the very basis of the proposed new system.

Fast track cases   In fast track cases the district judge would first have to consider whether there was any need for adjustments to the standard directions. This would not involve a hearing but he could consult with the parties over the telephone or otherwise (p 44, para 12).

In appropriate cases the judge should suggest to the parties that they discuss settlement or invite them to consider alternative dispute resolution mechanisms (p 44, para 13).

The procedure I have outlined above envisages a pro-active role for the district judge in communicating with the parties or, more often, their legal advisers by telephone, letter or fax . .. Where appropriate this should include tripartite discussions between the judge and the parties by means of a telephone conference facility. . .The fast track procedure is designed to dispense with any procedures which create uncertainty or unnecessary preparation or generate additional cost. Although there will be no case management conference or pre-trial review, the district judge will be able to ensure that the case is reasonably fit for the hearing by monitoring the checklist and the documentation. To enable district judges to fulfil this role effectively, it is essential that they are provided with appropriate information technology [pp 44, paras 14–15].

Multi track cases   In cases on the multi track the system would provide the necessary amount of case management. Such management would range from standard directions and a standard timetable for straightforward cases to full 'hands on' management by the trial judge from a very early stage (p 48, para 1).

The process of case management would begin with the initial scrutiny of the case by a procedural judge who would decide what level of case management was appropriate. In multi track cases case management would normally be provided through at least two interlocutory management hearings. The first would be a case management conference shortly after the defence is received. The second would be the pre-trial review about 8 to 10 weeks before the trial. The first would normally be conducted by the procedural judge, though in complex cases the trial judge would need to do it. The pre-trial review should be before the trial judge 'to ensure that it is an effective preparation for trial' (p 48, para 4).

At the hearings a full management review of the action would take place. Anything that could be determined at that stage would be dealt with there. The parties would be required to provide information for the hearings on a prescribed questionnaire (p 49, para 6).

The case management conference should be attended by a counsel or solicitor with responsibility for the conduct of the case and at the pre-trial review the counsel or solicitor instructed to attend the trial must appear. The lay client, or someone fully authorised to act on his behalf, would be required to attend both hearings (p 49, para 8).

At the case management conference the parties should be given directions as to the steps to be taken prior to the pre-trial review, including dates. The date of the pre-trial review would be set and there would be a target week for the trial (p 49, para 10).

Where appropriate, the process could be in a rolling programme (p 50, para 11).

The pre-trial review would be the opportunity to try to narrow the issues for the trial, to identify the witnesses who need to give oral evidence and the issues to which their evidence would be related. The management of the documentary evidence would be agreed and the form of expert evidence determined (p 50, para 12).

Procedural applications should be heard in chambers. This was not to achieve privacy or to exclude the press and a judge could always adjourn into court or allow members of the public or the press to attend the hearing in chambers.

Appeals from interlocutory decisions by masters and district judges should be only with leave and to a High Court judge unless a point of principle was involved in which case the judge should refer the application for leave to the Court of Appeal. Appeals from decisions by circuit judges or High Court judges should also require leave but they would always go to the Court of Appeal (p 52, paras 23–5).

(h) Delay

One of the most critical problems for all legal systems is that of delay in civil as much as in criminal cases. Whether or not the English system is better than others in this respect, there is no question that the problem is a serious one.

The problem of what to do about delay has been the subject of inquiries, in turn by the Winn Committee (1968), the Cantley Committee (1979), the Civil Justice Review (1986–9) and the Woolf Inquiry (1995). The approach of each was very different.

The Winn Committee Report

The Winn Committee expressed considerable concern about delays in civil litigation. Delay, it said, 'is a very great reproach'. It was 'a particularly deplorable aspect of delay that the disposal of fatal accident cases took so long. In a sample of 22 such cases, the interval between the accident and the date of disposal by trial or settlement averaged 20 months'.

Looking for the reasons, it discovered several:

(1) The injured person often did not seek legal advice at an early stage.

(2) Claims assessors sometimes held on to cases too long rather than handing them over to solicitors and so jeopardizing their commission.

(3) Trades unions sometimes allowed negotiations to drag on too long before handing them on to solicitors, or sometimes they did nothing because they were too busy.

(4) Many solicitors who handled litigation had little experience of it and because they did not have the procedure at their finger-tips it took them longer than it would an expert.

(5) There was delay in counsel's chambers.

(6) Insurance companies not infrequently delayed simply in order to hang on to their money (paras 46–62).

The Committee proposed various remedies. One was interest on damages–to encourage insurance companies to pay up quicker. This was implemented in the Administration of Justice Act 1969, s 22.

Another was the power to order interim payment of part of the damages in a case where it was reasonably clear that damages would ultimately be awarded. This was implemented in the Administration of Justice Act 1969, s 20.

Thirdly, the Committee thought delays should be reduced by keeping the procedure on tighter reins so far as time-limits were concerned. The need, it thought, was to increase the penalties for delays:

Inducements for users of the court machine–and sanctions
322. The need is to provide material inducements for progress in litigation and effective sanctions for delay, even if the latter be of such a character that they may be regarded by those apprehensive, by reason of their own frailty, of incurring them as swingeing and draconian.

323. It was truly said by our advisers that the negotiation as well as the litigation of personal injury claims is today an industry. We think that commercial, i.e. monetary, considerations should play a greater part in the conduct of these industries and that it should be made costly for defendants or their insurers to postpone the settlement of claims or for plaintiffs to delay their presentation or negotiation. It is a feature of industry and commerce that outstanding liabilities incur added interest whereas prompt payments earn a discount [*Winn Committee Report*, p 94].

But Master Jacob did not accept this approach. He doubted whether discipline was the right approach. Rules of court should not be framed on the basis of imposing penalties. (The function of Rules of Court is to provide guide-lines, not trip wires.) Similarly, the rules on costs were compensatory not penal and they should not be used as a means of punishment. Mr Robin Thompson, agreeing, said that costs orders against lay clients were totally ineffective as a way of promoting speedy dispatch by solicitors.

Cantley Committee Report

The problem of delay was considered again by the Cantley Committee in its 1979 report (*Report of the Personal Injuries Litigation Procedure Working Party*, 1979, Cmnd 7476). (For a full account of the report see the 6th edition of this work at pp 110–15.) Cantley analysed delay in all High Court personal injury cases from 1974 to 1977. It looked at the delay between the issue of the writ and the setting down of the case for trial and said that this occurred within a reasonable time–45 to 50 per cent in 12 months and 80 per cent within 24 months (Appendix B and p 2). But there was a minority of cases which appeared to be unduly delayed–of those set down, about 20 per cent were set down more than two years and 2 per cent were set down more than four years, after the issue of the writ.

In evaluating these figures the Committee thought it necessary to bear in mind certain important general considerations:

Report of the Personal Injuries Litigation Procedure Working Party, 1979, Cmnd 7476

8. The basic principle of litigation as at present conducted in our courts is that the litigation is the litigation of the parties: the court is there to assist the parties and finally to resolve the dispute between the parties if asked to do so, but the court does not intervene unless asked to do so by the parties. Some of the weaknesses of our system derive from this fact but so do many of its strengths and given a competent legal profession, which, with some exceptions, we have, one should not lightly interfere with this method of conducting litigation and encourage an undue degree of court intervention if to do so would lose the advantages of economy and flexibility which our system brings.

9. Secondly, most accidents which lead to claims do not lead to writs and most writs do not lead to trial and judgment. These cases are settled and settlement is an essential ingredient in our system of disposing of actions:

(i) A delay which enabled and encouraged the parties to settle their dispute on reasonable terms is not an undue delay;

(ii) A proposal or solution which brought cases to the point of trial more quickly but which brought more cases to trial than at present would have the double disadvantage of being more costly for those cases which might otherwise have settled: and, by bringing more cases to the point of trial, delay the trial itself;

(iii) Any solution which hurried the case along but which in consequence required more steps to be taken and taken earlier and taken in all cases might make the cost of settling a case higher than it is now by increasing the costs and expenses of the solicitor on each side.

The Cantley Committee considered a number of possible proposals for reducing delays:

(1) Automatic striking out The suggestion had been made that the court should by rule automatically strike out an action if the plaintiff had not reached a certain stated stage (say, summons for directions) by a certain time (say, 12 months) after the issue of a writ. The Committee rejected this proposal as being too draconian and unjust, since it would give the plaintiff no chance of explaining the delay. If the rule were that the plaintiff could move to restore the action on showing good cause, there would be

many applications which would often be hotly contested and would lead to more delays. Also it would place a great burden on the plaintiff whilst allowing the defendant to reap the advantage of delays. If the court had a rule imposing a new burden on the parties, it should apply equally to both. (But see on this further pp 89–91 below.)

(2) Court control–court file   Another suggestion was that the court might send the plaintiff a notice inviting explanation for the fact that the case was not making proper progress. This would require the court to monitor the state of each case. It would require new records. This would involve a great deal of extra work. But most cases were settled before setting down, so that the maintenance of a case file resulting in summonses from the court for apparent delay would often be abortive in that the case would actually have been settled. Even if it had not yet been settled, it would often settle in the ordinary course before summons for directions. The cost of employing large numbers of extra staff to manage 9,000 case files a year was not justified by the limited problem that existed.

(3) Adaptation of pre-trial review   The chief purpose of pre-trial review in the county court was similar to that of the summons for directions in the High Court. There was not much that it could do that was not already being done in the High Court.

(4) Court control–plaintiff to report   If within 18 months after the issue of a writ in a personal injury case the action had not been set down for trial, the plaintiff's solicitor would be required to report to the court the stage at which the proceedings had reached. The court could then, if so minded, issue a summons for the purpose of giving such directions as it thought fit. If proper records were kept, it would be relatively easy to see each week in which cases writs had been issued 18 months previously. A standard-form letter could then be sent to the plaintiff's solicitors. It was estimated that the office would have to send a total of some 3,000 form letters annually, including reminders. The master would have extra work in dealing with court summonses. The court would have to 'lean on' the parties in appropriate cases. It would also have to follow up its own orders. This procedure, the Committee thought, would be worth trying.

(5) Dismissal of action for want of prosecution   The courts had in recent years been readier than before to use the power to strike out an action for want of prosecution. The new policy was heralded in *Allen v McAlpine & Sons Ltd* [1968] 2 QB 229. In that case the Court of Appeal held that the power to dismiss should only be exercised where the court was satisfied either: (1) that the default had been intentional and contumacious, or conduct amounting to an abuse of the court; or (2) that there had been inordinate and inexcusable delay by the plaintiff or his lawyers; and that such delay would give rise to a substantial risk that it was not possible to have a fair trial of the issues in the action or it had caused or was likely to cause serious prejudice to the defendant. (See also *Sweeney v McAlpine & Sons Ltd* [1974] 1 All ER 474 and *Department of Transport v Chris Smaller (Transport) Ltd* [1989] 1 All ER 897.) These principles were approved by the House of Lords in *Birkett v James* [1978] AC 297. But the House of Lords said there that delay before issuing the writ did not count. Delay must have occurred since the writ was issued, though, if he had delayed at first, it was incumbent on the plaintiff to move with all due speed after the writ was issued.

The majority thought that the fact that the plaintiff might have an action for negligence against his solicitor was not a relevant consideration. If the plaintiff could issue a fresh writ within the time limit, that was a reason not to dismiss the action. See, however, M Beaumont, 'Want of Prosecution', *Law Society's Gazette*, 27 September 1989, p 14.

The Cantley Committee thought that the power to dismiss encouraged defendants to delay and then to take advantage of their own failure. The power to dismiss should only arise if the defendant could show that he had asked the court to make an order that, unless the next stage was undertaken by the plaintiff within a specified period, the action would be dismissed. This would enlist the defendant's assistance in preventing delay.

The Cantley Committee took the view that the court should not be expected to chivvy the parties along so as to promote greater speed in civil litigation. This is of course in line with the classic English and common-law principle that it is for the parties to decide how to conduct their own litigation—see, on this, more below in Chapter 4 on the adversary system.

Civil Justice Review

The General Issues Paper said that although delay in some areas was a real problem, there were some areas in which it was not. Debt, housing and small claims cases were much the largest part of all civil business of the courts. According to the Debt Study, the formal process of obtaining an undefended judgment for debt was on average completed within 47 days in the High Court and 55 days in the county court (para 28). In housing possession cases, the average time taken from summons to hearing was 7.2 weeks. None of the courts in the sample survey took more than an average of nine weeks to arrange a hearing (para 29). For small claims, the average time from issue of summons to arbitration hearing fell between 24 and 36 weeks, although there were rather wide variations between courts (para 30).

In personal injury cases, the problem of delay was greater. In the county court the study of such cases showed a median time of 13 months from start of proceedings to the stage of asking for trial by 'setting down'. The High Court median was 19 months. Commercial cases showed a median from start of proceedings to summons for directions of almost 16 months (para 31).

The Civil Justice Review's approach to delay was, however, conceptually very different from that of the Cantley Committee. Where Cantley emphasized that civil litigation was essentially a private matter between the parties, the Civil Justice Review thought of it rather as a matter of public concern. The *Personal Injuries Consultation Paper* stated why delay was objectionable (para 86):

(i) It caused personal stress, anxiety and financial hardship to plaintiffs and their families.

(ii) These pressures sapped the morale and determination of plaintiffs, resulting often in acceptance of low settlement offers.

(iii) It reduced the availability of evidence and eroded the reliability of the evidence which was available.

(iv) It led to inefficient business dealing with files opened and reopened over months and years.

(v) Compensation was delayed until long after it was most needed.

(vi) It lowered public estimation for the legal system.

The proposals put forward by the *Personal Injuries Consultation paper* for reducing delays were radical:

(1) To reduce the limitation period for personal injury cases to require a plaintiff to start the proceedings within 12 months rather than 3 years. (Most of those who commented on this proposal thought that 12 months would be too short a time.)

(2) To require that solicitors handling personal injury cases must first have a special qualification without which they would not be entitled to conduct such work. (This likewise was criticized by most commentators, including not only the Law Society but also the National Consumer Council and National Association of Citizens' Advice Bureaux, on the ground that it would unduly restrict the availability of solicitors able to handle such work.)

(3) To oblige a solicitor who was consulted by an accident victim to commence proceedings within a fixed period after the first consultation. (This evoked little or no support.)

(4) A system of paper adjudication for small cases up to £5,000. (This again met with considerable resistance on the ground that it would deprive the parties of the opportunity of a proper hearing.)

(5) For larger cases a timetable should be laid down by the court with appropriate sanctions for non-compliance. (There was no reference to the problems of imposing sanctions addressed in the Winn Committee Report and the objections of Master Jacob and Mr Robin Thompson, pp 84–85 above.)

(6) Litigants personally should have to sign applications for adjournments. (Commentators pointed out that this would not help much since they would normally sign if advised to do so by their lawyers.)

(7) Court administrators should be given targets for trials on the lines of circuit objectives which would apply to much of the business of the courts.

The *General Issues Consultation Paper* admitted that the price of earlier settlement might be higher costs in some cases, but thought that this would have to be accepted. ('The conclusion of this paper is that if necessary, the price of earlier disposal ought to be paid' (para 129).) Moreover, costs in personal injury cases tended to fall on insurance companies, trade unions and the legal aid fund rather than individuals. The proposals it made to reduce delay were as follows:

(1) Control of the time taken in the conduct of civil litigation 'should now be accepted as a function proper to the court, acting where appropriate of its own motion' (para 172).

(2) Monitoring by the court would relate to the overall time up to setting down. There would be a weekly search in the records for any case not set down or disposed of within the set period. The plaintiff's solicitor would be sent a form to fill out, reporting on the state of the case. A reminder would be sent 14 days later if no reply had been received (with a copy to the client). If this produced no response, the matter would be referred to a master or registrar (now 'district judge') who could either issue a summons requiring the solicitors to come to explain themselves, or make an order that unless particular steps were taken within a particular time the action would be struck out, or he could set the case down. Computerization of court records would make this process very easy.

(3) Sanctions for failure to comply with time limits would vary from order regarding costs either on the parties or on the lawyers, and in extreme cases striking out.

(4) Better management systems to speed the through-put of cases, including fuller information to be prepared on a regular basis about the progress of cases.

The *Final Report of the Civil Justice Review Body* confirmed the approach set out in the *Consultation Paper*. The method should be that worked out by the Cantley Committee. Once an action became defended there should be a fixed period within which the parties should be expected to set the case down for trial, unless it had been settled or withdrawn. Different kinds of business should have different periods. For personal injury cases it should be nine months from notice of intention to defend.

The court should have an effective case-monitoring system. Three months before the due date the court should send out reminders to the parties. A report form should be sent to the plaintiff's solicitor. If this was not answered to the satisfaction of the court, a summons should be issued for the solicitors on one or both sides to come to give explanations. Having given the parties an opportunity to be heard, the court should either set the case down for trial or make an 'unless' order that the action would be dismissed unless particular steps were taken within stated time limits (para 226).

Automatic striking out in the county court

In 1952 the county court rules were changed to give the court a power to strike out an action if 12 months had elapsed from the date of service of a default summons and no admission, defence or counterclaim had been delivered or judgment entered (now CCR Ord 9, r 10). The Court of Appeal held in 1995 that this does not happen automatically–not least because the court does not always know when 12 months have elapsed. The court will wait for the defendant to apply for the case to be struck out. If the defendant has agreed to an extension of time he cannot renege on that agreement and ask for the action to be struck out. (*Heer v Tutton, Pickles v Holdsworth, Lovell v Porter* [1995] 4 All ER 547, CA.) But if there is no agreement to give an extension the court has no discretion–striking out is automatic–*Webster v Ellison Circlips Group Ltd* [1995] 4 All ER 556, CA.

In October 1990 a new rule was suddenly introduced without warning in the county court–Ord 17, r 11–providing for *automatic* striking out of an action if a request for a hearing has not been made within the time limit. The time limit is six months from the close of pleadings. The pleadings are deemed to be closed 14 days after delivery of a defence or 28 days after the delivery of a counterclaim. Where a case has been transferred from the High Court, pleadings are deemed to be closed 14 days after transfer. The request for a date for the hearing to be fixed must be accompanied by a note giving an estimate of the length of the trial and the number of witnesses to be called, which if possible, should be agreed.

The rule permits the plaintiff to ask for a new timetable and for the court to extend the time in which a request to fix a hearing date can be made (Ord 17, r 11(4)). The other party cannot agree to an extension. Only the court has the power to extend the time limit.

Unless the court has already fixed a hearing, the action is automatically struck out if no request to fix a hearing is made within fifteen months of the close of pleadings.

A common misconception is that the plaintiff has fifteen months in which to set the case down. In fact he only has six months. The extra nine months is a period of grace. The rule applies to any default or fixed date action ie one begun by plaint. This means most actions.

The Civil Justice Review envisaged that the court would send out a warning notice but this does not happen–no doubt at present because the court lacks the technology to discover which cases are at risk of being struck out. Practitioners must therefore watch the diary to make sure that they do not fall foul of the rule.

Discretion to reinstate the action

Under CCR Ord 13, r 4 the court has a discretion to extend time limits retrospectively and so can reinstate an action which has been struck out. But in *Rastin v British Steel plc* [1994] 2 All ER 641 the Master of the Rolls giving judgment for the Court of Appeal held that the discretion should be exercised sparingly. The assumption that plaintiffs' advisers could be relied on to drive the case forward was unreliable. 'Too often they allow months and even years to pass with little or nothing done to press the case forward' (at p 646). Accordingly it was intended that the court should control the timetable if the plaintiff for whatever reason sought to delay the trial. The duty to request a hearing date was laid squarely on the plaintiff. There was no corresponding duty on the defendant. The object of the rule was to see that plaintiffs did not sleep on their oars. The test was not whether the defendant would suffer prejudice by having the action restored. It would be strange to concentrate on the position of the defendant when the object of the rule was to ensure diligent prosecution of the case by the plaintiff.

The plaintiff had to be able to show that he had prosecuted the case with reasonable diligence. That meant that he must be innocent of 'any significant failure to conduct the case with expedition'–his failure must be excusable (at p 647). Only if the plaintiff could discharge that burden should the court consider the interests of justice, the position of the parties and the balance of hardship in a more general way. For discussion of *Rastin* and later cases see in particular N Madge, 'Sudden Death in the County Court', *New Law Journal*, 14 October 1994, p 1409; D Oldham, 'Plaintiff Beware', *Law Society Gazette*, 21 September 1994, p 23; and articles by Gordon Exall in *Solicitors' Journal*, 16 December 1994, p 1284; 27 January 1995, p 70; 24 March 1995, p 272; 28 April 1995, p 398; 28 July 1995, p 748; 24 November 1995, p 1188; 26 January 1996, p 68. See also the March 1996 20-page special supplement to the *Solicitors' Journal* on automatic striking out by Gordon Exall.

If when an action has been struck out the limitation period within which an action must be started has expired the plaintiff's only remedy is to sue his solicitor for negligence. If the limitation period has not expired he can start afresh. Either way it is clear that the plaintiff is seriously penalised for the solicitors' failure. Some would say that this penalty is little deserved.

Note that a county court action must automatically be struck out also if 12 months from the service of a default summons the plaintiff has not entered judgment in default of defence or on an admission or has not accepted or rejected an offer made by the defendant. Moreover the 12 month period cannot be extended under CCR Ord 13, r 4 and the court therefore has no discretion to restore the action. A common situation where this striking out rule applies is where settlement negotiations drag on and the plaintiff's solicitors fail to move for judgment in default. (On the niceties of this rule see KC Browne, 'Automatic Striking Out: Another Trap' *Solicitors' Journal*, 10 February 1995 and G Exall, *Solicitors' Journal*, 18 August 1995, p 824.

In the latter article Mr Exall (at p 825) quotes Judge Hague QC on the amount of time spent on striking out and the *Rastin* principles:

No doubt those responsible for Ord 17, r 11 had the best of intentions, and the *Rastin* decision gives effect to those intentions. But the practical results of the automatic striking-out provisions and the *Rastin* principles seem to me to be highly unsatisfactory, to say the least. The cure has proved to be much worse than the disease. The courts are now inundated with cases on the rule. It has thrown up a myriad of difficult technical points and attracted its own specialised jurisprudence. Every month Mr Gordon Exall contributes valuable articles to SOLICITORS JOURNAL entitled 'Civil Litigation Brief' which these days consist almost entirely of points arising under the rule. Hours of court time are now spent either deciding these technical points or having a sort of judicial enquiry into the conduct of the case by the plaintiff's solicitors (usually on inadequate information) or both. The present case, which was most ably presented by both counsel took virtually the whole day to hear, through no fault of theirs; and the undue length of this judgment confirms the point.

Further, as is almost always the case, conspicuous by its absence has been the slightest consideration of the facts and merits of the action, and the arguments have centred round what are entirely 'lawyers points' of no interest to the parties. What a modern-day Charles Dickens would make of it all I shudder to think.

The purpose of r 11(9) is to prevent delay, which is said to be an enemy of justice. But to deprive a plaintiff of justice altogether (and perhaps confer a totally undeserved bonus on the defendant who is not prejudiced by the delay and who may indeed have contributed to it), simply by reason of the default of the plaintiff's lawyers, seems to me to be a far worse injustice. The fact that 'the interests of justice' only become relevant at a late stage of the *Rastin* principles is to my mind of itself a condemnation of the rule and its interpretation. Some individual plaintiffs have suffered some real and serious injustice as a result... The purpose of this rule is to force all litigants into a bureaucratic timetable, and the effect of the draconian automatic striking out is not to do justice between the parties but merely *'pour encourager les autres'*.

It is plain that the automatic striking out rule has caused a great deal of trouble. Mr Exall said that there were at that time no fewer than 170 appeals on issues arising out of Order 17 pending in the Court of Appeal! According to Judge Greenslade writing in 1995 there had been no fewer than an astonishing 34,000 cases where the automatic striking out rule had been applied–in *Reform of Civil Procedure–Essays on Access to Justice*, (ed AAS Zuckerman and R Cranston, Clarendon, 1995, p 122).

Heilbron-Hodge on the need for court management

The Heilbron-Hodge Report in June 1993 entitled *Civil Justice on Trial–the Case for Change* was prepared by a Working Party set up jointly by the Bar Council and the Law Society under the chairmanship of Ms Hilary Heilbron QC and Mr Henry Hodge. One of the key defects in the system they identified was that 'Progress of actions lies with the parties and their lawyers rather than the courts. This is often a recipe for unacceptable and otherwise avoidable delay as well as unnecessary cost' (p 5, para 1.7(iv)).

Heilbron-Hodge called for 'a radical reappraisal of the approach to civil litigation from all its participants' (p 6, para 1.8):

It is time for many of the deeply ingrained traditions to be swept away and for their replacement by pragmatic and modern attitudes and ideas. In essence what is needed is a change in culture.

This much needed new ethos in the civil courts was embodied in ten basic principles of reform. One was that 'Litigants and their lawyers need to have imposed upon them, within sensible procedural time-frames, an obligation to prosecute and defend their proceedings with efficiency and despatch. Therefore, once the process of the court is invoked, the court should have a more active and responsible role over the progress and conduct of cases' (p 6, para 1.8,(ii)). Judges should adopt a more interventionist role 'to ensure that issues are limited, delays are reduced and court time is not wasted' (p 6, para 1.8(iv)).

Under the heading of 'Court Control of Litigation' the Committee recommended that the issue of all originating process should be computerised. Each stage in an action should be computer monitored, triggering 'prompts' where the time prescribed by the procedural rules has expired without any extension of time being ordered or mutually agreed. The court should ensure that extensions of time agreed between the parties should only rarely be allowed beyond set limits (p 34, para 4.11).

The automatic striking out rule introduced in the county court under CCR Ord 17, r 11 (see above) should be applied to the High Court.

The proposed system of court control of litigation should incorporate powers to dismiss claims which are not expeditiously prosecuted. The existing rules on dismissal for want of prosecution would then become redundant (p 39, para 4.30(i)). Pending the introduction of such a system the decision in *Birkett v James* (p 86 above) should be reversed.

Within a short period of setting down an action a 'pre-trial review' should be fixed. This should be heard by a High Court judge and in some long and complex cases by the trial judge. The matters to be dealt with would include identification of all witnesses and of the extent of documentation to be presented at the trial, estimates of length of trial, the agreement of non-contentious facts, and the fixing of approximate trial date (pp 40–41, para 4.33(iii)).

For a descriptive note about the Heilbron-Hodge report see *Civil Justice Quarterly*, January 1994, pp 11–14.

The Lord Chief Justice's Practice Direction of January 1995

On 25 January 1995 Lord Taylor, the Lord Chief Justice, gave the following remarkable Practice Direction to apply in the Queen's Bench Division and the Chancery Division:

Practice Note (Civil Litigation–Case Management [1995] 1 All ER 385

1. The paramount importance of reducing the cost and delay of civil litigation makes it necessary for judges sitting at first instance to assert greater control over the preparation for and conduct of hearings than has hitherto been customary. Failure by practitioners to conduct cases economically will be visited by appropriate orders for costs, including wasted costs orders.

2. The court will accordingly exercise its discretion to limit:

   (a) discovery;
   (b) the length of oral submissions;
   (c) the time allowed for the examination and cross-examination of witnesses;
   (d) the issues on which it wishes to be addressed; and
   (e) reading aloud from documents and authorities.

3. Unless otherwise ordered, every witness statement shall stand as the evidence-in-chief of the witness concerned.

4. RSC Ord 18, r 7 (facts, not evidence, to be pleaded) will be strictly enforced. In advance of trial parties should use their best endeavours to agree which are the issues or the main issues, and it is their duty so far as possible to reduce or eliminate the expert issues.

5. RSC Ord 34, r 10(2)(a) to (c) (the court bundle) will also be strictly enforced. Documents for use in court should be in A4 format where possible, contained in suitably secured bundles, and lodged with the court at least two clear days before the hearing of an application or a trial. Each bundle should be paginated, indexed, wholly legible, and arranged chronologically and contained in a ring binder or a lever-arch file. Where documents are copied unnecessarily or bundled incompetently the cost will be disallowed.

6. In cases estimated to last for more than ten days a pre-trial review should be applied for or in default may be appointed by the court. It should when practicable be conducted by the trial judge between eight and four weeks before the date of trial and should be attended by the advocates who are to represent the parties at trial.

7. Unless the court otherwise orders, there must be lodged with the listing officer (or equivalent) on behalf of each party no later than two months before the date of trial a completed pre-trial check-list in the form annexed to this practice direction.

8. Not less than three clear days before the hearing of an action or application each party should lodge with the court (with copies to other parties) a skeleton argument concisely summarising that party's submissions in relation to each of the issues, and citing the main authorities relied upon, which may be attached. Skeleton arguments should be as brief as the nature of the issues allows, and should not without leave of the court exceed 20 pages of double-spaced A4 paper.

9. The opening speech should be succinct. At its conclusion other parties may be invited briefly to amplify their skeleton arguments. In a heavy case the court may in conjunction with final speeches require written submissions, including the findings of fact for which each party contends.

10. This direction applies to all lists in the Queen's Bench and Chancery Divisions, except where other directions specifically apply.

PRE-TRIAL CHECK-LIST

Setting down
1. Has the action been set down?

Pleadings
2. (a) Do you intend to make any amendment to your pleading?
   (b) If so, when?

Interrogatories
3. (a) Are any interrogatories outstanding?
   (b) If so, when served and upon whom?

Evidence
4. (a) Have all orders in relation to expert, factual and hearsay evidence been complied with? If not, specify what remains outstanding.
   (b) Do you intend to serve/seek leave to serve/ any further report or statement? If so, when and what report or statement?
   (c) Have all other orders in relation to oral evidence been complied with?
   (d) Do you require any further leave or orders in relation to evidence? If so, please specify and say when will you apply.

5. (a) What witnesses of fact do you intend to call? [Name]
   (b) What expert witnesses do you intend to call? [Name]
   (c) Will any witness require an interpreter? If so, which?

Documents
6. (a) Have all orders in relation to discovery been complied with?
   (b) If not, what orders are outstanding?
   (c) Do you intend to apply for any further orders relating to discovery?
   (d) If so, what and when?
7. Will you not later than seven days before trial have prepared agreed paginated bundles of full legible documents for the use of counsel and the court?

Pre-trial review
8. (a) Has a pre-trial review been ordered?
   (b) If so, when is it to take place?
   (c) If not, would it be useful to have one?

Length of trial
9. What are counsels' estimates of the minimum and maximum lengths of the trial? [The answer to question 9 should ordinarily be supported by an estimate of length signed by the counsel to be instructed.]

Alternative dispute resolution
    (See *Practice Note* [1994] 1 All ER 34, [1994] 1 WLR 14)
    10. Have you or counsel discussed with your client(s) the possibility of attempting to resolve this dispute (or particular issues) by alternative dispute resolution (ADR)?
    11. Might some form of ADR procedure assist to resolve or narrow the issues in this case?
    12. Have you or your client(s) explored with the other parties the possibility of resolving this dispute (or particular issues) by ADR?
    [Signature of the solicitor, date]
    Note This check-list must be lodged not later than two months before the date of hearing with copies to the other parties.

A similar practice direction was issued on 31 January 1995 by the President of the Family Division [1995] 1 All ER 586.

For a critical commentary on all three Practice Directions see a note by the country's leading expert in this field, Professor IR Scott in *Civil Justice Quarterly*, April 1995, p 93. In his view, although the Practice Directions demonstrated a significant change to disciplining lawyers, they fell considerably short of 'caseflow management' (CFM) which required a much more cohesive approach. 'Unfortunately, the recent Directions do not seem to form part of, what could be called, a well-planned, "total" case management system' (at p 95). There was much more to CFM than the disciplining of practitioners in the way provided for in these Directions. Moreover 'the manner in which the Directions were devised, the assumptions which appear to lie behind them, the limited scope of the procedural issues tackled, and the abruptness of their introduction, almost amount to a classic example of how not to effect change' (*ibid*).

For the procedure in the Commercial Court where case management has already been adopted see *Commercial Court Guide* in the *Annual Practice* (better known as the White Book), 1995, vol 1, paras 72/A1–72/A30.

Note–another view on delay

A study by the Rand Corporation found, perhaps surprisingly, that litigants seem more concerned about the fairness of the process than about delays, or even whether they won or lost. (See M Zander, 'What Litigants Think of the Tort System', *New Law Journal*, 20 October 1989, p 1422.) See also R Dingwall, T Durkin and WLF Felstiner, 'Delay in Tort Cases: Critical Reflections on the Civil Justice Review', *Civil Justice Quarterly*, October 1990, pp 353–65 which showed that for expert litigators delay was simply a resource to be managed in the best interests of the clients and Dingwall and Dinkin, 'Time Management and Procedural Reform: Some Questions for Lord Woolf' in *Reform of Civil Procedure–Essays on Access to Justice* (ed AAS Zuckerman and R Cranston, Clarendon, 1995, p 371–392).

Woolf on caseflow management and delay

The central theme of Lord Woolf's Interim Report was that the ills of civil litigation were due to a single cause–the uncontrolled nature of the litigation process: 'In particular there is no clear judicial responsibility for managing individual cases or for the overall administration of the civil courts' (p 7, para 1). The reason proposed is that without effective judicial control the adversarial process is 'likely to encourage an adversarial culture and to degenerate into an environment in which the litigation process is too often seen as a battlefield where no rules apply'. The consequence was that expense was often excessive, disproportionate and unpredictable and delay was unreasonable. This was because the conduct, pace and extent of litigation were left almost completely to the parties. There was no effective control of their worst excesses (p 7, para 5).

The remedy prescribed by Lord Woolf was court control. Thus the first of the 124 recommendations in his Interim Report was: 'There should be a fundamental transfer in the responsibility for the management of civil litigation from litigants and their legal advisers to the courts' (p 223).

As has been seen, Lord Woolf envisaged a three tier system: an increased small claims jurisdiction, a new fast track for cases in the lower end of the scale (£3,000–£10,000) and a new multi track for the remaining cases. All cases where a defence was entered would be examined by a procedural judge who would allocate the case to the appropriate track. The fast track would have a set timetable of 20 to 30 weeks, limited discovery, a trial confined to no more than three hours and no oral evidence from experts. It would have fixed costs. On the multi-track, case management would usually be provided through at least two interlocutory management hearings, the first conducted by the procedural judge, the second by the trial judge. Cases would work to a fixed timetable and initially to approximate and subsequently to a fixed date of trial. In fast track cases there would be a standard timetable, but district judges should have a discretion to vary the timetable. Where appropriate the overall period could be shortened or lengthened. Either of the parties could apply for summary disposal and the court could order it of its own motion.

In making his recommendations Lord Woolf was greatly influenced by the development of caseflow management by the courts in the United States.

The American approach to delay

On the US approach to case management and delay see Joyce Plotnikoff, 'Judges as Case Managers', *Civil Justice Quarterly*, April 1985, p 102–11, and 'Case Control as Social Policy: Civil Case Management Legislation in the United States', *Civil Justice Quarterly*, July 1991, pp 230–45. For an overall view by an American expert on the problem of delay, see Geoffrey Hazard, 'Court Delay: Toward New Premises', *Civil Justice Quarterly*, July 1986, p 236; see also Peter A Sallman, 'Observations on Judicial Participation in Caseflow Management', *Civil Justice Quarterly*, April 1989, pp 129–51.

For comments by American scholars on the 'managerial judging' proposals in Lord Woolf's Report see Richard Marcus, 'Deja Vu All Over Again', in *Reform of Civil Procedure–Essays on Access to Justice* (ed AAS Zuckerman and R Cranston, Clarendon, 1995) pp 219–43 and Samuel Issachoroff, 'Too Much Lawyering, Too Little Law', *ibid*, pp 245–51.

For parallel developments in the field of family proceedings see Dame Margaret Booth, *Delay in Public Law Children Act Cases*, 1995 and an assessment by D Richmond in 'Case Management: A Fresh Approach to Family Proceedings', *Justice of the Peace*, 23 December 1995, p 854, 30 December 1995, p 870.

For description of the Australian approach to case management see Peter McManus, 'Case Management in the Family Court of Australia', *Civil Justice Quarterly*, July 1990, pp 280–99 and BC Cairns, 'Managing Civil Litigation: An Australian Adaptation of American Experience', *Civil Justice Quarterly*, January 1994, p 67.

Reaction to Lord Woolf's Interim Report

Lord Woolf's Interim Report published in June 1995 provoked a great deal of comment. For the most part it was favourable. The Law Society welcomed the report as an 'imaginative, thoughtful and practical approach to the problems of the civil justice system'. The Chairman of the Bar called on the legal profession, the judiciary and the government to support Lord Woolf's work and urged the government to give the reforms legislative priority. (See *Law Society's Gazette*, 21 June 1995, p 6.) The *Solicitors' Journal* (23 June 1995, p 599) thought that the recommendations had been constructed 'to offer benefits to all the key players in the area of litigation'. It admitted that litigation lawyers were sceptical about yet more civil justice changes but said they were 'rather impressed at the public support which the Woolf Report has already received'. Clearly there was a momentum of change which was not quite present when the Heilbron-Hodge Report was released two years earlier in June 1993. The received wisdom, it suggested, was that that this was not a report that would be buried and that this time something would be done. The *New Law Journal* (23 June 1995, p 913) said that Lord Woolf's analysis of the problems afflicting civil justice in England and Wales 'cannot be faulted' and that his solution 'is refreshingly simple: take the management of cases out of the hands of litigants and their legal advisers and give it to the judges'. The report had 'received almost universal praise from consumer groups to City law firms'.

The only serious issue raised by these early commentators was the question of resources. Lord Woolf was confident that implementation of his Report would not require significant new resources but commentators questioned whether this was correct and suggested that insofar as considerable resources would be needed, they would probably not be forthcoming. The *New Law Journal* thought the opportunity for long term savings was clear but suggested that new resources would be needed for more information technology, more administrative staff to support a new cadre of procedural judges, 'and above all, the training of judges to become case managers all have significant short term resource implications'. In the current political climate it thought that it was difficult to conceive of Lord Woolf's reforms becoming a reality.

Some commentators, including the writer, took a much more critical approach. In the writer's view implementation of the Report would be likely to make matters significantly worse in terms of both cost and delay–see M Zander, 'Are There Any Clothes for the Emperor to Wear?, *New Law Journal*, 3 February 1995, p 154 and 'Why Lord Woolf's Proposed Reforms of Civil Litigation Should be Rejected' in *Reform of Civil Procedure–Essays on Access to Justice* (ed AAS Zuckerman and R Cranston, Clarendon, 1995, pp 79–95).

The writer's fear is that putting the court in control of the progressing of civil litigation is open to the following objections:

(1) It will make the system less rather than more efficient. One reason is that judges have no relevant management skills. This might be cured by training if the judges had any appetite for management, though this would be costly.

(2) More fundamental however is the objection that much of the additional pre-trial activity proposed by Lord Woolf in the interests of cutting cost and delay would be likely to generate greater cost and greater delay. This would be true especially in multi-track cases. Thus for example, experience suggests that pre-trial hearings designed to shorten trials and cut down costs tend to have precisely the opposite result. (On this see further the studies cited in *Reform of Civil Procedure–Essays on Access to Justice* (ed AAS Zuckerman and R Cranston, Clarendon, 1995) by Nick Armstrong at p 114 and by the writer at p 93.)

(3) Even in fast track cases Lord Woolf was proposing a great deal of new add-on pre-trial process. Thus for instance in all cases where a defence was entered, the procedural judge would have to allocate the case to the appropriate track, to consider whether the pleadings were in proper form and whether to vary standard directions, to play a pro-active role in pre-trial process, to deal with applications for extra discovery, to decide what witnesses can be called and cross-examined on the content of witness statements. The extra cost would fall on both the system and the litigants.

(4) Lord Woolf was relying mainly on American models of case management without taking account of the fact that there is little, if any, evidence that they have worked there and a good deal of evidence that they have failed.

(5) The Report called for a radical change of culture on the part of all concerned, which would, at best, be difficult to achieve.

(6) To impose a significant measure of pre-trial case management is unnecessary and therefore wasteful in most cases since 97 per cent of cases settle without such intervention.

(7) The judge inevitably knows less about the case than the parties. It should not be assumed that judicial intervention designed mainly to 'move things along' would necessarily be well attuned to the needs of the case or that it would necessarily be welcomed by litigants.

(8) There is research evidence (see p 95 above) that litigants are more concerned about fair procedures than about delays. It is by no means certain that they will consider the abbreviated procedure on the fast track as consistent with fair procedure.

Further concerns about the Woolf proposals were canvassed by many of the contributors to *Reform of Civil Procedure–Essays on Access to Justice* (ed AAS Zuckerman and R Cranston, Clarendon, 1995). These concerns were summarised by the writer in *New Law Journal*, 15 December 1995, pp 1866, 12 January 1996, p 29. For the Law Society's response to the 1996 Issues Paper see *Law Society's Gazette*, 30 May 1996, p 24.

The Vice Chancellor to oversee implementation of Woolf

The Lord Chancellor announced in January 1996 that Sir Richard Scott, the Vice Chancellor, head of the Chancery Division, would take on the civil justice responsibilities recommended in Lord Woolf's Interim Report to provide the leadership and authority needed to take forward the reforms. (See *Law Society's Gazette*, 24 January 1996, p 56.)

Delay in small claims cases

In a Report by the Audit Commission published in March 1996 it was stated that only 11 per cent of arbitration cases were completed within three months, that 49 per cent took over six months and that 21 per cent took over 12 months. (Handling Small Claims in the County Court, National Audit Office, 1996, p 30, Fig 19.)

Alternative dispute settlement

In the last few years there has been a dramatic upsurge in new schemes and systems of alternative dispute settlement (ADR) which now has a large literature of its own–see below–and much support. ADR has not yet become part of the court system– as has happened in the United States. But it is increasingly being brought into connection with the ordinary legal system.

A dramatic example was the Lord Chief Justice's Practice Direction (p 92 above) issued in January 1995 which gave official recognition to the importance of ADR. The Practice Direction gave the text of the pre-trial check list to be lodged with the court. This specifically asks the solicitors to state whether some form of ADR might 'assist to resolve or narrow the issues in this case' and whether there has been exploration with the client or the other side of the possibility of resolving the dispute (or particular issues) by ADR?

The Lord Chancellor Lord Mackay devoted a whole chapter of his Hamlyn Lectures entitled *The Administration of Justice* (Sweet & Maxwell, 1994, pp 69–88) to ADR.

Lord Woolf's Interim Report also devoted a chapter to ADR. He did not propose that ADR should be imposed compulsorily on parties to civil litigation but he greatly welcomed the development and the strengthening of ADR. He suggested that in multi track cases at the case management conference and pre-trial review the parties should be required to state whether the question of ADR had been discussed and if not, why not. In deciding on the future conduct of a case, the judge should be able to take into account the litigant's unreasonable refusal to attempt ADR. The Lord Chancellor and the Court Service should treat it as one of their responsibilities to make the public aware of the possibility offered by ADR.

Ombudsmen   deal with complaints in a variety of contexts in both the public and the private sector. The public sector ombudsmen include the Parliamentary Commissioner, the Local Government Commissioner, and the Legal Services Ombudsman. Private sector ombudsmen exist in a number of industries such as insurance, building societies, pensions, banking and estate agencies. Lord Woolf expressed the hope that the private ombudsmen system 'which has an impressive track record in relation to the service industries' should be extended to cover consumer complaints in the retail sector (p 139, para 16). They had many advantages including the fact that they are free and that complainants do not need the assistance of lawyers. Using the ombudsman did not prevent the complainant from taking legal proceedings if in the event the ombudsman was not able to provide a satisfactory outcome.

Lord Woolf proposed that there should be a closer relationship between ombudsmen and the courts. Ombudsmen should have the right to apply to a court for a ruling on a point of law without requiring the complainant to commence legal proceedings. It would also be an advantage if the courts were able to refer issues to an ombudsman, subject to the parties' consent and that of the ombudsman in question. In any subsequent proceedings, the ombudsman's findings of fact would be accepted as being correct in the absence of evidence to the contrary. This would involve changes to the statutory position of public ombudsmen. The same concept should be applied to private sector ombudsmen if they thought it acceptable (p 140).

Mediation   is a method of resolving disputes by having a neutral third party to guide the parties to their own solution. Lord Woolf's Report described it as a form of 'facilitated negotiation'. It can be used in a great variety of disputes including family disputes, neighbour disputes, industrial and commercial relations.[7]

The Government's White Paper, 'Looking to the Future: Mediation and the Grounds for Divorce', Cm 2799, 1995 proposed a significant change in the procedure for divorce based on a formal role for mediation. Mediation, it said, was effective at reducing bitterness and tension, for improving communication between couples and for helping couples reach agreement on a wide range of issues (p 40, para 5.15). The Government was satisfied that 'family mediation is a cost effective means for couples to make their own arrangements consequent upon marriage breakdown' (p 42, para 5.19). The Government was satisfied that even when mediators were paid more than had been the case in the pilot studies, 'family mediation will still prove to be more cost effective than negotiating at arms length through two separate lawyers and even more so than litigating through the courts' (*ibid*).

It had reached the view 'that a greater use of mediation as part of the divorce process will help it achieve the objectives of a good divorce system' (p 42, para 5.21). But mediation would not be compulsory. If both parties were not willing to give mediation a try 'then it is not likely to be successful and valuable resources would be wasted' (p 44, para 5.28).

The White Paper proposed that public funds to pay for mediation would be available subject to eligibility criteria similar to those for legal aid–a means test, payment of a contribution for those who could afford it and subject to the condition that those receiving it should behave reasonably in all the circumstances. The Legal Aid Board should be responsible for the funding of mediation.

If parties decided to mediate they might well still need some legal advice and assistance but it should not then be necessary for them to be legally 'represented' by

7   An umbrella organisation for promoting mediation is Mediation UK, 82a Gloucester Road, Bishopston, Bristol BS7 8BN. It publishes a Directory of Mediation and Conflict Resolution Services.

lawyers in arms length negotiations or litigation' (p 51, para 6.19). Access to necessary legal advice and assistance should be available subject to the usual means and merits tests (see p 453 below).

The White Paper said that the Government did not however envisage allowing either uncontrolled access to lawyer representation, as opposed to specific advice on specific issues, throughout the mediation process or for solicitors to be employed at the expense of the taxpayer to go over the ground already covered unnecessarily' (p 52, para 6.21).

The Legal Aid Board would grant block funded grants to local mediation services, provided they met the necessary quality standards.

The White Paper proposed a variety of changes in regard to the grounds for, and procedure of divorce. These recommendations formed the basis for the Bill introduced by the Lord Chancellor in November 1995.

The Law Society's briefing for peers for the Second Reading stated that the Government's proposals would put pressure on legally aided couples to mediate when it might not be appropriate for them. They would not have a free choice. Use of mediation would be compulsory unless the couple could show that they came within criteria for exemption or that the mediator does not believe that mediation would be appropriate for them. Also, there would be financial pressures to use mediation–for instance because the statutory charge would not apply. So one spouse could put pressure on the other to accept mediation in order to avoid the effect of the statutory charge. Use of mediation should be entirely voluntary for all couples.

For some basic reading on ADR see: Karl Mackie[8] (ed), *A Handbook of Alternative Dispute Resolution* (Routledge and Sweet & Maxwell, 1991); HJ Brown and AL Marriott, *ADR Principles and Practice* (Sweet & Maxwell, 1993); National Consumer Council, *Settling Consumer Disputes: A Review of Alternative Dispute Resolution*, 1993; JS Auerbach, *Justice without Law* (Yale University Press, 1983); RL Abel, *The Politics of Informal Justice* (Academic Press, 1982); AH Bevan, *Alternative Dispute Resolution* (Sweet & Maxwell, 1992); and the special issue of the *Modern Law Review*, '*Dispute* Resolution and its Alternatives', May 1993.

See also: R Williams, 'Should the State Provide Alternative Dispute Resolution Services?', *Civil Justice Quarterly*, April 1987, p 142; Richard Thomas, 'Alternative Dispute Resolution–Consumer Disputes', *Civil Justice Quarterly*, July 1988, p 206; R Young, 'Neighbour Dispute Mediation: Theory and Practice', *Civil Justice Quarterly*, October 1989, p 319; 'ADR in Commercial Disputes: CEDR', *Civil Justice Quarterly*, July 1991, p 210; 'Alternative Dispute Resolution, Courts and Legal Services Committee, The Law Society, 1991, 1992; Bar Council (Beldam) Committee on Alternative Dispute Resolution, *Report*, 1991; AF Acland, 'Simply Negotiation with Knobs On', *Legal Action*, November 1995, pp 8–9.

On some of the problems associated with the growth of ADR see J Resnick, 'Failing Faith: Adjudicatory Procedure in Decline', 53 *University of Chicago L Rev* , 1986, p 494; 'Many Doors? Closing Doors? Alternative Dispute Resolution and Adjudication', 10 *Ohio State Jrnl on Dispute Resolution*, 1995, p 212.

---

8   Dr Karl Mackie holds an appointment as special professor in alternative dispute resolution in the Faculty of Law, Birmingham University–the first of its kind in this country.

National Consumer Council/BBC survey of public opinion

In May 1995, the National Consumer Council with the BBC Radio 4's Law in Action programme published a survey they had jointly commissioned of over 8,000 adults in England and Wales to get their experience of civil law disputes. The survey included 1,019 interviews with persons who had a serious civil law dispute. All who had experienced a dispute were given three alternative ways in which a case could be resolved and asked which they preferred. The option favoured by 53 per cent was 'Sitting round a table with an independent expert who helps you reach an agreement between yourselves'. 23 per cent said they preferred 'Sitting round a table with an independent expert who makes the decision'. Only 8 per cent said they would prefer 'a full trial in court'.

Asked what they would have liked more information about, 'alternatives to going to court' was the option selected by 33 per cent, compared with 18 per cent who selected 'the cost of going to court' and 17 per cent who chose 'how to find a good lawyer'.

CHAPTER 3

Pre-trial criminal proceedings

This chapter deals with one of the most important aspects of any legal system–how suspects are dealt with pre-trial, and police powers. It offers a great deal of scope for discussion of matters of both principle and practice. Two Royal Commissions have recently addressed the issues dealt with here. It is also an area where a considerable volume of empirical work has been done.

The recent history of pre-trial criminal proceedings in England and Wales has been dominated by the enactment of the Police and Criminal Evidence Act 1984 ('PACE') a modern recasting of police powers. The Act was the product of the Philips Royal Commission on Criminal Procedure (1981, Cmnd 8092), which was established by a Labour Government in 1978 and reported to a Conservative Government in January 1981.

The Conservative Government broadly accepted the recommendations of the Philips Royal Commission. It introduced the Police and Criminal Evidence Bill for the first time in the House of Commons in November 1982. In May 1983 its further progress was interrupted by the General Election called by Mrs Thatcher. The Conservatives were returned and in October 1983 a slightly revised version of the Bill was introduced by the new Home Secretary, Mr Leon Brittan. This became law at the end of that session in 1984 and came into force on 1 January 1986.

The Act was accompanied by four Codes of Practice: Code A on Stop and Search; Code B on Search of Premises; Code C on Detention, Questioning and Treatment of Persons in Custody; and Code D on Identification. Subsequently a fifth Code E on Tape-recording of Interviews was added.

The Codes were the result of extensive consultation with interested bodies and persons. Before promulgation, they were debated and approved by both Houses of Parliament. They were reviewed in 1989/90 and re-issued in a revised version which came into force on 1 April 1991. They were further extensively revised in 1994–95 and the new version of the Codes came into force on 8 April 1995.

The Codes are not technically law,[1] nor can a breach of the Codes be made the subject of an action for damages or a criminal prosecution against a police officer (PACE, s 67(10)). Originally PACE (s 67(8)) provided that a breach of the Codes was automatically an offence against the police disciplinary code, but this section was

---

1   See, however, *McCay* [1991] 1 All ER 232 in which the Court of Appeal said that the Codes had the full authority of Parliament behind them and that therefore there was statutory authority (*sic*) for a breach of the normal hearsay rule!

repealed by the Police and Magistrates' Courts Act 1994. Hardly any disciplinary proceedings for breaches of PACE had in fact been brought.[2]

The main sanction behind the Codes is that a judge may exclude evidence obtained in breach of the rules and an appeal court may quash a conviction where the judge failed to do so (s 67(11)). As will be seen below (p 358), this has happened often.

There are a number of books on PACE. See especially the writer's, *The Police and Criminal Evidence Act 1984* (3rd edn, Sweet and Maxwell, 1995) which includes a full PACE bibliography and H Levenson and F Fairweather, *Police Powers* (Legal Action Group, 3rd edn, 1996). (Both books include the full text of the Act and of the revised Codes.)

See also generally M McConville, A Sanders and R Leng, *The Case for the Prosecution* (Routledge, 1991); A Sanders and R Young, *Criminal Justice* (Butterworths, 1994); M McConville, J Hodgson, L Bridges and A Pavlovic, *Standing Accused* (Clarendon, Oxford, 1994); Andrew Ashworth, *The Criminal Process: an Evaluative Study*, (Clarendon, Oxford) 1994, David Rose, *In the Name of the Law: The Collapse of Criminal Justice* (Jonathan Cape, 1996).

At various points in this chapter reference is made to the Eleventh Report of the Criminal Law Revision Committee on evidence in criminal cases (*Evidence, General*), published in June 1972 (Cmnd 4991). This report made a number of fundamental and highly controversial recommendations for changes in the rules of evidence and procedure in criminal cases. The Report was received with such a volume of criticism, notably on the problem of the right of silence, that its recommendations (including some that were not controversial) were not implemented at the time.[3] However many of its recommendations, including those on the right to silence, were eventually implemented–notably in the Criminal Justice and Public Order Act 1994 (CJPOA).

This chapter also deals extensively with the Report of the Runciman Royal Commission on Criminal Justice the appointment of which was announced on 14 March 1991, the day the Birmingham Six had their convictions quashed and were set free. Its Report (Cm 2263) was published in July 1993. The Commission also produced 22 separate research reports–listed in Appendix 4 of the Report at pp 254–55. (The writer was a member of the Royal Commission.)

The Runciman Commission's Report generated considerable controversy. For a critical assessment of the Royal Commission's Report see for instance *Criminal Justice in Crisis* (ed M McConville and L Bridges, Edward Elgar, 1994.)

Evaluating criminal justice systems

The terms of reference of the Philips Royal Commission asked it to examine, 'having regard both to the interests of the community in bringing offenders to justice and to the rights and liberties of persons suspected or accused of crime and taking into account also the need for the efficient and economical use of resources', whether changes were needed in the system. The Philips Commission referred frequently to the need to strike a fundamental balance between the interests of the suspect and of the prosecution.

2   See Report of the Runciman Royal Commission on Criminal Justice, 1993, p 48, para 102.
3   See M Zander, 'The CLRC Evidence Report – a Survey of Reactions', *Law Society's Gazette*, 7 October 1974. For parliamentary reactions, see House of Lords debate, *Hansard*, 4 February 1974, cols 891–997. See also AAS Zuckerman, 36 *Modern Law Review*, 1973, p 509 and RH Field, 11 *Journal of the Society of Public Teachers of Law*, 1970, p 66.

The terms of reference of the Runciman Royal Commission required it to 'examine the effectiveness of the criminal justice system in England and Wales in securing the conviction of those guilty of criminal offences and the acquittal of those who are innocent, having regard to the efficient use of resources'.

Superficially, Runciman's terms of reference might suggest a different agenda from that posed for Philips but essentially it was just the same. Sensible assessment of the criminal justice system unavoidably has to take account of the proper concerns of the prosecution and of the defence and of the need to achieve due economy and efficiency. On some topics primary weight is given to the interests of the prosecution (sometimes called the 'crime control' perspective on others to the interests of the suspect (sometimes called the 'due process' perspective), on others again to the need for economy and efficiency. The civil libertarian will strike the balance differently from the police officer. The task of a Royal Commission is to consider all the evidence and then reach a considered view as to the pros and cons of all the arguments. Both the fifteen-person Philips Royal Commission and the eleven-person Runciman Royal Commission consisted of a mixture of persons knowledgeable about the system (judges, lawyers, police officers etc) and lay people with no prior experience of the criminal justice system. Both were unanimous in the majority of their recommendations.

For the view that principle rather than a search for a proper balance should guide reform of criminal justice systems see Andrew Ashworth, above, especially chapter 10.

When a report from an official advisory body such as a Royal Commission or the Criminal Law Revision Committee is received by the Government of the day it must decide whether, and if so to what extent and in what way, to implement the recommendations. On evaluating criminal justice see further Sanders and Young (above) pp 1–26.

The first substantive topic dealt with here is the questioning of suspects.

1. QUESTIONING OF SUSPECTS BY THE POLICE

(a) The importance and quality of police questioning

The questioning of suspects nowadays plays a central part in the police handling of the functions of prosecution. (See for instance M McConville and J Baldwin, *Courts, Prosecution and Conviction* (Clarendon Press, 1981), ch 7; B Mitchell, 'Confessions and Police Interrogation of Suspects', [1983] *Criminal Law Review*, p 596; McConville *et al* (1991), ch 4.)

It was not always so. Thus the Royal Commission on Police Powers and Procedure in 1929 made it clear that at that time the law was that where an arrest was necessary the constable should make it clear that the person was under arrest on a specific charge and: 'thereafter he should not question the prisoner ... although he should make a note of anything he says and should bring him straight to the police station for formal charging' (para 137). The basic concept was that the police should somehow be ready to charge the suspect as he had been arrested! Presumably that principle was in practice ignored both by the police and by the courts. It was only very recently that the courts directly recognised that the police could hold a suspect for questioning–see p 160 below. However, as will be seen, the right is fully recognised by PACE.

The quality of police interviewing

Until recently the police received little or no training in questioning. Research conducted for the Home Office by Professor John Baldwin of Birmingham University showed that the results were not unduly impressive. The research was to inquire into video taping of interviews but a side product was the first independent assessment of the quality of police interviews. The study was based on 400 video recordings and 200 audio recordings of interviews conducted by the police in the West Midlands, West Mercia and London. All six hundred interviews were recorded in 1989–90. (J Baldwin, *Video Taping Police Interviews with Suspects–an Evaluation* (Home Office, Police Research Series, Paper No 1, 1992.)

In judging such interviews, Professor Baldwin said, 'one needs to exercise a certain charity'. It was not a question of looking for flaws but rather of seeing whether an interview overall, is fair and is conducted in a professional manner.

Overall, he found that 64 per cent of interviews were conducted 'competently', 25 per cent were 'not very well conducted' and 11 per cent were conducted 'poorly' (Table 3, p 14).

The main weaknesses identified were: 'a lack of preparation, a general ineptitude, poor technique, an assumption of guilt, unduly repetitive, persistent or laboured questioning, a failure to establish relevant facts and the exertion of too much pressure' (*ibid*).

The image of police interviewers as professional, skilled and forceful interrogators scarcely matched the reality. Officers sometimes emerged as nervous, ill at ease and lacking in confidence. Even in the simplest cases, they were unfamiliar with the available evidence, and the video cameras often showed them with their eyes glued to a written statement, clearly unacquainted with its contents ... Many officers enter the interview room with their minds made up. They treat the suspect's explanation, if they bother to listen to it at all, with extreme scepticism from the outset. They are not predisposed, either from training or temperament, to think that they might be wrong. The questions asked (often leading questions starting as they do, from an assumption of guilt) merely seek to persuade suspects to agree to a series of propositions. If this is unsuccessful, discussion tends to be unhelpfully polarised, with claims and counter-claims, allegations and denials following a familiar circular path, descending often into a highly repetitive series of questions ... Some officers adopted an unduly harrying or aggressive approach in interviewing, and though this arose in a relatively small number of cases, these were the ones in which the present writer felt greatest unease about the outcome, particularly where they involved juveniles and young persons.

Another part of the mythology is that the great majority of interviews are with suspects who are awkward or aggressive. There are of course some interviews which are of this nature, but the great majority are not. Most involve relatively simple and straightforward matters with reasonably compliant suspects. Because officers assume the opposite to be the case (as do most training manuals), training often fails to deal with the commonplace and the humdrum ... In only twenty seven cases (4.5% of the whole sample) did the officer's manner seem unduly harsh or aggressive. In almost two thirds of all cases, the style of interviewing could not even be described as confrontational, since no serious challenge was made to what a suspect was saying ... Fewer than one in eight suspects sought to exercise their right to remain silent in any significant way, and taking interviews as a whole, it emerged that four out of every five were with such cooperative or compliant individuals that they should have presented no serious difficulties to a moderately competent interviewer (pp 14–18).

Professor Baldwin suggested that 'The importance of this simple finding can scarcely be overstated' (p 18).

For other writings on this research by Professor Baldwin see *New Law Journal*, 8 November 1991; 'Police Interview Techniques: Establishing Truth or Proof?', *British Journal of Criminology*, 1993, pp 325–52.

Partly in response to this research, partly because of the same concerns about police malpractice that led to the setting up of the Runciman Royal Commission, the police service commissioned outside experts to help it design a new interviewing training package. In its report in 1993 the Royal Commission referred with approval to this development. The new approach had been signalled in a Home Office circular (22/1992, dated 20 February 1992) which stated, *inter alia*, 'The role of investigative interviewing is to obtain accurate and reliable information from suspects, witnesses or victims in order to discover the truth about matters under police investigation... Investigative interviewing should be approached with an open mind .... When questioning anyone a police officer must act fairly in the circumstances of each individual case.' (Royal Commission on Criminal Justice, Report, 1993, p 13, para 21.)

A new training package based on these principles was introduced in 1993. It involved a full week of training. All police officers were supposed to be exposed to the new course. (For an article on investigative interviewing by one of those most responsible for its introduction see Chief Supt Tom Williamson, *Policing*, Winter 1992, pp 286–99. See also the series of articles by Det Sergt Gary Shaw in nine consecutive issues of *Police Review* starting 5 January 1996.) The essence of the method, one might say, is less talking by the officer and more listening!

(b) The danger of false confessions

The phenomenon of false confessions is now widely recognised and accepted. One of the world's leading authorities on the subject has identified four different types of false confessions:

(1) False confessions borne of a desire to attract publicity or notoriety, or to relieve guilt about real or imagined misdeeds, or from an inability to distinguish between reality and fantasy.

(2) False confessions to protect others.

(3) False confessions to gain a short-term advantage such as respite from questioning, or bail.

(4) False confessions which the suspect is persuaded by the interrogator are true.

See further G H Gudjonsson, *The Psychology of Interrogations, Confessions and Testimony*, (Wiley, 1992); and 'The Psychology of False Confessions', *New Law Journal*, 18 September 1992, p 1277.

For most of this century the process of questioning suspects was governed principally by the Judges' Rules.

(c) The Judges' Rules

The Judges' Rules were rules formulated by the judges of the Queen's Bench Division in the form of a code. Technically they were not law, and breaches of the Judges' Rules did not necessarily give rise to any adverse consequence for the police. As will be seen below, evidence obtained in breach of the Judges' Rules could in theory be held to be inadmissible, but this hardly ever occurred unless the defendant's statements was held by the court to be 'involuntary' (pp 350–51). There was also the theoretical possibility that a breach of the Rules (especially one revealed in court) could be made the occasion for police disciplinary proceedings against the officer concerned. It is safe to assume, however, that that was very rare.

The Judges' Rules had three parts. There was, first, the preamble which set out five principles that were said to apply generally:

These rules do not affect the principles

(a)   That citizens have a duty to help a police officer to discover and apprehend offenders;
(b)   That police officers, otherwise than by arrest, cannot compel any person against his will to come to or remain in any police station;
(c)   That every person at any stage of an investigation should be able to communicate and to consult privately with a solicitor. This is so even if he is in custody, provided that in such a case no unreasonable delay or hindrance is caused to the processes of investigation or the administration of justice by his doing so;
(d)   That when a police officer who is making inquiries of any person about an offence has enough evidence to prefer a charge against that person for the offence, he should without delay cause that person to be charged or informed that he may be prosecuted for the offence:
(e)   That it is a fundamental condition of the admissibility in evidence against any person, equally of any oral answer given by that person to a question put by a police officer and of any statement made by that person, that it shall have been voluntary in the sense that it has not been obtained from him by fear of prejudice or hope of advantage, exercised or held out by a person in authority, or by oppression.

The principle set out in paragraph (e) above is overriding and applicable in all cases. Within that principle the following Rules are put forward as a guide to police officers conducting investigations. Non-conformity with these Rules may render answers and statements liable to be excluded from evidence in subsequent criminal proceedings.

There then followed the actual Rules dealing with the stages of questioning. Rule I stated that the police could question anyone. Rule II required the police to caution the person being questioned as soon as the police officer had enough evidence to afford reasonable grounds for suspecting that he had committed an offence. The caution warned him that he was not obliged to say anything. Rule III required a second caution when he came to be charged and stated that thereafter questions should only be put in exceptional cases. ('Such questions may be put where they are necessary for the purpose of preventing or minimising harm or loss to some other person or to the public or for clearing up an ambiguity in a previous answer or statement'.) But a third caution had to be given before such further questions were asked. Rule IV regulated the taking of a statement and required the officer to allow the suspect to put it in his own words.

In addition to the Judges' Rules there were Administrative Directions accompanying the rules, drafted not by the judges but by the Home Office. These dealt with a variety of matters concerning the handling of suspects in the police station. (For the full text of the Rules and the Administrative Directions, see Home Office Circular No 89/1978, [1964] 1 WLR 152.)

The Judges' Rules and the Administrative Directions were criticized on various counts. One was that there were many aspects of the process of detention and questioning which they did not cover at all. Another was that they were badly drafted and that in many important respects they were vague. A third ground of objection was that they did not have the status of law. It seemed to be widely accepted that they were frequently flouted by the police and that breaches were ignored by the courts.

The Philips Royal Commission on Criminal Procedure concluded that it was desirable 'to replace the vagueness of the Judges' Rules with a set of instructions which provide strengthened safeguards to the suspect and clear and workable guidelines for the police' (para 4.109). It called this a code of practice for the regulation of interviews, and suggested that it should be contained in subordinate legislation subject to affirmative resolution of Parliament and 'made by the Home Secretary after consultation with the police, the judiciary and persons with the relevant expert medical and psychological experience' (para 4.110).

As will be seen below, the Code of Practice on Detention, Treatment and Questioning of Persons by Police Officers (Code C under the Police and Criminal Evidence Act 1984) is a major development in regard to the regulation of questioning. It laid down a mass of detailed rules regulating most aspects of the process of questioning. (In the 1995 HMSO version of the Codes, Code C runs to no less than 54 pages.)

(d) Whom can the police question?

The police can ask questions of anyone both before and after arrest. This right continues after arrest (see p 160 below), though, as will be seen, according to the principles of the English system, questioning is normally supposed to cease after the suspect has been charged. From that moment he is notionally under the control of the court and the police should regard themselves as having completed their function.

(e) Is the citizen obliged to answer police questions?

The fact that the police are entitled to ask questions does not mean that the citizen must answer them. The rule of English law on this critical point is that there is normally no such duty. This is the citizen's so-called 'right of silence'. Thus a person who is silent in the face of questioning cannot be charged with obstructing the police in the exercise of their duties.

This fundamental rule was stated authoritatively by the Divisional Court in 1966 :

Rice v Connolly [1966] 2 QB 414 (Divisional Court)

The appellant was seen by officers in the early hours of the morning behaving suspiciously in an area where on the same night breaking offences had taken place. On being questioned he refused to say where he was going or where he had come from. He refused to give his full name and address, though he did give a name and the name of a road, which were not untrue. He refused to accompany the police to a police box for identification purposes, saying, 'If you want me, you will have to arrest me.' He was arrested and charged with wilfully obstructing the policy contrary to s 51(3) of the Police Act of 1964.

Lord Parker CJ:

. . . it seems to me quite clear that the defendant was making it more difficult for the police to carry out their duties, and that the police at the time and throughout were acting in accordance with their duties. The only remaining ingredient, and the one upon which in my judgment this case revolves, is whether the obstruction of which the defendant was guilty was a wilful obstruction. 'Wilful' in this context not only in my judgment means 'intentional' but something which is done without lawful excuse. Accordingly, the sole question here is whether the defendant had a lawful excuse for refusing to answer the questions put to him. In my judgment he had. It seems to me quite clear that though every citizen has a moral duty or, if you like, a social duty to assist the police, there is no legal duty to that effect, and indeed the whole basis of the common law is the right of the individual to refuse to answer questions put to him by persons in authority, and to refuse to accompany those in authority to any particular place; short, of course, of arrest.

Mr Skinner has pointed out that it is undoubtedly an obstruction, and has been so held, for a person questioned by the police to tell a 'cock-and-bull' story to put the police off by giving them false information, and I think he would say: well, what is the real distinction? It is a very little way from giving false information to giving no information at all. If that does in fact make it more difficult for the police to carry out their duties, then there is a wilful obstruction.

In my judgment there is all the difference in the world between deliberately telling a false story–something which in no view a citizen has a right to do–and preserving silence or refusing to answer–something which he has every right to do. Accordingly, in my judgment, looked upon in that perfectly general way, it was not shown that the refusal of the defendant to answer the questions or to accompany the police officer in the first instance to the police box was an obstruction without lawful excuse.

Marshall and James JJ concurred, though James J said he would not go so far as to say that silence combined with conduct could not amount to obstruction. Whether it did amount to obstruction would depend on the facts of the actual case.

But see *Ricketts v Cox* [1982] Crim LR 184 (Divisional Court). See also K Lidstone, 'Minding the Law's Own Business', *New Law Journal*, 14 October 1982, p 953. Silence together with awkward, abusive behaviour may constitute the offence of obstruction. But no one has yet doubted that silence itself cannot.

When the citizen is under a duty to answer

The general principle of the common law is therefore that it is not a criminal offence not to answer questions–and especially questions the answer to which would be incriminating. But there are some exceptions to this fundamental rule.

Motorists   In certain situations, for instance, the police have a right to arrest someone who refuses to give his name and address. The most common example is where the policeman has reasonable grounds for thinking that a vehicle has been involved in an accident or traffic offence. It is an offence not to give up one's driving licence and to state one's date of birth if one is driving a car and one is asked to do so by a police officer. The duty to provide information about the driver of a motorcar applies not only to the driver himself but also to 'any other person'. It has been held that this extends to a doctor who has treated a patient–see *Hunter v Mann* [1974] 2 All ER 414.

Official Secrets There is a provision in the Official Secrets Act 1911, s 6 (introduced in 1939), that if a chief constable is satisfied that there is reasonable ground for suspecting that an offence under the Official Secrets Act has been committed and for believing that someone is able to furnish information about the offence, he can ask the Home Secretary for consent to use powers of coercive questioning. If such permission is granted, an officer not below the rank of inspector can require the person concerned to attend at a stated time and place and to answer questions. Failure to comply is a criminal offence. If the matter is one of urgency, the powers can be exercised without the Home Secretary's prior consent, provided the facts are reported forthwith to him.

Companies Act, bankruptcy, insolvency, liquidations, banking There are extensive powers in the Companies Act 1985 (which repeat powers previously in the Companies Act 1948), to require officers and agents of companies to assist inspectors appointed to investigate the affairs of the company under ss 431, 432 and 447. In essence they are powers to require production of books and documents and explanations. But refusal to answer questions can be dealt with under ss 431 and 432 as contempt of court and under s 447 as a criminal offence. Also the answers can be used in a criminal prosecution against the person making the statement. Inspectors can also ask the courts for an order enabling them to question any other person on oath. There are similar powers relating to insolvency and bankruptcy.

The courts have held that these statutory powers take precedence over the common law privilege against self incrimination: see *Seelig* [1991] 4 All ER 429, CA (admissions made to a Department of Trade Inspector conducting inquiries under s 432 of the Companies Act 1985 held to be admissible in evidence in criminal proceedings against the person who made them notwithstanding that the inspector was not obliged to caution him before requiring him to give evidence or produce documents and that the information could be passed to the police or the Serious Fraud Office); *Bank of England v Riley* [1992] 1 All ER 769, CA (Bank of England acting under the Banking Act 1987, s 42 could insist on answers from someone who had obtained deposits from the public); *Re London United Investments plc* [1992] 2 All ER 842, CA (inspectors under s 432 of the Companies Act 1985 entitled to insist on answers from chief executive of company under investigation); *Bishopsgate Investment Management Ltd v Maxwell Mirror Group Newspapers* [1992] 2 All ER 856 (liquidators acting under ss 235–236 of the Insolvency Act 1986 entitled to insist on answers from insolvents office holders); *Kansal* [1992] 3 All ER 844, CA (answers given during public examination of a bankrupt can be used against him in criminal proceedings). See Stephen Gilchrist, 'Crime in Commerce', *Law Society's Gazette*, 19 June 1991, p 17, and the same author's 'Defendants' Rights in SFO and DTI Investigations', *Solicitors' Journal*, 18 October 1991, p 1140; P Phippen, 'Silent Right', *Law Society's Gazette*, 16 June 1993, p 17.

In their report on Fraud Trials, the Roskill Committee in 1986 had recommended that the police should be given powers such as those under s 447 of the Companies Act in connection with fraud investigations. The Government adopted this recommendation in the Criminal Justice Act 1987.

The 1987 Act set up the Serious Fraud Office suggested by the Roskill Committee. Under s 2 of the Act the Director of the Serious Fraud Office can require anyone he has reason to think has relevant information to attend to answer questions and to provide information, including the production of books and paper. A statement made under these powers cannot, however, itself be used in evidence against the person concerned unless the person goes into the witness box and gives evidence inconsistent with his earlier answer to the SFO. The powers do not require disclosure of material covered by legal professional privilege. Failure to comply is a criminal offence and can also result in an application for a magistrates' search warrant.

In 1994, the European Commission of Human Rights by 14–1 held that Mr Ernest Saunders had had his right to a fair trial under Art 6 of the European Convention infringed by being required to answer questions under section 2 which answers were then passed to the police for possible use in his prosecution in the first Guiness case. The issue was then argued in the European Court of Human Rights (see (1996) *Times*, 20 February), but at the time of writing the court had not yet decided the case.

The powers have been used very extensively. The Serious Fraud Office's Annual Report for 1994–95 stated that in the previous three years 931, 657 and 547 section 2 notices had been issued requiring persons to give information and/or produce documents. Just under one fifth of the recipients were classified as 'unwilling'.

In June 1992 the House of Lords held that the Serious Fraud Office could compel a person to answer questions relating to an offence notwithstanding that he had already been charged. It followed that in relation to such questions the suspect did not have to be further cautioned. (*R v Director of Serious Fraud Office, ex p Smith*, [1992] 3 All ER 456. See also *Re Arrows Ltd (No 4)* [1994] 3 All ER 814, HL.)

Terrorism and drugs trafficking   A power to require answers on pains and penalties for refusal exists also under the special legislation concerning terrorism and drug trafficking. Thus, s 11 of the Prevention of Terrorism (Temporary Provisions) Acts 1974 and 1976 made it an offence for a person who has information which he knows or believes might be of material assistance in preventing an act of terrorism or to secure the arrest, prosecution or conviction of anyone involved in terrorism offences to 'fail without reasonable excuse to disclose that information as soon as reasonably practicable'.

In his 1978 report on the operation of the Act, Lord Shackleton recommended that this provision be allowed to lapse on the ground that 'it has an unpleasant ring about it in terms of civil liberties' (*Review of the Operation of the Prevention of Terrorism Acts*, 1978, Cmnd 7324, para 133). However, the second inquiry into the operation of the Act reached the opposite conclusion. Up to the end of 1982 a total of only 14 people had been charged under s 11 and nine had been convicted. Seven of these received sentences that were non-custodial and one of those imprisoned got a sentence of under a year. Nevertheless Lord Jellicoe thought retention of the section was warranted (*Review of the Operation of the Prevention of Terrorism (Temporary Provisions) Act 1976*, Cmnd 8803. 1983, ch 9). The Prevention of Terrorism (Temporary Provisions) Act 1989 retained the provision–which is now s 18.

The 1993 Criminal Justice Act added a new s 18A making it a criminal offence to fail to disclose to the police as soon as practicable knowledge or suspicion acquired in the course of one's trade, profession, business or employment that someone is providing financial assistance for terrorism. The same Act added a similar new provision to the Drug Trafficking Act 1986–as s 26B. See now Drug Trafficking Act 1994, s 52.

Arrest for failure to give name and address

The Police and Criminal Evidence Act did not alter the law regarding the duty to answer questions. However, it did give the police a new power to arrest someone for a non-arrestable offence where the officer cannot find out the name of the suspect or his address for the purpose of serving a summons on him (s 25(3)(a), (b) and (c)). This is close to creating for suspects a duty to reveal one's name and address.

A similar but even stronger power exists in Scotland originally under the Criminal Justice (Scotland) Act 1980 and now under the Criminal Procedure (Scotland) Act 1995, s 13:

where a constable has reasonable grounds for suspecting that a person has committed or is committing an offence at any place, he may require (a) that person ... to give his name and address and may ask him for an explanation of the circumstances which have given rise to the constable's suspicion; (b) any other person whom the constable finds at that place ... who the constable believes has information relating to the offence, to give his name and address.

The officer can require such a person to remain with him for such time as may be necessary to note the name, address and explanation given and to verify the name and address. But he may only require the person to remain with him for this purpose briefly. The requirement ceases if there is unreasonable delay in obtaining verification of the name and address. Reasonable force may be used to ensure that the person does remain with the officer, and failing to give a name and address or failing to remain with the officer are both offences. But failing to proffer an explanation is not made an offence and to that extent the right of silence is preserved in Scotland (*ibid*).

Obstructing the police and self-reporting

The right of silence must be distinguished from the question of actively misleading or hindering the police. This can constitute an offence. In *Ingleton v Dibble* [1972] 1 All ER 275, for instance, it was held to be obstruction of the police in the execution of their duty for a motorist to take a swig of whisky to defeat a breathalyser test. In *Willmott v Atack* [1977] QB 498, it was held not to be obstruction for a person to intervene between a police officer and a motorist who was resisting arrest when the purpose of the intervention was to help the police officer by persuading the motorist to desist. The motorist did in fact obstruct the officer, but the Divisional Court held that it had to be shown that he had intended to impede the officer. In *Moore v Green* [1983] 1 All ER 663, by contrast, it was held to be obstruction for a probationer police officer to warn the landlord of a public house that his premises were under police surveillance and that a raid to enforce the licensing laws was to be made that evening. For two views as to the implications of *Moore v Green* and related cases, see Thomas Gibbons and KW Lidstone in *Criminal Law Review* [1983] 21 and 29. Gibbons took the view that the courts were significantly shifting the balance of power toward the police in the obstruction cases. Lidstone was more sanguine about the effect of the case.

The Criminal Law Act 1967, s 4, made it an offence to do anything intended to impede the apprehension or prosecution of someone who is known or believed to have committed an arrestable offence. See Glanville Williams, 'Evading Justice' (1975) *Criminal Law Review*, pp 430, 477, 608. Section 5 of the same Act also made it an offence to accept money or other consideration for not disclosing information that would lead to the prosecution of an arrestable offence. See also *Albert v Lavin* [1981] 3 All ER 878, in which the House of Lords held that it was not merely the right but also the duty of a citizen in whose presence a breach of the peace is being, or appears about to be, committed, to attempt to stop it, if necessary by detaining the person responsible.

(f) The legal consequences of silence in the face of police questioning

The citizen's right of silence in the face of police questioning was supported by two main rules of law. One was that already shown in *Rice v Connolly*–namely that silence cannot be made the subject of a charge of obstructing the police in the execution of their duties or, with a few exceptional instances, any other criminal offence. The second was that the prosecution could not comment on the fact of silence and the judge could not suggest to the jury that silence was evidence of guilt. The second, as will be seen below, has however now been abolished by the Criminal Justice and Public Order Act 1994.

The previous law regarding comment on silence

The precise extent of legitimate comment by the judge was the subject of many decisions. See in particular *R v Naylor* (1932) 23 Cr App Rep 177; *R v Littleboy* (1934) 24 Cr App Rep 192; *R v Leckey* (1943) 29 Cr App Rep 128; *R v Tune* (1944) 29 Cr App Rep 162; *R v Gerard* (1948) 32 Cr App Rep 132; and *R v Ryan* (1964) 50 Cr App Rep 144. The cases stated there was a 'clear dividing line'. In *Gerard*, for instance, the trial judge said of the defendant's silence: 'Of course he is not bound to say anything ... but it may occur to you to be perhaps a little curious with a man who has not yet been charged and who merely ran away because he lost his head, not knowing what was wrong ... It may be a little odd to you–I do not know–that he should say "I reserve my statement for the court" when, in fact, he has not been charged with anything or told he is going to come before a court.' The Court of Criminal Appeal held that this was a 'perfectly harmless, reasonable and true observation to make'. On the other hand, in *Davis* (1959) 43 Cr App Rep 215 the trial judge said: 'Members of the jury, a man is not obliged to say anything, but you are entitled to use your common sense. If Davis was in the position that he now would have you believe he was in ... would he say to the police: "I am saying nothing"? I direct that you can take this into consideration as a matter of common sense ... Can you imagine an innocent man who had behaved like that not saying something to the police ... He said nothing'. The Court of Appeal Criminal Division held that this went too far and amounted to a misdirection.

Most judges used the 'standard direction' approved by the Lord Chief Justice which stated: 'Any person suspected of a criminal offence or charged with one, is entitled to say nothing when he is asked questions about it. You must not hold his/her [silence/refusal to answer questions] against him/her'.

There was one situation, however, where the courts permitted the trial judge to suggest to the jury that silence could be taken as some evidence of guilt. That is where two persons were speaking on equal terms and one accused the other who made no attempt to deny the charge. Here the failure to deny the charge could be treated as amounting to an admission that the charge was true. See *R v Mitchell* (1892) 17 Cox CC 503; *R v Christie* [1914] AC 545; *Parkes v R* [1976] 64 Cr App Rep 25; and *R v Chandler* [1976] 1 WLR 585. In *Parkes* the accuser was the defendant's landlady: The Privy Council said that adverse inferences could be drawn from silence by the lodger who had been accused by the landlady of murdering her daughter. They were on the same level–not like a suspect being questioned by a police officer. In *Chandler* the suspect was questioned by a police officer in the presence of a solicitor. Both before and after being cautioned he answered some questions and refused to answer others. The trial judge, directing the jury, said it was a matter for them to decide whether the suspect had remained silent before being cautioned in the exercise of his common-law right of silence, or whether he had 'remained silent because he might have thought that if he had answered he would in some way have incriminated himself'. The defendant appealed from his conviction.

Lord Justice Lawton, giving judgment for the Court of Appeal, said that this had gone too far in suggesting that silence before a caution could be evidence of guilt. The court quashed the conviction. But it specifically accepted that some comment by the judge on the suspect's silence before he was cautioned was justified. The Court of Appeal said: 'We are of the opinion that the appellant and the detective sergeant were speaking on equal terms since the former had his solicitor present to give him any advice he might have wanted and to testify, if needed, as to what had been said. We do not accept that a police officer always has an advantage over someone he is questioning. Everything depends on the circumstances. A young detective questioning a local dignitary in the course of an inquiry into alleged local government corruption may be very much at a disadvantage. This kind of situation is to be contrasted with that of a tearful housewife accused of shoplifting or of a parent on being questioned about the suspected wrongdoing of his son. Some comment on the appellant's lack of frankness before he was cautioned was justified, provided the jury's attention was directed to the right issue which was whether in the circumstances the appellant's silence amounted to an acceptance by him of what the detective sergeant had said. If he accepted what had been said, then the next question should have been whether guilt could reasonably have been inferred from what had been accepted.'

In *Horne* [1990] Crim LR 188 the Court of Appeal applied the 'on equal terms' doctrine to silence in the face of an accusation by the victim of a 'glassing' in the presence of police officers. In circumstance where some protest or denial might be expected, a jury were entitled to take account of the fact that the accused had said nothing. See also *Henry* [1990] Crim LR 574, in which the Court of Appeal ruled that the trial judge had erred in suggesting that the jury could draw inferences adverse to the accused from the fact that some questions had not been answered.

(g) The recommendations of the Criminal Law Revision Committee, 1972

In its Eleventh Report (*Evidence (General)*), the Criminal Law Revision Committee (CLRC) recommended that failure during police questioning to mention any fact on which the defendant sought subsequently to rely at his trial could be made the subject of adverse comment by the prosecution and the court, and adverse inferences could be drawn against the accused from such silence or failure. The accused would still have the right to silence, but he would exercise it at the risk that adverse inferences might be drawn against him if the jury or magistrates thought that it would have been reasonable to expect him to have mentioned the facts in question whilst being questioned. This would apply not only to facts raised in his own evidence but equally to facts referred to in the evidence of any of his witnesses:

To forbid it seems to us to be contrary to common sense and, without helping the innocent, to give an unnecessary advantage to the guilty. Hardened criminals often take advantage of the present rule to refuse to answer any questions at all, and this may greatly hamper the police and even bring their investigations to a halt. Therefore the abolition of the restriction would help justice. ... [para 30]

The Committee said that if this proposal regarding silence under interrogation were accepted, it would mean a change in the caution required by the Judges' Rules. This would follow logically from its proposal that a person's silence to the police could result in adverse inferences being drawn. The Committee said that the caution was of no help to an innocent person, 'indeed it might deter him from saying something which might serve to exculpate him'. On the other hand the caution 'often assists the guilty by providing an excuse for keeping back a false story until it becomes difficult to expose its falsity'. The caution, it said, stemmed from the ancient fallacy that fairness in criminal trials required that a guilty person should not be allowed to convict himself too easily. It was illogical for the police to have to start an interrogation by saying that the suspect need not say anything (para 43).

The Committee's proposals on the right of silence and the caution provoked furious debate. Most of the comment was hostile (see footnote 3, p 104, above) and it was this above all that led at the time to the rejection of the CLRC's entire report. It was argued by the critics that to allow adverse comment on silence would amount almost to a reversal of the burden of proof. It would put a premium on a suspect's articulateness when most suspects were notoriously inarticulate as well as confused and frightened. The critics also denied that silence necessarily indicated guilt. There were many possible innocent reasons for silence, including a desire to protect someone else, fear, contempt for the accusation or failure to understand the accusation.

The matter was next considered by the Philips Royal Commission on Criminal Procedure.

(h) The Philips Royal Commission's proposals

The Royal Commission felt that basically the law should not be changed. In relation to the situation before an arrest, it regarded the decision in *Rice v Connolly* (p 109 above) as correct. ('We adhere to the decision in *Rice v Connolly* that the duty to assist the police is a social one and not legally enforceable' (para 4.47).) Once a suspect was arrested the situation was different since he then had to submit to being questioned. But if adverse inferences could be drawn from the fact of silence it might 'put strong (and additional) psychological pressure upon some suspects to answer questions without knowing precisely what was the substance of and evidence for the accusations against them' (para 4.50). This, in the Commission's view, 'might well increase the risk of innocent people, particularly those under suspicion for the first time, making damaging statements' (*ibid*). On the other hand a guilty person who at present remained silent would still tend to remain silent since it would be more prudent to hope that the case against him would not be proved in spite of any adverse inferences.

Moreover, 'to use a suspect's silence as evidence against him seems to run counter to a central element in the accusatorial system at trial' (para 4.51). There was an inconsistency of principle 'in requiring the onus of proof at trial to be upon the prosecution and to be discharged without any assistance from the accused, and yet in enabling the prosecution to use the accused's silence in the face of police questioning under caution as any part of the case against him at trial'.

A minority of the Commission agreed with the police view that the right of silence should be abolished, but the majority concluded 'that the right of silence in the face of police questioning after caution should not be altered' (para 4.53). The Government accepted this recommendation.

The caution

The Commission addressed itself also to the caution and felt that in various respects it should be improved. One factor was its timing. Under the Judges' Rules it came too late. The Commission proposed that the first caution should be administered not when the police had enough admissible evidence to justify suspicion but when they had enough evidence to justify an arrest (para 4.56). This was accepted by the Government. Code of Practice C (para 10.1) states that 'a person whom there are grounds to suspect' must be cautioned 'before any questions about it ... are put to him'.

Under the Code of Practice the suspect had to be cautioned again before he was interviewed at a police station. The text of the caution was: 'You do not have to say anything unless you wish to do so, but what you say may be given in evidence' (Code C, para 10.4).

The text of the caution has now changed to take account of the 'abolition of the right to silence' (see p 122 below) but the suspect still has to be cautioned and the rules as to when cautions are required have not changed.

If questioning is interrupted, the suspect must be made aware that he is still under caution when it is resumed (Code C, para 10.5, Note 10A). After he is charged he must again be cautioned (Code C, para 16.2). The Code of Practice continues the rule under the Judges' Rules that from that point he should be questioned only 'where questions are necessary for the purpose of preventing or minimising harm or loss to some other person or to the public or for clearing up any ambiguity in a previous answer or statement'. However, a new reason for continuing questioning after charge has been added: 'where it is in the interests of justice that the person should have put to him and have an opportunity to comment on information concerning the offence which has come to light since he was charged'. Before such questions are put he should be cautioned again (Code C, para 16.5).

The Runciman Royal Commission on Criminal Justice recommended that providing the suspect was cautioned and that he had the usual opportunity to consult a solicitor, questioning after charge should be permitted (Report, p 17, para 42). But this recommendation was premised on the continuation of the protection of the right to silence. When that was abolished the Chairman of the Royal Commission Lord

Runciman wrote to the Home Secretary telling him that he would not be able to claim that he had the Royal Commission's support for such a change. In the event, the recommendation has not been effected.

(i) The right to silence debate reopened, 1987–1989

The issue of the right of silence appeared to have been settled by the report of the Philips Royal Commission and the conclusion of the debates on the Police and Criminal Evidence Act. However, in July 1987 Mr Douglas Hurd, the Home Secretary, unexpectedly reopened the whole debate. Delivering the annual Police Federation lecture, he said:

A few forces have suggested that the strengthened right for an accused person to have a legal adviser present may have increased their difficulties in bringing the guilty to book. I understand this concern but I must make it clear that I do not think it would be right to change this arrangement; access to a legal adviser is a fundamental safeguard. However, in the light of changing circumstances, including the advent of tape recording and other safeguards, it is right to consider whether the right balance is being struck between the interests of a person suspected of crime and the interests of society as a whole in bringing criminals to justice. A case in point is the debate which has been conducted over many years about the use which can be made in court of a defendant's failure to answer police questions. Fifteen years ago the Criminal Law Revision Committee made a limited recommendation, confined to cases where the accused failed to mention to the police a fact on which he subsequently relied for his defence. The subject arouses strong feelings and ten years later it divided the Royal Commission on Criminal Procedure.

We should be ready to look at these questions every so often with fresh eyes. Is it really in the interests of justice, for example, that experienced criminals should be able to refuse to answer all police questions secure in the knowledge that a jury will never hear of it? Does the present law really protect the innocent whose interests will generally lie in answering questions frankly? Is it really unthinkable that the jury should be allowed to know about the defendant's silence and, in the light of the other facts brought to light during a trial, be able to draw its own conclusions? I shall not seek to provide answers now. But I think these are questions which informed public opinion might address over the coming weeks–without preconceptions or prejudice.

What was so unexpected about these remarks was that although the Home Secretary was not prepared to reopen the question of the suspect's access to a lawyer, on the ground that it was a 'fundamental safeguard', he was ready to reconsider the much more fundamental safeguard of the right of silence. It seemed to suggest that the carefully constructed balance between police and suspect struck by the Philips Royal Commission and the Government in the Police and Criminal Evidence Act was to be set aside in this way almost casually.

The Home Secretary's remarks unleashed a considerable volume of comment both pro and con, with the police urging that he act on the idea of abolishing the right of silence, and the legal profession, the Criminal Bar Association and the Law Society, urging that the right of silence be preserved.

At the end of September 1987 the Lord Chief Justice, Lord Lane, speaking at the Bar's conference, supported the police view (1987) *Times*, 26 September. He suggested that only very rarely would an innocent person have anything to fear from having to give an account of himself. Defendants, he said, were today more sophisticated than in former times and did not require the protection of this ancient rule.

In May 1988, in a Written Parliamentary answer Mr Hurd said that, having listened to the arguments for and against change, 'I am not convinced that the protection which the law now gives to the accused person who ambushes the prosecution can be justified. The case for change is strong ... But I am persuaded by some of the comments that have been made that more careful work needs to be done before we can bring forward with confidence a specific proposal for legislation.'[4]

He announced the setting up of a Working Party to consider not so much whether the change should be made, but 'the precise form of the change in law which would best achieve our purposes'.

Northern Ireland, 1988

In October 1988 the Secretary of State for Northern Ireland laid before Parliament the draft Criminal Evidence (Northern Ireland) Order 1988 which was first approved and then made on November 14 and came into force one month later.[5]

The Northern Ireland Order permits the court to draw adverse inferences from the accused's failure before being charged or on being charged to mention any fact relied on in his defence at trial. As recommended by the CLRC, the Order states that such silence can also be corroboration of other evidence.

But the Northern Ireland Order goes even further. Where a person is arrested and there is on his person, clothing, footwear or otherwise in his possession or in any place where he was at the time of arrest 'any object, substance or mark' and the officer reasonably believes that the presence of the object, substance or mark is suspicious he may request an explanation from the suspect. Failure to provide such an explanation can be the subject of adverse inferences by the court or jury and can again amount to corroboration (art 5).[6]

Similarly, if a person is found at the scene of the crime or at the time of the crime and his presence there reasonably seems suspicious he can be asked for an explanation. Failure to give such an explanation again can be made the subject of adverse inferences and can be corroboration of other evidence (art 6).

Home Office Working Group, 1989

The *Report of the Home Office Working Group on the Right of Silence* was published in July 1989.[7] It recommended changes that were similar but not identical to those already introduced for Northern Ireland.

It approved the recommendation of the CLRC in its 1972 Report that silence during police questioning should be capable of being the subject of adverse comment by the prosecution and the judge and adverse inference by the jury. The new rules should also apply to cases in magistrates' courts.

4   House of Commons, *Hansard*, 18 May 1988, cols 465–6.
5   House of Commons, *Hansard*, November 8, 1988, cols 184–2253; House of Lords, *Hansard*, 10 November 1988, cols 774–803.
6   The model for this provision was the Criminal Justice Act 1984 in Eire, ss 18 and 19.
7   The report is obtainable from the Home Office Library, 50 Queen Anne's Gate, London SW1A 9AT, price £1. ISBN 0 862 52424 5.

The primary inference which should be drawn from a defendant's failure to answer questions or to mention a fact later relied on at his trial was that the subsequent line of defence was untrue. It could also have an adverse effect on his general credibility. But unlike the position in Northern Ireland, silence would not be capable of being corroboration or otherwise constitute positive evidence of guilt.

Moreover, there would be certain additional safeguards not included in either the CLRC's Report or in the Northern Ireland Order.

The first was that statutory guidelines should specify the factors to be taken into account in relation to the inferences which may be drawn. The judge would have to invite the jury to consider: (1) whether the failure to mention a fact later relied on was capable of an innocent explanation; (2) whether the defendant knew the fact at the time; (3) whether it was reasonable to expect him to have disclosed it at that stage having regard to all the circumstances including the extent of his then knowledge of the case against him; and (4) any other relevant factors.

The judge should also have to ask the jury to take into account: (1) whether the suspect had been cautioned or further cautioned; (2) whether the police had noted anything said by the suspect prior to a tape-recorded interview and whether the accused was allowed to sign the record; (3) whether the accused had received legal advice before the start of an interview; (4) whether the police had delayed legal advice for the suspect or whether he had declined it himself; (5) whether the provisions of the Codes of Practice had been complied with; and (6) whether the interview was tape recorded or whether there had been a contemporaneous note.

In magistrates' courts the court would have to apply the same guidelines before deciding what inferences they could draw from the accused's failure to mention a fact.

The Working Party also recommended that in serious cases where there was a risk of an ambush defence the judge should be given power to order advance disclosure of the defence case either on his own initiative or at the suggestion of the prosecution. Failure to comply with the requirements of advance disclosure should enable the judge and counsel to comment adversely and the jury to draw adverse inferences.

(j) The Runciman Royal Commission's proposals

The Government, however, did not implement the recommendations of the Working Group, possibly out of a sense that it would be inappropriate in a climate dominated by the concern about miscarriages of justice generated in particular by the trio of IRA cases, the Guildford Four, the Maguires and the Birmingham Six. (As has already been seen, the establishment of the Runciman Royal Commission on Criminal Justice was announced on the same day that the convictions of the Birmingham Six were quashed by the Court of Appeal.)

In the evidence to the Runciman Commission those who wished the right of silence in the police station to be retained included the civil libertarian organisations, the Law Society, the Bar Council and the Magistrates' Association. Those who proposed substantial modification or abolition of the right of silence included the Police Service, the Crown Prosecution Service, HM Council of Circuit Judges, Lord Lane, the Lord Chief Justice and many of the senior judges.

The Runciman Royal Commission, like the Philips Royal Commission, re-commended by a majority that the traditional protection for the right to silence be retained. The majority of nine considered that to allow the prosecution and the judge to suggest that silence was evidence of guilt could produce false confessions and therefore more miscarriages of justice.

The majority of us, however believe that the possibility of an increase in the convictions of the guilty is outweighed by the risk that the extra pressure on suspects to talk in the police station and the adverse inferences invited if they do not may result in more convictions of the innocent. They recommend retaining the present caution and trial direction unamended. In taking this view, the majority acknowledge the frustration which many police officers feel when confronted with suspects who refuse to offer any explanation whatever of strong *prima facie* evidence that they have committed an offence. But they doubt whether the possibility of adverse comment at trial would make the difference which the police suppose. The experienced professional criminals who wish to remain silent are likely to continue to do so and will justify their silence by stating at trial that their solicitors have advised them to say nothing at least until the allegations against them have been fully disclosed. It may be that some more defendants would be convicted whose refusal to answer police questions had been the subject of adverse comment; but the majority believe that their number would not be as great as is popularly imagined.

It is the less experienced and more vulnerable suspects against whom the threat of adverse comment would be likely to be more damaging. There are too many cases of improper pressures being brought to bear on suspects in police custody, even when the safeguards of PACE and the codes of practice have been supposedly in force, for the majority to regard this with equanimity [Report, pp 54–55, paras 22, 23].

The Report then cited with approval the view of the Philips majority (cited above) to the effect that if adverse inferences could be drawn from silence it might put strong additional pressure on some suspects and might result in more false confessions.

The minority of two of the Runciman Commission however favoured the view that both the prosecution and the judge should be permitted to invite the jury to draw adverse inferences from silence. In the view of many police officers 'a significant number of suspects, by refusing to answer questions, seriously impede the efforts of investigators to fulfil their function of establishing the facts of the case.'

The initial aim of these suspects may be to avoid being charged but, if this is not successful, they may subsequently fabricate a defence which will not be revealed until their trial, at which point it may be impracticable to investigate and detect the fabrication. Alternatively, they may remain silent, offer no explanations and yet try to discredit the prosecution evidence or intimidate witnesses or victims in order to deter them from giving evidence [Report, p 51, para 7].

The minority recommended that only silence in response to questions 'asked in a room with audio or visual recording, preferably with a legal representative present, but at least after the suspect has been offered the opportunity of taking legal advice, would qualify for later comment at trial' (p 51, para 10).

(k) The Criminal Justice and Public Order Act 1994

The Home Secretary, Mr Michael Howard, made his position clear shortly after the Royal Commission reported. Speaking at the Conservative Party Conference that October he said:

As I talk to people up and down the country, there is one part of our law in particular that makes their blood boil...It's the so-called right of silence. This is of course a complete misnomer, What is at stake is not the right to refuse to answer questions. But if a suspect does remain silent should the prosecution and the judge or magistrates be allowed to comment on it? Should they have the right to take it into account in deciding guilt or innocence? The so-called right to silence is ruthlessly exploited by terrorists. What fools they must think we are. It's time to call a halt to this charade. The so-called right to silence will be abolished.

Mr Howard made good his promise in the provisions of the Criminal Justice and Public Order Act 1994 (CJPOA). There are five sections that are especially relevant.

Section 34 gives the court the power to invite the jury (or in the case of the magistrates, themselves) to draw an adverse inference from silence. The right arises only if the suspect has been cautioned and if he is being questioned by a constable 'trying to discover whether or by whom the offence had been committed'. The inference can be drawn if he 'failed to mention any fact relied on in his defence' or failed to mention any such fact on being charged, being a fact 'which in the circumstances existing at the time the accused could reasonably have been expected to mention when so questioned' or charged (s 34(1)). The inferences to be drawn can be 'such inferences from the failure as appear proper' (s 34(2)).

The new caution to take account of the change in the law in s 34 is more complex than the old caution: 'You do not have to say anything. But it may harm your defence if you do not mention when questioned something which you later rely on in court. Anything you do say may be given in evidence' (Code C, para 10.4). (The old much simpler caution was misunderstood by many suspects. The new more complex caution will pose even more difficulties. See I Clare and G Gudjunsson, *Devising and Piloting an Experimental Version of the "Notice to Detained Persons"* (Royal Commission on Criminal Justice, Research Study No 7, 1992) and Ed Cape, 'Mentally disordered suspects and the right to silence', *New Law Journal*, 26 January 1996, p 80.)

Section 35 deals with comment on the failure by the accused to give evidence at his trial–see pp 345–46 below.

Section 36, like the Northern Ireland rule (p 119 above), permits the court to invite adverse inferences from the accused's failure or refusal to account for suspicious objects, substances or marks. Section 37, again like the Northern Ireland rule, permits adverse inferences from the accused's failure or refusal to account for his presence at the scene of the crime at the time it was committed. In both cases the suspect must first have been cautioned by the constable. The caution under s 36 must advise the suspect that the objects, marks or substances found on his person, or his clothing or footwear seem suspicious and must ask for an explanation. Where the suspect is arrested at the scene of the crime at the time it is committed, the s 37 caution must inform him what offence is being investigated, what fact he is being asked to account for, that the officer believes that fact may be due to his having taken part in the offence and that failure to account for the fact could lead to adverse inferences being drawn at the trial.

Section 38(3) states that silence on its own can never be enough. There must always be a *prima facie* case before any adverse inference can be drawn.

The right of silence provisions in the CJPOA came into force on 8 April 1995. Prior to that the Law Society had advised its members about the implications. To the dismay of the police the basic advice was that the new regime did not necessarily mean that the suspect should be advised to cooperate with the police:

You should not be panicked into thinking that these changes mean that you have to adopt a completely different approach to formulating your advice to a client. In practical terms, the changes make little difference to the actual advice you give ... A judge will not always allow comment to be made about a suspect's silence. Experience will soon tell how judges exercise their discretion about this. The less articulate a client is, the less capable he or she is of understanding and making a reasoned choice about whether to remain silent or not and the less able he or she is of giving a good account in an interview, the more likely that a judge will not allow comment to be made [Law Society, Criminal Practitioner's Newsletter, October 1994].

The Law Society's guidance went on to suggest that talking to the police would pose a greater risk of conviction if the client was emotional, highly compliant, confused, likely to forget important details of his story or otherwise. There should equally be no comment on silence allowed if the suspect had an innocent explanation for his conduct—for instance that he was protecting someone else, or he was embarrassed about admitting discreditable conduct or the police had not been sufficiently forthcoming about the case to enable the lawyer to give advice.

For their part, the police were advised by a former Crown Prosecution Service barrister that whether the suspect spoke or did not speak it could now count as evidence for the prosecution. 'The police now have a situation where whatever a suspect does—lie, tell the truth or remain silent—can be evidence providing the interview is conducted properly.' (Neil Addison, 'Beat the defence', *Police Review*, 14 April 1995, p 21.)

How will the judges deal with the new provisions?

At the time of writing (early 1996) it was still much too soon to have any sense of how the new regime will settle down. The Northern Ireland case law on the right to silence provisions did not throw great light on the matter. (See Edward Rees, 'The Irish Experience of Silence in Court', *Counsel*, November/December 1994, p 16, March/April 1995, p 20.) The most important case from Northern Ireland is the House of Lords decision in *Murray* [1994] 1 WLR 1. Kevin Sean Murray was charged with the attempted murder of a part-time member of the Ulster Defence Regiment. The defendant had made a short statement about the shooting before he was arrested but after he was arrested he said nothing and he did not give evidence. It was the adverse inference drawn from his failure to give evidence that led to the appeal—a point that is more relevant in regard to the trial rather than the pre-trial stage. But what was said by Lords Slynn and Mustill applies also to adverse inferences drawn from pre-trial silence. They both stated that providing the prosecution established a prima facie case which required an answer, adverse inferences might be drawn from the defendant's failure to give an answer.

On the other hand, if aspects of the evidence taken alone or in combination with other facts clearly call for an explanation which the accused ought to be in a position to give, if an explanation exists, then a failure to give any explanation may as a matter of common sense allow the drawing of an inference that there is no explanation and that the accused is guilty [per Lord Slynn at p 11].

Here parts of the circumstantial evidence and certainly the cumulative effect of the circumstantial evidence had called for an answer. The case was being tried by a judge alone (in a Diplock court, see p 393 below). The trial judge had been entitled to infer that the defendant was guilty.

Lord Mustill, in a separate concurring speech, said (at pp 4–5) that a prima facie case meant a case that was strong enough to go to the jury 'ie a case consisting of direct evidence which, if believed and combined with legitimate inferences based upon it, could lead a properly directed jury to be satisfied beyond reasonable doubt ... that each of the essential elements of the offence is proved'. The fact finder was entitled 'as a matter of common sense to draw his own conclusions if a defendant who is faced with evidence which does call for an answer fails to come forward to provide it'.

The key phrase to be taken from both speeches is that adverse inferences may be drawn if they are suggested by the application of common sense.[8]

The first English case to be decided on the new provisions was *R v Cowan, Gayle and Ricciardi* [1995] 4 All ER 939 in which the Court of Appeal, not surprisingly, held that the plain words of s 35 did not permit it to be confined to exceptional cases. On the contrary, there had to be some evidential basis or some exceptional factors in the case before a court could direct or advise a jury *against* drawing an adverse inference. But the trial judge had a broad discretion to decide in all the circumstances whether any proper inference was capable of being drawn by the jury. The case concerned refusal to give evidence at the trial but it would be surprising if the court's decision would have been different had the case concerned silence (or failure to mention a fact) while being questioned by the police.

The question whether the new legislation on the right to silence breaches the European Convention on Human Rights was answered in February 1996 when the European Court of Human Rights gave judgment in the case of John Murray, a convicted IRA terrorist. By 14 to 5 the court held that the drawing of adverse inferences from silence at the time of arrest under the Northern Ireland 1988 Order was not a breach of Article 6(1) of the Convention which guarantees the right to a fair and public trial and the presumption of innocence. The House of Lords in the case of Sean Murray (above) had held that the Northern Ireland legislation only permitted common sense inferences. In the case of John Murray the prosecution had a formidable case. Having regard to the weight of the evidence against the accused, the drawing of inferences from his refusal at arrest, during the police questioning and at trial to provide an explanation for this presence at the house where the offence had taken place was a matter of common sense and could not be regarded as unfair or unreasonable. ((1996) *Times*, 9 February.) For comment, see Roderick Munday, 'Inferences from Silence and European Human Rights Law', *Criminal Law Review*, June 1996.

(1) What is the likely impact of the right to silence changes?

The likely effects of the changes made by the CJPOA in regard to questioning of suspects by the police are, at least for the time being, a matter of speculation. Such

---

8   The case of Kevin Murray is to be distinguished from that of *John Murray* which was being pursued in Strasburg under the provisions of the European Convention on Human Rights as to whether the Northern Ireland right to silence provisions were a breach of the Convention. In June 1994 the European Commission decided by 15 votes to 2 that the right to silence provisions did not constitute a breach of Article 6 which guarantees everyone charged with a criminal offence a fair and public hearing and the presumption of innocence. The case was then referred to the European Court which reached the same result by a majority of 14 to 5 in February 1996 – see 1996 Times, 9 February.

speculation can however be informed by assessment of the present state of knowledge regarding silence by persons being questioned. What follows is a drawing together of relevant research evidence:

The overwhelming majority of defendants plead guilty. For anyone who pleads guilty, whether he previously exercised his right to silence is ultimately unimportant.

The jury could previously not be prevented from drawing an inference of guilt from silence if they felt so inclined, so telling them that they can draw such an inference may not make all that much difference.

Empirical evidence shows that relatively few suspects actually rely on their right of silence. David Brown of the Home Office conducted an analysis of studies on the right of silence for the Runciman Royal Commission on Criminal Justice. His conclusion was that 'outside the Metropolitan Police District, between 6% and 10% of suspects exercise their right to silence to some extent, while within the Metropolitan police district the equivalent percentage is between 14% and 16%. The number of those who refuse to answer any questions at all is estimated at 5% at most in provincial police force areas and 9% at most in the Metropolitan police district' (Report, p 53, para 15).

Some studies show a strong correlation between legal advice and silence. Thus a study done by the Metropolitan Police[9] showed that 43 per cent of those who had legal advice exercised their right of silence in one form or another, while in a study done in the West Yorkshire force[10] the figure was 23 per cent. A study by Moston and Williamson[11] found that 33 per cent of those who had legal advice were silent to some extent, compared with less than 5 per cent of those who had no legal advice. These figures are striking, though they are very much at variance from those in a large study by Sanders *et al*[12] which showed only 7 per cent of those who had legal advice being silent, as compared with an overall 2 per cent. (As will be seen, however, only about a quarter of suspects in police stations have legal advice–though in more serious cases the proportion is higher (see p 132 below).

There is also evidence of a correlation between exercise of the right of silence on the one hand and both previous convictions and seriousness of the offence on the other. Thus in the study by Moston and Williamson suspects were silent in 23 per cent of serious cases compared with 8 per cent of minor ones. Twenty-one per cent of suspects with a criminal history used the right of silence compared with 9 per cent of those with no prior record.

But what is the effect of silence on the prosecution and conviction of suspects?

The effect of silence on the decision to charge

In a study by Stephen Moston, Geoffrey Stephenson and Tom Williamson of 1,067 CID interviews carried out in nine London police stations in 1989, the factors that predicted whether or not suspects were charged were the strength of the evidence, the

9   Referred to in *Report of the Working Group on the Right of Silence*, Home Office, 1989, App C.
10 *Ibid*.
11 S Moston and T Williamson, 'The Extent of Silence in Police Stations' in S Greer and R Morgan (eds) *The Right to Silence Debate: Proceedings of a Conference at the University of Bristol in March 1990* (Bristol, 1990).
12 Sanders et al, *Advice and Assistance at Police Stations and the 24-hour Duty Solicitor Scheme*, Lord Chancellor's Department, 1989, pp 135–6.

seriousness of the case, the sex of the suspect and the outcome of the interview. Silence did not have any direct impact, though, as will be seen, it did have an indirect effect in a surprising way:

(*1*) *Evidence*   When the evidence was weak only 23 per cent were charged, with moderately strong evidence 63 per cent were charged, and with strong evidence 92 per cent were charged.

(*2*) *Seriousness of the offence*   Seriousness made less difference. The percentages of suspects charged for trivial, moderately serious and very serious offences were approximately 62, 63 and 68 per cent respectively.

(*3*) *Sex*   The difference made by sex was somewhat surprising. Some two-thirds of male suspects were charged compared with 53 per cent of female.

(*4*) *Outcome of interview*   When suspects admitted the offence, 91 per cent were charged. When suspects denied the offence, 38 per cent were charged. When suspects neither admitted nor denied, 62 per cent were charged.

When there was weak evidence and the suspect admitted the offence, all the 27 suspects were charged. In both the other categories with weak evidence only about 14 per cent of suspects were charged. There was therefore no sign that silence made any difference to the likelihood of being charged when the evidence was weak.

When the evidence was moderately strong and the suspect made an admission about 87 per cent were charged; when the suspect denied the offence 45 per cent were charged; and when the suspect neither admitted nor denied 58 per cent were charged. When the evidence was strong about 92 per cent of suspects were charged, regardless of how they responded to the allegations.

The effect of the neither admit nor deny category on the decision to charge seemed therefore to be confined to those situations where there was moderately strong evidence against the suspect, but in the opposite direction to that suggested by what the police say about the right of silence. It seems that use of the right of silence makes it *more* rather than *less* likely that one will be charged, perhaps because the police regard silence as itself some evidence of guilt which makes them more inclined to lay charges.

The researchers said: 'Use of silence as such had no statistical effect on the decision to charge or release suspects.' One reason was that in a considerable number of cases in which the suspect was silent the police had significant evidence–in 76 out of 174 silence cases the evidence was strong.

The effect of silence on conviction rate

Of the 174 suspects who used silence, 111 (64 per cent) were charged. In order to test the issue the researchers found a matching 'control' group of comparable cases in which suspects did not use silence. The control group cases were matched for strength of evidence, severity of the offence, age, type of offence, outcome of interview (admit, deny, neither admit nor deny), and whether the suspect made damaging statements. It was only possible, however, to match 52 of the 111 cases.

A matched comparison of silence and control groups showed there was no difference as between the two categories in regard to the decision of the Crown Prosecution Service to proceed with the case.

But comparison showed that silence cases were more likely to plead guilty (67 per cent compared with 49 per cent). There was little difference as to the proportion found guilty (80 per cent of the silent group compared with 77 per cent of the control).

There was therefore no evidence that silence at the police station gave the suspect any advantage at court. The researchers commented:

The high proportion of 'silence' cases who ultimately plead guilty might be taken to suggest that use of silence is a ploy, adopted for the most part by previously convicted offenders, which having failed to secure release from custody is abandoned in favour of a guilty plea when prosecution, probable conviction and (especially) sentencing are nigh. In sum, the results as a whole suggest that the tactical advantages of using silence in response to police questioning are rather limited. They further indicate that whether guilty or not the tactic might backfire when the evidence the police have already gathered is no more than of moderate strength.

Their final conclusion was that 'Abolishing the right to silence might reduce the irritation felt by the police, but would probably do little to increase the number of successful prosecutions.' (The force of this conclusion is strengthened by the fact that one of the three researchers was a senior police officer.[13])

The Runciman Royal Commission (pp 53–4, para 19) said:

The research evidence may be summarised as follows. The right of silence is exercised only in a minority of cases. It may tend to be exercised more often in the more serious cases and where legal advice is given. There is no evidence which shows conclusively that silence is used disproportionately by professional criminals. Nor is there evidence to support the belief that silence in the police station leads to improved chances of an acquittal. Most of those who are silent in the police station either plead guilty later or are subsequently found guilty. Nevertheless it is possible that some defendants who are silent and who are now acquitted might rightly or wrongly be convicted if the prosecution and the judge were permitted to suggest to the jury that silence can amount to supporting evidence of guilt.

The conclusion of Roger Leng, a leading academic researcher on the right to silence was similar: 'At most abolition of the right to silence will lead to conviction in a very small proportion of cases which otherwise would have ended in no prosecution or acquittal. But that benefit will have its cost in terms of extended trials and more miscarriages of justice.' ('The Right-to-Silence Debate' in *Suspicion & Silence: The Right to Silence in Criminal Investigations* (ed D Morgan and G Stephenson, Blackstone, 1994, p 35.)

Further reading

For further reading on the right to silence see in particular: Roger Leng, *The Right to Silence in Police Interrogation: A Study of some of the Issues Underlying the Debate*, Royal Commission on Criminal Justice, Research Study No 10, London HMSO, 1993– including a bibliography of research studies; *Suspicion & Silence: The Right to Silence in Criminal Investigations* (above); Steven Greer, 'The Right to Silence: A Review of the Current Debate', 53 *Modern Law Review*, 1990, pp 709–30; David Dixon, 'Politics,

13 In 1991 Tom Williamson was Chief Superintendent and Commandant of the Police Training College at Hendon. 'The Incidence, Antecedents and Consequences of the Use of the Right of Silence During Police Questioning', *Criminal Behaviour and Mental Health*, 1993, p 3.

Research and Symbolism in Criminal Justice: The Right of Silence and the Police and Criminal Evidence Act', 20 *Anglo-American Law Review* 1991, pp 27–50; D Dixon, 'Common Sense, Legal Advice and the Right of Silence', *Public Law*, 1991, pp 233–54.

2. SAFEGUARDS FOR THE SUSPECT

The suspect in the police station is in a very vulnerable position. The question arises as to how he can be protected from police abuse of power. A variety of approaches have been developed in recent years, of which the most important are treated below: access to a lawyer; informing the outside world of the fact of arrest; tape-recording of the interview; and rules to regulate the regime in the police station and to prevent oppressive questioning.

(a) Access to a lawyer

The presence of a lawyer during questioning provides the accused with much-needed advice and at the same time helps to minimise the risk of oppressive interrogation.[14]

Until 1986 when the Police and Criminal Evidence Act came into operation, access to a solicitor in the police station was governed by the Judges' Rules and some judicial dicta. As has been seen, the Preamble to the Judges' Rules (c) stated that the Rules did not affect the principle: 'That every person at any stage of an investigation should be able to communicate and to consult privately with a solicitor. This is so even if he is in custody, provided that in such a case no unreasonable delay or hindrance is caused to the processes of investigation or the administration of justice by his doing so.' This appeared to give a qualified right of access to a solicitor in the police station. The Administrative Directions drafted by the Home Office supplemented the Rules by stating in para 7(a) that provided no hindrance was reasonably likely to be caused to the processes of investigation or the administration of justice, 'he should be allowed to speak on the telephone to his solicitor or to his friends'. Para 7(b) stated that not only should persons in custody be informed of their right orally, but notices describing this right should be displayed at convenient and conspicuous places and the attention of persons in custody should be drawn to them.

In practice, the police were reluctant to allow a suspect to summon a solicitor. All the studies that were done before PACE agreed that the proportion of suspects who actually saw a solicitor was very small. Softley, in a study done for the Philips Royal Commission, found that only one in ten suspects asked to speak to a solicitor and that a third of these requests were refused by the police (P Softley, 'Police Interrogation: An Observational Study in Four Police Stations', p 68). John Baldwin and Michael McConville reported that only a third of a sample of defendants who pleaded not guilty in Birmingham Crown Court said they had asked to see a solicitor and more than three-quarters of them had their request turned down by the police (J Baldwin

---

14 However in two of the most celebrated cases in which oppressive questioning led to confessions in murder cases being held to be inadmissible the suspect had had a legal adviser present throughout-see p 354 below.

and M McConville, 'Police Interrogation and the Right to See a Solicitor' (1979) *Criminal Law Review*, pp 145–52. See to like effect M Zander, 'Access to a Solicitor in the Police Station' (1972) *Criminal Law Review*, p 342 and 'The Investigation of Crime' (1979) *Criminal Law Review*, p 215; B Mitchell, 'Confessions and Police Interrogation' (1983) *Criminal Law Review*, pp 597, 599–600.)

The Benson and Philips Royal Commissions

The Benson Royal Commission on Legal Services in 1979 had proposed that suspects should normally have access to a solicitor in the police station immediately after being detained. The Commission accepted that 'this right may have to be restricted in certain cases for the purposes of the detection or prevention of crime, but the onus of establishing the need for restriction lies on those who seek it' (Cmnd 7648, 1979, para 9.11, p 94). The Commission said it had drawn the attention of the Philips Royal Commission on Criminal Procedure to its views. It was for that Commission to determine in what circumstances a suspect should and should not have access to legal services. For those who were entitled to have such assistance there ought to be a 24–hour emergency service provided by the local solicitors on a rota basis (*ibid*, para 9.12, p 95).

The Philips Royal Commission on Criminal Procedure in 1981 thought the availability of legal advice for suspects was a matter of considerable importance. Existing studies suggested that the problem of non-access to lawyers was as much to do with failure to ask for a lawyer as with refusal by the police. In the Commission's view a suspect should be informed of his right to have a lawyer but it would not be right to require him to have a lawyer. If he waived his right to have a lawyer, that fact should be recorded. Moreover, it would not be practicable (for resource reasons) to have a lawyer attend on the suspect whilst he was deciding whether or not to have a lawyer.

The Commission rejected the view that there should be an absolute right to have a solicitor. There were situations in which the police should be entitled to refuse access to a lawyer–for instance where a solicitor could alert associates of the arrested person. On the other hand, 'conferring the discretion to withhold access must not bring with it the risk that it will be used improperly' (para 4.90). In particular the Commission did not think it sufficient justification for withholding access that a solicitor might advise his client not to speak–that was the suspect's right. Nor should the police refuse access 'where secrecy is desirable but not imperative' (*ibid*).

The Commission summarized its view as follows:

4.91. Accordingly our general view is that the power to refuse access should be exercised only in exceptional cases. In the first place it should be limited to cases where the person in custody is suspected of a grave offence. Further, even in the case of such offences, the right should be withheld only where there are reasonable grounds to believe that the time taken to arrange for legal advice to be available will involve a risk of harm to persons or serious damage to property; or that giving access to a legal adviser may lead to one or more of the following: (a) evidence of the offence or offences under investigation will be interfered with; (b) witnesses to those offences will be harmed or threatened; (c) other persons suspected of committing those offences will be alerted; or (d) the recovery of the proceeds of those offences will be impeded.

Where the power to refuse access was exercised, it should be done only on the authority of a sub-divisional commander or above, and the grounds should be recorded on the custody sheet.

4.93. To sum up, all suspects other than those suspected of grave offences will have an unrestricted right to consult and communicate privately with a solicitor at any stage of an investigation, and even for the restricted group the circumstances in which the right may be withheld will be limited and the subject of record and review.

The Commission estimated the total cost of its proposals would be a maximum of £30m a year if all the 720,000 suspects interviewed at police stations in connection with indictable offences were to take up their right to see a solicitor. In fact, however, take-up would be much less. In police stations where suspects were at present informed of their rights to have a solicitor, take-up was of the order of one-fifth. If this proved to be typical for the system as a whole it would mean an annual cost of some £6m. The Commission thought that this expenditure would be warranted. (In 1994 the cost of legal advice to suspects in the police station was £68 million!)

PACE

The Police and Criminal Evidence Act provides that 'a person arrested and held in custody in a police station or other premises shall be entitled, if he so requests, to consult a solicitor privately at any time' (s 58(1)). The provision of the lawyer is free regardless of the suspect's means. A suspect who comes to the police station under arrest or is arrested there must be informed of the right to have free legal advice both orally and in writing. (Code C, paras 3.1, 3.2, 6.1.)

If a person makes such a request it must be recorded in the custody sheet and, subject to the exceptions that are mentioned, he must be allowed to have access to a solicitor 'as soon as is practicable' (s 58(2) and (4)). Delay in compliance with such a request is only permitted where (1) the detainee is being held in connection with a serious arrestable offence (as defined in the Act, see p 135); and (2) an officer of the rank of at least superintendent authorized delay.

Delay

The circumstances in which such authorization may be given are defined in s 58(8):

An officer may only authorise delay where he has reasonable grounds for believing that the exercise of the right [of asking for a solicitor]

   (a)   will lead to interference with or harm to evidence connected with a serious arrestable offence or interference with or physical injury to other persons; or

   (b)   will lead to the alerting of other persons suspected of having committed such an offence but not yet arrested for it; or

   (c)   will hinder the recovery of any property obtained as a result of such an offence.

If such a delay is authorized, the detainee must be told the reason for it, the reasons must be recorded on the custody record (see below) and, once the reasons cease to exist, he must be allowed to see a solicitor. The maximum period of delay is 36 hours, or in the case of terrorism suspects held under the Prevention of Terrorism Act, 48 hours. (Code C, Annex B, para 8)

There has been a consider able amount of case-law on the interpretation of s 58(8). Most of the cases have involved defence assertions that the police wrongly delayed access to a solicitor and that subsequent confessions or admissions should not be (or should not have been) admitted. (See further M Zander, *Police and Criminal Evidence Act 1984*, 3rd edn, Sweet and Maxwell 1995, pp 131–35, 238, 240.)

The leading case is *Samuel* [1988] QB 615. The suspect was being questioned in connection with robbery and burglary offences. He asked for a solicitor but the request was refused on the ground that the offences were serious and that there was a risk of accomplices being inadvertently alerted. Subsequently he confessed. The trial judge admitted the interview in which he confessed. The Court of Appeal quashed the conviction. The right of access to a solicitor, it held, was a 'fundamental right of a citizen' and if a police officer sought to justify refusal of the right he had to do so by reference to the specific circumstances of the case. It was not enough to believe that giving access to a solicitor *might* lead to the alerting of accomplices. He had to believe that it probably would. This would be very rare, especially where the lawyer called was the Duty Solicitor. (See to like effect *Parris* [1989] Crim LR 214.)

A Note for Guidance in Code C summarizes the case-law: the officer may authorize delaying access to a solicitor only if he has reasonable grounds to believe that the specific solicitor will, inadvertently or otherwise, pass on a message from the detained person which will lead to the alerting of accomplices, or interference with evidence (Code C, Annex B, Note B4). In the nature of things this is very unlikely to be the case and indeed research shows that the police hardly ever claim to be entitled to delay access to a solicitor. In a massive study carried out by David Brown of the Home Office Research Unit involving two samples each of 5,000 taken in 1991, there was only one case(!) of legal advice delayed.[15] Not surprisingly, in terrorism cases, delay is more frequent. A special study of this problem by David Brown showed that delay of access to a solicitor was authorised in 26 per cent of cases.[16]

The position may have been further affected by the ruling of the European Court of Human Rights in the case of *Murray (John) v United Kingdom*, (1996) Times, 9 February. The European Court of Human Rights held by 12 votes to 7 that John Murray had been deprived of his rights under the Convention because when he came to the police station under arrest a decision was taken to delay access to a lawyer for 48 hours. The majority judgment said that national laws could attach consequences to the attitude of an accused at the initial stages of police interrogation but in such circumstances article 6 of the European Convention would normally require that the accused be allowed to benefit from the assistance of a lawyer at that stage. The scheme under the Northern Ireland 1988 Order affecting the right to silence (p 119 above) was such that 'it was of paramount importance for the rights of the defence that an accused had access to a lawyer at the initial stages of police interrogation'. The fact that he had been denied access to a lawyer for the first 48 hours was a breach of the Convention. It seems that the court would have applied the same reasoning to a denial of access to a solicitor for 36 hours under the PACE provisions in s 58(8). At the time of writing the implications of the decision for the rule permitting delay of access to a solicitor were unclear.

The fact that there has been a breach of s 58(8) does not mean that the court will automatically exclude the resulting statement. It will depend on the court's evaluation

---

15 Brown *et al*, *Changing the Code: Police Detention under the revised PACE Codes of Practice* (Home Office Research Study, 1992), p 68.
16 D Brown, *Detention under the Prevention of Terrorism Provisions Act 1989: Legal Advice and Outside Contact* (Home Office Research and Planning Unit Paper No 75, 1993, p16).

of all the circumstances. Thus in *Dunford* [1991] Crim LR 370 the Court of Appeal took into account the fact that the suspect had a record and was therefore familiar with the police station. He answered several questions with 'No comment' and before reaching the police station he declined to answer any questions. The court held that the judge had been entitled to allow in the confession. In *Walsh* (1989) 91 Cr App Rep 161 the Court of Appeal said that to admit evidence obtained following a 'significant and substantial' breach of s 58 would inevitably have an adverse effect on the fairness of the proceedings within the meaning of s 78 (see p 358 below). But that did not mean it had necessarily to be excluded. The task of the court was not only to consider whether there would have been an adverse effect on the fairness of the proceedings but *such an adverse effect* that justice required the evidence to be excluded. Where the suspect knows his way around in the police station situation it is less likely that a breach of s 58 will result in exclusion of the evidence. (See also *Alladice* (1988) 87 Cr App Rep 380.)

It remains to be seen how the courts will deal with wrongful denial of access to a solicitor in the new situation where silence in the face of police questioning may count against the suspect.

Getting a lawyer

PACE required the Law Society to establish Duty Solicitor schemes for police stations and these are now run by the Legal Aid Board. If the detainee does not know of a solicitor, he must be told of the availability of a Duty Solicitor and be shown a list of solicitors who have indicated they are available for this purpose. In 1994–95, 1,828 out of 1,836 police stations had some kind of duty solicitor schemes and no fewer than 663,000 suspects received assistance under this scheme. In about two-thirds of all cases the suspect asks to speak to his own solicitor, rather than the Duty Solicitor. But the state pays the cost regardless of means in any event.

Research had showed that only about one-quarter of all suspects asked to have a solicitor in the police station and that about one-fifth actually get one.[17] The April 1991 revision of the Code specified that the suspect must be informed that legal advice is free and that posters advertising the fact must be displayed in police stations (Code C, para 6.3). Subsequent research showed that this did make a difference to take-up. In Brown's first 1991 sample of 5,000 taken before April, 24 per cent asked for legal advice. In his second sample taken after the April 1991 revision of the Code, 32 per cent asked for legal advice.[18]

The biggest jump was where the offence was medium serious. Where the offence was defined as 'Very serious' the proportion asking for a solicitor rose from 51 to 53 per cent; where it was 'Moderately serious' it rose from 27 to 36 per cent and where it was 'Less serious' it rose from 18 to 24 per cent.[19]

---

17 See in particular D Brown, *Detention at the Police Station under the Police and Criminal Evidence Act 1984* (Home Office, 1989); A Sanders *et al*, *Advice and Assistance at Police Stations and the 24 Hours Duty Solicitor Scheme* (Lord Chancellor's Department, 1989); and A Sanders and L Bridges 'Access to Legal Advice and Police Malpractice' [1990] Crim LR 494. See also M McConville, A Sanders and R Leng, *The Case for the Prosecution* (Routledge, 1991), pp 49–50.

18 See Brown *et al*, n 15 above at p 47.

19 *Ibid*, p 49.

Another factor in low take-up could be the way the police communicate the right to consult a solicitor. Sanders and his colleagues in the report (see footnote 17 above) identified a long list of 'ploys' used by the police to discourage suspects from asking for solicitors. These included speaking too quickly or saying that the charge was not very serious, that getting a solicitor would involve considerable delays, that the solicitor probably would not come anyway, or that one was unnecessary.

The Code as revised in 1991 now specifically states that no attempt may be made to dissuade a suspect from obtaining legal advice (Code C, para 6.4). Brown's research conducted before and after the 1991 change did not find much evidence of 'ploys' if that word is taken to connote conscious attempts to dissuade or discourage the suspect from seeking legal advice. (In the great majority of cases 'details of rights were given in exemplary fashion, both slowly and clearly'. But in some cases it was given too quickly or incompletely or the language used was not readily comprehensible. Strangely, this occurred in more cases after the April 1991 revision of the Code than before (26% compared with 16%[20])!

Often the solicitor does not actually go to the police station, he advises over the telephone. Code C, para 6.1, says the communication with the solicitor may be 'in person, in writing or on the telephone'. The Duty Solicitor rules were changed in light of research findings so as to require the solicitor normally to attend in person where (1) the police intend to interview the suspect for an arrestable offence under s 24 (see p 156 below), or (2) the police intend to hold an identification parade or (3) the suspect complains of serious maltreatment by the police. (Sanders *et al* found that 26% of advice was by telephone. Brown *et al*, 1992, found that advice was given by telephone in 36% of instances before April 1991 and 30% after April 1991, footnote 15 above, Table 4.3.)

But even if the solicitor advises in person it does not mean that he will necessarily stay while the suspect is interviewed. Brown *et al*, 1992, found there had been a significant decline between 1990 and 1991 in the proportion who stayed for the interview–from 84% to 57%, (footnote 15 above, Table 6.6).

The police may not refuse someone access to a solicitor because he might advise the suspect to be silent or because he has been asked to act by someone else–providing the suspect does actually want to see the solicitor (Code C, Annex B, A(a) 3).

Visits by solicitors 'may take place in the sight but shall take place out of the hearing of a police officer'. If a person has asked for legal advice he 'shall not be interviewed or continue to be interviewed ... until he has received such advice' unless an officer of the rank of superintendent reasonably thinks that delay 'will involve an immediate risk of harm to persons or serious loss of or damage to property', or that to wait would cause 'unreasonable delay to the processes of investigation' (Code C, para 6.6).

If a person who wanted legal advice changes his mind, an interview may take place if that person agrees in writing or on tape and an officer of the rank of inspector or above agrees (para 6.6 (d)).

The right to get legal advice under s 58 contemplates that the adviser will be a solicitor but in reality this is often not so. Lee Bridges and Jacqueline Hodgson (1995) said: 'it appears from the available research evidence that a significant proportion, probably between two-fifths and one-half, of all attendances at police stations by

20 *Ibid*, Table 2.5.

legal advisers are carried out by persons other than fully qualified solicitors'.[1] Often the adviser is a former police officer. The use of non-solicitors as police station advisers is particularly common when the firm used is the client's own solicitors (as opposed to the duty solicitor). (As has been seen, suspects in the police station call for their own solicitor in about two-thirds of all cases.)

The quality of legal advice in police stations has been criticised in several research studies. (For a review of this evidence see the same very useful article by Bridges and Hodgson.) Thus McConville and Hodgson in a study done for the Runciman Royal Commission found that in 86 per cent of cases, the adviser made no inquiries about the case of the custody officer. In half the cases the adviser spent under 10 minutes in private conversation with the client and many such consultations appeared cursory in nature.[2] Dixon *et al* reported that 'legal advisers are largely passive and non-interventionist in police interrogations'. The role of many was 'to act purely as witness to the proceedings.'[3] Baldwin, in a study of 182 audio or video tapes of police interrogations where a legal adviser was present, found that in two-thirds of these cases the adviser said nothing at all in the interview.[4]

Concern about the quality of the work done in police stations led the Law Society to produce an elaborate new training scheme for police station advisers. It led also to the Legal Aid Board insisting that it will only pay for advice done by persons who have qualified themselves under the new 'accreditation scheme'. As from February 1995 the Legal Aid only paid for police station work done by 'own solicitor' representatives if they were on the accreditation list. In January 1995 it was announced that duty solicitor representatives and trainee solicitors were also being brought into the new accreditation scheme, though introduction of this would be staggered to give practitioners time to adjust to it.[5]

For more details of the rules and the research data on the many aspects of legal advice to suspects in the police station see M Zander, *The Police and Criminal Evidence Act 1994*, 3rd edn, 1995, pp 124–42 and Bridges and Hodgson (1995).

Question

It has been found in the USA that the caution under *Miranda v Arizona* 384 US 436 (1966), advising the suspect of his right to have a lawyer present during questioning, does not result in many asking for a lawyer. In a study in Washington DC, for instance, lawyers were available to help suspects in the police stations around the clock seven days a week. In the first year it was used by only 7 per cent of those arrested for misdemeanours and felonies, and the numbers using it actually declined–see Medalie, Zeitz and Alexander, 'Custodial Police Interrogations in our Nation's Capital', 1968, *Michigan Law Review*, p 1352. The evidence in this country so far suggests a take-up rate overall of 'only' around 30 per cent. Is this acceptable? If not, are there further steps

1　Lee Bridges and J Hodgson, 'Improving Custodial Legal Advice' *Criminal Law Review* (1995), p 104.
2　M McConville and J Hodgson, *Custodial Legal Advice and the Right to Silence*, Royal Commission on Criminal Justice, Research Study No 16, 1993).
3　D Dixon *et al*, 'Safeguarding the Rights of Suspects in Police Custody' (1990) 1 Policing and Society, 124.
4　J Baldwin, *The Role of the Legal Representatives at Police Stations* (Royal Commission on Criminal Justice, Research Study No 3, 1992), p 49.
5　See *Law Society's Gazette*, 11 January 1995, p 29. For a detailed assessment see L Bridges and J Hodgson, op cit, n 1 above, pp 106–13.

that might be taken to increase the proportion of suspects who have legal advice in the police station?

Note–'serious arrestable offences' (PACE, s 116 and Sch 5)

'Serious arrestable offences' are defined in Sch 5 of the Act to mean any of certain named offences such as murder, manslaughter, rape, using explosives to endanger life or property, and possession of firearms with intent to injure or with criminal intent. Apart from the named offences, under s 116 an offence is a serious arrestable one if it is arrestable (see p 156 below) and it either has led or is likely to lead to serious harm to the security of the state, serious interference with the administration of justice or the investigation of offences, or death or serious injury or substantial financial gain or loss to anyone. Loss is serious if, having regard to the circumstances, it is serious for the person who suffers it (s 116(7)). This might cover £50 stolen from a pensioner– see *McIvor* [1987] Crim LR 409.

Research has shown that, according to the police, only about 2 per cent of suspects are identified as being involved in serious arrestable offences (D Brown, *Detention at the Police Station under the PACE Act 1984* (Home Office, 1989), pp 48–9). In Brown *et al*'s later study (1992) serious arrestable offences again constituted between 1 and 2 per cent of the samples (see footnote 15 above, p 68).

(b) Informing someone that one has been arrested

In 1977 a provision was inserted into the Criminal Law Act as the result of the initiative of a backbench Member of Parliament, Mr George Cunningham. It stated: 'Where any person has been arrested and is being held in custody in a police station or other premises, he shall be entitled to have intimation of his arrest and of the place where he is being held sent to one person reasonably named by him, without delay or, where some delay is necessary in the interests of the investigation or prevention of crime or the apprehension of offenders, with no more delay than is so necessary' (s 62).

Section 62 of the 1977 Act was recreated with minor modification in s 56 of the Police and Criminal Evidence Act. The person to be informed is now 'one friend or relative or other person who is known to him or who is likely to take an interest in his welfare'. Delay is only permitted where the offence in question is a serious arrestable one and is authorized by an officer of at least the rank of superintendent. The only permitted ground is that informing someone of the fact of the suspect's arrest 'will lead to interference with or harm to evidence connected with a serious arrestable offence or interference with or physical injury to other persons, or will lead to alerting of other persons suspected of having committed such an offence but not yet arrested for it; or will hinder the recovery of any property obtained as a result of such an offence' (s 56(5)). If delay is authorized, the person must be told the grounds and they must be recorded on his custody sheet (s 56(6)). The right to have someone informed of his whereabouts applies anew every time that the suspect is brought to a new police station (s 56(8)).

The Code of Practice (Code C, para 5) adds one or two further details. Thus the suspect has the right to have someone informed of his whereabouts at public expense. If one person cannot be reached he has the right to nominate someone else. The police right to delay informing someone does not apply in the case of a child or young person. Efforts must be made to notify his parent or guardian, or, where he is subject to a supervision order, his supervisor.

The Code of Practice also provides for a foreign national or Commonwealth citizen to be allowed to communicate with embassy or high commission or consulate at any time, and this right may not be suspended (para 7.1 and note 7A).

It seems that under one fifth of suspects seek to avail themselves of this right: D Brown, 'Detention at the Police Station under PACE', Home Office Research Study No 104, 1989, p 34. Delays are hardly ever imposed by the police. Brown *et al* (1992, p 68) found that delays were imposed in only 0.1 per cent of cases.

(c) Tape-recording of interviews

It would be a very unusual suspect who could take a note (let alone a coherent note), of the questioning he undergoes in the police station. The police on the other hand are well placed to make an official record of the process. For many years there was a serious issue as to the accuracy of this record. It happened not infrequently that the suspect claimed that he had (in the jargon) been 'verballed', meaning that an alleged admission or confession had been invented by the police.

The best way to safeguard the accused from police malpractice of this kind is obviously to have the entire transaction on tape. The tape also protects the police from false accusations of improper questioning or fabrication of evidence. Tape recording has been compulsory since January 1992 for all interviews in connection with all offences other than summary only offences. But it took a considerable period to reach this position.

In 1972, a majority of the CLRC thought the time was not yet ripe to make tape-recordings compulsory. It suggested, however, that the Home Office mount an experiment. The Philips Royal Commission in its 1981 report considered various options. It recommended the most modest–that only the final stage of police questioning be tape-recorded, namely the formal 'statement stage'. This is the stage when the police assist the suspect to put his previous more rambling account of the matter into a coherent statement. Taping of the whole interview, the Royal Commission thought, would prove too costly.

To its credit, the Conservative Government nevertheless went ahead with an experiment into taping the whole interview. The police were initially extremely hostile. The results soon convinced the police, however, and they became as enthusiastic about tape-recording as any civil libertarians. The reason was that the presence of tape-recordings seems to increase the proportion of guilty pleas and to reduce challenges to prosecution evidence. Moreover, police fears that tape-recording would diminish the flow of confessions or information about offences committed by suspects were not realized. Perhaps surprisingly, suspects seem just as ready to 'help the police with their inquiries' on tape as before. For an account of the sea-change in the attitude of the police see J Baldwin, 'The Police and Tape Recorders' (1985) *Criminal Law Review*, p 659.

Tape-recording is done under the procedure laid down in the fifth of the Codes of Practice under PACE (Code E). This makes provision for all the details. Thus it provides that tape-recording must be done openly. The master tape is sealed in the presence of the suspect. The second tape is the working copy. There should be a time coding to ensure that the tape is not changed by the police. The fact of breaks, with timings, is supposed to be recorded.

If the suspect objects to the interview being tape-recorded, the officer can, but need not, turn the recorder off.

The police have to make a record of the interview. The Home Office Circular to the police on tape-recorded interviews (39/1991) said that the summary was supposed to be a 'balanced, accurate and reliable summary of what has been said which contains sufficient information to enable the Crown Prosecution Service to decide whether or not a criminal prosecution is appropriate and whether the charges are appropriate'. The summary was supposed to include a verbatim written record of all questions and answers containing admissions by the suspect. (See, however, J Baldwin and J Bedward, 'Summarising Tape Recordings of Police Interviews' (1991) *Criminal Law Review*, p 671 and J Baldwin, 'Getting the Record Straight', *Law Society's Gazette*, 3 February 1993, p 28 to the effect that summaries are often inaccurate.)

The Home Office Circular suggested that in the majority of cases the summary should not take more than one side of paper. But in complex cases a much fuller account should be prepared. A transcript of the tape was only to be made with the approval of an officer of superintendent level, because of the resource implications.

The Runciman Royal Commission took the point made by the police that too much police time was used in making the summaries (technically called 'records of inter-view').It recommended that further work be done on the matter by the Home Office. Research by Price Waterhouse funded by the Home Office showed that summaries prepared by civilian employees were generally of higher quality than those prepared by police officers. They were more consistently free from bias either toward prosecution or defence and they were better in terms of coverage, accuracy, relevance and literacy. Also they were cheaper. The average cost was £13.61 as against £29.11 for summaries prepared by the police. The civilian model reduced police input on average from 82 minutes to 19 minutes. The Price Waterhouse report of the research concluded that the findings supported the case for moving increasingly to use civilians for this work. (See A Hooke and J Knox, 'Preparing Records of Taped Interviews', Home Office Research and Statistics Department, Research Findings No 22, November 1995.)

Based on this research all forces were advised by an efficiency scrutiny in July 1995 to implement a programme to employ civilians to prepare records of taped interviews.

The efficiency scrutiny led in November 1995 to further major changes, the main purpose of which was to cut down significantly on police paperwork. In straightforward cases where the defendant is likely to plead guilty in the magistrates' court the police are now supposed to send to the CPS an Abbreviated File with Short Descriptive Notes (SDNs) of taped interviews instead of a Record of Taped Interview (ROTI). The SDN should be brief, should refer to relevant tape counter times, and should use reported speech. The Abbreviated File would have a statement of the victim and of key witnesses. The full file has typed copies of all witnesses.

The defence have full access to the tape-recording. But ironically it seems that it is relatively rare for either the prosecution or the defence lawyers to listen to the actual tapes. They tend instead to work from the summary of the tape. In 1994 the Law Society laid down guidelines as to when solicitors should listen to the tape. (See *Law Society's Gazette*, 20 April 1994, p 29.)

Tape-recording does not apply to interviews with terrorism suspects. There has been a fear that giving the defence access to the tapes might result in the identification of the officers involved in questioning such suspects, with possible risk to their lives. But in March 1990 the Home Secretary announced a two-year experiment in London and Merseyside in which the police would tape-record summaries of interviews with terrorism suspects. The suspect would be given an opportunity to record his comments about the interview. The tapes would then be sealed and would be available to both the prosecution and the defence if the case resulted in charges, but not otherwise. No report of the results of this study has ever been published.

In January 1996, the Northern Ireland Secretary, Sir Patrick Mayhew announced that audio recording had been ruled out because of security concerns but that the Government planned to introduce silent video recording of interviews with suspected terrorists. (House of Commons, *Hansard*, 9 January 1996, col 34.)

For an account of a major study of tape-recording see Carole Willis, J Macleod and P Nash *The Tape Recording of Police Interviews with Suspects*, 2nd Interim Report, Home Office Research Study No 97, 1988. For an account of an equivalent study in Scotland see Scottish Home and Health Department, 'Tape Recording of Police Interviews: An Interim Report–the First 24 Months', 1982. On guidance to the courts on the handling of tape recordings see *Rampling* [1987] Crim LR 823, and *Practice Direction* (Crime: Tape Recording of Police Interviews) [1989] 1 WLR 631.

The next development will undoubtedly be video-recording of ordinary interviews. For an account of a successful Canadian experiment with videos, see Alan Grant, 'Video-taping Police Questioning: a Canadian Experiment' (1987) *Criminal Law Review*, p 375. Experiments are also taking place in this country, in the USA and in Australia. The Runciman Royal Commission made no recommendation on the matter (see Report p 26, para 5).

Exchanges that are not recorded

It is clear that exchanges will inevitably take place between suspects and police officers that are not recorded–whether in the street, in private homes or other premises, in the police car or even at the police station. Research done for the Runciman Commission showed that the arresting officers reported having interviewed suspects before arrival at the police station in 8 per cent of cases.[6] The Royal Commission called for more research on the pros and cons of attempting to tape-record such exchanges outside the police station (Report, pp 27–28). It is to be noted in this context that Code C, para 11.1 states that save for exceptional circumstances 'Following a decision to arrest a suspect he must not be interviewed about the relevant offence except at a police station'. No doubt this is because it is only when he gets to the police station that the suspect is advised of his full rights and, in particular, it is only then that he is told about and enabled to get legal advice. Now that silence after caution can 'count' for the prosecution it is at least possible that the courts will be faced with more situations where the police question (and therefore 'interview'–see below) suspects outside the police station.

6   S Moston and G Stephenson, *The Questioning and Interviewing of Suspects outside the Police Station* (Royal Commission on Criminal Justice, Research Study No 22, 1993).

The Royal Commission did recommend that the public parts of police stations should be under constant 24–hour a day surveillance through both audio and video recording. That would include the area around the custody officer's desk (the 'custody suite') and the corridors leading to the cells. It would not include the cells themselves. The purpose would be to reduce the danger of unauthorised and improper exchanges, as well as to monitor the nature of any physical interaction between suspects and police officers (Report, pp 33–34). The Government's Interim Response to the Royal Commission's Report in February 1994 indicated that this recommendation was accepted in principle.

(d) The regime in the police station–the Codes of Practice and the custody officer

As has been seen, the old Administrative Directions accompanying the Judges' Rules made some provision for the way the suspect was to be looked after in the police station. These dealt with such matters as the way the statement was to be taken and recorded, the record of the questioning, reasonable comfort and refreshment of suspects, special rules for questioning children, young persons and mentally handicapped persons, rules regarding the questioning of foreigners and access to writing materials.

The PACE Codes of Practice very significantly added to these rules and laid on the police a large number of detailed new requirements in regard to the way that suspects must be handled. The difference between the old Administrative Directions and the Codes may be seen from their respective length–the Directions ran to some two pages; as has been seen, Code C for the Detention, Treatment and Questioning of persons by the police runs to nearly sixty.

Code C starts with the statement that 'all persons shall be dealt with expeditiously and released as soon as the need for detention has ceased to apply' (para 1.1).

Most of the Code deals with the situation in the police station. It deals with the duties in particular of the custody officer the person in each police station designated to be responsible for the well-being of suspects. The Police and Criminal Evidence Act states there has to be a custody officer on duty in each police station and that normally he should be of the rank of sergeant or above. It is the custody officer's duty to ensure 'that all persons in police detention at that station are treated in accordance with this Act and any code of practice issued under it ... and that all matters relating to such persons which are required by this Act or by such codes of practice to be recorded are recorded in the custody records relating to such persons' (s 39(1)). The custody officer must, if possible, be someone other than the arresting or investigating officers. Where the arresting officer is higher in rank than the custody officer and there is some disagreement between them regarding the handling of the suspect, the custody officer has to refer the matter to an officer of the rank of superintendent or above responsible for that police station (s 39(6)).

The custody record

The Code requires the custody officer in each police station to maintain the custody record, which will contain the details of all the relevant events of the detention. The items that must be stated in the custody record include: the grounds of detention; the time when detention starts; the suspect's signature acknowledging receipt of a notice of his rights, or the custody officer's note that he refused to sign; any waiver by the suspect of his right to have legal advice; details of all visits to detained persons; the grounds for delaying access to legal advice; the grounds for starting to interview a suspect who has been allowed to call a solicitor before the solicitor arrives; details of any letters sent out by the suspect; details of any call made on behalf of a person from abroad to an embassy, consulate or High Commission regarding the fact of his detention; details of the times at which meals are served to the suspect; details of any exercise taken; the grounds why a child or young person is placed in police cells; details of any complaint by a suspect regarding his treatment; details of any medical treatment or action taken regarding a condition requiring medical attention; the time and place of any caution; the time at which the suspect is handed over by the custody officer for questioning; any decision to interview a mentally disordered person or child or young person without waiting for a responsible person who has been asked to come to be with him; the time at which the suspect is cautioned on being charged, and details of anything he said.

A person is entitled to a copy of any part of the custody record that the police are required to maintain and he must be told of his right to have a copy.

Information to the person in custody

One of the most important provisions in the Code relates to the information that must be given to the suspect. The custody officer, before any questioning of the suspect, must tell him the ground of his detention and tell him both orally and in writing of his right to have someone informed about his arrest, to have free legal advice and of his rights under para 5 to send messages to the outside world.

Para 5 permits the suspect at his own expense to send letters, or telegrams or make telephone calls, providing Annex B does not apply. (Annex B states that the implementation of certain rights may be delayed if an officer of the rank of superintendent or above has reasonable grounds to believe that it would lead to 'interference with or harm to evidence connected with a serious arrestable offence', or to the alerting of other persons suspected of having committed such an offence, or will hinder the recovery of property obtained in the course of such an offence.) If letters are sent from the police station, the police are permitted to monitor their contents–other than in the case of letters to a solicitor (para 5.7).

As has been seen, the custody record must show that the suspect has been told about his rights, either by his signed acknowledgement or a note that he refused to sign. If he wishes to waive the right to legal advice, this too must be signed (para 3.2).

The police must caution the suspect that anything he says in a letter, phone call or telegram may be used in evidence (para 5.7).

Records of interviews

The provisions in Code C regarding the process of keeping proper records of any interview with the suspect require records to be kept of the place of interviews, the time they begin and end, and the time of any breaks. The person interviewed must be given the chance to read the record and to sign it as correct or to indicate what he thinks is not accurate. Persons making statements must be allowed to make them in their own words. If the officer writes the statement he should use the words actually spoken by the suspect. (Paras 2.6, 11.5–11.13, Annex D.)

One important addition to the old rules is that records of interviews should so far as practicable be made contemporaneously, or failing this as soon as possible after the interview (para 11.5(c)). This has caused the police much concern. Also a full written record of the interview must be made and the suspect must be given a chance to read it and to sign it as correct. Where a third person is present at an interview, he has to be given the opportunity to read the written record of the interview and to sign it as correct or to indicate the aspects in which he thinks it is inaccurate. If he refuses to do so, this fact should be recorded (para 11.11).

For definition of an interview see Code C, Note 11A. But the definition is less important since a record must now be made of relevant comments even if they are made outside the context of an interview (para 11.13).

For an evaluation of the value of the recording rules see H Fenwick, 'Confessions, Recording Rules and Miscarriages of Justice: a Mistaken Emphasis', *Criminal Law Review* [1993], p 174.

Conditions of detention (paras 8 and 9)

The Judges' Rules and Administrative Directions made some, but only rather general, reference to the conditions of detention. The Code puts detailed flesh and blood on the existing skeleton.

So far as practicable there should be no more than one person per cell. Cells and bedding should be aired and cleaned daily. There should be reasonable access to toilet and washing facilities. Replacement clothing should be of reasonable standard and no questioning must take place unless the suspect has been offered clothing. There should be at least two light and one main meal per 24 hours and any dietary requirements should be met so far as possible. Brief outdoor exercise should be permitted daily, if possible.

A child or young person should not be placed in police cells unless he is so unruly as to be a danger to person or property or there is no other secure accommodation available. Only an inspector or above can authorize such detention.

No more than reasonable force may be used by a police officer to secure compliance with reasonable instructions, to prevent the suspect's escape, or to restrain him from causing injury to persons or damage to property or evidence.

If any ill-treatment or unlawful force has been used, any officer who has notice of it should draw it to the attention of the custody officer who in turn must inform an officer of at least the rank of inspector not connected with the investigation. He in turn must summon a police surgeon to examine the suspect. A complaint from the suspect to this effect must similarly be reported to an inspector or above.

Medical treatment (para 9(b))

The Code requires that appropriate action be taken by the custody officer to deal with any medical condition–whether or not the person in custody asks for it. This applies not only to obvious medical conditions but where the person is unable to appreciate the nature of the proceedings, or he is incoherent or somnolent and the custody officer is in any doubt as to the circumstances of his condition. The Code specifically warns that a person who appears to be drunk may in fact be suffering from the effects of drugs or some injury. The police should 'always call the police surgeon when in any doubt' (Note 9B).

If the suspect says he needs medication for a serious condition such as heart disease, diabetes or epilepsy, the advice of the police surgeon should be obtained. If the suspect is thought to be a drug addict, only a police surgeon can authorize the administration of drugs.

Conduct of interviews (para 12)

In any period of 24 hours the suspect is supposed to be given eight continuous hours for rest, free from questioning, travel or other interruption and, if possible, at night. If he goes to the police station voluntarily, the period is calculated from arrest.

Except where life is at stake, no one may be questioned if he cannot understand the significance of the questions through the effect of drink or drugs (para 12.3 and Annex C).

Interview rooms are supposed to be adequately heated, lit and ventilated. The suspect should not be required to stand. The interviewing officer should identify his name and rank (or in terrorism cases his number). In addition to meal breaks there should also be short breaks for refreshment approximately every two hours unless this would prejudice the investigation.

The questioning of mentally disordered persons, children and young persons (para 3(b) and Annex E)

There are detailed provisions in the Code regulating the questioning of persons who are mentally handicapped or disordered or youthful. Broadly, they require that normally questioning should only take place in the presence of an 'appropriate adult' who is either a parent or guardian or a person in whose care he is. If the adult thinks that legal advice should be taken, the interview should not commence until such advice has been taken. However, an interview may take place in the absence of the responsible adult or lawyer if an officer of the rank of superintendent or above reasonably believes that the delay in waiting would involve the risk of immediate harm to persons or serious loss of or damage to property. (Annex C.)

The Runciman Royal Commission (p 44, para 86) recommended that an expert working party be appointed to consider the role of the appropriate adult. The Home Office set up a Review Group which reported in June 1995. It recommended, inter alia, that local panels of appropriate adults should be set up and that guidance as to the role should be available in the form of leaflets.

Interpreters (para 13)

The Administrative Directions accompanying the Judges' Rules referred to statements made by those who could not speak English being translated by an interpreter. But they did not positively require the interpreter to be called. The Code remedies this deficiency and states categorically that a person who has difficulty in understanding English shall not be interviewed save in the presence of someone who can act as interpreter.

Questioning of deaf persons (para 13)

The Code also provides that where there is a doubt as to a person's hearing, arrangements should be made to have a competent interpreter. If he wishes, no interview should take place without the interpreter. On the other hand, if he does not insist on having an interpreter, the person should sign a waiver to that effect. If the deaf person is also mentally disordered or a child or young person, the interpreter should be someone different from the responsible adult whose presence is required under para 3(b).

See generally M Zander, *The Police and Criminal Evidence Act 1984*, 3rd edn, 1995, pp 174–92.

(e) Rules preventing improper pressure on suspects

It goes without saying that police officers may not use physical violence or the threat of violence against suspects. Any such action would of course constitute the criminal offence of assault (or worse). It would also be actionable in civil proceedings for damages. But civil and criminal proceedings are usually difficult to launch because of the problem of proving the allegations. The use or the threat of physical violence would also be the basis of a formal complaint against the officers concerned.

Apart from the inhibiting effect of these possibilities there is also the long-established principle that statements to be admissible in evidence must be voluntary. The requirement that all confessions or admissions be voluntary is considered in chapter 4. It will be seen there that the Philips Royal Commission proposed that the common-law rules be modified and that the Police and Criminal Evidence Act partly adopted the Commission's proposals and partly altered the common-law rules. Under the scheme of the Act, confessions obtained as a result of oppression, violence, the threat of violence, or inhuman or degrading treatment are wholly inadmissible. Likewise inadmissible are statements obtained in circumstances that make it likely that any confession obtained in those circumstances would be unreliable. Moreover it is for the prosecution to prove beyond reasonable doubt that the statement was not obtained as a result of such conduct. But if these conditions are met, the confession can be admissible even though it was obtained as a result of inducements. (See further pp 350–59.)

3. DETENTION AND ARREST

(a) Can a person be held in the police station if he is not under arrest?

It is common to read in the newspapers that a man is 'helping the police with their inquiries'. When asked, the police normally assert that he is not, however, under arrest. What is the legal status of a person in this situation?

The position is stated in s 29 of the Police and Criminal Evidence Act which provides that where a person attends a police station voluntarily 'for the purpose of assisting with an investigation', he is entitled to leave at will unless placed under arrest. Secondly, he must be informed 'at once that he is under arrest if a decision is taken by a constable to prevent him from leaving at will'. The only gap in the system is that there is no duty on the police to advise the person in question that he need not accompany the officer to the police station unless he wishes to do so. This would be the equivalent of the duty to caution him about his right of silence. But it does not exist and neither the Philips Royal Commission on Criminal Procedure nor PACE made any reference to the issue.

However if someone who is voluntarily helping the police with their inquiries, whether at a police station or elsewhere, is cautioned he must be informed that he is not under arrest, if that is the case (Code C, paras 3.15 and 10.2).

(b) In what circumstances can someone be stopped in the street?

The police can ask anyone any questions–but can they lawfully stop a citizen who does not wish to be stopped, without arresting him? This question has arisen in a variety of contexts. In 1967 the Divisional Court gave a clear response to this question:

Kenlin v Gardiner [1967] 2 QB 510 (Divisional Court)

Two schoolboys were going from house to house to remind members of their rugby team about a game. Two police officers became suspicious and, producing a warrant card, asked what they were doing. The boys did not believe they were police officers. One boy made as if to run away. The police officer took hold of his arm. The boy struggled violently, punching and kicking the officer. The other boy got involved and struck the other officer. Both were charged with assaulting a police constable in the execution of his duty.

Appeal by case stated.

Winn LJ gave the judgment of the court:
The boys undoubtedly assaulted the police officers: there cannot be any doubt about that, they struck them and kicked them, but the question is whether that was a justifiable or unjustified assault; and that again, as Mr Rogers agreed, depends entirely on whether the answer of self-defence was available to these two boys in the particular circumstances. ... So one comes back to the question in the end, in the ultimate analysis: was this officer entitled in law to take hold of the first boy by the arm–of course the same situation arises with the other officer in regard to the second boy a little later–justified in committing that technical assault by the exercise of any power which he as a police constable in the precise circumstances prevailing at that exact moment possessed?

I regret, really, that I feel myself compelled to say that the answer to that question must be in the negative. This officer might or might not in the particular circumstances have possessed a power to arrest these boys. I leave that question open, saying no more than that I feel some doubt whether he would have had a power of arrest: but on the assumption that he had a power to arrest, it is to my mind perfectly plain that neither of these officers purported to arrest either of these boys. What was done was not as an integral step in the process of arresting, but was done in order to secure an opportunity, by detaining the boys from escape, to put to them or to either of them the question which was regarded as the test question to satisfy the officers whether or not it would be right in the circumstances, and having regard to the answer obtained from that question, if any, to arrest them.

I regret to say that I think there was a technical assault by the police officer. From which it follows that the justification of self-defence exerted or exercised by these two boys is not negatived by any justifiable character of the initial assault. ...

For these reasons I think that this appeal should be allowed and this conviction quashed.

To the same effect see *Ludlow v Burgess* [1971] Crim LR 238, and *Pedro v Diss* [1981] 2 All ER 59. A case that seems at first sight to be at variance with *Kenlin v Gardiner* is *Donnelly v Jackman*.

Donnelly v Jackman [1970] 1 All ER 987 (Divisional Court)

TALBOT J gave the judgment of the court:

The facts found by the justices were these: at about 11.15 am on Saturday, 5 April, the appellant was lawfully walking along a pavement when PC Roy Grimmett in uniform came up to him for the purposes of making inquiries about an offence which the officer had cause to believe the appellant had committed or might have committed. The officer spoke to the appellant asking him if he could have a word with him. The appellant ignored that request, and continued to walk along the pavement away from the officer. The officer followed close behind him and apparently repeatedly asked him to stop and speak to him. At one stage the officer tapped the appellant on the shoulder, and apparently shortly after that the appellant turned round and in turn tapped the officer on the chest saying 'Now we are even, copper'.

It became apparent to the officer, so the finding proceeds, that the appellant had no intention of stopping to speak to him. The officer then again touched the appellant on the shoulder with the intention of stopping him, whereupon the appellant then turned round and struck the officer with some force. The finding is that the officer did not touch the appellant for the purpose of making any formal arrest or charge, but solely for the purpose of speaking to him. Following the striking of the officer, the appellant was arrested for assaulting the officer in the execution of his duty and taken to the police station. The justices convicted the appellant, finding the summons proved.

[The Divisional Court then distinguished *Kenlin v Gardiner* on the ground that there each officer had taken hold of one of the boys and had in fact detained him. They continued:]

Turning to the facts of this matter, it is not very clear what precisely the justices meant or found when they said that the officer touched the appellant on the shoulder, but whatever it was that they really did mean, it seems clear to me that they must have felt that it was a minimal matter by the way in which they treated this matter and the result of the case. When one considers the problem: was the officer acting in the course of his duty, in my view one ought to bear in mind that it is not every trivial interference with a citizen's liberty that amounts to a course of conduct sufficient to take the officer out of the course of his duties. In my judgment the facts that the justices found in this case do not justify the view that the officer was not acting in the execution of his duty when he went to the appellant and wanted to speak to him. Therefore the assault was rightly found to be an assault on the officer whilst acting in the execution of his duties, and I would dismiss this appeal.

The case of *Donnelly v Jackman* can perhaps, however, be reconciled with the principle of *Kenlin v Gardiner* (which Talbot J plainly accepted), on the basis that the interference with liberty there could be dismissed as *de minimis*. (Concern has, however, been expressed that this decision and one or two others reflected a new departure in extending police powers–see D Lanham, 'Arrest, Detention and Compulsion' (1974) *Criminal Law Review*, p 288.)

In a later case the Divisional Court, on facts virtually identical with those of *Donnelly v Jackman*, went the other way (*Bentley v Brudzinski* [1982] Crim LR 825). The respondent and his brother were stopped and questioned by a police officer at 3.30 am. They answered his questions truthfully and identified themselves. After waiting some ten minutes whilst the officer unsuccessfully tried to verify their identities by radio, they walked away. Another officer who came up at that point stopped the respondent by putting his hand on his shoulder and was punched in the face. The Divisional Court held that this was more than a trivial interference with the respondent's liberty and amounted to an unlawful attempt to stop and detain him. Accordingly the respondent was not guilty of assaulting an officer in the execution of his duty. Lord Justice Donaldson added, however, that the respondent would have had no defence to a charge of common assault if one had been laid. (For comment, see (1982) *Criminal Law Review* pp 481 and 826.) See also the contrasting cases of *Collins v Wilcock* [1984] 1 WLR 1172 and *Weight v Long* [1986] Crim LR 746.

Another type of exception to the general rule is under the Road Traffic Acts. Section 163 of the Road Traffic Act 1988 (formerly s 159 of the 1972 Act) gives the police the power to stop a vehicle on any ground whatever. It is an offence to fail to stop. This power of stopping the vehicle does not, however, give the police any right to search it unless the driver agrees. As has been seen, the officer can, however, demand to have the name and address of the driver or the owner. The Divisional Court held in 1972 that the power to demand that a motorist give his name and address includes the power to block his passage for the purpose–*Squires v Botwright* [1972] RTR 462.

The courts have held that the police have the right to detain motorists for a short period while they administer the breathalyser–see, for instance, *Coleman* [1974] RTR 359 or *Squires v Botwright* above. See also *Lodwick v Sanders* [1985] 1 All ER 577. The police stopped a lorry driver who had no excise licence, index plate or brake lights. In the course of the subsequent exchange, the police officer became suspicious as to whether the lorry was stolen. The officer took the ignition keys when the driver tried to leave. There was a minor fracas. The driver was charged with assault on the police, but was acquitted on the ground that the officer had not been acting within his duty. Held, on appeal, that this was incorrect. He was entitled to stop it in the first place and, being suspicious, to detain it for a reasonable period whilst checking out whether it was stolen. He had therefore been acting in the execution of his duty.

In its 1975 Report the Scottish Thomson Committee thought that a right of detention on suspicion should exist for such brief period as was necessary to ask for an explanation of suspicious behaviour; to take the name and address of the detainee and, where it can be done rapidly (eg by radio), to verify these; and to search outer clothing or baggage for stolen goods, tools of the crime or weapons. The detainee would have to be told immediately the reason for his detention (para 3.18). The Committee also proposed that there should be a legal duty on anyone the police reasonably believed to be a potential witness to give his name and address, and that failure to do so should be an arrestable offence (p 278).

As has been seen, in Scotland since 1980, (now under the Criminal Procedure (Scotland) Act 1995) where a constable has reasonable grounds for suspecting that a person has committed an offence he can ask him for his name and address and 'an explanation of the circumstances which have given rise to the constable's suspicion' (s 13(1)). He can also ask anyone whom he thinks has information relating to that offence to give his name and address. Secondly, the officer can require anyone whose name and address he has asked for to remain with him while he verifies the name and address–provided it can be done quickly. It is an arrestable offence not to comply (s 13(7)).

The Philips Royal Commission did not recommend that the police should have any power short of arrest to detain persons as suspects. It also specifically rejected the idea that witnesses should be liable to arrest if they refused to give their name and address (para 3.90). They preferred the approach that citizens should be left to make up their own minds as to whether to co-operate with the police. Only in one situation should the rule be otherwise. This was where there had been some grave incident (such as a murder on a train of football supporters). The police should then have the right to detain potential witnesses 'while names and addresses are obtained or a suspect identified or the matter is otherwise resolved' (para 3.93).

But the Police and Criminal Evidence Act contained no provision which gave the police any power to detain suspects other than through arrest. (See also the next section below.)

Note however that under the new Prevention of Terrorism (Additional Powers) Act 1996, s 4 the police can cordon off an area while they search for a bomb or collect forensic evidence following the discovery or the explosion of a bomb. People can be excluded for their own safety and for that of others. The schedule to the Act gives the police the power within the cordon to search premises for any device or other terrorist material and to collect any forensic evidence found. It is an offence to fail without lawful authority or reasonable excuse to leave the cordon when required to do so, to break the cordon or to obstruct an officer in the exercise of these powers. Prosecutions can only be brought by the Director of Public Prosecutions.

The power to stop and search persons arises solely under statute. There are a number of statutes which give the police this power. Pre PACE the best known of these was probably the power under s 66 of the Metropolitan Police Act 1839 to stop and search anyone in the metropolitan area reasonably suspected of carrying stolen goods. This power also existed by virtue of bye-laws in a few other cities. A similar power exists nationally in relation to drugs under the Misuse of Drugs Act 1971 and firearms under the Firearms Act 1968. There are also a variety of archaic powers to stop and search persons suspected eg under the Badgers Act, the Pedlars Act, the Poaching Prevention Act and the Protection of Birds Act. (For a full list see *Report of the Royal Commission on Criminal Procedure: Law and Procedure,* 1981, Cmnd 8092–1, pp 75–9.)

In *Daniel v Morrison* [1980] Crim LR 181, the Divisional Court held that the power under s 66 of the 1839 Metropolitan Police Act to stop, search and detain anyone suspected of having stolen goods included the power to question them as well, if only briefly. Similarly, in *Geen* [1982] Crim LR 604, the court held that the power to search someone suspected of carrying prohibited drugs under the Misuse of Drugs Act 1971 included a power to question him briefly.

The Report of the Philips Royal Commission gave some statistics as to the use of stop and search powers. Over the period 1972 to 1978 in England and Wales (excluding the Metropolitan Police District), the percentage of cases in which illegal possession of drugs was discovered ranged from a quarter (in 1976) to 33 per cent (in 1973). The Metropolitan Police supplied the Commission with the number of stops of persons and vehicles made under s 66 of the Metropolitan Police Act 1839 in regard to suspected stolen goods. The percentage of arrests flowing from such stops in the two sample periods in 1978 and 1979 was 13 per cent and 12 per cent.

Later figures confirmed this general picture but presented an even more striking contrast between the success rate of stops and searches under the drugs legislation as against other kinds of stops. In 1979, 10 per cent of all those stopped under various statutes other than the Misuse of Drugs Act were subsequently arrested. The proportion for those stopped under the drugs laws was as high as 47 per cent. (See *New Law Journal*, 25 June 1981, p 676, reporting on figures given in House of Commons, *Hansard*, 16 June 1981, vol 6, 1980–1, cols 298–9.)

(c) The Philips Royal Commission's proposals

The Philips Royal Commission on Criminal Procedure recommended that the police be given considerably broader powers to stop and search. It proposed that the power should be extended to cover reasonable suspicion that the person stopped was carrying stolen goods. It thought that it was illogical that certain police forces should have greater powers than others in this regard. If it had been right for the Metropolitan force to have had a power since 1839 to stop for reasonable suspicion of stolen goods, the same power should apply throughout the country. It also proposed a new power to stop and search for something possession of which was prohibited in a public place–such as offensive weapons (para 3.20).

A minority of the Royal Commission (Jack Jones, the trade-union leader, and Canon Wood, a black minister) objected to this recommendation on the ground that it would tend to worsen police-community relations and especially in areas where black youths were numerous. ('Some of us consider that because of the wide range of articles that can be classified as "offensive weapons" and the necessity to prove intent this extension of stop and search power brings with it a risk of random and discriminatory searches which could further worsen the relationship between the police and young people and particularly black youth' (para 3.21).)

The majority of the Royal Commission thought that the danger of abuse of power could be avoided by the incorporation of proper safeguards, together with the fact that search would only be possible where there were reasonable grounds for suspicion. ('If parliament has made it an offence to be in possession of a particular article in a public place, the police should be able to stop and search persons suspected on reasonable grounds of committing that offence' (para 3.21).) The safeguards proposed were: the officer should have to record every search and the reason for it; supervising officers should have a duty to collect and scrutinize figures of searches and their results for evidence that they were being carried out randomly, arbitrarily or in a discriminatory way; the person stopped should have a right to get a copy of the record; and numbers of stops and searches should be given to chief constables' annual reports (para 3.26). The Commission also thought that searches on the street should be limited to fairly superficial examination of a person's clothing and baggage.

Pre-PACE research on stop and search

The problems of the stop and search power were highlighted in a major piece of research by the Policy Studies Institute published before PACE. The four-volume report had been commissioned and largely paid for by the Metropolitan Police. It included a survey of the attitudes and experiences of a random sample of 2,420 Londoners. (David Smith, *Police and People in London: I.A. Survey of Londoners*, 1983.)

The study found that a substantial minority of the population (16 per cent) had been stopped by the police in the previous twelve months. Three-quarters of stops were of people in vehicles and one-quarter of people on foot. But some people were stopped much more often than others. Age, sex and ethnic group were the three characteristics that most strongly correlated with being stopped. The young were eleven times more likely to be stopped than the old. When the number of stops was taken into account, the difference increased to thirty to one. Men were twice as likely to be stopped as women. The group most likely to be stopped were young West Indians. Overall, the numbers of West Indians stopped was not so much greater than for whites– 24 per cent to 17 per cent. But West Indians who were stopped tended to be stopped nearly three times as often as whites. Among men aged 15 to 24, the proportion stopped was 63 per cent for West Indians, 44 per cent for whites and 18 per cent for Asians. Those young West Indians who had been stopped in the previous twelve months had been stopped four times on average, compared with two and a half times for the whites (pp 309–19).

In about three-quarters of the cases the person concerned thought that the police behaved in a polite, fair and reasonable manner. In about half the cases where the person thought they had not behaved well, the complaint was about an 'unpleasant manner'.

Three per cent of the stops led to the person being arrested and charged with an offence, 5 per cent to an offence being reported and in another 1 per cent the person was arrested but not subsequently charged. The total 'strike rate'–the proportion of stops leading to detection of an offence–was therefore about one in twelve, or 8 per cent. In aggregate it appeared that the Metropolitan Police made more than a million stops per year and that they discovered over 100,000 offences a year through stops and searches. The report said:

In a substantial minority of cases, people are unhappy about the way the police handle the incident; but perhaps most important, the more intelligently the police use their discretion, the more they come to concentrate on certain specific groups, a high proportion of which are stopped and stopped repeatedly. Even if these people have no objections to the way a particular stop is handled, they will come to object to being stopped at all, bearing in mind that most of them are innocent. Indeed, the survey shows that people who have been stopped, and especially those who have been stopped repeatedly, tend to have a much poorer opinion of the police than others; and this is in spite of the fact that they were usually happy with the way in which particular stops were handled [pp 311–12].

The study by the Policy Studies Institute also included a two-year period of observation of police in six Districts (David Smith and Jeremy Gray, *Police and People in London: IV. The Police in Action*, 1983). The two researchers considered in particular whether the use of the power to stop and search was exercised responsibly and in accordance with the requirement that there be reasonable suspicion. They concluded that in a high proportion of occasions when the power was used there had been no cause for suspicion of the individual concerned, though often there might be a higher-than-average chance that the individual had committed an offence–because of the area, or the group to which he belonged. Thus it might be reasonable to believe that young football supporters are carrying offensive weapons because some are, even though there is no reason to suppose that any particular youth attending a match is, because most are not. But if the law requires reasonable suspicion of the individual, then (perhaps not surprisingly) it was rarely present (pp 232–3). (For a discussion of 'reasonable cause' in this context, see LH Leigh, *Police Powers in England and Wales* (2nd edn, Butterworth, 1986), pp 129–40, and JL Lambert, 'Reasonable Cause of Arrest' [1973] *Public Law*, p 285. See also *Holtham v Metropolitan Police Comr* (1987) Times, 28 November, and (1982) *Criminal Law Review*, pp 475–6.

The researchers observed 129 stops. In 23 (18 per cent) the person was seen to commit a traffic offence. In 63 cases (49 per cent) the researchers thought the police had reasonable grounds for suspicion. The grounds for such suspicion they identified were: odd driving (eg fast acceleration or very slow driving, other than where a driving offence was involved); running or moving quickly; 'hanging about', moving very slowly especially at night; carrying valuables (eg a TV in the back of a car); being about in the small hours; following someone (eg a man following a woman at 3 am); or looking like the description of a suspect in a recently reported crime. In the remaining 43 cases (33 per cent) the researchers could see no ground for the stop at all (pp 232–3).

The authors said: 'It is clear from the way that police officers talk about stops that the question of what their legal powers may be does not enter into their decision-making except in the case of rare individuals' (p 233). The criterion of 'reasonable suspicion', they thought, 'does not act as an effective constraint on police officers in deciding whether to make a stop' (*ibid*). No one challenged the right of the police to stop, search or question them, nor did anyone ever refuse to answer questions (*ibid*). In the great majority of cases the encounter was fairly relaxed and friendly, though in about 5 per cent of cases the person concerned was clearly abusive or obstreperous, and in another 20 per cent of cases there appeared to be some resentment. Resentment was most common amongst those who said they had been stopped repeatedly (p 234). Some of the stops made without any basis for suspicion did nevertheless produce 'a result'.

The survey also had data on the extent to which the police kept the records they were meant to. Before the introduction of the Police and Criminal Evidence Act, Metropolitan Police officers were required by Force orders to take down the name and address of every person stopped and to record it in a special 'stop book' at the police station. (They no longer have this duty since it is not required by PACE.) The survey of Londoners showed that only 39 per cent of those stopped thought that their name and address had been taken. The observational study of the police in action broadly confirmed that this was about right–about half of all stops seemed to result in a record being made afterwards (p 236). It seemed to the researchers that a record was made where the stop caused some resentment, in case the citizen made a complaint.

See also the Home Office Research Unit's study, Carole Willis, *The Use, Effectiveness and Impact of Police Stop and Search Powers* (Home Office Research and Planning Unit, Paper 15, 1983). Like the Policy Studies Institute's study, this reported that young blacks were much more likely to be stopped than young whites (pp 13–14). It reported equally that the safeguard of reporting of stops and searches was apt to be undermined by the habit of police officers only to record some of the stops they made. The uniformed beat officers said they recorded 20 to 30 per cent of their stops, crime squad officers, plain clothes officers and special squad officers recorded 40 to 60 per cent, and probationers and young inexperienced officers recorded 70 to 80 per cent. Overall the recording rate in the two London districts was under a half and in the two provincial forces was only about 30 per cent (Carole Willis, *op cit*, p 10). The researcher suggested that it would not be useful to have a rule requiring recording of all *stops* not least because this would require a request for name and address which was likely to cause most resentment from the public. All *searches* should be recorded and stops that were resented should also be recorded (*ibid*, p 24).

The Royal Commission's recommendation that persons affected should be told the grounds on which the officer was acting, was also the subject of data in the research study. It appeared that grounds for stops were rarely recorded at present and many officers seemed to find it difficult to articulate the reasons why they stopped particular individuals. If the safeguard of reasons was to have the effect intended, 'special training may be required'. This training 'would need to be designed to ensure that officers did not use their discretion on whim, or worse, prejudice and that where their actions were justified, they could articulate the basis for them' (*ibid*).

The research found that supervising officers did not devote much effort to monitoring stop and search records except to see how individual officers compared on arrests. Implementation of the Royal Commission's recommendation for monitoring by senior officers would therefore involve a change in police practice (*ibid*, p 25).

(d) PACE

The Government did not wholly accept the Royal Commission's proposals on stop and search powers. It rejected the argument that there should be a general new power to stop and search anyone reasonably suspected of carrying something possession of which in a public place was forbidden. The police therefore have to continue to manage under the various specific statutes which give them stop and search powers.

But the Government did introduce into the Police and Criminal Evidence Act a new power to search someone reasonably suspected of carrying housebreaking implements or an offensive weapon. (An 'offensive weapon' is defined in the same way as under the Prevention of Crime Act 1953, s 1, as 'any article made or adapted for use for causing injury to the person, or intended by the person having it with him for such use by him or by some other person' (s 1(9)).) The Act also provides for the extension nationally of the power under s 66 of the 1839 Act to search persons suspected of carrying stolen goods.

Records of stops and searches

Under the Police and Criminal Evidence Act, s 2, the police officer who proposes to carry out a stop and search must state his name and police station, and the purpose of the search. A plain clothes officer must in addition produce documentary evidence that he is a policeman. The officer must give the grounds for the search. (This seems in fact to have been the common law already–see *McBean v Parker* [1983] Crim LR 399.) A search in the street must be limited to the outer clothing–the individual cannot be required to remove anything other than his jacket, outer coat or gloves. The police officer is required to make a record of the search immediately, or if this is not practicable, as soon as possible (s 3). The record is supposed to state the name of the officer, the name of the person stopped, if known, the object of the search, the ground of the search and its result (s 3).

There is nothing in the Act to give the police a power to detain witnesses not suspected of any involvement in the crime (s 4).

The Code of Practice for the exercise of powers of stop and search

Code A on stop and search warns that stop and search powers are to be used sparingly and responsibly.

The person stopped can be questioned prior to a search and, if such preliminary exchanges indicated that the suspicion is ill-founded, no search need take place. But a person cannot be stopped in order for grounds for a search to be found. There has to be reasonable suspicion that the person was carrying articles unlawfully obtained or possessed (para 1.5). Reasonable suspicion requires an objective basis. ('An officer will need to consider the nature of the article suspected of being carried in the context of other factors such as the time and the place, and the behaviour of the person concerned or of those with him.' Reasonable suspicion may exist for instance 'where a person is seen acting covertly or warily or attempting to hide something; or a person is carrying a certain type of article at an unusual time or in a place where a number of burglaries or thefts are known to have taken place recently'. (para 1.6.)

Reasonable suspicion can 'never be supported on the basis of personal factors alone' (para 1.7). So colour, age, hairstyle, dress or even that a person had previous convictions for possession of an unlawful article, either alone or in combination with others, cannot be the sole basis on which to search. Nor can a search be based on 'stereotyped images of certain persons or groups as more likely to be committing offences' (*ibid*).

It is also important to ensure 'that any person searched must be treated courteously and considerately'.

There is a striking contrast between the terms of the Code of Practice on the need for reasonable cause to legitimate a stop, and the decision of the Divisional Court in *Chief Constable of Gwent v Dash* [1985] Crim LR 674, in which it was held that random stopping of motorists to see whether they are driving with excess alcohol is not unlawful–though randomly requiring motorists to give a specimen of breath would be unlawful. The court said that, provided there was 'no malpractice, caprice, or opprobrious behaviour', there was no legal restriction on the stopping of motorists by a police officer in the execution of his duty.

For a long and helpful evaluation of the problem of police discretion and its control in arrest and stop and search, see CL Ryan and KS Williams, 'Police Discretion', *Public Law*, Summer 1986, p 285; see also D Dixon *et al*, 'Reality and Rules in the Construction and Regulation of Police Suspicion', 17 *International Journal of the Sociology of Law*, 1989, p 185.

There is one situation however where the police are permitted to stop and search without reasonable grounds to suspect–under the Criminal Justice and Public Order Act 1994, s 81 which added a new provision, s 13A, to the Prevention of Terrorism (Temporary Provisions) Act 1989. In order to prevent acts of terrorism the police are now permitted to designate a particular locality for periods of up to 28 days and stops and searches by officers in uniform can then take place randomly. The power covered the search of a vehicle and of things carried by pedestrians. It did not cover a search of the pedestrian him or herself.

But at the beginning of April 1996 the Government rushed new legislation through all its stages in two days, inter alia, to fill this gap. The Prevention of Terrorism (Additional Provisions) Act 1996 inserted a new section 13B into the Prevention of Terrorism Act giving the police the power to stop and search pedestrians within a designated area subject to the same safeguards as apply under section 13A above. An additional safeguard is that authorisation of the exercise of the new powers by the assistant chief constable must be confirmed by the Home Secretary within 48 hours failing which the authorisation lapses. The power is to stop any pedestrian in that area and to conduct a 'rub-down' search, which includes examining pockets. The officer may ask the pedestrian to remove his outer coat, jacket, footwear, gloves or headgear. It is an offence to fail to stop when asked to do so or to obstruct the police in the exercise of the new power. Prosecution for either of these offences can however only be brought by the Director of Public Prosecutions.

The Government acknowledged that the new power would provoke concern. Parliament was told that the Home Secretary would issue the police with guidance, that Code A would be amended to apply its procedural provisions and that in the meanwhile the police would apply those provisions voluntarily. Parliament would receive periodic reports about the operation of the new power. (See House of Commons, *Hansard*, April 2 1996, col 298; House of Lords, *Hansard*, 3 April, 1996, col 292.)

Voluntary searches–post-PACE research

PACE does not apply to 'voluntary searches'. But what is a 'voluntary search'? Obviously, if the concept is given a wide interpretation there is a danger that a 'coach and four' will be driven through the procedural safeguards of PACE. The Home Office Circular on PACE issued to police said 'Voluntary search must not be used as a way of avoiding the main thrust of the safeguards.' But it is not easy to assure the compliance by the police with this exhortation. In fact it seems that in many forces the concept of the voluntary search *does* undermine the safeguards. This emerges from research conducted on the operation of PACE by researchers from Hull University:

David Dixon, Clive Coleman and Keith Bottomley, 'Consent and Legal Regulation of Policing', 17 *Journal of Law and Society*, 1990, p 345

The major device which bridges the gap between the records and the reality is 'consent'. Suspects 'consent' to be stopped and searched: consequently, no power is employed and (subject to regulations to be noted below) no record need be made. In our search force, three-quarters of interviewed officers had done a consent stop/search since 1986, while only a quarter said that they had used statutory powers. Many distinguished between types of encounters. Some officers considered that a stop/search means a thorough search of the suspect's clothes: they classified simply looking in a bag as a (non-PACE) 'stop/check' for which legal authority was not provided and was, in any case, unnecessary, because 'consent' would be obtained. Several officers told us that they did not even bother to carry stop/search forms when they were on patrol. They, and many others, said that they would try to get consent from a suspect: if that was not forthcoming, they would arrest her or him. As elsewhere, the very process of trying to obtain consent allows officers to test their suspicion about a person. As the hoary truism insists, only the guilty have reason to refuse it. One officer explained: 'If they are decent law-abiding citizens they wouldn't mind being stopped because they'd appreciate the police being about.'

'Consent' here frequently consists of acquiescence based on ignorance. Many people assume that the officer who says 'What have you got in your pockets?' or 'Let's have a look in your bag' has a power to search. We asked officers how often people whom they stopped and searched knew their rights: seventy-nine per cent said rarely or never. Such lack of knowledge must mean that their 'consent' has little substance. Familiar strategies are used to deal with those who do raise questions about the authority to search. As a sergeant put it: 'A lot of people are not quite certain that they have the right to say no. And then we, sort of, bamboozle them into allowing us to search.' Such 'bamboozling' is done by appealing to the willingness of the innocent to be searched, by threatening arrest, or by claiming the authority of fictional powers.

This is certainly the way in which some people are handled: however, it is too legalistic as an account of how many interact with police. The reality for them may not be acquiescence based on ignorance, but submission rooted in an appreciation of the contextual irrelevance of rights and legal provisions. 'Rights' are seen by officers as properly belonging to some people, but not to the young and unrespectable whom they usually encounter in the street. An officer made the point in explaining what he would do if someone refused to show what was in a bag: 'If it was someone of reasonable intelligence, I'd leave it at that. If it was a scruff, I'd probably have a look myself.' For a 'scruff' to assert her or his rights is 'buggering about' and itself suspicious: reference to rights may be regarded as a challenge to police authority and/or an indication of previous contact with police, and therefore as worth further investigation. Account must be taken of the substantive reality of the police mandate in order maintenance on the street and of material relations between police and policed (see below). A strategy of rights and legal regulation which overlooks them will be misleading and ineffective.

In the circumstances, it would be reasonable to ask why *any* stop/searches get recorded. First, some are recorded for operational purposes, notably drugs intelligence. Secondly, records are more likely to be completed if a probationary constable carries out the stop/search, if a supervisory officer is present, or if senior officers have commented on the lack of recorded stop/searches. Thirdly, if a prohibited article is found and an arrest is made, officers may cover their backs by completing a record. Fourthly, a record would be completed if other 'comeback' was a possibility: an officer explained that if for example, a middle-class person who was aware of the law happened to be stopped, 'you would probably revert to the standard opening speech procedure' and complete a form. However, as suggested above, refusal of consent is a rare experience for officers. One commented: 'I have never had any problems with anyone refusing to be searched ... so I have never had to fall back on proving my reasonable suspicion.'

As these points suggest, stop/searches usually come to be recorded because of contingent factors, rather than statutory criteria. It is important to note that many of these operate retrospectively: an officer begins operating by 'consent' and may only later reinterpret the encounter as being a PACE stop/search. Indeed, several officers *defend* a PACE stop/search as being one in which the suspect does not consent.

No voluntary stop and search of juveniles etc

The Code of Practice, as revised in April 1991, states that 'Juveniles, persons suffering from a mental handicap or mental illness and others who appear not to be capable of giving an informed consent should not be subject to a voluntary search' (Note IE).

Statistics

The annual Home Office statistics for 1994 on stops and searches show that 38 per cent were made for stolen property and 31 per cent for drugs. The total number of recorded stops and searches was 576,000, 30 per cent more than in 1993 and more than five times as many as were recorded in 1986. Offensive weapons, the subject of so much of the controversy during the debates on PACE, accounted for only 5 per cent of the total. The 'hit rate' in the sense of arrests following a stop and search which was 17 per cent in 1986 and 1987, declined in each year from 1991 to 1994— 15,14,13,12 per cent. ('Operation of Certain Police Powers under PACE', Home Office Statistical Bulletin, June 1995, Table A, p 3).

It should be noted that the total number of recorded stops and searches represents less than five stops per police officer *per year*! This indicates massive under-recording, since officers may typically carry out several such stops in a day.

According to figures for 1994 issued by the Metropolitan Police, blacks, who were 10 per cent of the population in London of those aged 5 to 29, accounted for 28 per cent of all stops and searches, whites (75% of the population of that age), accounted for 61 per cent of stops and searches and Asians (9 per cent of the population of that age) accounted for 6 per cent. (The figures were based on over a quarter of a million stops and searches.)

The research showed that younger officers were more likely to cary out stop and searches that did not lead to arrests, whereas more experienced officers were much more likely to arrest. But the more experienced officers were unable to explain their better 'hit rate' in terms of arrest: 'They couldn't analyse exactly how they were reaching their decisions. It was more intuition based on their experience and that makes it difficult to identify and to teach and pass on to others.' (Cdr Mike Briggs quoted in *Police Review*, 26 January 1996, p 10).

(e) What constitutes an arrest?

There are two forms of arrest, lawful and unlawful. In *Spicer v Holt* [1977] AC 987, HL, Lord Dilhorne said (at p 1000): 'Whether or not a person has been arrested depends not on the legality of the arrest, but on whether he has been deprived of his liberty to go where he pleases.' (See to same effect, *R v Inwood* [1973] 2 All ER 645; *R v Bass* [1953] 1 QB 680). So, if a person is being detained by the police against his will, he is under arrest, but whether the arrest is lawful will depend on whether the conditions for a lawful arrest have been fulfilled. (*Dawes v DPP* [1995] 1 Cr App Rep 65.) If the arrest is not lawful there is a right to use reasonable force to avoid it, but this is clearly not a right to be lightly exercised since the legality of the arrest is best tested after the event when the dust has settled.

A lawful arrest is one authorized by law. There are three basic types of lawful arrest.

(1) Arrest under warrant

The normal procedure is laid down in s 1(1) of the Magistrates' Courts Act 1980, which gives a magistrate power to issue a warrant upon written information being laid before him on oath 'that any person has, or is suspected of having, committed an offence'. Under s 24(1) of the Criminal Justice Act 1967 it is provided that a warrant for the arrest of someone should not be issued unless the offence in question is indictable or is punishable with imprisonment. This reflects the policy that minor offences should be dealt with by summons rather than arrest.

(2) Arrest without warrant at common law

Until 1967 the law of arrest at common law revolved around the distinction between felonies and misdemeanours. But felonies and misdemeanours were abolished by the Criminal Law Act 1967 which created the concepts of arrestable and non-arrestable offences.

There is now only one remaining common-law power to arrest–where a breach of the peace has been committed and there are reasonable grounds for believing that it will be continued or renewed, or where a breach of the peace is reasonably apprehended. (See *Wershof v Metropolitan Police Comr* [1978] 3 All ER 540; *Hickman v O'Dwyer* [1979] Crim LR 309; *Howell* [1981] Crim LR 697.)

(3) Arrest without a warrant under statute

The general power of arrest which formerly was set out in the Criminal Law Act 1967, s 2, is now to be found in the Police and Criminal Evidence Act 1984, s 24. This provides that the police may arrest without a warrant for arrestable and certain other offences. An arrestable offence is one for which the sentence is fixed by law (ie murder and treason); any offence which carries a liability to five years' imprisonment or more; any offence specifically listed in s 24(2); and any attempt to commit any of the above. (The offences listed in s 24(2) relate to Customs and Excise, the Official Secrets Act, indecent assaults on women, and taking a motor vehicle without authority.)

The Act gave constables and ordinary citizens slightly different powers of arrest in relation to these various offences:

Police and Criminal Evidence Act 1984, s 24

(4) Any person may arrest without a warrant–

   (a) anyone who is in the act of committing an arrestable offence;
   (b) anyone whom he has reasonable grounds for suspecting to be committing such an offence.

(5) Where an arrestable offence has been committed, any person may arrest without a warrant–

   (a) anyone who is guilty of the offence;
   (b) anyone whom he has reasonable grounds for suspecting to be guilty of it.

(6) Where a constable has reasonable grounds for suspecting that an arrestable offence has been committed, he may arrest without a warrant anyone whom he has reasonable grounds for suspecting to be guilty of the offence.

(7) A constable may arrest without a warrant–

   (a) anyone who is about to commit an arrestable offence;
   (b) anyone whom he has reasonable grounds for suspecting to be about to commit an arrestable offence.

In addition to the powers of arrest under s 24, the Act also gave the police new powers of arrest in regard to non-arrestable offences. Section 25 provides that 'where a constable has reasonable grounds for suspecting that an offence has been committed or attempted, or is being committed or attempted, he may arrest any person whom he has reasonable grounds to suspect of having committed the offence or of being in the course of committing or attempting to commit it if it appears to him that service of a summons is impracticable or inappropriate because any of the general arrest conditions is satisfied'. The 'general arrest conditions' are that the officer does not know and cannot find out the suspect's name or address (or he has reasonable grounds to think that he has been given a false name or address), or he has reasonable grounds for believing that an arrest is necessary to prevent someone causing: physical harm to himself or someone else; or loss of or damage to property; or an offence against public decency; or an obstruction of the highway (s 25 (3) (*d*)).

The Royal Commission on Criminal Procedure went further in recommending that an arrestable offence should include any offence carrying a penalty of imprisonment (para 3.83). But, on the other hand, the 1984 Act went considerably further than the Royal Commission in relation to the power of arrest for non-arrestable offences– which the Commission thought should only apply where the officer did not know the name or address of the suspect when he actually saw him committing such an offence (para 3.86).

Section 27 of the Act also goes beyond what the Royal Commission recommended by giving the police the power to arrest someone for the sole purpose of fingerprinting him where he has been convicted of an offence for which convictions are recorded in national police records and who refuses to go to the police station for the purpose. The power to take fingerprints compulsorily in such circumstances arises under s 61(6) of the Act.

(f) Procedure on arrest

The law does not lay down any particular procedure to effect a lawful arrest. In *Alderson v Booth* [1969] 2 QB 216, Lord Parker CJ said:

... whereas there was a time when it was held that there could be no lawful arrest unless there was an actual seizing or touching, it is quite clear that that is no longer the law. There may be an arrest by mere words, by saying 'I arrest you' without any touching. ... Equally it is clear ... that an arrest is constituted when any form of words is used which in the circumstances of the case were calculated to bring to the defendant's notice and did bring to the defendant's notice that he was under compulsion.

(See *R v Inwood* [1973] 2 All ER 645 and *Dawes v DPP* [1995] 1 Cr App Rep 65.) See also Glanville Williams, 'When is an arrest not an arrest', 54 *Modern Law Review*, 1991, p 408.

The other requisite of a valid arrest is that the officer must ensure that the suspect knows immediately, failing which, as soon as practicable (1) that he is under arrest–*R v Inwood* [1973] 1 WLR 647 and *Pedro v Diss* [1981] 2 All ER 59–and (2) the ground of arrest–*Christie v Leachinsky* [1947] AC 573, HL; *Grant v Gorman* [1980] RTR 119; *Waters v Bigmore* [1981] Crim LR 408; *Pedro v Diss*, above. In the famous case of *Christie v Leachinsky* Viscount Simon in a classic statement said (at p 589):

... (1) If a policeman arrests without warrant upon reasonable suspicion of felony, or of other crime of a sort which does not require a warrant, he must in ordinary circumstances inform the person arrested of the true ground of arrest. He is not entitled to keep the reason to himself or to give a reason which is not the true reason. In other words a citizen is entitled to know on what charge or on suspicion of what crime he is seized. (2) If the citizen is not so informed but is nevertheless seized, the policeman, apart from certain exceptions, is liable for false imprisonment. ... If a policeman who entertained a reasonable suspicion that X has committed a felony were at liberty to arrest him and march him off to a police station without giving any explanation of why he was doing this, the prima facie right of personal liberty would be gravely infringed. No one, I think, would approve a situation in which when the person arrested asked for the reason, the policeman replied 'that has nothing to do with you: come along with me'. ...

The common law is now reflected in the Police and Criminal Evidence Act 1984, s 28 of which states that an arrest is not lawful unless, at the time of or as soon as practicable after the arrest, the person arrested is informed (a) that he is under arrest, and (b) of the ground of the arrest (see JD Lowe (1986) *Criminal Law Review*, p 49). Moreover it is specifically stated that this applies even where the fact of the arrest or its ground is obvious.

The problem of the legal consequences of failing to give grounds of arrest were considered by the Divisional Court in *DPP v Hawkins* [1988] 3 All ER 673 and by the Court of Appeal in *Lewis v Chief Constable of South Wales* [1991] 1 All ER 206. In *Hawkins*, the court held that failure to state the reasons for an arrest at the moment when it became practicable to do so had the effect of rendering the initially lawful arrest unlawful as from that moment and not as from the outset. The court therefore refused to allow the lawful arrest to be invalidated retrospectively. In *Lewis* the officers had told the plaintiffs of the fact of arrest but delayed telling them the grounds for 10 minutes in one case and 23 minutes in the other. The Court of Appeal (without referring to the *Hawkins* case) said that arrest was not a legal concept but was a matter of fact arising out of the deprivation of a person's liberty. It was also a continuing act and therefore what had been an unlawful arrest could become a lawful arrest. The remedy for the plaintiffs was merely the damages they had been awarded by the jury for the 10 minutes and 23 minutes of illegality–£200 each. (For critical comment see J Marston, 'The Reasons for an Arrest', *Justice of the Peace*, 2 March 1991, p 131. See also *Kulynycz* [1970] 3 All ER 881.)

Under s 30 of the Police and Criminal Evidence Act, a person who has been arrested must be taken to a police station 'as soon as practicable', unless his presence elsewhere is reasonably necessary for the investigation.

Summons or arrest

Accused persons will either have been charged after an arrest or they will have been summonsed by post, after an information has been laid before a magistrate or a justice's clerk.

The proportion arrested for categories of offences dealt with at magistrates' courts varies dramatically. In 1994, of those dealt with for indictable offences, no fewer than 90 per cent were arrested, compared with 25 per cent of those dealt with for summary offences other than motoring charges, and 15 per cent of those dealt with for motoring offences (*Criminal Statistics*, 1994, Cm 3010, Table 8.1, p 185).

But there are great variations in the policies of different police forces. A study done for the Philips Royal Commission showed, that in Cambridgeshire, Cleveland and the Metropolitan Police District only 1 per cent of adults accused of indictable offences were summonsed, compared with over 40 per cent in places such as Thames

Valley, West Yorkshire, Wiltshire and North Wales, (See R Gemmill and RF Morgan-Giles, 'Arrest, Charge and Summons', Philips *Royal Commission, Research Study No 9*, 1981, Appendix A, p 42.)

The Philips Royal Commission (para 3.77) urged that the less intrusive procedure of summons be used wherever possible. But, for whatever reason, the trend is moving instead in the opposite direction. In 1984 and 1986 the proportion of suspects summonsed for indictable offences was 22 per cent. (In 1985 it was 21%.) But since 1986 it has declined steadily each year to 10 per cent in 1994. (*Criminal Statistics*, 1994, above, Table 8.1.)

Note–remedies for unlawful arrest

A victim of an unlawful arrest has three possible remedies. First, he can attempt to initiate proceedings for habeas corpus. This is by no means simple. The writ can be applied for by the person unlawfully detained or by someone else on his behalf. There is always supposed to be a duty judge available at or through the Royal Courts of Justice to hear applications. In emergencies the initial application to the judge can even be by telephone. But many lawyers are not familiar with this procedure and legal aid may not be available. Moreover, the Divisional Court to whom application must be made is not easily persuaded to grant the writ. (For a practical guide, see Tony Gifford and Paddy O'Connor, 'Habeas Corpus', *Legal Action Group Bulletin*, August 1979, p 182.) On the rare occasions when habeas corpus proceedings are brought on behalf of someone who is allegedly detained by the police without charges, the normal response from the police is to charge him before the case comes to be heard.

The second remedy is to use the illegality as the basis of an argument that the subsequent proceedings should be declared null and void. This is unlikely to succeed because of the rule of English law (see p 356 below) that evidence illegally obtained can nevertheless be admissible. Similarly, *R v Kulynycz* (p 158 above) shows that the courts may be ready to cure an initial illegality if it was subsequently corrected.

The third remedy is to bring an action for damages for false imprisonment. In cases like *Christie v Leachinsky* or *R v Kulynycz* this is of little use since the amount of damages awarded would be purely nominal. But sometimes this can be a significant remedy. In *Wershof v Metropolitan Police Comr* [1978] 3 All ER 540, the plaintiff, a young solicitor, got £1,000 for being arrested and detained for about an hour before being released on bail. In *Reynolds v Metropolitan Police Comr* [1982] Crim LR 600, the Court of Appeal rejected an appeal against a jury's award of £12,000 damages for false imprisonment. The plaintiff was arrested in the early hours of the morning in connection with charges of arson for gain. The journey to the police station took two and a half hours. She was detained until 8 pm the same day, when she was told there was no evidence against her. She got home by around 11 pm. The trial judge in her action for damages against the police ruled that they had had reasonable grounds for suspecting her of involvement in the crimes. See also *Allen v Metropolitan Police Comr* [1980] Crim LR 441–damages of £1,115 for unnecessary force used in an arrest. See J Marston, 'Remedies for Wrongful Process', *Law Society's Gazette*, 17 November 1982, p 1458.

(g) Can an arrested person be held without charges?

An arrest has to be based on reasonable suspicion that the person arrested has committed, is committing or is about to commit the offence in question. This is, however, not the same as the degree of suspicion necessary to base a charge. In other words, the police may hold a suspect for questioning once they have validly arrested him in order to see whether their suspicions are warranted. The fact that English common law did permit questioning after arrest was recognized by the Privy Council in a case in 1969.

Lord Devlin, giving judgment, said: 'Suspicion arises at or near the starting point of an investigation of which the obtaining of prima facie proof is the end.... It is indeed desirable as a general rule that an arrest should not be made until the case is complete. But if an arrest before that were forbidden, it could seriously hamper the police' (*Shaaban Bin Hussein v Chong Fook Kam* [1969] 3 All ER 1626 at 1630). Also in *R v Houghton* (1978) 68 Cr App Rep 197, 205 Lord Justice Lawton said: 'Having made an arrest for a specific offence, they can hold the arrested person in custody while they make inquiries; but when they have enough evidence to prefer a charge they should do so without delay.'

Similarly in *Holgate-Mohammed v Duke* [1984] 1 All ER 1054, the House of Lords held that the police were entitled to hold a suspect for questioning without charges. The plaintiff was arrested after the theft of jewellery from premises where she was a lodger. She was detained for six hours but was not charged. She brought an action for damages against the police and at first instance won damages of £1,000. The judge held that detention had not been too long and she had been allowed to see a solicitor. Also there had been no improper pressure. But the purpose of detention had been to put her under greater pressure through having her in custody under arrest than would have existed if she had been interviewed without being arrested. The House of Lords confirmed the Court of Appeal's decision allowing the appeal, and said that it was legitimate for the police to question someone in order to dispel or confirm the officer's reasonable suspicion which led to the arrest.

The first explicit statutory reference to this period between arrest and charge in any English statute was in the Police and Criminal Evidence Act. Section 37(2) states that before an arrested person is charged the only ground for detaining him is that there are 'reasonable grounds for believing that his detention without being charged is necessary to secure or preserve evidence relating to an offence for which he is under arrest or to obtain such evidence by questioning him'.

(h) What are the time-limits on police detention without charges?

Before PACE the law on time-limits for detention without charges was in a state of muddle. There was a common belief that the police were required to bring a suspect before the courts within 24 hours of arrest. But this was based on a misunderstanding. The only relevant provision that mentioned a time-limit was the Magistrates' Courts Act 1980, s 43(1) (formerly Magistrates' Courts Act 1952, s 38(1)), which stated, in effect, that a person charged with an offence that was not serious who could not be brought before a magistrates' court within 24 hours had to be bailed from the police station to appear before the court. But there was no requirement in the section that he be brought before the court within 24 hours–only that if he was not, he should be bailed unless the offence was a serious one. (There was no definition of the concept of 'serious offence', which was therefore left to the police to define.)

The only statutory time-limit on police detention prior to 1984 was the provision in s 43(4) of the Magistrates' Court Act 1980 (formerly s 38(4) of the 1952 Act) that 'Where a person is taken into custody for an offence without a warrant and is retained in custody he shall be brought before a magistrates' court as soon as practicable'. But it was clear from police practice that this was interpreted by them to mean as soon as practicable after he had been charged and not as soon as practicable after being taken into custody. In his evidence to the Philips Royal Commission, the Commissioner of the Metropolitan Police suggested that the words 'as soon as practicable' were intended to recognize the need to keep some people in custody whilst inquiries were pursued in order to see whether there was enough evidence for a charge. A person aggrieved by the delay could apply to the Divisional Court for habeas corpus.

For common-law decisions on time-limits for detention, see *Houghton and Franciosy* (1978) 68 Cr App Rep 197; *Hudson* (1980) 72 Cr App Rep 163; *Re Sherman and Apps* (1981) 72 Cr App Rep 266, (sub nom *Holmes ex p Sherman*) [1981] 2 All ER 612 ; *Nycander* (1982) Times, 9 December.

In his evidence to the Royal Commission on Criminal Procedure, the Commissioner of the Metropolitan Police argued that the police should have the right to hold a suspect in the first instance for up to 72 hours.

The Commissioner's proposal may be contrasted with the position under the Prevention of Terrorism (Temporary Provisions) Act, where a suspect can be held for 48 hours in the first instance and then, with the written permission of the Home Secretary, for a further five days.

The Scottish Thomson Committee thought that a maximum of six hours should be allowed for detention in the police station. Some witnesses had argued that it should be as long as 24 hours and that 'there was a strong body of opinion in favour of twelve hours', but the Thomson Committee concluded that six hours would be right. 'This was the maximum period favoured by the police witnesses who considered that generally it would be adequate for their purpose' (para 3–25, p 16). In the Thompson Committee's view, the six–hour period would be an absolute maximum. There would be no right to apply for any extension.

The legislation giving effect to the report of the Thompson Committee, the Criminal Justice (Scotland) Act 1980, s 2, authorized detention only for up to six hours as proposed in the Committee's report.

The Australian Law Reform Commission in its 1975 report recommended a four–hour normal maximum. There could then be an application to a magistrate for an extension for a further eight hours. In exceptional cases a Supreme Court judge could grant yet further extensions (para 95). The Commission said it had fixed on four hours because on the evidence it was the shortest period within which, in the great majority of cases, the post-arrest investigation was brought to fruition and the suspect was either charged or released. American studies had suggested that as many as 97 per cent of cases were cleared in that time, and local research had produced figures of a similar order. Oral statements by police officers in the Commission's hearings had indicated that four hours was realistic (pp 40–2).

The Model Pre-Arraignment Code proposed in 1975 by the American Law Institute (sec 130.2) suggested a limit of two hours in the police station for minor offences and five hours for other cases. There would be no power to exceed this limit, even for exceptional cases.

The first English figures about the length of interrogation were those of the writer's study of 150 cases involving 286 defendants tried at the Old Bailey. This showed that 214 (76 per cent) made oral or written admissions or both. In 26 of the 214 cases there was no information as to how long the questioning lasted. This left 188 cases. In 66 (35 per cent of the 188) the admissions came immediately without any hesitation or denial at the very outset of questioning by the police. In 71 cases (38 per cent) the admissions were made within the first two hours of questioning, sometimes after initial denials. In 27 cases (14 per cent) they came after questioning had gone on for more than two hours. In most of these 27 cases it continued for three, four, five or six hours. In two cases it was between six and 10 hours. There were a further 24 cases (13 per cent), in which the admissions came only after the accused had been held in custody overnight. In some of these cases he was not interviewed at all on first being arrested. He was simply taken into custody, mostly late at night, and was seen the next morning. In some instances he was seen for a short while on the first day and then left until the next day to think things over in the cells. In the cases where questioning continued in stages, each stage tended to be short–10 minutes, 25 minutes, 15 minutes, half an hour, 50 minutes, etc ((1979) *Criminal Law Review*, p 21.).

These figures broadly support the view that in most cases questioning is either effective in a relatively short period of time or is not effective at all. In the writer's Old Bailey sample, 20 per cent of the suspects denied the charges altogether, 4 per cent were silent in the face of questioning and the remaining 76 per cent made admissions.

The study of confession evidence conducted for the Philips Royal Commission by Baldwin and McConville found similarly that 'most interrogations lasted less than two hours, and only about two per cent of them continued beyond four hours' ('Confessions in Crown Court Trials', Research Study No 5, 1980, p 21). In another study for the Philips Royal Commission based on 187 interviews in the police station, four-fifths were concluded within half an hour and only 5 per cent lasted more than 45 minutes (P Softley, 'An Observational Study in Four Police Stations', *Royal Commission Research Study No 4*, 1980, p 77). Fifty-nine per cent of the persons being interviewed made admissions or confessions in the initial interview (*ibid*, p 80). Only a quarter of the total sample were interviewed on any subsequent occasion (*ibid*, p 82).

The Philips Royal Commission

The impression that most suspects spend relatively short periods in police custody was confirmed by the Royal Commission on Criminal Procedure. It said that the empirical data showed that overall about three-quarters of all suspects were dealt with in six hours or less, and about 95 per cent within 24 hours. Virtually none were held for more than 48 hours. A study based on nearly 50,000 detainees in the Metropolitan Police District showed that the proportion held for more than 72 hours was 0.4 per cent. (*Report of the Royal Commission*, para 3.96, p 52.) Statistics gathered by the Metropolitan Police for the third quarter of 1982 showed that during that period

1,000 suspects, being 1.6 per cent of all those arrested, were detained for more than 24 hours without charge and of these a mere 24 were detained more than 48 hours and only 4 were held for between 72 and 96 hours (House of Commons, *Hansard*, 25 July 1983, col 279).

In the Royal Commission's view the proper length of police detention before a suspect had to be brought before a court was a maximum of 24 hours. It proposed a scheme under which after six hours the custody officer in the police station would review the need for further detention. Within 24 hours the suspect would either have to be charged or released or an application would have to be made to a magistrates' court for permission to hold him for another 24 hours. The suspect would have a right to be present at any such hearing and he would equally be permitted legal representation on legal aid. Thereafter the police would be entitled to go back to the magistrates for further extensions of 24 hours at a time. After 48 hours' detention, there would be a right of appeal to a judge against continued detention. The Royal Commission did not propose any upper limit of time for such extensions. In theory the magistrates would be free to grant any number of 24-hour extensions.

PACE

The Government did not wholly accept the Royal Commission's scheme. When the first Police and Criminal Evidence Bill was published it provided that a suspect could be held without charges for a maximum of 24 hours before the police had to apply for permission from a magistrate to hold him for up to a further 24 hours. Such an application could have been made to the magistrate in his home. The suspect would have had no right to be present or to be legally represented. He would, however, have had the right to make written representations. After 48 hours the police would have had to get authority for further detention from a magistrates' court after a proper hearing (in private) at which the suspect would have had the right to be present and to be legally represented. The magistrates could then allow detention for a further period of 48 hours–making a total of 96 hours in all. There would be no right of appeal to a judge.

In the light of criticisms of this scheme the Government amended the legislation and the new scheme re-emerged in the 1984 Act, which provides that the review after 24 hours should be by a senior police officer at least of the rank of superintendent (s 42). (The 24-hour period is measured from arrival at the police station. If he is arrested by another force, it starts from the moment he arrives in the police station in the area where he is wanted. If he comes from outside England and Wales the 24-hour period has in any event to start within 24 hours of his first arrest (s 41).) If the superintendent authorizes further detention, this can continue for up to the 36-hour point (s 42(1)). After 36 hours from the beginning of detention, there has to be a hearing in the magistrates' court with the suspect present and, if he wishes, legally represented (s 43). The magistrates can grant a warrant of further detention for up to a further 60 hours–making a total of 96 hours, as under the original version of these proposals (ss 43 and 44). But the maximum period of time allowable by magistrates is 36 hours at a time. It follows that if the police want to ask for the full 96 hours they have to return to the magistrates for a second hearing (ss 43(12) and 44).

The magistrates can only authorize further detention if the offence in question is a serious arrestable offence (see p 135 above), is being investigated diligently and expeditiously, and if further detention is necessary to secure or preserve evidence relating to an offence for which the suspect is under arrest or to obtain such evidence by questioning him (s 43(4)).

The Act specifically preserves habeas corpus (s 51(*d*)). But such applications will presumably fail if detention has been properly authorized by the magistrates and the conditions for further detention still apply. If they no longer apply, further detention will be unlawful and habeas corpus is available.

The time for which a suspect can be held is, under the Police and Criminal Evidence Act, affected by the following provisions:

(1) Under s 34 of the Act, the custody officer is under a duty to order the immediate release of an arrested person if the grounds for holding him cease to apply and there are no other valid grounds for holding him.

(2) When the suspect first comes to the police station, the custody officer has to decide whether there is at that stage enough evidence to charge him and, if so, he should be charged forthwith (s 37(1) and (7)). But research has shown that this duty is not performed. Custody officers rubber-stamp the arresting officer's decision to bring the suspect in for questioning. (See I McKenzie, R Morgan and R Reiner, 'Helping the Police with their Inquiries: The Necessity Principle and Voluntary Attendance at the Police Station (1990) *Criminal Law Review*, pp 23–4, and M McConville, A Sanders and R Leng, *The Case for the Prosecution* (Routledge, 1991), pp 42–4, 119.

(3) After being charged the arrested person must be released, with or without bail, unless:

(i)   it is necessary to hold him so that his name or address can be ascertained; or
(ii) the custody officer reasonably thinks that it is necessary to hold him for his own protection or to prevent him from causing physical injury to anyone or from causing loss of or damage to property; or
(iii) the custody officer reasonably thinks that he needs to be held because he would otherwise fail to answer to bail or to prevent him from interfering with witnesses or otherwise obstructing the course of justice; or
(iv) if he is a juvenile, he needs to be held 'in his own interests' (s 38(1)).

(4) If charged and not released, he will have to be brought before a magistrates' court, as soon as practicable, and not later than the first sitting after being charged (s 46(2)). If no court is sitting on the same day as he is charged or the next day (other than Sunday), the custody officer is under a duty to inform the clerk to the justices so that a court sitting can be arranged (s 46(3)).

(5) If the suspect is not charged, the maximum time he can be held is 96 hours, provided that the magistrates authorize 'further detention' beyond the initial period of up to 36 hours during which the police themselves can authorize detention (ss 42 and 43).

(6) The necessity for further detention has to be reviewed regularly by the police– after six hours in the police station and thereafter at intervals of not more than nine hours (s 39).

Note–'holding charges'

The police commonly lay charges in regard to relatively minor offences whilst pursuing inquiries over more serious matters. Under the revised Code C they may now delay charging the suspect until they are ready to charge him on the other matters. ('When a person is detained in respect of more than one offence it is permissible to delay bringing him before the custody officer until [he has been asked whether he has anything more to say] in respect of all the offences', para 16.1). However, the rules still state that once they have enough evidence to justify a charge the police must not question the suspect about an offence, save for clarifying ambiguities or dealing with *new* matters (paras 11.4, 16.5).

Statistics on length of detention and charges

The annual Home Office statistics on length of detention give no clear picture. (The Runciman Royal Commission recommended that they be put on a better basis–p 30, para 21.) The best evidence of average periods of detention is in the two Home Office studies by David Brown, *Detention at the Police Station under the Police and Criminal Evidence Act 1984* (HMSO, 1989) and Brown *et al, Changing the Code: Police Detention under the revised PACE Codes of Practice* (HMSO, 1992). The 1989 report showed (p 62) that only 1 per cent of all suspects in the sample of some 5,500 were held for more than 24 hours. As many as 32 per cent were out of the police station within two hours, 59 per cent in four hours and 76 per cent in six hours. Eleven per cent were held more than twelve hours. The mean length of detention was 5 hours 10 minutes with a median of 3 hours 19 minutes. The later study showed that the position had basically not changed. The mean period in 1990 was five hours one minute, and in 1991, five hours 18 minutes. The median in 1990 was three hours 13 minutes and in 1991 was three hours 20 minutes (pp 104–105).

Not surprisingly, in terrorism cases the period is distinctly longer. A study of 253 persons detained under the Prevention of Terrorism Act, again by David Brown, found an average period of detention of nearly 29 hours with a median of 16 hours 24 minutes. But just under 40 per cent of the detainees had been released within 12 hours and nearly two-thirds within 24 hours. (D Brown, *Detention under the Prevention of Terrorism Act 1989: Legal Advice and Outside Contact* (HMSO, 1993, p 50.)

In the study by McConville, Sanders and Leng likewise it was found that the proportion held beyond 24 hours was tiny–1.2 per cent of 720 adults and none of the 360 juveniles. Half the adults and 72 per cent of the juveniles were held for under 4 hours; 71 per cent and 87 per cent for under 6 hours; and 90 per cent and 96 per cent for under 12 hours. (*The Case for the Prosecution*, Routledge, 1991, p 46.)

However, the study by McConville *et al* showed that, for one reason or another, no further action was taken in regard to 26 per cent of 720 cases involving arrests of adults and 24 per cent of 360 arrests involving juveniles in their sample. The arrested adult was charged in 58 per cent of cases, compared with only 35 per cent of arrested juveniles. The arrested adult was cautioned or warned informally in 14 per cent of cases, compared with 38 per cent of juveniles. (*Ibid*, Table 10, p 104.)

4. POLICE POWERS OF SEARCH AND SEIZURE

(a) On arrest

Searching the arrested person

When someone is arrested, it is normal police practice to search him. At common law there was no general right to make such a search unless there were reasonable grounds for believing that he was carrying a weapon or had about him evidence which was material to the offence in connection with which he had been arrested (see especially *Dillon v O'Brien and Davis* (1887) 16 Cox CC 245). Technically a search that did not fall within such limits would be unlawful and could give rise to an action for damages. In practice, however, such an action would be difficult to bring since the police would normally be able to justify the search on the ground that they had reasonable grounds to think that he might be carrying evidence implicating him in the crime.

However, in *Lindley v Rutter* [1981] QB 128, the Divisional Court quashed the conviction of a young woman, Janet Lindley, on the ground that the police had exceeded their powers in removing her brassiere 'for her own protection'. She had been arrested in a drunken state and taken to the police station. She refused to allow herself to be searched. During a struggle she scratched the police officer's hand and kicked her. Another police officer intervened and eventually they got her bra off. The magistrates found that Janet Lindley had not threatened to injure herself or anyone else, but that she had used more force than was necessary to resist the attempts to remove her underclothing. She was charged with assaulting an officer in the execution of her duty. On appeal Lord Justice Donaldson said that it was the duty of an officer to take all reasonable steps to ensure that a prisoner did not escape or assist others to escape, did not injure himself or others, did not destroy or dispose of evidence, and did not commit further crimes such as damage to property. The measures that could reasonably be taken in discharge of that duty depended on the circumstances of each case. Searches involved an affront to the dignity and privacy of the individual–especially a body search. The removal of a brassiere required considerable justification. It was not likely that the bra would have been used for improper purposes. The officers had been acting in accordance with the chief constable's standing order as to how to deal with female prisoners. It was impossible, he said, to justify such an order, since it was not adapted to the circumstances of the case. The officers therefore had not been acting in the execution of their duty and the conviction had to be quashed.

In *Eeet* [1983] Crim LR 806, the Teeside Crown Court directed the jury to acquit the defendant on a charge of assaulting a police officer by biting his thumb while three officers were forcibly searching him to establish his identity. He had been validly arrested under the Road Traffic Act after running away from his car when stopped. He had refused to give his name and address, which caused them to suspect (wrongly) that he had stolen the car. At the police station he maintained his refusal to identify himself. The police were carrying out the procedures in regard to breath testing under s 9 of the Road Traffic Act. The court held that it was not essential for the police to establish the motorist's identity at that stage and that the police had therefore not been entitled to use force in order to search him. The search was therefore unlawful and amounted to an assault on him by the officers.

A third pre-1984 case that went against the police was *Brazil v Chief Constable of Surrey* [1983] 3 All ER 537, in which a woman twice assaulted police officers while trying to resist a search in the police station. Her appeal against conviction was allowed by the Divisional Court on two grounds. In the case of the first assault, the ground was the same as that in *Lindley v Rutter*, that there was no evidence that the police had considered whether a search was necessary; they had simply applied a general rule that persons should be searched for their own safety. In the case of the second assault, which was to resist a search for drugs, she had not been given any reason for the search. Because a search involved an affront to the dignity of the person, a police officer was not normally entitled to carry out a search without first telling the suspect why it was necessary in the particular case. There was no evidence that there were any special grounds for exempting the police from this requirement and accordingly the officer had not been acting in the execution of her duty when she was assaulted.

Searching the arrested person's home

It was for a long time common police practice after arresting someone to go to his home and to search there. Surprisingly there was no judicial decision which made this lawful. The Royal Commission on the Police in 1929 said it was unlawful and should be either permitted by statute or stopped. In *Jeffrey v Black* [1978] 1 All ER 555, the defendant was arrested in a pub for allegedly stealing a sandwich. The police then searched his home and found drugs. The Lord Chief Justice said that the search might have been lawful if the police had been looking for evidence relating to the theft of stolen sandwiches. This was not, however, the case. He therefore did not decide the point but indicated that if it came up for decision the law might permit a search for evidence of the same crime. There was also the dictum of Lord Denning in *Ghani v Jones* ([1969] 3 All ER 1700, 1703) that where the police officers arrest a man, 'I take it to be settled law, without citing cases, that the officers are entitled to take any goods which they find in his possession or in his house which they reasonably believe to be material evidence in relation to the crime for which he is arrested'. But in fact there *were* no cases that stood for this proposition. It was also said obiter, since the case did not relate to an arrest.

In *McLorie v Oxford* [1982] QB 1290, the Divisional Court (Donaldson LJ and Webster J) took a very restrictive view of the powers of the police to search on arrest and they specifically disapproved the dictum of Lord Chief Justice Widgery in *Jeffrey v Black*. The case arose on an appeal by Malcolm McLorie against conviction for assault on a police officer at his own home. The police had gone there to look for a motorcar which according to them had been used on the previous day by the appellant's brother Marcus in an attempt to murder someone. (Marcus was later charged with attempted murder and pleaded guilty to causing grievous bodily harm for which he was sentenced to two years' imprisonment.) Marcus was arrested late in the evening on 1 June 1981 at the home where he lived with his brother and his father. A few hours later the police saw the car in the back yard of the house and asked Mr McLorie senior for permission to remove it for forensic examination. Mr McLorie refused permission and said it could not be taken without a warrant.

Subsequently, when the police returned with reinforcements they removed the car forcibly. Malcolm resisted them and was charged with assaulting an officer in the execution of his duty. But the Divisional Court quashed the conviction on the ground that, although the police were on duty, they were not acting lawfully. The police could certainly have followed a motorist onto his own property if it had been a case of 'hot pursuit'. This would also have permitted them then to remove the car as evidence. But this was not a case of hot pursuit. Lord Justice Donaldson continued:

Such is the importance attached by the common law to the relative inviolability of a dwelling house that we cannot believe that there is a common law right without warrant to enter one either in order to search for instruments of crime, even of serious crime, or in order to seize such an instrument which is known to be there. Certainly if there were, we would expect it to be reflected in the books and it is not.

Counsel for the respondent submits correctly that the common law evolves, or is discovered, in relation to changing social conditions. However, evolution, or discovery, is a delicate process and what he proposes would, in our judgment, constitute a violent change. For our part, we are unable to agree to it.

It has also been held that where the police are searching premises under a search warrant they are not permitted to search *persons* there unless the warrant so states (*King v R* [1969] 1 AC 304, PC).

The Philips Royal Commission's view and PACE

The Philips Royal Commission thought that the police should not routinely make full searches of all suspects and that the question of how far a search should go should be considered by the station officer. A superficial search should always be permissible. Strip searches, on the other hand, should be rare. If they required search of intimate parts of the body they should be permitted only in grave offences and only on the authority of a senior officer, and should always be conducted by a doctor.

Search of the arrested person's premises and vehicle should be allowed subject to safeguards. The chief safeguard should be that there must be reasonable suspicion that evidence material to the offence may be found on those premises. Search of any other premises should have to require a warrant. The reasons for any search should be recorded by the station officer before the search, in order to minimise the risk of 'fishing expeditions' (para 3.121). Evidence of other offences found in the course of such a search should be admissible if a warrant could have been obtained to look for it, even though no such warrant had been obtained. Searches should be conducted in a manner appropriate to what was being searched for (para 3.122).

The Police and Criminal Evidence Act 1984 broadly enacted these recommendations. Section 18 empowers a constable to enter premises occupied or controlled by a person arrested for an arrestable offence to search for evidence relating to that or connected offences. He must have reasonable grounds for believing that there is evidence on the premises that relates to the offence in question or to some offence 'which is connected with or similar to that offence' (s 18(1)). Authorization must normally be given in advance by an officer who is at least an inspector.[7] The officer who authorizes such a search in advance (or approves one after the event) must make a written record of the grounds for the search and of the nature of the evidence sought.

Section 32 authorizes search of an arrested person and any premises (including a vehicle) on which the arrest took place in which he was when arrested or immediately before. It cannot be used to justify a search several hours after the arrest.[8] A search under s 32 can be for anything that can be used to assist an escape or for evidence relating to *any* offence (s 32(2)).

Section 19 authorizes an officer who is lawfully searching any premises (whether after an arrest or not) to seize any article (other than one covered by legal professional privilege) if he reasonably believes that it is evidence relating to the offence which he is investigating 'or any other offence', and that 'it is necessary to seize it in order to prevent its being concealed, lost, damaged, altered or destroyed'.

---

7 See *Badham* [1987] Crim LR 202.
8 *Ibid*. See also *Churchill* [1989] Crim LR 226.

Intimate searches

Section 55 of PACE permits a search of bodily orifices (called an 'intimate search'). An intimate search can only be for a weapon or other article that might be used to cause injury or for Class 'A' drugs (eg not for 'evidence'), and it has to be conducted by a doctor or nurse or, in the case of a weapons search only, a police officer of the same sex provided that a superintendent or above reasonably considers that it is not practicable for the search to be by a doctor. In practice virtually all such searches are carried out by doctors. A full record has to be kept of such searches. In most years the total number of intimate searches is between 40 and 100 or so. In David Brown's 1989 Home Office study (see p 165 above) intimate searches were found in only seven cases of 5,519 (0.1%) (p 53). The Home Office annual statistics ('Operation of Certain Police Powers under PACE') show the number of intimate searches as 104 in 1986 and in each year thereafter at considerably lower figures ranging from a high of 77 to a low of 41. In 1994 there were 77 intimate searches, only three of which were carried out by a police officer. Forty two were made in connection with Class A drugs (in eight cases drugs were found) and in 36 cases the search was for a weapon (one was found). One person was searched for both drugs and a weapon.

Intimate and non-intimate samples

PACE also made provision for the taking of bodily samples from the suspect as part of the process of criminal investigation. With the development of DNA analysis this power is assuming increasing importance.

The Act distinguishes between two kinds of sample—'intimate' samples (s 62) and 'non-intimate' samples (s 63). The main practical difference is that intimate samples, other than urine, may only be taken with written consent, and only by a doctor. Non-intimate samples may in some circumstances be taken without consent and by a police officer.

Intimate samples may only be taken if an officer of the rank of superintendent or above gives permission. The 1984 Act defined intimate samples as samples of blood, semen, other tissue fluid, urine, saliva, pubic hair or a swab taken from a body orifice. The Runciman Royal Commission (Report, pp 14–15, para 29) recommended that the definition be changed so as to permit the taking of saliva by mouth swab without consent. This was done in the Criminal Justice and Public Order Act 1994 (CJPOA) by making saliva a non-intimate sample. Previously intimate samples could only be taken if the investigation concerned a serious arrestable offence. Now under the CJPOA it need only be a recordable offence which means an offence carrying a penalty of imprisonment.

Non-intimate samples are defined (s 65) as a sample of hair, other than pubic hair, a sample taken from a nail or under a nail, a swab taken from any part of the body including the mouth, other than a body orifice, saliva and a footprint or similar impression of part of a body. A non-intimate sample can be taken without the written consent of the person concerned if an officer of the rank of superintendent or above has authorised compulsory taking of the sample. The offence must be a recordable one and there must be reasonable grounds for believing the sample will tend to confirm or deny the person's involvement. A non-intimate sample may also now be taken from someone, whether or not he is in custody, who has been convicted after April 1995 of a recordable offence.

The police expect the database for DNA samples eventually to hold some 5 million records. The CJPOA added a new requirement for both intimate and non-intimate samples that the person from whom the sample is taken must be informed that it can be made the subject of a search (called 'a speculative search') against other records.

(b) Powers to enter premises other than after an arrest

At common law

There is no general common law power to enter private premises in order to investigate criminal acts:

Davis v Lisle [1936] 2 KB 434 (Divisional Court)

The respondent, a police officer, believing that an offence had been committed by the servants of the appellant in causing an obstruction in the highway with a motor lorry, followed the lorry into the appellant's garage to make inquiries as to the person responsible for the supposed obstruction. The respondent did not obtain the appellant's permission to enter the garage, nor had he a warrant authorizing him to enter it. The appellant directed the respondent to leave the premises, but the respondent claimed to be entitled to remain on them and the appellant assaulted him by striking him in the chest and stomach. The appellant was convicted of assaulting a police officer in the execution of his duty. Appeal by case stated:

Lord Hewart CJ: The point which is raised here with regard to the appellant's first two convictions is whether the officers were at the material time acting in the execution of their duty. In my opinion, they were not, and there are no grounds on which they can be held to have been so acting. The only ground which is put forward in support of the contention that they were so acting seems to me to be quite beside the point. I feel a difficulty in envisaging the legal proposition that because the police officers had witnessed an offence being committed on the highway they were acting in the execution of their duty in entering and remaining on private premises because the offenders then were on those premises. Admittedly, the officers had no warrant entitling them to search the premises. It is one thing to say that the officers were at liberty to enter this garage to make an enquiry, but quite a different thing to say that they were entitled to remain when, not without emphasis, the appellant had said: 'Get outside. You cannot come here without a search warrant. ... From that moment on, while the officers remained where they were, it seems to me that they were trespassers.'

I think that the conclusion of quarter sessions was erroneous and that, with regard to those two convictions, which are the real pith and substance of this case, the appeal ought to be allowed and the case go back to the court of quarter sessions with the direction that at the material time the respondent was not acting in the execution of his duty.

Du Parcq and Goddard JJ agreed.

See, to like effect, *Lambert v Roberts* [1981] 2 All ER 15, in which the Divisional Court held that a police officer was not entitled to administer a breathalyser test on a motorist he had followed home when the motorist asked him to leave. The motorist and his family told the officer that he was on private property and asked him to leave.

This was a revocation of the officer's implied licence to be on the drive. The officer should thereupon have left. But in *Snook v Mannion* [1982] RTR 321, on virtually identical facts the decision went the other way. The officers followed the motorist home after observing his erratic driving. They asked him to take a breathalyser test which he refused, and he told them to 'fuck off'. The magistrates held that this was mere abuse, not a revocation of their implied licence to be on his drive. He was therefore convicted of driving with an excess of alcohol in his blood and the Divisional Court upheld the decision. See also *Morris v Beardmore* [1981] AC 446, HL; *Clowser v Chaplin, Finnigan v Sandiford* [1981] Crim LR 643, HL; *Hart v Chief Constable of Kent* [1983] Crim LR 117.

The particular problem in relation to motoring law was altered by the provisions of the Transport Act 1981. Section 25 of that Act stated: 'for the purposes of arresting a person under the power conferred by s 5 [driving, or being in charge of a motorcar whilst unfit] a constable may enter (if need be by force) any place where that person is or where the constable, with reasonable cause, suspects him to be. 'This power may not, however, cover the situation where the officer wishes to administer a breathalyser test. The 1981 Act also gave the police a power of entry where an accident has taken place–see Schedule 8. But these statutory provisions confirm that at common law there is no such power. On the force that can be used by the police in effecting entry, see *Swales v Cox* [1981] 1 All ER 1115.

A police officer who enters premises without lawful excuse commits a trespass. Prior to PACE, there were various kinds of lawful excuse.

(1) Under the authority of a search warrant   There are many statutory provisions that permit the police to ask magistrates for a search warrant. In dealing with an application for a search warrant, the magistrate is supposed to satisfy himself that in all the circumstances of the case it is reasonable to grant it. But in the nature of the situation it is difficult for the magistrate to differ from the police officer's view. The search warrant must, however, specify the correct premises. If it says Flat 45, the police cannot lawfully search Flat 30 even though that was what they actually intended when they asked for a search of Flat 45–*R v Atkinson* [1976] Crim LR 307.

(2) To execute an arrest without warrant   This power which arose formerly under the Criminal Law Act 1967, s 2(6), now arises under the Police and Criminal Evidence Act 1984, s 17(1).

(3) To deal with emergency situations   There was a common-law power to enter premises to deal with, or prevent, a breach of the peace–see *Thomas v Sawkins* [1935] 2 KB 249. The power also extended to saving life or limb.

It was held by the Divisional Court in 1985, that once the police were on premises lawfully for one purpose, they were there lawfully for any purpose. They could therefore search persons for drugs (which was their real object in being there) even though they had not got a warrant under the Misuse of Drugs Act, because they were lawfully on the premises to check out the premises under the Greater London Council (General Powers) Act 1968: *Foster v Attard* [1986] Crim LR 627.

According to survey evidence given by the police to the Philips Royal Commission, most searches of premises were under warrant. The survey showed that 61 per cent of such searches in London (compared with only 24 per cent in the provinces) were backed by a warrant and, overall, 43 per cent were deemed to be successful on one criterion or another (*The Investigation and Prosecution of Criminal Offences in England and Wales: The Law and Procedure*, Cmnd 8092–1, 1981, pp 126–9). But when members of the public were asked for their experiences, the position appeared in rather different light. In a survey in Notting Hill the overwhelming majority of searches were said to have been without warrant and in most cases no reason had been given to the householder. Only about one-fifth of the searches led to any prosecution. (M McConville, 'Search of Persons and Premises: New Data from London' (1983) *Criminal Law Review*, pp 605, 606.)

However, by far the fullest study of the operation of the search-warrant power pre-PACE was published in August 1984 (KW Lidstone, 'Magistrates, Police and Search Warrants' (1984) *Criminal Law Review*, p 449). The survey by Mr KW Lidstone of Sheffield University showed that the three courts studied issued 688 search warrants over a six-month period for stolen or prohibited goods. This was a mere 8 per cent of all the search warrants issued in that period. (No less than 86 per cent were issued to the Gas and Electricity Boards.) The London court issued the highest proportion of warrants for criminal investigation purposes (almost a quarter of its warrants, compared with 7 per cent in one provincial court and 4 per cent in the other). This was in line with the research done for the Royal Commission (above). In all, twelve statutes were relied on. In order of use, they were the Theft Act (58 per cent), the Misuse of Drugs Act (24 per cent), and the Obscene Publications Act (10 per cent). These three therefore accounted for over 90 per cent of all the warrants issued.

The researchers observed 32 warrant applications. The magistrate asked questions of the police officer in only four and in only two were the questions directed to the grounds for the application. It does not appear, therefore, that the power is exercised with much care. (Stipendiary magistrates were no more likely to ask questions than lay magistrates.)

The information supplied to magistrates was usually minimal–limited to the name of the police officer, the name of the occupier, the address and the nature of the case. The grounds for the application were rarely stated. (Usually it was 'As a result of information received, there is reason to believe' or something similar.) Only occasionally was there any indication that the police had verified the information or had supporting evidence. (The Lord Chancellor's guidance to magistrates is that police officers should not be required to identify an informant but that it is legitimate to ask whether he is known to the officer and whether it has been possible to make other inquiries.)

The comment from Mr Lidstone was that:

The reality is then that the judicial hurdle of the warrant application is no more than a stepping stone. Magistrates see the 'information from a reliable source' formula as an impenetrable barrier beyond which they cannot or will not go. This, together with an almost unquestioning trust in the police, the clerk, or both, allied to a lack of knowledge of how the police actually operate and an over-glamorised view of specialist squads, combine to impair the proper exercise of the independent judicial function [pp 452–3].

The study conflicted with the police evidence to the Philips Royal Commission on the extent to which searches under warrant occurred. There were 289 entries on premises, 201 for searches and 88 to make an arrest. Only 34 of the searches were backed by a warrant. Seventy-nine per cent of the entries were without a warrant. Of these, 30 per cent were with consent before an arrest and 44 per cent with consent after an arrest. The impression gained by the researchers was that the police only troubled to get a warrant where for some reason they expected 'bother'. Normally they expected to be able to get into premises by a combination of 'front' or 'bluff'.

The success rate for searches under warrant varied from offence to offence. Obscene publications searches were 100 per cent successful, two-thirds of those for drugs were successful, while those for stolen goods were only successful in a quarter of cases.

The Philips Royal Commission

The Royal Commission on Criminal Procedure recommended that existing powers to get a search warrant to look for prohibited goods such as stolen goods, drugs, firearms, explosives, etc should be confirmed (para 3.39). In addition, however, there should be a new power to search for evidence whether from guilty persons or from persons totally unconnected with the offence. But this power, it thought, should be used very sparingly and subject to strict controls:

3.42. A compulsory power of search for evidence should be available only as a last resort. It should be granted only in exceptional circumstances and in respect only of grave offences. The seriousness of the intrusion could also be marked by making the issuing authority a circuit judge. The procedure for obtaining access to evidence might have two stages. The appropriate initial step would be for the police to apply for an order of the court on a procedure analogous to the witness summons under the Criminal Procedure (Attendance of Witnesses) Act 1965 or to the orders for the discovery and production of evidence available in civil proceedings. The order, if the court were satisfied of the conditions set out in the next paragraph, would operate to require the person to whom it was addressed to provide or to allow the police to inspect or have access to the items specified in the order (if they were in the form of documents, this might be done by providing copies or taking photographs). It should be provided that the person could appeal to the court against the order in the same way as a witness summons can now be objected to. If the court were not satisfied with the grounds of appeal and if the person still refused access, a warrant to search and seize could be issued on proof of deliberate refusal to comply with the order. It would also be necessary to provide for the order procedure to be dispensed with and for a warrant to be issued forthwith where there is reason to believe that the evidence will disappear, or be disposed of if the person concerned is alerted to the police interest in it.

PACE

The Government, however, took a different approach on this issue. When the first Police and Criminal Evidence Bill was published it provided for two different procedures. The normal method for getting permission to search for evidence in premises was to be by getting an ordinary warrant from the magistrates. The Government said it took the view that the magistrates already granted search warrants in so many different situations that there was normally no need to require a judge's permission to search in this class of case. But where the material sought was held in confidence and related to a serious arrestable offence (p 136 above) an order from a circuit judge would be required. Application to the judge would normally be made in the absence of the other side by the police.

These proposals provoked a great outcry of protest from a variety of quarters– notably from doctors, priests, journalists and Citizens' Advice Bureaux–claiming that the police would be given the right to search through confidential files and records. As a result the Government made a number of major changes in the proposals. First it was provided that any hearing before a judge (called a 'special procedure' application) would be *inter partes* unless the police had reason to suspect that the person from whom the material was sought was implicated in the crimes in question. Secondly, categories of 'excluded material' were defined which would be exempt from any kind of search by the police. (Though if the material could pre-PACE have been the subject of a search warrant it could be made the subject of a special procedure application[9] (see below).) Excluded material covers:

(1) Personal records held in confidence and acquired in the course of any 'trade, business, profession or other occupation'. 'Personal records' for this purpose means documents or records concerning individuals relating to their physical or mental health, spiritual counselling, social work or similar work involving counselling or assistance and other activities relating to a client's personal welfare or counselling and assistance given by voluntary organizations (ss 11–12). Thus the files and records of doctors, priests, social workers and Citizens' Advice Bureaux are normally exempt from any kind of police search under PACE (but see p 175 below). Excluded material also covers human tissue or tissue fluid taken for the purpose of treatment or diagnosis. But if a doctor has the gun used in the crime or the patient's bloodstained clothing, the police would be able to ask a judge for an order requiring it to be produced. They would not be excluded material because they are not 'records' (s 12).

(2) Journalistic material in the form of documents or records held in confidence. 'Journalistic material' for this purpose means material acquired or created for the purposes of journalism. It is not required that the material be for publication in a national newspaper or that the person holding it be a member of one of the journalists' unions. The material is only 'journalistic material', however, if it is held in confidence and is in the possession of someone who acquired or created it for the purposes of journalism (ss 11 and 13).

PACE also provided that items held subject to legal professional privilege could not be made the subject of a search warrant application to magistrates (s 8(1)(d)). Nor can such material be made the subject of a special procedure application or even seizure under s 19 if actually found during a lawful search.

(3) Items covered by legal professional privilege consist of material exchanged between the client and his lawyer or anyone else acting for the client regarding legal advice; material exchanged between the client and the lawyer or anyone else acting for the client or between the client and such other person in connection with legal proceedings; and items enclosed with or referred to in such communications. Items held with the intention of furthering a criminal purpose are not, however, items subject to legal privilege (s 10). See on this issue the House of Lords' decision in *R v Central Criminal Court, ex p Francis & Francis* [1989] AC 346, which established that the criminal intent need not be that of the client or the solicitor. It can be that of a third party. Note also *R v Crown Court at Inner London Sessions, ex p Baines & Baines* [1987] 3 All ER 1025, in which it was held that material consisting simply of records of the financing and purchase of a house was not covered by privilege because they

9   Also under the Prevention of Terrorism (Temporary Provisions) Act 1989, Sch 7, para 3, even excluded material can be the subject of an access order by a court. Only material covered by legal professional privilege is protected from such an order (ed).

were not concerned with the giving of legal advice. (See L Alt, 'Raids: Against the Law', *Solicitors' Journal*, 15 November 1991, p 1248.)

If the police seek evidence that is held in confidence but which is not excluded material, they must go to a circuit judge for permission to seek *special procedure material*. The special procedure for getting permission to seek such evidence is set out in Schedule 1 of PACE. This requires that the judge be satisfied: (1) that there are reasonable grounds for thinking that a serious arrestable offence has been committed; (2) that there is 'special procedure material' on premises specified in the police application; (3) that it is likely to be of substantial value to the investigation and that it is likely to be relevant evidence; (4) that other methods of obtaining the material either have been tried or have not been tried because they would be bound to fail; and (5) that it is in the public interest that the material should be produced having regard, on the one hand, to the benefit likely to accrue to the investigation and, on the other, to the circumstances in which it is held.

If so satisfied, the judge would order the person who appears to be in possession of the material to produce it to the police or to give them access to it, within seven days from the date of the order. The person against whom the order is sought must normally be given due notice of the application so that he can appear to contest the application. Once a person is served with an order to produce the material, he must not conceal or destroy it. If he disobeys the order he can be dealt with by proceedings for contempt but not normally by the issue of a search warrant.

Special procedure applications have been made very frequently by the police, especially against banks and other financial institutions. Usually they are uncontested hearings. Ken Lidstone reported over 2,000 such applications between 1986 and 1989– see 'Entry, Search and Seizure', 40 *Northern Ireland Legal Quarterly*, Winter 1989, p 333 at 342.

In certain circumstances the police can ask the judge for a search warrant instead of an order to produce and in that case the hearing is *ex p ante* not *inter partes*.

One is where service of notice of the proceedings would seriously prejudice the investigation. The 1984 Act also provides that the special procedure applies to any search for excluded material or special procedure material under previous statutes. In other words, insofar as the previous law already allowed any search for confidential material on a magistrates' warrant or otherwise (for instance, under the Official Secrets Act), the police now have to get a judge's order authorizing such a search. But the judge will be required to issue a warrant if he is satisfied that it is appropriate to do so. He cannot apply all the other tests that he has to apply before authorizing access to other special procedure material. (See Schedule 1, ss 3, 4, 11 and 12.)

See further Ken Lidstone, 'Entry, Search and Seizure', 40 *Northern Ireland Legal Quarterly*, 1989, pp 333–62. See generally Richard Stone, *Entry, Search and Seizure*, (2nd edn, Butterworth, 1989). For criticism of the way the courts have dealt with the seizure of journalistic material see R Costigan, 'Fleet Street Blues: Police Seizure of Journalists' Material' [1996] *Criminal Law Review*, pp 231–39.

(c) Getting a search warrant

The Philips Royal Commission on Criminal Procedure proposed (paras 3.46–7) that new rules should be laid down to regulate the procedure for getting a search warrant, and these recommendations were adopted in PACE. This provides (s 15) that an application for a warrant must state the grounds for making the application, the statutory authority covering the claim and, in as much detail as possible,[10] the object of the warrant and the premises concerned. The application must be supported by an information in writing. The constable must answer any questions put by the justice of the peace on oath. Each warrant can authorize only one entry. The warrant must specify the name of the person applying for it, the date of issue, the statutory power under which it is issued, and, so far as possible, the articles sought and when the search is to take place. The Act also requires a report to be made by the police to the issuing judicial authority (s 16(9)). If it is executed, it must be endorsed with a statement showing whether the articles specified or any other articles were seized. This must be made forthwith after the search. If the warrant is not executed within one month, it must be returned at that point (s 16(10)).

The utility of these requirements must, however, be somewhat undermined by the evidence of the study by Mr Lidstone (p 172 above) showing how magistrates actually grant search warrants. He argued that the police were much more likely to use their powers under s 32 of the Act (search after an arrest) or s 19 (general power of seizure of evidence found incidental to a lawful search), than the power to get a search warrant. Since the police could normally get access to and the right to search premises without having to get a search warrant they would presumably prefer that.

(d) Executing a search warrant and search by consent

Where the occupier of the premises to be searched is there, PACE requires that the constable identify himself, produce a copy of the warrant and give him a copy (s 16(5)). If he is not in uniform, the officer must produce documentary evidence that he is a constable (s 16(5)(*a*)). Code B on the searching of premises requires that, where it is proposed to search by consent without a warrant or arrest, the police must, if it is practicable, get the occupier's consent in writing before the search (para 4.1) and they must tell him that he is not obliged to give such consent (a new caution) and that anything taken may be produced in evidence (para 4.2). Under the April 1991 revised Code B the police must, unless it is impracticable to do so, give the occupier a Note of Powers and Rights stating whether the search is under warrant or with consent, explaining the rights of the occupier and the powers of the police (para 5.7). If the person is not suspected of an offence he should be told so (para 4.2).

The officer may use such force as is reasonable but no more than the minimum degree of force is to be used (Code B, para 5.6). Searches must be conducted 'with consideration for the property and privacy of the occupier searched, and with no more disturbance than necessary' (para 5.10). If the occupier wishes to have a friend to witness the search, he should not be prevented or discouraged from this (para 5.11).

---

10 In *IRC v Rossminster Ltd* [1980] 1 All ER 80, the Inland Revenue obtained a search warrant to look for evidence of suspected tax fraud from the homes of two directors of Rossminster Ltd and its offices. Piles of documents were taken away for inspection. The House of Lords, reversing the Court of Appeal, held that the warrant was sufficiently detailed since it stated that the search was for evidence of tax fraud. It was not necessary, and might be impossible, to be more specific before the documents had been examined. See also *Reynolds v Metropolitan Police Comr* [1984] 3 All ER 649.

If the search was for special procedure material under Schedule 1 of the Act, the officer should ask the occupier to produce it. He may also ask to see any index to files and to inspect files which according to the index appear to contain any of the material sought. But a more extensive search of the premises can only be made if it appears that the index is inaccurate or incomplete, or if 'for any other reason the officer in charge has reasonable grounds to believe that such a search is necessary in order to find the material sought' (para 5.14).

Post-PACE research

Research on the operation of PACE has shown, however, that the rules in Code B regarding searches of premises by consent are not necessarily working as intended:

D Dixon, C Coleman, and Keith Bottomley, 'Consent and the Legal Regulation of Policing', 17 *Journal of Law and Society*, 1990, pp 345, 352–54

We found that many consent searches were not recorded.

The main reason for this is simply that the legal requirements cannot be easily reconciled with standard practice in searching premises. Our observational research found that the police often rely on a potent combination of three factors–householders' ignorance of the law; their unquestioning belief in the power of the police; and their implied guilt if they refuse access. A requirement for officers to tell a householder that they do not have the power to do what they want (and, more to the point, intend) to do is seen as being quite unrealistic. A serious loss of face would be threatened if a suspect decided not to consent to a search. Two officers summed up the police perspective admirably:

'If you ask people for consent, they seem to think that they have the right to say no. By asking someone for consent, you immediately infer that they have the right to say no. So, if they are happy in their ignorance, I confess I would use that to my advantage.'

One incident was observed in which consent was refused; however, its particular characteristics reinforce the general point. Two detectives wanted to search rooms in a hostel for property which, they had been informed, was being kept there after a burglary. The warden refused to allow them to search: she was experienced and confident in dealing with the police, and knew that they had no power to do so. The senior detective accepted her refusal. However, the junior tried, unsuccessfully, to slip away from the warden while she was talking to the senior officer. He was angry at the loss of face suffered when the warden insisted that he did not attempt to enter and search rooms. He told the researcher that he would have searched irrespective of the warden's consent if the senior officer (whom he thought too cautious) had not been there.

Like stop/searches, search of premises is resistant to legal regulation because of its processual, fluid nature. Consent and power are often not clearly distinct. Officers will typically attempt to get consent even when a power is available to them, for example, if they have obtained a warrant. Indeed, ninety-five per cent of officers in our interview sample said they would do this. They prefer to search 'by consent' because it makes dealing with householders easier. This is illustrated by one detective's comments:

'The thing is, particularly in the CID, we tend to deal with the same people all the time, and if you knock on somebody's door and say, 'Under section so-and-so of the Police Act we're coming in to search, like it or not', you antagonize them, and if you are back there a few weeks later, you are going to pay for that. That is why I, and most CID lads try and do it with an air of consent and try and do it friendly. You still get your search done but it's much easier if everybody gets on, isn't it?

This reference to an 'air of consent' suggests that what is at issue here is civility rather than consent. As in the case of stop/search, an officer's 'request' is not really a question, but rather an easing tactic, a way of handling the situation in a non-conflictual manner.

Furthermore, decisions and requests to search are often not distinct incidents to which legal regulation can more appropriately be applied. Officers are often in premises for various reasons (such as talking to or taking statements from parents, suspects or witnesses) before the issue of search arises. They may then ask for a 'look around' before they go. Just as they differentiate types of stop/search, so officers typically distinguish 'a quick look around' from a full house search. The former would usually not be recorded: only the latter is considered to need either written consent or legal authority. The result was that consent searches amounted to only fifteen per cent of those recorded: our observations and interviews made clear that this was a substantial under-representation.

When they felt that recording was necessary, many officers in our research force had developed a simple method of coping with the requirement that consents should be obtained in writing. Entry would be gained in the traditional way, beginning with a 'request' such as: 'We'll just have a quick look around, OK?' The consent would only be put in writing at the *end* of the search. Typically, this involved officers asking householders to 'sign for the search' in the officer's notebook immediately before they *left* the premises. The householder usually had little appreciation of what she or he was signing. Legal requirements were fulfilled but in a way which was clearly against the intentions of Parliament and which effectively emptied them of usefulness.

The revision of Code B counters this tactic by clearly requiring [para 4.1] that 'the consent must, if practicable, be given in writing before the search takes place.' In a section which illustrates some of the problems of terminology in the area, it goes on to provide [para 4.3] that an 'officer cannot enter and search premises or continue to search premises under 4.1 above' [that is, by consent] 'if the consent has been given under duress or is subsequently withdrawn before the search is completed'. More importantly, the code includes a new general requirement that officers must provide occupiers of premises (normally before the search begins) with a standard notice stating, among other things, whether the search is by consent or under a power, and summarizing powers of search and occupiers' rights. Welcome as this provision may be, it seems unlikely that police officers will stand waiting at the front door while the householder reads the notice provided.

It has been a basic rule for centuries that the police may not ransack a person's home looking generally for evidence against him. Any lawful entry upon premises for the purposes of a search must always be for a specified reason and the search must be consistent with that reason.

The common-law rule against 'general warrants' was laid down in *Entick v Carrington* (1765) 2 Wils 275. PACE now provides that 'a search under warrant may only be a search to the extent required for the purpose for which the warrant was issued' (s 16(8)). This would obviously make unlawful a search for stolen refrigerators under the floor-boards. But if the search was for drugs, such a search would presumably be permitted. The same section also states that entry and search must be at a reasonable time of day 'unless it appears to the constable executing it that there are grounds for suspecting that the purpose of a search may be frustrated on an entry at a reasonable hour' (s 16(4)). Code B adds that a search under warrant may not continue once the things specified in the warrant have been found or the officer in charge is satisfied that they are not there (para 5.9).

(e) Bugging by MI5 and the police

The Security Service, known as MI5, has traditionally been used in response to national security issues such as espionage and terrorism. Because of the nature of their work they have been allowed to operate with a minimum of the normal controls that apply to the police. (For an insider's account of their activities see the celebrated best-seller, *Spycatcher, 1987,* the memoirs of MI5 officer Peter Wright.)

Entry on premises by MI5 is covered by the Security Service Act 1989, s 3(1) which provided: 'No entry on or interference with property shall be unlawful if it is authorised by a warrant issued by the Secretary of State'. The warrants in question are mainly to authorise entry for the purpose of bugging.

The ordinary police have no statutory power to enter premises for the purpose of bugging. Instead the position is governed by Guidelines issued by the Home Secretary in 1984. Under the Guidelines a chief constable or assistant chief constable can authorise 'encroachment on privacy' through the use of surveillance devices. Though not formally published, the Guidelines were cited extensively by the Lord Chief Justice, Lord Taylor giving the judgment of the Court of Appeal in *R v Khan* [1994] 4 All ER 426 at pp 430–31, a case that arose from the placing of a bug on the exterior wall of a house which enabled the police to tape record a conversation inside the house about drug smuggling.

As a result of the end of the Cold War, MI5 has been seeking new roles–and employment for its staff of about 2,000. In 1996 the Government introduced the Security Service Bill to amend the Security Service Act 1989 by extending MI5's functions to 'act in support of the prevention and detection of serious crime'. The move alarmed not merely civil libertarians but the police who had not been consulted. Behind-the-scenes lobbying by the police and others persuaded the Government to amend the Bill at the start of its Committee stage in the House of Commons. The new function for MI5 of the prevention and detection of serious crime was amended to be only if 'in support of the activities of police forces and other law enforcement agencies'. The Home Office Minister Mr David Maclean during the Committee Stage emphasised the significance of the word 'activities'.

If the amendment merely said 'in support of the police' it would not achieve the desired effect ... To use the words 'in support of the police' would not require the active involvement of the police. It could mean support for their general functions, which include the prevention and detection of crime... Just about anything done to prevent crime could be interpreted as general support for the police. By contrast, tying the service to support 'for the activities of' the police and other law enforcement agencies indicates that some active involvement of the police is required, in terms of planning, strategic direction or practical involvement on the ground. The wording also mirrors the arrangements provision in clause 1(2), which emphasises that whenever the Security Service gets involved under its new function it will be tied to and coordinated with the law enforcement agencies that it is supporting. [House of Commons, Standing Committee A, 30 January 1996, col 28].

In answer to a question, the Minister said that 'of course, in the normal course of coordination, the chief constable will know' of the involvement of the Security Service (*op cit,* col 29).

The power to get an entry to premises warrant from the Home Secretary in regard to property in the UK could theoretically be exercised in relation to a wide range of offences. The 1996 Bill defines these as conduct which 'involves the use of violence, results in substantial financial gain or is conduct by a large number of persons in pursuit of a common purpose' or the offence is one for which someone over 21 with no previous convictions could expect to get a term of three years' imprisonment or more. This definition (taken from the Interception of Communications Act 1985) is a very broad one, but Mr David Maclean assured the House of Commons that the Security Service would only be used against what the ordinary citizen would understand to be organised and serious crime. (House of Commons, Standing Committee A, 1 February 1996, col 44.)

The Minister also stated that the Government intended to introduce legislation to regulate the position regarding police surveillance and bugging operations. He acknowledged that it was not satisfactory that the Security Service should be subject to the requirement of getting a warrant for a bugging operation from the Home Secretary whilst the police could authorise it themselves. (*op cit,* col 78). (See P Leach, 'The Security Service Bill', *New Law Journal*, 16 February 1996, p 224.)

(f) Seizure of evidence

The law of seizure is closely related to, but is nevertheless separate from, the law of search. Traditionally, the common law required that search be by warrant and that the warrant be particular and faithfully followed. Thus in *Entick v Carrington* (1765) 2 Wils 275 it was held that the police could not ransack a man's house on a general warrant looking for evidence of a crime. In *Price v Messenger* (1800) 2 Bos & P 158, it was said that a constable who finds goods whilst searching under a warrant, which are not covered by the warrant, commits a trespass by seizing them.

However, the common law on this crucial topic had considerably modified this strict rule. See *Elias v Pasmore* [1934] 2 KB 164; *Chic Fashions (West Wales) Ltd v Jones* [1968] 2 QB 299; *Ghani v Jones* [1969] 3 All ER 1700; *Garfinkel v Metropolitan Police Comr* [1972] Crim LR 44; *Frank Truman Export Ltd v Metropolitan Police Comr* [1977] 3 All ER 431. See also *R v Waterfield, R v Lynn* [1964] 1 QB 164; *Jeffrey v Black* [1978] 1 All ER 555; and *McLorie v Oxford* [1982] QB 1290.

The Philips Royal Commission's approach and PACE

The Philips Royal Commission dealt with the problem posed by seizure of evidence not covered by the search warrant:

Restrictions upon seizure for evidential and other purposes
   3.48. Restriction on seizure of goods provides another method of controlling the execution of warrants. We do not think it desirable to limit seizure only to prohibited goods or to the evidence specified in the warrant. It defies common sense to expect the police not to seize such items incidentally found during the course of a search. At the same time the risk that premises may be ransacked as soon as a warrant is granted in respect of any offence must be minimised. The present law seems to us to be uncertain and of little help in this respect.
   3.49 We wish to preclude a specific warrant being used to legitimise general searches. Accordingly when the police have lawful authority to enter premises upon one of the warrants proposed in paragraphs 3.39 and 3.42, they should be entitled to seize the items specified in that warrant and any other prohibited goods or evidence of a grave offence (that is items for

which they could have obtained a warrant) which they find incidentally in the course of a lawful search, that is one conducted in accordance with the terms of the warrant and in the manner appropriate to the items being searched for. The procedure for giving a receipt should apply to such additional material that is seized and the receipt should specify the suspected offence in respect of which the material has been seized. Items seized otherwise than in this way may not be used in evidence. We appreciate that the obligatory exclusion of evidence at trial may appear an inflexible restriction, but the right of members of the public to be free from general searches must be respected.

However, the Government did not wholly accept the Royal Commission's recommendations in this regard. Section 19 of the Police and Criminal Evidence Act 1984 gives the police power to seize articles where a search is carried out lawfully either with the consent of the occupier or under any statutory power. The article may be seized if the officer reasonably believes that it is evidence in relation to an offence which he is investigating *or any other offence* or that it has been obtained in consequence of the commission of an offence and that it is necessary to seize it in order to prevent its concealment, loss or destruction. The only articles exempted are those covered by legal professional privilege (s 19(6), pp 174–75 above). It is immaterial whether an arrest has or has not taken place and equally whether the occupier is suspected of any involvement in criminal activity. An article may be held for use as evidence at the trial, for forensic examination or, where it appears to be stolen, for restoration to its lawful owner (s 22(2)). If requested by the occupier or the person having possession of the article, the police must give that person a record of what was seized (s 21(1)) or a photocopy or photographs of items seized (s 21(3)). Alternatively, the officer should be prepared to grant access, under supervision, to the items in question (s 21(3)). But neither photographs, nor photocopies nor access need be granted if 'the officer in charge of the investigation has reasonable grounds for believing that to do so would prejudice the investigation' (s 21(8)).

Note–the inadmissibility of evidence illegally obtained

The problem dealt with here arises again below on the admissibility of evidence–see Chapter 4 below. The House of Lords held in *R v Sang* [1980] AC 402 (see p 356 below) that the courts did not have any general discretion to exclude illegally obtained evidence. Prior to *Sang* it was generally accepted that the courts did have such a discretion–though it was very rarely exercised. But now under the Police and Criminal Evidence Act 1984, s 78, the court does have a general power to exclude improperly obtained evidence–see p 358 below.

(g) The power to freeze the suspect's assets

A new development in the law in recent years has been the power to freeze assets of a defendant prior to a trial. It is similar to developments in civil procedure, especially of Mareva injunctions (p 65 above).

The first step was taken in *West Mercia Constabulary v Wagener* [1981] 3 All ER 378, where the police used civil process to seize and preserve property of a suspect. The High Court judge granted the police an injunction to restrain the alleged proceeds of fraud from being withdrawn from a bank account. The court said that since magistrates could not issue a search warrant to deal with proceeds of an alleged crime held in a bank account, the High Court would fill the gap. The new power was applied by the Court of Appeal in *Chief Constable of Kent v V* [1982] 3 All ER 36, even though the alleged proceeds of crime had been mingled with the defendant's own moneys. But in *Chief Constable of Hampshire v A Ltd* [1984] 2 All ER 385, the mingling of the alleged proceeds of crime with other moneys proved fatal to the police request for the same injunction. The Court of Appeal distinguished the earlier decision. In that case there was one victim of fraud and the fraud was easily identifiable. In the Hampshire case there were large numbers of transactions and much of the money in the relevant accounts would not be the result of fraud. The Court of Appeal in the Hampshire case seemed concerned to restrict the ambit of the new doctrine to cases where it could be shown that they were the proceeds of crime and could be identified. See similarly *Chief Constable of Leicestershire v M* [1988] 3 All ER 1015, *per* Hoffmann J holding that the *proceeds* of crime could not be the subject of an interlocutory injunction.

But the common-law power to freeze the defendant's assets was supplemented by the Drug Trafficking Offences Act 1986. The basic scheme of the 1986 Act was to give the court powers to freeze property or assets, whether in the hands of a defendant or a third party, which might subsequently be needed to satisfy the confiscation order for which the Act made provision. (Under the 1986 Act the court is required to make a confiscation order on every person convicted of a drug-trafficking offence who has received any payment or reward in connection with drug trafficking at any time. The requirement is mandatory. The confiscation order is in addition to any sentence including a fine. The amount is the amount assessed by the court to be the full value of the offender's drug-trafficking activities. For this purpose the court can assume that, unless the contrary is shown, all the offender's assets plus any assets he has had in the previous six years, represent the proceeds of drug trafficking.) The similar powers under Part VI of the Criminal Justice Act 1988, by contrast, apply only to offences where the court is satisfied that the proceeds of the crime were more than £10,000.

The power to confiscate the proceeds of crime was hugely expanded by the Proceeds of Crime Act 1995 which is not restricted to offences involving more than £10,000. The Act provides extraordinary ancillary civil powers which permit the High Court to make a restraint order preventing any dealing with the defendant's assets. Such an order is similar to a Mareva injunction, and the prosecutor is given priority over unsecured creditors. The High Court can make disclosure orders requiring disclosure by affidavit of the nature and extent of assets. (See *Re O* [1991] 1 All ER 330.) It can also make receivership orders to manage assets or to realise them to enforce payment of a confiscation order made by the crown court. (See K Talbot, 'The Proceeds of Crime Act 1995', *New Law Journal*, 15 December 1995, p 1857.)

5. THE PROSECUTION PROCESS

(a) Who prosecutes?

Until 1986, England was one of the few countries in the world which left a major prosecution function to the police. In most countries the police start criminal proceedings but they are then continued (or not) by some form of public prosecution service such as the district attorney in the United States, the procurator fiscal in Scotland, or the procureur in France.

In England, until 1986, the police themselves prosecuted in a great number of cases tried in the magistrates' courts, though they would often use lawyers. In cases dealt with at the higher level, the police, like solicitors, have never had a right of audience and must therefore instruct both solicitors and barristers.

From 1986 onwards, under the Prosecution of Offences Act 1985, the police have no longer had any role in continuing prosecutions beyond the stage of charge. Once a suspect has been charged the papers go to the Crown Prosecution Service (CPS), which decides whether to proceed, and, if so, on what charges. It is then the CPS which carries the prosecution forward. The change represented a revolution in the actual practice of prosecutions, especially in magistrates' courts.

At the time when the Philips Royal Commission examined the problem, there were basically five separate forms of prosecution:

(1) The police

By far the largest number were brought by the police. There are 43 police forces in England and Wales. Each had its own prosecution policy. Most but not all forces had prosecuting solicitors' departments; eleven used firms of solicitors in private practice.

(2) The law officers

The Attorney-General (assisted by the Solicitor-General) had (and has) two main functions in respect of prosecutions. First, he possessed the power to enter a *nolle prosequi* in cases tried on indictment, which had the effect of stopping the proceedings. Secondly, he could (and still can) give or refuse his permission (known as *fiat*) in the considerable number of cases where by statute his consent was required for a prosecution.

(3) The Director of Public Prosecutions

The DPP had a statutory duty to prosecute in any case punishable by death (now obsolete), in cases brought to him by government departments where he thought he should prosecute, and in 'any other case which appears to him to be of importance or difficulty or which for any other reason requires his intervention' (Prosecution of Offences Regulations 1946, reg 1). He also advised the police and government departments as to whether they should prosecute. In addition, there are some 60 statutes which specify that no prosecution can be started without the consent of the DPP. (There are some 40 statutes that require the consent instead of the Attorney-General.) The DPP prosecuted in about 2,000 cases a year. (Note: he also had (and has) the power to intervene to stop a prosecution–see *Raymond v A-G* [1982] QB 839. The power applied to summary as well as to indictable offences. It operated through taking over the case and then offering no evidence. See JK Bentil, 'Private Criminal Proceedings and the Director of Public Prosecutions', *Solicitors' Journal*, 5 August 1983, p 516.)

(4) Public bodies

Many prosecutions were (and are) conducted by government departments, nationalized industries, local authorities and other statutory bodies. A study done for the Philips Royal Commission on Criminal Procedure showed that they amounted to something like one-quarter of all prosecutions. Prosecutions were conducted, in order of frequency, by: the Post Office (mainly for television-licence offences); the British Transport Police (eg for non-payment of fares); the Department of the Environment in relation to vehicle excise licences; the Department of Social Security (for social security frauds); HM Customs and Excise; and Regional Traffic Commissioners, for offences connected with the use of heavy lorries. Other public bodies with some prosecution functions included the Health and Safety at Work Inspectorate, Water Authorities, the Inland Revenue, Department of Trade, and Ministry of Agriculture. (See KW Lidstone, R Hogg and F Sutcliffe, 'Prosecutions by Private Individuals and Non-Police Agencies', *Royal Commission on Criminal Procedure, Research Study No 10*, 1980, Table 2.3, p 15.)

(5) Private prosecutions

A private person could bring a prosecution even though he had no direct interest in the matter. He had, however, to persuade a magistrate to issue a summons which would be refused if it appeared to be a vexatious or improper proceeding. He would also normally have to bear his own costs and if the prosecution failed he might in addition have to pay something in respect of the costs of the defence. As has been seen, the DPP had the right to take over a private prosecution and the Attorney-General had the power to stop one by entering a *nolle prosequi*. Private prosecutions were very rare, save for two types of case–shoplifting, where the store was often left to bring its own prosecution, and common assault, where, for instance, wives quite frequently brought prosecutions against husbands. There are also private bodies such as the NSPCC or the RSPCA which bring prosecutions. Most of the evidence to the Philips Royal Commission urged that the right of private prosecution be preserved.

A study done for the Philips Royal Commission showed that the proportion of defendants prosecuted by private individuals was 2.4 per cent (Lidstone, Hogg and Sutcliffe, *op cit*, Table 2.13, p 23). The great majority of these were for common assault. In some areas the police had a policy of not prosecuting in shoplifting cases and all prosecutions for this offence were brought by retail stores. The Commissioner of the Metropolitan Police said in his evidence to the Royal Commission that it was his policy 'to encourage supermarkets and other large stores to undertake their own prosecutions and most are prepared to do so' (Part II, para 15.15, p 192). On private prosecutions see further pp 207–08 below.

(b) Who should prosecute?

The JUSTICE Report

The whole debate on this issue was begun in 1970 by JUSTICE, the prestigious British Section of the International Commission of Jurists, in a report which argued that the police role in prosecutions should be restricted to very minor cases or should be eliminated altogether (*The Prosecution Process in England and Wales*, 1970). The main thrust of the JUSTICE report was that even the honest, conscientious police officer may become psychologically committed to successful prosecution. 'He wants to prosecute and he wants to win.' He is therefore more likely to continue with a prosecution where the evidence may be weak. Also the police were not well suited to evaluate the public-policy aspects of the discretion not to prosecute. The police should not both collect the evidence and conduct the proceedings.

The Committee concluded:

9. ... that there is substance in the criticism set out in the previous section of this Report, and that the present system fails to match up to what we regard as the principles and practice which ought to regulate a matter of such importance. In particular, we think that two basic points can legitimately be made against the existing procedure:

(*a*) It confuses two quite distinct and disparate functions and responsibilities, namely the vigorous investigation of crime; and the cool, careful objective assessment of the whole of the evidence and probabilities needed for a correct decision as to whether a prosecution should be started or, if started, continued.

(*b*) It offends against the principle that the prosecution should be–and should be plainly seen to be–independent, impartial and fair: concerned only with the pursuit of truth and not with winning or losing. This is of cardinal importance in an accusatorial system. ...

The Committee recommended the introduction of the Scottish system where the decision to prosecute in all but very minor cases is taken by prosecutors, known as procurators fiscal, under the Lord Advocate who are wholly independent of the police. The police report all cases to the procurators fiscal, who decide whether a prosecution is warranted.

Evidence to the Philips Royal Commission

The problem was specifically referred to the Royal Commission on Criminal Procedure which was set up in 1978. The evidence of police organizations, predictably, was against the notion of any transfer of power in regard to prosecutions to any other agency. It might have been expected that the Director of Public Prosecutions would argue for implementation of the JUSTICE scheme with himself as the centre of the new system of public prosecution. This proved not to be the case. On the whole he thought there was little real evidence of any abuse or criticism of the present system. Moreover, insofar as there were criticisms, it was by no means certain that the problems would be cured by a national public prosecution system. ('Even a system dealing with all cases would not eliminate human error or laziness and with it unsatisfactory prosecutions' (para 247).)

He thought that his own role should continue to be confined to the small range of important and especially difficult cases. He did not therefore favour any significant change from the present position.

The Philips Royal Commission's Report

The Commission suggested that the prosecutor should be accountable for his policies and for his efficiency, but not for decisions to prosecute or not to prosecute in individual cases. Under the present arrangement the lack of any systematic basis for the funding and supervision of prosecuting solicitors' departments meant that there was no proper accountability in regard to efficiency. Equally, accountability in regard to policies was insufficient. At a national level the lack of power in the DPP to issue general advice on prosecution policy limited his role in securing consistency to those cases for which he was responsible. At the local level few police authorities interested themselves in the chief constable's exercise of his prosecutorial discretion.

On efficiency, the Commission thought the existing arrangements left much to be desired:

Not all forces have prosecuting solicitors' departments. In those that do, the status, size and function of the departments differ widely. Some report to the county council, some to the police authority; some control their budgets and staffing, others do not; funding arrangements differ; some prosecute all cases in magistrates' courts, others only a proportion; a few advise the police on the prosecution decisions in all cases, others do so rarely. As the Prosecuting Solicitors' Society put it in their evidence: 'There are no national organisational arrangements and in the sense in which the word is generally understood, there is no system. The dissimilarity in arrangements from area to area does not in general result from different needs or conditions but from the different approaches of county councils, their chief executives and from the different personalities of chief constables and county prosecuting solicitors' [para 6.63].

The Philips Royal Commission's proposals

The Philips Royal Commission proposed a new system based on the following features:
The initial decision to charge a suspect should continue to be taken by the police. Thereafter all decisions would be taken by a prosecution agency, including any decision to alter or drop the charges. Each area would have a prosecuting solicitors' department presided over by a Crown Prosecutor of equal status to the chief constable and answerable to the same authority. Each police authority area should have a new committee to be known as the Police and Prosecution Authority, to which the crown prosecutor and the chief constable would both be accountable. The Minister responsible for the prosecution system should be either the Home Secretary or the Attorney-General.

Private prosecutions should continue but with different rules. If a private citizen wished to bring a prosecution, he should have to apply to the crown prosecutor in the first instance. If the prosecutor agreed that the case should be brought, he should take it himself. If not, the citizen should have the right to ask the magistrates for leave to commence the proceedings. But the crown prosecutor should be represented at the application before the magistrates. If leave was given, this should automatically carry a right to have all reasonable costs borne out of central funds. Any balance would have to be paid by the private prosecutor.

The Government's reaction

The Government rejected the Royal Commission's view that the new prosecution system would be based on local committees. (For the history see the 6th edition of this work, p 220.) The Government proposed that there should be a single prosecution service, controlled and directed by the DPP. The investigation of criminal offences would remain with the police and they would continue to lay the initial charges but thereafter the responsibility for all prosecution decisions (including the dropping or alteration of charges) would be that of the prosecution service. The Government said it believed 'that the establishment of an independent prosecution service on this basis would promote consistency and fairness; would reduce the proportion of cases pursued despite lack of sufficient evidence; would improve the preparation and presentation of cases in court; would provide an attractive career structure; and would lead to greater efficiency and better accountability for the use of resources' (White Paper, *An Independent Prosecution Service for England and Wales*, Cmnd 9074, 1983 para 6).

The Government stated that no change would be made in regard to the rules regarding private prosecutions. (See further pp 207–08 below.)

(c) Establishment of the Crown Prosecution Service (CPS)

The Crown Prosecution Act 1985 established the Crown Prosecution Service (CPS) as a national prosecution service for the whole of England and Wales under the general direction of the Director of Public Prosecutions (DPP).

The country was originally divided into areas–29 in England and 2 in Wales–with each area headed by a chief crown prosecutor, responsible to the DPP for the operation of his area. In 1993 this structure was altered. The 31 areas were amalgamated into 13 larger areas, including one for the whole of London.

The function of the CPS is to conduct all criminal cases against both adults and juveniles (apart from minor motoring offences which have been excluded from the system) that are instituted by or on behalf of the police.

It is also given a power in s 23 to discontinue proceedings which is used very often (see further below). This is in addition to the power not to start proceedings where charges have been laid. In summary cases before the court has heard any evidence, and in proceedings in the crown court before it or the magistrates' court has heard any evidence, the proceedings can be stopped by notice to the court with reasons. They can also be stopped where someone has been arrested without a warrant before the court has been informed of the charge by notice to the suspect.

The service does not, however, have its own investigation machinery or facilities. It relies for that role on the police. Unlike the procurator fiscal in Scotland, the CPS cannot direct the police to carry out an investigation or further investigations. It can only request. The Runciman Royal Commission considered whether the CPS should be given such a power but by a majority of 10 to 1 decided against it. Any dispute between the CPS and the police as to such a question should, it thought, be resolvable between the two agencies, if necessary with the help of the Chief Inspector of Constabulary (Report, p 74, para 26).

A rocky start

The CPS started operation in 1986. At the outset it was plagued by desperate problems caused by insufficient funds and insufficient manpower. There were countless media stories about the serious problems faced by the service due to these factors. In October 1986 the service was several hundred lawyers short of its proper complement. In a written parliamentary answer on 11 March 1987 the Attorney-General said that there was a shortfall at the time of 22 per cent. In Inner London it was close to 50 per cent.

But in the course of time the staffing problem has been solved. The manpower situation of the CPS is affected by employment prospects in private practice. When private practice is booming, the CPS finds it difficult to get enough recruits. When the economic situation for the profession has been more difficult, as has been the case in recent years, the CPS finds no lack of good quality entrants. (In 1994, there were 1,300 applications for 20 legal trainee posts.)

Partly because of the shortfall, use has always had to be made of 'agents'–barristers and solicitors in private practice working on an ad hoc, fee-for-case basis with little possibility of supervision and at great cost. The annual report for 1990–1 stated that the use of agents ranged from a high of 38 per cent in the first quarter of the year to a low of 30 per cent in the last. Continuing efforts are made to reduce reliance on private practitioners. The 1993–94 annual report stated (p 34) that the proportion of half-day magistrates' court sessions done by private practitioners fell to 16 per cent compared with 20 per cent in the previous year. In 1994–95 the percentage was down to 13 per cent.

In the early years of the service there were many media stories of muddle and confusion, of lost files, delays and cases bungled. There is general agreement that operational efficiency of the service has greatly increased. Such stories are now rare. But the CPS continues to be the butt of criticism, often coming from the police because of decisions to discontinue cases, on which see further below (pp 201–04).

There has also been a continuing problem of staff morale–due largely to issues of management. A survey in November 1993 by the First Division Association (FDA) the union which represents three-quarters of CPS lawyers, found that their morale was at an all-time low and that the majority had no confidence in the senior management. A poll of the entire membership of the union in November 1995 found the lowest morale and highest dissatisfaction was in the CPS section. Members complained that management was poor and that government-imposed efficiency and economy drives had put intolerable pressures on them. Disaffection in this latest survey was especially pronounced among senior staff. (See D Bindman, 'Crown Jewels', *Law Society's Gazette*, 7 February 1996, p 22).

Statements on the subject from the Director of Public Prosecutions are invariably upbeat and cheerful. (For instance, she dismissed the results of both FDA surveys as 'unrepresentative'.) For a caustic assessment of the position see however Neil Addison, 'What's Wrong with the CPS?', *Counsel*, January/February 1995, p 14. (Mr Addison, a barrister, had been sacked by the CPS after eight years' service for writing an article for *The Times* about rights of audience for CPS lawyers without permission.) In the Bar's journal *Counsel* he said (p 14) that after a disastrous start 'things had settled down somewhat and between 1989 and 1992, the CPS improved and became more accepted by police, lawyers and the courts–with improving morale and pride. Since 1992, however, the CPS has deteriorated rapidly into an increasingly centralised bureaucratic and demoralised organisation, governed by an inefficient, autocratic and self-obsessed headquarters ...'.

He had several major points of criticism: One was the restructuring which reduced 31 areas to 13 which made it impossible for Chief Crown Prosecutors to forge good relations with their local Chief Constables because the areas were not coterminous. (One covered five police forces.) The reorganisation, he said, had also helped to destroy the staff's feeling of local involvement and local management. Staff were disillusioned with the new system of 'team working'. At first they were told that this was designed to check on the viability of the idea. However, he wrote, 'it has become obvious that team-working did not work at all: the pilot branches were in a shambles, while CPS HQ staff steadfastly ignored local management warnings'. Dan Bindman (op cit, above), said that 'team working', the most recent change in the name of efficiency had provoked particular discontent among prosecutors. 'This involves working together in "units", usually in an open plan office and side by side with case workers and administrative staff. Privacy and quiet contemplation were not possible.'[11] For a stout reply to Neil Addison see C Metherell, 'What's Right with the CPS', *Counsel*, March/April 1995, p 24 written by a Branch Crown Prosecutor.

(d) The police have a wide discretion

A vital question is how is the decision to prosecute taken, on what criteria, subject to what principles and controls? The decision to prosecute is taken initially by the police and is then subjected to review by the CPS.

Many aspects of the great scope of police discretion have already emerged in this chapter–in relation to questioning of suspects and their treatment, search and seizure, detention and arrest. But the police also have a major field of discretion in deciding whether to prosecute–whether to ignore the conduct, to caution or to charge and, if to charge, then for what.

A former police officer turned journalist described once how he had walked from Waterloo Station to Holborn in order to see how many criminal offences he could identify:

CR Rolph, 'Police Discretion', *New Statesman*, 2 February 1969

I got the following bag:

A girl feeding the pigeons inside Waterloo Station.
Two cars with expired Excise Licences
Three cars with none at all.
Twenty-three cars parked wholly or partly on the footway.
One lorry with its lowered tailboard hiding the rear number plate while in motion.
A furniture van with its rear number chalked on the back.
One flag-day girl shaking a collecting box in people's faces.
One boy throwing a half-eaten egg sandwich into the roadway.
Three shop awnings that you had to duck under.
A cycling window cleaner carrying a ladder on his shoulders.
And a painter on a window-sill wearing no means of preventing a fall.

I would say it was a typical lot. And among the things too numerous to count were cars bearing advertising 'stickers', vehicles waiting on double yellow lines, and disembarking bus passengers throwing their tickets away.

I've known policemen who would have hated to let any of these escape. They would all have been seen as personal affronts. But even a policeman like that couldn't have coped with

11 *Ibid.*

more than one of them. If he chose the cycling man with the ladder, who was actually the most dangerous, all the rest would have got away. So perhaps he would have chosen the three shop blinds, on the ground that they might have knocked his helmet off (they ought to be 8ft 6in from the ground).

But it has to be faced that the great majority of policemen would have chosen none of them. Which in itself would have been a choice. And the chief constable's 'discretion' is merely the same choice writ large, with the difference that chief constables, who have no time to go around looking for car licences, number plates, flag-day offences, litter bugs, men on window-sills, don't exercise their choice until an offence is actually reported and the papers come before them.

A more systematic exploration of the discretionary element in policing was part of a study of policing conducted in the late 1960s by John Lambert. What he wrote then is as relevant today:

John Lambert, 'The Police Can Choose', *New Society*, 18 September 1969

The policeman is not, and never has been, simply a 'law-enforcement officer'. He has *discretion*, in almost all circumstances except catching a murderer actually on the job, about whom he will arrest, investigate or harass, and whom he won't. In this sense, the problem is that of 'normal' policing, because in this exercise of discretion, which is central to all his work, the policeman's own private view of the world comes into play: his opinion, as a citizen, of other citizens; his reaction, as a member of one class or race, towards other classes or races.

The part that discretion plays, necessarily, in British police work is seldom acknowledged publicly. The legal philosophy of a democratic society sees police activities as potentially threatening to individual liberty. So the police, in enforcing the law, are themselves bound by numerous regulations. The theory is that laws apply to all men and the police must enforce the law always, everywhere equally.

Yet *full* enforcement is not possible. Law-breaking is so common that to investigate every infringement, to prosecute every known offender, would require police forces of a size, and involve expenditures on a scale, that would be impracticable and intolerable. So small police forces with small budgets have to enforce laws selectively. Both as an organization and as individuals, the police have considerable choice about how to organize, which crimes and criminals to prosecute, how to allocate what number of men to different law enforcements tasks, and so on. It's almost a question of artistry, and certainly it's craftsmanship ...

Crime occurs unevenly in different neighbourhoods of towns and cities. This puts more policemen in some areas than others, with different opportunities to discover offences and to find offenders to process as clients. Opportunities abound for legalistic policemen to cram police cells with the drunk and disorderly and police offices with papers relating to motoring offences. In practice, many are seen but few are processed. How the drunk or the motorist reacts to the policeman's intervention determines the outcome.

What matters is whether the client shows deference or respect to the policeman. And which of these is shown depends very much on a two-way perception of status, rank, position and power between policeman and client. Thus law enforcement depends quite precisely on relations between police and public. The legal role of the police is defined by the perceptions of policemen and their ability to manage relationships.

Police work comprises a great variety of business, particularly when making the sort of contacts that go into the traditional peacekeeping job.

In his day-to-day duties the uniformed policeman meets many people who seek some service from him in a wide variety of situations. Seldom is the person a suspect: the policeman is more advisory than authoritarian. The uniformed policeman usually meets a complainant or a victim, not a suspect or an offender. And other social duties–diverting traffic, crowd control, helping pedestrians, advising on crime prevention, road-safety liaison with schools, conveying messages from hospitals and for other bodies, helping fire departments during alarm calls: such tasks, arising from the patrolling presence of the uniformed officer, require the police to engage in fairly straightforward 'helping' relationships.

But a more ambiguous situation confronts the uniformed officer who is summoned to solve a dispute between families, neighbours, landlords and tenants, pub landlords and customers, café owners and customers. One party in the dispute often makes a demand for the backing of authority: the story is seldom clear-cut: both parties can justify a bid for police support. An appeal to the law is frequently unhelpful. The police are expected to find a way to mediate between the disputants.

Custom and tradition suggest a number of techniques. A very common one is a plain denial of competence–'This is not a police matter'–followed by a plea for calm and reason, sometimes supported by a warning about breaching the peace. The police task is to get the disputants to behave reasonably. The presence of an authoritarian stranger, a few words of advice, a warning, some reassurance, are all the sanctions possible. The policeman's ultimate authority, his power of arrest, is here a threat rather than reality. Even if an arrest for drunkenness or disorder in a public place could be made, the policeman will often ask the man to come outside 'for a word'. Anything else would be a failure of 'reasonableness'.

A policeman, to be successful, must learn how to 'handle people'. He has to sum up a person very quickly, and fix on what is a suitable manner for that situation. He must try and judge the person's response, and mould his manner to achieve his purpose. At its simplest, this means that the policeman cannot begin to treat everyone the same. Depending on his perception of someone's class status, occupation, education or bearing, the policeman fits him into a stereotype and behaves accordingly.

In his dealings with black citizens in poor neighbourhoods, however, the stereotypes that a policeman uses are especially unhelpful for creating the sort of relationship he needs and expects. Not surprisingly, the white policeman does not automatically win from black immigrants the 'respect' he values, and indeed needs, in 'normal' transactions. Nothing in his upbringing or experience has taught him to handle a relationship with someone who denies him the traditional and customary British police role. He falls back on his own attitudes as a citizen–derogatory, prejudiced, perhaps racist.

The various techniques of bonhomie or bombast, and the stylized deference that the police adopt towards 'better-class' whites, are all right for their traditional clientele, but they don't work in this new situation. Moreover, the black man's experience of the police in his homeland may lead him to fear actual police violence or hostility. So both parties to the relationship share expectations of uncertainty and unpredictability. Hostility is inevitable.

Policemen themselves rate some kinds of work above others. The most obvious division is the most significant–the position of the CID and its influence on the work of the uniformed patrolmen.

Few reported crimes are amenable to much detective work. All the CID can do is to hold on to cases in the hope that someone caught red-handed in a crime will admit his part in a series of other offences which can then be taken into consideration by the court. Much of the recorded clear-up rate comes from talkative officers rather than from the skills of detectives. Routine CID work is highly administrative; it is the effective processing of offenders, caught by uniformed patrolmen, in a way that will reveal a maximum number of offences. The crime rate is slightly inflated by this. Crimes that were never reported by a complainant are admitted by offenders; one offence can reveal others.

Of course, there are the highly skilled organized and technically complex crime-squad investigations of major crimes. But in general local CID men have an impossible task, with huge caseloads of unsolvable crimes. Yet their work provides the only measure of success the police use–the clear-up rate.

The whole business of policing suffers by this distortion. The need to have a good clear-up rate makes the CID depend on effective criminal-catching operations. The uniformed patrolman services the CID with suspects, this is what constitutes 'good' police work. A policeman knows that his success within the force will depend on his record of 'good' arrests, ie arrests of persons who contribute to a good clear-up rate. So uniformed police tend not to attach much value to many of the advising/helping tasks they are asked to perform. In the main, they are on the lookout for suspects. This is not a detective function so much as a search for people who can be defined as offenders, who merit police attention.

Anyone definable as a 'suspect' will be approached in a certain way to see if the definition will stick. The police discriminate against those who look guilty. And police organization and culture provide a set of definitions of those who look guilty. Thus, by definition, anyone who has been 'in trouble' before is scrutinized continually, and liable to be brought in or approached for questioning. The police discriminate against those known to have been guilty in the past. 'Problem areas' are also useful. Opportunities for offender-labelling abound; and problem areas are often coloured areas.

The prosecution case is a construct'

A book published in 1991 based on a survey of over 1,000 cases argued that discretion runs through, and indeed dominates, every aspect of the prosecution case. Michael McConville, Andrew Sanders and Roger Leng in *The Case for the Prosecution* (Routledge, 1991) make a powerful case for their thesis.

The gist of their thesis is that the prosecution case is 'constructed' not in the sense of consciously fabricated, but in the sense of being built up by a process that detaches it from the 'truth'. No one can know what 'really happened'. The prosecution's version of reality is only a poor approximation of the truth because all those involved in the process are fallible human beings prone to see things from the perspective that best suits their own interests. This is true of those who first report the crime (usually ordinary members of the public), the police and the crown prosecution lawyers. The largest role in the process of 'construction', however, is played by the police, who very definitely have their perspective on how the case should develop:

The preceding chapters have demonstrated the power of the police over all other competing institutions and persons. ... This power is at its height in setting the terms of the charge and in creating the information relevant to that charge. How can the CPS act 'fairly' when the only information which forms the basis of its actions comes from the police? ... And defence lawyers are in thrall to the police and CPS in other ways.

When we argue that the case for the prosecution is a construction we are making the following statement. The case is a product of (a) low level officers operating under conditions of low visibility, enforcing (b) particular socio-economic and political policies, through (c) socially (rather than legally) constructed criteria which incorporate and produce structural bias, within (d) a permissive institutional and legal framework riddled with contradictions, in which (e) rule breaking is sanctioned in a graded manner, allowing a large amount of rule breaking when the law is insufficiently permissive to the police [p 182].

Class bias in prosecutions

Research conducted by Andrew Sanders then of Birmingham University explored the question of how far prosecution policy was influenced by class bias. He took 1,200 (non-motoring) cases from six police divisions (two from a large metropolitan county force, two from a small rural force and two from a force that policed both rural areas and a city). He compared police decisions with those of non-police agencies and especially the Factory Inspectorate (HMFI). (See A Sanders, 'Class Bias in Prosecutions', *The Hansard Journal*, vol 24, 1985, p 176.)

He found:

(1) That the police cautioned very little–in about 4 per cent of cases; whereas the HMFI used cautions as the norm–in the period 1978 to 1982 cautions were used in 65–73 per cent of cases.

(2) The overwhelming majority of HMFI prosecutions are directed at the middle class, that is companies and managers, whereas most police prosecutions are of working-class or unemployed (previously working-class) persons. Despite considerable demographic differences, the police divisions produced very similar class patterns with around 5 per cent from the middle or upper class. (Also a statistically significant difference emerged in the ability of middle-class persons suspected of crime to avoid prosecution by the police.)

(3) In the police, the decision to prosecute is taken at a relatively junior level (inspector), while the decision not to prosecute is made at a relatively high level (superintendent or above). In the HMFI it is the other way round. The junior (inspector) can caution but it requires a more senior officer to institute a prosecution. Prosecutions are only started by the HMFI for what are regarded as the most serious of the serious cases, whereas the police often prosecute trivial cases.

(4) The police do not take poverty into account when deciding whether to prosecute. By contrast, if a factory owner or trader says he broke the law because he could not afford to comply, it would be taken into account and would be regarded as a valid reason for not prosecuting.

(5) Whereas in the police there was an institutional bias in favour of prosecution (reflected in the phrase 'let the court decide'), the HMFI regarded prosecutions as a last resort. The role of HMFI officials was one more of advice and persuasion, getting firms to comply with the law. The police saw their role in prosecutions as such.

In Sanders' view the different decisions of the agencies were the result not of the people concerned but rather of the perspective of the agencies. The police in some circumstances behaved in a similar way–eg in fraud cases where it was widely agreed that prosecution was thought of as a last resort for the real rogues.

In tax evasion, too, very few are prosecuted. In 1980 there were 22,000 serious cases of tax evasion. One in 122 was prosecuted. By contrast there were 107,000 social security frauds, of which one in four were prosecuted. The total value of social security fraud was estimated at some £108m in 1979 compared to £3–3.5 billion in tax evasion in the same year. Tax evasion therefore resulted in 30 times more loss to the public purse and yet there were far more prosecutions of social security fraud.

On class bias see also the research sample reported by McConville, Sanders and Leng in *The Case for the Prosecution* (Routledge, 1991), p 123.

Cautioning as an alternative to prosecution

An important form of police discretion is whether to caution or to prosecute offenders. A police caution is a formal warning, given orally by a senior police officer in uniform, to a person who admits his guilt. This is distinct from an informal warning. The caution becomes part of that person's record and can be referred to in subsequent court proceedings. An informal caution does not become part of the offender's record and cannot be mentioned in later proceedings. A caution cannot be made dependent on the offender complying with some requirement or performance of some task. It is technically not a sentence. (In some force areas there are 'caution plus' schemes under which the suspect agrees voluntarily to make reparation or pay compensation or to undertake counselling or other help but these schemes are not yet official.)

Cautioning of juveniles has been a part of the system for many years. It has only recently started to be important for adults as well. Thus in 1984 the cautioning rate for indictable offences for offenders between the ages of 10 and 14 was 75 per cent. By 1994 the proportion had risen to 87 per cent. For offenders between 14 and 18 the proportion cautioned in 1984 was 36 per cent. By 1994 this had risen to 59 per cent. For those between 18 and 21 it was 4 per cent in 1984 and 33 per cent in 1994. For those over 21 it was 5 per cent in 1984 and 25 per cent in 1994. (*Criminal Statistics*, 1994, Cm 3010, Table 5.3, p 106).

The proportion cautioned for summary non-motoring offences is always lower. The reason is that a very large proportion of summary non-motoring offences are social security, tax and TV licence offences where police involvement is rare and where there is therefore no possibility of a police caution. The cautioning rate for summary non-motoring offences remained constant at around 18 per cent from 1988 to 1994.

In the mid-1980s the Home Office officially encouraged cautioning. (See Home Office, 'Cautioning by the Police', Consultative Document, 1984.) A Home Office circular in 1985 said: 'There is no rule of law that suspected offenders must be prosecuted. It has long been recognized in the case of juveniles that there may be positive advantages for society as well as for the individual in using prosecution as a last resort. Cautioning provides an important alternative to prosecution in the case of juvenile offending; it also represents a possible course of action in the case of adults.' (Home Office Circular, 14/1985, *The Cautioning of Offenders*.)

But practice varies considerably from force to force. This was shown by research done for the Philips Royal Commission (1981, Cmnd 8092–I, App 23, p 203.) See also annual *Criminal Statistics* and H Giller and Norman Tutt, 'The Police Cautioning of Juveniles: The Practice of Diversity' (1983) *Criminal Law Review*, pp 587–95; *ibid* (1987) pp 367–74.) The Runciman Royal Commission on Criminal Justice recommended that cautioning practice should be 'subject to national guidelines and applied more consistently across police force areas than appears to be the case' (Report, p 82, para 57). Police cautioning, it thought, should be governed by statute, under which national guidelines, drawn up in consultation with the CPS and police service among others, should be laid down in regulations (*ibid*).

A news item, indicating the development of police discretion in regard to prosecution policy, reported a representative of the Police Federation in January 1984 as saying that the police tended to take an increasingly lenient view of cannabis smoking. Mr Tony Judge, a Federation spokesman, was quoted as saying: 'The police do not have the resources to control possession of cannabis. The law on possession is fairly unenforceable and it points to a growing lack of conviction that it is a sensible law.' A spokesman for the South Yorkshire police said that first offenders caught in possession of small amounts of cannabis were more likely to be cautioned than charged. (*The Times*, 19 January 1984.)

The Home Office guidelines on cautioning were changed in 1990, largely because of the research showing wide variations in cautioning rates between forces. They were also partly the result of a drop in cautions of persons over 17. Under the new guidelines cautioning was supposed to be considered where there was evidence of guilt sufficient to give a realistic prospect of conviction and an admission of guilt and consent to the caution by the offender or in the case of a juvenile by his parent. The criteria for cautioning were the same as before: the nature of the offence, the likely penalty, the offender's age and health, and his or her criminal record and attitude towards the offence. The presumption in favour of not prosecuting juveniles and the elderly was now to be extended also 'to other groups—young adults and adults alike— where the criteria for caution are met'.

However, Mr Michael Howard, who became Home Secretary in 1993, took a less positive view of cautioning at least for more serious offences. His tougher approach was reflected in a new circular (18/1994) issued in March 1994 which replaced and cancelled the 1990 circular. Its purpose was to provide guidance on cautioning and in particular 'to discourage the use of cautions in inappropriate cases, for example for offences which are triable on indictment only; to seek greater consistency between police forces; and to promote the better recording of cautions' (para 1).

The circular said that, despite earlier discouragement of cautions for the most serious offences, cautions had been administered for offences as serious as attempted murder and rape. This 'undermines the credibility of the disposal' (para 5).

Cautions should *never* be used for the most serious indictable-only offences such as these, and only in exceptional circumstances (one example might be a child taking another's pocket-money by force, which in law is robbery) for other indictable only offences, regardless of the age or previous record of the offender [para 5].

Other offences, less grave in themselves, may nevertheless be too serious for a caution to be appropriate. The factors which will be relevant in making this judgment ... include the nature and extent of the harm or loss resulting from the offence, relative to the victim's age and means; whether the offence was racially motivated; whether it involved a breach of trust; and whether it was carried out in a systematic and organised way... [para 6].

Research ... indicates that 8 per cent of [the sample] had already received two or more cautions. Multiple cautioning brings this disposal into disrepute... It is only in the following circumstances that more than one caution should be considered: where the subsequent offence is trivial; or where there has been a sufficient lapse of time since the first caution to suggest that it had some effect [para 8].

The Home Office circular was first issued in draft in October 1993. The 1994 *Criminal Statistics*, published in November 1995, said 'Following the latest Home Office circular on cautioning there was a decrease in the numbers cautioned for the most serious indictable-only offences and in the percentage of offenders cautioned with past criminal history' (Cm 3010, 1994, p 91). It also said: 'Research into the criminal histories of those cautioned in 1985, 1988, 1991 and 1994 shows that the effectiveness of cautioning appears to decline after the first caution (*ibid*, p 93, para 5.3).

See further C Wilkinson and R Evans, 'Police Cautioning of Juveniles' (1990) *Criminal Law Review*, p 165; D Westwood, 'The Effects of Home Office Guidelines on the Cautioning of Offenders' (1991) *Criminal Law Review*, p 591; R Evans, 'Police Cautioning and the Young Adult Offender' (1991) *Criminal Law Review*, p 598; M McConville and A Sanders, 'Fairness and the CPS', 31 January 1992, p 120; S Uglow, A Dart, A Bottomley and C Hale, 'Cautioning Juveniles-Multi-Agency Impotence' (1992) *Criminal Law Review*, p 632.

(e) The CPS decision whether to prosecute

The CPS decision as to whether to continue a prosecution begun by the police is informed by the Code for Crown Prosecutors. In the CPS 1994–95 annual report the DPP stated that the aim of the Code 'is to promote independent and consistent decision making in the conduct of criminal prosecutions'. In June 1994 the CPS published the third revised edition of the Code. The following text gives key passages:

Code for Prosecutors, June 1994

2.3 Crown Prosecutors must be fair, independent and objective. They must not let their personal views of the ethnic or national origin, sex, religious beliefs, political views or sexual preference of the offender, victim or witness influence their decisions. They must also not be affected by improper or undue pressure from any source. . .

4 The Code Tests
4.1 There are two stages in the decision to prosecute. The first stage is *the evidential test*. If the case does not pass the evidential test, it must not go ahead, no matter how important or serious it may be. If the case does pass the evidential test, Crown Prosecutors must decide if a prosecution is needed in the public interest.

4.2 This second stage is *the public interest test*. The Crown Prosecution Service will only start or continue a prosecution when the case has passed both tests.

5 The Evidential Test
5.1 Crown Prosecutors must be satisfied that there is enough evidence to provide a 'realistic prospect of conviction' against each defendant on each charge. They must consider what the defence case may be and how that is likely to affect the prosecution case.

5.2 A realistic prospect of conviction is an objective test. It means that a jury or bench of magistrates, properly directed in accordance with the law, is more likely than not to convict the defendant of the charge alleged.

5.3 When deciding whether there is enough evidence to prosecute, Crown Prosecutors must consider whether the evidence can be used and is reliable. There will be many cases in which the evidence does not give any cause for concern. But there will also be cases in which the evidence may not be as strong as it first appears.

6. The Public Interest Test
6.1 In 1951, Lord Shawcross, who was Attorney General, made the classic statement on public interest, which has been supported by Attorneys General ever since: 'It has never been the rule in this country, I hope it never will be, that suspected criminal offences must automatically be the subject of prosecution'. (House of Commons Debates, vol 483, col 681, 29 January 1951.)

6.2 The public interest must be considered in each case where there is enough evidence to provide a realistic prospect of conviction. In cases of any seriousness, a prosecution will usually take place unless there are public interest factors tending against prosecution which clearly outweigh those tending in favour. Although there may be public interest factors against prosecution in a particular case, often the prosecution should go ahead and those factors should be put to the court for consideration when sentence is being passed.

Factors stated to militate *in favour* of prosecution: (1) the likelihood of a significant sentence; (2) a weapon was used or violence was threatened; (3) the offence was committed against someone who serves the public such as a police or prison officer or a nurse; (4) the accused was in a position of authority or trust; (5) the accused was the ringleader or an organiser; (6) the offence was premeditated; (7) that it was carried out by a group; (8) the victim was vulnerable, or was put in fear or suffered personal attack, damage or disturbance; (9) the offence involved discrimination on grounds of ethnic or national origin, sex, religion, political belief or sexual preference; (10) a marked difference between the actual or mental ages of the accused and the victim, or if there is an element of corruption; (11) the relevance of the accused's record; (12) whether the accused was subject to a court order; (13) the likelihood of repetition; (13) the offence, though not serious in itself, is widespread in that area.

Factors stated to militate *against* prosecution: (1) the likely penalty would be very small or nominal; (2) the offence was committed as a result of a mistake or misunderstanding; (3) the loss or harm is minor; (4) long delay between the offence and the trial, unless the offence is serious or it has only just come to light; (5) prosecution will have a very bad effect on the accused's physical or mental health, always bearing in mind the seriousness of the offence; (6) the accused is old, suffering from significant mental or physical ill health, unless the offence is serious or there is a real possibility of it being repeated; (7) the accused has already made reparation or paid compensation ('but defendants must not avoid prosecution simply because they can pay compensation'); (8) details may emerge at the trial which could harm sources, international relations or national security. The interests of the victim must also be very carefully considered.

The Code states that in regard to young offenders the CPS must have in mind that the stigma of a conviction can cause very serious harm to the prospects of such an offender and they can sometimes be dealt with without going to court. 'But Crown Prosecutors should not avoid prosecuting simply because of the defendant's age. The seriousness of the offence or the offender's past behaviour may make prosecution necessary.'

For analysis of the 'public interest element' as it was then defined see Andrew Ashworth, 'The "Public Interest" Element in Prosecutions' (1987) *Criminal Law Review* p 595. Professor Ashworth made the point that the CPS 'has the opportunity to take steps toward a major re-orientation of criminal justice' (p 596).

For a strongly argued view that the evidential requirement in the Code is misconceived, see Glanville Williams, 'Letting off the Guilty and Prosecuting the Innocent' (1985) *Criminal Law Review*, p 115. Professor Williams' contention was that if the test for proceeding is whether a conviction is likely to succeed (the '51 per cent rule'), many prosecutions that ought to be brought will not be. The test rather should be whether the prosecutor is satisfied on the evidence that the suspect is guilty, subject to the public interest questions as to whether a prosecution is desirable. Certainly there must at the least be a reasonable possibility of a conviction. But the effect of the rule that there must be a reasonable probability of a conviction means, for instance, that corrupt police officers may not be prosecuted because it is notoriously difficult to get a jury to convict a police officer. Where the prosecutor does not believe that the accused is guilty, he should drop the case. An exception to this principle might be where failure to charge someone may bring about a loss of public confidence in the integrity of the prosecution service.

On the new Code for Prosecutors see the DPP, Mrs Barbara Mills, *New Law Journal*, 1 July 1994, p 899 and Andrew Sanders, *ibid*, 8 July 1994, p 946. See also A Ashworth and J Fionda, 'Prosecution, Accountability and the Public Interest' (1994) *Criminal Law Review*, p 894; and Roger Daw 'A Response', *ibid*, p 904.

However it is not only the Code for Crown Prosecutors that influences the decision whether or not to continue a prosecution started by the police. Another consideration is the CPS staff member's concern to maintain his employer's approval by not having too many cases that go wrong–ie end in acquittal. That will tend to militate in favour of dropping cases. The same tendency is promoted by the current concern to reduce costs which affects the CPS like all other public agencies. It should be borne in mind that in addition to the published Code CPS staff also work under the influence of the unpublished *Policy Manual* which is for internal use only. There is also now a new factor called 'charging standards'.

Reducing discretion by new 'charging standards'

In August 1994 the police and the CPS introduced a new piece of machinery, 'charging standards', designed to standardise the decision to charge throughout the country. The first such standards were for assault. (The standards were published in *Justice of the Peace*, 20 August 1994, pp 554–55.)

The standards defined the degree of injury that would justify charges respectively of common assault (Criminal Justice Act 1988 s 37), assault occasioning actual bodily harm (s 47 of the 1988 Act, 'ABH'), unlawful wounding/inflicting grievous bodily harm (Offences Against the Person Act, s 20 1861, 'GBH') and wounding/causing grievous bodily harm with intent (s 18 of the 1861 Act).

But although the motive for this innovation was stated to be to increase consistency of decision making it seemed likely that there were other more questionable reasons behind the decision. One was to minimise the occasions when the CPS incur the anger of the police by reducing charges. If they are reduced initially by the police this problem does not arise. Another, probably much more important, was to reduce costs especially by increasing the number of cases charged as common assault which can only be tried summarily. The concern expressed in some quarters was that the overall effect would be to downgrade offences. (See for instance FG Davies, 'CPS Charging Standards: A Cynic's View', *Justice of the Peace*, 1 April 1995, p 203.) Another concern expressed is that in many cases police officers may now arrest someone for ABH knowing full well that he will be charged only with common assault which is not an arrestable offence. This would be an abuse of power. 'The charge should relate to the evidence available, not to a set of instructions. Parliament intended the custody officer to charge according to the evidence. If there is to be a change in this, it is to be made by Parliament not by an agreement between the police and the prosecutor.' (J Woods, 'The Metropolitan Police Assault–Charging Offences–Are they Based on Law?', *Justice of the Peace*, 21 January 1995, p 43.)

Guide to case disposal

A further step in the direction of reducing both discretion and prosecutions came in 1995 with the issue to the police of a new Case Disposal Manual. This ranks every offence, motoring, criminal and alcohol-related, on a scale of points from one to five. *Five-point offences*, such as murder, would always be prosecuted. *Four-point offences* have what the manual terms 'a high probability of prosecution'. This category includes

GBH, forgery, arson, perjury, burglary and perverting the course of justice. *Three-point offences* include indecent assault, theft, handling stolen goods, buggery, prostitution offences, resisting arrest, criminal damage and ABH. In three-point offences the decision whether to charge is to be made by listing the 'aggravating' and the 'mitigating' factors. The manual lists general factors, for instance, the impact on the victim, the accused's prior criminal record, the likelihood of penalty and whether the crime is a prevalent offence causing local concern. The manual also indicates factors specific to particular offences. So possession of drugs (even Class A substances such as cocaine, crack and heroin) will usually be cautioned if only 'small amounts, for personal use' are involved! The possessor of an offensive weapon will not be prosecuted under the manual's guidelines if there was 'no risk, weapon not on display, mistaken belief that there would be no offence if carried for protection only'. Deception offences will not be prosecuted if they were 'committed over a short period, low value' or 'driven by poverty/personal need'. ABH would not be prosecuted if it is a single blow causing only superficial injury. *Two-point offences* are those where there is a high probability of a caution and the decision maker needs to be able to justify the decision not to caution. This category includes begging, kerb-crawling and being drunk and incapable in a public place. A charge for this offence will only be laid if the offender is arrested four times for the same offence within a four-week period. One-point offences are minor offences for which a Formal Warning is appropriate or where there is a decision not to proceed with a prosecution. They include such things as throwing litter in the street or sending someone to buy liquor for a person who is under-age.

David Rose, Home Affairs Correspondent of *The Observer*, described and commented on this remarkable development in his powerful new book *In the Name of the Law: The Collapse of Criminal Justice* (Jonathan Cape, 1996, pp 163–64):

The Case Disposal Manual, introduced at first in London and several counties, with others rapidly following suit, enlarges police discretion on an unprecedented scale. It requires that officers of junior rank take fundamental decisions with massive implications for the lives of those they arrest, without reference to any court or outside authority. The judgments it demands are even more subjective than some of those required by the Code for Crown Prosecutors. How, for example, do you measure whether a sexual assault is 'trivial'? It is inescapable that many of those judgments will be shaped by factors which have nothing to do with the true merits of the case: the officer's workload; his opinion of the suspect; and the possibility that he may, in return for non-prosecution, become a useful informant in future.... The Manual, drawn up after consultation between the Metropolitan Police, the Association of Chief Police Officers and the CPS, alters institutionalised police practice significantly, but its introduction took place without any trace of public or parliamentary debate.

(f) Is the prosecutor genuinely independent of the police?

A central part of the case for the establishment of the CPS was that it should be more independent of the police. Has this objective been realized?

In the formal sense, the answer is yes. The CPS is independent of the police in that it is the CPS that takes the decision whether to proceed with a case. Also, the police are no longer in a client-lawyer relationship with the prosecutor able to direct the decision.

But there are a variety of reasons for doubting whether in fact the independence of the prosecution is as great as the change to the new system implied.

(1) The fact that the police continue to take the initial decision to charge puts them in a powerful position. Unless the police ask the CPS for advice as to whether to bring charges, the CPS will usually see only the cases where proceedings have been instituted.

(2) The entire investigation of the offence is in the hands of the police. The CPS gets the file prepared by the police and nothing much else. (Also, the amount of material in the file supplied to the CPS by the police is being reduced as an economy measure.)

The Philips Royal Commission clearly envisaged that the CPS would supervise and check the work of the police but in practice this does not happen and, as has been seen, the Runciman Royal Commission did not recommend any change in that regard. One reason is simply the lack of manpower resources to engage in this work. Another is that it would generate tensions between the two agencies. Thirdly, since the CPS has no investigatory powers under the Act, technically it lacks the technical standing to do so. The role of the CPS is simply to vet the work done by the police and this is inconsistent with the function of performing an active role of supervision. It is much more likely that they will broadly continue to play much the same role *vis-à-vis* the police of simply processing the cases put to them by the police and advising when asked by the police for advice. This is the more so since they need the cooperation of the police and will not therefore want to be thought by the police as excessively negative.

The study of over 1,000 cases by M McConville, A Sanders and R Leng, *The Case for the Prosecution* (Routledge, 1991) supports this view:

Police influence over a case is said to be confined to the investigation and case preparation stages with ultimate decision making by the prosecutor applying rigorous tests of public interest and evidential sufficiency. The reality is a system of routinized decision making embodying an overwhelming propensity to prosecute, bolstered by the presumption that earlier decisions were properly made and should not be overturned. The system is dominated throughout its stages by the interests and values of the police, with the CPS playing an essentially subordinate and reactive role [p 126].

The image of the proposed prosecution service conjured by both sides of the debate was of a body which would *displace* the police from their central role in prosecution decision making and relegate the police to a new subservient role in investigating crime and preparing cases for the new prosecution service. The reality is of a Crown Prosecution Service which is in many respects subordinate to the police. The police retain total control over many key decisions, such as decisions to take no further action, informally warn and caution. The police also decide whether or not to consult the CPS prior to making their initial charge/caution/No Further Action decision [p 141].[12]

Even in Scotland where the prosecutors have investigatory powers they tend to 'rubber stamp' most police prosecution decisions. Research as to how the Scottish system actually works showed that the fiscals prosecute in about 92 per cent of cases referred to them. They act almost invariably on the basis of information supplied by the police. They have the power to ask for further information but rarely do so, in the study in only 6 per cent of cases. In other words the police largely determine the

12 Advice was sought in only 51 of the 711 prosecution decisions taken after the establishment of the CPS –and in 48 cases the advice was sought by one force which was simply continuing its pre-CPS practice of consulting lawyers (p 142) (ed).

exercise of the fiscal's discretion as to whether to prosecute. In most cases the papers make it clear and the decision-making is largely routine. (In 63 per cent of cases the decision was taken on the same day that the fiscal received the papers.) The real discretion of the fiscal came in the 'trial avoidance arrangements'–bargaining over a guilty plea to lesser charges in return for other more serious charges being dropped. (See S Moody and J Tombs, *Prosecution in the Public Interest*, Scottish Academic Press, 1982.)

At the time when the CPS was established it was regarded as vital that the new organisation be moved physically into its own buildings away from the police. In 1996 it was announced that an experiment would be tried–of having CPS lawyers in police stations to advise the police and improve liaison! The first pilot scheme was set up in Darlington Police Station. Five others would be established and the experiment would then be evaluated (*New Law Journal*, 2 February 1996, p 115).

(g) Discontinuance by the CPS

One of the stated objectives for setting up the CPS was better and earlier identification of cases that for any reason should not go forward to prosecution. The 1983 White Paper *An Independent Prosecution Service for England and Wales* said the objectives of the CPS included the promotion of greater consistency of policy and uniformly high standards of case preparation and decision-making across the country. The effect, it was said:'should be that cases which are unlikely to succeed should be weeded out at an early stage' (Cmnd 9074, p 14). But the CPS' power to drop a prosecution has given rise to much controversy. The Code for Prosecutors states:

Prosecutors may decide to continue with the original charges, to change the charges or sometimes to stop the proceedings.

Review, however, is a continuing process so that Crown Prosecutors can take into account any change in circumstances. Wherever possible, they talk to the police first if they are thinking about changing the charges or stopping the proceedings. This gives the police the chance to provide more information that may affect the decision. The Crown Prosecution Service and the police work closely together to reach the right decision, but the final responsibility for the decision rests with the Crown Prosecution Service. (1994, paras 3.1–2)

Broadly, the CPS drops around 12 per cent of the cases but this tells us nothing as to whether that is about the right proportion. The police tend to complain that the CPS drops too many cases, but there is also some evidence that it drops too few.

The Crown Court Study done for the Runciman Royal Commission showed that in the view of both prosecuting and defence barristers and of judges, the prosecution was weak in about one-fifth of contested cases and that over 80 per cent of these cases ended in acquittal.[13]

The other relevant evidence is from the acquittal statistics. There are three kinds of acquittals–ordered acquittals, directed acquittals and jury acquittals. 'Ordered acquittals' are where the prosecution offers no evidence at all. It is dropped at court because the prosecution have decided at the last moment not to pursue the case, perhaps

13 M Zander and P Henderson, *The Crown Court Study* (Royal Commission on Criminal Justice, Research Study No 19, 1993, pp 184–5, Table 6.20, 6.21).

because a crucial witness fails to turn up or refuses to give evidence. (The rules do not permit the CPS to discontinue a case between committal for trial by the magistrates and trial at the crown court. They must therefore go through the process of formally offering no evidence even in cases which their process of review has identified as too weak to continue.) 'Directed acquittals' are where the judge in effect stops the case–usually after the defence submits that the prosecution's case is not strong enough to require a response. Jury acquittals are where the jury has deliberated and found the defendant not guilty. At first sight ordered and directed acquittals would seem to be in the category of weak cases that arguably could and should have been aborted earlier.

In the six years leading to the establishment of the CPS the proportion of acquittals that were either ordered or directed acquittals ranged from a low of 43 per cent in 1982 to a high of 48 per cent in 1985. It might have been expected that with the establishment of the CPS and its presumably better screening methods, the proportion of ordered and directed acquittals would go down. In fact however they went up. In fact the proportion has risen from 52 per cent in 1986 to 62 per cent in 1994. This is a puzzling phenomenon. (See annual *Judicial Statistics*. See also M Zander, 'What the Annual Statistics tell us about Pleas and Acquittals' (1991) *Criminal Law Review*, p 252 at 255–57).

What has changed is the balance between ordered and directed acquittals. In each of the six years just before the establishment of the CPS (1980 to 1985) the two kinds of non-jury acquittals were more or less similar proportions. In each year since the establishment of the CPS the ratio of ordered acquittals has greatly exceeded that of directed acquittals by a ratio of more than two to one. (In 1994 for instance 41% of acquittals were ordered, 17% were directed.)

From the defendant's point of view it is clearly better that the case against him should be dropped from the outset than that it should go forward. That is also better from the point of view of the system in terms of cost and effort.

But it would be better if the weak cases could be identified even earlier. This raises the question of the reasons for cases being dropped.

A Home Office study by D Crisp and D Moxon looked at nearly 1,300 magistrates' court cases terminated in 1991 in seven areas involving thirteen CPS branches (*Case Screening by the Crown Prosecution Service: How and Why Cases are Terminated*, Home Office Research Study 137, 1994). Fifty-eight per cent of non-motoring and 47 per cent of motoring cases were dropped on evidential as opposed to public interest grounds. The most common reasons were lack of supporting or corroborative evidence; problems with witnesses (availability, reliability or willingness to give evidence); and insufficient evidence of a key element of the offence. Other evidential problems were conflicts of evidence between witnesses, the strength of the defence and the inadmissibility of evidence.

Thirty five per cent of non-motoring and 24 per cent of motoring cases were dropped on public interest grounds. The main factors found by the researchers were that a nominal penalty was thought likely, the complainant did not wish to proceed, and the triviality of the offence. Less frequently mentioned factors included the youth of the defendant, the fact that the offence was stale, that the defendant was mentally ill or suffering acute stress, that the defendant had already suffered enough, that recompense had been made or that the case was suitable for a caution instead of prosecution.

The most common grounds of termination other than evidential or public interest grounds was inability to trace the defendant which accounted for 24 per cent of motoring terminations, though only 3 per cent of non-motoring cases.

There were no significant differences between cases terminated and those which went to court in terms of the age or sex of the accused or whether they had previous convictions. But cases in the terminated sample were more likely to involve a family dispute, reflecting the reluctance of the complainant to give evidence or the fact that reconciliation had been achieved or was being attempted.

Interviews with police officers and crown prosecutors confirmed that the police were sometimes unhappy about termination of cases they felt were strong enough to succeed in court. The CPS for their part sometimes felt that more could have been done by the police to meet their requests for additional information. But in general, communication between the CPS and the police appeared to be satisfactory, but reasons for dropping cases did not always filter through to the officers most directly concerned with the case, which 'could leave them uneasy about decisions and undermine morale' (p viii).

Only 5 per cent of the terminated cases were dropped before the first court appearance. Seven per cent were dropped at the first court appearance and a further 37 per cent were dropped between the first and the second court appearance. The majority were dropped at the second or subsequent court appearance. In more than one-third of terminated cases (37%) the defendant had no advance notice and in some other cases less than 48 hours' notice was given. In 29 per cent of cases where no advance notice was given it was because the defendant's whereabouts were unknown.

A study of a large national sample of over 11,000 discontinuances by the CPS in 1994 showed that 11.7 per cent of cases finalised by the CPS were discontinued—43 per cent for evidential reasons, 28 per cent for public interest reasons, 19 per cent for inability to proceed and 10 per cent because motoring documents were produced. (CPS Annual Report, 1994–95, pp 7–8) The survey established that the police were consulted in 99 per cent of cases where consultation was possible (74% of all the discontinued cases). Where there was consultation with the police, objections to discontinuance were advanced in 4 per cent of cases. Where it had been impossible to consult it was usually because the reason for having to discontinue only emerged on the day of the court hearing (*ibid*).

The Runciman Royal Commission recommended that more efforts be made to drop cases in time to save the defendant, the victim and the other witnesses the need to attend court (Report, p 76, para 35). It also recommended that the CPS be given power to discontinue proceedings up to the beginning of the trial both in the magistrates' and in the crown court (p 77, para 37).

For an account of new initiatives in Scotland to provide alternatives to prosecution see J Tombs and S Moody, 'Alternatives to Prosecution: The Public Interest Redefined', [1993] *Criminal Law Review*, p 357.

Research carried out for the Runciman Commission looked at 100 ordered and directed acquittal cases in two CPS areas, one urban, one provincial. The researchers concluded that 45 of these 100 acquittals were unforeseeable, over half of them because the victim or key witnesses disappeared or refused to testify. Twenty seven were classified as foreseeable and another 28 as possibly foreseeable. In a quarter of the cases the evidential weakness was present and foreseeable before, at or just after committal. At a minimum, they considered that 15 per cent which were foreseeably weak prior to committal should have been discontinued or manifest defects in the evidence rectified. (B Block, C Corbett and J Peay, *Ordered and Directed Acquittals in the Crown Court*, Royal Commission on Criminal Justice Research Study No 15, 1993.)

The Royal Commission recommended that where counsel was briefed, he or she should be required to read the papers in good time and to inform the CPS in writing that the case met the criterion of the Code for Prosecutors in that there was a realistic prospect of conviction, or that further evidence was required, or that it should be discontinued or no evidence offered. The Bar should take steps necessary to ensure that when work comes into chambers it is allocated to someone of appropriate seniority and that that counsel provides the advice and signs it in good time. ('The system must not be allowed to fail because no one knows who is the counsel in the case. We recommend that the Bar ensures that suitable procedures are put in place, failing which steps should be taken through legal aid legislation to impose them', (p 78, para 39).)

The Royal Commission also said that it agreed with the suggestion made by Block, Corbett and Peay that instead of allocating case files to whichever prosecutor happens to be free, every case should be assigned to one prosecutor or team of prosecutors for the period when it is passing through the magistrates' court. This was already happening under the CPS new system known as 'National Operational Practice'. It also welcomed the CPS plans to extend the practice to crown court cases as well.

Team working is now increasingly a formal part of the CPS method—see *Annual Report, 1994–95*. Prior to the introduction of this new method, staff worked either on magistrates' courts or on crown court cases and the case was sent 'down the line' a little like a factory production line. The change was designed by the CPS to bring prosecutors, caseworkers and administrative staff into a more effective pooling of their skills and involvement with the case. Prosecutors and caseworkers are to become responsible for cases throughout their duration. This would 'improve focus and continuity, provide clearer accountability and ownership, and a consistent point of contact for the police and the courts' (*ibid*, p 15). The new system was being brought in in 1995–96 with implementation by the end of 1996. The change was also designed to put more lawyers into the crown court to support prosecuting counsel where previously the CPS used unqualified clerks. As has been seen, however this new system has not necessarily proved popular with the CPS staff.

It is likely that there are a much larger number of cases that could be discontinued if the CPS had more information about the accused. There are now a number of courts where such information is being provided by the Probation Service with the full cooperation of the police. This method of providing information to the system was pioneered by the Vera Institute of Justice of New York working initially in Horseferry Road Court in London. (See S Elliman, 'Independent Information for the Crown Prosecution Service', *New Law Journal*, 8 June 1990, pp 812 and 864.)

(h) Judicial control of police discretion in prosecution policy

The problem of controlling police discretion in regard to prosecuting has only rarely come before the courts. The first modern examples of importance were the cases brought by a private citizen, former Member of Parliament Mr Raymond Blackburn, to compel the police to enforce the gambling and then the obscenity laws.

R v Metropolitan Police Comr, ex p Blackburn [1968] 2 WLR 893 (Court of Appeal)

In April 1966, a confidential instruction was issued to senior officers of the Metropolitan Police. Underlying this instruction was a policy decision not to take proceedings against clubs for breach of the gaming laws unless there were complaints of cheating or they had become the haunts of criminals. The applicant, being concerned at gaming in London clubs, brought proceedings for mandamus to get the Commissioner to withdraw the confidential instruction.

Lord Denning MR:–the result of the police decision of 22 April 1966, was that thenceforward, in this great metropolis, the big gaming clubs were allowed to carry on without any interference by the police ...

The duty of the Commissioner of Police of the Metropolis
I hold it to be the duty of the Commissioner of Police in the Metropolis, as it is of every chief constable, to enforce the law of the land. He must take steps so to post his men that crimes may be detected; and that honest citizens may go about their affairs in peace. He must decide whether or not suspected persons are to be prosecuted; and, if need be, bring the prosecution or see that it is brought. But in all these things he is not the servant of anyone, save the law itself. No Minister of the Crown can tell him that he must, or must not, prosecute this man or that one. Nor can any police authority tell him so. The responsibility for law enforcement lies on him. He is answerable to the law and to the law alone. That appears sufficiently from *Fisher v Oldham Corpn*,[14] and *A-G for New South Wales v Perpetual Trustee Co Ltd*.[15]

Although the chief officers of police are answerable to the law, there are many fields in which they have a discretion with which the law will not interfere. For instance, it is for the Commissioner of Police of the Metropolis, or the chief constable, as the case may be, to decide in any particular case whether inquiries should be pursued, or whether an arrest should be made or a prosecution brought. It must be for him to decide on the disposition of his force and the concentration of his resources on any particular crime or area. No court can or should give him directions on such a matter. He can also make policy decisions and give effect to them, as, for instance, was often done when prosecutions were not brought for attempted suicide. But there are some policy decisions with which, I think, the courts in a case can, if necessary, interfere. Suppose a chief constable were to issue a directive to his men that no person should be prosecuted for stealing any goods less than £100 in value. I should have thought that the court could countermand it. He would be failing in his duty to enforce the law.

A question may be raised as to the machinery by which he could be compelled to do his duty. On principle, it seems to me that once a duty exists, there should be a means of enforcing it. This duty can be enforced, I think, either by action at the suit of the Attorney-General: or by the prerogative writ of mandamus ... No doubt the party who applies for mandamus must show that he has sufficient interest to be protected and that there is no other equally convenient remedy. But once this is shown, the remedy of mandamus is available, in the case of need, even against the Commissioner of Police of the Metropolis.

Can Mr Blackburn invoke the remedy of mandamus here? It is I think an open question whether Mr Blackburn has a sufficient interest to be protected. No doubt any person who was adversely affected by the action of the commissioner in making a mistaken policy decision would have such an interest. The difficulty is to see how Mr Blackburn himself has been affected. But without deciding that question, I turn to see whether it is shown that the Commissioner of Police of the Metropolis has failed in his duty ...

14 [1930] 2 KB 364; 46 TLR 390.
15 [1955] AC 457.

... On 30 December 1967, the Commissioner issued a statement in which he said: 'It is the intention of the Metropolitan Police to enforce the law as it has been interpreted.' That implicitly revoked the policy decision of 22 April 1966; and the Commissioner by his counsel gave an undertaking to the court that the policy decision would be officially revoked. We were also told that immediate steps are being taken to consider the 'goings-on' in the big London clubs with a view to prosecution if there is anything unlawful. That is all that Mr Blackburn or anyone else can reasonably expect.

See also *R v Metropolitan Police Comr, ex p Blackburn (No 3)* [1973] 1 All ER 324 and *R v Chief Constable of Devon and Cornwall, ex p Central Electricity Generating Board* [1981] 3 All ER 826. In the second *Blackburn* case the applicant was asking again for mandamus to require the police to enforce the law–this time in respect of pornography. The application was refused on a showing by the Commissioner that he was doing his best to stem the tide of obscene publications. (A series of trials of senior members of the Obscene Publications Squad on corruption charges later suggested that the Court of Appeal had not been put wholly in the picture regarding the zeal with which the police discharged their duties in this area. But at the time nothing was known of this.)

In the second case, mandamus was sought by the Electricity Board to require the police to help clear squatters off ground that the Board wanted to survey as a site for a nuclear power station. The site had been occupied by protesters and Chief Constable John Alderson refused to help the Board to remove them on the ground that he had no statutory power of arrest in the circumstances nor any common-law power of arrest since there had been no breach of the peace and none was anticipated, nor was there any unlawful assembly to disperse. The Court of Appeal held that the Board were entitled to use the remedy of self-help to remove the obstructing demonstrators and the police had power to enter on the land at the invitation of the Board to assist them either to prevent actual or apprehended breaches of the peace occurring when the removal took place, or (per Lord Denning) because the conduct of the protesters in unlawfully obstructing the survey was itself a breach of the peace. However, since it was for the police on the spot and not the Court to decide when and how to exercise that power, mandamus would not be issued. In the event the police did move in a few days later with the Board, and the protesters were removed peaceably.

A third case in which the issue of the limit to police discretion was raised was *Coxhead* [1986] Crim LR 251. The appellant was a police sergeant in charge of a police station. He had recognized a motorist brought in to be 'breathalysed' as the son of a police inspector. The inspector was known to him to be suffering from a bad heart condition. In order not to exacerbate this condition the sergeant did not administer the test and allowed the motorist to go free. He was subsequently prosecuted and convicted for conduct tending and intended to pervert the course of justice.

His defence was that his decision came within the legitimate scope of discretion exercised by a police officer.

The crown court judge ruled that the extent of any discretion depended on the facts and was a matter for the jury to determine. The jury convicted. On appeal the Court of Appeal agreed. There were minor cases where the police had very wide discretion and major cases where effectively they had none or virtually none. It was eminently a matter for the jury to decide where on the scale a particular case fell. As the commentator in the *Criminal Law Review* said, the decision is odd in making it 'entirely' a question for a jury to decide whether an officer has a discretion lawfully to stop a case. Whether such a discretion exists must surely be a matter of law.

See also *R v General Council of the Bar, ex p Percival* [1990] 3 All ER 137, 149–52 (Div C):–the decision whether to prosecute is reviewable by the courts; it is not right that strictly defined limits should be set to the judicial review of decisions of a prosecution authority. In *R v Chief Constable of Kent County Constabulary, ex p L* and *R v DPP, ex p B (a minor)* [1993] 1 All ER 756 the Divisional Court held that the decision to prosecute a juvenile as opposed to cautioning him could be challenged by judicial review, but that such an action would rarely succeed. See to same effect *R v IRC, ex p Mead* [1993] 1 All ER 772, regarding a decision by the Inland Revenue to prosecute an adult.

In *R v DPP, ex p C* [1995] 1 Cr App Rep 136 the Divisional Court, most unusually, allowed an application for judicial review of the decision of the CPS *not* to prosecute for buggery of a wife by a husband on the ground that the prosecutor had not had in mind certain relevant considerations.

Private prosecution as an alternative

If the CPS decide not to prosecute (or brings charges felt to be too lenient), there is still the possibility that the victim or a relative may try to bring a private prosecution. In *R v Tower Bridge Metropolitan Stipendiary Magistrate, ex p Chaudhry* [1994] 1 All ER 44 the mother of the deceased victim of a driving accident tried to get a summons for causing death by reckless driving. The driver had been charged with summary only traffic offences. The Divisional Court held that the decision whether to allow a private prosecution to go forward should be based on consideration of various matters. One was whether the case had already been investigated by a responsible prosecuting authority which was pursuing what it considered to be appropriate charges. Regard should be had to para 7 of the Code for Crown Prosecutors–whether the charges reflect the seriousness of the offence, give the court sufficient sentencing powers and whether the charges can be presented in a clear and simple manner. A second consideration would be whether the issue of a summons for a more serious offence would override the discretion of the CPS in a way that would be oppressive to the defendant. Thirdly, the court should bear in mind that the DPP could always intervene to discontinue the proceedings under s 6(2) of the Prosecution of Offences Act 1985 or to reduce the charges under s 23. Lord Justice Kennedy suggested that there would have to be special circumstances 'such as apparent bad faith on the part of the public prosecutor' (at p 51). The court refused the application for judicial review. See also *R v Bow Street Stipendiary Magistrate, ex p South Coast Shipping Co Ltd* [1993] 1 All ER 219.

In 1995 the family of 18-year old Stephen Lawrence succeeded in launching a private prosecution for murder after the CPS dropped charges against two teenagers who had been charged with the killing. It was believed to be the first time that a private prosecution had been brought in this country in a murder case. Stephen Lawrence, who was black, was stabbed by a white gang while waiting for a bus in South East London in April 1993. The murder aroused much public attention and a fund was established to pay for the private prosecution. However, in the event, the trial of the three defendants collapsed after the judge ruled that crucial eye witness evidence for the prosecution was too unreliable to be put before the jury. (See national press 26 April 1996.) (For discussion of the legal issues see Edward Saunders, 'Private prosecutions by the victims of violent crime', *New Law Journal*, 29 September 1994, p 1423.) See further on this subject, J Kodwo Bentil, 'The Unenviable Task of Seeking to Institute a Private Prosecution', 154 *Justice of the Peace*, 26 May 1990.)

See also *Elguzouli-Daf v Metropolitan Police Comr* [1995] 1 All ER 833, CA, holding that the CPS owes no duty of care toward defendants such that they could sue for failure to dismiss charges earlier where the forensic evidence had been discredited.

(i) Duties of prosecuting lawyers

In the context of the establishment of the new Crown Prosecution Service, the Bar set up a committee on the duties and obligations of counsel when conducting a prosecution. The chairman, appointed by the Lord Chief Justice, was Mr Justice Farquharson as he then was. The Committee's report was published in the *Law Society's Gazette*:

'The Role of Prosecution Counsel', Report of the Farquharson Committee, *Law Society's Gazette*, 26 November 1986, p 3599

There is no doubt that the obligations of prosecution counsel are different from those of counsel instructed for the defence in a criminal case or of counsel instructed in civil matters. His duties are wider both to the court and to the public at large. Furthermore, having regard to his duty to present the case for the prosecution fairly to the jury he has a greater independence of those instructing him than that enjoyed by other counsel. It is well known to every practitioner that counsel for the prosecution must conduct his case moderately, albeit firmly. He must not strive unfairly to obtain a conviction; he must not press his case beyond the limits which the evidence permits; he must not invite the jury to convict on evidence which in his own judgment no longer sustains the charge laid in the indictment. If the evidence of a witness is undermined or severely blemished in the course of cross-examination, prosecution counsel must not present him to the jury as worthy of a credibility he no longer enjoys. Many of the important decisions counsel for the prosecution has to make arise during the trial itself, and then because he has the conduct of the prosecution case, he is the person best fitted to make them. Information will be available to him and not, for example, to the judge of the reliability and background of the witnesses he is proposing to call. It is for these reasons that great responsibility is placed upon prosecution counsel and although his description as a 'minister of justice' may sound pompous to modern ears it accurately describes the way in which he should discharge his function.

Those instructing counsel also have important public duties. The Crown Prosecution Service has a statutory obligation to take over the conduct of all prosecutions initiated by the police (save for some minor traffic cases) and one of its primary objectives is to secure greater consistency in prosecution policy. Other bodies, including government departments and local authorities will continue to strive for consistency in their own prosecution policy. These responsibilities must be reconciled as far as possible with the duties of prosecution counsel.

The Relationship between Prosecution Counsel and his Instructing Solicitor/the Crown Prosecutor
Generally speaking, a prosecuting solicitor is in the same position as any other solicitor instructing counsel. This will be the case when instructions are received from the Crown prosecutor, acting as instructing solicitor. He will not brief counsel whose competence he doubts and in whose judgment he has no faith. Moreover, he has available the ultimate sanction of the professional client that, if he does not like the way his work is done, he can brief other counsel thereafter. There will remain rare occasions when an experienced prosecuting solicitor is not prepared to accept the advice of counsel upon whose judgment he would normally rely. If the difference of

opinion is about an unimportant aspect of the prosecution, then it will be resolved by the usual give and take which informs discussion between members of the profession. Sometimes the difference is more fundamental as, for example, where there is a conflict between prosecution counsel, wishing to accept a manslaughter plea in a murder case, and his instructing solicitor who does not. In such circumstances, it is the view of the majority of us that the prosecuting solicitor/Crown prosecutor should be in the same position as other instructing solicitors: if he feels it is necessary, he should be entitled to take a second opinion, either by taking in a leader to advise or by withdrawing the instructions from counsel originally briefed and instructing other counsel. There will come a point before the commencement of the trial, however, when it will cease to be practicable for him to withdraw his instructions. It is fundamental to our thinking that, from this point, prosecution counsel must be accepted as being in control of the case. In the vast majority of trials, prosecution counsel will not normally be attended by an experienced prosecuting solicitor/Crown prosecutor: he is more likely to be attended by an unqualified clerk.[16] The only other person in court equipped to give an opinion on a matter requiring decision is likely to be the police officer in the case. Whilst it is proper for counsel to seek and consider their views, they can be no substitute for the view of counsel himself.

We have suggested that the moment from which prosecution counsel's control should start is the point, before the commencement of the trial, when it becomes impracticable for his instructions to be withdrawn. This seems to us to allow for the present common experience of pleas to different or lesser counts being offered by the defence and considered by prosecution counsel when the parties are at court but before the trial has begun. There has been a measure of dissension in the committee about this with one view being advanced that prosecution counsel's authority to consider and accept pleas should run from the time that he receives his brief to prosecute. Whilst recognising both the force and the convenience of that view, the majority of the committee has concluded that the prosecuting solicitor has authority to withdraw his instructions for proper cause up to the point which we have indicated. Once the case reaches court, so that it becomes impracticable as well as undesirable for instructions to be withdrawn (other than in the extreme circumstances of counsel being unable to continue for physical or mental reasons), it is for counsel to make the necessary decisions on all matters relating to the general conduct of the trial. These will include, for example: what evidence should be called; which witnesses, in the event, are to be relied upon and which are to be abandoned; what submissions are appropriate to be made to the judge on matters of law and/or to the judge and jury on the existence and strength of the evidence required and available to prove the count(s) in the indictment.

We recognize that there is a significant distinction between decisions on matters of 'policy' and other decisions which have to be made. We refer to the latter hereafter as 'evidential' decisions. We do not regard any of the decisions referred to in the examples just given as being 'policy' decisions. In our view, 'policy' decisions should be understood as referring only to non-evidential decisions on: the acceptance of pleas of guilty to lesser counts or groups of counts or available alternatives; offering no evidence on particular counts; and the withdrawal of the prosecution as a whole.

On 'policy' matters, we consider that the proper practice is and should continue to be that prosecution counsel should act contrary to his instructions only in circumstances which give him no alternative. Before reaching that stage, he will have to consider his duty to those for whom he acts, his duty to the court and his duty to do only that which he considers to be proper. If those considerations lead him to a different view from that held by those who instruct him, he will have to act accordingly. Consideration of the views of the prosecuting solicitor/Crown prosecutor, important at every stage when any kind of decision has to be taken, is crucially important with regard to 'policy' decisions.

---

16 But note that in 1995 the CPS decided to increase the number of lawyers in the crown court so as to provide better quality decision making in the interaction between counsel and the CPS (ed).

Prosecution Counsel and the Judge

It is a matter of curiosity that the respective rights and duties of the judge and prosecution counsel have never been clearly defined. The most likely explanation is that whenever a difference has arisen between the two as to which course to take in particular circumstances, it has usually been resolved by discussion. Such authority as there is suggests that there had been some change of view on the topic by the Court of Appeal over the last thirty years.

In the case of *R v Soanes* (1948) 32 Cr App Rep 136 prosecution counsel, in an indictment for murder, agreed with defence counsel to accept a plea of guilty to infanticide. The judge, Singleton J, refused to accept it on the grounds that there was nothing on the depositions which could justify such a course. As a matter of history the trial proceeded on the charge of murder and the jury convicted of infanticide. In the Court of Criminal Appeal Goddard LCJ said this:

'… it is impossible to lay down a hard and fast rule in any class of case in which a plea for a lesser offence should be accepted by counsel for the Crown … and it must always be in the discretion of the judge whether he will allow it to be accepted …'

… [However] in *R v Coward* (1979) 70 Cr App Rep 70 at p 76 Lawton LJ said:

'It is for prosecuting counsel to make up their own minds what pleas to accept. If the judge does not approve he can say so in open court and then the prosecution will have to decide what course to take.'

We approach the problem by considering whether counsel acting on behalf of the prosecution may or should decide to offer no evidence on any particular count in an indictment or on the indictment itself, without the approval of the judge. When taking such a decision it is usual for counsel to explain his reasons for doing so to the judge. It is open then to the judge to express his own views and if he disapproves of the course taken by counsel he will no doubt say so. In those circumstances, counsel is under an obligation to reconsider the matter, both personally and with his junior, if he has one, and his instructing solicitor. Whilst great weight should be given to the judge's view, if counsel still feels that the prosecution's decision is the correct one then he must persist in the course he originally proposed. He will have much more information about the background and weight of the case than the judge who will only have the depositions and exhibits. Counsel is therefore in the best position to make the decision and although one would expect that counsel would rarely have to take the course of offering no evidence in defiance of the opinion of the judge, in the final analysis the decision must be his.

The Committee cited *R v County London Quarter Sessions, ex p Downes* (1953) 37 Cr App Rep 148, for the proposition that the judge cannot stop a case being brought by the prosecution because he thinks the case is too weak. See also *Grafton* [1993] QB 101.

If counsel had the right not to offer any evidence at all, he must equally be able to decide whether to accept a guilty plea to a lesser count. However, if counsel submitted his decision to the judge's approval (for instance to reassure the public) he must follow the judge's view. Where the judge thinks that the prosecutor's decision is completely wrong, he could refuse to sentence before counsel has sought the approval of the DPP or the Attorney-General.

The Runciman Royal Commission (Report, p 78, para 42) referred to widespread dissatisfaction amongst counsel revealed by the Crown Court Study with the requirement to consult with the CPS as to the decision to drop the case or to reduce the charges. Typically the barrister would be able to consult only indirectly with a CPS lawyer through the unqualified CPS clerk attending at the crown court. Typically he would telephone a lawyer at the office and would pass his decision back to counsel.

The DPP, for her part, considered however that since the CPS were accountable for the conduct of the case they must be able to take these crucial decisions. She told the Royal Commission that she was working towards an arrangement whereby a qualified lawyer would be present at all crown court centres in order to be able to settle matters of this kind direct with counsel. (Such a CPS lawyer would however have to deal with several, and in some crown centres many, courts.)

The Royal Commission (p 79, para 43) said that it assumed that problems would nevertheless continue to arise and that the best way forward would be to reconvene the Farquharson Committee and to ask it to consider whether its 1986 guidelines needed refinement. No action had however been taken on this recommendation by early 1996 and it appears as if it will be left to develop without such intervention.

(j) The duties of defence counsel

The duties of the defence were considered in the extract that follows, which was provoked by the decision of the Court of Appeal in *Edwards* (1983) 77 Cr App Rep 5. The judge in a rape case failed through an oversight to tell the jury about the burden of proof. Defence counsel noticed but said nothing. The Court of Appeal refused to quash the conviction on the ground that there had been ample evidence of guilt. But the court was critical of the defence for keeping silent.

Mr Munday argues that although the Court of Appeal's view may have been contrary to the traditional view, it was in the public interest and right:

Roderick Munday, 'The Duties of Defence Counsel' (1983) *Criminal Law Review*, p 703

'Defending counsel owes a duty to his client and it is not his duty to correct the judge if the judge has gone wrong.'

This declaration of James LJ in *Cocks*[17] echoed faithfully in the Code of Conduct promulgated by the Senate of the Inns of Court and the Bar,[18] has for some time been considered to represent the limits of defending counsel's obligations in a criminal case. Whereas the Crown may be required to prosecute in an even-handed manner, the defence's role by tradition has been viewed differently. As the late Christmas Humphreys observed, 'The Crown is interested in justice;[19] the defence in obtaining an acquittal within the limits of lawful procedure and bar etiquette[20] ... James LJ's dictum in *Cocks*, which states that defence counsel is under no duty to correct a judge who has 'gone wrong' in his summing-up to the jury, contrasts sharply with Edmund Davies J's judgment in the Court of Criminal Appeal in the earlier case of *Southgate*.[1] In this

17 (1976) 63 Cr App Rep 79, 82.
18 If some procedural irregularity comes to the knowledge of Defence Counsel before the verdict is returned, he should inform the Court as soon as practicable and should not wait with a view to raising the matter later on appeal. Defence Counsel is not under any duty to draw matters of fact or law to the attention of the Court at the conclusion of the summing-up, but he may do so if he believes it would be to the advantage of his client: *Code of Conduct for the Bar of England and Wales* (July 1980), para 154.
19 It is the duty of Prosecuting Counsel to assist the Court at the conclusion of the summing-up by drawing attention to any apparent errors or omissions of fact or law which, in his opinion, ought to be corrected: *Code of Conduct for the Bar of England and Wales* (July 1980), para 162.
20 The Duties and Responsibilities of Prosecuting Counsel (1955) *Criminal Law Review*, pp 739, 746.
1   [1963] 2 All ER 833.

latter case, which appears to have been overlooked by the Court of Appeal in *Edwards*, a trial judge, in directing the jury on the issue of provocation, inadvertently departed from the statutory language of s 3 of the Homicide Act 1957. Defence counsel (a certain AE James QC) with some diffidence took it upon himself to draw this crucial error to the judge's attention and the appellate court, dismissing the appeal, expressed the view that defence 'counsel had, in the circumstances, adopted a course which was commendable and desirable'.

Of course, what is commendable and desirable need not be obligatory and, indeed, according to *Cocks* and *Edwards* is only a matter for professional conscience. It is interesting that in the most recent case of *Edwards* defence counsel seem to have had doubts as to where their duty lay. Only after consulting *Archbold* did they feel entitled to place their client's particular interests before the general interests of justice. Whilst accepting that this course was justified by *Archbold* and, furthermore, by an entry in the current *Rules of Conduct for the Bar*, Robert Goff LJ in the Court of Appeal still had doubts as to the propriety of this practice. As he circumspectly pointed out, had it not been that defence counsel must have felt, like their Lordships, that the prosecution evidence was quite overwhelming, it would have been inconceivable that they, acting in the best interests of their client, could have failed discreetly to draw that serious omission in the summing-up to the attention of the judge. The court felt that nothing less could explain counsel's decision to deprive their client of the benefit of the jury hearing the direction on the standard of proof from the lips of the judge himself. Furthermore, Goff LJ went on to add, if ever counsel again found themselves in a similar predicament, they might find the judgment in *Edwards* of assistance. The import of this remark is tolerably plain: despite the dictum in *Cocks*, defence counsel in future will not be expected deliberately to remain impassive whilst the judge makes an elementary and easily corrected error of law in his summing-up. This, it is submitted, is the desirable practice. Although it may mean that defence counsel occasionally finds himself embarrassed, it does accord more closely than *Cocks* with that elevated view of counsel's obligations expressed in recent times in the House of Lords[2] and, moreover, it tempers the more unseemly tactical possibilities inherent in English criminal procedure

The Runciman Royal Commission recommended that the Bar's code of conduct should be amended to make it clear that where the judge has plainly overlooked or misinterpreted a legal matter, defence counsel should intervene to point it out. (Report, p 124, para 24.)

6. BAIL

There are many reasons for concern as to whether accused persons should be held in custody while their cases are still pending. Remand in custody for someone who has not yet been convicted is despite the fact that he is formally presumed to be innocent. To be remanded in custody is in many ways a serious matter for the person concerned.

Remand prisoners are disadvantaged in preparing their cases for trial. The remand prisoner will be hindered in getting access to lawyers to prepare his defence, in looking for witnesses and collecting evidence or preparing evidence in mitigation of sentence. If the prison where he is held is remote, he may find that lawyers are not willing to

---

2   For instance, Lord Reid in *Rondel v Worsley*: 'Every counsel has a duty to his client fearlessly to raise every issue, advance every argument, and ask every question, however distasteful, which he thinks will help his client's case. But, as an officer of the court concerned in the administration of justice, he has an overriding duty to the court, to the standards of his profession, and to the public, which may and often does lead to a conflict with his client's wishes or with what the client thinks are his personal interests' ([1969] 1 AC 191, at 227).

come there at all. Even when it is relatively close to main centres of population he will find it difficult to have the kind of access to advisers that would be possible if he were at liberty. If someone is sent to the prison it is often a clerk rather than a qualified solicitor just because of the amount of time involved in making the visit.

There is evidence that, *other things being equal*, those who are held in custody are more likely to plead guilty, to be found guilty and to be given a custodial sentence than those who are on bail. In other words, the mere fact of being imprisoned seems to have an effect on one's prospects in the criminal justice system. (See AK Bottomley, *Decisions in the Penal Process*, Martin Robertson, 1973, pp 88–93.)

Also, the defendant in custody is unable to continue with his normal life, may lose his job, may fall behind in paying rent and both he and his family may suffer other financial and other practical difficulties, as well as obvious emotional upset or even trauma. The National Association for the Care and Resettlement of Offenders (NACRO) carried out a study based on interviews in 1991 and 1992 with 3,449 prisoners in eight male and two female prisons. Nearly one third of the sample (31%) were on remand. Two-fifths of the remand prisoners had lost their homes as a result of being in prison. Over one third (35%) of the remand prisoners had lost jobs through being imprisoned. ('Bail-Some Current Issues', Penal Affairs Consortium, October 1995, p 2–referred to here as the 'Penal Affairs Consortium Paper, 1995'). A Home Office study of 415 unconvicted prisoners at Brixton, Holloway and Feltham stated that the prisoners reported problems with depression (59%), loneliness (49%), relationships with partners (45% of those who had partners). ('The Welfare Needs of Unconvicted Prisoners' 1994, Home Office Research and Planning Unit Paper No 81–cited in the Penal Affairs Consortium Paper, 1995, pp 2–3.)

The suicide rate of remand prisoners is significantly higher than the rate for prisoners who are not on remand. Between 1990 and 1994, remand prisoners were between a fifth and a quarter of the prison population but they accounted for over half the suicides (122 out of 240)–Penal Affairs Consortium paper, 1995, p 3. It is generally assumed that the reason is the anxiety and uncertainty of the situation of awaiting trial or sentence, the higher proportion of mental disturbance among remand prisoners and the depressing effect of the poor conditions and restricted regimes in which remand prisoners are held–see below.

Remand prisoners are a serious issue also from the point of view of prison overcrowding. In 1994 remand prisoners who had not yet been convicted or were awaiting sentence made up as much as 25 per cent of the prison population. (In 1984, the proportion was 20 per cent.) Because of the rapid turn-over of remand prisoners, they are, of course, an even higher proportion of all *receptions* into prison. Many remand prisoners are held in police station cells for lack of space in the prisons.

Remand prisoners as a proportion of the total prison population has been rising as a result of various factors. A paper presented in 1992 to the Criminal Justice Consultative Committee prepared by the Director General of the Prison Service (para 2.7–the paper is referred to here is 'The Director General's paper') suggested that the steady increase in persons remanded 'would seem to be the result of steadily fewer cases over the period being dealt with on first appearance and, consequently, being adjourned at least once'. Previously it had been suggested by a Home Office paper that the explanation was more defendants being committed for trial and more delays in bringing cases on for trial. (See Rachel Pearce, 'Waiting for Crown Court Trial: The Remand Population', Home Office Research and Planning Unit, Paper 40, 1987.)

Conditions in prisons for remand prisoners are theoretically better than for convicted prisoners. They are allowed more visits; they can send more letters; they can wear their own clothes and be attended by a doctor of their own choice (provided they meet the cost); they can work if they wish like convicted prisoners but cannot be required to do so; they cannot be required to have their hair cut; they can have more cigarettes and may use private cash for purchases from the prison shop. But in practice the regime for remand prisoners is in most ways worse than for those who have been convicted. (The Director General's paper states: 'Taken as a whole, however, the regime for unconvicted prisoners in practice far from satisfactory, and is often worse than for the convicted. A variety of factors contribute to this, including antiquated accommodation, a transient and sometimes volatile population, and the pressures placed on establishments by the demands of courts and other work' (para 4.3). In many prisons they are locked in their cells as much as 23-hours a day.

The Director General's paper included a Statement on Unconvicted Prisoners which he said reflected a model regime that had been agreed by the Prisons Board and Ministers (para 7.9). It said that unconvicted prisoners 'are presumed to be innocent'. It continued:

Subject to the duty to hold them and deliver them to court securely and to the need to maintain order in establishments, they will be treated accordingly and, in particular, will be allowed all reasonable facilities to: seek release on bail; preserve their accommodation and employment; prepare for trial; maintain contact with relatives and friends; pursue legitimate business and social interests; obtain help with personal problems. They will receive health care appropriate to their needs. They will have opportunities for education, religious observance, exercise and recreation and, where possible, for training and work.

But the Director General candidly admitted that this represented hope not reality:

The model regime has been agreed by the Prisons Board and Ministers. But it is important to be clear about its status. It represents the sort of regime we believe that we ought to offer prisoners, not what we feel fully equipped to offer them at the moment.

It is unfortunately the case that the model regime bears little, if any, relation to the situation in the prisons today.

Length of remand period   The number of remand prisoners who as at 30 June 1995 were awaiting trial or sentence for different periods of time was stated by the Prison Service to be:

Less than 3 months	6,380
More than 3 months, up to 6 months	2,343
More than 6 months, up to 12 months	1,542
Over 12 months	341

(Source: House of Commons, *Hansard*, 4 December 1995, vol 268, col 18.)

(a) Bail from the police station

The problem of bail first occurs at the police station. If a person is arrested on a warrant, the warrant will state whether he is to be held in custody or released on bail.

But if he is arrested without a warrant the police will have to decide whether or not to release the suspect after they have charged him. Their duties used to be those set out in s 43 of the Magistrates' Courts Act 1980. This distinguished between 'serious' cases and ones that were not regarded by the police as serious. Section 43 required the police to inquire into any case where it would not be practicable to bring the suspect before a court within twenty-four hours and, unless the case appeared to the officer to be a serious one, to grant him bail subject to a duty to appear before a magistrates' court at a time and place appointed by the officer. The statute did not define what for this purpose was to be regarded as a serious case. Subsection (3) permitted the police to grant bail to a suspect to come back to the police station where the inquiry could not be completed forthwith and to ask the suspect for a surety (ie some person willing to promise to pay money if the suspect himself failed to comply with the duty to come back to the police station). The surety's promise ('recognisance') would then be enforceable by a magistrates' court.

The provisions of s 43 of the 1980 Act have, however, been replaced by the scheme of the Police and Criminal Evidence Act. The 1984 Act, as has been seen, lays on the custody officer the duty to consider in relation to all cases (other than those where the arrest warrant is endorsed for bail) whether further detention is appropriate. Before a suspect has been charged, he can only be detained in the police station if the custody officer reasonably thinks that such detention is 'necessary to secure or preserve evidence relating to an offence for which he is under arrest or to obtain such evidence by questioning him' (s 37(2)). There is no distinction drawn between serious and non-serious offences.

After a person has been charged, he has to be released from the police station unless his name and address are not known or the custody officer reasonably thinks his detention is necessary for his own protection or to prevent him causing injury to a person or damage to property or because he might 'skip' or interfere with the course of justice (s 38(1)(*a*)). A juvenile can be held in custody, in addition, 'in his own interests' (sub-s (*b*)).

The Criminal Justice and Public Order Act 1994 gave the police the power to grant bail subject to conditions very similar to the power to grant bail subject to conditions enjoyed by the court. (On the courts' power to set conditions for bail see p 218 below.) The power, established by CJPOA, s 27, followed a recommendation of the Runciman Royal Commission (Report, p 73, para 22) based on the belief that it would result in release of far more persons from police custody. (The Government estimated that giving the power to grant bail subject to conditions could reduce the numbers held overnight in police custody pending production in court by up to 40,000 out of a current total of around 100,000.) But whereas the Runciman Commission envisaged that it would apply to arrested persons regardless of whether they had been charged, the power to impose conditions under CJPOA, s 27 only applies to persons who have been charged.

Conditions should only be imposed if it appears to the custody officer that they are necessary to secure that the defendant (a) surrenders to custody, (b) does not commit further offences while on bail, (c) does not interfere with witnesses or otherwise obstruct the course of justice (CJPOA, s 27(3)). The police, unlike the court, cannot order reports to be prepared nor can the police order the defendant to live in a bail hostel.

The conditions of bail can be made more onerous or less onerous by the original or another custody officer (*ibid*).

The CJPOA, s 29 gave the police for the first time a power to arrest someone who did not answer to police bail.

Police bail is important not least because it has been found that the courts seem to be influenced in their decisions on bail by whether the accused has had bail from the police station. In a study by the Home Office Research Unit it was found that the factor which was most highly correlated with the bail rate in courts was whether the police had given the defendant bail from the police station (F Simon and M Weatheritt, *The Use of Bail and Custody by London Magistrates' Courts Before and After the Criminal Justice Act* (HMSO, 1984), p 15).

Not surprisingly, the great majority of those arrested are in fact bailed by the police. In 1994 the proportion was 86 per cent of those arrested in connection with indictable offences and 90 per cent of those arrested for summary offences other than motoring offences. (Ten years earlier, in 1984, the proportions were marginally lower–81 per cent and 84 per cent respectively.) (*Criminal Statistics*, 1994, Cm 3010, Table 8.1). Of those committed for trial to the crown court in each of the past ten years the proportion released on bail has ranged between 77–81 per cent (*ibid*, Table 8.7.)

(b) Bail decisions by courts

When a court adjourns a case–whether overnight or for a week or a month–it has to decide whether the defendant should be remanded on bail or in custody. Until the Bail Act 1976 the system of bail was to permit the release of the defendant, usually on his own recognisance (his promise to pay a stated sum of money if he absconded and was caught) and often also the promise by sureties that they too would pay a stated sum of money in the same event. (No money had to be provided by the surety unless the defendant did 'skip'.) Bail could be granted either with or without conditions. Police objections to bail could be based on a variety of grounds–for example, the likelihood that the defendant would abscond, would interfere with witnesses, or would commit further offences.

Historically the chief reason for refusing bail was that the accused might abscond. In fact in the nineteenth century it seems to have been the sole reason (*In Re Robinson* (1854) 23 LJQB 286) and this remained the case well into this century. But gradually the courts began to accept other grounds as well. In 1955 Lord Goddard changed the position by recognizing the notion that persons with a bad record and especially those who were housebreakers should not normally be granted bail. (*Pegg* [1955] Crim LR 308; *Wharton* [1955] Crim LR 565; *Gentry* [1956] Crim LR 120.) One of the main justifications for this new approach was that it would help to prevent the defendant from committing further offences whilst on bail.

The Home Office Working Party

In June 1971, in response to mounting debate about bail, the Home Secretary set up a Working Party to inquire into the problem. Its report (*Bail Procedures in Magistrates' Courts*, 1974) made a number of proposals which were in due course implemented in the Bail Act 1976. (For a critical review of the Working Party's report, see Michael King, 'Bail Reform: The Working Party and the Ideal Bail System' (1974) *Criminal Law Review*, p 451.)

The Bail Act 1976

The Bail Act 1976 created a statutory presumption of bail for remand cases (including remands after conviction for reports to be made). This means that the court *must* grant bail unless one of the statutory exceptions applies–even if the defendant does not apply for bail (s 4). (The importance of the presumption was shown by the results of one study carried out over six months in Cardiff. There were almost 500 cases (496). In 395 the police did not object to bail, nothing was said about bail on behalf of the defendant and bail was simply granted. (MJ Doherty and R East, 'Bail Decisions in Magistrates' Courts', 25 *British Journal of Criminology*, 1985, Table 2, p 256.)

The main exceptions are set out in the Bail Act itself, Sch 1. They provide that a court need not grant bail to a person charged with an offence punishable with imprisonment if the court is satisfied that there are substantial grounds for believing that, if released on bail, the defendant would (a) fail to appear, (b) commit an offence while on bail, or (c) obstruct the course of justice. Bail also need not be granted if the court thinks he ought to stay in custody for his own protection (or, in the case of a juvenile, for his own welfare), or if there has been insufficient time to obtain enough information about the defendant for the court to reach a decision, or he has previously failed to answer to bail (Sch 1, Pt 1, paras 2–6).

In determining whether it is likely that the defendant would skip or commit an offence or obstruct justice, the court should have regard to (a) the nature and seriousness of the offence (and the probable way the court will deal with the defendant), (b) the character, antecedents, associations and community ties of the defendant, (c) his record in regard to any previous grant of bail and, (d) except where the remand is for reports, the strength of the evidence against him (Sch 1, Pt 1, para 9). (For criticism of the structure of the Bail Act provisions see *Criminal Law Review* (1987) p 438–9, and (1993) p 1.)

In the case of someone charged with an offence punishable with imprisonment who is remanded for reports, bail need not be granted if it appears to the court impracticable to complete the inquiries or make the report without keeping the defendant in custody (Pt 1, para 7).

Where the defendant is charged with an offence not punishable with imprisonment, the permissible grounds for refusing bail are narrower. He can be refused bail if he has previously failed to answer to bail and if the court believes, in view of that failure, that he will again fail to surrender to custody if released on bail (Sch 1, Pt 2, para 2).

Further exceptions to the statutory presumption for bail were introduced by Mr Michael Howard as Home Secretary. The most severe is for anyone on a charge of murder, attempted murder, manslaughter, rape or attempted rape who has previously been convicted for one of those offences. Such person cannot now be given bail (CJPOA, s 25(1) and (2)). (In the case of manslaughter the rule only applies however if the defendant received a prison sentence.)

Of greater practical significance is s 26 of Mr Howard's CJPOA 1994 which removed the statutory presumption of bail in regard to anyone charged with an offence which is not a purely summary offence where the alleged offence occurred whilst the defendant was on bail. This was to deal with the alleged scandal of so called 'bail bandits'–see p 223 below. The court is not bound to refuse bail in such cases; it simply is not subject to the statutory presumption.

If bail is granted, it can be conditional or unconditional. Unconditional bail means that the defendant must simply surrender to the court on the appointed date. Failure to do so without reasonable cause is an offence (s 6(1)), punishable in the magistrates' court with three months' imprisonment and/or a fine, or in the crown court with twelve months' imprisonment or a fine.

Conditions can be attached where the court thinks it is necessary to ensure the defendant's presence at court, or so that he does not commit further offences or interfere with witnesses or obstruct the course of justice, or to ensure that he makes himself available for reports (s 3(6)).[3] But the statute gives no guidance as to what sort of conditions may lawfully be imposed. The most common relate to such matters as reporting to the police daily or weekly, handing in one's passport, living in particular premises or with particular persons, or *not* associating with particular persons or not going to particular places. An appeal can be lodged against unreasonable conditions, but this is extremely rare. (See generally JN Spencer, 'Bail Conditions: Logical or Illogical?' (*Justice of the Peace*, 24 March 1990, p 180.) For an account of a study of the use made by courts of the power to impose conditions see JW Raine and MJ Willson, 'The Imposition and Effectiveness of Conditions in Bail Decisions', *Justice of the Peace*, 3 June 1995, p 364–67. The study which was commissioned by the Home Office, was based on five courts. The most frequently used conditions in a sample of 1,050 cases in which conditions were imposed was a residence requirement (79%), no contact with a named person (46%), keep away from a specified address ((24%), curfew (21%), reporting (17%). No other condition was imposed in more than 4 per cent of cases. The study suggests that magistrates pay little regard to the Bail Act's requirement that the conditions be framed so as to be related to the four statutory reasons for imposing conditions–set out at the start of this paragraph. Instead they tend to focus on the conditions without much attention to the grounds for imposing them.

The study suggests that enforcement in regard to compliance with conditions is poor. For example the CPS typically do not inform witnesses that the defendant's bail has been made subject to his not contacting the witness. Nor was it necessarily the case that the police officer handling the case would be informed about the conditions subject to which bail had been granted. Even curfew orders were rarely backed by spot checks. Nevertheless many of the defendants told the researchers that the conditions had helped them keep out of trouble.

One such occasion occurred, however, during the long-drawn-out and bitter miners' strike in 1984. Nine miners sought judicial review in October 1984 of the conditions of bail imposed by justices. The common condition complained of was that they should 'not visit any places or place for the purpose of picketing or demonstrating in connection with the current dispute, other than peacefully to picket or demonstrate at his usual place of employment'. The Lord Chief Justice said that the justices only had to decide that that condition was necessary to prevent the commission of an offence (as opposed to the requirement that they have substantial grounds when considering whether to refuse bail altogether). There was no requirement for formal evidence. The justices were entitled to use their own knowledge of the situation. ('They were entitled to use their knowledge of events at local collieries during preceding weeks'.) See *R v Mansfield Justices, ex p Sharkey* [1985] Crim LR 148.

---

3   Section 3(6).

The Bail Act did not create an offence of breaking conditions imposed by the court. The sanctions for breach in the Act are under s 7(3), which give the police a power to arrest a defendant on conditional bail where they reasonably suspect that he is likely to break the conditions or that he has already done so. Anyone arrested under this subsection must be brought before a justice of the peace within 24 hours. The justice of the peace may then reconsider the question of bail.

However the 1994 Criminal Justice and Public Order Act gave the police a new power to arrest a person failing to answer to police bail.

The 1976 Bail Act abolished personal recognisances whereby the defendant agreed to pay a sum of money if he failed to appear on the appointed day. The only exception was where the court thinks there is a danger the defendant may go abroad, in which case he can be asked to give monetary security. But the Act did preserve the ancient right of the court to ask for sureties as a condition of bail. The sureties promise to pay in the event that the defendant does not turn up. The court then has a discretion as to whether to order that the amount put up by the sureties be forfeited (technically called 'estreated'). (For the principles on which the courts should act, see *R v Uxbridge Justices, ex p Heward-Mills* [1983] 1 WLR 56; *R v Southampton Justices, ex p Green* [1976] QB 11; and A Eccles, 'New Developments in the Law of Forfeiture of Recognisance' (1982) *Justices of the Peace*, p 146.) Standing surety for someone can have catastrophic consequences. In a case in December 1982, for instance, Bow Street magistrates' court demanded payment of £120,000 from a travel agent who promised that amount as surety for two men he hardly knew charged with VAT frauds of over £20 million. See also *R v Bow Street Magistrates' Court, ex p Hall and Otobo* [1986] NLJ Rep 1111.

It does seem from some recent decisions however, that the courts may now be more inclined to give a blameless surety the benefit of the doubt—see in particular the Court of Appeal's decision in *R v Crown Court at Reading, ex p Bello* [1992] 3 All ER 353. The Divisional Court had upheld the judge's order that the surety lose £5,000, which was half the sum he had agreed to stand for, even though he was entirely blameless. In the view of the Divisional Court it was not necessary to show that the surety was at fault. But the Court of Appeal disagreed. The court should always consider the question of fault. ('If it was satisfied the surety was blameless throughout it would then be proper to remit the whole of the amount of the recognisance'.) But in *R v Crown Court at Maidstone, ex p Lever* [1995] 2 All ER 35 the Court of Appeal held that the absence of culpability on the part of the surety was not by itself a reason to reduce or remit entirely the forfeiture of a recognisance if the defendant absconded. It upheld forfeiture of £35,000 out of £40,000 and of £16,000 from £19,000 even though the surety had been in no way at fault. In *ex p Bello* the Court of Appeal also held that the surety had to be informed of the date when the defendant was required to attend at court. Since he had not been so informed that was in itself sufficient ground to allow the appeal. See also *R v Crown Court at Wood Green, ex p Howe* [1992] 3 All ER 366 holding that courts should consider the surety's ability to pay when deciding how much of the sum promised should be forfeited.

In 1990 the financier Asil Nadir fled Britain for Cyprus after he had been arraigned at the start of his trial for fraud offences. The trial judge Mr Justice Tucker required a Mr Guney who had stood as surety in the amount of £1 million to forfeit £650,000. The Court of Appeal (the Master of the Rolls dissenting) held that since from the moment that the defendant was arraigned at the start of the trial the surety was no longer at risk, the decision to forfeit the surety's money had been wrong (*R v Central Criminal Court, ex p Guney*, [1996] 2 All ER 705).

The Bail Act, s 9, specifically made it a criminal offence to agree to indemnify a surety–for example, where the defendant or his associates agree to reimburse the surety if he is asked by the court to pay the money he has promised to pay. This is treated as a conspiracy to pervert the course of justice.

The Act provides that a surety can be relieved of his obligations if he notifies the police that the bailed person is unlikely to surrender. The police can then make an arrest without a warrant. *R v Crown Court at Ipswich, ex p Reddington* [1981] Crim LR 618, established that the surety was not automatically relieved simply by going to the police. Mrs R had stood surety in the amount of £2,000 on condition that the accused reside with her and report daily to the police station. She feared that the accused was not reliable and went to the police to say that she thought he might not surrender to his bail. When in fact the accused did not appear, the court ordered that half of her surety be estreated. On appeal, it was held that the crown court judge had not sufficiently taken into account the efforts she had made and he had erred in law in saying that she had done the wrong thing to have gone to the police station. Also there should have been an inquiry as to her means. The case was sent back for re-hearing.

There is some authority that the surety can himself make an arrest but in practice this is hardly likely to be done–see (1981) *Criminal Law Review*, p 619.

The Act requires that the bail decision be recorded and that reasons must be given to the defendant if it is refused or conditions are attached to the grant of bail. If the defendant is unrepresented and is refused bail, he must be told of his right to apply to a higher court for bail (s 5).

(c) How many bail applications?

Until recently, an unconvicted person could not be remanded in custody for more than eight days. This ensured that his case would be reconsidered every week and repeated applications could be made to have him released by the magistrates.

However, in 1980 the Divisional Court held in *R v Nottingham Justices, ex p Davies* [1980] 2 All ER 775, that no fresh application for bail could be made to magistrates unless the circumstances had in some way changed since the last application.

One effect of the decision in the *Nottingham Justices'* case was that even competent defence counsel delayed making an application for bail lest the client was prejudiced by the rule. As a result, a client might be remanded in custody much longer than would otherwise have been the case. See B Brink and C Stone, 'Defendants Who Do Not Ask For Bail' (1987) *Criminal Law Review*, p 152. This article led to Criminal Justice Act 1988, s 154, which requires courts to consider bail at *each* hearing (s 154 added a new Part IIA to Sch I of the Bail Act 1976).

Moreover, under s 154, at the first hearing after the defendant has been remanded in custody his lawyers can deploy any arguments they please, whether or not they have been advanced previously. But at any subsequent hearing the court need not hear arguments heard previously. This helped to defuse part of the problem created by the *Nottingham Justices* case. But there is a doubt as to whether if the defence do not advance any argument regarding bail at the first hearing they are restricted to two hearings or whether the first 'unargued' hearing should be disregarded and not count.

It seems that many courts adopt a strict approach and in effect hold that the defendant who does not utilise his first opportunity of arguing for bail has wasted it. (See M Hinchcliffe, *Law Society's Gazette* 1 July 1992, p 19)

Length of periods of remand

The Criminal Justice Act 1982, s 59 and Sch 9, provided for the longer remand in custody of defendants over 17 who are legally represented even though they are not physically before the court. The defendant could be remanded in custody for three one-week periods providing this was explained to him when he was first remanded in custody and he gave his consent. This meant that he had to be produced at least every four weeks. But if he wished to change his mind during that period, he could. His lawyer would not normally appear for him in his absence either.

At first this was introduced as an experiment (Criminal Justice Act 1988, s 155 but in July 1991 the Home Office laid before Parliament an order extending to all courts the power to remand defendants for up to 28 days. The purpose is to reduce court hearings, to reduce time taking prisoners to and from courts and prisons, and to save legal aid money. The new order became effective in December 1991 (Magistrates' Courts (Remand in Custody) Order 1991, SI 1991/2667).

(d) Appeals against a refusal of bail

There are three alternative methods of appealing against a refusal of bail–other than applying again to another bench of magistrates, which was considerably restricted by the *Nottingham Justices* decision.

The first is to apply to the judge in chambers through a barrister or a solicitor. This is fairly costly unless legal aid can be obtained. Criminal legal aid cannot be obtained for this purpose, but in 1981 the Law Society announced that it would entertain applications for civil legal aid for applications to the judge in chambers (*Law Society's Gazette*, 18 and 25 November 1981, pp 1281 and 1321). The basic procedure for such applications is set out in RSC Ord 79, r 9. (For a detailed description see *LAG Bulletin*, May 1982, p 56.)

The alternative is to apply for assistance to the Official Solicitor. The prisoner simply fills out a form in prison which requests the Official Solicitor to forward an application to the judge in chambers. There is no oral argument. The papers are simply presented to the judge by an official. On the other hand, there is no charge for the service.

The chances of success are much greater through an oral argument presented by lawyers than in appeals by the Official Solicitor. According to a Parliamentary Answer, the success rate for Official Solicitor applications in 1980 was 9 per cent compared with 69 per cent for those privately represented (House of Commons, *Hansard*, 23 November 1981, Written Answers, cols 274–5). (See to like effect Nan Bases and Michael Smith, 'A Study of Bail Applications Through the Official Solicitor to the Judge in Chambers' (1976) *Criminal Law Review*, p 541.)

The third method of seeking to obtain bail after it has been refused by magistrates is through the crown court. This was previously regulated by the Supreme Court Act 1981, s 81 of which said that the crown court may grant bail in relation to anyone who has been committed for trial or sentence to the crown court or who is appealing to the crown court. These provisions date back to the Courts Act 1971. But since May 1983 under the provisions of the Criminal Justice Act 1982, s 60, it became possible to apply to the crown court for bail before committal. In order for this procedure to be available, the magistrates have to issue a certificate saying that they heard full argument on the application for bail before they refused bail. Such appeals can be made in summary cases as well as in cases that are indictable. If the applicant is legally aided the legal aid order covers an application under this procedure. If not, neither the crown court nor the magistrates' court have the power to issue a legal aid order for the purposes of a bail application alone.

(e) Appeals against a grant of bail

The Bail (Amendment) Act 1993 gave the prosecution a right of appeal where a magistrates' court grants bail to a person who is charged with or convicted of an offence carrying a sentence of five years' imprisonment, or an offence of taking a conveyance without the owner's consent (contrary to the Theft Act 1968, s 12), or aggravated vehicle taking (contrary to the Theft Act 1968, s 12A). The right of appeal is against the grant of bail only, and therefore cannot be used to challenge conditions imposed.

In order to exercise the right the prosecution must strictly follow the set procedure. First, the prosecution must have objected to bail during the bail hearing (s 1(3)). At the conclusion of the bail hearing the prosecution must immediately state in open court that it proposes to exercise its right of appeal (s 1(4)). The clerk of the court announces the time at which this oral notice was given and issues a warrant of detention authorising the detention of the defendant for the time being. This is also recorded in the court register.

If the defendant is unrepresented, the clerk has to tell him that he has the right to ask the Official Solicitor to represent him at the appeal.

The prosecution must serve written notice on the court and the defendant (not his legal representative). If this is not done within two hours, the appeal is deemed to have been dropped (s 1(7)).

The appeal hearing must start within 48 hours of the day on which oral notice of intention to appeal was given, not counting weekends and public holidays (s 1(8)). The hearing is before a single judge in chambers in the crown court (s 1(9)). The defendant has no right to be present.

See further *Solicitors' Journal*, 8 October 1993, p 1000 and 15 July 1994, p 715; *New Law Journal*, 3 June 1994, p 745, *Legal Action*, August 1994, p 21.

Note

1. Time spent in custody pre-trial or pre-sentence can generally be deducted from the ultimate sentence. This is by virtue of s 67(1) of the Criminal Justice Act 1967. But this is not always the case–see N Yell, 'Credit for Time Spent Remanded in Custody', *Justice of the Peace*, 1982, p 275; *Criminal Law Review* (1986) pp 270–1; *New Law Journal*, 3 October 1980, p 937.

2. No compensation is paid to persons who have been remanded in custody and then are found not guilty. (By contrast in West Germany, France, Holland and Sweden, persons who are detained and then acquitted can sometimes be compensated.)

(f) Causes for concern

Bail/remand in custody is a subject that perennially seems to attract critical comment from all quarters.

The civil libertarians are concerned especially that:

(1) A high proportion of those remanded in custody pre-trial receive non-custodial penalties. (In 1994, of those remanded in custody at some stage either during proceedings in the magistrates' courts or in crown court cases, 'an estimated 43 per cent are given a custodial sentence, 34 per cent are given a non-custodial sentence and 23 per cent are acquitted' (*Criminal Statistics*, 1994, p 184, para 8.9.

(2) There are considerable variations in the policy of different courts in remanding defendants on bail or in custody.

(3) Bail decisions are too hasty. Research has showed 62 per cent of bail hearings lasted less than two minutes, and 96 per cent less than 10 minutes. Even when bail was refused, 38 per cent were heard in under two minutes and 87 per cent in less than 10 minutes. (MJ Doherty and R East, *op cit*, p 217 above at p 262.)

(4) As has been seen, remand prisoners tend to be held in highly unsatisfactory conditions in prisons or in police cells. Mr Leon Brittan when Home Secretary in July 1983 promised to end the use of police cells by the end of that year, but this has not occurred. When they are not held in police stations remand prisoners tend to be held in local prisons, the oldest part of the prison estate and also the most overcrowded prisons.

At the same time, other discontents and anxieties are expressed by the police and the media:

(1) 'Too many people get bail who then go out and commit offences whilst on bail'–the problem of what the media call 'bail bandits'. In 1992 the Home Office produced a study of the results of the then available research studies. ('Offending While on Bail: a Survey of Recent Studies', Home Office Research and Planning Unit Paper No 65). This concluded that the percentage of offenders who were convicted of offences committed whilst on bail had varied little over the previous decade. The studies consistently showed that 10 to 12 per cent of persons granted bail were convicted of offences committed whilst on bail. One study which included offences for which the offender was cautioned and offences 'taken into consideration' (on which see below p 250), produced a total figure of 17 per cent. However, even when the defendant is released on bail after police objections the great majority are not convicted of an offence committed whilst on bail. (A study conducted by the Metropolitan Police showed that 18% of defendants granted bail despite police objections were convicted of offences committed on bail.)

The legislature has recently taken a number of steps directed at the problem of offences committed whilst on bail. Thus a provision in the Criminal Justice Act 1991 required magistrates to give reasons for rejecting police objections to bail in murder, manslaughter or rape cases (s 29(2)). The Criminal Justice Act 1993 provided that an offence committed by a person on bail should be treated by the court sentencing for that offence as an aggravating factor (s 66). The Criminal Justice and Public Order Act 1994, as has already been seen (p 217 above), removed the power to grant bail in certain cases (s 25) and removed the presumption in favour of bail where the defendant is accused of offences committed whilst on bail (s 26).

(2) 'Too many people skip'. (In 1994, of the 1.3 million persons summoned, an estimated 5 per cent failed to appear at court. But the proportion for indictable offences was considerably higher (17%). About 9 per cent of those arrested and bailed and 10 per cent of those bailed by magistrates failed to appear. An estimated 7 per cent of those on bail to appear at the crown court fail to do so. (*Criminal Statistics*, 1994, Cm 3010, p 184, paras 8.10–11.)

The prison authorities are concerned about the cost of remand prisoners, the burdens they create for the prison system including the burden of escorts for prisoners going to court, the rapid turnover in receptions and discharges, and in terms of the problem of prison overcrowding and providing a tolerable regime whilst they are in custody.

(g) New developments

One helpful recent development is the Bail Information Scheme now operating in over a hundred magistrates' courts. (They began in the mid-1980s as a result of the initiative of the Vera Institute of Justice of New York.[4]) Under these schemes probation officers provide the CPS and the court with verified information about the defendant— his employment status, where he lives, his family situation and other community roots and the like. Research has shown that the provision of bail information has a significant effect. Thus a Home Office study of three schemes at magistrates' courts showed, for instance, that at Hull the CPS made no objection to bail in 39 per cent of cases where bail information was provided, compared with 13 per cent where it was not provided. The equivalent figures at Blackpool were 19 per cent, compared with 15 per cent and at Manchester (where the scheme concentrated on the most serious cases), 58 per cent and 40 per cent. The figures for court decisions were even more striking. At Hull, when information was provided, 69 per cent of decisions favoured bail, compared with 38 per cent where no information was provided. In Blackpool the figures were 58 per cent, compared with 38 per cent and in Manchester 80 per cent, compared with 50 per cent. Seventy two per cent of homeless defendants who had information presented were bailed (mostly to bail hostels), compared with 15 per cent where no information was provided. ('Bail Information Schemes: Practice and Effect', Home Office Research and Planning Unit, Paper No 69, 1992.)

There are now a growing number of similar bail information schemes in prisons. In October 1995 there were 45–50 local prisons and remand centres with such schemes operating. The Prison Service Business Plan for 1995–96 stated that the Service aimed to 'continue the development of prison based bail information schemes, with a view to ensuring that all unconvicted prisoners have access to a scheme by 1997'.

One of the beneficial side-effects of this development is that the schemes have promoted an inter-agency approach to one of the major problems of the criminal

4   The concept, based on pioneering work by the Vera Institute in New York, was first proposed in this country by the writer in the late 1960s–see M Zander, 'Bail: A Reappraisal', *Criminal Law Review*, March 1967.

justice system. A new step in the same direction was the start in 1993 by the Home Office of pilot 'bail process' projects. The projects established in five areas were intended to examine the mechanics of the whole bail decision-taking process with a view to improving the content and sharing of information and advice between agencies. The first phase of the projects was to obtain a detailed description in each area of how information about defendants was obtained, with proposals for improvements. (See 'Improving Bail Decisions: the Bail Process Project, Phase 1', Home Office Research and Planning Unit, Paper No 90, 1994.) The second phase was for the local steering committee to try to effect the recommended improvements.

Another helpful development has been the establishment of bail hostels and other facilities where defendants can be sent by courts. At the end of 1995 there were 16 approved bail hostels with 370 places and 89 combined probation/bail hostels with some 2,000 places. About three-quarters of these places were being used by persons on bail. The number of places was however reduced when the Government decided in 1993 to close 11 hostels with 270 places and to abandon a planned expansion programme.

There are also a growing number of bail support schemes usually run by probation involving arrangements to help defendants on bail–through contact with bail support workers, residence requirements, volunteer befriending schemes, debt counselling and the like.

But these more hopeful developments must be seen against a background of a continuing huge remand population in prison, held for the most part in their cells, as had been seen, for 23 out of 24 hours a day.

Note–Woolf Report on the prisons

The Woolf Inquiry into the prison system (*Prison Disturbances April 1990*, 1991, Cm 1456) proposed that 'there should be a clear expectation that magistrates should not make a final decision to remand a defendant in custody until they have received at least the information which will be available to the Crown Prosecution Service in areas where a Bail Information Scheme is in operation' (para 10.83). Also magistrates should pay considerable attention to the question whether the defendant is charged with an offence for which he might realistically be imprisoned if convicted (para 10.84). Magistrates should be supplied with information as to where remand prisoners should be detained in custody–and what regime was in operation there.

See generally Rod Morgan, 'Remands in Custody: Problems and Prospects' (1989) *Criminal Law Review*, p 481; NACRO, *Legislation on Bail: What Should be Done?*, 1992, commented on editorially in *Criminal Law Review* (1993) p 1 and resulting correspondence, *ibid*, pp 324–27; 'Bail: Some Current Issues' by the Penal Affairs Consortium, October 1995.

7. INFORMATION SUPPLIED TO THE OPPONENT

(a) Evidence the prosecution intend to call or use

If a case was to be committed for trial to the crown court, the prosecution was under an obligation to provide the defence prior to the committal with copies of enough of the prosecution evidence to constitute a prima facie case (*R v Epping and Harlow Justices, ex p Massaro* [1973] QB 433; *R v Grays Justices, ex p Tetley* (1979) 70 Cr App Rep 11). Before the trial took place or at least before the end of the prosecution's case, any other evidence the prosecution intends to call must also be handed over.

In 1996, committal proceedings had been on the point of being abolished and new arrangements for transfer of cases to the crown court were due to be implemented. In the event, however, the new scheme was scrapped–see p 265 below. The rule remains that the prosecution must supply the defence with copies of enough of the prosecution case to constitute a prima facie case. A copy must also be served on the accused (sub-s (4)).

The prosecution's duty to disclose its case in advance may even apply to material it plans to use in cross-examination to challenge the evidence of defence witnesses. In *Phillipson* [1990] Crim LR 407, the Court of Appeal quashed a conviction because the prosecution had failed to disclose letters which could be and were used in cross-examination to rebut the defence case of duress. The prosecution must have realized that duress would be the defence.

Where the case is tried by magistrates, the rules distinguish between summary-only offences and either-way offences. For summary offences, there is no duty of prior disclosure at all, other than the details on the information setting out the charge. (However see p 236 below for a new duty laid on the prosecution under the Criminal Procedure and Investigations Bill introduced in November 1995 to provide the defence with 'unused material' (material the prosecution do not intend to use) which in the opinion of the prosecutor undermines the defence case. The duty applies to contested cases regardless of whether they are dealt with in the magistrates' court or the crown court. But it is not clear whether and if so, how this new duty will in practice operate in regard to summary only offences.

Formerly there was no duty of prosecution disclosure of its case in regard to either way offences tried summarily. But in 1985, after much debate, (for the history see the 6th edition of this work at pp 265–66), the Magistrates' Courts (Advance Information) Rules 1985, SI 1985/60 were promulgated. These required that the prosecution disclose its case in all either-way offences if requested to do so by the accused or his representative. The prosecution can choose whether to make disclosure by handing over copies of its witnesses' statements or by making summaries. Most opt for summaries. The actual process is now handled by the Crown Prosecution Service. It appears to be widely accepted that if the Government were to require that full statements be handed over in all cases, the burden on the CPS would be intolerable.

In 1989, Home Office concern that advance disclosure was causing unnecessary delays resulted in new guidelines to defence solicitors issued by the Law Society. (See *Law Society's Gazette*, 30 August 1989, p 3.) The guidelines said that normally a solicitor should not ask for advance disclosure until after having got his client's instructions as to the likely plea and choice of venue. If the client intended to plead guilty or the case was to go to the crown court, there would be no need for advance disclosure.

Practitioners, commenting on these guidelines (*Law Society's Gazette*, 27 September 1989, p 9), suggested that one did not know whether one needed advance disclosure until one had received it. It was the defence lawyer's duty normally to ask for it, in case it revealed something of advantage to the client. Also, often one should not advise the client on plea and choice of venue until after receiving advance disclosure.

(b) Evidence the prosecution do not intend to use ('unused material')

The rules regarding disclosure to the defence of material the prosecution do not intend to use were formerly a mixture of common law and guidelines laid down by the Attorney General. They are now however statutory.

The common law rules 1946–1981

In *R v Bryant and Dickson* (1946) 31 Cr App Rep 146, it was held that where the prosecution took a statement from a witness who they knew could give material evidence but whom they did not intend to call as a witness, they were obliged to supply his name and address to the defence. Failure to comply with this duty led to the conviction being quashed for a breach of natural justice in *R v Leyland Justices, ex p Hawthorn* [1979] 1 All ER 209.

But did this duty extend to making witnesses' statements available to the defence? The position was not clear. In *Dallison v Caffery* [1964] 2 All ER 610 at 618, Lord Denning said:

The duty of a prosecuting counsel or solicitor, as I have always understood it, is this: if he knows of a credible witness who can speak to material facts which tend to show the prisoner to be innocent, he must either call that witness himself or make his statement available to the defence. It would be highly reprehensible to conceal from the court the evidence which such a witness can give. If the prosecuting counsel or solicitor knows, not of a credible witness, but a witness whom he does not accept as credible, he should tell the defence about him so that they can call him if they wish.

Danckwerts LJ said he agreed with Lord Denning, but Diplock LJ (as he then was) indicated (at p 622) that in his view the duty of prosecution counsel did *not* extend to supplying the defence with statements of such witnesses. It seems that Lord Justice Diplock's view was the correct one at law, whilst that of Lord Denning represented the then best practice. (See also Christmas Humphreys, 'The Duties and Responsibilities of Prosecuting Counsel' (1955) *Criminal Law Review*, p 739, in which he strongly endorsed Lord Denning's view.)

In *R v Hennessey* (1978) 68 Cr App Rep 419, the Court of Appeal did not refer to either *Bryant and Dickson* or *Dallison v Caffery*. However, it said (at p 426):

... those who prepare and conduct prosecutions owe a duty to the courts to ensure that all relevant evidence of help to an accused is either led by them or made available to the defence. We have no reason to think that this duty is neglected;[5] and if it ever should be, the appropriate disciplinary bodies can be expected to take action. The judges for their part will ensure that the Crown gets no advantage from neglect of duty on the part of the prosecution.

5 In the light of subsequent events in some of the notorious 'miscarriage of justice cases' this was to prove a very inappropriate statement (ed).

It is uncertain to what extent the prosecution were obliged to tell the defence if a prosecution witness gave evidence in court that was inconsistent with a prior statement to the police. It seems clear that they have to inform the defence of the fact (*Baksh v R* [1958] AC 167), but there is no clear ruling that they must also supply the actual prior statement.

The Attorney-General's Guidelines

The rules about disclosure by the prosecution were significantly affected by Guidelines issued in December 1981 by the Attorney-General. They concerned all cases to be tried on indictment. These stated that all 'unused material' should normally be made available to the defence solicitor 'if it has some bearing on the offence(s) charged and the surrounding circumstances of the case'. 'Unused material' for this purpose was defined to mean (1) all witness statements and documents not included in the committal bundles served on the defence; and (2) where edited statements are included in the committal bundle, the unedited version of such statements or documents. The Guidelines indicated that disclosure should be made if possible before committal or otherwise as soon as possible after committal. If the material was less than fifty pages, copies should be provided. If it was longer, the defence should be given the chance of inspecting the material and of taking copies.

There was, however, a discretion not to disclose documents in certain circumstances: (1) where there was reason to fear that it might lead to improper pressure being brought on a witness to alter or retract a statement, nor to appear in court or to intimidate him; (2) where the statement was from someone close to the accused and was untrue, in which case it might be very useful to the prosecution in any cross-examination of the witness if he were called by the defence; (3) where the statement was favourable to the prosecution or was neutral but it was thought that the witness might give the defence a very different story out of loyalty or fear. If this should happen and he were called by the defence, the original statement would be valuable for the prosecution as a basis for cross-examination. In any of such cases the names and addresses of the witnesses should, however, normally be supplied.

The other ground of withholding a statement, according to the Guidelines, was where it was against the public interest on account of being 'sensitive'. Examples included: (1) where it dealt with matters of national security; (2) where it disclosed the identity of an informer and might place the person concerned in danger; (3) where it identified a witness who might become the victim of intimidation or even violence; (4) if it alerted someone that he was a suspect or revealed some unusual form of surveillance or method of detecting crime; (5) if it related to serious allegations against someone who was not an accused or disclosed prejudicial material about him; (6) if it disclosed matters of 'private delicacy' to the maker and/or might cause domestic strife.

In the case of any doubt, the material ought to be submitted to counsel for advice. A balance should then be struck between the competing values. If, for instance, the material established the accused's innocence or even if it only tended to show him to be innocent, it should either be disclosed in full or at least with the sensitive passages excised. Any doubt should be resolved in favour of disclosure. If the material was too sensitive to show to counsel, it must be sent to the DPP. (The Guidelines were set out in full in *Practice Note* [1982] 1 All ER 734 and in 74 Cr App Rep 302.)

Technically, the Guidelines were not law but the courts treated failure to comply with them as the basis for quashing convictions–see for instance *R v Lawson* (1989) 90 Cr App Rep 107.

Strictly, the Guidelines only applied to trials on indictment, but in 1987 the Attorney-General told the House of Commons that in summary trials the prosecution were under a general duty of being fair, which required them, *inter alia*, to supply to the defence any materially inconsistent statement, written or oral, of any prosecution witness of which the prosecutor became aware at any stage (House of Commons, *Hansard*, 5 November 1987, col 713). The Divisional Court held that this view was correct in *R v Bromley Magistrates' Court, ex p Smith and Wilkins, R v Wells Street Magistrates' Court, ex p King* [1995] 4 All ER 146. The court asserted the principle that 'An accused is as much entitled to the safeguards designed to ensure a fair trial in the magistrates' court as in the crown court' (p 149). The court was told that, except in non-imprisonable, summary only traffic offences, after a not guilty plea the routine practice was for the CPS to provide disclosure either by way of the material itself or by way of a schedule inviting access to the disclosable material.

The duties laid down by the Guidelines also applied even when the prosecution was private, provided the case had been committed for trial. Cf *R v Gregory Pawsey* [1989] Crim LR 152 with *R v DPP, ex p Hallas* [1988] Crim LR 316.

Whether the Attorney-General's Guidelines were being followed was another question. A JUSTICE Committee in December 1987 said that it was the experience of the Committee that the spirit of the Attorney-General's Guidelines on disclosure to the defence was frequently ignored and that the practice of disclosure varied considerably from area to area (JUSTICE, *A Public Defender*, 1987, para 25).

Common law 1989–1995

The law relating to prosecution disclosure of unused material developed rapidly in the years after 1989 so that in effect the Attorney General's Guidelines were to a significant extent displaced. This process began with the decision of Mr Justice Henry, as he then was, in the first of the so-called Guinness prosecutions in August 1989 (*Saunders*) when he ruled that unused material included all preparatory notes and memoranda which led to the making of witness statements. The breadth of this ruling caused consternation amongst prosecution agencies.

In June 1992 the Court of Appeal developed the rule further in quashing the conviction of Judith Ward (*R v Ward* [1993] 2 All ER 577). The judgment (which was over 60 pages long) held that the accused should have the same opportunity of reviewing all the available material as the crown has. It followed that copies of all police officers' notebooks should be provided to the defence *without request*, as should observation logs, crime reports, photofits, artists impressions from all witnesses, notes of oral descriptions and car registration numbers.

In *R v Preston* [1993] 4 All ER 638 the House of Lords held that the test for the disclosure of unused material was materiality not admissibility. Lord Mustill giving the lead judgment said (at p 664):

The fact that an item cannot be put in evidence by a party does not mean that it is worthless. Often, the train of inquiry which leads to the discovery of evidence which is admissible at a trial may include an item which is not admissible, and this may apply, although less frequently, to the defence as well as to the prosecution. As the Court of Appeal pointed out in *R v Ward* (above) at 601, it is of help to the accused to have the opportunity of considering all the material evidence which the prosecution have gathered and from which the prosecution have made their own selection. In my opinion the test is materiality, not admissibility.

The material ought to be made available by the prosecution to prosecution counsel for him to decide what should be disclosed to the defence. In *Preston* the Attorney General had advised that prosecuting counsel should not receive the product of the tapping of the defendants' phones because it was inadmissible in evidence. The House of Lords held that the Attorney General had been wrong so to advise. Prosecution counsel's role as arbiter between the adversarial interests of the prosecution and the broader dictates of justice could not be performed effectively unless he knew everything material.

In *Ward* (above) the Court of Appeal said that although the Attorney General's Guidelines created an exception for material that was 'sensitive' or subject to public interest immunity, neither ground for withholding could be used without informing the defence of its nature or getting a ruling of the court.

Sensitive material and public interest immunity

The issue of how the courts should deal with disclosure of sensitive material came before the Court of Appeal directly a few months after the decision in *Ward*. In *R v Davis* [1993] 2 All ER 643 prosecution counsel had handed the court a document which was so sensitive that it had not been shown even to defence counsel (Michael Mansfield QC). He asked the Court of Appeal to deal with the matter in camera either in the absence of the defence or in the presence of Mr Mansfield only if he gave an undertaking that he would not disclose what took place to his instructing solicitors or his clients. Mr Mansfield refused to give such an undertaking and voluntarily withdraw. The hearing then took place in camera with only the prosecution present.

The Court of Appeal held that if the prosecution wished to rely on sensitivity to justify non-disclosure (a) they had to give the defence notice that they were applying for a ruling, (b) they had to indicate to the defence at least the category of the material held and (c) the defence had to be given the chance of making representations to the court. But where to give notice even of the category of material would arguably not be in the public interest, the prosecution would merely have to tell the defence that an application was to be made ex p ante to the court. If the court, having heard the argument, thought it wrong to proceed with an ex p ante hearing it would so order. In rare cases it might be contrary to the public interest even to reveal that an ex p ante application was to be made. In that situation the prosecution could apply to the court ex p ante without telling the defence.

In *R v Keane* [1994] 2 All ER 478 the Court of Appeal held that if the disputed material might prove the defendant's innocence or avoid a miscarriage of justice the court should always order disclosure.

But by 1995 the pendulum had begun to swing back a little. In *R v Turner* [1995] 1 WLR 264, the Court of Appeal, per Lord Taylor the Lord Chief Justice, urged judges faced with defence requests for disclosure to adopt a fairly tough approach:

Since *R v Ward* there has been an increasing tendency for defendants to seek disclosure of informants' names and roles, alleging that those details are essential to the defence. Defences that the accused has been set up, and allegations of duress, which used at one time to be rare, have multiplied. We wish to alert judges to the need to scrutinise applications for disclosure of details about informants with very great care. They will need to be astute to see that assertions of a need to know such details, because they are essential to the running of the defence, are justified. If they are not so justified, then the judge will need to adopt a robust approach in declining to order disclosure.

Recommendations of the Runciman Royal Commission

The Runciman Royal Commission was persuaded by evidence given mainly by the police that the disclosure regime introduced by Mr Justice Henry's decision in Guinness I and by the Court of Appeal's judgment in *Ward* resulted in some cases in excessive burdens on the prosecution.

41. ... Even in some straightforward cases the amount of material collected during the course of the investigation can be voluminous. In major inquiries, even with computerised logs of all the information collected during the investigation, it is scarcely possible to be sure that all the material that has been generated has been listed.

42. Against this background, the defence can require the police and prosecution to comb through large masses of material in the hope either of causing delay or of chancing upon something that will induce the prosecution to drop the case rather than to have to disclose the material concerned. The defence may do this by successive requests for more material, far beyond the stage at which it could reasonably be claimed that the information was likely to cast doubt upon the prosecution case. Although it may be time consuming and wasteful of resources for the police to check all the material requested, they may have to do so if they are to be sure that they can properly be released. For example, the information may have been given to the police in response to a broadcast appeal promising confidentiality to those providing the information. Or some witnesses may have given statements to the police naming third parties... The police may well feel that the information should not be divulged and may in some cases decline to divulge it even if it means dropping the case. This does not seem to us to be in the interests of justice.

43. These problems were particularly acute where informants or undercover police officers were concerned. 'Their lives may be at stake if their existence, let alone their identities, are suspected' (Report, p 93, para 43).

The Attorney General's Guidelines had left it to the prosecution, in consultation with prosecution counsel when necessary, to decide whether material should be withheld on public interest or sensitivity grounds. In *Ward* the court said it was not for the prosecution to be judge in its own cause. But where sensitivity was not the issue the present position was not satisfactory.

49. ... We strongly support the aim of the recent decisions to compel the prosecution to disclose everything that may be relevant to the defence's case. But we accept the evidence that we have received that the decisions have created burdens for the prosecution that go beyond what is reasonable. At present the prosecution can be required to disclose the existence of matters whose potential relevance is speculative in the extreme. Moreover, the sheer bulk of the material involved in many cases makes it wholly impracticable for every one of what may be hundreds of thousands of individual transactions to be disclosed.

50. In our unanimous view a reasonable balance between the duties of the prosecution and the rights of the defence requires that a new regime be created with two stages of disclosure. The first stage of primary disclosure, would, subject to appropriate exceptions, be automatic.

The second stage, of secondary or further disclosure would be made if the defence could establish its relevance to the case. Where the prosecution and defence disagreed on this aspect, the court would rule on the matter after weighing the potential importance of the material to the defence.

51. We envisage, therefore, that the prosecution's initial duty should be to supply to the defence copies of all material relevant to the offence or to the offender or to the surrounding circumstances of the case whether or not the prosecution intend to rely upon that material. Material relevant to the offender includes evidence which might not appear on the face of it to be relevant to the offence but which might be important to the defence because for example it raises questions about the defendant's mental state, including his suggestibility or propensity to make false confessions (as happened in the case of Judith Ward). In addition, the prosecution should inform the defence at this stage of the existence of any other material obtained during the course of the inquiry into the offence. This part of its duty should be discharged by the CPS or other prosecuting authority disclosing to the defence the lists [which could in many cases be by reference to categories, such as 'house-to-house inquiries on a housing estate'] or schedules which it had obtained from the police and other key participants in the investigation such as expert scientific witnesses. This would enable the defence to go through the lists and see whether there was any material which might be relevant to the defence but which the prosecution had not thought to be relevant in its initial selection of items for full disclosure.

Thereafter, if the defence wanted more disclosure it should be under an obligation to justify such a request by reference to the case it intended or hoped to present. As will be seen below, the Commission by a majority of 10–1 recommended that the defence should be required to give outline details of the defence in all cases. The dissenter was the writer. But the writer agreed with the other ten members of the Royal Commission that in the probably quite rare case where the defence wanted further disclosure that should be on the basis of disclosure of enough of the defence case as to persuade a judge that such an order should be made.

Disclosure of scientific evidence

In *R v Ward* (above) the Court of Appeal dealt specifically with the duty of disclosure in regard to scientific evidence (at p 628):

> We believe that the surest way of preventing the misuse of scientific evidence is by ensuring that there is a proper understanding of the nature and scope of the prosecution's duty of disclosure ... [The court then dealt with the Advance Notice of Expert Evidence Rules, 1987 which enabled the defence to ask the prosecution to provide a copy or an opportunity to inspect 'the record of any observation, test, calculation, or other procedure on which [any] finding or opinion is based'.] The new rules are helpful. But it is a misconception to regard them as exhaustive; they do not in any way supplant or detract from the prosecution's general duty of disclosure in respect of scientific evidence. That duty exists irrespective of any request by the defence. It is also not limited to documentation on which the opinion or findings of an expert is based. It extends to anything that may arguably help the defence ... Moreover, it is a positive duty, which in the context of scientific evidence obliges the prosecution to make full and proper inquiries from forensic scientists in order to discover whether there is discoverable material. Given the undoubted inequality as between prosecution and defence in access to forensic scientists, we regard it as of paramount importance that the common law duty of disclosure, as we have explained it, should be understood by those who prosecute and defend.

The Runciman Royal Commission also emphasised the crucial importance of prosecution disclosure to the defence where exhibits are sent to a lab for analysis. Sir

John May's inquiry into the case of the Maguires[6] and the Court of Appeal's judgment in the Judith Ward case (above) had demonstrated the serious risk of a miscarriage of justice if there were not full disclosure of scientific evidence to the defence. 'Forensic scientists are therefore under a categorical obligation to disclose to the police, and the police to pass on to the CPS, all the scientific evidence that may be relevant to the case' (Report, p 154, para 45). This duty of disclosure it said extended to anything that might help the defence.

Following disclosure, the defence are entitled to access to notebooks and test results and to information about similar evidence discovered in other or related cases, especially where this tends to undermine the identification of the defendant as the offender. We interpret the Court of Appeal judgment in *Ward* as meaning that, if expert witnesses are aware of experiments or tests, even if they have not carried them out personally, which tend to disprove or cast doubt upon the opinions that they are expressing, they are under an obligation to bring the records of them to the attention of the police and prosecution.

The Commission said that it had 'no hesitation in endorsing the main thrust of the Court of Appeal's judgment in *Ward* as regards the disclosure of scientific evidence and it was pleased to be able to say 'that this is also accepted by the public sector laboratories concerned' (p 154, para 47). If the defence thought there might be material at the laboratory which threw doubt on the prosecution's test results, 'they should in our view be entitled to have access to the original notes of the experiment in order to test that belief'. It continued:

We believe that this is in fact the position, since we have been told by defence experts that they now have full access to everyone and everything relevant to the case in question.

The Royal Commission recommended that when exhibits were taken for analysis by the prosecution, regard should be had to the potential desire of the defence in due course to carry out their own tests on the material. Where practicable sufficient material should be collected for the purpose and, so far as practicable, the scene of the crime should remain undisturbed. After a suspect had been charged the defence should have an enforceable right to observe any further scientific tests carried out or the right to remove some of the material for their own analysis (Report, p 155, para 52).

The Government's Consultation Paper on Disclosure

In May 1995 the Government published its Consultation Paper on Disclosure (Cm 2864). Broadly it accepted the recommendations of the Runciman Royal Commission but both in regard to prosecution and in regard to defence disclosure it proposed certain changes from what the Commission had recommended.

The Government proposed first that there should be a new statutory duty on the investigator to preserve material until the outcome of the case and for an unspecified period thereafter.

The investigator would not have to make all the material available to the prosecutor. Instead, he would be required to sort the material into three categories: (1) material expected to support the prosecution's case; (2) 'specified category material'; and (3) all other material.

6 *Interim Report on the Guildford and Woolwich pub bombings*, (HMSO) 1990, (HC 556) and *Second Report on the Maguire Case*, 1992 (HC 296).

Specified category material would include material relevant to the issue of the accused's legal responsibility (relating for instance to his mental condition); statements by potential witnesses containing a description of the offender; inconsistent statements by potential witnesses; material affecting the reliability of a confession; material going to the credibility or reliability of potential witnesses whose evidence goes to the substantive issues; statements showing the results of forensic tests or other material provided by material witnesses (para 35).

Material expected to support the prosecution's case and material in the specified categories would be supplied to the prosecutor, together with a schedule of all other material.

Primary prosecution disclosure   The prosecutor would always be under a duty to disclose to the defence material which constituted the prosecution's case. He would be under a duty to disclose to the defence unused material in the specified categories and any other material which had been brought to his attention which in his view might undermine the prosecution case. The prosecutor would make that judgment on the basis of what *he believed* the issues to be, based on the evidence contained in the prosecution case (para 39).

Primary disclosure would take place as soon as possible after either a not guilty plea has been entered by the defendant in summary proceedings, or after committal where the case is to be tried in the crown court.

The effect of the test proposed by the Government, the Document stated, was to return to the prosecutor the initial decision whether material in his possession might undermine the prosecution case. There should be no room for fishing expeditions by the defence, and no role for the court at this stage, unless the prosecutor brings material before it.

The prosecutor would not at that stage have to disclose the schedule of unused material provided by the investigator. The Government acknowledged that this represented a significant change from the existing position. It would put heavy reliance on the investigator to identify material that ought to be disclosed–'given that the material itself will not necessarily be scrutinised by the prosecutor' (para 44.) The investigator would have to ensure that an officer of appropriate seniority was responsible for the compilation of the schedule. The system would demand a significant degree of liaison between the prosecutor and the investigator.

Secondary prosecution disclosure   The defence would only be entitled to ask for further disclosure if it first complies with the obligation to disclose sufficient details of its case to identify the issues in dispute. (For the legislation as regards defence disclosure see p 245 below). The prosecution would then have to re-check their material in the light of what has been disclosed by the defence and, subject to considerations of sensitivity, to disclose any further unused material 'which might reasonably assist the particular line of argument disclosed by the defence' (para 57).

Any dispute would be resolved by the court but the court would not have the power to order disclosure of the schedule of unused material (paras 60–62).

The Government considered that there would not be a right of appeal against decisions of the court on disclosure disputes (para 63).

Sensitive material   If the prosecution wished not to disclose sensitive material that would otherwise have to be disclosed, the procedure should be that laid down in *R v Davis* (sometimes called *Johnson, Davis and Rowe*–p 230 above.)

The draft Code of Practice which will accompany the new rules stated that the person responsible for making disclosure (to be known as 'the disclosure officer') should list and number each item of material separately and the description 'should make clear the nature of the item and should contain sufficient detail to enable the prosecutor to form a judgment on whether the material needs to be disclosed'. The disclosure officer would in addition give the prosecutor a copy of any material in the following categories: (1) information from witnesses containing a description of the alleged offender which does not conform to the defendant's description; (2) information from the accused person giving an explanation; (3) any material casting doubt on the reliability of a confession or on the reliability of a witness; and (4) any other material which the investigator believes may fall within the test for primary disclosure.

After the defendant has put in his defence statement the disclosure officer must look again at the material and must draw the attention of the prosecutor to any material that might reasonably be expected to assist the defence disclosed by the accused. The disclosure officer must certify to the prosecutor that to the best of his knowledge and belief the duties under the Code have been complied with.

Reactions to the Consultation Document

The proposals in the Consultation Paper were criticised not only by the main civil liberties bodies but by the Law Society–see Roger Ede, 'Law Society Attacks Government's Disclosure Plans', Criminal Practitioners Newsletter, No 24, 1995, p 2. The Law Society said that it was only in very few cases that unused material was voluminous. These cases should not be allowed to shape the system. The Government's proposals did not deal adequately with disclosure by the police to the prosecution. ('This is a fatal flaw as they do not ensure that the police make proper disclosure to the prosecution in the first place' (*ibid*).) The proposal gave the police and the prosecution a defence role–'suggesting that they know what the defence need more than the defence themselves' (*ibid*). The Law Society suggested that the schedule should always be disclosed to the defence and that there should be minimum standards set for its contents. Only the defence were in a position to judge what the defence required, though a judge should decide issues of public interest immunity. A police investigator could not be expected to look at the case from the defence point of view and was not trained to be impartial. ('Nor can the officer be expected to help to dismantle a case which he or she has just constructed or reveal wrongdoings by the police' (*ibid*).)

The Law Reform Committee of the Bar Council, in its response in July 1995, argued that the Government had failed to strike the right balance. The Government's paper had for instance paid insufficient attention to how the investigator could be made to perform his duties properly. This was surprising 'when one considers that those found to be at fault in some of the miscarriage of justice cases based on failure to disclose have been investigators who have deliberately avoided making or negligently omitted to make proper disclosure' (para 34). The Bar Council said: 'We do not believe it to be appropriate for the police to be taking decisions as to disclosure' (para 35). It fundamentally disagreed with the proposal that the investigator would not have to make available to the prosecutor all the material which had been preserved. This 'ignores the lessons to be learnt from recent history' (para 36). The investigator should be under a (continuing) duty to make available to the prosecutor all the material gathered or generated during the investigation. It would then be for the prosecutor to discharge the (continuing) duty of disclosure. Also the investigator should be under a duty to prepare a schedule of all material in his possession and all other possible sources of material which might be relevant to the investigation and such schedule should be disclosed to the defence and the court, at the latest on defence disclosure taking place. ('We strongly disagree with the Government's proposal, which is contrary to the views of the Royal Commission, that neither the defence or the court would have any right to see the schedule' (para 37)). Sensitive material could be listed on a separate schedule which would go to the prosecutor but not to the defence.

The Bar suggested that the schedule of unused material should be on a prescribed form, signed by the investigator which should bear a warning that it is to be used for criminal proceedings and spelling out the disclosure duties of the investigator. It should also state that it is a criminal offence knowingly to provide a schedule that is false or misleading. The importance of the matter should be emphasised. ('Further, the point has validly been made to us that the approach of the police to disclosure is one which has led to problems in the past, and is the product of a "culture" or approach in certain quarters which will not change or be encouraged to do so by the Government's present proposals' (para 38).) (For the Bar Council's views on what disclosure should be required of the defence see below, p 245.)

The Criminal Procedure and Investigations Act

The Government's response emerged in November 1995 with the publication of the Criminal Procedure and Investigations Bill. The Bill received the Royal Assent on 4 July 1996. Disclosure is dealt with in Parts I and II of the Act which replace common law disclosure rules and the Attorney General's Guidelines. The Act (ss 23–26) provides for a Code of Practice regarding disclosure.

Primary prosecution disclosure　Section 3(1) requires the prosecutor to disclose to the accused any prosecution material 'which *in the prosecutor's opinion* might undermine the case for the prosecution against the accused' (emphasis supplied), or alternatively to give the accused a written statement that there is no material of that description. (Attempts in both the House of Lords and the Commons to get Ministers to accept that this subjective test should be changed to an objective test were unsuccessful.)

This is to be compared with the definition of what the Lord Chief Justice in *Keane* (p 230 above at p 184) said had to be disclosed at common law: 'material which on a sensible appraisal was judged (1) to be relevant or possibly relevant to an issue in the case; or (2) to raise or possibly raise a new issue whose existence is not apparent from the evidence the prosecution propose to use; or (3) to hold a real (as opposed to fanciful) prospect of providing a lead on evidence which goes to (1) or (2)'. In *R v Brown (Winston)* [1994] 1 WLR 1599 it was made clear that the phrase 'an issue in the case' must be given a broad rather than a narrow interpretation and that the duty of disclosure applies to oral as well as to written statements.

Under the Act, the duty to give primary disclosure would arise with a period to be prescribed measured from 'the relevant day'. For cases dealt with in the magistrates' court the relevant day is the day the defendant pleads not guilty and for cases dealt with at the crown court, it is the day the proceedings are committed to the crown court (ss 3(8), 12 and 13(1)).

The periods were to be prescribed by regulations under the new Act. However, it will be possible for the prosecution to ask for an extension. If the prosecution fails to meet the time limits, this does not necessarily constitute grounds for staying the proceedings, for abuse of process but it can do so if 'it involves such delay by the prosecutor that the accused is denied a fair trial' (House of Commons Standing Committee B, 16 May 1996, col 157.)

Under the new disclosure rules the defence do not have the advantage of even primary prosecution disclosure before deciding whether to plead guilty in the magistrates' court. It is predictable that in many cases defence lawyers would advise a plea of not guilty, at least initially, in order to get the benefit of primary prosecution disclosure. The Government position in the debates on the Bill was that even if that were to happen it would still be less costly than providing primary prosecution disclosure in all cases.

Worse is the fact that in cases where the police anticipate a guilty plea in the magistrates' court, under the Act they will not have to pass information to the prosecution lawyers as to the weaknesses of the prosecution's case. The duty on the police to prepare a disclosure schedule for consideration by the prosecution lawyers only arises if the accused is likely to be tried in the crown court or is likely to plead not guilty in the magistrates' court. The Law Society suggested in April 1996 that this might result in some defence lawyers recommending a client to plead not guilty rather than guilty simply in order to get that information. (Law Society, *Criminal Practitioners' Newsletter*, April 1996, p 1.)

The Act requires the prosecutor when making primary disclosure, at the same time to give to the accused (a) a document indicating the nature of any prosecution material which relates to the offence, which has not been disclosed to the accused, and which the prosecutor believes is not sensitive, or (b) a written statement that there is no material of that kind.

Secondary prosecution disclosure   After defence disclosure has been made under sections 5 or 6, the prosecutor must make secondary disclosure of any prosecution material not already disclosed which 'might be reasonably expected to assist the accused's defence as disclosed by the defence statement given to the prosecutor under section 5 or 6' or give the accused a written statement that there is no such material (s 7(2)).

If the accused thinks the prosecution have not complied with their obligation to disclose he can apply to the court for an order requiring such disclosure (s 8(2)). The court need not make such an order if it does not think such disclosure to be in the public interest (s 8(5)). This decision must however be kept under continuing review by the court (s 15(3)).

The prosecutor too must keep the question of what should be disclosed under continuing review (s 9(2)).

For a critique of these proposals see, for instance, T Wyn and C Foster, 'If it ain't broke, don't fix it', *Solicitors' Journal*, 19 January 1996, p 50.

(c) Other issues of prosecution disclosure

Where a prosecution witness is of known bad character, the prosecution is under a duty to inform the defence of the fact (*R v Collister and Warhurst* (1955) 39 Cr App Rep 100). In *Paraskeva* [1983] Crim LR 186, the Court of Appeal quashed a conviction because the prosecution had failed to comply with this duty. The complainant in a charge of robbery and assault had had a conviction for theft. The Appeal Court said that the defence should have been told, since either the prosecution or the defence were lying and the jury should have had this information in making up their minds which it was. It has been laid down in a Practice Statement that details of the previous convictions of the accused himself must be supplied by the prosecution to the defence— *Practice Direction* [1966] 1 WLR 1184.

See also *Edwards* (1991) 93 Cr App Rep 48, where the Court of Appeal quashed convictions because disciplinary findings against police witnesses had not been made known to the defence or the court. The court held that the defence were entitled to cross-examine police officers not only about disciplinary findings but also about any earlier trial in which their evidence had been rejected by the jury in circumstances suggesting that they were not believed. The Runciman Royal Commission thought this went too far. It recommended that the prosecution should only be required to disclose disciplinary findings against police witnesses insofar as those records were relevant to an allegation by the defence about the conduct of the witness in the present case. The Royal Commission thought that the prosecution should also not be required to disclose cases in which there has been an acquittal following evidence given by an officer where it would seem that his evidence must have been disbelieved by the jury. Since research in the jury room was not permitted there was no way of knowing why the jury had rejected particular evidence (Report, p 97, para 56).

The prosecution must disclose to the defence copies of any statement or report made by any prison doctor as to the mental capacity of the defendant. Also the results of any examination carried out by the Home Office Forensic Science Laboratory should be handed over to the defence. But generally the prosecution are not under an obligation to disclose material that goes solely to the credibility of defence witnesses–*R v Brown (Winston)* [1994] 1 WLR 1599. For a report of the case, comparison with *R v Rasheed* (1994) 158 JP 941 and comment see also *New Law Journal* 8 July 1994, p 939.

Defence access to scientific or forensic material and testing

A JUSTICE Committee said in December 1987 that although the police theoretically made their forensic science laboratory facilities available to the defence, 'in practice little or no use can be made of them'. The police would not permit re-examination of an exhibit already examined by one of their own scientists. They would allow their own scientists to conduct tests for the defence or a defence scientist to use their laboratories. But they insisted that their own scientists had to be present, which meant that the prosecution were fully apprised of the experiments and the results. This was 'wholly unacceptable' and 'an erosion of the principle that it is for the prosecution to establish their case' (JUSTICE, *A Public Defender*, 1987, para 30). Generally the defence did not take advantage of the possibility of using police facilities. Indeed if they did, and if evidence favourable to the prosecution emerged, it would be a gross breach of duty by the defence solicitor to the client.

In 1989 the House of Commons Home Affairs Committee reported on the Forensic Science Service ('The Forensic Science Service', 1988–9, HC 26–1). On the issue of access for the defence it thought that it was valuable that defence lawyers had a choice of using independent scientists or the Forensic Service.

In April 1991 the Forensic Science Service (FSS) became an Executive Agency of the Home Office as part of the Thatcher Government's policy for making public bodies somewhat independent and financially accountable. It started to charge the police and others using its services. (Previously even the defence experts had the use of the facilities free of charge.) The Framework Document provided that the Agency was free to take on work for the defence. But it seems that this will develop slowly. (See Russell Stockdale. 'Running with the Hounds', *New Law Journal*, 7 June 1991, p 772, raising the question of how to provide adequate forensic scientific services to the defence.)

The problem of provision of adequate scientific facilities for the defence was in the terms of reference of the Runciman Royal Commission. The Royal Commission said that the public sector forensic science laboratories were prepared to work for the defence for its normal charges–provided the same lab was not already working on the case for the prosecution. The exception was the Metropolitan Police Forensic Science Laboratory, and it intended to change this policy. But it was rare that the defence were dissatisfied with tests carried out for the prosecution. It was more likely to be a matter of interpretation of the results. Defence scientists were allowed to use the public sector facilities (Report, p 146, para 11).

The Commission proposed that 'all the public sector laboratories should look upon themselves as equally available to the defence and the prosecution and we would expect to see considerable development of the provision of services to the defence as time goes by' (Report, p 149, para 24).

The Royal Commission thought that the defence should have complete freedom to choose between public sector and private sector forensic scientists (Report, p 156, para 55). It did not think that public funds should be devoted to establishing separate facilities for the defence.

(d) Disclosure by the defence

It has been a fundamental principle that the defendant's right of silence in the police station (p 114 above) extended also to the preparatory stages before the trial and to the trial itself. Subject to a few exceptions, the defence was not under any obligation to give advance notice of its case. But this has now changed.

The first exception was the Criminal Justice Act 1967, which in s 11 laid down that an alibi defence must be notified to the police in advance of the trial, so that it could be checked.

In 1975, the James Committee (p 18 above), in spite of its strong recommendations for more disclosure by the prosecution, did not think that the defence should be asked to disclose more–or at least not without more detailed consideration. It observed that: 'there is considerable strength in the argument that it is wrong in principle, in a system which presumes innocence until guilt is proved, to require disclosure of the defence before the details of the evidence for the prosecution are disclosed' (para 229).

The Philips Royal Commission on Criminal Procedure also considered whether the principle of disclosure accepted in alibi defences should be extended to other forms of evidence. It did not think that the defence should generally be required to disclose its case. It thought there was an 'objection of principle' to any formal requirement of general disclosure by the defence because the burden of proof was upon the prosecution (para 8.20). It considered that it would be impossible to devise effective sanctions against a defendant who failed to comply with the requirement, since it seemed unlikely that in practice courts would be prepared to prevent a defendant from introducing evidence that demonstrated his innocence. (The experience with the alibi defence rule is that courts are normally lax about insisting on compliance by the defence and in reality the sanction is the comment permitted to prosecution and judge on failure to comply.) The Commission cited research evidence that even police officers thought that new facts introduced at the trial resulted in unjustified acquittals only in about 1 per cent of cases (para 8.21). But it agreed with the Scottish Thomson Committee in its report in 1975 (Cmnd 6218, para 37.11) that special defences should be notified to the prosecution in advance. The obvious examples, it thought, were defences depending on medical or forensic evidence on which the prosecution would wish to consider calling expert testimony.

Section 81 of PACE granted power to make crown court rules to require any party to proceedings before the crown court to disclose to the other party any expert evidence which he proposes to adduce in the case.

The new rules (Crown Court (Advance Notice of Expert Evidence) Rules, SI 1987/716) provide for the disclosure, as soon as practicable after committal, of a statement in writing of any finding or opinion of an expert upon which a party intends to rely. Failure can be penalized by the court refusing permission to adduce the expert evidence, but, like alibi notices, it is not strictly enforced by the courts.

Roskill Report

The problem of disclosure by the defence was also considered by the Roskill Committee in its report on Fraud Trials (HMSO, January 1986). It said that the evidence it had received disagreed on the subject. Some argued that at least in fraud cases there should be something like pleadings in a civil case so as to define the issues. A great deal of time was wasted at fraud trials on evidence over which in the end there proved to be no dispute. Trials could be shorter if the defence were disclosed in advance. (The Committee also thought that the jury would be greatly assisted if at the outset, after the prosecution had outlined its case, the defence were to be asked to clarify what part of the prosecution's case it intended to dispute.)

The main objection was that it was an infringement of the principle of the right of silence, the burden of proof and the protection against self-incrimination. It also alluded to the problem of finding an effective sanction. It thought that the sanction of not allowing the defendant to give that evidence or possibly any evidence was either too draconian or unworkable or both. A costs sanction would hardly ever be effective. Those on legal aid would have no cause to worry about such a sanction and the wealthy could ignore it. But the threat of critical comment by the prosecution and the judge would, it thought, be a useful sanction (paras 6.67–6.81).

It concluded, subject to one dissent, that the defence should be required to outline its case in writing at the preparatory stage. Failure to do so should be capable of attracting adverse comment from the prosecution and the judge, and the jury could be invited to draw adverse inferences (para 6.82).

It also considered, but ultimately rejected, the case for advance disclosure by the defence of the names of its witnesses and for advance notification to the prosecution as to whether the defendant himself intends to give evidence (paras 6.83–4).

In his Note of Dissent, Mr Merricks said that he would restrict the use that could be made of the defence outline of its case at the trial. No reference to it should be permitted during the trial save with the leave of the judge. This would be to avoid the danger that prosecution counsel would use the defence advance disclosure statement in examining his own witnesses, so as to discredit the defence. By the same token, there would be a danger that the defence might be hampered in cross-examining the prosecution witnesses. It was a normal aspect of cross-examination that counsel would probe and test the veracity and credibility of the other side's witnesses. But if the defence were revealed in advance the judge might rule irrelevant any line of questioning which was not germane to the defence as outlined.

The Government, however, accepted the majority's recommendation. The Criminal Justice Act 1987, which was rushed into law before the General Election in June 1987, provided that in serious fraud case investigations notices can be given under s 2 requiring persons to give information and to produce documents. This power has been used extensively. But in addition under s 7 a crown court judge can order a special preparatory hearing in cases of 'fraud of such seriousness and complexity that substantial benefits are likely to accrue from' such a hearing, for the purpose of identifying the issues, assisting the comprehension of such issues, expediting the proceedings or assisting the judge's management of the trial. An order for a preparatory hearing may be asked for by either the prosecution or the defence.

The judge can order the prosecution to 'prepare and serve any documents that appear to him to be relevant' and having made such an order and the prosecution having complied with it, the judge can then make an equivalent order for the defence to provide relevant documents (s 8).

The judge can order the prosecution to supply the defence with a 'case statement' of the following: (1) the principal facts of the prosecution case; (2) the witnesses who will speak to those facts; (3) any exhibits relevant to those facts; (4) any proposition of law on which the prosecution intends to rely; and (5) the relationship between any of the above and the charges (s 9(4)(*a*). He can also require the prosecution to give notice of documents the truth of the contents of which ought, in the view of the prosecution, to be admitted by the defence and of any other matters which ought to be agreed (s 9(4)(*c*)).

When the prosecution have complied with such an order, the judge can order the defence to give the court and the prosecution: (1) a statement in writing setting out in general terms the nature of his defence and indicating the principal matters on which he takes issue with the prosecution; (2) notice of any objections he has to the prosecution's case statement; (3) notice of any points of law he intends to take, including any on the admissibility of evidence; and (4) notice of the extent to which he agrees with the prosecution as regards documents and other matters under s 4(*c*) and the reason for any disagreements (s 9(4)(*c*)).

Section 10 provides that, in the event of any departure from the case disclosed at the preparatory hearing or any failure to comply with the obligation to make advance disclosure, the judge and, with the judge's leave, the other party, may make such comment as he thinks appropriate. (In deciding whether to give such leave the judge is required to have regard to the extent of any departure and whether there was any justification for it.) When making an order to the defence to make advance disclosure, the judge must warn the defence of the possibility of such comment (s 9(6)).

For a report on how the powers under the 1987 Act have been utilised see M Levi, *The Investigation, Prosecution and Trial of Serious Fraud*, Royal Commission on Criminal Justice, Research Report No 14, 1993.

A high-powered Working Group chaired by the Lord Chancellor's Department recommended in 1991 that legislation should be introduced requiring the defendant to state the nature of his defence at a plea and directions hearing in the Crown Court (*Working Group on Pre-Trial Issues*, November 1991[7], para 244). The Working Group included representatives of the CPS, the Home Office, the Justices' Clerks Society, the Legal Secretariat to the Law Officers and the police. The report said that it was not suggested that a defendant should specify the substance or detail of his case or the evidence he will call to establish his defence, but he should be asked to reveal the essential issues in dispute and the principal facts (*ibid*). This could achieve substantial savings in court time.

Runciman Royal Commission on Criminal Justice

The Runciman Royal Commission too, by a majority of 10–1, recommended that after the prosecution had produced its case, the defendant should be asked to indicate in outline the nature of his defence:

59. With one dissentient, we believe that there are powerful reasons for extending the obligations on the defence to provide advance disclosure. If all the parties had in advance an indication of what the defence would be, this would not only encourage earlier and better preparation of cases but might well result in the prosecution being dropped in the light of the defence disclosure, an earlier resolution through a plea of guilty, or the fixing of an earlier trial date. The length of the trial could also be more readily estimated, leading to a better use of the time both of the court and of those involved in the trial; and there would be kept to a minimum those cases where the defendant withholds his or her defence until the last possible moment in the hope of confusing the jury or evading investigation of a fabricated defence [p 97].

The majority thought this would not infringe the right of defendants not to incriminate themselves–anymore than this right was infringed by the duty to advance one's defence at trial. Moreover defendants would still be entitled to remain silent throughout (pp 97–8, para 60). It was true that 'ambush defences' were relatively rare but the present system encouraged late preparation of cases which was undesirable.

68. In most cases disclosure of the defence should be a matter capable of being handled by the defendant's solicitor (in the same way that alibi notices are usually dealt with at present). Standard forms could be drawn up to cover the most common offences, with the solicitor having only to tick one or more of a list of possibilities, such as 'accident', 'self-defence', 'consent', 'no dishonest intent', 'no appropriation', 'abandoned goods', 'claim of right', 'mistaken identification' and so on. There will be complex cases which may require the assistance of counsel in formulating the defence. Where counsel are involved, they should if practicable stay with the case until the end of the trial: where this is impracticable, the barrister who has been involved

---

7   The Report, which made 165 recommendations, was not published in the normal sense. The work of this committee was taken over in January 1996 by a new Trial Issues Group–see p 281 below.

with the pre-trial work should pass on his or her preparation to the barrister who is to present the case at trial [p 98].

The writer dissented:

1. The most important objection to defence disclosure is that it is contrary to principle for the defendant to be made to respond to the prosecution's case until it has been presented at the trial. The defendant should be required to respond to the case the prosecution makes, not to the case it says it is going to make. They are often significantly different.

2. The fundamental issue at stake is that the burden of proof lies throughout on the prosecution. Defence disclosure is designed to be helpful to the prosecution and, more generally, to the system. But it is not the job of the defendant to be helpful either to the prosecution or to the system. His task, if he chooses to put the prosecution to the proof, is simply to defend himself. Rules requiring advance disclosure of alibis and expert evidence are reasonable exceptions to this general principle. But, in my view, it is wrong to require the defendant to be helpful by giving advance notice of his defence and to penalise him by adverse comment if he fails to do so.

3. Moreover, the majority provides no evidence that there is a problem that requires action. The chief reason for wanting defence disclosure is to assist the prosecution's preparation and to avoid 'ambush defences', sprung without notice. But, as the majority itself admits, ambush defences are rare, and when they occur they usually do not pose much of a problem.

6. Other reasons advanced by the majority[8] to justify introducing a requirement of defence disclosure are:

– That advance disclosure of the nature of the defence may lead to the prosecution dropping the case;
– That it may lead to an early guilty plea;
– That it may lead to fixing of an earlier trial date;
– That it would permit more accurate estimates of the length of the trial.

7. Each of these propositions seems unconvincing. All that is to be required of the defendant is that he disclose the broad nature of his defence (ie that it will be self-defence, provocation, consent, etc). It is difficult to visualise such limited disclosure having any of the above effects. Such limited disclosure would give little real help to the prosecution which wants to know what witnesses the defence intends to call and what they are likely to say. But it is not (yet) suggested that the defence would have to reveal such information. If therefore there is a problem about ambush defences, the majority's proposal would barely touch it. (One can foresee that if this limited form of defence disclosure proves largely useless to the prosecution, the next thing will be a call for much more defence disclosure.)

8. In serious fraud cases under the Criminal Justice Act 1987 the defence can be required by the judge to produce a case statement setting out the defence 'in general terms'. But a study done for the Royal Commission by Professor Michael Levi shows that this has proved largely ineffectual because it is not sufficiently specific.[9] If it does not work in the serious fraud area, it probably will not work in other areas.

9. Moreover, a general requirement of defence disclosure would involve significant extra delays, costs and inefficiencies. The lay client would have to be seen to take his instructions. Getting the lay client to come into the solicitor's office or going to see him in prison is often troublesome. Counsel would quite frequently be involved both to advise and often actually to settle the defence disclosure. It could hardly be expected that defence lawyers would go out of their way to be helpful to the prosecution. The prosecution would therefore often find it right to ask for 'further and better particulars', with resulting further delays and costs. These extra costs

8 Report, p 97, paragraph 59.
9 Michael Levi, *The Investigation, Prosecution and Trial of Serious Fraud*, Royal Commission on Criminal Justice Research Study No 14, 1993, pp 104, 182.

would apply not only to cases that ended as trials but also to those that ended as last-minute guilty pleas ('cracked trials').

10. The present much criticised lack of continuity in counsel's involvement in the case would pose even greater problems than in relation to ordinary pre-trial matters. From the defendant's point of view, the last minute appearance of a barrister he has never seen before would be even more upsetting in a regime where pre-trial defence disclosure was a requirement. It is bad enough that the client should so often be faced on the day of the trial with a new barrister. It would be worse if he knew that the new barrister's ability to represent him was restricted by decisions regarding defence disclosure made by another barrister at an earlier stage whether on paper or at a pre-trial hearing.

11. Moreover it is extremely unlikely that defence disclosure rules would be enforced. The rule requiring advance notice of an alibi defence is honoured more in the breach than in the observance. Where there has been a breach of the rule the judge can refuse to allow the alibi defence to be put. But breaches are generally not penalised by the judges–because they are understandably reluctant to prevent a defendant from putting forward his defence. The judges would I believe be equally slow to penalise failure to make this new form of defence disclosure, whether by adverse comment or by sanctions imposed on the lawyers.

12. In summary, I am against defence disclosure because it is wrong in principle, and because it would cause extra delay, cost and general inefficiency in the system, to little, if any, purpose [pp 221–23].

The Government's Consultation Document on Disclosure

The Government adopted the view of the majority, but it was minded to go even further than the Royal Commission. In its May 1995 Consultation Document on Disclosure (Cm 2864) it proposed that after the prosecution had served the unused material in its possession (see above), the defence should be required to 'provide sufficient particulars of its case to identify the issues in dispute between the defence and the prosecution before the commencement':

51. The defence would be required to provide sufficient particulars of its case to identify the issues in dispute between the defence and the prosecution before the commencement of the trial. It would also enable the prosecutor or investigator to assess whether they had any additional unused material which might assist that case. The exact details of what would need to be disclosed by the defendant in each case would depend on the particular defence to be advanced. The Government envisages that the details will include, as they currently do in an alibi defence, the name and address of any witnesses the defendant proposes to call in support of that defence, or a written statement of fact or opinion which the defendant proposes to adduce as expert evidence, or any evidence which might support a defence of, for example consent or self-defence or duress.

52. The Government believes that the defence should be expected to assist the prosecutor to identify material which is genuinely helpful to the defence case if it is seeking further prosecution disclosure, and that disclosure of the defence case is in the interests of justice and should assist the better management of trials [p 16].

The sanction for non-compliance would be that the jury could be invited to draw adverse inferences. Such inferences could be drawn where the defendant made no response, or where he disclosed two or more mutually inconsistent defences or where he disclosed a defence pre-trial and then at the trial presented a different defence. The Consultation Document added:

56. These proposals will not penalise the defendant who has a genuine defence, who discloses it at the appropriate stage and maintains that defence at trial. Nor does the Government believe that these proposals affect the principle that it is the duty of the prosecution to establish the guilt of a defendant beyond reasonable doubt, and that the defendant may not be compelled to incriminate himself. The burden of proof will remain upon the prosecution. Furthermore, as with the existing provisions on inferences from silence, no-one will be convicted simply on the basis of an inference drawn by the court from the response of the defence at this stage of the proceedings.

In its response to the Consultation Document the Bar Council said that it supported defence disclosure along the lines of the regime in serious fraud cases. But neither party should be permitted to amend their case statements without good cause being given to the court. But the Bar Council opposed the Government's proposal that the defence be required to provide the names and addresses of defence witnesses. The Law Society took a similar line, accepting a limited form of defence disclosure but objecting to disclosure by the defence of the names and addresses of its witnesses.

The Criminal Procedure and Investigations Act

The Criminal Procedure and Investigations Act introduced in November 1995 provided for a new regime of compulsory disclosure by the accused in response to primary disclosure by the prosecution (on which see p 236 above). Section 5 says that the accused must give a defence statement to the prosecutor–

s 5 (6) For the purposes of this section a defence statement is a written statement–

    (a) setting out in general terms the nature of the accused's defence,

    (b) indicating the matters on which he takes issue with the prosecution, and

    (c) setting out, in the case of each such matter, the reason why he takes issue with the prosecution.

In the case of an alibi the particulars to be provided include the name and address of any such witness, failing which, information as to how to find him (s 5(7)). But apart from this the Act did not include the proposal in the Consultation Document that the defence would as a matter of rule have to give the police advance notice of the names and addresses of their witnesses. In this respect therefore the Government heeded the advice received, *inter alia*, from the Bar Council and the Law Society.

If the defendant fails to comply with the obligation to give a defence statement or does so late, or sets out inconsistent defences, or at his trial puts forward a defence inconsistent with what appeared in the defence statement, or advances an alibi of which he has not given advance notice, the judge and, with leave of the court, the prosecution 'may make such comment as appears appropriate' (s 11(3)(*a*)). Also 'the court or jury may draw such inferences as appear proper in deciding whether the accused is guilty' (s 11(3)(*b*)).

The Runciman Royal Commission and expert evidence

The Royal Commission unanimously recommended that if the defence propose to contest the prosecution's scientific or other expert evidence they should give advance notice of the grounds on which they dispute that evidence–*whether or not they intend to call expert testimony of their own* (Report, p 157, para 60). The Crown Court Study done by the writer for the Royal Commission showed that the defence called an expert in only one third of the cases in which they contested the prosecution's scientific evidence. In two thirds of cases, the challenge was purely in the form of cross-examination. But it is very common in that situation for the defence to be advised by an expert even though he is not called at the trial. The present rules only require advance disclosure of evidence one intends to adduce at the trial. The defendant does not have to give notice of tests done which support the prosecution theory of the case.

The Royal Commission recommended that where the defence were calling an expert at the trial, the experts for both sides should be required to meet 'in order to draw up a report of the scientific facts and their interpretation by both sides' (Report, p 158, para 63). That document would then be available at the trial as a statement of what was agreed and what remained in dispute. If substantial disagreement on scientific issues was recorded, a preparatory hearing should be held in front of the trial judge to see whether disagreement could be narrowed before the trial unless both sides certify that this is unnecessary (Report, p 159, para 68). (The Commission did not refer to the problem identified in Lord Woolf's Interim Report (p 183, para 9) of experts being instructed by the lawyers not to agree anything.)

Where the defence intended to dispute the prosecution's scientific evidence without calling their own expert they should be required to indicate what was in dispute. Five members of the eleven-member Commission would have gone further to require the defence experts to participate in pre-trial discussion with the prosecution expert. But the majority did not support that recommendation.

The Commission considered, but rejected a proposal that the judge should be given the power to order that further scientific tests be done or that a third independent expert be asked for his opinion. It concluded that that 'might well add greater complexity to the pre-trial and trial phases, because it would be necessary for the third expert to be subjected to examination and cross-examination by both sides, without necessarily bringing about any decisive answer to the questions in issue' (p 158, para 67). But the judge should have a power to direct the experts on both sides to meet to discuss and to try to resolve their differences (*ibid*). (As has been seen, (p 75 above) Lord Woolf's Interim Report was more radical in recommending that, at least in some cases, the court should appoint an independent expert even though the parties would also have their own experts (p 187, para 23).)

7. THE GUILTY PLEA

The guilty plea plays a critical role in the criminal process since the great majority of defendants do plead guilty. In the crown court the proportion is currently a little under 70 per cent. (According to the *Judicial Statistics*, in 1994, 66% pleaded guilty to all charges and 4% pleaded guilty to some charges.) In the magistrates' courts there are unfortunately no official figures. Obviously, in the great mass of minor motoring cases the accused pleads guilty in virtually all cases. But even in categories of more serious offences, most plead guilty. Thus in a sample of 3,000 cases in five offence categories–shoplifting, assaulting a police officer, possession of cannabis, criminal damage and social security fraud–as many as 83 per cent of the defendants pleaded guilty ('Report of a Survey of the Grant of Legal Aid in Magistrates' Courts', Lord Chancellor's Department, 1983, p 5).

One very curious aspect of the statistics on guilty pleas is how they consistently show very different patterns in different parts of the country. Thus the guilty-plea rate nationally in 1994 was 66 per cent but it varied from a high of 78 per cent on the North Eastern circuit to a low of 49 per cent in London.

It seems likely that the main reason why accused persons plead guilty is that they *are* guilty, they know they are guilty, they believe that the police know it and can prove it, and they cannot see any advantage in pleading not guilty. Frequently they have made a tape-recorded or signed statement admitting the facts alleged against them in the police station, and this in turn has followed from admissions made in the course of the earlier period of questioning by the police. (A study of a large sample of cases tried in the crown court in Birmingham and London showed that 88 per cent of those who made statements confessing to the charges pleaded guilty in Birmingham and two-thirds in London–see J Baldwin and M McConville, 'Confessions in Crown Court Trials', *Royal Commission on Criminal Procedure, Research Study No 5*, 1980, p 14.)

Sometimes, however, innocent persons plead guilty.

(a) The innocent who plead guilty

There have been three formal studies which have produced substantial evidence that this is a real issue. The first was that of Mr Clive Davies, a barrister, who conducted interviews with 418 men charged with burglary in the course of a study of the bail system. Of these, eight men volunteered the information that although they were not guilty they intended to plead guilty to the charges. A further 21 either said that they were not guilty or said they intended to plead not guilty, but subsequently pleaded guilty. Davies concentrated his focus on the eight who said they would plead guilty from the outset:

Clive Davies, 'The Innocent who Plead Guilty', *Law Guardian*, March 1970, pp 9, 11

AB, a man with no previous convictions of crime, was walking home from a dance late at night with a friend. In the High Street they were stopped by three policemen, who pointed out a broken shop door and accused AB and his friend of having broken it with intent to steal. AB (who declares that until that moment he had no knowledge whatsoever of the broken door) and his friend were cautioned, taken to the police station and charged with the offence of burglary. After four hours at the police station (11 pm to 3 am) they both agreed to 'do a deal' by pleading guilty to causing malicious damage in return for the charge of burglary being withdrawn. AB insisted to me that he had nothing whatever to do with the broken door, and agreed to admit the charge because: (1) No one would believe his word and that of his friend against the word of the three police officers, who, he said, were going to testify that they caught the two men in the act of pushing against the shop door; (2) His wife, who resented his being out late, would be staying up awaiting his arrival home, and would be 'doing her nut' at the lateness of the hour; (3) The case, with a plea of guilty, would entail the loss of only two days' work through appearance in court, while a plea of not guilty, especially if taken to Quarter Sessions, would involve the loss of many day's work, spread over several weeks or months, and possibly of

AB's job, a matter of some importance to him, because he had a wife and family to support and numerous hire-purchase payments to keep up; and (4) As a first offender, he could expect to escape with a fairly small fine. He did plead guilty, and fines and compensation amounted to some £30, rather less than the probable total cost of even a successful defended case.

CD, also a man without previous convictions, left a public house at about eleven o'clock with EF, a friend with a long criminal record. Both were fairly drunk and both wanted to urinate. They went into an alley, where they saw an open outhouse door and (with the logic of the drunken) thought it would be a good idea to relieve their aching bladders in the darkness and privacy of the outhouse. They came out to find two plain-clothes policemen waiting for them in the alley, and they were subsequently charged with being found on enclosed premises with intent to steal a motor-cycle, even though neither of them knew how to ride one. CD's solicitor strongly advised him to plead guilty, as did a fellow employed at CD's place of work 'who used to be the clerk of the Court': no one, said these well-informed persons, would believe him, especially in view of EF's previous convictions. When I saw him, CD had firmly made up his mind to plead guilty–'to get it over with' as he said, and to bring an end to the intolerable state of anxiety that was depriving him of his appetite and sleep. It is a cardinal rule of social research that the investigator must not intervene so as to alter the situation he is studying, but most rules have their exceptions, and in this case it seemed essential to try to intervene. ... So I spent upwards of an hour trying to make him see the folly of pleading guilty if he was not: in this I was supported by his mother, who shared my views, but had succumbed in their two-week period of misery to CD's own mood of hopelessness. Whether or not as a result of this persuasion, CD pleaded not guilty, and both he and EF were acquitted. They were bound over to keep the peace, presumably on account of their undoubtedly illegal and somewhat offensive trespass. According to CD there were unsavoury undertones in his case which never came to the attention of the court. He has the appearance and manner of a 'female' homosexual, and was found to be carrying a perfume bottle when given a routine search after arrest. ... He said that he was told at the police station that unless he pleaded guilty to the garage-breaking charge he would be charged with something very much more serious, from which he inferred (as well he might) that allegations of a homosexual offence would be made.

On the basis of this study Davies calculated that some thousands of persons each year pleaded guilty to charges of which they were innocent. In a study based on interviews with women in Holloway prison it was found that a significant number pleaded guilty to offences they claimed not to have committed. Of 527 women who had been tried at magistrates' courts, there were 56 such cases. The reasons they gave were similar to those mentioned by Davies–police advice or pressure, to save time and avoid remands, fear that pleading not guilty would lead to harsher penalties or the feeling that there was no point, when the police evidence would inevitably be preferred (Susanne Dell, *Silent in Court*, Occasional Papers in Social Administration, Number 42 (Bell, 1971), p 30).

In a later study by John Baldwin and Michael McConville of last-minute change of plea cases tried at the Birmingham crown court, 'over half of the sample made some claim to be innocent, and often very vehemently, either of the whole of the indictment to which they pleaded guilty or of individual counts within it' (*Negotiated Justice* (Martin Robertson, 1977), p 61). No fewer than 70 of the 121 defendants interviewed (58 per cent) claimed to be innocent. Some of these claims according to the researchers were somewhat limp, others were scarcely believable and seemed far-fetched to the interviewer. Others were based on a misunderstanding of the law. But there were some whose stories could not be so lightly dismissed. The reasons given for pleading guilty were variations on a few themes–'the feeling of hopelessness at attempting to rebut the evidence of police officers and the severity of sentence they anticipated if they failed to do so; the weariness caused by the case dragging on for months on end and the consequent anxiety and social disruption caused by frequent remands (especially if in custody); the attractiveness of the bargain held out to them or perhaps merely the negative pressure exerted by counsel' (p 65).

No fewer than a third of the defendants who claimed innocence alleged that the police had falsely attributed verbal admissions to them. Some of these allegations the researchers found credible, others less so. Another factor in the decision to plead guilty was the advice of counsel. Some defendants said that their barristers had made it clear that they had no real prospect of an acquittal (p 70). The independent assessors who examined the cases concluded that in 79 per cent of these cases the likelihood was that the defendant would be convicted; but in 21 per cent they thought there was some chance of an acquittal and in some instances that the chances of an acquittal were good (p 74).[10]

One of the main contentions of the Baldwin and McConville study was that some guilty pleas are induced by *improper pressure* by the barrister. This suggestion produced a strong and angry response from the Bar. But a later piece of analysis of the same data by the same two authors revealed the very significant fact that the proportion of guilty pleas varied dramatically from one barrister to another (*New Law Journal*, 27 October 1977, p 1040). Some apparently like a fight more than others and some may be more inclined to exert pressure on the client to plead guilty. No doubt the barrister honestly believes this to be in the best interests of his client but, because of his psychological 'set', he may take insufficient notice of the client's protestations of innocence.

It has already been seen that guilty-plea rates vary also as between different circuits. Ole Hansen (in the *New Law Journal*, 27 June 1986, p 601) reported on an informal inquiry into the reasons behind these marked and remarkable variations. Michael Huebner, Circuit Administrator in Leeds, said that the abnormally high guilty-plea rate in his (North Eastern) circuit reflected the robustness of the bench and the legal profession 'and a good dollop of northern common sense'.

But, Hansen suggested, what seemed like robustness to a circuit administrator might look rather different from the defendant's perspective. A Leeds solicitor had told him that 'the local bar was not prepared to fight enough cases'. One of the reasons that he used London counsel a lot was that they were more ready to fight–and they usually won their cases.

Moreover the problem was not confined to the Bar. 'Many solicitors had a similar attitude. They did not believe their client's defences were valid and therefore did not investigate cases fully–preferring instead to maximise their fee income from magistrates' court advocacy. The end result was a client under pressure to plead guilty in the crown court'.

In Newcastle a further reason was that the local lay magistrates were so punitive that many solicitors would advise clients to go to the crown court for a more lenient sentence.

10 The *Crown Court Study* conducted by the writer for the Runciman Royal Commission on Criminal Justice appeared at first to be a fourth such study. In a pre-publication lecture about the early results of the study, the writer suggested that the study included 53 such cases. (M Zander, 'The Royal Commission's Crown Court Study' *New Law Journal*, 11 December 1992.) However further analysis of these cases showed that very few, if any, were in reality cases of innocent persons pleading guilty. (For further details see M Zander, 'The "Innocent" who Plead Guilty'. *New Law Journal*, 22 January 1993, p 85. See also the Royal Commission's Report, p 11, para 43.)

Another explanation for the high guilty-plea rate was that the judge, the defending and the prosecuting barristers all frequently came from the same chambers, which made defence counsel 'anxious not to appear to "waste" the courts' time'. Also, in the provinces, if a barrister had a number of guilty-plea cases in a session he could get a higher level of remuneration than if he only had the one not-guilty-plea case. He might therefore have a financial incentive to get his client to plead guilty.

Note–fabricated TICs

There is a very different form of 'confession'–the admission by someone who either pleads guilty or is found guilty that he committed *other* offences. If this happens before the court case, they are mentioned in court and 'taken into consideration' for the purpose of sentencing. (Hence they are called TICs.) The advantage for the accused is that they cannot later be brought up against him. The advantage for the police is that they can 'clear the books'–the success rate of cleared-up crime in that force area improves.

In recent years the police on some forces have taken this one step further by visiting defendants in prison after they have been sentenced to see whether they can get them to admit to other offences.

It is of course quite possible that not all of these admissions are in fact true. In August 1986 detectives from Scotland Yard investigating allegations that police officers in Kent had been falsifying crime statistics with bogus confessions, made an unprecedented series of surprise raids on 13 police stations in Kent. It was the sort of police operation usually directed against leading criminals, complete with a 6 am briefing at the Yard and a simultaneous swoop on target stations at 10 am. Teams of officers from the Serious Crime Branch were investigating allegations made by a serving Kent officer, PC Ron Walker, that detectives in the area had been 'cooking the books'. He had alleged that the fake confessions were boosting the clear-up rate in some areas by as much as 50 per cent. He also claimed that in return for making false confessions, some criminals were given a licence to commit further crimes on release from prison.

(b) The sentence discount

One of the most powerful incentives to pleading guilty (whether one *is* guilty or not) is the prospect of a lighter sentence if one pleads guilty than if one contests one's guilt and is then convicted. The judges have made it abundantly clear that a person who pleads guilty is entitled to expect some 'sentence discount'.

There are many cases that make the point that a guilty plea can legitimately result in a lower sentence. In *Turner* (p 254 below), Lord Parker CJ said that counsel for the defence was entitled to advise his client ('if need be in strong terms') that a guilty plea 'showing an element of remorse is a mitigating factor which may well enable the court to give a lesser sentence than would otherwise be the case'. In *Cain* the Court of Appeal stressed that defendants should appreciate that, in general, a plea of guilty attracts a lesser sentence and that this was 'a glimpse of the obvious'. Lord Widgery said: 'Everybody knows that it is so and there is no doubt about it. Any accused person who does not know about it should know about it. The sooner he knows the better' ([1976] Crim LR 464). In *Davis* in 1978 the Court of Appeal said: 'It is common knowledge, that it is an almost universal practice for some such discount to be made on a plea of guilty' ([1979] Crim LR 327).

For later decisions on the question of the extent of the discount for a guilty plea, see *Williams* [1983] Crim LR 693 and commentary at p 694. See also *Pyne* [1984] Crim LR 118, and *Barnes* [1984] Crim LR 119.

The usual range of discount from the notional appropriate sentence is in the region of 25 to 30 per cent. One would assume that this must act as an incentive to plead guilty in a proportion of cases. For a practitioner's view, see James Morton, 'Plea Bargaining', *New Law Journal*, 10 May 1985, p 457; 24 May 1985, p 515; 7 June 1985, p 564.

Although almost all the literature and case-law on the sentence discount relates to the crown court, the concept applies equally in the magistrates' court. The Magistrates' Association's Sentencing Guidelines (1993), state, for example, that the sentence starting-points indicated in the Guidelines should be reduced by approximately one third where there has been 'a timely guilty plea'.

Of the many hundreds of memoranda of evidence received by the Runciman Royal Commission on Criminal Justice the writer does not remember a single one that argued for the abolition of the sentence discount. One can say therefore that the sentence discount seems to be accepted by just about everyone–even though it presumably causes some innocent persons to plead guilty. But see further discussion below of the dangers of increasing the temptation to plead guilty.

Note–supergrasses and other informers

A rare but important situation is where an accused is given total immunity from prosecution in return for evidence for the Crown. A celebrated instance of this was the case in 1974 of Bertie Smalls, who was charged with taking part in a number of robberies. In return for a guarantee of immunity he promised to tell the police about a whole series of robberies. As a result, 26 defendants were arrested, charged and ultimately convicted on Smalls' evidence of robberies involving £1.2m in stolen money. Smalls was arraigned at the Old Bailey but the prosecution offered no evidence against him and a verdict of not guilty was entered.

The Court of Appeal said that undertakings of immunity to criminals might have to be given in the public interest. They should, however, never be given by the police. They should be given only by the Director of Public Prosecutions, and then only most sparingly. In serious cases it would be prudent of him to consult the Law Officers (*The Times*, 25 March 1975, p 18).

After the Smalls case the practice in England seemed to be to prosecute in such cases and hope that a combination of a recommendation from the prosecutor, a lenient judge and an even more lenient Home Office would secure a sufficiently short sentence for supergrasses to make the advantages of adopting this course outweigh the pressures the other way.

In Northern Ireland, however, total immunity was still being given at least so long as the supergrass was not himself directly linked to murder. In 1982 and 1983 the security forces and police were having more and more success largely due to the assistance of supergrasses. In autumn 1983 this led to considerable press publicity for various groups and individuals who expressed unease about this development. The campaign was triggered largely by the case of Joe Bennett, whose evidence led to 14 people being given sentences of some 200 years. *The Sunday Times* wrote on 11 September 1983 that Bennett had in reality been involved in at least one murder. According to the *Sunday Times* story, there were at that date some 300 people awaiting trial on 700 charges arising out of the activities of 26 supergrasses.

The main concern about supergrasses was that they were being allowed to get away with it, that the courts were relying on their uncorroborated evidence and that, in Northern Ireland, charges in terrorism cases are dealt with in the special 'Diplock courts' without juries. (On Diplock courts, see pp 393–94 below.) Even the Rev Ian Paisley, a hard-line opponent of the IRA, was quoted as saying that the use of supergrasses was 'undermining the rule of law'. The concern was heightened when it became known in October 1983 that supergrasses were being offered significant financial inducements in the form of cash and resettlement grants. In October 1983, the then Attorney-General Sir Michael Havers in a written parliamentary answer said that the DPP had given instructions that the chief constable would in every case 'furnish him with a statement of all financial arrangements for the support of the witness and his family and any arrangements for future financial payment to the witness or for his benefit, and that these particulars will be disclosed to the defence and will be available to the court of trial' (House of Commons, *Hansard*, 24 October 1083, vol 47, cols 3–5). So far as was known, no such disclosure had until then ever been made either to the defence or to the judge.

On the very day when the Attorney-General made his statement, the case against eight alleged terrorists based entirely on the evidence of supergrass Patrick McGurk collapsed when McGurk announced that he would not after all be giving evidence. Crown counsel read a statement to the court in which McGurk said he had lost his nerve after waiting for 20 months for the trial to come on. Only a few days earlier another major supergrass, Robert Lean, had withdrawn his evidence against no fewer than 28 people. He had previously been given immunity against prosecution in regard to any crimes he admitted and therefore could not be prosecuted for the many serious terrorist acts he had himself committed.

The case of Robert Lean marked a turning point. After that everything seemed to go wrong for the authorities in these cases. In 1985 the DPP decided not to proceed with a case against Terry Davis, a supergrass who had implicated 40 to 50 other people in serious burglaries. Many had been picked up but in the end they were released without charges being brought. In 1986 the convictions of 18 defendants on the evidence of supergrass Christopher Black were quashed by the Criminal Appeal Court. Black had been given immunity for a murder charge in exchange for evidence against 38 people charged with 184 terrorist offences. The case against 20 defendants accused on the evidence of William Allen collapsed when the trial judge described his evidence as 'unworthy of belief'. The 14 men convicted on the evidence of Joseph Bennett all had their convictions quashed on appeal. In October 1986 the DPP decided not to offer any evidence against 19 defendants accused of terrorist offences on information given by Northern Ireland's first woman supergrass Angela Whoriskey. It seemed that the whole policy of using supergrasses in Northern Ireland had fallen apart.

See generally A Jennings, 'Supergrasses and the Northern Ireland Legal System', *New Law Journal*, 1983, p 1043; Tony Gifford, *Supergrasses*, Cobden Trust, 1984; E Grant, 'The Use of "Supergrass" Evidence in Northern Ireland 1982–1985', *New Law Journal*, 8 November 1985, p 1125; Steven C Greer, 'The Rise and Fall of the

Northern Ireland Supergrass System' (1987) *Criminal Law Review*, p 663; D Bonner, *Modern LR* 1988, p 23; Steve Greer, 'Supergrasses and the Legal System in Britain and Northern Ireland', 102 *Law Quarterly R*, 1986, p 198.

There is no doubt that many guilty pleas result from skilful handling of the suspect by the police. See B Smythe, 'Police Investigation and the Rules of Evidence' 117 *Solicitors' Journal*, 5 October 1973, p 718 written by a former police officer. See further McConville, Sanders and Leng, *The Case for the Prosecution* (Routledge, 1991), pp 60–65.

Sometimes a guilty plea occurs when the prosecution do not have enough evidence to prove the case. (See J Baldwin and M McConville, *Negotiated Justice* (Martin Robertson, 1977), p 74; S Moody and J Tombs, *Prosecution in the Public Interest* (Scottish Academic Press, 1982), p 307; and McConville, Sanders and Leng, *op cit*, p 159.)

In the Crown Court Study done for the Royal Commission on Criminal Justice prosecution barristers in guilty plea cases were asked: 'If the defendant had pleaded not guilty but the prosecution had gone forward, do you think he/she would have stood a fair chance of an acquittal?' There were 767 responses. In 9 per cent it was 'Yes, the defendant would have had a fair chance of an acquittal' (*op cit*, p 188, para 6.5.5).

In the United States discussions regarding plea are assisted by the fact that the prosecutor is permitted to make recommendations to the court as to the appropriate sentence. He can therefore state in the 'plea bargaining stage' that if the suspect agrees to plead guilty he will ask for a lesser sentence, and actual figures can be mentioned. In the English system this is not possible since the prosecutor does not recommend any particular sentence. However, the prosecutor can promise to 'put in a good word' for the defendant. He can also change the charges, by dropping the most serious.

(c) The judge's involvement in plea discussions

The courts have tried over the years to arrive at an acceptable approach to the problem of communication regarding the plea between the defendant and his lawyers, on the one hand, and the prosecution lawyers and the judge, on the other. The defendant speaks to his lawyer who in turn may have had discussions with counsel for the prosecution, with the judge or with both as to plea. Such discussions are normally designed to see whether there is a basis for advising the defendant to plead guilty on the understanding that he will get a certain kind of sentence. Thus if the judge indicates that he will not send the defendant to prison, his counsel may be able to get him to change his plea to guilty and thus bring the proceedings to an early halt. These discussions are generally referred to as plea (or charge) bargaining.

Whatever is agreed between the lawyers, the judge has the final word. He can reject the 'deal' struck between the lawyers. This was illustrated in the 'Yorkshire Ripper' case in 1981. The prosecution and defence agreed that Peter Sutcliffe would plead guilty to manslaughter on the grounds of diminished responsibility. But the judge refused to accept the plea and there was then a long trial, at the end of which the jury found the accused guilty of murder and rejected the diminished responsibility defence.

In a minority of cases the judge himself becomes directly involved in the bargaining process. This has certain dangers, and the courts in recent years have had many occasions to express views on the subject. The *locus classicus* of advice to counsel on the practice of discussing these issues with the judge is *R v Turner*.

R v Turner [1970] 2 QB 321 (Court of Appeal, Criminal Division)

The defendant pleaded not guilty at his trial on a charge of theft. He had previous convictions, and during an adjournment he was advised by his counsel in strong terms to change his plea; after having spoken to the trial judge, as the defendant knew, counsel advised that in his opinion a non-custodial sentence would be imposed if the defendant changed his plea, whereas, if he persisted with the plea of not guilty, with an attack being made on police witnesses, and the jury convicted him there was a real possibility of a sentence of imprisonment being passed. Repeated statements were made to him that the ultimate choice of plea was his. He thought that counsel's views were those of the trial judge; nothing happened to show that they were not and the defendant changed his plea. He did not receive a custodial sentence but still appealed against his own plea.

Lord Parker CJ gave the judgment of the court:

... The court would like to say, with emphasis, that they can find no evidence here that Mr Grey exceeded his duty in the way he presented advice to the appellant. He did it in strong terms. It is perfectly right that counsel should be able to do it in strong terms, provided always that it is made clear that the ultimate choice and a free choice is in the accused person.

The matter, however, does not end there, because albeit it may be sufficient in the majority of cases if it is made clear to a prisoner that the final decision is his, however forcibly counsel may put it, the position is different if the advice is conveyed as the advice of someone who has seen the judge, and has given the impression that he is repeating the judge's views in the matter. As I have said, the court is quite satisfied Mr Grey was giving his own views and not the judge's at all. But it had been conveyed to the appellant that Mr Grey had just returned from seeing the deputy chairman. What was said gave Mr Laity the impression that those were the judge's views, and Mr Grey very frankly said that in the circumstances the appellant might well have got the impression that they were the judge's views. ...

Accordingly, though not without some doubt, the court feels that this appeal must succeed. ...

Before leaving this case, which has brought out into the open the vexed question of so-called 'plea-bargaining', the court would like to make some observations which may be of help to judges and to counsel, and, indeed, solicitors. They are these:

1. Counsel must be completely free to do what is his duty, namely to give the accused the best advice he can and, if need be, advice in strong terms. This will often include advice that a plea of guilty, showing an element of remorse, is a mitigating factor which may well enable the court, to give a lesser sentence than would otherwise be the case. Counsel of course will emphasize that the accused must not plead guilty unless he has committed the acts constituting the offence charged.

2. The accused, having considered counsel's advice, must have a complete freedom of choice whether to plead guilty or not guilty.

3. There must be freedom of access between counsel and judge. Any discussion, however, which takes place must be between the judge and both counsel for the defence and counsel for the prosecution. If a solicitor representing the accused is in the court, he should be allowed to attend the discussion if he so desires. This freedom of access is important because there may be matters calling for communication or discussion, which are of such a nature that counsel cannot in the interests of his client mention them in open court. Purely by way of example, counsel for

the defence may by way of mitigation wish to tell the judge that the accused has not long to live, is suffering maybe from cancer, of which he is and should remain ignorant. Again, counsel on both sides may wish to discuss with the judge whether it would be proper, in a particular case, for the prosecution to accept a plea to a lesser offence. It is of course imperative that so far as possible justice must be administered in open court. Counsel should, therefore, only ask to see the judge when it is felt to be really necessary, and the judge must be careful only to treat such communications as private where, in fairness to the accused person, this is necessary.

4. The judge should, subject to the one exception referred to hereafter, never indicate the sentence which he is minded to impose. A statement that on a plea of guilty he would impose one sentence but that on a conviction following a plea of not guilty he would impose a severer sentence is one which should never be made. This could be taken to be undue pressure on the accused, thus depriving him of that complete freedom of choice which is essential. Such cases, however, are in the experience of the court happily rare. What on occasion does appear to happen however is that a judge will tell counsel that, having read the depositions and the antecedents, he can safely say that on a plea of guilty he will, for instance, make a probation order, something which may be helpful to counsel in advising the accused. The judge in such a case is no doubt careful not to mention what he would do if the accused were convicted following a plea of not guilty. Even so, the accused may well get the impression that the judge is intimating that in that event a severer sentence, maybe a custodial sentence, would result, so that again he may feel under pressure. This accordingly must also not be done.

The only exception to this rule is that it should be permissible for a judge to say, if it be the case, that whatever happens, whether the accused pleads guilty or not guilty, the sentence will or will not take a particular form, eg a probation order or a fine, or a custodial sentence.

Finally, where such discussion on sentence has taken place between judge and counsel, counsel for the defence should disclose this to the accused and inform him of what took place.

Questions

1. In Rule 1 the court indicated that counsel could inform his client that a guilty plea could be a mitigating factor. In Rule 4 it said that the judge must not give any indication that the plea could make any difference to his judgment. Are these two propositions consistent?

2. In Rule 2 the court said that the accused must have complete freedom of choice as to whether to plead guilty or not. Is this realistic? Is his freedom of choice not seriously qualified by the pressure of the advice to plead guilty?

3. The court is prepared to countenance solicitors at discussions about plea and sentence with the judge, but there is clearly no thought that the defendant himself might be there. Is this justifiable?

The final words of the extract from *Turner* emphasized the duty of counsel to relay to his client what had happened in the judge's room. This critical issue came up for more detailed scrutiny in *Cain* [1976] Crim LR 464. At the trial Mr Justice Melford Stevenson had sent for counsel for both sides and had said that he thought the defendant had no defence at all. If he persisted in his not-guilty plea he said that he would get a very severe sentence indeed but that a change of plea would make a considerable difference. Counsel reported this to the accused who eventually agreed to plead guilty to three counts, the prosecution having agreed to accept those pleas. The judge gave him four years' imprisonment. Cain then appealed on the ground that he had been pressured into pleading guilty. The Court of Appeal quashed the conviction and ordered a new trial. Lord Widgery referred to Lord Parker's remark in *Turner* about counsel passing on to his client what the judge had said. That statement admitted exceptions, for example where counsel who did not know the judge and was not familiar with the tariff, wished to obtain guidance as to the sentence the judge had in mind so he could properly advise the defendant. If he had to disclose what the judge had said, the confidentiality between judge and counsel would be broken.

This decision gave rise to considerable confusion as to what counsel was and was not permitted to say to his client, and in July 1976 the Court of Appeal issued a Practice Direction which stated that insofar as *Cain* and *Turner* were inconsistent, *Turner* should prevail–[1976] Crim LR 561. This did little to clarify matters.

Since then there have been further decisions: *Llewellyn* (1978) 67 Cr App Rep 149; *Bird* [1978] Crim LR 237; *Atkinson, ibid,* 238; *Ryan, ibid,* 306; *Eccles, ibid,* 757; *Davis* [1979] Crim LR 167; *Winterblood, ibid,* 263; *Smith* [1990] Crim LR 354; *Keily, ibid,* 204. The principles that can be distilled from these cases are, first that the judge should not engage in over-precise indications, let alone bargaining as to what he intends, and, secondly, private discussions between counsel and the judge should not take place unless it was absolutely necessary. The Court of Appeal has said the decisions should take place in open court in the absence of the jury.

In *R v Harper-Taylor and Bakker* [1988] NLJR 80, the Court of Appeal warned that one of the dangers of going into chambers was that the more relaxed atmosphere of the private room could blur the formal outlines of the trial. The fact that the accused was not present meant that he had to be informed of what had happened at second hand. The lawyers for either side might hear things that they would rather not hear that would put them into conflict between their duty to the client and their duty to preserve the confidentiality of the private room.[11]

This passage was cited by the Court of Appeal in *R v Pitman* [1991] 1 All ER 468 in which Lord Lane LCJ said that there continued to be a steady flow of appeals to the Court of Appeal arising out of visits by counsel to the judge. ('No amount of criticism and no amount of warnings and no amount of exhortation seems to be able to prevent this happening' p 470.) The court quashed a conviction because of undue pressure by the trial judge on the accused by saying to counsel in chambers that there seemed to be no defence to the charge (although counsel had advised the client to plead not guilty), and that he would get substantial credit for a guilty plea. The plea was a matter for the defendant and if he was accepting blame for the incident (death of a motorist in a collision) and was contrite, his plea was the best evidence of that. The defendant changed his plea and was given a nine months' prison sentence.

A learned commentary on *Pitman* sums up the effect of the case-law in this vexed area as follows:

Patrick Curran, 'Discussions in the Judge's Private Room' (1991) *Criminal Law Review*, pp 79, 85–6

It is submitted that the following principles may be identified in the case law which has developed from the original guide-lines in *Turner*:
1. An accused person must have a completely free choice of plea.[12]
2. Defending counsel must be quite free to do his duty, which is to give the accused the best advice he can, if need be in strong terms. He is entitled to tell the accused that a plea of guilty

11 But see *Agar* (1990) 90 Cr App Rep 318.
12 *Inns* (1974) 60 Cr App Rep 231; *Barnes* (1970) 55 Cr App Rep 100; *Quartey* [1975] Crim LR 592; *Turner*; *Cain*; *Ryan*; *Llewellyn*; *Atkinson*; and *Smith*.

is a mitigating factor which may result in a lighter sentence than would otherwise be imposed. Counsel must however emphasise that the accused must not plead guilty if he has not committed the offence.[13]

3. There must be freedom of access between counsel and the judge.[14] However, a judge should not initiate discussions in private.[15] Both prosecuting and defence counsel must be present at any private discussion.[16]

4. Such discussions should not take place unless they are really necessary.[17] Pre-trial reviews should take place in open court.[18]

5. A judge should only give an indication of sentence (a) when he is in possession of all the material facts;[19] and (b) when he is of the view that a particular form of sentence is appropriate irrespective of plea. Any suggestion of different kinds of sentence following a guilty plea on the one hand and a conviction by the jury on the other is fundamentally wrong.[20] This applies even where the judge is silent as to the alternative sentence after conviction by the jury.[1]

6. No discussion should take place in the judge's private room without the presence of a shorthand writer or tape-recorder to record exactly what is said.[2]

The fundamental problem is that the Court of Appeal wants to have it both ways. On the one hand, it wants defendants to appreciate that if they plead guilty they will get a lesser sentence. On the other hand, it does not want judges to provide defendants with solid information as to how great the discount will be.

The courts have given two reasons for refusing to provide a defendant with this information. One is that it will create undue pressure on him to plead guilty. But the pressure is already created by the fact of the sentence discount. To quantify the discount can hardly increase the pressure—on the contrary, it may reduce it by making it clear that the defendant's fears about the penalty for pleading not guilty are exaggerated. The second reason is that it is thought unseemly for the court to be in any sense bargaining or haggling with the defendant. As was said in *Cain*, 'What was being condemned was a more precise offer because the judge was then inviting the defendant to bargain with him.'

Should plea bargaining be more explicit?

Should the process of 'bargaining' be explicit or implicit, detailed or vague? Is it better for the judge to give a general indication of the kind of sentence he has in mind which is conveyed to the accused without too detailed an account of what the judge has in mind, or should the accused be told more precisely what his options are?

The judges and barristers who took part in the Crown Court Study done for the Runciman Royal Commission were asked 'Do you think that *Turner* should be reformed to permit full and realistic discussion between counsel and the judge about plea and especially sentence?' Eighty six per cent of prosecution barristers, 88 per cent of defence barristers and 67 per cent of judges answered this question 'Yes' (*op cit* p 145, para 4.13.1).

13 *Turner; Bird* (1977) 67 Cr App Rep 203.
14 *Turner; Harper-Taylor and Bakker; Pitman.*
15 *Llewellyn; Bird; Cullen* (1984) 81 Cr App Rep 17; *Pitman.*
16 *Turner.*
17 *Turner; Bird; Winterflood* (1978) 68 Cr App Rep 291, *Harper-Taylor and Bakker.*
18 *Keily.*
19 *Ryan.*
20 *Turner; Cain; Quartey; Atkinson; Smith; Keily.*
1 *Ryan.*
2 *Smith; Keily; Cullen* [1984] 81 Cr App Rep 17; *Pitman.*

For the early literature on plea bargaining, see the 6th edition of this work, page 299. In 1992 a committee of the Bar Council chaired by Mr Robert Seabrook QC recommended that unofficial plea bargaining should be replaced with a formal system with graduated sentence discounts depending on the stage at which the guilty plea was entered. The report included a table which proposed that a guilty plea at the committal stage should receive a minimum of 30 per cent discount, while those who waited longer would get less–a minimum of 10 per cent was suggested for a plea made between the first crown court listing and arraignment (*The Efficient Disposal of Business in the Crown Court*, June 1992. For a fierce critique of the Seabrook proposals see M McConville and C Mirsky, 'To Plea or not to Plea', *Legal Action*, February 1993, p 6.)

(d) The Runciman Royal Commission Report

The Runciman Royal Commission said of the sentence discount:

Provided that the defendant is in fact guilty and has received competent legal advice about his or her position, there can be no serious objection to a system of inducements designed to encourage him or her so to plead (p 110, para 42).

It thought that the system of sentence discounts should remain but that it should be made more effective, in particular by promotion of earlier guilty pleas so as to reduce the very high proportion of last minute guilty pleas (known as 'cracked trials'). In the Crown Court Study, of the total of cases listed, 39 per cent were listed as guilty pleas, 26 per cent were listed as not guilty pleas but 'cracked' (ie. became guilty pleas), 31 per cent were contested and 3 per cent ended without a plea when the defendant was bound over or the case was allowed to lie on the file (Royal Commission Report, p 111, note 15).

Cracked trials create serious problems, principally for all the thousands of witnesses, police officers, experts and ordinary citizens, who come to court expecting a trial only to find that there is no trial because the defendant pleads guilty at the last minute. This causes unnecessary anxiety in particular for victims whose evidence has up to that point been disputed (*ibid*, p 111, para 45).

The Court of Appeal had stated that other things being equal, an earlier plea ought to attract a higher discount:

This court has long said that discounts on sentence are appropriate, but everything depends on the circumstances of the case. If a man is arrested and at once tells the police that he is guilty and cooperates with them …, he can expect to get a substantial discount. But if a man is arrested in circumstances in which he cannot hope to put forward a defence of not guilty, he cannot expect much by way of a discount. In between come this kind of case, where the court has been put to considerable trouble as a result of a tactical [late] plea. The sooner it is appreciated that defendants are not going to get a full discount for pleas of guilty in those circumstances, the better it will be for the administration of justice' (*R v Hollington and Emmens* (1985) 82 Cr App Rep 281).

The Royal Commission said it agreed with the view expressed by the Court of Appeal that, other things being equal, the earlier the plea the higher the discount (p 111, para 47).

This recommendation was given statutory effect in the Criminal Justice and Public Order Act 1994, s 48(1) which provides that when determining what sentence to pass on an offender who has pleaded guilty the court shall take into account (a) the stage in the proceedings for the offence at which the offender indicated his intention to plead guilty and (b) the circumstances in which this indication was given'. Section 48(2) states that if the court, in consequence of taking into account the matters referred to in subs (1), 'imposes a punishment on the offender which is less severe than the punishment it would otherwise have imposed, it shall state in open court that it has done so'.

For a comment on the worrying implications of s 48 see B Davies and G Dingwall, 'Defendants' Guilty Pleas and Section 48', *Legal Action*, February 1996, p 8.

In January 1996 *Police Review* reported that an MP had called for the withdrawal of a leaflet, headed *Guilty Plea Discounts*, prepared by Newcastle-Upon-Tyne Magistrates' Court and circulated by the local police which informed defendants about the sentence discount system under the CJPOA, s 48 (12 January, p 9). The leaflet said that an early plea could lead to two months being knocked off a six-month sentence or a £200 fine being lowered to £140.

'Sentence canvass'

The Runciman Royal Commission recommended a new system of formalised plea bargaining. Under this system, which the Commission called 'sentence canvass', the defendant's lawyer would be permitted to ask a judge at a hearing in chambers what sentence he would impose on a guilty plea. Prosecution and defence would present the case to the judge who would, if he felt able and willing, give an indication as to sentence. If the defendant accepted that sentence, the case would be adjourned into open court and the parties would go through it all again in public. If the defendant did not accept it he would be free to contest the case in the normal way. (See Runciman Report, pp 113–14, paras 50–55.) The proposal was based on a recommendation in the report of the Bar Council Working Party chaired by Robert Seabrook QC (see p 258 above). But it was not well received. In particular, the Lord Chief Justice, Lord Taylor, indicated that he opposed the proposal. It seemed unlikely that this recommendation of the Runciman Royal Commission would be implemented.

(e) Taking a plea before mode of trial decision

As a way of reducing the numbers of cases going to the crown court the Government's Consultation Document on Mode of Trial issued in July 1995 (Cm 2908) put forward a new idea that had not been considered by the Runciman Royal Commission. This was to oblige the defendant to enter a plea before the mode of trial decision was taken. The Consultation Document stated that this procedural innovation had long term potential for retaining significantly more work at magistrates' courts.

Under the then existing procedure the law did not permit the defendant to enter a plea when magistrates decided to commit a case for trial. Under the system proposed by the Government this would change. The defendant would be required to enter a plea before the magistrates decided whether to commit/transfer the case to the crown court. In respect of defendants who pleaded guilty, the magistrates would then hear a recital of the facts of the case by the prosecution. If the magistrates thought their sentencing powers were insufficient, the defence would be given an opportunity to try to persuade the court to retain the case. If the magistrates decided to retain the case, they would then move to sentence.

In the year ending June 1993 it was estimated that about 38,000 defendants who pleaded guilty in the crown court received a sentence which magistrates could have imposed. Home Office research had shown that nearly three-quarters (73%) of defendants who had been dealt with at the crown court because magistrates declined jurisdiction, would, had they had the choice, have chosen to be dealt with at a magistrates' court and another 4 per cent had no preference (D Moxon and C Hedderman, *Magistrates Court or Crown Court? Mode of Trial Decisions*, Home Office Research Study, Paper No 125, 1992, p 21).

Of the 73,800 either way cases sent to the crown court in 1992, 63 per cent (about 46,500 defendants) were sent there because magistrates declined jurisdiction. This suggested that something like 25,000 defendants at the crown court might have been willing to plead guilty at the magistrates' court and either be sentenced by magistrates or have their cases transferred for sentence to the crown court. The Government said that it saw attraction in this proposal and invited views (Consultation Document, *Mode of Trial*, Cm 2908, 1995, p 5).

It did not take the Government long to conclude that this idea should be pursued and a modified version was included in the Criminal Procedure and Criminal Investigations Bill introduced in the House of Lords in November 1995.

The main modification was that, instead of the new procedure being compulsory, it is merely optional. The second modification is that asking the defendant to indicate how he would plead would not technically constitute taking a plea.

Section 49 of the Act provides that the magistrates' court must explain to the accused charged with an either way offence that 'he may indicate whether (if the offence were to proceed to trial) he would plead guilty or not guilty'. If he indicates that he would plead guilty the court then proceeds as if it had been a summary trial–either to sentence him or to commit him to the crown court for sentence only. The guilty plea is taken into account by magistrates together with the matters that they would previously have taken into account (set out in s 19 of the Magistrates' Courts Act 1980) in considering whether their powers of sentencing were sufficient. The defendant however does not have to give an indication of his likely plea before receiving advance disclosure from the prosecution–on which see p 236 below.

If the case is sent to the crown court the defendant remains free to change his plea to one of not guilty, at the risk of that raising his sentence if he is convicted.

The Law Society stated in January 1996 that it had told the Home Office that it had no objection to what it called this 'major change to procedure in the magistrates' court' because although it considered that the accused should be able to choose which court *tried* the charges against him, this did not apply to the court that sentenced him. But it had told the Government that solicitors would not advise their clients to take advantage of the new provision 'unless charges have been finalised and sufficient evidence has been disclosed to enable them to assess the strength of the prosecution case' (Roger Ede, *Criminal Practitioner's Newsletter*, Law Society, January 1996, p 1). As has been seen, the same Act deals with the new disclosure rules which require the prosecutor to make primary disclosure in the magistrates' court of material which might undermine the prosecution case together with a schedule of non-sensitive unused material–but this is only to be triggered by the accused pleading not guilty.

9. COMMITTAL [NOT TRANSFER] PROCEEDINGS

If the charge is one on which there is a choice between the magistrates' court and the crown court, the defendant must be told of his right to ask for trial at the higher level. As has been seen, most then opt for summary trial. If the defendant asks for trial at the higher level, his preference always prevails. If, however, he asks for summary trial and the prosecutor prefers to have the case tried at the crown court, the court will decide. The court can also override the defendant's choice of summary trial if it thinks the case too serious for trial in a magistrates' court.

Hitherto, if the case was to be tried in the crown court, the defendant had to be committed for trial by the magistrates' court. In other words, even cases that are dealt with in the crown court must start in the magistrates' court.

The history of committal proceedings was set out by the Royal Commission on Criminal Procedure in *The Investigation and Prosecution of Criminal Offences in England and Wales: The Law and Procedure* (1981, Cmnd 8092–1, pp 67–8):

a. Historical background

184. Before the establishment of regular police forces it was the duty of magistrates to pursue and arrest offenders and it was the magistrates who could be referred to as 'detectives and prosecutors'. They had responsibility for the taking of depositions as long ago as the 16th century. These were equivalent to the statements taken from witnesses by the police today. The examination of the witnesses took place in private and the accused had no right to be present. In the early part of the 19th century the responsibility for enquiring into offences began to pass to the police. In 1848 changes were made in the procedure. The Administration of Justice (No 1) Act of that year set out to consolidate the law relating to the duties of magistrates in relation to the functions of investigating and inquiring into offences, with such changes as were deemed necessary. The most important change was a provision whereby the accused was entitled, for the first time, to be present at the examination of the witnesses against him. But the inquiry was not required to be in open court, that is in public. The nature of the inquiry by the magistrates was changing before 1848 and continued to do so after that year. During this transitional period, the position of the police as investigators and prosecutors was becoming more clearly established. During the same period, the magistrates' inquiry became a judicial instead of an investigative function. Indeed, by 1848, or soon after, the magistrates' examination (that is committal proceedings) usually took place in open court. As a result of these changes there became grafted onto the system a preliminary judicial hearing.

b. Committal proceedings in the modern era

185. This preliminary judicial hearing continues today, with modifications, as committal proceedings. The link with the magistrates' former investigative functions is evidenced by the statutory reference to committal proceedings as an inquiry into an offence by examining justices, and by the procedure which envisages that the charge will not be formulated until after the 'examining justices' have heard the evidence of the prosecution and that it is the magistrates who will decide upon what charge the accused will be committed for trial. These terminological and procedural relics have no practical effect today. As the police became the principal investigators of crime, so the magistrates' inquiry became a judicial function with the object of

ensuring that there was sufficient evidence for the accused to stand trial. In 1848 when this practice was codified (in the Administration of Justice (No 1) Act 1848) all crimes proper were triable only at assizes or quarter sessions so it may be said that the normal criminal procedure envisaged a preliminary judicial hearing before a person could be put on trial.

186. From 1848 until the present time there has been a continuous tendency to confer jurisdiction on magistrates' courts to try criminal offences. Today, those courts try as many as 80 per cent of all indictable offences. Consequently, a preliminary judicial hearing is held in only the 20 per cent of such cases which are committed for trial at the crown court.

c. Purpose of committal proceedings

187. The purpose of committal proceedings now is to ensure that no person shall stand trial at the crown court unless there is a *prima facie* case against him. It is not a purpose of committal proceedings that the defence may hear all the prosecution witnesses, or any particular witness or witnesses, give their evidence in chief or that such witnesses shall be made available for cross examination. The prosecution are not required to call all their witnesses at committal proceedings; if they can make out a *prima facie* case without calling any particular witness or witnesses, even an important witness, they are entitled to do so and neither the defence nor the court can require any witness to be called.[3] It follows that committal proceedings are not necessarily a means whereby the defence may obtain full disclosure of the prosecution case before trial. In most cases, however, the prosecution do present all their evidence at the committal proceedings, and if they do not, they should give notice before the trial of any additional evidence they propose to call.

The introduction of 'paper committals' in 1967

Before the Criminal Justice Act 1967, committal proceedings were lengthy affairs in which all the evidence had to be taken laboriously, translated into depositions and then signed. In the overwhelming proportion of cases the defendant was committed for trial. The Criminal Justice Act 1967 introduced changes designed to abbreviate this procedure and thus save the time of courts, lawyers, police and witnesses. Instead of the witnesses having to come to the magistrates' courts to have their statements taken down, the statements were now sent to the defence. If the defendant was legally represented, he could agree to be committed for trial on the basis of the prosecution statements. The procedure in that event lasted only a few minutes. If, however, he wanted all or some of the prosecution witnesses to be called for examination and cross-examination, this was open to him. (The procedure was to be found in Magistrates' Courts Act 1980, s 6(1)–paper committals and s 6(2)–old style full committals.)

In a large Home Office study in 1985 it was found that there was no evidence that full committals resulted in the weeding out of a higher proportion of weak cases than paper committals. The rate of acquittals directed by the judge was considerably higher in the full committal cases–15 per cent as against 5 per cent (P Jones *et al*, 'The Effectiveness of Committal Proceedings as a Filter in the Criminal Justice System' (1985) *Criminal Law Review*, p 355, 360). Also, full committals resulted in considerably greater delays.

---

3   *R v Epping and Harlow Justices, ex p Massaro* [1973] QB 433; *R v Grays Justices, ex p Tetley* (1979) 70 Cr App Rep 11. See also *R v Governor of Pentonville Prison, ex p Osman* [1989] 3 All ER 701; and *Galbraith* [1981] 2 All ER 1060, CA (ed).

Abolition or reform?

The Philips Royal Commission on Criminal Procedure thought that committal proceedings were an inadequate filter against weak cases. It proposed the abolition of full committal proceedings and the institution of a new procedure ('application for discharge') whereby the defence could ask for a hearing before the magistrates at which to make a submission of no case to answer. The Royal Commission also proposed the abolition of paper committals, on the ground that sifting of weak cases would be done by the proposed new independent prosecution service. The defence should, however, be able to apply to the magistrates for rulings on bail, witness orders, mode of trial, etc (paras 8.24–8.31).

The Roskill Committee on Fraud Trials in its report in January 1986 also recommended that something drastic should be done about committal proceedings. With regard to full committals, they were time-consuming. Sometimes in complicated cases they lasted for weeks and occasionally even months. The defence desire to use the committal stage as a dress-rehearsal for the trial could be an abuse. Sometimes, for instance, the defence would cross-examine prosecution witnesses simply in the hope of turning up something that would assist the defence.

The Committee recommended a new procedure whereby fraud cases could be sent for trial direct to the crown court by the new prosecution authorities recommended by the report. They would issue a 'transfer certificate' subject to the right of the accused to apply to a judge for a discharge on the ground that the prosecution's evidence failed to disclose a *prima facie* case. (See paras 4.31–4.40.)

This recommendation was implemented in the Criminal Justice Act 1987, ss 4–6. A transfer certificate can be issued under s 4 by the DPP (and therefore anyone in the Crown Prosecution Service), the Director of the Serious Fraud Office, the Commissioners of Customs and Excise or the Home Secretary. The basis of a transfer certificate is (1) that in the opinion of one of the above the evidence of the offence would be sufficient for the person charged to be committed for trial and (2) that it reveals a case of fraud 'of such seriousness and complexity that it is appropriate that the management of the case should without delay be taken over by the crown court' (s 4(1)(*b*)).

Further erosion of the value of committal proceedings occurred in the 1991 Criminal Justice Act, s 55(7), which removed the right of the accused personally to cross-examine a child victim in sex and assault cases at the committal stage. The debate as to what to do about committals continued. (For the history between 1986 and 1992 see the 6th edn of this work, pp 304–06.)

In 1992 a study of some 3,000 either-way cases in five crown court areas and interviews with magistrates and justices' clerks showed that they thought that full committals rarely achieved any useful purpose. (Carol Hedderman and David Moxon, *Magistrates' Court or Crown Court? Mode of Trial Decisions and Sentencing*, Home Office Research and Planning Unit, Paper No 125, 1992.) Occasionally they were useful but the resources they absorbed were quite out of proportion to any benefits. Equally there was a strong view that 'paper committals' served no judicial purpose and that there was no point in retaining them in their existing form.

The Runciman Royal Commission

The Runciman Royal Commission, like the Philips Commission and the Roskill Committee, recommended that committal proceedings be abolished on the grounds that paper committals were a waste of time and that there were better ways of achieving the objective of weeding out weak cases than by old style full committals. It commented on the cumbersome procedure of full committals. The Commission said that it did think however that there ought to be a way for the defendant to argue that the case against him was so weak that it should not be allowed to proceed. The defendant ought therefore to have the right to submit that there was no case to answer. Such a submission should be considered on the papers, without calling any evidence. The parties should however be permitted to present oral argument. In indictable only cases the submission of no case to answer should be made to the crown court; in either way cases it should be made to the magistrates' court but they should be heard by stipendiary magistrates rather than lay justices. (Report, pp 90–91, paras 25–32.)

Apparent abolition–Criminal Justice and Public Order Act 1994, s 44

The Government accepted the recommendation. Committal proceedings were seemingly abolished by s 44 of the Criminal Justice and Public Order Act 1994. Instead cases were to be transferred under provisions set out in Sch 4 of the 1994 Act.

Transfer proceedings applied to all indictable-only offences and all either way offences which the magistrates decided were more suitable for crown court trial or where the defendant had not agreed to summary trial. Section 5(1) of Sch 4 required the prosecutor, within the prescribed period, to serve on the court and the defendant 'a notice of the prosecution case'. This had to specify the charges and include a set of documents containing the evidence on which the charges were based (s 5(2)). If transfer was not contested, the magistrates' court would transfer the case without any hearing to the crown court for trial.

If the defence wished to oppose transfer they had to do so in writing. The defence could only apply for an oral hearing on the grounds that oral argument was warranted because of the difficulty or complexity of the case. But if the defendant was unrepresented, he had an absolute right to make oral representations (s 6(5)).

If the defendant was legally represented, oral representation could be made by his representative if such a request was included in his application to dismiss (s 6(6)). The prosecutor could oppose both the application for dismissal and the request for oral representations. The rules also permitted an application to extend the prescribed time limits.

If oral representations were allowed, no witnesses could be called by either side. If oral representations were not permitted the court decided on the basis of the papers alone. Having considered what it had before it, the court had to dismiss a charge against the defendant 'if it appears to the court that there is not sufficient evidence against the accused to put him on trial by jury for the offence charged' (s 6(10)).

Dismissal of the charge had the effect of barring any further proceedings on that charge on that evidence other than by a voluntary bill of indictment–see below.

The draft rules originally gave the prosecution six weeks to serve their case on the defence but as a result of lobbying by the CPS this was extended to ten weeks, or longer if an application for an extension of time was granted by the court. If the defendant wrote to the court that he did not intend to apply for dismissal, the case could then be transferred. If the defence wished to apply for dismissal they had to do so within two weeks. If no application was made within that time the case would then be transferred to the crown court.

The government changes its mind   It had originally been intended that the transfer provisions would come into force in May 1995 but major snags were discovered in the drafting of Sch 4–which caused successive post-ponements, first to July 1995, then to September 1995 and then to a date in 1996 and then to a later date in 1996. Finally, to the Government's considerable discomfiture, the difficulties raised by the Law Society and others proved insurmountable. On 25 April 1996 the Home Office wrote to the relevant interested parties that it had decided to move amendments to the Criminal Procedure and Investigations Bill totally abandoning the whole idea of transfer proceedings!

Instead, uncontested 'paper committals' under s 6(2) of the Magistrates' Courts Act 1980 were to be retained without change. Contested 'old style committals' under s 6(1) were to be reformed by the removal of the right to call witnesses to give oral evidence. Contested committal proceedings will therefore proceed simply on the basis of witness statements and other documentary material presented by the prosecution and oral argument by both prosecution and defence. The letter said 'We believe that it will guarantee a system which will work, which has the confidence of practitioners, and which achieves the essential aim of sparing witnesses the possible distress of giving evidence at contested hearings, was well as some savings in time and resources'. (For the amendments, see Criminal Procedure and Investigations Act, ss 44, 45 and Sch 1.)

10. THE VOLUNTARY BILL OF INDICTMENT

There is one procedural device to avoid committal proceedings–the voluntary bill of indictment. This is an application to commit a defendant direct to the crown court without going via the magistrates' court. The application is made to a High Court judge. Normally it is made when the committal proceedings are already completed and subsequently a further defendant emerges. Instead of starting the committal proceedings again, the defendant is belatedly sent for trial on the basis of the evidence already available. The applicant supplies the judge with the committal papers, including proofs of all witnesses, depositions and witness statements. The defendant can ask for leave to oppose the application but he has no right to do so and usually leave is not given. The High Court judge simply considers the papers. There is no hearing unless he calls for the applicant or some or all of the witnesses to attend.

See generally Charles Lewis, 'The Voluntary Bill of Indictment', *Law Society's Gazette*, 16 December 1981, p 1442. For the procedure see now *Practice Direction (Crime: Voluntary Bills)* [1990] 1 WLR 1633. See also *Blackstone's Criminal Practice*, D7.3.

There are no statistics as to the extent of the use of the procedure. The Roskill Committee on Fraud Trials said that it had been told that it was used at the Central Criminal Court in about 6 to 12 cases each year (p 53, n 24).

11. PRE-TRIAL COURT HEARINGS

(a) Plea and directions hearing (PDH)

In 1990 a report issued by the Pre-Trial Issues Working Group, representing all relevant criminal justice agencies, recommended that soon after a case was sent to the crown court it should have a short plea and directions hearing. Recommendation 92 of the Report said: 'Magistrates' courts should commit the defendant to appear on a specific date in the crown court and all cases should initially be listed there for a plea and directions hearing'.

The main purpose of the plea and directions hearing (PDH) was to try to identify the cases that could be dealt with either immediately or very quickly, especially those in which the defendant intended to plead guilty. Where a not guilty plea was confirmed, the judge would question counsel for both sides with a standard questionnaire with a view to identifying the issues and giving directions that would assist preparation for trial.

Recommendation 92 was then put to the test by a pilot study in three courts—Leeds, Plymouth and Croydon. The experiment demonstrated that a PDH did have the hoped for effects. (Report of the National Steering Group on the Pilot Study of Recommendation 92 issued by the Lord Chancellor's Department, February 1994.) In particular, it significantly increased the number of early guilty pleas and, by the same token, significantly reduced the number of 'cracked trials', (cases that are listed for trial where the defendant pleads guilty at the last minute.) The average drop in the cases listed for trial that then cracked was from 58 per cent before the pilot, to 45 per cent after. Of even more significance was the reduction in cracked trials as a proportion of all cases—from 31 per cent pre-pilot to 18 per cent during the pilot.

The proportion of all cases which proceeded to an effective trial did not change significantly from pre-pilot to pilot, which suggested that PDHs did not lead to defendants pleading guilty when they would not otherwise have done so.

Ideally, counsel who appears at the trial should be the same as counsel who appears at the PDH. The pilot study showed however that this rarely happens. The same prosecution counsel appeared at both in only 8 per cent of cases; for defence counsel the proportion was 21 per cent.

The pilot experiment also showed that the length of effective trials was reduced slightly—from 4 hours 41 minutes in the pre-pilot, to 4 hours 12 minutes in the pilot. Almost 50 per cent of trials in the pilot, compared with only 30 per cent of those in the pre-pilot, were concluded within 4 hours. Also, for guilty pleas, the interval between committal and disposal was shorter under the pilot. For cases that went to trial the PDH lengthened the time from committal to the trial by two to three days but the Report said that this had to be viewed against the national picture of lengthening waiting times in the crown court. (The PDH itself typically lasted 15 to 30 minutes.)

The Runciman Royal Commission reported before the final report on Recommendation 92 was available. (It had available an interim report.) However the Commission by 10–1 opposed implementation of Recommendation 92. Instead the majority proposed a new, mainly paper-based, pre-trial regime for all cases, involving a series of steps designed to streamline the trial. The CPS would serve a form on the defence certifying that they had made full disclosure. The defence would then serve on the CPS a form indicating whether the defence intended to defend and, if not, to what charges the accused was prepared to plead guilty. If the defendant was prepared to plead guilty, the CPS would then indicate on a form whether it was prepared to accept the plea to those charges. If the plea was not guilty, the defence would serve on the CPS a form making pre-trial disclosure and dealing with other pre-trial matters. All notices would also have to be served on the court, which would be required to monitor compliance with the new procedural requirements. The court would remind the parties by telephone of time-table lapses. If there was serious delay the judge would be informed so that he could take action. Either side would have the right to call for a preparatory hearing (PTR). If there was no PTR, a date would be fixed for trial. Prior to the trial counsel for both sides would confer informally to sort out whatever could be sorted out pre-trial. Both counsel would be under a duty to certify that they had discussed the case and with what result. If no PTR were sought, counsel's 'certificate of readiness' would record that fact, contain an estimate of the likely length of the case and indicate dates when counsel and witnesses would not be available for a trial.

The writer did not support this proposal. In a lengthy dissent he argued that even if the majority's proposal worked as intended it would make the system less rather than more efficient and would increase both delay and costs, and that in any event it was unlikely to work as intended (Report, pp 223–33). Instead, he argued for implementation of Recommendation 92.

The final Report on Recommendation 92 was published in February 1994. The National Steering Group which had overseen the pilot study recommended that Recommendation 92 be introduced generally.

One of the essentials for success of the new system it said was firm use by the judge of the Judge's Questionnaire for not guilty plea cases which both the prosecution and defence have to respond to at the PDH hearing. (Will the not guilty plea be maintained? The numbers of witnesses and their availability. What facts and exhibits are admitted? What issues are to be raised as to admissibility of evidence? What points of law will be argued? Is there an alibi defence? If so, has it been disclosed? etc.)

The Report advised against proceeding with the proposal of the majority of the Royal Commission for a paper-based system as an alternative to Recommendation 92.

Replying to a Parliamentary Question on 5 July 1994, the Lord Chancellor announced that Recommendation 92 would be implemented nationwide. A Practice Direction extending PDHs to all crown court centres was handed down by the Lord Chief Justice on 27 July 1995. (See [1995] 4 All ER 379 and *New Law Journal*, 15 September 1995, p 1331.) The Practice Direction states that where the defendant intends to plead guilty, probation, the CPS and the court should all be notified as soon as possible. (Probation can then proceed to prepare a pre-sentence report.) The PDH must be held in public.

In his Note of Dissent to the Royal Commission Report the writer suggested that implementation of Recommendation 92 would benefit not only the system (in terms of earlier identification of guilty pleas and a reduction in the number of cracked trials), but also, and even more important, the defendant:

Any of these forms of assistance should have the effect of improving the quality of preparation of cases. The Interim Report on the pilot experiment states:

'The indications are that Recommendation 92 is improving the preparation and disposal of Crown Court cases. The extent of this will not be clear until completion of the pilot... It is however already clear that the key to any improvement is early and adequate preparation by both prosecution and defence ...'.[4]

This is extremely important–considerably more important than 'clarifying issues for the jury' or 'streamlining the trial' or 'saving costs'. It is central to whether justice is done because it directly concerns the question whether the defendant's case is properly put to the court by his lawyers. Critical to that is whether the case has been properly prepared by the solicitors. (Sir Patrick Hastings QC, one of the greatest advocates of the century, said 'at least 90 per cent of cases win or lose themselves and the result would have been the same whoever the counsel'[5]– meaning that preparation is much more often the basis of success than advocacy.)

One of the most serious defects in the existing system is inadequate preparation of routine cases by defence lawyers.[6] Among the many reasons for this is that the work in most solicitors' firms is done by clerks, with insufficient guidance from solicitors in their own firms and, too often, with no guidance from a barrister. The early opportunity of a face-to-face consultation with a barrister for both the defendant and the representative of the solicitors' firm is therefore one of the potentially most valuable aspects of the automatic Plea and Directions Hearing for cases that end as trials.[7]

By contrast, under the majority's scheme, in a significant proportion of cases there would have been no pre-trial conference *with any barrister*.[8] If Recommendation 92 made a dent on that problem, it would be worthwhile for that alone [p 231].

(b) Preparatory or pre-trial hearings

The majority of the Runciman Royal Commission placed considerable weight on the value of preparatory hearings for the more complex cases. In such cases it proposed that either side should have the right to require a preparatory hearing in front of a judge in order to secure rulings on the main issues. It should also be possible for the court itself to direct that such a hearing take place (Report, p 102, para 4). These views were supported in evidence to the Royal Commission by the Bar Council, the Criminal Bar Association, the Law Society, the CPS and the police service.

Such a hearing, the Royal Commission said, should be treated as part of the trial itself so that decisions made by the judge would be binding throughout (Report, pp 104–05, para 16).

The Royal Commission suggested that practice directions be issued to the effect that in cases of a certain length a preparatory hearing should normally occur. The Lord Chancellor's Department had suggested that as a general rule a preparatory

---

4   Para 23 at p 9.
5   P Hastings, *Cases in Court*, Pan Books, 1953, p 250.
6   See for instance, M McConville and J Hodgson, *Custodial Legal Advice and the Right for Silence*, Royal Commission on Criminal Justice Research Study No 16, 1993, and M McConville, J Hodgson, L Bridges, *Standing Accused*, OUP, 1994.
7   It is appreciated that at many court centres the present facilities for such consultations are woefully inadequate.
8   According to the defence barristers in the Crown Court Study (sect 2.6.1) there was no pre-trial conference with counsel in 58% of cases. According to defence solicitors there was none in 59%. Not surprisingly, it was considerably more common to have had no conference when the defendant ended by pleading guilty. But, according to the barristers, there was no pre-trial conference in 37% of contested cases, and according to defence solicitors in 46%. Whichever figure was correct, the proportion is considerable.

hearing should only be considered necessary in cases expected to last for more than two and a half days. That would cover around 6 per cent of contested trials. The Royal Commission thought that this was going too wide and that at least initially cases likely to last longer than a week would be sufficient. But it added that 'it should be open to either of the parties or the court to require a hearing in shorter cases for reasons other than the expected length of the trial' (Report, p 105, para 17).

The writer in his Dissent (Report, pp 223–33) expressed considerable reservations about the value of preparatory hearings and suggested that they should be restricted to the narrowest possible category of cases. (The rule of thumb at the Old Bailey was that a case should have a preparatory hearing if it was likely to take more than four weeks. That might provide a sensible test.) Certainly it should not be possible for a party to *demand* such a hearing. The reason for viewing preparatory hearings sceptically was that the empirical evidence suggested that far from simplifying and shortening trials, they tend to have the opposite effect of lengthening trials and making them more costly:

52. Worse, the existing empirical evidence about pre-trial hearings of whatever kind suggests that, contrary to what common sense would suggest, instead of simplifying trials or saving costs, such hearings tend to do the opposite. They increase costs and lengthen trials. The evidence for this proposition is now extensive:

- In the Crown Court Study, judges were asked whether they thought the pre-trial review had saved much time and money. As many as two-thirds (66%) said No. A quarter (24%) said that a little time and money had been saved. In 8% a fair amount of time and money had been saved. A 'great deal' had been saved in only 1%.[9]
- Professor Michael Levi's study of serious fraud cases stated in regard to ordinary pre-trial reviews:[10] 'none of the defence lawyers I interviewed argued that pre-trial reviews had any significant effect on the development of the case... The problem is that the judge in the pre-trial reviews is seldom the trial judge, has seldom read the papers, and therefore understandably does not wish to become embroiled in complex matters.'[11]
- The fate of the more formal preparatory hearings under the Serious Fraud regime is equally discouraging. The Roskill Committee said that a full day should be set aside for preparatory hearings.[12] In fact, however, in many of the cases brought by the Serious Fraud Office, preparatory hearings have taken weeks or even months. (In Guinness I, the preparatory hearing took three months)
- The only proper study of the impact of pre-trial conferences, using *matched* samples, conducted in 3,000 personal injury cases in New Jersey,[13] concluded that although they improved preparation,[14] they did not shorten trials. The researchers concluded that they therefore lowered rather than raised the efficiency of the system by absorbing a great deal of court and judge time without any compensating saving in the time required for trials.

9   Sect 2.8.9.
10 Pre-trial reviews are not the special preparatory hearings envisaged for serious fraud cases by the Roskill Committee which were established by the Criminal Justice Act 1987.
11 Royal Commission Research Study No. 14, 1993, p 105.
12 Fraud Trials Committee Report, 1986, HMSO, para 6.52.
13 M Rosenberg, *The Pre-Trial Conference and Effective Justice*, 1964, Columbia University Press, p 68.
14 Civil cases are of course not the same as criminal. But if pre-trial conferences do not achieve their intended results in civil cases, it is arguable that they are even less likely to work in criminal cases where the adversarial nature of the proceedings is greater and the defendant is understandably therefore even less inclined to be co-operative or helpful.

*The Government's Consultation Document and the Criminal Procedure and
Investigations Act 1996*

Pre-trial rulings   The Government's Consultation Document *Improving the
Effectiveness of Pre-Trial Hearings in the Crown Court*, issued in July 1995 (Cm
2924) proposed that judges should have a power to make binding rulings at any point
after the transfer of a case to the crown court. This proposal was to be implemented
by section 31 of the Criminal Procedure and Investigations Act. The section would
enable a judge to make a ruling as to the admissibility of evidence or any other question
of law before the trial, whether on application or on its own motion. The start of a trial
is defined to mean when the jury is sworn (s 30). This will in future avoid swearing a
jury and then having to send them away for hours or days while lawyers argue legal
points.

   Section 31 would enable a judge who makes a ruling under the section to order
that the ruling is binding, but then goes on to say that such a ruling can be varied by
the trial judge 'if it appears to him that it is in the interests of justice to do so' (s 31(11)).
Neither party can seek to obtain a variation in a binding pre-trial ruling unless there
has been some material change in circumstances.

Extension of preparatory hearings   The Government's Consultation Document
proposed that, subject to a satisfactory pilot, a scheme of preparatory hearings similar
to those that operate in serious fraud cases under the Criminal Justice Act 1987 should
be introduced for other complex and potentially lengthy cases tried in the crown court.
Section 29 of the Bill enables a judge, on application or otherwise, to order a preparatory
hearing in a long or complex case if it appears to him that substantial benefits will
accrue from such a hearing. The purpose of such a hearing would be to identify material
issues, to assist the jury's comprehension of the issues, to expedite the trial or to assist
the management of the trial

12. PREPARATION OF CASES BY THE DEFENCE

An exceedingly depressing picture of the way cases are prepared by defence lawyers
emerged from the research conducted by Professor Michael McConville and colleagues
Jacqueline Hodgson, Lee Bridges and Anita Pavlovic, published as *Standing Accused*,
Clarendon Press, Oxford, 1994. The study was the first to try to explain what defence
lawyers actually do. It was based on examination of files, attending police stations,
sitting in on legal advice sessions in police stations, attending questioning of suspects
by police officers; interviews with clients; attending interviews with clients in the
solicitors' office and at court and conferences with counsel. Interviews were also
conducted with the lawyers and their staffs.

   The main research was conducted over a three-year period starting in October
1988. In that period the researchers observed the practices of 22 firms of solicitors in
cities and towns in the South West, East Anglia, the South, Central and North Midlands,
the North West and the North East of England. 'The firms were chosen for the most
part because of their status as mass deliverers of legal services in criminal cases in
their localities' (p 15). In some cases the researcher spent several months with the

firm. For most the observation period lasted between four and eight researcher weeks. Shorter periods were spent with firms with smaller practices. The average time spent with each firm was six and a half researcher weeks. In addition to this main sample, another twenty six firms and three independent agencies were targeted by police station advice and interrogation observation. The average period spent observing this sample of firms was about two weeks. In total therefore there were 48 firms in the study and the research covered 198 researcher weeks of observation.

The research came to the following conclusions:

Almost all those interviewed in the firms 'came to see criminal defence practices as geared, in cooperation with the other elements of the system, toward the routine production of guilty pleas' (p 71). ('In the process, any notions they have carried with them into practice of criminal defence work being based in an adversarial process and involving careful investigation and construction of the individual's case are disabused' (*ibid*).)

Many suspects in the police station do not appreciate the significance of the right to free legal advice, some are dissuaded by the police, and some are confronted by solicitors who do not want to attend the police station. Many of those who do police station work are former police officers. Non-solicitor clerks generally cannot offer legal advice. 'Advisers of all grades fall in with police routines and are responsive to police expectations that the private interview with the client will be over in a matter of minutes. Consultations are hurried and produce only an outline of the client's account sufficient to enable the adviser to slot the case into one of the "typical case" categories with which advisers are familiar' (p 100).

Defence advisers present during interviews conducted by the police make few if any objections to the way the interview is conducted.

Looked at as a whole, advisers who attend police stations accept uncritically the propriety and legitimacy of police action, even where what they witness themselves, what they hear from clients, and what they suspect goes on, leaves them convinced that the police break the rules and in other ways are beyond the law. The reason for this is that many advisers, like the police, instinctively believe, without requiring substantiation through evidence, that there is a case to answer, and that it is the client who must give the answer. This in turn springs from a working assumption that the client is probably factually guilty' [pp 126–7].

'Defence-advisers, most of whom are non-qualified staff, are less concerned with establishing the circumstances relating to the alleged offence than with securing from the client a promise to plead guilty.' ('Their dealings with the clients, based in personal relationships, operate on the principle that the client has done something and should plead' (p 159).) Clerks do not assiduously test for the existence of defences or satisfy themselves that all legal requirements of guilt are met, nor do they have the skills to undertake such an inquiry ... many solicitors are court-based, keep a distance from clients and delegate all tasks short of advocacy to non-qualified staff on an ungraded and unsupervised basis' (*ibid*).

Legally aided clients are not generally encouraged to tell their stories. Insofar as their version emerges they are taught that it is not worth recording, that it will not persuade any court, and should be abandoned in the face of police evidence. Statements of clients are routinely disregarded. The adviser persuades the client that his case is not worth pursuing. Those that survive to trial do so despite not because of the process. 'Conviction is achieved in the office of their own adviser through a process whose methodologies most nearly resemble those of the police themselves' (p 160).

Plea settlement and pleas in mitigation are dealt with in a routine manner. Magistrates' courts are seen by solicitors as places where clients can be processed through guilty pleas. Defence solicitors fail to see their own central role in the production of guilty pleas.

In magistrates' courts, the principal strength of prosecution cases lies in their heavy reliance upon evidence from the police. Such evidence assumes legitimacy because it is practised, assertive and depersonalised. Supported by notebook entries and the testimony of fellow officers, the self-legitimating and mutually supporting character of police evidence commends itself to magistrates ... Against this there is often no separate, competing case for the defence. 'The general lack of investigation and preparation by solicitors and their staff, throws the burden of the defence onto the defendant' [p 237] 'So far as conviction or acquittal is concerned, any success defence solicitors have at trials themselves tends to be a product of what they can achieve "on their feet" in court and whatever "turns up" on the day' [p 238].

For crown court cases a few firms were exceptional in employing competent and experienced staff:

'Here the case was prepared well in advance and a real effort made to engage in proactive defence work. Witnesses were sought and pursued until contacted; enquiry agents were sent to draw up plans of the scene of the crime; and forensic experts were employed in response to the client's assertion of inaccurate or fabricated evidence. However, these individuals were quite exceptional, even within the firms in which they were employed. In the majority of practices much preparatory work is undertaken by non-qualified staff, and solicitors themselves have little contact with routine crown court cases ... In an unacceptably high number of cases, evidence is still being gathered long after the time when it was first available, sometimes during the trial itself ... The role definition applied to staff, leads solicitors to employ junior, casual or part-time individuals who are not otherwise involved in the case at all. The fact that the rates of remuneration are so low shows that it is not just solicitors who undervalue these tasks but the state itself ... With occasional outstanding exceptions, the average solicitor has little involvement in preparing these cases, and what work is done is often too little and too late [pp 267–8].

A few barristers were strongly committed to cases and were careful to test the underlying basis of a guilty plea, but most barristers were not:

'Strikingly on the hearing day at court, but also in conferences in chambers, barristers evince little interest in scrutinising the evidence or in attempting to convince the defendant of its weight and probative value. Rather, conferences are treated as "disclosure interviews", the purpose of which is to extract a plea of guilty from the client. In this process, what the prosecution alleges, what witnesses may say, and what the client wishes to say, are not discussed ... In place of evidence, a whole gamut of persuasive tactics is deployed against clients enabling barristers to take control of cases and to prevent most clients from becoming, in any real sense, defendants' [pp 268–9].

For a different picture given by participants in the process see M Zander and P Henderson, *Crown Court Study*, (Royal Commission on Criminal Justice, 1993). This confirmed that a high proportion of briefs are received by the barrister in the case at the last minute—40 per cent of prosecution barristers and 25 per cent of defence barristers got the brief in contested cases after 4pm of the day before the trial (p 30). Fifty nine per cent of prosecution barristers and 44 per cent of defence barristers said it was a returned brief (p 32). A quarter of all barristers said the brief was not adequate (p 33). But almost all the barristers thought they had enough time to prepare the case (pp 30–31) and seventy one per cent of prosecution barristers and 83 per cent of defence barristers said they had been able to rectify inadequacies in the brief (p 33).

The judges were asked whether counsel was well-prepared. Nearly half the judges (47%) thought the prosecution counsel was 'Very well prepared' and the same proportion thought counsel was 'Adequately prepared'. The remaining 6 per cent thought counsel was 'Not well prepared' (p 47). The judicial assessment of defence counsel was precisely the same (pp 59–60).

Bar/CPS Service Standards

In August 1994 the CPS distributed to all barristers' chambers involved in prosecution work standards to which members of the Bar were requested to adhere. The aim was to encourage early preparation of cases by the Bar in order to reduce last minute consultations at court and the number of adjournments. The standards laid down time periods within which counsel would be expected to have read his instructions and, where appropriate, to have advised the CPS in writing. For cases likely to take up to 3 days the target time was 7 days; for trials lasting 3 days or more and guilty pleas in serious cases, it was 14 days; and for heavy cases 21 days. Whether or not formal written advice was given, when counsel had read the papers within the time laid down for the type of case, the CPS have to be notified that this had been done. Likewise failure to meet the target dates has to be notified to the CPS.

The sanction for repeated failure to meet the new standards was not stated, but clearly the CPS could take individual barristers, or even whole chambers, off its list of prosecution counsel.

13. PUBLICITY AND CONTEMPT OF COURT

It is a principle of fundamental importance that the trial of an accused person should not be prejudiced by inappropriate pre-trial publicity or by publication of prejudicial material during the trial itself. Traditionally, English law controlling the media in regard to publication of pre-trial material has been strict; in practice in recent years it has become far less so. There are two main different kinds of approach to the problem— to prohibit certain kinds of publication and to penalise breaches by proceedings for contempt of court or, alternatively, to grant a stay or to quash proceedings in the case which is the subject of the publicity. Until very recently almost all English law has been of the former kind. But in recent years there has emerged also the question whether proceedings should be stayed in advance or retrospectively annulled because of excessive media publicity.

Under the Contempt of Court Act 1981 it is unlawful to publish anything which 'creates a substantial risk that the course of justice in the proceedings will be seriously impeded or prejudiced' (s 2(2)). The rule takes effect from the moment when proceedings are active, which in criminal cases is from the moment of arrest without a warrant, or from the issue of a warrant or from the charging of a suspect (Sch 1, ss 3–5).

Before criminal proceedings are active   Publication of prejudicial material at a point in time where there is as yet no suspect would therefore not fall foul of the statutory rule though it could still be common law contempt of intending to prejudice potential criminal proceedings. This was held to apply to *The Sun* newspaper in 1988 when it delayed laying an information before magistrates for a private prosecution it was funding until after it had published its story about a doctor allegedly raping an 8-year old girl. The *sub judice* period did not begin until the information was laid so that the 1981 Act had not been breached. But after the doctor had been acquitted, the paper was held to have committed a common law contempt by proclaiming the doctor's guilt. A fine of £75,000 was imposed. (*AG v News Group Newspapers plc* [1988] 2 All ER 906.) By contrast in *AG v Sport Newspapers Ltd* [1992] 1 All ER 503, *The Daily Sport* published the previous convictions of a man the police suspected of kidnapping a girl, after the police asked the media not to publish the information. No warrant had yet been issued for the arrest of the man. The editor said that he got the message about the police request not to publish the information too late. The court held that there would not be liability for common law contempt unless there were overwhelming evidence of intent to prejudice the proceedings. The court criticised the paper but did not find such intent. The decision was somewhat surprising as the paper knew that the man was likely to be arrested and obviously knew that publication of his previous convictions would be highly prejudicial.

When criminal proceedings are active   Once criminal proceedings are 'active' (see above) the media publish prejudicial material at their risk. They are liable for contempt even though it cannot be proved that they intended to prejudice a fair trial. There is an exception however if they can show that they did not know and had no reason to know that criminal proceedings were active (s 3(1)). It is also a defence if it can be established that publication was part of a discussion of public affairs or matters of public interest, if the risk of prejudice to the proceedings is incidental to the discussion (s 5).

Proceedings to enforce the law are brought by the Attorney-General. In recent years the standard of compliance with the spirit of the law of contempt in criminal cases has slipped considerably. The media now frequently publish material in the early stages of a case which in former times would have resulted in severe penalties on editors. In the case of the Yorkshire Ripper, for instance, most of the press published quotes from the police on the day of the arrest of the suspect, Peter Sutcliffe, indicating that the police were jubilant at having caught the man they were hunting. The search for the Ripper was over. One or two papers even published photographs of him in spite of the fact that there might well have been issues of identification evidence. The Attorney-General happened to be out of the country at the time. The Solicitor-General merely issued a letter to editors reminding them of the law of contempt, but no proceedings followed.

Another huge wave of media publicity followed the arrest of Michael Fagan in 1982 after he had been found in the Queen's bedroom at Buckingham Palace. This time proceedings *were* brought against several newspapers for publishing material about Fagan that showed him to be feckless, that he had been a 'junkie' and had marriage problems and that other criminal proceedings were pending against him. As *The Times* said (12 February 1983): 'It was fortissimo and it was as lurid as the pettiness of the material permitted. Any idea that while a man has a criminal charge outstanding against him his character is in baulk[15] was thrown to the wind.' But, to general surprise, the Divisional Court, with the Lord Chief Justice presiding, rejected all but one of the charges against the papers. It therefore set a lower standard of conduct for the press than would have been thought right before (*A-G v Times Newspapers* (1983) Times, 12 February).

In 1994 the Court of Appeal quashed the conviction for murder of two sisters Michelle and Lisa Taylor because of prejudicial pre-trial publicity and material irregularities at the trial. (*R v Taylor and Taylor* (1993) 98 Cr App Rep 361.) The Court of Appeal referred the case to the Attorney General and asked him to consider bringing proceedings for contempt against the newspapers concerned but the Solicitor General declined to do so. In December 1994 the two sisters were given leave to bring proceedings for judicial review against the Attorney General's failure to take proceedings against the newspapers. But in August 1995 the Divisional Court dismissed the proceedings on the ground that, even though some of the newspaper reports crossed the acceptable limits of fair and accurate reporting, the Attorney General's discretion could not be reviewed by the courts.

In March 1995, the trial judge refused to stay the proceedings against the Maxwell brothers, Kevin and Ian (sons of Robert Maxwell), who had been the subject of a great deal of adverse pre-trial publicity before their trial for fraud. As will be seen, however, (p 365 below) the judge did take steps to see that the jury selection process should so far as possible eliminate any individual who was biased against the accused. In the event, the jury acquitted the defendants. Mr Justice Phillips spoke of the way in which, especially in a long case, all the participants in the case are dominated by the experience:

> It is something that it is impossible to exaggerate. As the weeks go by the trial becomes not merely part of life, but the dominant feature of it so that the stage is reached when one can hardly see behind or beyond it, and I am quite sure that this is true of all who are involved in the trial. The responsibility of reaching verdicts is a heavy one in any case, but in a case such as this it is one of which the jury will be particularly aware. I do not believe that their verdicts will be influenced by anything they may have read about individual defendants before the trial begins.

In October 1995 a trial judge stopped a trial of Geoff Knights, partner of *EastEnders* star Gillian Tayforth, because of what the judge called 'unlawful reporting and scandalous reporting'. (Knights was charged on 17 April 1995. On the following day the *Daily Mail* and *Today* published interviews with witnesses, the *Daily Star* said he 'had gone berserk with an iron bar after catching Miss Tayforth with another man' and a few days later the *Daily Mail* published a lengthy interview with a potential witness along with an account of Knights' previous convictions.) The case was believed to be the first where the trial was abandoned before it started simply because of pre-trial publicity. (See national newspapers 5 October 1995 and E Crowther, 'Publish and Then be Damned', *Justice of the Peace*, 13 January 1996, p 26.)

The Attorney General in a Parliamentary Answer in October 1995 said that at least five trials, including that of Knights, had been halted in the previous three years because the trial judge decided that media coverage would make a fair trial impossible. (House of Commons, *Hansard*, 26 October 1995, vol 264, col 797/807.)

15 A billiards term meaning 'out of play' (ed).

Committal proceedings   Until 1967 the committal proceedings before magistrates provided much lurid material for the press which was lawful since it amounted to reporting of court proceedings. But it was often said that such reporting prejudiced the prospects of a fair trial since the jury might remember what they had read and be affected by it. This was the more so since the normal practice was for the prosecution to present its case at the committal stage but for the defendant to refrain from revealing his defence. The press accounts of the case would therefore inevitably be very one-sided.

The matter came to a head after the trial of Dr Bodkin Adams in 1957 for the murder of one of his elderly patients. The prosecution at the committal proceedings led evidence of the circumstances in which two other patients had died but this was not introduced at the trial. The massive newspaper coverage of the case from the arrest of the doctor to his ultimate acquittal gave the impression that he had been guilty of several murders. As a result of the case, in June 1957 a Departmental Committee under the chairmanship of Lord Tucker was appointed to consider whether there should be restrictions on reports of committal proceedings.

The report of the Committee (*Proceedings Before Examining Magistrates*, 1958, Cmnd 479) recommended that restrictions should be imposed, and these recommendations were eventually enacted in the Criminal Justice Act 1967, s 3 (see s 8 of the Magistrates' Court Act 1980), which made press reporting of the evidence at committal proceedings unlawful save where asked for by the defence. The press could only publish the formal basic facts and not the evidence (8(4)): the identity of the court; the names, addresses and occupations of the parties and witnesses and the ages of the accused and witnesses; the offence or offences, or a summary of them, with which the accused was charged; any decision of the court to commit the accused for trial and the charges.

It was held that where one defendant wanted publicity and the others did not, they all had to suffer publicity (see *R v Russell, ex p Beaverbrook Newspapers* [1968] 3 All ER 695 interpreting the former s 3(2)). The decision was applied by the magistrates at Minehead in November 1978 in the sensational trial of the leader of the Liberal Party Jeremy Thorpe for conspiracy to murder, when one of the defendants wanted publicity and Mr Thorpe and his two other co-defendants did not.

The case gave rise to a change in the rule. The Criminal Justice (Amendment) Act 1981 allowed an application to be made to the court where one co-defendant objects to pre-trial publicity. The court is required to make an order 'if, and only if, it is satisfied after hearing representations of the accused, that it is in the interests of justice to do so'. This provision became s 8A of the Magistrates' Courts Act 1980. The Divisional Court held in October 1982 that the burden of satisfying the magistrates lay on the defendant who wanted publicity and that the burden was a heavy one. No order should be made unless powerful reasons were given. (See *R v Leeds Justices, ex p Sykes* [1983] 1 All ER 460.)

The restrictions regarding reporting of committal proceedings were to be applied to transfer proceedings to take account of the abolition of committal proceedings by the Criminal Justice and Public Order Act 1994, Sch 4 but as has been seen, p 264 above, this is now not happening.

The 1981 Contempt of Court Act, s 4(1) states that a person is not guilty of contempt of court under the strict liability rule in respect of a 'fair and accurate report of legal proceedings held in public, published contemporaneously and in good faith'. Section 4(2) gives the court the power to order that publication of a report of the proceedings of any court be postponed for such period as the court thinks 'where it appears to be necessary for avoiding a substantial risk of prejudice'. The power is very rarely used by magistrates but it has been used quite often by crown courts–see C Walker *et al*, 'The Reporting of Crown Court Proceedings and the Contempt of Court Act 1981, *Modern Law Review*, September 1992, p 647.

The Court of Appeal held in 1982 that this power applied to committal proceedings. It held, however, that the only risk the court could take into account was a risk of prejudice to the committal proceedings–not any possibility of risk of prejudice to the later trial. (See *R v Horsham Justices, ex p Farquharson* [1982] 2 All ER 269.)

During the trial The media are not permitted to publish evidence held to be inadmissible. This would normally preclude publication of what takes place in the absence of the jury even though it is fair and accurate and contemporaneous. It would not be published 'in good faith'–since it would normally be obvious that it was not intended to be seen by jurors and if published might prejudice a fair trial. The contrast with the comparable rule in the USA emerged clearly in the televised trial of OJ Simpson during which viewers around the globe frequently saw evidence not seen by the jury.

Anonymity for victims of sexual offences

Since 1976 the victim of rape has been given a measure of anonymity. The Sexual Offences (Amendment) Act 1976 provided anonymity for the victim after someone had been accused of rape, but not earlier. Also the judge could lift the protection pre-trial if he thought that would cause witnesses to come forward or if the accused's defence would otherwise be prejudiced. At the trial he could lift the protection if satisfied that it was an unreasonable restriction on reporting and that it was in the public interest.

The 1976 Act also gave the defendant the same protection.

The Criminal Justice Act, 1988, s 158 extended the protection of anonymity to the victim from the moment of the allegation but withdrew the protection of anonymity from the defendant.

The 1976 and 1988 Acts dealt with rape, attempted rape, incitement to rape and accomplices to such offences. They did not deal with conspiracy to rape or burglary with intent to rape. But the Sexual Offences (Amendment) Act 1992 extended the statutory anonymity of rape victims to other sexual offences. The 1992 legislation was a Private Members' Bill implementing a recommendation of the Calcutt Committee on Privacy (Cm 1102), with Government support.

Under the 1992 Act the accused can ask for the prohibition to be lifted if he can satisfy the judge that it is necessary to induce witnesses to come forward because the conduct of the defence would otherwise be substantially prejudiced. At the trial, the prohibition can be lifted if the judge considers that the effect of the prohibition is to impose a substantial and unreasonable restriction on reporting and that it is in the public interest to remove it.

14. DELAYS IN CRIMINAL CASES

The modern approach to the problem of delay in criminal proceedings can be referred back to the report of the Streatfield Committee in 1962. It recommended that defendants tried in the higher courts should not have to wait more than eight weeks from committal to trial. Ever since, this has been used as the yardstick to test the extent of delay.

There are various indications of the extent of delays. One is the proportion of cases in which the defendant waited for under eight weeks from committal to trial. In 1975 this was just over half of all defendants (56 per cent). In the 1980s it declined to around one-third. In 1990 it was improved somewhat to 48 per cent but then it declined again and in 1994 was back down to one third.

The proportion of defendants who had to wait for more than 16 weeks was 24 per cent in 1990 and 36 per cent in 1994.

The average waiting time from committal to crown court trial in 1994 was 16.7 weeks, with variations regionally from 12.3 weeks on the Wales and Chester circuit to 19.4 weeks on the Northern Circuit. In London the average was 15.8 weeks. For those pleading guilty it was 14 weeks nationally compared to 21.4 weeks for those pleading not guilty. For those in custody it was 13.5 weeks, compared with 17.7 for those out on bail. (*Judicial Statistics*, 1994, chapter 6.) (There are no figures for the period from first appearance in the magistrates' court to committal.)

But some defendants inevitably wait much longer than the average. In 1989, for instance, there were over 100 prisoners who had to wait more than a year from committal to trial (Woolf *Report on Prison Disturbances*, 1990, Cm 1456, para 10.51).

Solutions to the problem of delay include more courts and more judges or magistrates. Another approach is through procedural reform, such as the introduction of Plea and Directions Hearings (pp 266–68 above).

Another attempt at procedural reform to reduce delay was tried in magistrates' courts as a result of another initiative by the Vera Institute of Justice. Its research had shown that magistrates too often face adjournments without any knowledge as to the previous history of the case including the number and reason for previous adjournments. It was suggested that this problem might be resolved if each case had a case file, so that the bench could see the previous history when they came to consider an application for an adjournment. (See generally *Report of the Working Group on Magistrates' Courts*, Home Office, 1982, Part III; Vera Institute of Justice, London, 'Waiting Time in Magistrates' Courts', 1979; John Bates and C Heal, 'Delays in the Magistrates' Courts', *Justice of the Peace*, 5 June 1982, p 334; TW Church, 'The Costs of Adjournments in Magistrates' Courts', *Justice of the Peace*, 24 July 1982, p 445.)

A new attack on the problem of delay was launched by the Pre-Trial Issues Working Group chaired by the Lord Chancellor's Department and including representatives of the Home Office, the CPS, the police and the Justices' Clerks Society (see p 242 above). Their report in November 1990 made a long list of recommendations designed to speed up criminal proceedings. They included:

(1) National time guidelines as to the different stages of the process. (So for the period between the completion of an investigation and the laying of an information they suggested three weeks or, if the advice of the CPS was sought, five weeks. For

the period between laying of informations and the first court listing, they recommended five weeks, etc.)

(2) Things should happen as a matter of course rather than it being necessary to ask for them–eg advance information should be sent routinely to the defence solicitor or, when there is no information as to the name of the defence solicitor, it should be prepared routinely for the first court hearing.

(3) The courts and the police should make local arrangements to limit the number of cases given a hearing date.

(4) Realistic dates should be fixed when adjournments are granted. Courts should specify the reasons for the adjournment and what they expect to happen at the next hearing.

(5) Detailed case histories should be available to the court whenever an adjournment is asked for.

(6) Temporary stipendiary magistrates should be appointed to clear local backlogs. There should be secondment of staff to other courts to help clear backlogs.

Time-limits

When Mr Leon Brittan was Home Secretary he became enthusiastic about time-limits for different stages of the procedure as a way of speeding up justice. Such a system operated in Scotland (the so-called 110–day rule) and in the United States. For the US approach and experience, see Julie Vennard, 'Court Delay and Speedy Trial Provisions' (1985) *Criminal Law Review*, p 73, which showed that the results were not outstanding. Miss Vennard concluded that it was vital that the courts themselves take an active part in promoting speedy trial through a mixture of judicial activism, a commitment to enforce deadlines and improved communication between the crucial actors. (See also Roger Tarling and Julie Vennard, 'Speeding up Justice', In *Managing Criminal Justice*, ed D Moxon, HMSO, 1985, p 118.)

In Scotland the 110–day rule is that the defendant must be brought to trial within 110 days of his committal for trial. If not, he is a free man, unless an extension of time is given, which is rare. In summary cases there is also a rule that a person must not be kept in custody for more than 40 days. Failure to start the trial within 40 days has the same result as failure to observe the 110 day rule. (See 'Time Limits for Prosecutions', *Justice of the Peace*, 15 December 1984, p 788.)

An experiment with time-limits was authorised by the Prosecution of Offences Act 1985, s 22. An experiment starting in April 1987 was approved by the Prosecution of Offences (Custody Time Limits) Regulations (SI 1987/299). It related to the period for which someone could be kept in custody while awaiting trial or committal for trial.

The time limits are now standard for the whole country: 56 days between first appearance and summary trial; if a decision to go to summary trial has not been made within 56 days the limit is 70 days. The time limit from first appearance to committal/transfer is 70 days and from committal/transfer to crown court is 112 days.

The effect of not keeping to the time-limits in custody cases is not that the case is brought to an end but only that a defendant who was in custody has to be released on bail.

Where the time-limit relates to cases on bail, the result of a failure to observe the limit means, however, that the accused is entirely free. But both in relation to custody and bail cases, the prosecution can ask for an extension of time.

Under the regulations, an application for an extension has to be made *before the time-limit expires* after two days' notice had been given.[16] This has given rise to considerable difficulties. In *R v Sheffield Justices, ex p Turner* [1991] 1 All ER 858 the accused was charged with murder. Both the CPS and the defendant's solicitor miscalculated the time-limit and thought it ended on 23 August when in fact it ended the previous day. The application for an extension of the time-limit which was granted on 23 August was therefore technically too late. The Divisional Court ruled that the accused was held unlawfully from 23 August until his committal on 20 September, but that from 20 September he was again held lawfully because on that date he had been committed for trial. The fact that the time limit had expired on 22 August did not invalidate the committal on 20 September.

An extension will not be granted where the prosecution has failed to act expeditiously in regard to supplying the defence with material–in that instance tape recordings: *R v Central Criminal Court, ex p Behbehani* [1994] Crim LR 352.

In *R v Governor of Winchester Prison, ex p Roddie* [1991] 2 All ER 931, the accused was charged with robbery. The prosecution asked for an extension of time because of delays in getting the papers ready due to the police being drastically understaffed. The Divisional Court held that neither the seriousness of the offence, nor the fact that the extension was for a short period, nor that the police were understaffed constituted good and sufficient grounds for an extension of time. Once the time-limit had expired there was no discretion to extend it. The accused was held unlawfully for six weeks until the date of his committal. For three recent cases see *R v Crown Court at Maidstone, ex p Hollstein* [1995] 3 All ER 503; *R v Crown Court at Maidstone, ex p Clark* [1995] 3 All ER 513; *R v Crown Court at Leeds, ex p Hussain* [1995] 3 All ER 527.

Stay of prosecution because of delay

If delay in bringing the prosecution is excessive it may be stopped ('stayed') as an abuse of the process of the court. But the courts are very reluctant indeed to entertain such an application. See *A-G's Reference (No 1 of 1990)* [1992] 3 All ER 169.

Computerisation of Crown Court Listing etc (CREST)

The Lord Chancellor's Department has introduced a computerised case management system (the Crown Court Electronic Support System or CREST). The system became operational in all the crown court centres in 1993. It enables courts to produce automatically warned lists and cases for fixed dates. It will record information about availability of court-rooms, judges, counsel and witnesses. It will also generate management information.

---

16 In *R v Governor of Canterbury Prison, ex p Craig* [1990] 2 All ER 654, the Divisional Court held that the notice requirements are directory not mandatory and the court can give an extension if satisfied that there is a good and sufficient reason to do so.

There are also computerization programs being developed for magistrates' courts–known as MASS–and for the CPS–known as SCOPE. SCOPE was intended to be fully operational by the end of 1996. MASS was not likely to be fully operational for some years.

New inter-agency group formed

The Lord Chancellor's Department announced in January 1996 the establishment of a new inter-agency group to be known as the Trial Issues Group (TIG) to improve the efficiency of the criminal justice system. The group would oversee initiatives to cut waste and to improve the quality of service to victims, witnesses and other court users. The group would take over the work previously being done by the Pre-Trial Issues Steering (or Working) Group which brought together representatives of the key agencies including the CPS, the Home Office, the Justices' Clerks Society, the Lord Chancellor's Department and the police. They had been working to improve performance, cooperation and communication. Now it would include also re-presentatives of the Bar Council, the Law Society and the Magistrates' Association. It would soon also add members of the Prison and Probation Services and the private sector.

Specific projects on which it would work immediately were:

* New style case files to reduce forms that had to be filled in by police officers in cases likely to end as guilty pleas in the magistrates' courts. The guilty plea files would include typed key witness statements to establish the elements of the offences charged, 'short descriptive notes' summarising admissions made by the accused, any mitigating or aggravating factors and other relevant material. They would replace the 'record of taped interview' (a verbatim account of the accused's admissions and other material), the accused's criminal record, the victim's compensation claim and other forms.

* Joint performance management for monitoring the quality and delivery of police files, the reasons for discontinuing cases and for acquittals in the crown court.

* More effective communication through greater use of information technology.

CHAPTER 4

The trial process

This chapter deals with the trial itself. The first section considers the particular characteristics of the English, adversary method of trial as compared with the inquisitorial method followed on the Continent, and examines the role of the judge. The second and third sections concern the advantages of representation and the difficulties faced by the unrepresented person in an English trial. The following sections look at the orality of procedure and the evidence of social psychologists that evidence on questions of fact is more apt to be unreliable than the participants appear to realize. The sixth section deals with the most important problems of the rules of evidence.

1. THE ADVERSARY SYSTEM COMPARED WITH THE INQUISITORIAL

The common-law method of trial is often described as 'adversary' or 'accusatorial'—as distinct from the continental 'inquisitorial' method. The essence of the distinction is that, whereas in the inquisitorial system the dominant role is played by the court, in the adversary system it is played by the parties. In the adversary system the judge is supposed to remain a passive and mainly silent umpire, listening to the evidence produced by the two parties. The parties decide what witnesses to call and in what order, the parties examine and cross-examine the witnesses and, if both sides decide not to call a witness who has potentially relevant evidence, there is nothing the court will do about it. The burden of preparing the case and of presenting it falls on the parties themselves, which means that a party without a lawyer is at a distinct disadvantage. (On the problems of the unrepresented in the adversary system, see pp 301–02 below. On Lord Woolf's recommendations that would drastically alter this system see pp 290–91 below.)

By contrast, in the inquisitorial system the judge calls the witnesses and examines them, while the parties or their lawyers play a supporting or subsidiary role.

(a) The adversary system

Judicial intervention

Jones v National Coal Board [1957] 2 QB 55, CA

Appeal against decision of trial judge (Hallett J) in an action arising out of a fatal accident in a coal-mine, on the ground that the judge had intervened excessively.

Lord Denning MR, giving the judgment of the court, said:

We are quite clear that the interventions, taken together, were far more than they should have been. In the system of trial which we have evolved in this country, the judge sits to hear and determine the issues raised by the parties, not to conduct an investigation or examination on behalf of society at large, as happens, we believe, in some foreign countries. Even in England, however, a judge is not a mere umpire to answer the question 'How's that?' His object, above all, is to find out the truth, and to do justice according to law; and in the daily pursuit of it the advocate plays an honourable and necessary role. Was it not Lord Eldon LC who said in a notable passage that 'truth is best discovered by powerful statements on both sides of the question'? See *ex p Lloyd*.[1] And Lord Greene MR who explained that justice is best done by a judge who holds the balance between the contending parties without himself taking part in their disputations? If a Judge, said Lord Greene, should himself conduct the examination of witnesses, 'he, so to speak, descends into the arena and is liable to have his vision clouded by the dust of conflict': see *Yuill v Yuill*.[2]

Let the advocates one after the other put the weights into the scales–the 'nicely calculated less or more'–but the judge at the end decides which way the balance tilts, be it ever so slightly ... The judge's part in all this is to hearken to the evidence, only himself asking questions of witnesses when it is necessary to clear up any point that has been overlooked or left obscure; to see that the advocates behave themselves seemly and keep to the rules laid down by law; to exclude irrelevancies and discourage repetition; to make sure by wise intervention that he follows the points that the advocates are making and can assess their worth; and at the end to make up his mind where the truth lies. If he goes beyond this, he drops the mantle of a judge and assumes the robe of an advocate: and the change does not become him well. Lord Chancellor Bacon spoke right when he said that:[3] 'Patience and gravity of hearing is an essential part of justice; and an overspeaking judge is no well-tuned cymbal.'

The *Jones* case happened to be a civil one but the court would have taken precisely the same view if it had been a criminal matter. See *R v Perks* [1973] Crim LR 388. In *Gunning* [1980] Crim LR 592, the conviction was quashed where the judge asked 165 questions compared with 172 from counsel. But in *Matthews* (1983) 78 Cr App Rep 23, the Court of Appeal declined to quash a conviction where the judge put 524 questions to counsel's 538. On any view, the court said, the number of judicial interventions and questions was excessive but they did not quite go so far as to divert counsel from his own line of questioning. The court said that a large number of interruptions put the court on notice of the possibility of a denial of justice but the critical issue was not the number but the quality of the interventions. 'The critical aspect of the investigation is the quality of the interventions as they relate to the attitude of the judge as might be observed by the jury and the effect that the interventions have either upon the orderly, proper and lucid deployment of the case for the defendant by his advocate or upon the efficacy of the attack to be made on the defendant's behalf upon vital prosecution witnesses by cross-examination' (at pp 32–33). Nor will the court interfere merely on the ground that the judge has been guilty of discourtesy, even gross discourtesy, to counsel: *R v Ptohopoulos* [1968] Crim LR 52.

In *Hamilton* [1969] Crim LR 486 (quoted more fully in (1973) 58 Cr App Rep 378 at 382), Lord Parker LCJ said the Court of Appeal would overturn a conviction on account of excessive intervention (a) where the interventions invited the jury to

1   (1822) Mont 70, 72 n.
2   [1945] P 15, 20, [1945] 1 All ER 183, 61 TLR 176.
3   'Of Judicature', *Essays or Counsels Civil and Moral*.

disbelieve the defence evidence in such strong terms that they could not be cured by the usual formula that the facts are for the jury; (b) where they prevented defence counsel from carrying out his duty to present the case for the defence; and (c) where the defendant himself was prevented from telling his own story. (See, for instance, *Rabbitt* (1931) 23 Cr App Rep 112; *Clewer* (1953) 37 Cr App Rep 37; *Renshaw* [1989] Crim LR 811; *Sharp* [1993] 3 All ER 225; and generally Sean Doran, 'Descent to Avernus', *NLJ*, 1 September 1989, p 1147.)

For the role of the judge in influencing or directing the jury to convict or acquit, see pp 397–98 below.

The nature of the role of the judge described in Lord Denning's judgment in *Jones v National Coal Board* is not accurate, however, for legal argument, only for that part of a case which concerns the establishment of the facts. Legal argument in a common-law case involves the judge very actively. Counsel makes his points and submissions but the judge will feel free to engage him in discussion by asking questions, raising objections, putting contrary points. The process may sometimes almost resemble a seminar. The higher in the system, the more extensive the exchanges between counsel and the court. (In his book *The Law Lords* (Macmillan, 1982) Professor Alan Paterson reports that in the argument in *Cassell v Broome* there were 99 judicial interventions on the first day alone, 61 of which came from the presiding judge (at p 70).)

Even on points of law however the adversary system works on the basis that the court is not supposed to undertake its own research and is not supposed to go beyond the arguments presented by the parties. For consideration of the weaknesses of this rule see NH Andrews, 'The Passive Court and Legal Argument', *Civil Justice Quarterly*, 1988, p 125.

Calling witnesses

The basic common-law rule is that it is for the parties, not for the court, to call and to examine the witnesses. The parties decide what witnesses to call, in what order, and what questions to ask them. In civil cases the court cannot call a witness unless the parties agree–see for instance *Briscoe v Briscoe* [1966] 1 All ER 465 (Div Ct). In criminal cases the judge technically has the right to call a witness but virtually never does so. For a rare example that was upheld by the Court of Appeal see *Bowles* [1992] Crim LR 726. By contrast, in *Grafton* [1992] Crim LR 826 the judge's decision led to the conviction being quashed. After evidence by the defendant and a friend of his the prosecution said it would offer no further evidence. The judge decided to go ahead and call the remaining witness for the Crown. Prosecution counsel took no further part. The jury convicted. The Court of Appeal said that the judge's role was to hold the ring impartially and to direct the jury on the law. By acting as he had done, he had taken over the prosecution. But see *R v Haringey Justices, ex p DPP* [1996] 1 All ER 828 where the Divisional Court held that if magistrates considered that it would be unfair to the defence if a witness were not called they should call the witness rather than dismiss a case as an abuse of process.

The rules about the calling of expert witnesses are basically the same. Under RSC Ord 40, r 1(1) the court can, on the application of either party, appoint an expert 'to inquire and report upon any question of fact or opinion not involving questions of law or construction' but the power is virtually never used. (See A Jack, 'Lord Woolf and Expert Evidence', *NLJ*, 5 August 1994, p 1099.)

See J Basten, 'The Court Expert in Civil Trials–A Comparative Appraisal', 40 *Modern Law Review*, 1977, p 174.

In 'The Expert Witness in the Criminal Trial' (1987) *Criminal Law Review*, p 307, the author DJ Gee, Professor of Forensic Medicine at Leeds University, argued that the position of the expert witness in the adversary system was most unsatisfactory. The adversary system, he suggested, was inimical to the presentation of expert evidence in a way that was scientific. ('Indeed a real danger lies in the possibility that the scientist could become more concerned to be an effective witness than a conscientious scientist', p 308.) The scientist prepared his report without knowing what the other side would say. He gave his report to the lawyers for his side. He will have had a brief consultation with his own counsel, usually just before he gave evidence. He would have only a slight idea of the facts of the case and would rarely attend for longer than his evidence. It was rare for him to see the depositions of the other witnesses. He often would not know what precisely counsel wanted to elicit from him. Inadequate knowledge of the facts could affect the way in which he presented his evidence.

Professor Gee suggested that the expert should be more fully informed of the facts and the court should be able to appoint an independent expert (nominated by the appropriate Royal College) to review the expert evidence given on behalf of the two sides. As has been seen (pp 74–77, above), a similar view was expressed by Lord Woolf in his Interim Report.

On the problem of the expert witness in the adversary system see further MN Howard QC, 'The Neutral Expert: A Plausible Threat to Justice' (1991) *Crim Law Review*, p 98, and JR Spencer, 'The Neutral Expert: An Implausible Bogey' *ibid*, p 106. On experts in children's cases see V Smith, 'Use of Experts in Children's Cases', *Justice of the Peace* 23 September 1995, p 635 and 30 September p 648.

The Court of Appeal held that the fundamental principles of the adversary system, including the right to cross-examine witnesses, apply even in small claims cases–see *Chilton v Saga Holidays plc* [1986] 1 All ER 841, described more fully on p 305 below. (On the implications see F Miller, 'The Adversarial Myth', *New Law Journal*, 19 May 1995, p 734.) But Lord Woolf in his Interim Report, (p 179, para 18) proposed that cross-examination should only be permitted to the extent allowed by the judge– a proposal that has attracted sharp criticism.

For a dramatic case illustrating the limits of the adversary system see however *Crozier* [1991] Crim LR 138, where the Court of Appeal held that a psychiatrist instructed by the defence in a criminal trial might in exceptional circumstances be justified in showing his report to the prosecution–even though that would be contrary to the wishes of the defence. The circumstances must be such that the public interest in the disclosure of his views to the prosecution was stronger than his duty of confidentiality to his patient. The defendant had pleaded guilty to attempted murder of his sister. The psychiatrist thought that the defendant was a serious danger to his family and should be detained in Broadmoor. When he came into the court room, to his consternation he found that the judge was in the process of imposing sentence–a nine-year term. He told prosecution counsel of his report and as a result the prosecution applied for the sentence to be altered. The judge quashed his own sentence of imprisonment and substituted a hospital order with an unlimited restriction of time on release. The Court of Appeal held that the public interest in having the information divulged was greater than in the confidential relationship between doctor and patient. (See to like effect *W v Egdell* [1990] 1 All ER 835.)

The rule is that each party is bound by the evidence of his own witness. One cannot impeach the evidence of a witness one has called by cross-examination to show that he is in error, save where the court is persuaded to allow cross-examination on the ground that the witness is 'hostile'. (See M Newark, 'The Hostile Witness and the Adversary System' (1986) *Criminal Law Review*, p 441.) This means that each side may have an interest in suppressing a witness for fear of what he may say.

In research conducted in crown courts for the Royal Commission on Criminal Justice judges were asked 'Were you aware of any important witness(es) who were not called by either side?' In as many as 19 per cent of 743 cases the judge answered Yes, (M Zander and P Henderson, *The Crown Court Study*, Royal Commission on Criminal Justice, Research Study No 19, para 4.3.12). The Royal Commission recommended that judges be prepared in suitable cases, where they become aware of a witness who may have something to contribute, to ask counsel in the absence of the jury why the witness has not been called and, if they think appropriate, urge them to rectify the situation. In the last resort, however, judges must be prepared to exercise their power to call the witness themselves.

Subject to certain exceptions, the parties may suppress evidence that they do not intend to call. This was illustrated in *Causton v Mann Egerton* [1974] 1 All ER 453. The plaintiff was considering suing his employers for injuries to his eye suffered through their alleged negligence. He agreed to be examined by the insurers' doctors. They were pessimistic about the prospects of his regaining his sight. He was also examined by doctors on his own behalf. On request from the defendants' solicitors, the reports of his doctors were disclosed to them. But when the plaintiff's solicitors asked for reciprocal disclosure of the reports prepared by the insurers' doctors, this was refused.

The Court of Appeal (Lord Denning dissenting) held that the refusal was legitimate in law. Disclosure could be compelled if a party was intending to rely on the evidence. But neither the opposite party nor the court could require a party to produce privileged testimony which it did not intend to call. Lord Denning said that the defendants' doctors apparently took a more serious view of the plaintiff's injuries than did his own doctors. The defendants accordingly wished to keep their own reports away from the court and the plaintiff. This would be unfair. 'Counsel for the defendants sought to excuse their conduct by saying that litigation in this country is based on the adversary procedure. By that he means, I suppose, that it is permissible for an insurance company to refuse to cooperate in the doing of justice. It can play with a poker face with the cards hidden from view. I cannot subscribe to that view. Although litigation is based on the adversary procedure, we require the adversaries to play it fairly and openly. The defendants have made the plaintiff put his cards on the table. They should put theirs too' (at p 458). But Lord Denning was overruled by his two fellow judges. Lord Justice Roskill said that to decide otherwise would be to ride roughshod over the clear rule that in the absence of the parties' consent, the court could not order the production of privileged documents. ('So long as we have an adversary system a party is entitled not to produce documents which are properly protected by privilege if it is not to his advantage to produce them and even though their production might assist his adversary or his solicitor were aware of their contents or might lead the court to a different conclusion from that to which the court would come in ignorance of their existence' (at p 460).) See also *Air Canada v Secretary of State for Trade (No 2)* [1983] 1 All ER 910.

(b) Exceptions to the rules of the adversary system

There are, however, some exceptions to the general rule that the court leaves it to the parties to make their case.

Prosecution disclosure

As has been seen, there are rules requiring the prosecution to reveal to the defence material that tends to undermine the prosecution's case (see pp 228–37 above)

Court acting of its own motion

There are also a considerable number of situations where the rules specifically permit the court to act 'of its own motion' as well as on application by the parties. Thus under RSC Ord 15, r 6(2), the court may order anyone who has improperly or unnecessarily been a party to cease to be a party or to order anyone who ought to have been a party to be joined–though no one can be made a plaintiff without his consent. Under Ord 20, r 8(1), the court may order any document in the proceedings to be amended 'for the purposes of determining the real question in controversy between the parties'. (For an unusual example of this power being exercised, see *Liverpool Roman Catholic Archdiocesan Trustees Inc v Gibberd and Co* (1986) Con LR 113 and noted in *Civil Justice Quarterly*, July 1986, p 181), where the court, without any application by the plaintiff, ordered the writ and statement of claim to be amended by adding a new cause of action and back-dated it so as to permit the plaintiffs to claim damages for breaches of duty that they pleaded late. The writ claimed damages against the architects and engineers relating to the design and construction of a cathedral. The plaintiffs gave further and better particulars of fresh breaches of duty arising after completion of the building, whereas the claim had been pleaded so as to be limited to the period before completion. The judge said that it would be unusual hardship on the plaintiffs not to allow them to pursue these additional causes of action and of his own motion ordered the amendment of the statement of claim.

Under Order 43 (which deals with accounts and inquiries) the court can require a party to explain delay (r 7(1)). Under Order 34, r 5(5), the court may change the venue of the trial if it thinks the action cannot conveniently be tried where it would otherwise take place. There is also the 'own motion' power of the High Court to transfer a case to the county court and of the county court to transfer a case to the High Court. (See Supreme Court Act 1981, s 149 (1) and Sch 3.) Courts have a duty to refuse to enforce a contract tainted with illegality regardless of whether the point is taken by a party. A court is also responsible for preventing abuse of its own process.

Another exception was the requirement in undefended divorce cases that the judge satisfy himself about the arrangements made for minor children (now in s 41 of the Matrimonial Causes Act 1973.) But research has showed that this duty was being largely neglected by the judges. In almost half the cases observed, the judge asked no question at all regarding the children. The majority of cases were completed within ten minutes. The conclusion was that the judges regarded their inquisitorial function somewhat perfunctorily. (E Elston, J Fuller and M Murch, 'Judicial Hearing of Undefended Divorce Petitions', 38 *Modern Law Review*, 1975, pp 609, 618, 619,

626.) See now Children Act 1989, Sch 12. See also J Masson, 'The Role of the Judge in Children's Cases', *Civil Justice Quarterly*, 1988, p 141.

Today most divorces are obtained under the Special Procedure whereby there is no hearing at all. The registrar simply considers the papers submitted by the petitioner and, if they seem to be in order, the judge pronounces the divorce in open court. The only obligation of the parties to attend for a hearing arises in connection with the children, since the court still retains the duty to satisfy itself regarding the arrangements for the children. But although the parties now commonly attend without their lawyers and therefore confront the judge directly, he still rarely questions them closely on the arrangements that have been made. Research by the same Bristol team showed that the judge typically has some fifty appointments with parents in a day! The researchers concluded that normally the appointment did not serve any very useful purpose in terms of checking on the arrangements made. (See G Davis, A McLeod and M Murch, 'Undefended Divorce: Should s 41 of the Matrimonial Causes Act 1973 be Repealed?', 46 *Modern Law Review*, 1983, p 121.)

Professional rules of conduct

Another exception to the rule that it is for the parties to make their case is the rule of professional conduct which places limits on the extent to which a lawyer can knowingly lend himself to deception of the court. If, for instance, his client confesses his guilt to his own barrister, the barrister is not required to report the fact to the authorities nor need he give up the case. But he may not 'assert that which he knows to be a lie'. He may take points by way of objection to the jurisdiction of the court, to the admissibility of evidence, or to the form of the proceedings. But he may not call evidence which he knows to be false. He is entitled to test the prosecution's case by cross-examination and he may argue that the prosecution have failed to produce enough evidence to establish their case. Further than that he should not go. (*Code of Conduct of the Bar of England and Wales*, 1994, Annex H, paras 3.1–3.5.)

In 1962 sentence of suspension from practice was confirmed on a prominent Queen's Counsel, Mr Victor Durand, for misleading the court in an action for damages against the police. Mr Durand had put his witness, a police officer, on the stand and examined him as Mr G without alluding to the fact that he had been demoted for misconduct. The original sentence of three-year suspension from practice was later reduced to one year. (See *Times*, 24 November 1961 and 12 January 1962.)

Note–settlements and guilty pleas avoid the adversary system

The pure model of the adversary system assumes a trial whereas, as has been seen, a trial is as rare in criminal cases as in civil. The overwhelming majority of civil cases are settled. The concept of settlement in criminal cases is obviously very different– though plea bargaining (pp 253-58, above) has some features which suggest similarities. But, for whatever reason, the accused does normally end by pleading guilty and thus there is no trial. This in itself is significant. In the inquisitorial system the prosecution must prove its case regardless of whether the accused pleads guilty. In the adversary system, if the defendant pleads guilty, the prosecution is under no such duty.

Lord Woolf's and the Runciman Royal Commission on the adversary system

Lord Woolf's Interim Report *Access to Justice* published in June 1995 blamed the excesses of the adversary for much of the cost, delay and complexity of the civil justice system (p 7):

3. By tradition the conduct of civil litigation in England and Wales, as in other common law jurisdictions, is adversarial. Within a framework of substantive and procedural law established by the state for the resolution of civil disputes, the main responsibility for the initiation and conduct of proceedings rests with the parties to each individual case, and it is normally the plaintiff who sets the pace. The role of the judge is to adjudicate on issues selected by the parties when they choose to present them to the court.

4. Without effective judicial control, however, the adversarial process is likely to encourage an adversarial culture and to degenerate into an environment in which the litigation process is too often seen as a battlefield where no rules apply. In this environment, questions of expense, delay, compromise and fairness may have only low priority. The consequence is that expense is often excessive, disproportionate and unpredictable; and delay is frequently unreasonable.

5. This situation arises precisely because the conduct, pace and extent of litigation are left almost completely to the parties. There is no effective control of their worst excesses. Indeed, the complexity of the present rules facilitates the use of adversarial tactics and is considered by many to require it. As Lord Williams, a former Chairman of the Bar Council, said in responding to the announcement of this Inquiry, the process of law has moved from being 'servant to master, due to cost, length and uncertainty'.

At various points in the Report, Lord Woolf calls for the parties to behave in a more co-operative and less combative or adversarial manner. He states that one of the objectives of judicial case management would be 'the encouragement of a spirit of co-operation between the parties and the avoidance of unnecessary combativeness which is productive of unnecessary additional expense and delay' (p 30, para 17(c)).

Sir Jack Jacob has written 'the passive role of the English court greatly enhances the standing, the influence and the authority of the judiciary at all levels and may well account for the high respect and esteem in which they are held' (*The Fabric of English Civil Justice*, 1987, p 12). Lord Woolf, by contrast, proposed that the judge should exercise control both before and during trial not only to marshall the case but to control the quantity and quality of evidence received by the court. Thus, in both fast track and multi track cases the judge would decide which witnesses he wished to be called (p 178, paras 14,15); 'Cross-examination on the content of witness statements should only be allowed with leave of the judge' (p 179, p 22); 'The court is perfectly capable of deciding which cases would be appropriate for a court expert and then of appointing an expert with the necessary qualifications and ensuring that he is used effectively' (p 187, para 23); 'The calling of expert evidence should be subject to the complete control of the court' (p 192, para (1)).

In the view of some this would imperil both the search for truth and the court's appearance of impartiality–see for instance the severe criticisms of Conrad Dehn QC 'The Woolf Report: Against the Public Interest?' in *Reform of Civil Procedure–Essays on Access to Justice* (ed Zuckerman and Cranston, Clarendon, OUP, 1995), p 162; and of Neil Andrews, 'The Adversarial Principle: Fairness and Efficiency Reflections on the Recommendations of the Woolf Report', *ibid*, pp 171–183.

By contrast with the view of Lord Woolf, the Runciman Royal Commission on Criminal Justice did not call for any fundamental move towards a less adversary procedure–though it did make some relatively minor proposals for alterations in the way that expert evidence is prepared–see pp 245–46 above. Thus, it rejected the idea of the court calling its own expert. (Report, p 160, para 74.) It equally rejected the concept of judicial supervision of the pre-trial stage of a criminal investigation.

Partly its reason was cultural, but partly it was substantive:

Every system is the product of a distinctive history and culture, and the more different the history and culture from our own the greater must be the danger that an attempted transfer will fail. Hardly any of those who gave evidence to the Commission suggested that the system in another jurisdiction should be adopted in England and Wales; and of those who did, none argued for it in any depth or with any supporting detail [Report, p 4, para 13].

Our reason for not recommending a change to an inquisitorial system as such is not simply fear of the consequences of an unsuccessful cultural transplant. It is also that we doubt whether the fusion of the functions of investigation and prosecution, and the direct involvement of judges in both are more likely to serve the interests of justice than a system in which the roles of police, prosecutors, and judges are as far as possible kept separate and the judge who is responsible for the conduct of the trial is the arbiter of law but not of fact. We believe that a system in which the critical roles are kept separate offers a better protection against the risk of unnecessarily prolonged detention prior to trial [*ibid*, para 14].

For the research evidence on the inquisitorial system done for the Royal Commission, see p 296 below.

(c) The inquisitorial system compared

In the continental inquisitorial system the main burden of presenting the case at court falls on the court itself. The court calls the witnesses and there is, therefore, not the same danger as exists in the common-law systems of the evidence of a particular witness being suppressed because neither side wishes to call him. The witnesses are questioned ('examined') by the presiding judge.

The role of the lawyers is supplementary. They can suggest the names of further witnesses that the court should call. They can ask questions of witnesses after the court has finished asking its questions. But the lawyers play a subsidiary role.

Obviously there has to be some method whereby the court in the inquisitorial system masters the details of the case so that it knows what witnesses to call and what questions to pose. The method used is the preparation of a written *dossier* which contains the fruits of the pre-trial investigation of the case. The *dossier* is read prior to the trial by the presiding judge who uses it as his text for first calling and then questioning the witnesses.

In the English-language literature about the inquisitorial system it is usually stated that in criminal cases the *dossier* is prepared by an examining magistrate (in France called *le juge d'instruction*, in Italy the *giudice istruttore*), whose job it is to see all the potential witnesses and take their statements. But the idea that the inquisitorial system normally, let alone invariably, uses an examining magistrate/*juge d'instruction* is mistaken. Moreover, even in countries such as France which use the *juge d'instruction*, it is relatively rare for one actually to be used even in cases where in theory he could be used.

Criminal offences are divided in France into three categories of gravity–*crimes*, which carry a penalty of five or more years' imprisonment; *delits*, which carry a term of imprisonment of two months or more; and *contraventions*, which are minor summary-trial matters. The *juge d'instruction* functions in relation to all *crimes* and some *delits*. This means that even in France the *juge d'instruction* can play a role in only a small minority of cases estimated to be around 10 per cent.

The decision whether the *juge d'instruction* is to play a role in a particular case is generally for the prosecutor. One reason the prosecutor decides to bring in a *juge d'instruction* is because the exercise of certain powers (such as the granting of a search warrant, the taking of fingerprints, the authorization of telephone tapping and the like) requires the authority of a *juge d'instruction*. (In cases where the accused has been apprehended red-handed '*flagrant delit*' and the case is serious, the prosecutor has wider than usual powers to investigate himself and through the police without the authority of the *juge d'instruction*.)

If the *juge d'instruction* is functioning, his legal powers are formidable. He can totally dominate, direct and control the police inquiry. Constantin's feature film *K* of some years ago about an actual political murder carried out in the time of the Greek Colonels was a vivid demonstration of the way in which a courageous and persistent *juge d'instruction* can surmount even the obstruction of the highest organs of state. But the vast powers of the *juge d'instruction* can also be abused and there is no doubt that the way in which the powers are exercised is sometimes extremely controversial. In a *cause célèbre* the *juge d'instruction* can become a figure of national consequence attracting vast media attention.

Indeed one of the criticisms of the system in France is that the *juge d'instruction* not infrequently leaks to the press the details of his investigation as it develops which then results in widespread pre-trial publication of material that in England would be regarded as grossly prejudicial to the prospects of a fair trial. Continental systems, however, take a much more relaxed view than common-law systems of the danger of prejudice to judicial proceedings through press publication–largely perhaps because they make much less use of the lay jury. In continental countries there is generally no equivalent of our proceedings for contempt of court in relation to pre-trial publication.

The role of the *juge d'instruction* has come under severe criticism in several continental countries. In Germany it was abolished in 1975. In Italy it was abolished in 1988 as part of a dramatic and radical reform of the criminal justice system which represented a flight from the inquisitorial system toward the adversary model.[4] There has even been a serious call for the abolition of the *juge d'instruction* in France–see the 1991 Report of the Delmas Marty Commission Justice Penale et Droits d'homme entitled *La Mise en Etat des Affaires Pénale*.[5]

But, as has been said, even where the *juge d'instruction* exists, he operates in only a tiny minority of cases. How then is the *dossier* prepared in the majority of cases where there is no *juge d'instruction* and in the countries where no such office exists?

4   For a description of the reform by two of its chief authors, see Ennio Amodio and Eugenio Selvaggi, 'An Accusatorial System in a Civil Law Country: The 1988 Italian Code of Criminal Procedure', 62 *Temple Law Review*, 1989, p 1211; for a brief description see M Zander, 'From Inquisitorial to Adversarial–The Italian Experiment', *New Law Journal*, 17 May 1991, p 678.
5   For a brief account see Jennifer Monahan, 'Sanctioning Injustice', *New Law Journal*, 17 May 1991, p 679.

The answer is that the *dossier* is prepared either by the police or by the prosecutor or by a combination of the two. In most continental countries prime responsibility for the *dossier* in all but minor cases lies with the public prosecutor. This is true, for instance, in Germany and Holland and since 1988 in Italy.

An important part of the continental system is that the suspect is supposed to have full access to the *dossier* not only when it is completed, but also as the inquiry goes along. In practice this does not always work as it should. It is common for the defence lawyers to be told that the *dossier* is not yet ready, is not available or is not complete. It is difficult for the defence to be sure that the *dossier* actually includes all that it should—and especially all the material potentially helpful to the accused. Also, the arrangements for enabling defence lawyers to see the *dossier* and to copy extracts are not always what they might be. The lawyers are often poorly paid under legal aid for studying the *dossier*, and legal aid does not necessarily extend to the copying of documents.

The accused in the continental system is himself directly involved in the process of developing the *dossier*. One of the results is that it is quite common for him to be held in custody for lengthy periods while the pre-trial process takes its often weary course. It is not that pre-trial detention without charges is a necessary part of the inquisitorial system. The suspect could perfectly well be allowed to stay at home and attend periodically for hearings by the examining magistrate. This can be and is done. But the inquisitorial culture tends to assume that the easiest way of ensuring that the suspect is readily available to the examining magistrate is to have him in custody—and as a result very lengthy periods of pre-charge incarceration are not uncommon.

Another attribute of inquisitorial systems is said to be that the accused has a lawyer to assist him. But in many continental countries this only applies in more serious cases and does not even then apply to the crucial earliest stages of the investigation. In France, for instance, the *garde à vue* during which the suspect is held incommunicado, lasts 48 hours. There seems to be no inquisitorial system which provides any equivalent of the right of access to a solicitor normally available under PACE, s 58, from the first stages of a person's period in custody or of the Duty Solicitor scheme for police stations.

In the inquisitorial system the decision to send the accused for trial, save in very minor cases, is not necessarily taken by the same person who prepared the *dossier*. There is commonly a process of review by a different person or body to determine whether the *dossier* discloses sufficient evidence and reason for a prosecution to go ahead. In France, for instance, the *dossier* prepared by the *juge d'instruction* is submitted to the *chambre des accusations* for the review. As has been seen, there is great variation in continental systems as to how much discretion exists *not* to proceed with prosecutions.

One myth about the inquisitorial systems is that they have no equivalent of the common-law presumption of innocence in a criminal case. This is untrue. In fact, if anything, they take the presumption even more seriously in that there they do not allow the accused to plead guilty. Regardless of what he says and even when he has signed a written confession the case must be proved by evidence (whereas in the common-law systems a guilty plea is sufficient on its own). But, understandably, when the accused does admit the offence the degree of proof required is not great.

Some inquisitorial systems (such as the French) use juries, others (such as the Dutch and German) do not. But jury trial in an inquisitorial system has a completely different meaning from jury trial in the common-law systems. In particular the jury deliberates together with the professional judge (or judges). Also the jury is commonly not drawn randomly from the electoral register, but is selected from some form of special list of persons thought to be appropriate for this function. They do not necessarily serve for a brief two weeks as in the typical common-law system. Instead, they may serve for a period of months. They therefore become much more integrated into the administration of justice than common-law juries.

One significant difference between the inquisitorial and common-law systems is that the accused's antecedents–including any prior criminal record–are part of the *dossier* and are brought out in evidence from the outset of the trial. Since the court therefore has a full picture about him there may be no separate stage of a plea in mitigation of sentence. When the court announced its decision that the accused is guilty it will commonly also announce the sentence.

Another difference between the inquisitorial and the adversary systems is that the former commonly have a procedure whereby the victim can play a part both at the pre-trial and at the trial stage. The victim is allowed to join the criminal proceedings as *le parti civile*. The English system does also now permit an award to be made by a criminal court of compensation to the victim over and above any penalty by way of fine or other appropriate sentence. But the victim in English criminal proceedings has no recognized status. He cannot be heard on the subject either of guilt or of sentence.

For a highly critical view of the French system in operation see the account of a young solicitor, Claire Johnstone, in the *Law Society's Gazette*, 6 February 1991, p 41. She had been sent to France by the London Criminal Courts Solicitors' Association to study the French system. Her main concerns were:

(1) That in serious cases the suspect was held without access to lawyers for up to 48 hours.
(2) That, still without a lawyer, he would then be brought before the *juge d'instruction* to be interviewed.
(3) That the system led to long remands in custody–some 50 per cent of the prison population was on remand (compared with around 20 per cent in Britain). About one-half of those subject to the *instruction* process were remanded in custody.
(4) That there were no time-limits on remands in custody. In assize court matters, the *juge d'instruction* only had to review the detention warrant 'every 12 months'!
(5) That although in theory the suspect had a right of silence, it was exceedingly difficult (almost impossible) for him to exercise it.
(6) The delays. She reported on the delays in the five cases heard by the Versailles Assize Court during its two-week session in November 1990:

Course of cases at Versailles Assizes, November 1990

Case	Arrest to close of instruction	Close of instruction to trial	Total (arrest to trial)	Time in custody
A	1 yr 3 wks	9.5 mths	1 yr 10 mths	1 yr 10 mths
B	1 yr 2 wks	1 yr 2 mths	2 yrs 2.5 mth	1 yr 2 mths
C	1 yr 2 wks	8 mths	1 yr 8.5 mths	1 yr 8.5 mths
D	1 yr 8 mths	11 mths	2 yrs 7 mths	2 yrs 7 mths
E	3 yrs 5 mths	1 yr	4 yrs 5 mths	4 yrs 5 mths

She continued:

Long delays are not unusual in French assize courts. Leaving aside the issue of lack of court time for hearings, which exists in our own system, it is clear that the process of the instruction itself, the post-charge investigation conducted by a solitary state employee, adds immeasurably to the period elapsing between arrest and disposal.

Having conducted the enquiry and periodically made any necessary judicial orders authorizing remands in custody, searches, seizures or even telephone taps, the instruction judge will (at last) decide to close the instruction. She can now make orders either discharging the accused or sending the *dossier* to the committal court. In practice, the committal court will almost automatically endorse the instruction judge's conclusions. It is simply a fact that by the time the famous *dossier* arrives at the assize court the case has literally been pre-judged.

Hearing

Before the assize court hearing the president (who sits with two junior judges and nine jurors) will study every detail of the *dossier*. Even in a contested matter, there is no obligation on the prosecution to produce oral evidence. At the centre of the trial will lie two question-and-answer sessions between president and defendant; the first in relation to background matters and especially the defendant's previous convictions, the second in relation to the facts of the case. The president bases the discussion on the information in the *dossier*. The defence lawyer takes no part in these sessions. The president has inherited the instruction judge's function and is seeking out the truth. The defence lawyer cannot help with that. Nor can the defendant pre-empt it by entering a plea, as there are no pleas in French courts.

The defendant speaks from the dock and unsworn. Refusing to answer is hardly an option. A French defendant who refuses to speak to the instruction judge or the president of the trial court is striking at the heart of the system. It is very rare. Quite explicitly, the instruction judge and the president will object to such silence, press for answers to their questions and take sustained silence as evidence of guilt. The defence lawyer, meanwhile, sits silent and powerless. The lawyers can put questions to witnesses or defendants only by suggesting the questions to the president; the French have no word for 'cross-examination.'

The 1991 Delmas-Marty report on the system (p 292 above) recommended:

(1) That the investigation and the judicial functions of the *juge d'instruction* should be separated. The investigative functions should be transferred to the prosecutor while the judicial powers should be performed by a judge in open court.

(2) That at the trial the prosecutor, not the president of the court, should question the accused. The position of the prosecutor in the court room should be brought down from the raised desk at the level of the judges to the same level as the defence.

(3) That questioning should deal only with the facts of the case. Background matters and prior convictions should not be dealt with until after conviction–at the sentencing stage, as in the English system.

(4) That lawyers should be allowed to ask direct questions of witnesses and defendants.

(5) That provision should be made for entering guilty pleas.

See also C Johnstone, 'Trial by Dossier', *New Law Journal*, 21 February 1992, p 249 and Torquil D Erikson, 'Confessions in Evidence: A Look at the Inquisitorial System', *New Law Journal*, 22 June 1990, p 884.

The Runciman Royal Commission on Criminal Justice invited Professor Leonard Leigh and Dr Lucia Zedner to advise it upon the suitability of the French or German models of procedure for adoption or adaptation in England and Wales'. In their report (*A Report on the Administration of Criminal Justice in the Pre-trial phase in France and Germany*, Royal Commission Research Study No 1, 1992) they rejected the notion that the inquisitorial model was 'better' or that it should be adopted: 'We do not believe that adoption, certainly in the crude form which is sometimes suggested in respect of the examining magistrates, is either feasible or desirable' (p 67). In some respect the protections afforded to the suspect in England and Wales were already more extensive than those in France and Germany. 'To reproduce the best features of a foreign system in this country would require much more than the introduction of an office found in the foreign jurisdiction. It would be expensive and time-consuming and would not in our submission, produce better results than could be achieved by an intelligent adaptation of the existing English system' (*ibid*).

Comparisons

The differences between the two systems were commented on from a different point of view more than forty years ago by the Evershed Committee in its *Final Report on Supreme Court Practice*, 1953, Cmnd 8878:

250. (a) There is no doubt that the difference between the English and the continental systems in regard to evidence, ie in regard to the rules of evidence and the way in which evidence is taken, is very marked; and equally there is no doubt that the difference is one of the main reasons for the fact that litigation in England is substantially more costly than (for example) in France or Germany.

(b) In both France and Germany all (oral) witnesses are the court's witnesses, though generally speaking they are tendered by the parties. In both countries the system is (as has been said), unlike the English system, 'inquisitorial'. There is substantially no cross-examination and for practical purposes none at all by the parties or their legal representatives. The witness in effect makes a deposition before the examining judge who decides what witnesses shall be summoned. The process of taking evidence is almost invariably at an early stage of the proceedings, long before the 'trial' proper.

(c) The witness makes his statement in his own words–there being no 'hearsay' rule. It is for the court to decide the value of what has been said. It is, however, to be noted that the parties themselves are, generally, not competent witnesses in Germany; and in France parents, relatives and servants of the parties and certain other categories of persons are not competent.

(d) In Both France and Germany, oral testimony is regarded as of far less significance than in England (as will be apparent from the preceding paragraph). The main emphasis is on written evidence including notarially attested records of every sort of transaction. This point is of the greatest significance and is later referred to.

(e) The adoption here of continental rules and practice in regard to evidence would mean a new kind of judiciary with many hundreds of local examining magistrates. It would mean also (at any rate if the French model were followed) the creation of a system of notaries all over the country before whom every transaction of any significance would have to be recorded if it were to be legally enforceable in practice. We are not prepared to recommend such changes even if they were within our terms of reference.

One of the points frequently made in comparisons between the English and the civil law systems of trial is their different approach to the 'search for the truth'. This was the theme of a leading academic-practitioner who favours the inquisitorial model in a book about a famous English murder case:

Louis Blom-Cooper, *The A6 Murder*, 1963, pp 72, 80–2

In the Continental trial system the starting point of the trial is the accused man. The first thing the court learns about is his medical and criminal antecedents; the court then feels more able to adjudge the man's conduct in relation to the crime, both for testing his culpability in arriving at a verdict and his responsibility for the crime in assessing the treatment he should receive.

The English form of trial is more professional, more aseptic, than the Continental system, a kind of surgical operation, a great deal less painful to the public who are immune from the range of a Continental system of inquiry. The English trial is precise and coldly analytical within the narrow confines marked out by the accusatorial system. Every piece of the puzzle is fitted into a framework which is delineated by the nature of the trial, an accusation on a specific charge against a specific person with all else ruthlessly excluded. The rapier of the prosecution is thrust out; the defence's task is merely to parry it, with no concern other than that the rapier thrust should not strike home. A successful parry means an acquittal and that is that. This precision is claimed to be the English virtue, and certainly the construction of the English trial system does mean that the rules of the game are well defined, and that an accused can prepare himself for it. A more roving inquiry means that the accused may find himself outflanked and may mean also that other suspects may find, in the course of the judicial process, that the pointer of guilt as it swings away from the major suspect shifts towards them.

The Continental system of law, called by contrast the inquisitorial system, believes that a human being is on trial and that the acts of a human being, judged to be criminal, are highly complex. To affix criminal responsibility on an accused, it is not enough to inquire: did this man do the specific act alleged against him? The Continental lawyer wishes to probe deeper in order to determine the full criminal responsibility and the certainty, so far as certainty can be achieved, that the crime is laid at the door of the right perpetrator. It is in essence a search for the truth about the crime.

If your system searches for the truth of the crime, what better start can be made than that the chief suspect 'the accused' should be examined by the court? He must, if any one does, know most about the crime. And so immediately at the outset the scope of the trial is altogether wider. The stage of the trial is taken a step further by the defence and prosecution being allowed to show the real, extended context of the act with which the accused is charged. This intense search for the truth is wholly commendable, since the public, through the agency of the judicial system, is entitled to know not only the criminal but the nature of the crime. For to find out the crime is to make absolute at one fell swoop the nature of responsibility without qualification, and to hamstring the power of the court when determining the sentence. In English law the two functions are kept quite distinct. The mitigating features of the accused's acts are kept away from the eyes and ears of the court–except when, as in Hanratty's case, the defence chooses to put in a record of the accused's character.

In the Continental system, the form of the court's verdict is fashioned by the mixture of evidence touching on both the substantive defence and any plea of mitigation.

The Continental system is therefore fairer to the public, in whose name the trial is being conducted, than it is to those who are the personalities engaged in the trial.

The inquisitorial system in civil litigation

The basic model of the inquisitorial system as it operates in criminal cases–with an active court and relatively passive lawyers–applies also to civil cases. The great difference in the procedure between civil and criminal cases is that in civil cases typically the same judge presides at both the pre-trial and the trial. In fact there is less difference between the two stages than in common-law systems. The procedure has been described by an English lawyer writing about the German system:[6]

John Ratliff, 'Civil Procedure in Germany', 2 *Civil Justice Quarterly*, July 1983, p 257

The absence of a 'day in court'[7]
There is no single, continuous, oral hearing in German law. Instead proceedings take the form of a series of meetings interwoven with the taking of evidence. German law adheres to the principle that officials should direct the case. This means that the court itself, or an office thereof, is responsible for the initial service of the writ and subsequent exchange of pleadings. Pleadings are sent to the court, which keeps one copy for the official file and sends on two copies to the opposing side, one for the party and one for his lawyer. There is an initial meeting at which the court, after discussion with the parties and on the basis of the written pleadings, decides on what points it will take evidence. The court is not bound to take evidence in any particular order and often hears what it considers to be the decisive evidence first. The actual examination of witnesses takes place in a separate hearing. After the taking of evidence there will be a discussion on what the evidence proves and further appointments for the taking of evidence may be made. This process of taking evidence in instalments succeeded by discussion continues until the court considers the case adequately clarified. One judge is delegated the task of 'reporting' the case, compiling a factual summary of the evidence. At the final hearing the court asks the parties' lawyers if they wish to make any concluding remarks, however, usually a lawyer makes only a 'ritualized reference' to his pleadings. A short discussion on one or two points may follow. The court then retires to come to judgment. The principle of collegiality renders judgment 'off the cuff' impossible. Judgment is later given in court and sent to the parties or their lawyers by registered post or placed in the 'postboxes' which many lawyers' firms have at the courts for receipt of official communications.

In recent years it has increasingly been appreciated in Germany that there may be value at least in some cases in having a trial more in the English sense instead of a series of meetings and written communications between the parties, their lawyers and the court. A new method of handling civil cases (called 'the Stuttgart procedure') was

6   For other accounts in English see EJ Cohn, *Manual of German Law* (2nd edn, 1971), vol 2, pp 162–260; B Kaplan, A von Mehren and R Schaefer, 'Phases of German Civil Procedure' (1957–58) 71 *Harv L Rev*, pp 1193, 1443; B Kaplan, 'Civil Procedure–Reflections on the Comparison of Systems' (1959–60) 9 *Buffalo L Rev*, p 409; N Horn, H Kötz and HG Leser, *German Private and Commercial Law–An Introduction*, translated by Tony Weir (1982), Oxford, Clarendon), pp 45–8; K Suhr, 'Forum Shopping in Relation to Germany,' *International Bar News*, April–May 1981, pp 22–4.
7   Code of Civil Procedure (*Zivilprozessordnung*).

therefore developed. Its essence is to prepare the case so thoroughly beforehand that it can be determined conclusively in one hearing–possibly with the support of a single preliminary meeting. Under the Code of Civil Procedure the judge can if he wishes adopt this mode of proceeding.

See also CN Ngwasiri, 'The Role of the Judge in French Court Proceedings', *Civil Justice Quarterly*, April 1990, p 167.

Further reading

For further reading about the English system of trial, see: Glanville Williams' classic work, *The Proof of Guilt* (3rd edn, Stevens, 1963); Sybille Bedford, *The Faces of Justice* (Collins, 1961) and *The Best We Can Do* (Collins, 1963; Penguin, 1961); see also Richard du Cann, *The Art of the Advocate* (revised edn, Penguin, 1993); Patrick Devlin, *The Judge* (Oxford University Press, 1979), pp 54–85; Stephen Landsman, 'The Decline of the Adversary System', 29 *Buffalo Law Review*, 1980, p 487; S. Landsman, 'A Brief Survey of the Development of the Adversary System', 44 *Ohio St LJ*, 1983, p 713; and Sir Jack Jacob, *The Fabric of English Civil Justice* (Sweet and Maxwell, 1987), pp 5–19.

On the inquisitorial system, see Sybille Bedford, *The Faces of Justice, op cit;* B Kaplan *et al*, 'Phases of German Civil Procedure', 71 *Harvard law Review*, 1957–8, pp 1193, 1443; B Kaplan, 'Civil Procedure–Reflections on the Comparison of Systems', 9 *Buffalo Law Review*, 1959–60, p 409; M Damaska, 'Evidential Barriers to Conviction and Two Models of Criminal Procedure: A Comparative Study', 121 *University of Pennsylvania Law Review*, 1973, p 506; 'Structures of Authority and Comparative Criminal Procedure', 84 *Yale Law Journal*, 1975, p 480; and John Langbein, 'The German Advantage in Criminal Procedure, 52 *University of Chicago Law Review*, 1985, p 230. Langbein's article provoked SR Gross 'The American Advantage: The Value of Inefficient Litigation' (1987) 85 *Michigan Law Rev* 734; and RJ Allan *et al*, 'The German Advantage in Civil Procedure: A Plea for More Details and Fewer Generalities in Comparative Scholarship' (1988) 82 *Northwestern Law Rev* 705 and his reply 'Trashing the German Advantage' (1988) 82 *Northwestern Law Rev* 763.

For an American view that the two systems are not in fact as different as is often thought, because the *juge d'instruction* is only rarely involved and, even when he is, there is still much scope for independent police action, see A Goldstein and M Marcus, 'The Myth of Judicial Supervision in Three Inquisitorial Systems: France, Italy, and Germany', 1977 *Yale Law Journal*, pp 240–83. For a comment on this article and a reply to the comment, see *Yale Law Journal*, 1978, pp 1549, 1570. See also Abraham Goldstein, 'Reflections on Two Models: Inquisitorial Themes in American Criminal Procedure', 26 *Stanford Law Review*, 1974, pp 1009, 1016–25, and Patrick Devlin, 'The Judge in the Adversary System', in *The Judge* (OUP, 1979), p 54. For further basic information about the two systems see Alain Cornec, 'You Can Say Accident in French', *Law Society's Gazette*, 28 November 1984, p 3328; P Dugdale, 'The West German Court System', *Law Society's Gazette*, 10 September 1986, p 2665. See also H Kötz, 'The Role of the Judge in the Court Room: The Common Law and Civil Law Compared' (1987–91) *Journal of South African Law*, p 35.

Tribunals and the adversary system

For an evaluation of the tribunal system as to its 'adversary' and 'inquisitorial' features see Gabrielle Ganz, *Administrative Procedures* (Sweet & Maxwell, 1974), pp 29–35. For a very critical view of the decision-making process in industrial tribunals, see Alice Leonard, *Judging Inequality* (Cobden Trust, 1987). Miss Leonard studied 300 industrial tribunal cases relating to sex discrimination and equal pay over a three-year period. Her conclusions were disturbing. She found considerable ignorance and misunderstanding about the relevant legislation in the decisions. Many tribunals applied the wrong legal standard. Tribunals were found to be superficial in their analysis of the evidence, too ready to accept vague and generalized statements even when these were inconsistent with other evidence or based on irrelevant considerations. There was a great lack of uniformity in the quality of decision-making as between different tribunals. Some were much more expert than others. The lack of uniformity applied also to the expertise of those assisting applicants. Most claims failed because of the failure by the complainant and his representative to present relevant evidence. The usual pattern was for the parties to present only oral evidence with no more than one or two pre-existing documents. They failed to call supporting witnesses, failed to cross-examine witnesses effectively and made little or no use of statistical or comparative evidence. Complainants who had representatives who were more experienced and knowledgeable about the legislation had much better success rates.

Miss Leonard adopted the view of a previous study[8] that the tribunal should perform an inquisitorial rather than an adversarial function. But in addition to an expert tribunal there would be a need for some form of expert to help the tribunal by organizing the presentation of the cases, 'an individual expert in the legislation who in each case reviews the available information, determines what evidence and witnesses would be appropriate and ensures that they are produced by the parties' (p 147).

2. THE ADVANTAGES OF BEING REPRESENTED

It would appear obvious that in an adversary system the party who is unrepresented is likely to be at a distinct disadvantage. But until recently there has not been much statistical evidence one way or the other on this crucial question.

The problem is mainly one that affects the lower courts and proceedings in tribunals since in the higher trial courts it is rare for the parties to be unrepresented. One set of figures for the magistrates' courts were those of a small study in London courts conducted by the writer in 1972. This showed that out of 111 defendants who pleaded not guilty, of those who were unrepresented 30 per cent were acquitted as against 64 per cent of those who were represented by lawyers. In other words, the represented were statistically more than twice as likely to be acquitted as the unrepresented (M Zander, 'Unrepresented Defendants in Magistrates' Courts, 1972', *New Law Journal*, 23 November 1972, p 1042).

---

8   J Corcoran and E Donnelly, 'Report of a comparative analysis of the provisions for legal redress in member states of the EEC in respect of Article 119 of the Treaty of Rome and the Equal Pay, Equal Treatment and Social Security Directive', 1984.

In a larger study done by the Lord Chancellor's Department in some 60 magistrates' courts there were 566 cases in which the defendant pleaded not guilty. The proportion acquitted for those who were granted legal aid was 42 per cent, for those who refused legal aid but were represented privately was 52 per cent, and for those who were not represented was virtually the same, 51 per cent. This suggested that representation was not necessarily so significant. (See Lord Chancellor's Department, 'Report of a Survey of the Grant of Legal Aid in Magistrates' Courts', 1983, Table 17.)

Another set of statistics showing the advantage of representation relates to proceedings before national insurance tribunals and supplementary benefit appeals tribunals. In a study by Professor Kathleen Bell and colleagues, conducted in Scotland and the northern region of England, it was found that out of 4,456 cases in national insurance tribunals, the appellant was represented in just over 20 per cent. Representation in three-quarters of the cases was by a trade-union representative, in 19 per cent by a relative or friend and in only 3 per cent by lawyers. Overall, the success rate of appeals was 21 per cent, but the success rate was distinctly higher for those who had been represented, regardless of who was the representative. (Kathleen Bell, 'National Insurance Local Tribunals', 4 *Journal of Social Policy*, 1975, p 16.) See to like effect vol 885 House of Commons, *Hansard*, 1 May 1973, cols 264–5.

The Benson Royal Commission on Legal Services in 1979 cited new evidence to similar effect in regard to the success rate in over 50,000 supplementary benefit appeal tribunal cases in 1976. (Cmnd 7648, 1979, para 15.9, p 169).

The most sophisticated inquiry into the issue is, however, the study by Hazel and Yvette Genn carried out for the Lord Chancellor's Department ('The Effectiveness of Representation at Tribunals' July 1989, published by the Lord Chancellor's Department).

The data showed that the presence of a representative 'significantly increases' the probability that cases will be won. In social security appeals the presence of a representative increased the probability of success from 30 per cent to 48 per cent. In hearings before Immigration Adjudicators it went up from 20 per cent to 38 per cent. In Mental Health Review Tribunals it increased the success rate from 20 per cent to 35 per cent. In Industrial Tribunals the impact depended on whether the respondent was represented. When he was not the presence of a representative for the applicant pushed the success rate up from 30 per cent to 48 per cent. Where the respondent was represented and the applicant was not the success rate went down to 10 per cent.

3. HANDICAPS OF THE UNREPRESENTED

The formality of English proceedings is often referred to by commentators. Where both parties are legally represented, as they normally are in High Court or the higher criminal courts, this may not be quite so important. But where they are not legally represented it may be of great significance. The essence of the situation was captured by Mrs Susanne Dell's study based on interviews with a random sample of 565 prisoners at Holloway prison:

(a) In the lower courts

Susanne Dell, *Silent in Court*, 1971, pp 17–19

Many of the women who were unrepresented were seriously handicapped by the lack of legal help. An inexperienced defendant is at a disadvantage in court even if well educated and articulate,[9] but for those who have little education, who are scared, nervous and unable to express themselves in the kind of language they believe is expected in court, the handicap can be crippling, particularly if they wish to deny the offence or to plead mitigating circumstances.

... when the unrepresented defendant first appears in court, she is in several ways at a disadvantage. The proceedings may be bewildering and unintelligible to her to an extent the court can hardly appreciate. One remanded girl, when asked by the interviewer whether she had asked for bail in court, replied 'What is bail? Is it the same as legal aid?' Many others, even by the time they were interviewed, were confused about the correct meaning of terms like 'remand' and 'bail'. This kind of ignorance was not restricted to first offenders, although for them the position is particularly difficult; they do not know what to expect, how to behave, when to speak, and when to be silent. As one girl put it, 'I kept being told to get up and sit down.' It is not easy in such circumstances to do justice to one's own defence.

Frequently, the women said that they had not been able to catch what was being said: a typical comment was 'The Judge mumbles away, and you don't know whether or not he's supposed to be speaking to you'. Many remanded women said they had left the court room without realizing what the magistrate had decided: and it was then the police who had had to explain to them that they could not go home, as they had been remanded to Holloway. One first offender who caught the words 'two weeks' thought she was being put on probation for that period, until the police disabused her in the cells. This ignorance and lack of understanding can be a practical handicap to the unrepresented person: if a woman who has been remanded in custody is not aware of the fact before she leaves the court room, she cannot ask for bail, nor can she ask for it if she does not understand the meaning of the term. If she is remanded in custody for medical reports while unaware 'as virtually all such women were' that bail could be granted for such a purpose, she is also precluded by her ignorance from asking for it. When a person is represented, her ignorance on such matters is immaterial: her solicitor will ask for bail, and present what arguments there may be against the use of custody. But it is unrealistic to assume that most unrepresented persons can properly look after their own interests in these matters. ... The impossibility of expressing themselves in court weighed heavily on many women: not infrequently those who had given the interviewer full accounts of the background to their offences, said that the court had not known of the mitigating circumstances, as they had found themselves tongue-tied and silent at the appropriate moment. ... A few women complained that they never had a chance to explain themselves in court: this, no doubt, reflected their failure to understand the procedure, since they had probably been interrupted when trying to speak at the wrong moment. But the most common situation among the unrepresented was that when invited to do so, they failed to give the court any explanation of their behaviour. When asked 'What have you to say?' they seemed to think that the response expected was a short stereotype like 'I'm sorry' and they felt it impossible and inappropriate in the formality of the atmosphere to talk about the background to their offence. One woman described her feelings when she was invited to speak in court and failed to respond, much as she wished to: 'I was too over-awed and frightened–I didn't want to make a fool of myself–I would only have cried.'

9   Not many women in the sample fell into that category, but an example was a professional woman, who was arrested with others at a political demonstration. She appeared in court with the others, unrepresented, and was remanded in custody untried. When asked by the interviewer why bail had not been allowed, she said she did not know. She knew the police had opposed it, but said that all she heard was a policeman saying that the reason was 'the same as before'. It had not occurred to her to ask in court what bail meant.

A somewhat similar impression of the situation of the defendant in the magistrates' court was given in a book based on observation in magistrates' courts–Pat Carlen, *Magistrates' Justice*, 1976, pp 83–5.

The complexity of bringing even a county court case was made the main focus of the Consumer Council's argument in 1970 for a new, less formal procedure for consumer claims. As has been seen, the Consumer Council's paper was influential in causing the Lord Chancellor's Department to initiate the so-called 'arbitration' procedure for small claims (see below). But the description in the piece that follows remains relevant to a large number of cases tried in the county court.

Consumer Council, *Justice Out of Reach*, 1970, pp 19–20 and 30–34

'The county courts . . . are adapted to the needs of the great masses of the population by the maximum of . . . simplicity of procedure, suitors being able in fact to obtain relief and to defend themselves without legal assistance.' This sentiment in its nineteenth-century prose appears each year in that bible of the county courts, the County Court Practice book. Afterwards, for the direction of these 'suitors' the 1969 edition of the practice book printed 319 pages of annotated County Court Rules and 204 pages of Forms, not to mention over 2,000 more pages of acts, tables of costs and fees, and rules relating to special jurisdictions.

The truth is that, although to lawyers the county courts are the acme of informality, to the layman they are surrounded by a bewildering maze of rules and practices. The solicitors we interviewed in our survey were unanimous in saying that it was a rare person who could successfully fight a case of any complexity unrepresented. Simple debt claims they can manage, but not disputed cases where evidence and law need to be marshalled to present a coherent case. Some do struggle through but, because of their ignorance of the law, both substantive and procedural, they waste a great deal of time and are the bane of courts and lawyers.

(b) Special procedure for small claims–'arbitration' in county courts

Responding to the pressure of the Consumer Council's pamphlet *Justice Out of Reach*, the Lord Chancellor's Office in 1973 introduced a new scheme for handling small claims in the county courts. It had four main features: the pre-trial review (already mentioned on p 80 above); a no-costs rule (see p 435 below); hearings in private and informal procedure. (For a brief overview description see J Pyke, 'Well done Philadelphia', *Solicitors' Journal*, 23 September 1994, p 964.)

Initially the scheme (somewhat confusingly called 'arbitration') applied where the amount of dispute was under £75. This figure has been progressively increased: in 1979 to £200, in 1981 to £500 and in October 1991 to £1,000. Lord Woolf's Interim Report of June 1995 recommended that save in personal injury cases, the figure be raised to £3,000 and this recommendation was implemented as from January 1996.

In *Joyce v Liverpool City Council* [1995] 3 All ER 110 the Court of Appeal held that the small claims system was not restricted to monetary claims. It could apply for instance to applications by tenants to get a landlord to carry out repairs. The judgment made it clear that in the small claims cases judges could give the same remedies as in their normal trial work including specific performance, injunctions and declarations.

From 1981 arbitration has applied *automatically* to all such cases where a defence is filed. It is therefore no longer necessary to ask for arbitration. The only circumstances in which an ordinary trial can be ordered is where the district judge is satisfied that a difficult question of law or a question of fact of exceptional complexity is involved or a charge of fraud, or that the parties have agreed that the dispute should be tried in court or 'that it would be unreasonable for the claim to proceed to arbitration having regard to its subject matter, the circumstances of the parties or the interests of any person likely to be affected by the award' (CCR Ord 19, r 1(5)).

In *Afzal v Ford Motor Co Ltd* [1994] 4 All ER 720 the Court of Appeal said that the court should not rescind an automatic reference to arbitration under CCR Ord 19 merely because a question of law was involved or the facts were complex. The question of law had to be difficult, the question of fact had to be of exceptional complexity.

The decision in that case concerned 22 actions brought by employees in respect of personal injuries. The unions argued that if the cases were dealt with as small claims and therefore no costs were recoverable, the unions would no longer be able to support their members. Many injured plaintiffs would be denied access to justice. Even if employees did bring their own claims, they would be hopelessly outgunned by the lawyers acting for the employers. But Lord Justice Beldam giving judgment for the Court of Appeal said that the hardship of an employee representing himself against his legally represented employer was one likely to be faced in all cases where the financial resources of the parties were unequal and was a matter for the judge to take into account in the procedure to be adopted, rather than a decisive factor in the decision whether to transfer the case from the small claims system. Inequality of representation was not something that could be taken into account when deciding whether a case should be taken out of the small claims system.

The hearing in arbitrations is normally in private. It is usually taken by the district judge. The County Court Rules for arbitrations provide that 'Any hearing *shall* be informal and the strict rules of evidence *shall not* apply' (Ord 19, r 2.7(3), emphasis supplied). At the hearing, 'the arbitrator may adopt any method of procedure which he may consider to be convenient and to afford a fair and equal opportunity to each party to present his case' (*ibid* (4)). The arbitrator, with the consent of the parties, is allowed to consult with an expert either before or after the hearing (*ibid* (6)).

The number of cases dealt with under the arbitration procedure has risen dramatically. In 1974 there were just under 5,000. In 1989 the number was just under 50,000, in 1994 it was 87,800. In fact there are now far more arbitrations than other forms of hearing leading to judgment in the county court. (In 1994 the total of such other hearings was some 24,200.)

Contrary to the recommendations of the Consumer Council, legal representation is permitted, though, as will be seen (p 435 below), it is discouraged through the 'no-costs rule'. According to official figures in the 1970s, in about half the cases neither side was represented, in about a third the plaintiff alone was represented, in less than 10 per cent only the defendant was represented and in about the same proportion both sides were represented (*Statistical Report on Arbitration in County Courts*, 1974, 1975, 1976). But the report has unfortunately not been published since 1976 and there have been no official figures on this aspect of the system since then. In a study conducted in 1994 by Professor John Baldwin for the Office of Fair Trading based on interviews with 262 small claims litigants in 16 county courts throughout the country, only a tiny proportion were represented.

One of the chief objectives of the system is to provide for a less formal hearing process than that typical in the county courts. A study of 30 courts by a member of the

Institute of Judicial Administration at Birmingham University found that practice varied considerably from court to court. Some courts adopted an inquisitorial technique, asking questions even when the parties were legally represented; some used such methods only when the parties were unrepresented; others again followed the normal adversarial methods. Some took the rules of evidence seriously, others did not. Most of the registrars interviewed said they valued the increased informality of the new system. (George Appleby, *Small Claims in England and Wales*, Birmingham Institute of Judicial Administration, 1978 pp 30–3.)

However, *Chilton v Saga Holidays plc* [1986] 1 All ER 841 held that the special rules for small claims did not mean that the basic principles of the adversary system could be set aside. The registrar in the case had refused to allow solicitors for the defendants to cross-examine the plaintiff and his wife. (He gave his ruling as follows: 'In cases where one side is unrepresented, I do not allow cross-examination. All questions to the other side will be put through me.') The county court judge upheld the decision of the registrar. But on further appeal the Court of Appeal held that their view was wrong. The Master of the Rolls said that, although the procedure was designed to be informal, it was fundamental to the adversary system 'that each party shall be entitled to ask questions designed to probe the accuracy or otherwise, or the completeness or otherwise, of the evidence which has been given'.

In the study by George Appleby, the types of case brought were found to be very similar to those brought in ordinary county court procedure. Moreover, individuals were not by any means the main category of plaintiff. About half the claims were brought by companies and firms, and this proportion was unaffected by the size of the claim. Firms were defendants in about a quarter of the cases.

A somewhat similar picture emerged from an unpublished study of cases processed by one county court in 1984. Private individuals were defendants in 59 per cent of the cases brought in the court but in only 14 per cent of the cases that were defended. By contrast firms, traders and companies were defendants in 41 per cent of the cases filed, but accounted for 86 per cent of the cases in which a defence was filed. It was also found that individuals brought only 12 per cent of small claims under £500. (See the account of the study by R Bowles, in Dr C Whelan's article in *Civil Justice Quarterly*, July 1987, p 237 at pp 240–1.) The 1994 study of 262 small claims litigants in 16 county courts by Professor John Baldwin of Birmingham University found that individuals were plaintiffs in 36 per cent of the cases and defendants in 55 per cent. (Office of Fair Trading Consumer Redress Symposium, 27 September 1955; see monograph by Professor Baldwin to be published by OUP in 1997.) In a new study by the National Audit Office individuals were plaintiffs in 20 per cent of arbitration cases and defendants in 60 per cent. (*Handling Small Claims in the County Court*, 1996, p 12, Fig 6.) The impression that arbitration is used mainly by individuals, for whom it was chiefly intended, is therefore wrong. But it may nevertheless be the case that some individuals are using the procedure who would not have come to the county court previously.

Professor Baldwin said that in the main the litigants were middle class. ('If small claims procedures have been devised to enhance the rights of the poor, then they cannot be said to have achieved that objective'.)

The Final Report of the Civil Justice Review (HMSO, Cm 394, 1988) recommended that these cases should be called 'small claims cases' and that there should be a separate and self-contained set of small claims rules (paras 510–11). The court should have the right on its own motion to transfer a case for trial in the ordinary way, but the parties should have a right to object (para 517). (This was implemented in October 1990.)[10] Normally there should be no preliminary hearing. The aim should be wherever possible to dispose of the case at a single hearing. (But the Government decided not to abolish the preliminary hearing.)

The registrar should conduct the hearing according to the circumstances of each case and should 'adopt an interventionist role, dispensing with the rules of evidence and procedure, and assuming control of the questioning of the parties and their witnesses' (para 527).

The Courts and Legal Services Act 1990, s 6, has a provision that county court rules may prescribe the procedure and rules for small claims arbitrations and that such rules 'may, in particular, make provision with respect to the manner of taking and questioning evidence'. The Notes on Clauses in the Bill specifically related this provision to the problem created by the Court of Appeal's decision in *Chilton v Saga Holidays plc* (p 305 above). The right to cross-examine lay on the border between procedural rules and the law of substantive evidence, and an enabling power was therefore needed to permit a rule to be made which gave the court the right to dispense with the right.

As has been seen in 1992 the County Court Rules were amended. CCR Order 19, r 7 now provides that the arbitrator can 'adopt any method of proceeding which he may consider fair and which gives each party an equal opportunity to have his case presented'. Having considered the circumstances of the parties and whether and to what extent they are represented, the arbitrator '(a) may assist a party by putting questions to the witnesses and the other party; and (b) should explain any legal terms or expressions which are used.'

The Courts and Legal Services Act also has a provision (s 11) permitting the Lord Chancellor to abolish restrictions on who may appear as an advocate or who may conduct litigation in specified proceedings in the county court. A Consultation Paper issued by the Lord Chancellor's Department in May 1992 suggested that in the first instance lay representatives would be given only a right of audience to act as advocates. The operation of such extended rights of audience would be monitored to see how they worked in practice. (Under the Act 'right of audience' means addressing the court, 'right to conduct litigation' means issuing proceedings and performing the ancillary functions in relation to proceedings (s 119(1)). The Lay Representation (Rights of Audience) Order 1992 gave effect to this proposal. It provided that a lay representative may however not exercise his right of audience unless his client attends the hearing (r 2(2)).

Woolf on small claims

Lord Woolf's Interim Report made a number of recommendations regarding small claims. One, as has been seen, was to increase the jurisdiction to £3,000–save for personal injury (PI) cases involving claims of more than £1,000. In regard to PI cases Lord Woolf accepted that there was justification for an exception because the costs rule applicable to small claims had the effect of depriving plaintiffs of the benefits of help from lawyers because the loser did not have to pay costs. (On this see p 436 below.)

10 County Court (Amendment No 3) Rules 1990, SI 1990/1764.

Lord Woolf said (p 104, para 11) that where both sides were represented the more attention the judge should pay to the parties' agreed view that the case should be taken out of the small claims track. Conversely, the smaller the claim, the stronger the presumption that it should stay in the small claims track even if the parties agreed otherwise. He did not however say what the court's attitude should be in regard to inequality of representation as such.

Lord Woolf proposed that the district judge should have a discretion to transfer cases out of the small claims system where they involved complex questions of fact (as opposed to the requirement that the issues be of *exceptional* complexity).

Professor John Baldwin's research had identified four different styles of judicial approach to small claims work: 'going for the jugular' (identifying the central issues and sticking to them); 'hearing the parties' (allowing the parties to develop their arguments in their own way); 'passive' (talking to each of the parties like a solicitor interviewing clients); 'mediatory' (encouraging the parties to agree their own solution).

Professor Baldwin had also shown that the judges differed considerably in the way in which they dealt with evidence and applied the substantive law. In regard to evidence, some made an active attempt to fill in gaps in the evidence presented by the parties, or half-hear the evidence and give directions for further evidence to be obtained. Others were prepared to decide the case on the basis of what was available. In regard to the law, some saw it as their duty to apply the law strictly, whilst others spoke of a wider responsibility to 'do justice', even if that meant disregarding the strict requirements of the law.

Research in England and Wales, in Scotland and in the United States had shown that the most crucial element affecting litigants' perceptions of small claims was their treatment by the judge. It was essential to secure greater consistency of judicial approach. The variation in the way that different judges conducted small claims hearings should be dealt with by training.

Lord Woolf did not think there was any need for a wholly separate set of rules for small claims. This was an area, he said, 'where a robust judicial approach is required to curtail and disallow adversarial tactics and to ensure speedy progress, the avoidance of unnecessary expense and above all fairness' (p 107, para 22). He thought there was a case for introducing 'paper arbitrations' where the matter would be resolved without a hearing–but only as an option where the parties wanted it, and subject to the court's approval.

In regard to expert testimony, Lord Woolf recommended that in appropriate cases the court should appoint its own expert assessor to assess the problem and to report to the judge.

Are litigants satisfied with the small claims system?

The Touche Ross report on small claims for the Civil Justice Review said that most litigants were well satisfied with the system. No less than 81 per cent of plaintiffs interviewed said they would 'very likely' or 'quite likely' to use the system again.

Professor Baldwin equally found in his 1994 study that 'a substantial majority of all types of litigants expressed satisfaction with the way that their cases had been dealt with'–whether they won or lost. Most said they would use the procedure again. Professor Baldwin said that it was his impression that most litigants managed quite well. These findings, he thought, 'provide impressive testimony to the efficacy of small claims procedures as they currently operate in this country and to the skill and sensitivity of district judges'. In his view, 'in the vast majority of small claims hearings litigants are well able to represent themselves'. The main advantages of the system were 'low cost in initiating process, personal participation in the resolution of the dispute, absence of lawyers and the attendant formality, simplicity of procedures, a pragmatic and direct judicial approach, courtesy and politeness of judges and court staff, an absence of long delay and finality of result'.

But in the minority of cases where there was dissatisfaction it was more often the business litigants who thought the judges favoured the individual than the opposite. Baldwin said 'It was surprising to hear these views since they run counter to much of the received wisdom surrounding small claims procedures.' It suggested that the view expressed in much academic literature that the individual was likely to get a raw deal with traders and businesses able to exploit legal processes to their own advantage was somewhat overstated. Few of the business litigants were regulars (in the jargon, 'repeat players'). Few of the parties 'lay, business or other' used the county courts regularly. Indeed, Baldwin said that those who used the system were 'the tip of a very large iceberg of "unmet legal need". The evidence suggests that, no matter how informal legal procedures might be and no matter how sympathetic or interventionist judges might be, most people shy away from the prospect of a court appearance'. Whatever the merits, the temptation was either to forget the whole thing or to pay up whatever sum was claimed.

(c) In the tribunals

The 1957 Franks Committee on the Tribunal System said (p 9) that tribunals had certain characteristics which distinguished them from courts cheapness, accessibility, freedom from technicality and expert knowledge of the tribunal members. It identified three main objectives for the system: namely, openness, fairness and impartiality. But as H Genn and Y Genn ('The Effectiveness of Representation at Tribunals', Lord Chancellor's Department, 1989, p 111) point out, the Franks Committee did not acknowledge that, to an extent, there is a conflict between the two sets of objectives. Cheapness and informality may be in conflict with fairness and impartiality.

They found that tribunals were decidedly 'more informal and procedurally more flexible than courts' (p 112). But the price was paid in quality of decision making, since much of the law dealt with in tribunals is difficult and to present a coherent case on fact and law is not easy. The notion that tribunal cases were straightforward and that therefore there was no great need for a representative was unrealistic (*ibid*, ch 4).

The experience of unrepresented appellants and applicants is overwhelmingly of feeling ill-equipped to present their case effectively at their hearing. They are intimidated, confused by the language and often surprised at the formality of the proceedings. Those who are subjected to cross-examination find the experience stressful, and feel unable to conduct cross-examination themselves. It is difficult to convey the degree of incomprehension common among appellants and applicants who appear unrepresented at tribunals, or the extent of the difficulties experienced by ordinary people trying to present their case in a legal forum.

Representatives perform a number of functions. They prepare the case, act as a mouthpiece, and protect and support appellants and applicants. They act as a physical buffer between the appellant and the tribunal, and between the appellant and the opposing side. Most importantly, representation reduces the sense of being at a disadvantage experienced by unrepresented appellants. It increases the likelihood that those who appear before tribunals will perceive the process as fair.

(d) Litigants in person

A litigant always has the right to represent himself in any court. But if he is not legally represented, can he come with some other kind of person to assist him? This issue came up in the case of *McKenzie v McKenzie* [1971] P 33, CA. The husband petitioner in a defended divorce case appeared in person. His former solicitors sent a young Australian barrister to assist him gratuitously by sitting beside him and prompting him. The judge told him that he must not take part in the proceedings, which was understood by the barrister as meaning that he must not assist the husband by prompting, and he left the court. The judge granted the wife her decree nisi and rejected the husband's petition. On appeal.

Davies LJ: Mr Hanger was there voluntarily in order to assist Mr McKenzie in conducting his case Mr Hanger was not there to take part in the proceedings in any sort of way. He was merely there to prompt and to make suggestions to the husband in the conduct of his case, the calling of his witnesses and, perhaps more importantly, on the very critical and difficult questions of fact in this case, to assist him by making suggestions as to the cross-examination of the wife and her witnesses.

The court cited the words of Chief Justice Tenterden in *Collier v Hicks* (1831) 2 B & Ad 663 at p 669:

'Any person, whether he be a professional man or not, may attend as a friend of either party, may take notes, may quietly make suggestions, and give advice; but no one can demand to take part in the proceedings as an advocate, contrary to the regulations of the court as settled by the discretion of the justices.'

... Mr Payne submitted, in my opinion rightly, that the judge ought not to have excluded Mr Hanger from the court, or, rather, ought not to have prevented Mr Hanger from assisting the husband in the way that he proposed to do. And, goes the submission, justice was not seen to be done in those circumstances.....

This decision led to the start of a new form of assistance in courts known as the 'McKenzie man'. But for an indication that the *McKenzie* concept might not extend to advocacy, see *Mercy v Persons Unknown* (1974) 231 Estates Gazette 1159, CA. Notwithstanding this judicial discouragement. 'McKenzie men' were permitted to appear as advocates in the discretion of individual courts. But by the end of the 1970s it seemed that the McKenzie-man concept was unlikely to develop into a major source of representation in courts. It flourished briefly for a few years but then seemed to go into decline.

The question came up again in the early 1990s in the context of hearings for non-payment of community charge (poll tax). In *R v Leicester City Justices, ex p Barrow* [1991] 2 All ER 437 the Divisional Court held that no party to court proceedings had a 'right' to the assistance of a 'McKenzie friend'. It was a matter for the judge or justices to decide whether or not such assistance should be permitted as an exercise of discretion. But on appeal the Court of Appeal [1991] 3 All ER 935 disagreed. It held that in civil proceedings to which the public had a right of access, the court, as part of its duty to administer justice fairly and openly, was under a duty to permit a litigant in person to have all reasonable facilities for exercising his right to be heard in his own defence. This included quiet and unobtrusive advice from another member of the public accompanying him as an assistant or adviser. A litigant did not need leave from the court for this. But in the exercise of its inherent jurisdiction the court could restrict the assistance of an adviser or even require him to leave the court if it became apparent that his assistance was unreasonable or not *bona fide* and was harmful to the proper and efficient administration of justice. Here there was no evidence that either the applicants or the person who was helping them had any intention of disrupting the court proceedings and the court should have allowed such assistance. The Master of the Rolls, Lord Donaldson, concluded his judgment by saying that he hoped fervently that the term 'McKenzie friend' would go the way of 'Piltdown man' into decent obscurity. (For an account of this litigation see PA Thomas, 'From McKenzie Friend to Leicester Assistant: the Impact of the Poll Tax', *Public Law*, 1992, pp 208–20.)

The Otton Working Party on Litigants in Person in the Royal Courts

In June 1995 a committee established by the Judges' Council reported on the problem of litigants in person in the Royal Courts of Justice.[11] It said there had been significant increase in the number of such litigants in the RCJ. The largest number and proportion were in the civil division of the Court of Appeal. In 1993–94, litigants in person were one in three of applicants for leave to appeal but only 10 per cent of actual appellants. The litigant in person was ultimately successful in only 4 per cent of cases–a much lower rate than litigants who have representation (p 10). One reason was that some simply had no case at law. Others were prejudiced by the complexity of the proceedings, their lack of knowledge of procedure, and the non-availability of low cost or free legal advice and assistance. Court staff gave as much assistance as they could but they could not become legal advisers without prejudicing the independence of the court.

The Working Party endorsed the call by Lord Woolf in his Interim Report for additional support for the Citizens' Advice Bureau in the Royal Courts of Justice in the Strand which handled 18,000 inquiries in 1994. Also the Bar and the Law Society should each have a scheme for the provision of free advisory services for such litigants. (See B McConnell, 'Watch these LIPs', *New Law Journal*, 20 October 1995, p 1549–52).

4. ESTABLISHING THE FACTS IN COURT: THE UNRELIABILITY OF HUMAN TESTIMONY

Law teachers often make it appear that most of the courts' time is taken up with legal problems. This is far from the case. The majority of trials on both the civil and the criminal side involve issues of fact, not problems of law. One of the difficulties faced by the courts is the danger of perjury by those giving evidence.

---

11   The report is obtainable from the Courts Business Section, Supreme Court Group, Room W08, Royal Courts of Justice, Strand London WC2A 2LL.

Perjury

This is an area where little is known–though everyone connected with the justice business would agree that perjury is not infrequent. The number of prosecutions is small. In each of the years from 1984 to 1994 it was under 300 a year. This is undoubtedly only the tip of the iceberg. An attempt to get some kind of line on the problem was reported by a practising barrister in 1986 (*New Law Journal*, 28 February 1986, p 181). David Wolchover had been at the Bar since 1971. His aim was to discover how much perjury was committed by police officers. His method was to inquire of his fellow barristers. He accepted that it was far from ideal as a basis for an assessment, but said he thought that there was none better and that it might not be wildly wrong.

He considered that having practised for many years he 'had sufficient experience and acumen to be capable of making a reasonably confident judgment from the details of facts and circumstances in a given case whether police officers were committing perjury'. It had become apparent to him that 'police perjury occurs with great frequency in London' where he practised. His belief that this was so 'was reinforced by hearing, in chambers, in the robing room and Bar mess, the casual and matter of fact way in which the Bar tends to refer to police perjury. It was regarded as commonplace' (p 183). Over a two-year period he conducted an informal and statistically haphazard poll of fellow barristers to ask how many shared that view. In the large majority it was shared. Most were between five and twenty years since call to the Bar and took part in prosecution and defence work in about equal proportions.

In Mr Wolchover's estimation, perjury took place in as many as three out of every ten criminal trials both summary and on indictment. Forty-one of the 55 barristers (75 per cent) he asked thought that this was 'a reasonable estimate with which they could readily concur'. Eight thought it occurred in only one or two out of ten. Four thought its frequency was less than one in ten. Two thought it happened in as many as 50 per cent of their cases (one of these did more prosecution than defence work). Averaged out roughly, this would mean that police perjury was observed to occur in a little over a quarter of all trials.

Mr Wolchover observes that this figure relates only to perceptible lying under oath. There would be many other cases (possibly more) where the police officers lied in ways that were not perceptible to the barristers in the case or where the issue of police perjury never became relevant because the defendant pleaded guilty. There would almost certainly be cases where innocent defendants pleaded guilty to trumped-up charges (see p 247 above) or where some of the prospective evidence was invented–the gilding on the lily.

Human fallibility

Almost certainly the problem of perjury in the courts is minor by comparison with the problems created by the fallibility of honest witnesses. There is now a mass of evidence based on the experiments conducted by psychologists and others showing how deplorably inaccurate human beings are in their powers of observation, recall and reporting. (See in particular DS Greer, 'Anything But the Truth?–The Reliability of Testimony in Criminal Trials', 11 *British Journal of Criminology*, 1971, p 13; Dr Eliot Slater, 'The Judicial Process and the Ascertainment of Truth', 24 *Modern Law Review*, 1961, p 721; Dr LRC Haward, 'Some Psychological Aspects of Oral Evidence', 3 *British Journal of*

Criminology, 1962–3, p 342; LRC Haward, 'A Psychologist's Contribution to Legal Procedure'. 27 *Modern Law Review*, 1964, p 656; D Farrington, K Hawkins and S Lloyd-Bostock, *Psychology, Law and Legal Processes* (Macmillan, 1979), especially Part IV; D Yamey, *The Psychology of Eye-Witness Testimony* (Free Press, 1979).

Professor Greer, for instance, said (*op cit*):

On the whole, it seems, psychological theory in the field of perception is fairly well advanced. It is now generally recognized that there is an important distinction between 'actual' and 'perceived' characteristics of the environment. In other words, 'We all live in a world of our own psychological reality, a world of personal experience separated from the real world (whatever we choose to mean by that) and from the psychological world of others by a complex neuro-physiological process.. . . .This process selects, organizes and transforms objective information according to conditions existing in the observer at the time' (Haward, 1964, *op cit*, p 663). In short, what a witness recognizes perceptually is not necessarily an exact reproduction of the data presented and for legal purposes at any rate the most important finding in this area is that there can be a very considerable discrepancy between the two.

Many of the causes of this discrepancy are already well known, eg the adverse effect on accuracy of testimony of poor lighting, long distance, short duration of exposure, etc Less well-known factors influencing perception include emotion, interest, bias, prejudice, or expectancy, on the part of the perceiver. Take, for instance, the effect of 'expectancy' or 'set'. It is a well-documented fact that we frequently perceive what we expect to perceive. If we expect to see an individual performing a particular action we are more likely than not to interpret a stimulus which is in fact ambiguous as evidence that the person is performing the expected action.

One example of this is provided by a Canadian case where a hunter was mistaken for a deer and shot by his companions. The hunters, who were eagerly scanning the landscape for deer, perceived the moving object (the victim) as a deer. Before the trial, the police recreated the scene under the same conditions, using another man in the place of the deceased. They reported at the trial that the object was clearly visible as a man. But the important psychological difference between the first and second 'shooting' was that the hunters, expecting to see a deer, 'saw' a deer; the police expected to see a man and therefore 'saw' a man.

More recently, a psychologist was called in by the defence in an English case where two men were charged with having committed an act of gross indecency in a public convenience. Complaints had been made to the police that the convenience was being used for indecent purposes and the accused were apprehended by two policemen who were keeping the convenience under secret observation. The defendants denied that any criminal acts had taken place. The psychologist reproduced the defence version of the facts (ie no criminal act) in a series of photographs and he showed these to twelve adults under different conditions of light, for varying lengths of time, and with reference to three different question: In A they were merely asked to say what they saw in the pictures; in B they were asked if they could see any crime being committed in any of the pictures; in C they were told that some of the pictures actually portrayed criminal acts being committed and they were asked to identify the pictures concerned.

The result was that the number of errors increased considerably from A to B to C. In other words, the witnesses most frequently erred in asserting that a crime was being committed when they were led to expect to see this criminal behaviour. The police, therefore, expecting to see an indecent act being committed might well have put an erroneous interpretation on innocent facts. In the event, the accused were acquitted.

A revealing account of a personal experience of being a witness was written in 1973 by *New Society's* legal correspondent (now a distinguished Queen's Counsel):

'Diogenes', *New Society*, 31 August 1973

Just over two years ago, I witnessed a minor accident. It happened in this way. I was riding in a bus which had new automatic doors at its exit. On reaching the bus stop where I wanted to get off, I found myself behind an old lady who was stepping onto the pavement with some caution. The bus driver evidently had his view of the exit in the mirror blocked because, before she had completed her manoeuvre, he started the bus up. Her arm was caught in the closing doors. Fortunately, my shouts caused the bus driver to stop and the old lady was saved from nothing worse than slight shock, bruises to her arm, and a cut on her shin.

At the time, with a barrister's instinct for a possible civil claim by the old lady against the city bus company, I gave her my name (as a witness, not an advocate), and on my return to my parents' house, some ten minutes later, I wrote out a statement of what I had seen. I was, in other words, the perfect witness. I was on the spot. I had appreciated at once the need for an accurate account of what had happened. I was trained to understand what was and what was not relevant to a claim for negligent driving. And I made a statement within minutes.

Yet, even within that short space of time I found myself forgetting certain details. Had I been directly behind the old lady, or were there other passengers between us? Where had her arm been when it was trapped? How fast was the bus going before it stopped? I argued several points with my wife, who had been with me; and, later that evening, when I furnished another statement to the police, I found myself making minor modifications to my account.

A magistrates' court hearing followed a few months later, I gave my evidence as well as I could; but, by that time, I could not honestly say that I remembered more than the bare outlines of the event, and would have been lost without an ability to refer to my contemporary record–something admissible in evidence like the policeman's notebook. The driver was, however, convicted, in my view quite properly. I felt sorry for the defence solicitor.

I have not been summoned to give evidence in civil proceedings. Nowadays, once a driver has a conviction in respect of an accident, the fact of which can be adduced in evidence, his chances of defending a civil claim are slim indeed. And, I assume, the claim has been settled by the city bus company's insurers.

But, in the ordinary run of things, a trial of a personal injury claim two years after the event would be nothing unusual; slow for a county court, but average for the high court. And, if I am called on as a witness at this length of time, what do I really retain except a memory of the kind of accident that it was and a feeling that it was the driver's fault?

The point of this reminiscence? Only that every day witnesses purport to give truthful accounts, in the box, of accidents that occurred in split-second circumstances, and in which they were often themselves involved; and that thousands of pounds, indeed an individual's future, may depend on the outcome of the case.

Research has been done on both sides of the Atlantic to discover whether different groups of people are aware of the factors that influence the accuracy of eye witness evidence. To an alarming extent they do not. Even police officers have little appreciation of the relevant factors–and length of service, rank or nature of employment (in uniform or CID) seem not to affect the matter one way or the other (Peter Bennett and Felicity Gibling, 'Can We Trust Our Eyes?' 5 *Policing*, Winter 1989, p 313 and p 320).

For the (entertaining and instructive) reflections of an experienced judge on the problems of finding the facts in civil cases, see T Bingham, 'The Judge as Juror', *Current Legal Problems*, 1985, p 1.

5. THE PRINCIPLE OF ORALITY

One of the fundamental features of an English trial has been the oral examination of witnesses. The principle of orality has always been at the heart of the English trial, partly because of the dominant role played for centuries by the jury. There are, however, exceptions–and these are increasing.

One minor exception is the evidence of someone who cannot come to the trial– because of age, infirmity or physical distance. The court can order that his evidence be taken by an examiner on behalf of the court with both sides present.

Another more important exception is evidence given on affidavit, a procedure that is common, for instance, in the Chancery Division. The evidence in interlocutory injunction cases is normally taken on affidavit, eg in trade-union disputes. So, too, is the evidence on the basis of which the Divisional Court decides applications for judicial review of administrative action, under Order 53 of the Rules of Supreme Court. In theory, the person whose evidence is being read to the court (the deponent) can be asked to come to court to be cross-examined. But this is very rare. This means that the procedure is not well adapted to dealing with disputes as to the facts.

The concept of evidence on affidavit has recently been developed in a different way by the Practice Directions issued in 1995 for the Queen's Bench Division, the Chancery Division and the Family Division each of which state that 'unless otherwise ordered, every witness statement or affidavit shall stand as the evidence-in-chief of the witness concerned': [1995] 1 All ER 385, para 3; [1995] 1 All ER 586, para 3.

Virtually all divorces are obtained through the 'special procedure', which is effectively divorce by post under which the court simply looks at the petition and the supporting affidavits and, if they are in order, pronounces the divorce.

Another exception to the principle that evidence must be given orally in open courts is in relation to criminal cases. The Magistrates' Courts Act 1980, ss 6 and 102, provided for the committal stage to be shortened by the acceptance as evidence of written statements of witnesses, providing that they were signed, that they had been sent in advance to the other side and that the other side did not object. Even if the other side did not object, the court retained an overriding discretion to call a witness whose statement had been produced as evidence, but in practice this was rarely exercised. Committal proceedings were to have been abolished and the same concept applied to transfer proceedings under the Criminal Justice and Public Order Act 1994. But as has been seen, (p 265 above) the legislation purporting to abolish committal proceedings was scrapped on the launch pad. Committal proceedings broadly in their existing state were to be retained save that in old style committals no oral evidence can be given. The court will deal with the issue of committal simply by reference to the written witness statements and oral submissions from counsel.

Section 9 of the Criminal Justice Act 1967 has an even wider provision since it relates to any criminal case whether tried summarily or on indictment. It permits the admission as evidence of a written statement subject to the same conditions as applied committal proceedings under the Magistrates' Courts Act 1980.

Legal argument has also been affected by the requirement of 'skeleton arguments' which have to be made available both to the court and to one's opponent ahead of the hearing. They were first introduced for appeal hearings. But in 1995 the Practice Directions that dealt with witness statements in the QBD, the Chancery and the Family

Divisions (above) stated that whenever practicable and in any matter estimated to last five days or longer each party should lodge with the court and deliver to the other parties a case chronology and skeleton arguments summarising the party's legal submissions and citing the authorities relied upon.

An English criminal trial remains essentially an oral hearing but the exceptions to the general rule especially in civil proceedings have diminished the principle of orality and Lord Woolf's Interim Report threatens a major further reduction in orality in fast track cases through the proposal to restrict the oral hearing to three hours.

See generally C Glasser, 'Civil Procedure and the Lawyers–the Adversary System and the Decline of the Orality Principle', 56 *Modern Law Review*, 1993, pp 307–24.

Trials are normally continuous. Once the case comes on, it continues until it is finished. The only important exception is in the county court, where fixed dates for trial are usually not given for more than one day. Where the trial is not concluded on the day it starts, the next day for the case to be continued may be weeks later. But since the extension of the jurisdiction of the county court as a result of the Civil Justice Review, more and more county courts do have facilities for continuous trial.

6. JUSTICE SHOULD BE CONDUCTED IN PUBLIC

It is an old adage that justice must not only be done but must be seen to be done. It is therefore axiomatic that judicial business should be transacted in public.

However, there are situations where this basic maxim gives way to other even more important considerations. An obvious example is where a case is heard *in camera* because of the national security implications of the evidence.

But there are other situations where for one reason or another the public and the press have no access to the proceedings. The list is long and seems to be growing.

Pre-trial proceedings are generally not truly accessible to the public. In regard to committal proceedings, as has been seen, although the proceedings are held in public, a person in the public gallery would normally have no idea what is the nature of the case since the evidence is not read out. It was only in the rare case of a full old-style committal that the notion of the open court had much meaning. Now that oral evidence is banned even in old style committals the position is, if anything, even less 'open'.

In pre-trial civil matters, most interlocutory proceedings are conducted behind closed doors in the chambers of masters and district judges. There is no admission for the public or the press.

Even when the matter is dealt with by a High Court judge, it is often heard in chambers. This is true, for instance, of injunctions in the Queen's Bench Division– whereas injunctions in the Chancery Division are heard in open court. There is no logical reason for this difference, which is the more curious since, if the matter goes on appeal, it is always heard in open court by the Court of Appeal. The judge can adjourn the matter into open court for his decision and does so if he considers that it deserves to have publicity, but the decision is one for him and there is no doubt that many matters of high importance are heard behind closed doors.

Trials are generally open to the public and the press. But there are some exceptions.

In *Scott v Scott* [1913] AC 417, the House of Lords held that normally a court must sit in public but it can sit in camera if this is necessary to achieve justice. The rule has been applied, for instance, to protect a secret trade process, or national security, or the affairs of the mentally ill or to prevent tumult or disorder. Convenience however is not sufficient reason to sit in camera. In 1982 the Divisional Court ruled that magistrates in Reigate had erred in going into camera for a hearing of charges against a 'supergrass' who had committed his offences *after* he had been given a light sentence for informing. Both defence and prosecution asked for the matter to be dealt with in camera but the Divisional Court said the decision to comply was wrong (*R v Reigate Justices, ex p Argus Newspapers* (1983) 5 Cr App Rep (S) 181). Nor is the protection of public decency a sufficient basis for proceeding in private–see *Scott v Scott* above at p 439. But in *R v Malvern Justices, ex p Evans* [1988] 1 All ER 371 (Div Ct) the court held the magistrates in a criminal case had been entitled to sit in camera to spare the defendant from giving embarrassing evidence about her husband that could affect her pending divorce case. See also *A-G v Leveller Magazines* [1979] AC 440, HL.

See generally James Michael, 'Open Justice: Publicity and the Judicial Process', 46 *Current Legal Problems*, 1993, pp 190–203.

Wardship, guardianship and adoption cases are usually heard in chambers. In undefended divorce cases no evidence is heard in open court. Ancillary proceedings concerning maintenance and custody of children are normally heard in chambers. Domestic proceedings in magistrates' courts are in private.

In the Family Division a commentator has observed that, since 'chambers' hearings are the rule and open court hearings the exception, a situation has been created which is causing concern even among some judges'. So little in the way of reported decisions were emerging from this quarter that 'lawyers specialising in divorce related cases are faced with a virtual famine of modern day case law': Roger P Pearson, 'Open Justice', *Solicitors' Journal*, 19/26 December 1986, p 969.

Press reports of judicial proceedings

The question of reporting of court proceedings is a separate issue. Normally proceedings can be reported. Thus the Contempt of Court Act 1981, s 4 states: 'subject to this section, a person is not guilty of contempt of court under the strict liability rule in respect of a fair and accurate report of legal proceedings held in public, published contemporaneously and in good faith'.

Section 4 of the Act gives the courts the power to direct that publication be postponed 'where it appears to be necessary for avoiding a substantial risk of prejudice to the administration of justice'. Such orders must be formulated with precision–see *Practice Direction (Contempt: Reporting Restrictions)* [1982] 1 WLR 1475. On s 4 orders see especially *R v Horsham Justices, ex p Farquharson* [1982] QB 762; *R v Leveller Magazines Ltd*, above.

Under s 11 of the Contempt of Court Act 1981, a court, having power to do so, may direct that a name or other material not be published if it appears to the court to be necessary. Use of this power by the courts has proved very controversial. Until 1988 there was no right of appeal against the exercise of the power by the crown court or higher courts, but this was changed by s 159 of the Criminal Justice Act 1988. There have, however, been a number of decisions mainly by the Divisional Court on challenges to s 11 orders made by magistrates. From these it seems clear that the courts should not, for instance, prevent publication of the name of a witness or party simply to protect them from embarrassment. Thus in 1987 the Divisional Court held that justices in Malvern and Evesham had been wrong to prohibit publication of a former Conservative MP's name and address when he appeared on a motoring charge. He had claimed that publication of the details would expose him to harassment by his wife. Lord Justice Watkins said that s 11 of the 1981 Act was not enacted 'for the benefit of the comfort and feelings of defendants' (*R v Evesham* Justices, *ex p McDonagh* [1988] 1 All ER 371.) But it would be legitimate to ban reporting of a witness's name in a blackmail case.

Even chambers' hearings to which the public are not admitted are generally capable of being reported. The Administration of Justice Act 1960, s 12(1), states: 'The publication of any information before the court sitting in private shall not of itself be contempt of court'. So if reporters can find out what happened in chambers they can publish it. The exceptions are for matters affecting juveniles, national security, secret processes and where the court, having power to do so, has specifically prohibited publicity.

Reporters who attend the youth court in the magistrates' courts (which again is not open to the public) cannot report anything which would lead to the child being identified unless the court permits it. (Children and Young Persons Act 1933, s 49 (as amended). By contrast, by virtue of s 39 of the same Act, in the crown court and the magistrates' court the press can identify a juvenile unless the court prohibits such publication.

See further Geoffrey Robertson and Andrew Nicol, *Media Law* (Penguin, 3rd edn, 1992).

Protecting the witness

In child abuse cases child witnesses have been allowed to give their evidence from behind a screen, but the identity of the witness is known. It is simply a device to spare the child the trauma of giving evidence in the face of the court and, more especially, of the accused.

Courts have also had to decide whether in exceptional circumstances the identity of witnesses such as members of the security service can be concealed even from the other side.

In a trial in Belfast in June 1989 Hutton LCJ held that in the particular circumstances of the case such an order could be made, but in that instance the defence raised no objection. The defendants Murphy and Maguire were accused of taking part in the gruesome murder of two British army corporals who became entangled in an IRA funeral in March 1988. The prosecution asked the court to rule that some 27 media witnesses could give their evidence without being identified and that they should not be seen by the accused, the public or the press, but only by the court and the lawyers for each side. Their evidence mainly concerned television footage. The judge held that the witnesses could give their evidence behind a large curtain. (For critical comment see Gilbert Marcus, 'Secret Witnesses', *Public Law*, Summer 1990, p 207.)

7. THE TAKING OF EVIDENCE

In a civil case the case starts with an opening speech for the plaintiff. In a criminal case tried in the crown court the case opens with a speech from prosecution counsel.

(In the magistrates' court the prosecution will not necessarily make an opening speech beyond a statement as to the nature of their case.) The purpose of the opening speech is to set out that side's case and what the witnesses will establish. In Scotland, by contrast, the case starts right away with the prosecution's first witness–no opening speech is permitted. The danger of the English system is that the jury will be prejudiced against the accused by counsel's address, and the more so because, in the event, the prosecution may not actually succeed in proving what counsel's opening speech foreshadowed.

The Runciman Royal Commission on Criminal Justice proposed that unless the judge gave leave, the prosecutor's opening speech should not be longer than 15 minutes and that opening speeches should be limited to an explanation of the issues at trial. They should refer to the evidence to be called only if that was essential to the jury's understanding of the case. The prosecution should not seek to suggest that particular matters will be proved by the prosecution (p 120, paras 8, 9).

The Royal Commission also proposed (p 121, para 10), that the defence should have the option of making their opening speech immediately after the prosecution's opening. This is in fact occasionally done.

The prosecution then call their witnesses in turn. Each witness is examined-in-chief by the prosecution. Examination-in-chief consists of taking the witness through his story stage by stage. The advocate will base his examination of the witness on the information supplied by his instructing solicitors based on their meetings with the witness, which they have reduced to his statement or 'proof'. Barristers are not generally permitted to speak about the evidence to their own witnesses prior to the trial. The only general exceptions are the client and an expert witness.

Examination-in-chief should not generally include 'leading questions'. A leading question is one that suggests the answer ('Did you see the accused at that point raise his arm in a threatening way?' as opposed to 'What did you see then?'). Leading questions are, however, permitted for matter that is wholly uncontroversial ('Is your name John Smith and do you live at ?'). They are also allowed when the purpose is to elicit a denial from the witness ('Did you kill the deceased?').

In civil cases, witness statements that have been compulsorily exchanged now normally stand as the witness' evidence-in-chief–see p 92 above.

At the end of the examination-in-chief the witness is offered to the other side for cross-examination. Cross-examination is the attempt to show that the witness was lying or mistaken, or that he is not a person who can be relied on to tell the truth. It may also be used to establish evidence favourable to the cross-examiner's side. Leading questions are permitted. The witness can be cross-examined about his previous convictions, his bias and his reputation for untruthfulness. But the Bar's *Code of Conduct* says that a barrister must not suggest that a witness or other person is guilty of crime fraud or misconduct or attribute the crime to someone else unless such allegations go to a matter in issue (including the credibility of the witness) which is material to the lay client's case 'and which appear to him to be supported by reasonable grounds' ((para 610(h)). Also a barrister must not make statements or ask questions which 'are merely scandalous or intended or calculated only to vilify insult or annoy either a witness or some other person' (*ibid*, para 610(e)).

In rape cases the Sexual Offences (Amendment) Act 1976, s 2 requires the consent of the judge for questions to be put on behalf of the defendant regarding the complainant's sexual experience with other persons.

The general rule is that evidence is not admissible to contradict answers given in answering questions put in cross-examination. The reason is to confine the scope of the case within reasonable limits. But if the witness has made a prior statement which is inconsistent with his evidence he can be cross-examined about it.

Occasionally, effective cross-examination can be based simply on what the witness has said, by pointing up inconsistencies or improbabilities; usually, however, it requires other material based on work done by those responsible for preparation of the case. Cross-examination is a difficult art and it is not very often that it significantly dents the witness's evidence.

One of the duties of the cross-examiner is to 'put his client's case'. This is because of the technical rule that one cannot call evidence to contradict the opponent's case unless one has challenged the disputed evidence in cross-examination. That is why one so frequently hears counsel say to the witness 'I put it to you that ...'–to which the usual reply is 'No, that is not so.' Nothing much is achieved by such exchanges other than fulfilment of the requirement that the case be 'put' to the witness.

For an assessment of the rules on cross-examination of police witnesses by the defence so as to bring out past discreditable incidents, see David Wolchover, 'Attacking Confessions with Past Police Embarrassments' (1988) *Criminal Law Review*, p 573.

At the close of cross-examination, the witness is offered back to the opponent for re-examination. The purpose of re-examination is not to go over the same ground again, but to clarify or to explain evidence that has emerged during cross-examination. Thus, if in cross-examination reference has been made to part of a conversation favourable to the cross-examiner, questions could be put to draw out other parts of the conversation which put a very different gloss on the matter.

This process of examination-in-chief, cross-examination and re-examination is repeated for each witness in turn. When that process is complete, each party makes a closing speech. In a criminal case the defence has the last word (Criminal Procedure (Right of Reply) Act 1964). In a civil case it is the plaintiff who goes last.

Historically the courts have allowed counsel to take as long as they need to present their case. But increasingly this relaxed attitude is giving way to a new concern to see that litigation does not take more time than is necessary. Thus, the Practice Directions issued in 1995 for proceedings in the Queen's Bench Division and the Chancery Division and for the Family Division stated that the court would increasingly exercise its discretion to limit the length of opening and closing oral submissions, the time allowed for the examination and cross-examination of witnesses, the issues on which it wished to be addressed and reading aloud from documents and authorities. ([1995] 1 All ER 385, para 2; [1995] 1 All ER 385, para 2.)

The final stage is the process of actual decision. In a case with a jury, the judge sums up on the facts and the law (see pp 396–400 below) and the jury then decides. In a criminal trial with a jury the question of sentence is solely for the judge. Juries, as will be seen, are rare in civil cases. Usually, therefore, it is simply a matter of the court reaching and announcing its decision. In the High Court (but not always in the county or magistrates' court) it will normally also give a reasoned judgment.

See further: Richard du Cann, *The Art of the Advocate* (Penguin, revised edn, 1993).

The role of the justices' clerk

One of the peculiarities of the English legal system is the role of the justices' clerk. Most magistrates are laymen and it is therefore right that the system provides them with expertise in the shape of the clerk. The position of clerk comprises many duties. He runs the court, helps to train the new magistrates, administers the legal aid system in his court and is chief legal adviser to the bench. In almost all courts the clerk himself is a lawyer.

But the clerk to the justices has in fact so many administrative duties that he rarely finds time to be in court. The task of guiding the justices from day-to-day in court actually falls on his assistants, known as court clerks. Some of these have professional qualifications as barristers and solicitors but many more have not. (It seems that in 1987, of the 1,300 or so court clerks, only about a quarter had a professional qualification as a barrister or solicitor.) They may be law graduates, but many court clerks come to the job straight from school. Under Regulations which came into force in 1980 all court clerks are supposed to possess a minimum of legal education (at least a Diploma of Magisterial Law, available from certain former polytechnics). If not exempt by virtue of experience, a court clerk must be a barrister or a solicitor or have been employed in a magistrates' court for not less than two years and have passed a preliminary exam.[12] But the fact of the matter is that a large number of court clerks have only the slenderest of qualifications. Since the bench itself is composed of lay persons, this is plainly a highly unsatisfactory situation.

The function of the clerk has undergone certain changes in the past decade. In the 1950s it was laid down that the clerk must be, and be seen to be, subservient to the bench and that although the clerk could for instance retire with the bench when they went to consider their decision, he should do so only on invitation and should emerge before the justices. See *Practice Direction* [1953] 2 All ER 1306.

But in more recent years the crucial role played by the clerk has increasingly been recognized and the courts have now rather changed their emphasis when dealing with the delicate balance of power between the clerk and the bench.

In July 1981 a Practice Direction was issued giving the latest official statement of the role of the clerk. This appeared to approve consultation with the clerk even more than before:

Practice Direction [1981] 2 All ER 831

1. A justices' clerk is responsible to the justices for the performance of any of the functions set out below by any member of his staff acting as court clerk and may be called in to advise the justices even when he is not personally sitting with the justices as clerk to the court.

2. It shall be the responsibility of the justices' clerk to advise the justices as follows: (a) on questions of law or of mixed law and fact; (b) as to matters of practice and procedure.

3. If it appears to him necessary to do so, or he is so requested by the justices, the justices' clerk has the responsibility to (a) refresh the justices' memory as to any matter of evidence and to draw attention to any issues involved in the matters before the court; (b) advise the justices generally on the range of penalties which the law allows them to impose and on any guidance relevant to the choice of penalty provided by the law, the decisions of the superior courts or

---

12 Justices' Clerks Qualifications Rules 1979, SI 1979/570.

other authorities. If no request for advice has been made by the justices, the justices' clerk shall discharge his responsibility in court in the presence of the parties.

4. The way in which the justices' clerk should perform his functions should be stated as follows: (a) The justices are entitled to the advice of their clerk when they retire in order that the clerk may fulfil his responsibility outlined above. (b) Some justices may prefer to take their own notes of evidence. There is, however, no obligation on them to do so. Whether they do so or not, there is nothing to prevent them from enlisting the aid of their clerk and his notes if they are in any doubt as to the evidence which has been given. (c) If the justices wish to consult their clerk solely about the evidence or his notes of it, this should ordinarily, and certainly in simple cases, be done in open court. The object is to avoid any suspicion that the clerk has been involved in deciding issues of fact.

There is no requirement that the clerk advise the justices in open court on the law. For a strong argument that this should be changed, see A Heaton-Armstrong, 'The Verdict of the Court and its Clerk? Can Justice be Seen to be Done Behind Closed Doors?', *Justice of the Peace*, 31 May 1985, p 340; 7 June 1985, p 357.

In recent years there has in fact increasingly been a suggestion that the role of the clerk might expand to include actual judicial functions. The first step in that direction was taken in the Justices' Clerks Rules of 1970, which allowed clerks to hear applications for summonses. But it has been suggested that they should be allowed to rule formally on the admissibility of evidence and to sum up points for the justices. They would then be acting very much like the judge with a jury. One strong argument for such a development is that it would make the administration of justice more open,. The parties would be able to see on what basis the case was being approached and what law was being applied.

For further reading on the role of the justices' clerk, see especially Brian Harris, 'Role of the Justices' Clerks', *New Law Journal*, 1973, pp 360 and 384; Cecil Latham, *Justice of the Peace* 22 February 1975, p 106; March 1, 1975, p 120; 8 March 1975, p 130; Mervyn Burton, 'May it Please Your Clerkship', *New Law Journal*, 28 July 1977, p 728; Elizabeth Burney, *Magistrate, Court and Community* (Hutchinson, 1979), ch 9; Sir Thomas Skyrme, *The Changing Image of the Magistracy* (Macmillan, 1979), ch 12; Penny Darbyshire, 'The Role of the Magistrates' Clerk in Summary Proceedings', *Justice of the Peace*, 29 March 1980, p 186; 5 April 1980, p 201; 12 April 1980, p 219; 19 April 1980, p 233; Darbyshire, *The Magistrates' Clerk* (Barry Rose, 1984); and Andrew Pote and Elaine Houlton, 'Proactive Clerking or "Sans Peur et sans Reproche" ', *Justice of the Peace* 11 April 1992, p 227.

8. THE EXCLUSIONARY RULES OF EVIDENCE

One of the chief differences between the English and the continental systems is that the English excludes various categories of evidence in spite of the fact that they are relevant to the matters in dispute. The exclusionary rules of evidence fall into three main categories: (*a*) evidence excluded because it might be unduly prejudicial; (*b*) evidence excluded because it is inherently unreliable; and (*c*) evidence excluded because it is against the public interest that it be admitted.

(a) Evidence excluded because it might be unduly prejudicial

Bad character and prior convictions

The basic English rule is that the court in a criminal case should not receive evidence of the accused's bad character or of his 'disposition' to commit the offence of which he is charged. (Note that in the United States the rule is very different–a defendant's prior convictions can generally be proved there if he takes the witness stand.) In civil-law countries the accused's character and background, including previous convictions, are regarded as fully admissible on the question of whether or not he is guilty.

The impact of the English rule is typified by the case which follows.

R v Coombes (1960) 45 Cr App Rep 36 (Court of Criminal Appeal)

The appellant was charged with indecent assault on a married woman. His defence was accident and the absence of guilty intent. With permission of the court, prosecuting counsel asked the appellant whether a few months before he had pleaded guilty to indecent assault on a twelve-year-old girl. The appellant admitted this but no further evidence about the affair was produced.

Lord Parker CJ, giving the judgment of the court, said:

'It is perfectly clear that evidence of a previous offence is admissible to rebut a defence of innocent intent; but the offence which it is sought to adduce in evidence must be of similar character [see p 325 below for this exception (ed)]. There is no clear authority as to how similar the offence must be to make it admissible;' but there must be some nexus both in time and in the nature of the offence. In the present case the Chairman was not told in detail what the offence was, except that it involved a young girl. ...

If the prosecution had called the police officer and if he had given detailed evidence of the nature of the previous offence, would not any chairman have said: 'This is just the sort of evidence which will inflame the jury, where the prejudicial value would far exceed the probative value', and on that ground excluded it? The Chairman did not have that evidence before him when he ruled. In these circumstances the court feels that it is possible to interfere with the Chairman's discretion and hold that the evidence ought not to have been admitted. ...

The court has considered whether this is a case where the proviso to section 4(1) of the Criminal Appeal Act, 1907, should be applied.[13] It follows from what I have said that this is not the sort of case where the proviso could be applied. If, as we hold, this evidence was likely to inflame the jury, it is quite impossible to say that without it they must have come to the same conclusion. In those circumstances the court feels that it is unsafe to let this conviction stand and it must be quashed.

Even when the evidence of previous convictions is technically admissible (see below), the court has a general discretion to refuse to permit cross-examination about past convictions where it believes the prejudicial effect outweighs the probative value of such evidence: *Selvey v DPP* [1968] 2 All ER 497. See generally R Pattenden, 'The Purpose of Cross-Examination under s 1(*f*) of the Criminal Evidence Act 1898 (1982). *Criminal Law Review*, p 706.

Exceptions to the general rule

There are, however, four main exceptions to the general rule that evidence of past misconduct is not admissible in evidence against the accused:

13 See p 566 below (ed).

(1) Asserting good character

Where the accused asserts his good character the prosecution are entitled to show that this is a misrepresentation. For consideration of what amounts to putting one's character forward, see *Stronoch* [1988] Crim LR 48.

(2) Imputations about prosecution witnesses

Where the accused makes imputations about the character of prosecution witnesses, the prosecution can, in the discretion of the court, introduce his previous convictions. This was established in the Criminal Evidence Act 1898, s 1(*f*)(ii), which provides an exception to the general rule where 'the nature or conduct of the defence is such as to involve imputations on the character of the prosecutor or the witness for the prosecution'. The rationale of the rule is that where there is a conflict of evidence between the prosecution and defence and the defence makes allegations about the character of the prosecution witnesses, it is right that the jury or magistrates should know what kind of a person the accused is in order better to judge who is telling the truth. Alto the rule helps to protect the witnesses from totally unfounded attacks which might otherwise serve as the accused's only form of defence. On the other hand, the rule creates a difficult dilemma for the accused with a record. Moreover, where the attack is entirely justifiable, it is arguably wrong to penalize the defendant for making it. It is perhaps also wrong to have a rule the effect of which may be to inhibit well-founded attacks on prosecution witnesses. If it is right generally to withhold evidence of past misconduct from the court on the ground that it is unduly prejudicial, it does not become any the less prejudicial simply because the accused has attacked prosecution witnesses.

In the case of *R v Britzman and Hall* [1983] 1 All ER 369, the Court of Appeal tried to settle the circumstances in which the imputations would entitle the prosecution to introduce evidence of the defendant's convictions from those which would not have this result. Lord Justice Lawton said (at p 373) that it might be of assistance to judges and counsel if the court set out some guidelines as to how the judges should exercise their discretion:

First, it should be used if there is nothing more than a denial, however emphatic or offensively made, of an act or even a short series of acts amounting to one incident or in what was said to have been a short interview. Examples are provided by the kind of evidence given in pickpocket cases and where the defendant is alleged to have said: 'Who grassed on me this time?' The position would be different however if there were a denial of evidence of a long period of detailed observation extending over hours and, just as in this case and in *R Tanner*, where there were denials of long conversations.

Second, cross-examination should only be allowed if the judge is sure that there is no possibility of mistake, misunderstanding or confusion and that the jury will inevitably have to decide whether the prosecution witnesses have fabricated evidence. Defendants sometimes make wild allegations when giving evidence. Allowance should be made for the strain of being in the witness box and the exaggerated use of language which sometimes results from such strain or lack of education or mental instability. Particular care should be used when a defendant is led into making allegations during cross-examination. The defendant who, during cross-examination, is driven to explaining away the evidence by saying it has been made up or planted on him usually convicts himself without having his previous convictions brought out. Finally, there is no need for the prosecution to rely on s 1(*f*)(ii) if the evidence against a defendant is overwhelming.

On the facts the court did not interfere with the judge's exercise of discretion. The defendants had denied having made admissions to a police officer and denied having had a shouted conversation from one cell to another with each other which included some further admissions. These denials necessarily meant that the officers had given false evidence. Lord Justice Lawton said: 'On the facts of this case there could be no question of mistake, misunderstanding or confusion' (at p 372). They must have committed wilful perjury. The conversation reported by the officers was long 'and of a kind which could have appeared in a television script for a crime series'. The only possibility was that they had made the evidence up and this allowed the prosecution to introduce their previous convictions. The Court of Appeal agreed.

One of the peculiarities of the rule is that when previous convictions or other evidence of bad character are admitted it is only evidence as to the creditworthiness of the accused. It is not supposed to be considered by the jury as evidence tending to show a propensity to commit the offence in question. This was laid down by Viscount Dilhorne in *Selvey v DPP* [1968] 2 All ER 497, HL, at 508. It seems unlikely, however, that the average juror can perceive the difference between considering previous convictions as evidence of a disposition to commit the offence in question (forbidden) and evidence showing the defendant to be a person of dubious credibility (legitimate). Once the prior convictions are in, the jury are likely to draw adverse inferences—especially if the prior convictions are of a similar kind.

Until quite recently, prior convictions of a similar kind were banned even when they went to creditworthiness, unless they qualified for admissibility under the similar facts rule (below). But the latest cases changed this rule.

In *R v Watts (Idwal)* (1983) 77 Cr App Rep 126, the defendant was accused of indecent assault on a young married woman in an underpass. According to police officers, the accused made an oral admission and later dictated a confession which he signed. The accused, who was of low intelligence and suffered from epileptic fits, later denied the offence and set up an alibi defence. In effect he said the police evidence was fabricated. The prosecution was given leave to cross-examine him on his previous convictions for sexual assaults on his two nieces aged five and three. The Court of Appeal allowed his appeal and quashed the conviction on the ground that the judge had wrongly exercised his discretion. The jury had been correctly instructed that they were only to consider the previous convictions on the question of credibility and that it was not relevant on the question whether it made it more probable that the accused committed the offence. But it would have been practically impossible for the jury to have performed such intellectual acrobatics.

However, in two more recent cases the Court of Appeal effectively changed its mind. In *Burke* [1985] Crim LR 660, the accused was charged with offences of supplying drugs. He made blatant imputations on the character of the prosecution witnesses and was cross-examined on previous drug offences. Lord Justice Ackner said that in *Watts* the Court of Appeal's attention had not been drawn to the House of Lords decision in *Selvey* and especially to the fact that in that case the judge had specifically confined cross-examination to prior convictions of a similar kind–and the House of Lords had not commented adversely on the fact, which should be taken to be implicit approval of the judge's exercise of his discretion.

In *Powell* [1985] 1 WLR 1364, Lord Lane, who had also taken part in *Watts*, in effect said that *Watts* had been wrongly decided in the light of *Selvey* (as now reinterpreted). P was convicted of living off immoral earnings of prostitution. He claimed that police officers had lied about their observations of him with prostitutes. The prosecution got permission to cross-examine him about prior convictions for allowing the premises to be used for prostitution. The judge said he would not have permitted it simply to counter the attack on the police witnesses, but he did so on the ground that the defendant had put his character in issue. The fact that the prior convictions were for similar offences was a matter to be taken into account by the judge when deciding how to exercise his discretion but it did not oblige him to disallow the proposed cross-examination.

For a statement of the principles to be followed in these cases see *McLeod* [1994] 3 All ER 254. For a comment suggesting that the law on this issue is now in a hopeless muddle, based on a lack of logic, a lack of commonsense and a lack of intellectual rigour, see Roderick Munday, 'Stepping Beyond the Bounds of Credibility: The Application of s 1(*f*)(ii) of the Criminal Evidence Act 1898' (1986) *Criminal Law Review*, p 511. See also comment on *Powell* in (1986) *Criminal Law Review*, p 176, and on *Burke* in (1986) *Criminal Law Review*, p 662; and S Seabrooke, 'Closing the Credibility Gap: A New Approach to s 1(*f*)(ii) of the Criminal Evidence Act 1898' (1987) *Criminal Law Review*, p 231. See also in particular AAS Zuckerman, *The Principles of Criminal Evidence* (Clarendon, 1989), ch 13.

The Criminal Law Revision Committee in its 1972 report made a proposal (by a majority) for an important change in the rule, whereby it would only apply if the main purpose of the attack was to challenge the credibility of the witness. If the attack was necessary in order to put the defence case, it would not expose the accused to cross-examination on his record. So a person charged with assault could with impunity put forward the defence that the alleged victim himself was the aggressor. Similarly, a defendant would be able to say that the police extorted his confession or planted evidence on him because in both cases the main purpose would be to challenge not the credibility of the witness but the prosecution's evidence (Criminal Law Revision Committee, 'Evidence (General)', *Eleventh Report*, 1972, Cmnd 4991, paras 123–30). The proposal was supported by the Runciman Royal Commission on Criminal Justice in its 1993 Report (Cm 2263, p 127, para 33). However, the proposal has not been implemented.

(3) Similarity of facts

A third exception to the general rule is where the facts in the present case are sufficiently similar to the facts in previous incidents to make it legitimate for them to be made known to the jury. This rule used to apply only where the similarity was very striking, so as virtually to rule out the possibility of coincidence:

R v Straffen [1952] 2 QB 911 (Court of Criminal Appeal)

Appellant was found guilty of strangling a small girl. At his trial the prosecution were allowed to prove that he had previously been charged with two similar murders to which he was found unfit to plead by reason of insanity. On appeal it was argued that this evidence should not have been admitted.

Slade J, giving the judgment of the court, said:

The evidence with regard to the Bath murders was tendered and admitted for the purpose of showing that the same person killed all three little girls; that is to say, that the person who strangled Brenda Goddard and Cicely Batstone, in the circumstances described, also manually strangled Linda Bowyer in similar circumstances as regards the method of death, the precision of the strangulation, and the other similar circumstances to which I have referred. In the opinion of the court that evidence was rightly admitted, not for the purpose of showing, to use Mr Elam's words, that the appellant was 'a professional strangler', but to show that he strangled Linda Bowyer; in other words, for the purpose of identifying the murderer of Linda Bowyer as being the same individual as the person who had murdered the other two little girls in precisely the same way.

I can see no distinction in principle between the present case and *Thompson v R*[14] to which we were referred, and, indeed, I think one cannot distinguish abnormal propensities from identification. Abnormal propensity is a means of identification. In the *Thompson*'s case evidence was admitted to prove his identity which showed that he was a person who suffered from the abnormal propensity of homosexuality. It is an abnormal propensity to strangle young girls and to do so without any apparent motive, without any attempt at sexual interference, and to leave their dead bodies where they can be seen and where, presumably, their deaths would be detected. In the judgment of the court, that evidence was admissible because it tended to identify the person who murdered Linda Bowyer with the person who confessed in his statements to having murdered the other two girls a year before, in exactly similar circumstances.

Mr Elam asked: 'How far does the admissibility of such evidence go? Would it extend to the case of a burglar, housebreaker, thief, and so on?' Speaking for myself, I think that if the question of identity arose in a case of housebreaking and it were possible to adduce evidence that there was some hallmark or other peculiarity in relation to earlier housebreakings which were also apparent in the case of the housebreaking charged, so as to stamp the accused man, not only with the housebreaking charged but with the earlier housebreakings, and there was a confession or other evidence that he had committed the earlier housebreakings, that would fall within the same principle of admissibility, not to prove his propensity for housebreaking, but to prove that he was the person who had committed the housebreaking charged.

In a case of bizarre and unique facts like that of *Straffen* the possibility that a different person might have committed both murders is so improbable as to be completely discounted. But the courts have not always been so scrupulous in applying the principle. Thus, for instance, in *Barrington* [1981] 1 All ER 1132 the Court of Appeal upheld a conviction of indecent assault where the similar facts were that the accused had in each case lured young girls to a house on the pretext that they were required as baby-sitters when in fact he showed them pornographic pictures and photographed them in the nude. The Court of Appeal allowed the conviction to stand even though in the previous three 'similar' instances the girls had not actually been indecently assaulted. It was sufficient that there was similarity as to the 'surrounding circumstances'!

In *Makin v A-G for New South Wales* [1894] AC 57, Lord Herschell LC laid down a two-pronged test for dealing with similar-fact evidence. First the prosecution was forbidden to adduce evidence of prior convictions in order to show that the accused was a person likely because of his criminal conduct or character to have committed the present offence. Such evidence would be admissible, however, if it was 'relevant to an issue before the jury' and it might be so relevant if 'it bears upon the question whether the acts alleged, were designed or accidental, or to rebut a defence which would, be open to the accused' (at p 65). Other examples allowed by the judges include to show system or to rebut a defence of innocent association.

14 [1918] AC 221.

But in *Boardman v DPP* [1974] 3 All ER 887, the House of Lords considerably broadened the test. B, a schoolmaster, was charged with counts of buggery with two boys in the school. Their accounts of the incidents were similar but there was nothing to make the circumstances 'strikingly similar' or unusual. Nevertheless the House of Lords ruled that the evidence of both cases could fairly be put to the jury at the same time. It sought to protect the vulnerability of the accused to multiple false accusations based on potentially contaminated evidence by proposing severance of counts relating to the different witnesses, or if they were to be tried together, to exclude the evidence relating to any such witness, unless the judge was satisfied that there had been no contamination.

The ruling in *Boardman* was applied in 1991 in *R v P* [1991] 3 All ER 337, where P was charged with rape of and incest with his two daughters. The trial judge had allowed the jury to hear the allegations of both sisters in the same case. The Court of Appeal quashed the convictions on the ground that there had not been such striking similarities between the girls' accounts of their father's behaviour toward them to permit the evidence of one girl properly to be admitted on the trial of the counts relating to the other.

The House of Lords allowed an appeal by the prosecution. In a speech given by the Lord Chancellor, Lord Mackay, the House of Lords held that evidence of an offence against one victim could be admitted at the trial of an allegation against another if the probative force of the evidence to be admitted was sufficiently great as to make it just to admit it notwithstanding that it was prejudicial to the accused. It was not essential to show that the similarities were 'striking' or that the circumstances were unusual. It was not even necessary to show that there was similarity beyond the stock-in-trade of offenders of that kind. The probative force of the evidence could come from an infinite variety of circumstances. But where the identity of the perpetrator was in issue there would normally need to be some evidence of his 'signature' or other special feature.

In the particular case both girls described a prolonged course of conduct. Force was used in both cases. Both girls were threatened if they told anyone. The father paid for abortions for both girls. Here the identity of the perpetrator was not in issue. It was simply a question of whether the father had committed these offences. Lord Mackay said (at p 347): 'In my view these circumstances taken together gave strong probative force to the evidence of each of the girls in relation to the incidents involving the other, and was certainly sufficient to make it just to admit that evidence, notwithstanding its prejudicial effect.'

The issue was considered again by the House of Lords in *R v H* [1995] 2 All ER 865, again a case concerning sexual offences allegedly committed by a father against an adopted daughter, over a period of two years starting when she was nine and against a step-daughter over the same period starting when she was 14. There had been no complaint for five years. The prosecution accepted that there was a danger of contamination of the evidence by collusion between the two girls. There was no particular similarity in the offences charged. The House of Lords held that where similar fact evidence was put forward as corroboration and there was a risk of contamination by collusion (whether deliberate or through the unconscious influence of one witness by another), the admissibility of such evidence should first be considered, without reference to the risk of collusion, by the judge applying the test of whether, if assumed to be true, the similar fact evidence was so probative of the crime that it ought to be admitted notwithstanding its prejudicial effect. If the evidence was admitted it was then for the jury to determine its credibility after it had been warned by the judge that they had to be satisfied that it was not tainted by collusion or other defects. If it became apparent that no reasonable jury could regard the evidence as free from collusion the judge should rule that it could not be regarded as evidence against the accused.

For commentary on the decision in *H* see the note by Professor John Smith in [1995] *Criminal Law Review*, 718–20. For a devastating critique of the decision see Colin Tapper, 'The Erosion of *Boardman v DPP*', *New Law Journal*, 11 August 1995, p 1223 and 18 August, p 1263. Professor Tapper concluded: 'The result in *H* was to remove the last vestiges of the breakthrough made by *Boardman* in relation to the admissibility of similar fact evidence. After *P* it seems that the relevance of evidence of allegations of other offences is to be assumed without explanation of the reasoning process involved, and after *H* the evidence is to be assumed to be true' (at p 1264). In light of this there was little if anything to be weighed in the balance on the probative force side of the balance. The result was authorisation of 'the most unfair evidence'.

Prior convictions in handling cases

There is a statutory exception to the general rule of non-admissibility of previous convictions in s 27(3)(b) of the Theft Act 1968, which permits the prosecution to introduce the accused's previous convictions for handling stolen goods where the prosecution evidence has established that he had stolen property in his possession or that he had arranged for its disposal. The judge retains a discretion not to permit this where its effect would be more prejudicial than probative (*Herron* [1967] 1 QB 107). See R Munday, 'Handling Convictions Admissible under s 27(3) of the Theft Act 1968', *Justice of the Peace*, 8 April, 1995, p 223, 22 April, p 261. Dr Munday's article is a comment on the decision of the House of Lords in *Hacker* [1994] 1 WLR 1659. He suggests that the law lords gave the subsection 'a new lease of life, encouraging courts to admit evidence under a renegade provision which offends against what orthodox lawyers would count fundamental principles of the law of evidence' (p 223).

For discussions of the cases more generally, see DW Elliot, 'The Young Person's Guide to Similar Fact Evidence' (1983) *Criminal Law Review*, pp 284, 352; and PB Carter, 'Forbidden Reasoning Permissible: Similar Fact Evidence a Decade after *Boardman*', 48 *Modern Law Review*, 1985, p 29. See also Adrian Zuckerman, 'Similar Fact Evidence: The Unobservable Rule' [1987] 104 *Law Quarterly Review*, p 187, or chapter 12 of his book *The Principles of Criminal Evidence* (Clarendon, 1989). See also *Cross on Evidence*, 7th edn (1990) pp 353–360.

(4) Evidence by co-accused

The fourth exception to the general rule is that, where one co-accused (A) gives evidence against another co-accused (B), B can cross-examine A about his previous convictions. The rationale here is that from B's point of view A has virtually become a witness for the prosecution. The Criminal Evidence Act 1979 extended this exception to the general rule to cases where the co-accused are not charged with the same offence. (See on this exception R Munday, 'The Wilder Permutations of s 1(f) of the Criminal Evidence Act 1898', *Legal Studies*, July 1987, p 137. See also Zuckerman, *Principles of Criminal Evidence, op cit*, pp 280–3.)

It seems that the court has no discretion provided that such cross examination is relevant to the accused's credibility as a witness. See *Murdoch v Taylor* [1965] AC 574; *Reid* [1989] Crim LR 719.

The CLRC's modest proposal

The 1972 Report of the Criminal Law Revision Committee (paras 92–4) proposed a further, fifth situation in which previous convictions or other past misconduct should be admissible in evidence. This was where the accused did not deny that the conduct complained of had occurred, but maintained that he did not have the requisite criminal intent: that he entered the building but did so in a state of automatism or that he took the little girl into the bushes but only to show her some wild flowers. In such a case the prosecution should be permitted to prove similar previous convictions to show that the intent was in fact guilty. The proposal was supported by the Runciman Royal Commission on Criminal Justice in its 1993 report (Cm 2263, p 126, para 31).

The apparent importance of this recommendation became clear when it emerged from research that this was the type of defence in no fewer than seven out of ten cases of acquittal in a sample of 115 acquittals at assizes and quarter sessions. In one half of the cases where this was the defence, the accused had had previous convictions. (See Sarah McCabe and Robert Purves, *The Jury at Work*, Occasional Papers No 42 (Blackwell, 1972), pp 40–1, and, to same effect, M Zander, 'Are Too Many Professional Criminals Avoiding Conviction?' 37 *Modern Law Review*, 1974, p 59, n 50.)

But later research on a large sample of cases in London and Birmingham by Drs Baldwin and McConville suggested that in fact the recommendation was not after all so significant. In each city about 40 per cent of the defendants admitted the act but denied the *mens rea* or intent. But in about seven out of eight of these cases, the accused either had no similar previous convictions (in which case, the CLRC's recommendation would not operate), or was convicted at the trial (in which case it was unnecessary). (See Michael McConville and John Baldwin, *Courts' Prosecution and Conviction*, 1981, p 120.)

Law Commission review

The Runciman Royal Commission recommended that the whole question of the use in evidence of the defendant's prior convictions or other evidence of past misconduct be reconsidered by the Law Commission. The Law Commission published its Consultation Paper *Evidence in Criminal Proceedings: Previous Misconduct of a Defendant* on 10 July 1996.

Use of prior convictions in civil proceedings

Previous convictions could not until fairly recently be admitted in evidence in civil proceedings arising out of the same facts. A conviction for dangerous driving was therefore not admissible in subsequent proceedings for damages resulting from the same incident. This rule, known as the rule in *Hollington v Hewthorn* [1943] KB 587, was abolished by the Civil Evidence Act 1968, s 11. The conviction is now rebuttable evidence of the facts involved in the offence, save in libel proceedings where the conviction is deemed to be irrebuttable evidence of the facts.

(b) Evidence excluded because it is inherently unreliable

(1) Evidence of children

The law affecting the evidence of children has recently undergone major reform.

The common-law rule was that a witness must not be allowed to give evidence unless he had sworn the oath (or affirmed). There was no precise age at which a child was allowed to take the oath; this was a matter for the judge to determine after talking to the child. In *Campbell* [1983] Crim LR 174 the Court of Appeal quashed the conviction where a judge had allowed the ten-year-old victim of a sexual assault to give sworn testimony without any inquiry as to whether she understood the nature of the oath or of the necessity to speak the truth. In *Brasier* (1779) 1 Leach 199, the court said that a child as young as seven could be sworn. In *Hayes* [1977] 1 WLR 234, the court said the dividing line was probably between eight and ten. The question was whether there was an appreciation of the solemnity of the occasion and the special responsibility to tell the truth conveyed by the oath.

But in criminal cases there was statutory power to receive unsworn evidence from children provided that the judge thought the child had 'sufficient intelligence to justify the evidence being taken and understood the duty of telling the truth' (Children and Young Persons Act, 1933, s 38). In *Wallwork* (1958) 42 Cr App Rep 153, Lord Goddard LCJ expressed astonishment that the trial judge had allowed a child of five to give evidence. That view was supported by the Court of Appeal in *Wright* (1987) 90 Cr App Rep 91. But in February 1990 the Lord Chief Justice in *R v Z* [1990] 2 QB 355 upheld the trial judge's decision to hear evidence from a six-year-old. (The judge said she seemed to be a perfectly intelligent girl able to give her account of events.) Lord Lane said that the decision in *Wallwork* had to some extent been overtaken by events– notably by the new possibility of children giving their evidence by video link and the abolition of the requirement of corroboration of the evidence of children (see below).

The recent reforms followed growing concern in the late 1980s about the difficulty of securing convictions in serious sex abuse cases involving young children. Also they were premised on a sense that the evidence of young children was by no means necessarily as unreliable as had previously been thought. One reason is that very young children (unless they have seen pornographic videos) would not have the knowledge about sex to invent the stories they tell. There is now a body of research data that conflicts with the traditional view that the evidence of young children is less reliable than that of adults.[15]

---

15 For a review of empirical research evidence, see JR Spencer and Rhona Flin, 'Child Witnesses–Are They Liars?', *New Law Journal*, 24 November 1989, p 1603. Their conclusion was that the evidence did not support the traditional view that children are more likely to tell lies than adults, and it contradicted the view that the younger the child, the more likely it is that he or she will lie. On the empirical evidence see also Ray Bull, 'Children as Witnesses', 4 *Policing*, 1988, p 130.

One piece of research was reported by G Davies, A Tarrant and R Flin, 'Close Encounters of the witness kind: children's memory/a simulated health inspection', *British Journal of Psychology*, 1989. The study tested 128 boys and girls split into age groups of 6 to 7 and 10 to 11. The test involved direct confrontation between the child and an adult stranger in which the child was touched and an article of clothing (shoes) removed. The two age groups did not differ in their ability to help produce a photofit of the man. The report says 'Even the youngest subjects tested could have provided evidence on a number of points relevant to the main theme of events which would have been accurate in essentials and of interest to the court.'

The Criminal Law Revision Committee recommended in its 1972 Report that children under 14 should always give evidence unsworn and that children over 14 should always give sworn evidence. The Pigot Committee (*The Report of the Advisory Group on Video Recorded Evidence*, Home Office, December 1989[16] agreed. The Pigot Committee thought that if a child's account of the matter was available it should be heard. The question of what weight to place upon it should be one for the jury. This would, however, be subject to the overriding discretion of the judge to rule the witness incompetent if he or she 'became incoherent' or failed 'to communicate in a way that makes sense' (para 5–13).

This recommendation was adopted by the Government for criminal cases. Section 52 of the Criminal Justice Act 1991 (adding a new s 33A to the Criminal Justice Act 1988) requires all witnesses under 14 in criminal cases to give unsworn evidence. The competency test for child witnesses was therefore put on the same basis as for adults. The judge has a right to stand down a witness who seems to lack the knowledge or intelligence necessary to understand the nature of the oath. It was suggested that this could therefore lead to a reintroduction of pre-examination of children by the judge, which is what the reform was supposed to abolish.[17] But in the Criminal Justice and Public Order Act 1994 new words were added to s 33A(2) the effect of which is to provide that a child's evidence shall be received save that the court can exclude any evidence of a witness under the age of 14 'where it appears to the court that the witness is incapable of giving intelligible testimony' (CJPOA, 1994, Sch 9, para 33). In *R v D* (1995) Times, 15 November, the Court of Appeal, Criminal Division held that in deciding the competency of a child witness in a criminal trial, the court should ask if he could understand questions and respond coherently and intelligibly, though it remained relevant to inquire as to his ability to distinguish between truth and fiction and between fact and fantasy as part of that test.

The second reform was in regard to the requirement that the unsworn evidence of children in criminal cases had to be corroborated (Children and Young Persons Act, 1933, s 38). This was joined with a further rule that the unsworn evidence of one child could not corroborate the unsworn evidence of another child, however cogent the evidence (*Hester* [1973] AC 296). The effect of these rules was to make it impossible in some cases to get convictions of offenders in extremely serious sexual abuse cases.

The requirement of corroboration for the unsworn evidence of children was abolished by the Criminal Justice Act 1988, s 34(1). Section 34(3) also provided that unsworn evidence could corroborate the evidence, whether sworn or unsworn, of anyone.

Prior to 1988 the sworn evidence of a child did not technically require corroboration but the judge had to warn the jury of the danger of relying on such uncorroborated evidence. The requirement of that warning has now also been abolished by s 34(2) of the 1988 Act–unless such a warning is required in relation the evidence of an adult witness.

---

16 See Jennifer Temkin, 'Child Sexual Abuse and Criminal Justice', *New Law Journal*, 16 March 1990, p 352, and 23 March 1990, p 410. For an article expressing some concerns about the report see K Stevenson and U Sood, 'Pigot: The Need for a Good Look at Videos', *Law Society's Gazette*, 16 May 1990, p 23. There is also an important Scottish report by the Scottish Law Commission ('The Evidence of Children and Other Potentially Vulnerable Witnesses', Discussion Paper No 75, June 1988). For an evaluation of this report in the light of English law and practice, see Jenny McEwan, 'Child Evidence: More Proposals for Reform' (1988) *Criminal Law Review*, p 813.
17 This point was made by JR Spencer in *New Law Journal*, 14 December 1990, p 1750.

The third area of reform is to permit children to give evidence by live video link instead of in the actual courtroom. Another recent innovation made by s 32(1) of the Criminal Justice Act 1988 was to allow children under 14 in crown court cases of violence, sexual assault or cruelty to give evidence by a live closed circuit television so that they do not have to face the allegedly abusing adult.[18]

The reform did not go so far as to permit *pre-recorded* video interviews to be admissible–though the Pigot Committee thought this would be desirable. The Committee thought that the child should be interviewed as soon as possible after the report of the incident by a trained interviewer who would follow an official code of practice. A tape of the interview would then be shown to a judge who would decide if it was suitable to be admitted. If the judge decided that it should be admitted, the defence would see the tape and decide whether they wanted to carry out a cross-examination. This could be done as soon as possible at a preliminary hearing held privately in chambers with only the judge, the advocate, the child and a 'support person' there. The defendant would be physically absent, but would be able to watch the proceedings by closed-circuit television, communicating with his lawyer by means of an inconspicuous audio link. The child would be shown the tape and would be questioned on that in order to spare him or her the ordeal of repeating the harrowing story again from memory. The child would then not appear at the trial. A video tape of the initial interview would replace the child's evidence-in-chief, and a tape of the hearing before the judge would replace live cross-examination.[19]

The chief objections to the Pigot Committee's proposal are that it interferes with the defendant's right to confront prosecution witnesses directly, and that it is hearsay evidence. It is one thing to have the defendant removed from the courtroom slightly by a screen and wholly by a closed-circuit television link. It is something quite different to make it impossible for the defendant to question his accuser at the trial.[20]

The Pigot Committee's recommendation was not accepted. But the Criminal Justice Act 1991 did contain two sections that represented a compromise approach to this vexed issue. Section 54 permits the crown court or a youth court at the trial of a case to which s 32 of the 1988 Act (above, adding a new s 32A) applies to admit as evidence-in-chief a video-recording of an interview with a child unless: (a) the child is not available for cross-examination; or (b) there has been a failure to comply with rules about disclosing the circumstances in which the recording was made; or (c) it would not be in the interests of justice to admit the recording. The child must be called and can be cross-examined, but not by the accused himself (s 55(7)).

18 For a description of how this procedure operates and of some of its problems, see C Champness, 'Children's Evidence in Criminal Proceedings', *Law Society's Gazette*, 8 March 1989, p 14.
19 For discussion of rejection of this proposal by the Government, see Jennifer Temkin, 'Doing Justice to Children', *New Law Journal*, 8 March 1991, p 315.
20 The pros and cons of this have been fiercely contested. See, for instance, Glanville Williams, 'Video-taping Children's Evidence' *New Law Journal*, January 30 1987, p 108; April 10, 1987, p 351; April 17, 1987, p 369; JR Spencer, 'Child Witnesses, Video-technology and the Law of Evidence' (1987) *Criminal Law Review*, p 76. See also David PH Jones, 'The Evidence of a Three-year-old child' (1987) *Criminal Law Review*, p 677. For the contrary view, see for instance James Morton, 'Videotaping Children's Evidence–A Reply', *New Law Journal*, 6 March 1987, p 2126. See on this issue Chapness, 'Children's Evidence', op cit, which gives some information about the approach to the problem in the USA.

The effect of this provision could be that eventually video-recordings replace the evidence-in-chief of children in such cases. Note that under s 55 the video-recording would not have to be one prepared specifically for criminal proceedings. (It might even therefore be one made for therapeutic purposes!) But the judge would have to give leave for it to be admitted.

The Home Office and the Department of Health jointly produced a *Memorandum of Good Practice on Video Recorded Interviews with Child Witnesses for Criminal Proceedings* (HMSO, 1992). For description see Brian Ward, 'Children's Evidence', *Solicitors' Journal*, 3 July 1992, p 644 and by the same author, 'Interviewing Child Witnesses', *New Law Journal*, 6 November 1992, p 1547.

As has been seen, there was also a new procedure under the 1991 Act, s 53, to enable the DPP in cases of violence, sexual assault or cruelty to send a case direct to the crown court without committal proceedings. The DPP needed only to certify his opinion that the case falls within the criteria and the onus then fell on the defendant to apply for a discharge on the ground that there was not sufficient evidence. This complemented a further change made in the 1988 Criminal Justice Act, s 33, under which the evidence of children witnesses at 'old-style' full committals in cases of violence, cruelty or sexual assault was to be given by written statements rather than oral evidence unless the defence objected or the child was needed at court by the prosecution for identification purposes. The power to transfer cases direct to the crown court applies generally to victims under 14. But the age limit rises to 18 if a video has been made of the child's evidence (s 53 (6)).

For further reading see especially JR Spencer and Rhona Flin, *The Evidence of Children–The Law and the Psychology* (Blackstone Press, 1990); Alex Samuels, 'Child Witnesses in Criminal Cases', *Law Society's Gazette*, 27 November 1991, p 25. See also a report published by the Home Office in 1992 which showed that child witnesses using video links gave more consistent evidence, more audibly and were less unhappy than those giving evidence in open court. The facility was already available in 36 of the 72 main Crown Court centres and this number would soon rise to 44 (Graham Davies and Elizabeth Noon, *An Evaluation of the Live Link for Child Witnesses*, Home Office, 1992).

(2) Persons of defective intellect

Where it is alleged that a witness lacks the mental capacity to testify, it is for the judge to decide whether he understands the nature of the oath.

(3) Parties

Until modern times both in civil and criminal cases the parties themselves were not permitted to give evidence, because it was thought that their evidence would be unreliable. This was changed for civil cases in 1851 by the Evidence Act of that year. In criminal cases defendants were not permitted to give evidence on oath until 1898, though before that date the judges allowed accused persons to make an unsworn statement from the dock. The present rules regarding occasions when parties need not give evidence fall under the different heading of evidence excluded for reasons of public policy–see below.

(4) Spouses of parties

The spouse of a party was incompetent as a witness on the same basis as the party himself on the grounds of the likely unreliability of the evidence. It was not until the Evidence Amendment Act 1853 that a spouse became a competent witness in a civil case and in the 1898 Criminal Evidence Act that a spouse became a competent witness for the defence in a criminal case. (As will be seen (p 343 below), the spouse is not normally competent for the prosecution.) It seems, however, that a spouse is not a compellable witness for the defence. See TMS Tosswill, 'The Accused's Spouse as a Defence Witness' (1979) *Criminal Law Review*, p 702, and Michael Cohen, 'Are Wives Really so Incompetent?' (1980) *Criminal Law Review*, p 222.

(5) Hearsay evidence

Hearsay evidence is excluded mainly on the ground that it is inherently unreliable. Hearsay evidence very simply defined is that of someone who is not present in court as a witness. If A is the witness, what B said to A is first-hand hearsay; whilst what B said to C, who told A, is second-hand hearsay. A document is hearsay evidence unless its author is there to introduce it in evidence.

The rule has been regarded as one of the essential features of the basic common-law principle that a trial, especially in a criminal case, should be based on evidence given by live witnesses in (open) court subject to cross-examination.

At the Nuremberg trial of the Nazi war criminals there was a clash between the continental systems which permit hearsay evidence, for what it is worth, and the common-law systems which basically reject it. In that situation the common-law countries agreed to accept hearsay evidence.

A dramatic example of the impact of the exclusion of hearsay evidence is *Sparks v Reginam*:

Sparks v R [1964] 1 All ER 727 (Judicial Committee of the Privy Council)

A girl of three was sexually assaulted. The mother asked what the person who did it looked like. She said, 'It was a coloured boy.' The defendant, a staff sergeant in the US Air Force, was a white man. The trial court ruled that the mother could not give in evidence her daughter's statement. On appeal, *inter alia*, against this ruling, Lord Morris, giving the judgment of the Board, said (at p 733):

It becomes necessary therefore to examine the contentions which have been advanced in support of the admissibility of the evidence. It was said that 'it was manifestly unjust for the jury to be left throughout the whole trial with the impression that the child could not give any clue to the identity of her assailant'. The cause of justice is, however, best served by adherence to rules which have long been recognized and settled. If the girl had made a remark to her mother (not in the presence of the appellant) to the effect that it was the appellant who had assaulted her and if the girl was not to be a witness at the trial, evidence as to what she had said would be the merest hearsay. In such circumstances it would be the defence who would wish to challenge a contention, if advanced, that it would be 'manifestly unjust' for the jury not to know that the girl had given a clue to the identity of her assailant. If it is said that hearsay evidence should freely be admitted and that there should be concentration in any particular case on deciding as to its value or weight, it is sufficient to say that our law has not been evolved on such lines, but is firmly based on the view that it is wiser and better that hearsay should be excluded save in certain well-defined and rather exceptional circumstances. [The appeal was allowed on other grounds.]

In an even more remarkable case, *Myers v DPP* [1965] AC 1001, the prosecution foundered because of the hearsay rule. The accused took part in a conspiracy involving the purchase of wrecked cars with their log books, then disguising stolen cars so as to make them conform to the log books of the wrecked cars and selling them as renovated wrecks. In order to prove that the cars were the stolen rather than the wrecked ones, the prosecution called an officer in charge of the records of the manufacturers of the stolen cars to produce microfilms of the cards filled in by workmen showing the numbers of the cylinder blocks which coincided with the cylinder block numbers of the cars sold by the defendants. The majority of the House of Lords held that the admission of the records would be a breach of the rule against hearsay evidence because, as Lord Reid said, 'The entries on the cards were assertions by the unidentifiable men who made them that they had entered numbers which they had seen on the cars'. The problem was dealt with almost immediately by statute in the Criminal Evidence Act 1965, which made admissible business or trade records. (For a striking more recent case, see also *R v Kearley* [1992] 2 All ER 345, HL.)

There have always been a variety of exceptions to the hearsay rule, some statutory, some common law, and in recent years there have been a succession of statutory exceptions and amendments of the rule. As will be seen, p 339 below, in 1995, on the re-commendation of the Law Commission the hearsay rule was effectively abolished in civil cases. In the same year the Law Commission published a report recommending drastic reform of the rule for criminal cases (see p 341 below).

The rule only applies if the statement in question is to be introduced in order to establish the truth of its contents. If it is to be introduced for some other purpose, it does not count as hearsay evidence. This is confusing not only for the student. It causes confusion even for the courts. The distinction drawn is between 'hearsay' and 'direct evidence'. Thus, for instance, the printout from an intoximeter measuring blood alcohol level has been treated not as hearsay but as direct ('real') evidence of the mechanical process. (*Castle v Cross* [1985] 1 All ER 87). In *Taylor v Chief Constable of Cheshire* [1987] 1 All ER 225, the prosecution case depended in part on what three police officers had seen in a video-recording allegedly showing the appellant committing theft from a shop. But the video had mistakenly been erased before the trial. The evidence of what was on the video was held by the Divisional Court not to be hearsay at all but rather direct evidence of what was seen happening at a particular time and place. Similarly, the courts have held that a sketch made by a police officer from a description given by a witness was not hearsay (*Smith, Percy* [1976] Crim LR 511), that a photofit picture compiled by a police officer was not hearsay (*Cook* [1987] Crim LR 402), and that in some circumstances computer printout is not hearsay– *Wood* [1982] Crim LR 667.[1]

However, in *Townsend* [1987] Crim LR 411, the court refused to extend this to a piece of paper on which a victim of a mugging had written the assailant's car number with a defective ball-point pen which only made indentations. The police had been able to blow up the indentations which matched the defendant's car number, but they

---

1   See 'The Admissibility of Statements by Computer' (1981) *Criminal Law Review*, p 387; WMS Tildesley, 'The Admissibility of Computer Print-Outs', *Justice of the Peace*, 15 October 1983, p 661; and generally C Tapper, *Computer Law*, (4th edn, London: Longman, 1989).

had lost the original piece of paper. (The commentator in the *Criminal Law Review* on *Cook* and *Townsend* points to the unsatisfactory nature of these cases.)

Another form of evidence which looks as if it should be treated as hearsay evidence is where it is introduced simply to permit a witness to refresh his memory (for instance in the very common situation where a police officer is permitted to 'refresh' his memory from his notebook), or to show a previous inconsistent statement or a prior consistent statement. Another example of non-hearsay is where the statement is introduced not to show the truth of the statement but rather to show a person's mental state. Thus in *Subramaniam v Public Prosecutor* [1956] 1 WLR 965, the court allowed evidence of threats allegedly made by terrorists to the appellant to be admissible not to show that they intended to carry out those threats but to demonstrate his state of mind where his defence to the charge was duress. (Cf *Blastland* [1986] AC 41 where the House of Lords ruled that the out-of-court statement could only be introduced to show a state of mind where the state of mind was in issue. The charge was murder and buggery. The defence was that the offences had been committed by someone else. The defence wished to introduce statements made by that person to others revealing knowledge of the murder at a time when it was not generally known. The House of Lords held that the purpose of introducing the statement was not to show the other person's state of mind but to show that he had committed the murder. It was therefore not admissible.)

A cynical comment on these examples of 'non-hearsay' is to see them all as ways simply of avoiding the rule–a view expressed by Adrian Zuckerman in his *Principles of Criminal Evidence* (Clarendon, 1989) at p 197:

The methodology just described illustrates a fairly common tendency in this area. A certain type of statement is taken to be reliable. To avoid exclusion the court searches for a convenient tag which may be given to this type of evidence so that it may pass for something other than hearsay. To fulfil its function the tag or label must be associated with admissible evidence ... Once the label is attached to a piece of evidence, the inhibiting effect of the hearsay rule disappears as if by magic.

There are in addition a long list of exceptions to the rule.

Exceptions to the hearsay rule

At common law, an early exception recognized was that a deposition taken before a coroner or justice of the peace might be read at a subsequent trial if the witness was *dead, or too ill* to travel. The exception did not, however, extend to cases where the witness was simply untraceable, even if it could be shown that diligent efforts had been made to find him. (These exceptions are now in the Criminal Justice Act 1925 s 13 (4) (*a*), which provides also for the situation where the witness whose deposition is to be read is proved to be insane or kept out of the way by means of the procurement of the accused or on his behalf.)

Another common-law exception was for the *dying declaration*. This allowed the prosecution in a murder or manslaughter case to introduce in evidence a statement made by the deceased purporting to identify his assailant, providing he had a 'settled and hopeless expectation of death'. If he believed he had a chance of recovery the exception did not apply. For a modern example of the rule, see *Nembhard v R* [1982] 1 All ER 183, where the Judicial Committee of the Privy Council upheld a conviction for murder where the only evidence against the accused was the deceased's alleged statement to his wife that he was going to die and that the defendant had shot him.

A much more important common-law exception in criminal cases is for *admissions or confessions*. If it were not for this exception, a police officer would not be able to tell the court about the accused's alleged self-incriminatory statement. The rationale for the exception was that people do not make false statements to the police to their own detriment; therefore there would be an inherent probability that the statement was true, which would avoid the vice of hearsay statements that they are inherently unreliable and not subject to cross-examination. The rationale is patently unconvincing. First, as is nowadays well known, people do make untrue confessions and admissions— whether to protect others or out of some form of pressure or psychological weakness. Secondly, the issue in regard to confessions in a contested case is often not whether the confession was true or false but whether it was made at all. The real reason for the exception is the need for it if criminals are to be brought to book.

Another common-law exception was for a statement made so close to the event as in effect itself to be part of the event (the '*res gestae' rule*). It used to be thought that the statement had to be actually contemporaneous with the event. Thus in *Bedingfield* (1879) 14 Cox CC 341 the court refused to admit under the *res gestae* doctrine a statement by the victim who came out of her house with her throat slit ('See what Harry's done') because it was not made at the moment of the murderous attack. But this requirement has now been abandoned. See the House of Lords decision in *Andrews* [1987] 1 All ER 513. A was charged with murder by stabbing. The victim was found bleeding heavily a few minutes after the stabbing. A police officer arrived a few minutes later. The victim told the police that the defendant had carried out the stabbing. This statement was admitted as part of the *res gestae* and the ruling was upheld by the House of Lords. Lord Ackner's judgment said that a *res gestae* statement was admissible if it was made in circumstances which were sufficiently spontaneous and contemporaneous with the event to preclude the possibility of concoction or distortion. It had to be so closely associated with the event that the victim's mind was still dominated by it. The decision in *Bedingfield* was overruled. (See to like effect *Turnbull* (1984) 80 Cr App Rep 104, where the court admitted a statement made in a pub some 200 yards away from the scene of the attack and some 45 minutes after it had occurred.)

The common law also allowed statements in *public documents* such as a birth or marriage certificate to be admitted without requiring that the author of the document has to come to court to give evidence. At common law, however, the rule required that the document be available for public inspection. So in *Lilley v Pettit* [1946] KB 401 the court held inadmissible the regimental records of the army unit of the defendant's husband where she had been charged with falsely entering her husband's name as father of her child.

The prosecution wanted to prove that the husband had been abroad at all material times. The evidence was not admissible because the records were not public.

There is another, somewhat odd, category of common-law exception to the hearsay rule–for family-law matters especially where they affect children. The attitude of the courts has been somewhat erratic. In several cases the courts decided that in family-law cases the strict hearsay rule can be relaxed. (See for instance *Official Solicitor v K* [1965] AC 201; *Hurwitt v Hurwitt* (1979) 3 FLR 194; *Edwards v Edwards* [1986] 1 FLR 187; *Thompson v Thompson* [1986] 1 FLR 212; *Webb v Webb* [1986] 1 FLR

541.) But in other cases the courts have insisted on strict compliance with the rules. (See especially *H v H*; *K v K* [1990] Fam 86 in regard to custody and access disputes and *Bradford City Metropolitan Council v K and K* [1990] Fam 140 ('the *Bradford* case').[2]

Concern over the last two of these decisions prompted a last-minute amendment to the Children Act 1989 enabling the Lord Chancellor to provide by order for the admissibility of hearsay evidence in children's proceedings. This was done by the Children (Admissibility of Hearsay Evidence) Order 1990, which was then repeated in the 1991 Order of the same name (SI 1990/1115). The 1990 Order provided that the hearsay rule will not apply in civil proceedings before the High Court or a county court concerning the upbringing, maintenance or welfare of a child. This therefore reversed the effect of *K v K* and the *Bradford* case. The Order also provides that the hearsay rule will not apply in relation to such proceedings in juvenile courts. This refers in particular to care and related proceedings. The 1991 Order extended the new rule to magistrates' courts.

Civil cases

In civil cases the main statutes until 1995 were the Civil Evidence Acts of 1938, 1968 and 1972. Under the 1938 Act, statements in original documents could be admitted to establish a fact of which direct oral evidence would be admissible if the maker of the statement had personal knowledge of the matter or it was part of a continuous record in the performance of a duty and the witness could not attend because he was dead, ill or abroad, or if all reasonable efforts to find him had been made without success. It also allowed the statement to be admitted if the witness was present to avoid delay or cost. The maker of the statement had to have personal knowledge of the facts stated and there were specific requirements that he authenticate the document. Also the statement had to be one made in writing.

The Civil Evidence Act 1968 broadened admissible hearsay to oral statements and also to mechanically recorded statements made by someone under a duty to record such information supplied to him by someone with personal knowledge of the facts. Procedural safeguards required notice to be given in advance to the other side, with full particulars of the hearsay statement in question. If the other party objected, the person whose statement was to be given had to be called in person, unless he was dead, ill or abroad or could not reasonably be expected to remember the matter. The Civil Evidence Act 1972 made the evidence of expert witnesses admissible in the form of their reports without having to call them.

In January 1991 the Law Commission proposed that the hearsay rule should be completely abolished for civil proceedings. The proposal was made in a Consultation Paper ('The Hearsay Rule in Civil Proceedings', Consultation Paper No 117). The proposal was a provisional one, subject to the consultation exercise. The alternative would be to reform the Civil Evidence Act 1968 and procedural rules of court so as to simplify the rule. The Law Commission suggested that, despite reform of the hearsay rule, it was not only difficult to understand but increasingly difficult to reconcile with recent procedural developments such as pre-trial exchange of witness statements. The Commission also drew attention to the fact that the hearsay rule in civil proceedings had already been abolished in Scotland by the Civil Evidence (Scotland) Act 1988.

2   See generally 'Hearsay in Children's Proceedings', 9 *Civil Justice Quarterly*, 1990, p 228.

There was still a case for keeping the hearsay rule in criminal proceedings, especially in jury trials. But jury trials in civil cases were now exceedingly rare. (In 1989 there were only 104 in county courts out of 22,259 trials (para 3.19, p 52).)

The Law Commission said that the chief advantage of abolition of the rule was to simplify the rules of evidence and the elimination of technical objections to the admissibility of relevant evidence. It should be for the parties to decide what evidence would assist their case. In practice they would resort to hearsay evidence only where it was the best they could find.

The Law Commission's views were broadly confirmed in its final report published in 1993 ('The Hearsay Rule in Civil Proceedings', (Law Com No 216)). The Government implemented the recommendations of the report in the Civil Evidence Act 1995. The guiding principle in the Act is that evidence is not to be excluded on the ground that it is hearsay but the court will decide what weight to give to the evidence. The concept of hearsay evidence remains and will likely be regarded as less persuasive than direct evidence. But it will now no longer be excluded on that ground.

Parties are under a duty to give each other notice of their intention to adduce hearsay evidence but this requirement can be waived by the party concerned or by agreement. Rules of court will specify proceedings in which the requirement of notice does not apply. Failure to give such notice does not mean that the evidence cannot be introduced but the court can take that failure into account in considering what weight to place on the evidence and when making costs orders (s 2).

A party can call for cross-examination a person whose statement has been tendered as hearsay evidence and who has not been called to give oral evidence (s 3). Section 4 guides the court as to what factors to weigh in such evidence. These include factors such as whether it would have been reasonable and practicable to have called the maker of the statement, and when the statement was made eg was it made contemporaneously, or whether there was any motive to conceal or misrepresent matters.

See D O'Brien, 'The Rule Against Hearsay RIP', *New Law Journal*, 2 February 1996, p 153 and I Grainger, 'Hearsay Evidence Admissible', *New Law Journal*, 31 May 1996, p 536.

Criminal cases

In criminal cases, too, the hearsay rule has gradually been weakened by statute, though not hitherto as much as in the civil field.

The Criminal Justice Act 1967, s 9, made admissible written witness statements where they are signed, a copy has been served in advance on the other party and no counter-notice has been served objecting to the statement being tendered in evidence. This is very frequently used. Section 2 of the 1967 Act (now s 102 of the Magistrates Courts Act 1980) made written statements admissible in committal proceedings on a similar basis–namely, that they are written, signed and tendered in advance. Again, this is used all the time.

As has been seen, the Criminal Evidence Act 1965 was passed to reverse the House of Lords decision in *Myers v DPP* (p 335 above), by making business and trade records made under a duty to record the information admissible. But this legislation has now been superseded by the much wider provisions of the Police and Criminal Evidence Act 1984, which in turn has been superseded by the even wider provisions of the Criminal Justice Act 1988.

The Police and Criminal Evidence Act, s 68, made admissible statements in any document that form part of a record compiled by a person under a duty or on the basis of information supplied by someone acting under a duty, where the maker of the document is unavailable to give evidence. The supplier of the information must be dead, ill or physically unable to give evidence, abroad or not known, or it must be a situation where it would not be reasonable to expect him to remember the matters recorded.

Section 68 of PACE has, however, now been replaced by Part II and Schedule 2 of the Criminal Justice Act 1988. The purpose of Part II was to establish a new basis for the admissibility of documentary hearsay in criminal proceedings. It classifies documents into three categories: first-hand hearsay, business documents and documents which may fall into either category which are prepared specifically for the purpose of criminal proceedings. The 1988 Act, s 23 made any first-hand hearsay admissible provided the maker is unavailable to give evidence because he is dead or unfit or abroad and it is not reasonably practicable to secure his attendance; or that he cannot be found in spite of all reasonable steps taken. These provisions are similar to those in s 68 of the 1984 Act, but it is no longer possible to tender someone's hearsay statement on the basis that he cannot reasonably be expected to remember the matter. Nor can the maker's statement be admitted when he could not be identified after reasonable efforts made. So documents prepared by unidentified workmen seem now not to be admissible under s 23.

For a dramatic example of the use of s 23 see *R v James* (1995) 160 JP 9, Case No 93/6215/Y2. The defendant was convicted of murder. A crucial witness was R a prostitute who witnessed the killing. She made two statements to the police. In the first she described how the defendant had stabbed the deceased and then with another man (who at the time had been her boy friend) had dragged the body onto some grass and robbed him. Later she made a second statement denying the truth of important parts of the original statement. On the day of the trial R failed to appear. The judge adjourned the case for three days. It transpired that she had gone to Cyprus in order not to have to give evidence. The judge allowed both her statements to be introduced in evidence under s 23. On appeal in March 1995, the Court of Appeal held that the judge had been entitled to reach the decision he did and it upheld the conviction.

Section 24 considerably widened the previous exception for business records by no longer requiring that the business document have been made by someone acting under a duty. It is only necessary to prove that the information contained in the document was supplied by someone who had or might reasonably be supposed to have had personal knowledge of the matter.

Where a statement was prepared for the purposes of a criminal investigation or prosecution it can be introduced in evidence on proof regarding the absence of the maker that he is dead, unfit, abroad, etc, or that he does not give evidence 'through fear or because he is kept out of the way'. See further DJ Birch, 'The Criminal Justice Act–The Evidence Provisions' (1989) *Criminal Law Review*, pp 15–31.

The Runciman Royal Commission on Criminal Justice (Cm 2263, 1993) expressed the view that 'in general, the fact that a statement is hearsay should mean that the court places rather less weight on it, but not that it should be inadmissible in the first place' (p 125, para 26). The probative weight of the evidence should, it thought, 'in principle be decided by the jury for themselves' (*ibid*). It recommended that 'hearsay evidence should be admitted to a greater extent than at present' (*ibid*). But because of the complexity of the hearsay rule it thought that the issues needed thorough exploration by the Law Commission.

The Government referred the question of the hearsay rule to the Law Commission in April 1994 and in July 1995 the Commission produced Consultation Paper No 138, *Evidence in Criminal Proceedings: Hearsay and Related Topics*. The Consultation Paper, which was 266 pages long, suggested that it was right to retain the rule in criminal cases as a protection to the accused. In civil cases the finders of fact were judges; in criminal cases they were jurors and magistrates. But the rules needed reform– 'The rule is excessively complex; this complexity leads to confusion, anomalies and wasted time, both for the court and for the parties. The rule results in the exclusion of cogent evidence even when it is the defence that seeks to adduce it' (para 9.2).

The Commission proposed that as a general rule hearsay should remain inadmissible subject to listed statutory exceptions. These would be first hand oral or documentary hearsay other than the statements of unidentified witnesses. They also would not extend to evidence of any fact of which the witness' oral evidence would not be admissible. The categories of exception would be: (1) where the witness was dead or too ill to attend court; (2) where such steps had been taken as were reasonably practicable to secure his attendance but without success and he was abroad or could not be found; or (3) where the witness refused to give evidence although physically available.

The Commission proposed that there should be a residual discretion to admit hearsay falling outside the stated categories and other preserved exceptions which would extend to multiple as well as first hand-hand hearsay. This should be available only if it appeared to the court that (1) the evidence was so positively and obviously trustworthy that the opportunity to test it by cross-examination could safely be dispensed with, and (2) the interests of justice required that it be admitted.

The Commission also recommended that s 69 of PACE regarding computers should be repealed. In the absence of evidence to the contrary it should be assumed that a computer or other mechanical instrument was functioning properly.

(6) Evidence of identification

Possibly the most notorious source of miscarriages of justice is identification evidence. It has therefore been suggested by some that such evidence ought to be wholly excluded in criminal cases unless corroborated. The question was examined by the Devlin Committee on *Evidence of Identification in Criminal Cases*. In its report (House of Commons paper 338, 1976) it rejected this view but recommended (pp 94–5) that the judge should be required to warn the jury that it was unsafe to convict on the basis of eyewitness evidence unless the circumstances of the identification were exceptional or there was substantial evidence of some other sort. A judge who gave such warning should indicate the kind of case where exceptionally it might be reasonable to rely on eyewitness evidence. Failure to give the warning would be grounds to quash the conviction. So too would a finding by the Court of Appeal that the case was not such as to justify reliance on eyewitness evidence or that there was insufficient supporting evidence.

Only a few weeks after the report was published, the Court of Appeal in *R v Turnbull* [1977] QB 224 acted on the report but it did not give full effect to the Committee's recommendation. The Court, sitting with five judges, laid down new guidelines for trial judges in cases involving disputed identification evidence. Lord Widgery for the court said that the trial judge should warn the jury of the special need for caution before relying on identification evidence. He should instruct them as to the reason for such warning and should refer to the possibility that a mistaken witness was a convincing one and that even a number of such witnesses could be mistaken. Secondly, he should direct the jury to examine very closely the circumstances in which the identification came to be made: 'How long did the witness have the accused under observation? At what distance? In what light? Was the observation impeded in any way, as for example by passing traffic or a press of people? Had the witness ever seen the accused before? How often? If only occasionally, had he any reason for remembering the accused? How long elapsed between the original observation and the subsequent identification to the police? Was there any material discrepancy between the description of the accused given to the police by the witness when first seen by them and his actual appearance?' (at p 228). If there were such discrepancies, the prosecution should inform the defence.

The court said that in setting out its guidelines it had tried to follow the recommendations of the Devlin Committee. A failure to follow the guidelines was likely to result in a conviction being quashed. (For cases in which convictions were subsequently quashed as a result of a failure to follow the guidelines, see, for instance, *R v Hunjan* (1978) 68 Cr App Rep 99; *R v Raphael* (1978) Times, 13 October; *Bentley* [1991] Crim LR 620.) See also E Grayson, 'Identifying Turnbull' (1977) *Criminal Law Review*, p 509; and JD Jackson, 'The Insufficiency of Identification Evidence Based on Personal Impression' (1986) *Criminal Law Review*, p 203.

The rules for identification parades are now to be found in the Code of Practice on Identification Evidence (Code D) promulgated under PACE. (See M Zander, *Police and Criminal Evidence Act 1984* (3rd edn, Sweet & Maxwell, 1995, pp 489–92. See also A Heaton Armstrong and D Wolchover, 'Exorcising Dougherty's Ghost', *New Law Journal*, 1 February 1991, p 137.

Judicial warnings regarding uncorroborated evidence

Until very recently the judges were required to give the jury a warning about the danger of relying on the uncorroborated evidence of children (see p 331 above), accomplices giving evidence for the prosecution, and complainants in a sexual offence. The Law Commission recommended in 1991 that the present rules *requiring* such warnings should be abolished–*Corroboration of Evidence in Criminal Trials*, Cm 1620, 1991. This was effected in the Criminal Justice and Public Order Act 1994, s 32(1). Such a warning is therefore no longer required, but the judge still has a discretion to give such a warning if the facts of the case seem to him to call for it. (For explication of how courts should now approach the matter see *R v Makanjuola* [1995] 3 All ER 730, CA.)

Section 33 of the same Act abolished the requirement of actual corroboration for a number of offences under the Sexual Offences Act 1956.

(c) Evidence excluded because its admissibility would be against the public interest

There are various categories of excluded evidence that can conveniently be collected under this head:

(1) The evidence of spouses in criminal cases

A spouse was generally not able to give evidence for the prosecution in a criminal case even if willing to give evidence (see *R v Mount* (1934) 24 Cr App Rep 135). She was not competent as a witness. There were some exceptions where the wife was permitted to give evidence but was not compellable, mainly involving offences against the wife herself, her property or against their children. In *Hoskyn v Metropolitan Police Comr* [1978] 2 All ER 136, the House of Lords held that a woman who married the defendant two days before the trial could not be *compelled* to give evidence against her new husband in a case arising out of a serious assault on her! See also *R v Pitt* [1982] Crim LR 513, in which the Court of Appeal said a wife who was competent but not compellable to give evidence for the prosecution against her husband remained free to decide whether to give evidence until the moment that she entered the witness box, and was unaffected by whether she had previously given a statement to the police or had given evidence at the committal proceedings. But once she decided to give evidence she became like any other witness and had to answer all questions save those that might incriminate her. Moreover, she could be treated as a hostile witness if that would be legitimate with an ordinary witness. But this ought to be explained to her before she started to give evidence. The general exclusionary rule applied even after judicial separation and possibly after divorce in regard to matters that occurred during the marriage.

In its 1972 Report, the Criminal Law Revision Committee said the question of the continuation of this exclusionary rule involved a balancing of the need to get the right verdict, on the one hand, and, on the other hand, the objection that such evidence would disturb marital harmony and be harsh on the spouse compelled to testify. It thought that the rule should at least be modified to make the wife *competent* to give evidence for the prosecution if willing to do so. She should also be compellable (as opposed to being merely competent) in cases involving violence against her or against children of the household under 16 (paras 149–50). If the parties were divorced, the Committee thought that they should be treated for all purposes as if they had never been married–even in regard to matters occurring during the marriage. (But see M Cohen, 'Are Wives Really So Incompetent?' (1980) *Criminal Law Review*, p 222.)

The Police and Criminal Evidence Act, 1984, s 80, broadly carried into effect the proposals of the Criminal Law Revision Committee. It provides, first, that a spouse is always competent for the prosecution save where he or she is charged jointly with the same offence. (The exception does not apply, however, where he or she is no longer liable to be convicted for that offence by virtue of having pleaded guilty or otherwise.) The new Act, secondly, made the spouse always compellable for the defence–save for the same exception where she is charged jointly with him. The Act extended the CLRC's proposals by making a spouse *compellable* for the prosecution not only in cases of violence to children of the family under 16, but also in cases of violence or a sexual offence against anyone under 16 whether or not they were family members. Fourthly, the Act adopted the CLRC's proposal that a spouse should be competent for a co-accused regardless of whether his or her spouse consented. Fifthly, the Act laid down that after the marriage has been terminated both spouses become competent and compellable as if they had never been married–and this applies even to events that occurred during the marriage.

(2) Evidence of a witness that might incriminate him

Any witness in any case, other than the defendant himself, is entitled to refuse to answer a question that might expose him to a criminal charge. If the privilege is invoked, it is for the judge to decide whether the questions have to be answered. It seems that the privilege may extend to cover answers that could incriminate a spouse, but it does not go beyond that to protect other family members.

In *Re O (disclosure order)* [1991] 1 All ER 330 the Court of Appeal held that convicted persons could be required to make full disclosure of their assets for the purposes of potential confiscation proceedings under the Criminal Justice Act 1988, but because of the principle of not requiring a person to incriminate himself the order would be subject to a condition that no disclosure made in compliance with the order should be used as evidence in the prosecution of an offence alleged to have been committed by the person required to make the disclosure.

(3) The accused is not a compellable witness

An accused person in a criminal case has a right to remain silent in the dock. That was and remains the case. In fact the great majority of defendants who plead not guilty do give evidence. (In the Crown Court Study done for the Royal Commission on Criminal Justice over 70 per cent of defendants gave evidence.[3]

Until 1995 the prosecution were not permitted to comment on the fact that the defendant chose not to go into the witness box. (Criminal Evidence Act 1898, s 1(*b*)). (But see *R v Brown and Routh* [1983] Crim LR 38 where it was held the rule had not been infringed even though the prosecution counsel did comment on the defendants' failure to give evidence in the sense that he said the prosecution's case was uncontradicted.)

The judge was allowed in his discretion to draw the jury's attention to the fact but he could not suggest that silence constituted evidence against him. The position was explained by the Lord Chief Justice Lord Taylor in *R v Martinez-Tobon* [1994] 2 All ER 90 concerning the importation of cocaine. The trial judge had told the jury in his summing up that that they were not to conclude from the fact that the defendant had not given evidence that he was guilty but that they might think that if he had thought that D was bringing in emeralds rather than cocaine that he would have been very anxious to say so. The Court of Appeal upheld the conviction. Provided the judge told the jury that they should not assume guilt from a refusal to give evidence at least in some circumstances comment was permitted. Where the defence case involved facts which were at variance with the prosecution's case and which were within the defendant's knowledge such comment might be legitimate. The nature and strength of such comment was a matter for the judge.

Until 1982, if the defendant chose to give evidence he could either go into the witness box and thereby subject himself to cross-examination or he could make a statement from the dock on which he could not be cross-examined.

The Criminal Law Revision Committee in its 1972 report recommended drastic reform of the rules:

---

3   M Zander and P Henderson, *The Crown Court Study* (Royal Commission on Criminal Justice, Research Study No 19, 1993, p 114).

(1) That if the prosecution had established a *prima facie* case, the accused should formally be asked to go into the witness box and told that, if he failed to do so, adverse inferences could be drawn. Failure to do so could also amount to corroboration where corroboration was required. In the view of the Committee the existing rule was much too favourable to the defence. Normally it should be incumbent on the accused to give evidence, but it would not become contempt of court to refuse.

(2) The prosecution and judge should be entitled to comment on the accused's failure to give evidence. The prohibition on comment was wrong in principle and entirely illogical.

(3) The right to make an unsworn statement from the dock should be abolished. It was rarely exercised in trials on indictment save in cases where the accused wanted to attack prosecution witnesses without making himself liable to the revelations of his own prior convictions. (See on this point, p 323 above.) It was wrong to give the accused this choice (Criminal Law Revision Committee, 'Evidence (General)', *Eleventh Report*, 1972, Cmnd 4991, paras 102–13). These proposals were received with much less criticism than those made by the Criminal Law Revision Committee in regard to the right of silence in the police station.

The Philips Royal Commission on Criminal Procedure disagreed with the CLRC on the first two points. It did not favour putting pressure on the accused to give evidence or allowing comment on his refusal to testify. But it did agree that the right of the defendant to make an unsworn statement from the dock should be abolished. It was anomalous that a defendant should be able to give evidence without being subject to the possibility of perjury proceedings. He should be required to submit himself to the oath and cross-examination. (Cmnd 8092, 1981, paras 4.63–7.)

The Government followed the same line. The Criminal Justice Act 1982, s 72, abolished the right of the defendant to make an unsworn statement from the dock. However, it preserved the right of an unrepresented accused to address the court in the same way that counsel could, by way of submissions or in mitigation of sentence.

The Runciman Royal Commission on Criminal Justice said that the balance was held correctly in the standard direction given to juries:

The defendant does not have to give evidence. He is entitled to sit in the dock and require the prosecution to prove its case. You must not assume that he is guilty because he has not given evidence. The fact that he has not given evidence proves nothing one way or the other. It does nothing to establish his guilt. On the other hand, it means that there is no evidence from the defendant to undermine, contradict, or explain the evidence put before you by the prosecution.

Where the defendant did not give evidence, the prosecution could question and the judge could comment on the explanation given by counsel but 'neither the prosecution nor the judge should invite the jury to draw from the defendant's failure to give evidence the inference that his or her explanation is less deserving of being believed' (Report, p 56, para 27).

The Government however rejected the view of the two Royal Commissions and instead implemented the recommendation of the CLRC made in 1972. The Criminal Justice and Public Order Act 1994 (CJPOA), s 35 states that in a trial of someone over the age of 14, at the conclusion of the prosecution's case, the court must 'satisfy itself ... that the accused is aware that the stage has been reached at which evidence can be given for the defence ... and that, if he chooses not to give evidence, or having been sworn, without good cause refuses to answer any question, it will be permissible for the court or jury to draw such inferences as appear proper from his failure to give evidence or his refusal without good cause to answer any question' (s 35(2)). The court or jury may draw such inferences as appear proper from the failure to give evidence or refusal to answer questions (s 35(3)).

The new rule does not apply if it appears to the court that 'the physical or mental condition of the accused makes it undesirable for him to give evidence' (s 35(1)(*b*)).

A Practice Direction issued by the Lord Chief Justice dealt with the procedure to be followed (*Practice Direction* (Crown Court: evidence: advice to defendant) [1995] 1 WLR 657). If the defendant is legally represented and the court is informed that he does not intend to give evidence the judge should, in the presence of the jury inquire of the lawyer: 'Have you advised your client that the stage has now been reached at which he may give evidence and if he chooses not to do so, or, having been sworn, without good cause refuses to answer any questions, the jury may draw such inferences as appear proper?' If this assurance is given the case proceeds. If not, the case should briefly be adjourned for that to be done.

If the accused is not legally represented the judge should say to the defendant:

You have heard the evidence against you. Now is the time for you to make your defence. You may give evidence on oath, and be cross-examined like any other witness. If you do not give evidence, or having been sworn, without good cause refuse to answer any question, the jury may draw such inferences as appear proper. That means they may hold it against you. You may also call any witness or witnesses whom you have arranged to attend court. Afterwards you may also, if you wish, address the jury by arguing your case from the dock. But you cannot at that stage give evidence. Do you now intend to give evidence?

It remains to be seen to what extent unrepresented defendants will be able to understand this.

(4) Legal professional privilege

Communications between a client and his legal adviser generally cannot be given in evidence by the lawyer without the permission of the client if they were made either (1) with reference to proceedings in being or then contemplated, or (2) to enable the client to receive, or the lawyer to give, legal advice. The privilege is that of the client not the lawyer and can only be waived by the client. (There is no equivalent privilege for communications between doctor and patient, priest and penitent, or journalist and his source, though, as has been seen (p 174 above), these categories do now have a comparable immunity under the Police and Criminal Evidence Act in regard to certain pre-trial police searches.) The privilege is intended to promote candour between a client and his lawyers.

As has been seen (p 174) the House of Lords held in *R v Central Criminal Court, ex p Francis & Francis* [1989] AC 346 that legal professional privilege did not apply for the purposes of PACE where the material sought by the police was intended to further a criminal purpose *by anyone*. It has not yet been decided whether the same principle applies at common law to applications to waive privilege made in a court room.

But is the privilege absolute even where the material would help to establish someone's innocence? In 1988 the Court of Appeal, Criminal Division held in *Ataou* [1988] 2 All ER 321 that it was not and that in such a situation the court must undertake a balancing exercise. The appellant (A) was jointly charged with two others with conspiracy to supply heroin. The co-defendants pleaded guilty. One (H) gave evidence for the prosecution against A. All three had originally had the same solicitors. During H's evidence a representative of the solicitors passed to A's counsel an attendance note recording that H had said that A had not been involved. The judge refused to allow H to be cross-examined on the previous inconsistent statement on the ground that H refused to waive his legal privilege.

The Court of Appeal quashed A's conviction because the judge had failed to investigate and determine the balance of competing interests. ('The judge must decide whether the legitimate interest of the defendant in seeking to breach the privilege outweighs that of the client in seeking to maintain it.') For critical comment see TRS Allen, 'Legal Privilege and the Accused: An Unfair Balancing Act', *New Law Journal*, 16 September 1988, p 668.

But in June 1995 the House of Lords said that *Ataou* had been wrongly decided. Lord Taylor, the Lord Chief Justice, giving the unanimous decision of their lordships in *R v Derby Magistrates' Court, ex p B* [1995] NLJR 1575 said that the privilege was always absolute, no matter what the circumstances. The case concerned a murder charge brought against the appellant's step-father after the appellant himself had been acquitted of the murder. He had first confessed but had then retracted his confession and had blamed the step-father. The step-father applied to the magistrates' court for an order that all notes made by the solicitors of interviews with the appellant should be handed over.

The client must be sure that what he tells his lawyer in confidence will never be revealed without his consent. Legal professional privilege is thus much more than an ordinary rule of evidence, limited in its application to the facts of a particular case. It is a fundamental condition on which the administration of justice as a whole rests... Putting it another way, if a balancing exercise was ever required, it was performed once and for all in the sixteenth century and since then has been applied across the board in every case, irrespective of the client's individual merits... it is not for the sake of the appellant alone that the privilege must be upheld. It is in the wider interests of all those hereafter who might otherwise be deterred from telling the whole truth to their solicitors. For this reason I am of the opinion that no exception should be allowed to the absolute nature of legal professional privilege.

The privilege could only be waived by the client. Subject to that 'once privileged always privileged'. It was the same rule for civil and criminal cases and for both prosecution and defence.

It has been held that in the case of expert witnesses, legal professional privilege attaches to confidential communications between the solicitor and the expert, but it does not attach to the chattels or documents on which the expert based his opinion, or to the independent opinion of the expert himself: *Harmony Shipping Co SA v Davis* [1979] 3 All ER 177 at 181. This rule applies to criminal as well as to civil cases. Therefore in a criminal trial the Crown can subpoena as a witness a handwriting expert whom the defence has consulted but does not wish to call as a witness, and is entitled also to production of documents sent to the expert for examination and on which he based his opinion provided they are not covered by legal professional privilege: *R v King* [1983] 1 All ER 929. Lord Justice Dunn said: 'It would be strange if a forger could hide behind a claim of legal professional privilege by the simple device of sending all the incriminating documents in his possession to his solicitors to be examined by an expert' (at 931).

In the Police and Criminal Evidence Act 1984 legal professional privilege is defined to include not only communications but also documents and other articles mentioned in or enclosed with privileged communications if the communication was in connection with the giving of legal advice or in connection with or contemplation of legal proceedings and for the purpose of such proceedings (s 10). It also includes not only communications for these purposes between the client and the lawyer, but also with third persons such as accountants or others involved in legal advice or legal proceedings. (See TRS Allen, 'Legal Privilege and the Principle of Fairness in the Criminal Trial' (1987) *Criminal Law Review*, p 449.)

(5) Evidence obtained at a 'trial within a trial'

It is a common feature of crown court cases that the admissibility of evidence is considered by the judge, usually in the absence of the jury. This is known technically as a *voir dire*, or, less formally, as a 'trial within a trial'. (But sometimes the defence ask for the *voir dire* to be held in the presence of the jury. For a consideration of this and other aspects of the issue, see P Rowe, 'The Voir Dire and the Jury' (1986) *Criminal Law Review*, p 226 and *Solicitors' Journal*, 19 July 1991, p 827.) It may be that this option no longer exists because of the provisions of s 76 of the Police and Criminal Evidence Act 1984–see *Millard* [1987] Crim LR 196 and comments, pp 197–8.

If the accused makes admissions during the *voir dire*, can the prosecution give evidence of them once the trial resumes? The point came up in *R v Brophy* [1981] 2 All ER 705, an appeal to the House of Lords from Northern Ireland. B was accused of 49 counts of terrorism offences including 12 murders by explosions. There was no evidence against him other than admissions made during interrogations. He challenged the admissibility of these statements. During the trial within a trial on this issue, he admitted he had for years been a member of the IRA. The trial judge ruled that the statements made in the interrogations were inadmissible as having been obtained improperly. This meant that there was no evidence against B on any of the first 48 counts. But the 49th count was being a member of the IRA. This was allowed to be proved by reference to the admissions made by the defendant during the *voir dire*. On appeal, the House of Lords held that this was not proper, even though it had been a voluntary admission in answer to questions from his own counsel. Anything which emerged only at the *voir dire* and was relevant to the *voir dire* could not be admissible at the trial: 'if such evidence, being relevant, were admissible at the substantive trial, an accused person would not enjoy the complete freedom that he ought to have to contest the admissibility of his previous statements' (at p 709, per Lord Fraser). He would not feel free if what he said at the *voir dire* could be used against him at the trial.

If, however, he used the *voir dire* to boast of having committed the offences in question or used the occasion to make a political speech, that would be irrelevant to the issue of admissibility and different considerations would apply.

When the trial is in the magistrates' courts, a challenge to the admissibility of a confession cannot easily be conducted in the same way. There is no jury to withdraw while the court makes up its mind on the question of admissibility. On the other hand, it is not satisfactory for the magistrates to consider admissibility at the same time as considering the question of weight and truth. In *F (an infant) v Chief Constable of Kent* [1982] Crim LR 682, Lord Lane CJ said: 'where matters are being conducted before magistrates, there is no question of a "trial within a trial" because magistrates are judges of both fact and law and determine questions of guilt and innocence'. But this does mean that, where a confession is to be challenged, the chances of a fair trial are inevitably greater in the crown court than in the magistrates' court. (See, for discussion of this issue, WMS Tildesley and WF Bullock, 'Challenging Confessions in the Magistrates' Courts', *Justice of the Peace*, 16 April 1983, p 243.)

In *R v Liverpool Juvenile Court, ex p R* [1987] 2 All ER 668, it was argued on behalf of the juvenile accused that the *Chief Constable of Kent* case had in effect been displaced by the provisions of s 76 of the Police and Criminal Evidence Ace 1984 which dealt with the admissibility of confessions (see below). The Divisional Court upheld the contention. It ruled that, where the question of the admissibility of a confession is raised by the accused, the magistrates must hold a trial within a trial at which the defendant would be entitled to give and call evidence relating purely to the question of admissibility. (For comment see B Gibson, 'Justices and Trials Within Trials Yet Again', *Justice of the Peace*, 2 May 1987, p 275.)

(6) To protect police informers, etc

The courts have for decades recognized the principle that the identity of police informers should, if possible, be kept secret and that surveillance methods should not necessarily become known to the defence. As long ago as 1890 Lord Esher MR referred to the rule protecting the disclosure of the name of an informant as a rule in public prosecutions.[4] In *Rankine* [1986] QB 861 the appellant argued on appeal that his conviction was unsafe and unsatisfactory because he had not been allowed by the trial judge to cross-examine the police witnesses as to the location of the observation point from which they had allegedly seen him repeatedly selling drugs. The Court of Appeal refused to quash the conviction. See to same effect *Johnson* [1988] 1 WLR 1377.

However, this principle of public interest exclusion of evidence may have to give way to the even higher principle that the defendant should not be unfairly impeded from establishing his innocence. Thus in *Brown* (1987) 87 Cr App Rep 52 the Court of Appeal quashed convictions because the trial judge had refused to allow police officers to be questioned about the details of their surveillance operation.

Note that no equivalent tenderness toward the defendant is shown when his case on appeal is that the jury considered material that should not have been known to them. The principle in such cases is that the Court of Appeal will not permit such a contention to be urged in an attempt to undermine the conviction (see *Thompson*, p 406 below).

See generally JA Andrews, 'Public Interest and Criminal Proceedings', 104 *Law Quarterly Review*, 1988, pp 410–21.

(7) Evidence obtained by improper means

The common law made a distinction between *confessions* that were improperly obtained and other kinds of evidence obtained in regular ways. Broadly, confessions were liable to be excluded, whilst other evidence was normally admitted in evidence.

4   *Marks v Beyfus* (1890) 25 QBD 494.

(a) Confessions

The common law

There was a well-established common-law rule going back some two hundred years that a confession could not be admitted in evidence if it was 'involuntary', which was defined to mean obtained as the result of a threat or promise held out by a person in authority.[5]

The rule was expressed in the Judges' Rules, principle (e) of the preamble of which stated: 'it is a fundamental condition of the admissibility in evidence against any person ... that it shall have been voluntary in the sense that it has not been obtained from him by fear of prejudice or hope of advantage, exercised or held out by a person in authority or by oppression.' An example of the principle being applied is *R v Smith*, decided in 1959:

R v Smith [1959] 2 QB 35 (Courts Martial Appeal Court)

The appellant, a soldier, was charged with the murder by stabbing of a soldier of another regiment during a barrack-room fight. Immediately after the fight the appellant's regimental sergeant-major put his company on parade and indicated that the men would be kept there until he learnt who had been involved in the fighting. At the trial the judge-advocate admitted in evidence a statement made by the appellant to the sergeant-major at that parade, confessing to the stabbing. Evidence was also given of a subsequent confession made the following day to a sergeant of the Special Investigation Branch after a caution had been administered.

Lord Parker CJ, giving the judgment of the court, stated the facts and continued:

The court is quite clear that while there was nothing improper in the action taken by the regimental sergeant-major, the evidence of what took place was clearly inadmissible at the prisoner's trial. What the sergeant-major did might well have been a very useful course of action in order to enable further inquiries to be made, but the court is satisfied that if the only evidence against the prisoner was a confession obtained in those circumstances, it would be quite inadmissible at his trial. It has always been a fundamental principle of the courts, and something quite apart from the Judges' Rules of Practice, that a prisoner's confession outside the court is only admissible if it is voluntary. In deciding whether an admission is voluntary the court has been at pains to hold that even the most gentle, if I may put it in that way, threats or slight inducements will taint a confession. To say to all those on parade, 'You are staying here and are not going to bed until one of you owns up' is in the view of this court clearly a threat. It might also, I suppose, be looked upon as an inducement in that the converse is true, 'If one of you will come forward and own up, the rest of you can go to bed'; but whichever way one looks at it, the court is of opinion that while the action was perfectly proper and a useful start no doubt to inquiries, evidence in regard thereto was clearly inadmissible.

---

5   This was held to include a father–see *R v Moore* (1972) 56 Cr App Rep 373; and *R v Cleary* (1963) 48 Cr App Rep 116. In *R v Thompson,* (1978) Times, 18 January, it was held to include also a social worker who said: 'Do not admit something you have not done but it is always the best policy to be honest. If you were concerned tell him about it and get the matter cleared up for your own sake.' The judge excluded the accused's confession. On the concept of the person in authority, see P Mirfield, 'Confessions–the "Person in Authority" Requirement' (1981) *Criminal Law Review*, p 92.

The court then considered the second confession made by the accused the next morning. It ruled that this was admissible because the effect of the threat or inducement was then spent.

The *Smith* case did not end in the defendant's conviction being quashed. An even more striking case was that of *R v Zaveckas* [1970] 1 All ER 413 because the court there did quash the conviction when it found that the confession had followed upon an improper promise. The case was even more remarkable in that the promise came as the result of a request from the accused. He was told by the police that an identification parade had been arranged and if he was not picked out he would be allowed to go. He asked whether he would be given bail at once if he made a statement. The officer said 'yes' and he then made a statement admitting guilt. The Court of Appeal Criminal Division ruled that the statement should have been held inadmissible because it was an inducement held out by a person in authority. With regret, the court said, it had to quash the conviction. Similarly, in *Northam* (1967) 52 Cr App Rep 97, the Court of Appeal quashed a conviction based on a confession after the accused had asked a police officer whether it would be possible for a second offence to be taken into consideration at his forthcoming trial rather than being the basis of a later separate trial. The police officer said the police would have no objection. The Court of Appeal said this amounted to a fatal inducement.

The common-law objection to the admissibility of confessions obtained through *oppression* appears to be more recent than for confessions obtained by threats or promises. The preamble to the Judges' Rules mentioned 'oppression' as one reason for a confession being found 'involuntary'. For judicial statements on the subject see for instance *Prager* [1972] 1 WLR 260; *Westlake* [1979] Crim LR 652; *Hudson* [1981] *ibid*, 107; *Gowan* [1982] *ibid*, 821; and see generally John D Jackson, 'Confessions and the Doctrine of Oppression', *New Law Journal*, 15 March 1979, p 264.

Confessions obtained as a result of threats, promises or oppression were inadmissible in law. Once they were classified in this way the judge had no discretion. Confessions obtained in breach of the Judges' Rules, by contrast, were only inadmissible in the judge's discretion, though it was not easy to get the judges to exercise this discretion. In *Prager* [1972] 1 WLR 260, Lord Justice Edmund Davies dealt with the submission by counsel that a statement was inadmissible because the police had not cautioned the defendant before questioning him, even though they plainly had plenty of evidence justifying reasonable suspicion, and that the questioning was therefore in breach of Rule 2 which required a suspect to be cautioned when the police had sufficient admissible evidence reasonably to suspect him. (The defendant was taken from his house in the early hours of the morning and on arrival at the police station was questioned at length about complicity in espionage activities.) The Court of Appeal refused to hold that the confession should have been excluded.

See, to same effect, *Conway v Hotten* [1976] 2 All ER 213 and *Greaves v D* [1980] Crim LR 435. A breach of the Judges' Rules alone was not therefore likely to commend itself as a reason for excluding evidence. For a recent application of the doctrine in dramatic circumstances see however the Privy Council's quashing of a murder conviction in Hong Kong (*Lam Chi-ming* [1991] 3 All ER 172) because of mis-behaviour by the police.

Later changes in the admissibility rules regarding confessions

In its 1972 Report, the Criminal Law Revision Committee recommended by a majority that confessions should only be excluded where it was likely that the threat or inducement would produce an unreliable confession. It would be for the judge to imagine that he was present at the questioning and to consider in the light of all the evidence 'whether at the point when the threat was uttered or the inducement offered, any confession which the accused might make as a result of it would be likely to be unreliable'. The test applied not to the confession actually made but 'to any confession which he might have made in consequence of the threat or inducement' (para 65). The Committee did not make it clear whether the test should relate to the reasonable defendant in that situation or to the accused himself–ie whether it should be objective or subjective.

This proposal was not at first implemented by legislation but in the period between the CLRC's Report and the Police and Criminal Evidence Act 1984 the common law changed and came somewhat into line with the approach adopted by the CLRC.

This was mainly achieved by two cases. In the first, *DPP v Ping Lin* [1975] 3 All ER 175, the defendant confessed after the officer in the case had assured him 'If you show the judge that you have helped the police to trace bigger drug people, I am sure that he will bear it in mind when he sentences you.' The House of Lords upheld the trial judge's decision to allow the confession to be given in evidence. The question of voluntariness, the law lords held, was one of fact and causation.

The second case, *Rennie* [1982] 1 All ER 385, went even further. The officer admitted that the defendant confessed in return for a promise from the officer that he would in that event not bring the suspect's sister and mother into the affair. The Court of Appeal upheld the trial judge's decision to admit the confession. Giving judgment Lord Lane LCJ said it was for the court simply to take a commonsense view of whether the confession had been of the defendant's own free will. The fact that his confession was induced wholly or in part because he hoped the police would then not involve his mother or his sister did not make it involuntary.

Plainly, the test of whether a confession was voluntary had undergone a sea-change since decisions like *Smith* in 1959 and *Zaveckas* in 1970.

The Philips Royal Commission

The Royal Commission on Criminal Procedure (1981) criticized the common-law rule in regard to confessions (as it then stood), on the ground that it was unrealistic. It assumed, first, that suspects in the police station could be free from fear of prejudice or hope of advantage and, secondly, that it was possible to tell to what extent any particular suspect was affected by such fear or hope. Both assumptions, the Commission said, were false. Research conducted for the Commission by Dr Barrie Irving showed that even a trained psychologist present at the questioning of suspects could not tell what pressures were responsible for suspects making statements. But fear of prejudice and hope of advantage were in the very nature of the situation–regardless of what precisely was said or done by the police. (*Report of the Royal Commission*, 1981, para 4.73; based on B Irving, 'Police Interrogation: A Case Study of Current Practice', *Royal Commission Research Study No 2*, 1980.)

The Commission thought it would be better to abandon the vain attempt to distinguish between voluntary and involuntary confessions and to concentrate instead on the behaviour of the police officer. If the suspect was subjected to torture, violence, the threat of violence or inhuman or degrading treatment, any subsequent confession should be inadmissible. This would mark society's 'abhorrence of such conduct' (*Report*, para 4.132). But any lesser breach of the rules of questioning should only be liable to the consequence that the trial judge would warn the jury of the danger of relying on the resulting confession if there was no independent evidence (*Report*, para 4.133).

PACE

The proposal that the voluntariness test should be abolished met with considerable opposition, and the Conservative Government did not accept it. The Police and Criminal Evidence Act instead based its approach on the inadmissibility of any confession obtained as a result of oppression (as defined) or which was obtained in consequence of something 'likely in the circumstances to render unreliable any confession which might be made by the accused in consequence thereof':

Police and Criminal Evidence Act 1984, s 76

(1) In any proceedings a confession made by an accused person may be given in evidence against him in so far as it is relevant to any matter in issue in the proceedings and is not excluded by the court in pursuance of this section.

(2) If, in any proceedings where the prosecution proposes to give in evidence a confession made by an accused person, it is represented to the court that the confession was or may have been obtained–

(a) by oppression of the person who made it; or
(b) in consequence of anything said or done which was likely, in the circumstances existing at the time, to render unreliable any confession which might be made by him in consequence thereof,

the court shall not allow the confession to be given in evidence against him except in so far as the prosecution proves to the court beyond reasonable doubt that the confession (notwithstanding that it may be true) was not obtained as aforesaid.

'Oppression' as defined in s 76(8) 'includes torture, inhuman or degrading treatment, and the use or threat of violence'.

Various points arise:

(1) The burden of proof on questions of the admissibility of confessions lies on the prosecution–s 76(2).

(2) When any question of the admissibility of a confession arises it is for the judge to rule as to whether the evidence is admissible and for the jury to decide on whether it is to be believed (see *McCarthy* (1980) 70 Cr App Rep 270; *Ragho Prasad s/o Ram Autar Rao v R* [1981] 1 All ER 319).

(3) There is supposed to be a trial within a trial to determine the admissibility of a confession–even in the magistrates' court (see *R v Liverpool Juvenile Court, ex p R* [1988] QB 1). Moreover, the Court of Appeal has said *obiter* that the question of its admissibility cannot be considered by the court after the confession has been given in

evidence (*Sat-Bhambra* (1988) 88 Cr App Rep 55, [1988] Crim LR 453). But this seems questionable.[6]

(4) There have now been a few cases in which the courts have held that there was oppressive conduct by the police (s 76(2)(*a*)). In *Fulling* [1987] QB 426 the Court of Appeal made it clear that oppression would exist only very rarely. It gave the word its meaning in the *Oxford English Dictionary* as 'The exercise of authority or power in a burdensome, harsh or wrongful manner; unjust or cruel treatment of subjects, inferiors etc; the imposition of unreasonable or unjust burdens'.

In *Beales* [1991] Crim LR 118 the trial judge in the Norwich Crown Court found that questioning of the suspect for 35 minutes (!) 'stepped into the realm' of oppression because the police officer deliberately misled the suspect as to the existence of evidence of the offence. But the judge said that even if the police conduct was not oppressive under s 76(2)(*a*) the confession was certainly unreliable under s 76(2)(*b*). It seems unlikely that the Court of Appeal would have upheld the trial judge's finding that there was evidence of oppression on the facts of the case.

In *Davison* [1988] Crim LR 442, where there had been a whole series of breaches of the Act and the Codes of Practice, the judge held that the prosecution had failed to discharge the burden of proof on it to show that the confessions in a series of interviews had not been obtained as a result of oppression. He seemed to regard the unlawful detention of the suspect as of prime significance.

In the case of Timothy West in 1988 the trial judge held that police had been oppressive in constantly interrupting the defendant, shouting at him, using foul language to indicate that he was lying, and making it clear that they would continue questioning him until he confessed.

In *Paris, Abdullahi and Miller* (1992) 97 Cr App Rep 99 (the case of the 'Cardiff Three'), the Lord Chief Justice in the Court of Appeal said the court had been horrified by the hectoring and bullying manner of the police questioning of Miller who denied the murder charge over 300 times before making admissions. ('Short of physical violence, it is hard to conceive a more hostile and intimidating approach to a suspect. It is impossible to convey on the printed page the pace, force and menace of the officer's delivery.') The Court of Appeal quashed all three convictions.

In the George Heron case in November 1993, Mr Justice Mitchell ruled that confessions and admissions to the murder of a seven year old girl were inadmissible because they had been obtained by oppression. The questioning had been conducted without any hectoring or shouting. But the judge held that oppression existed in falsely telling the accused that he had been identified, in pounding him with being a killer and with sexual motives for the killing and in telling him that it was in his interest to tell the truth when it had been made clear that the police regarded the truth to be that he had done the killing. The police had been engaged in breaking the defendant's resolve to make no admissions.

In both the Cardiff Three case and the George Heron case the suspect had had his legal adviser present throughout the interviews.

Unreliability (s 76(2)(b))

The formula adopted in s 76(2)(*b*) (p 353 above) was effectively that recommended by the Criminal Law Revision Committee in its 1972 Report. The fact that the new

6   See Professor JC Smith in a comment on the case after the report in the *Criminal Law Review*.

test abandons the previous law as reflected in decisions like *Zaveckas* (p 351 above) is confirmed by the provision in Code C that if a suspect asks an officer 'what action will be taken in the event of his answering questions, making a statement or refusing to do either, the officer may inform him what action he proposes to take in that event provided that the action is itself proper and warranted (Code C, para 11.3). But officers are still admonished not to indicate 'except in answer to a direct question' what action will be taken if the person being interviewed answers questions, makes a statement or refuses to do either (*ibid*).

The issue of reliability of confessions has given rise to a number of different points:

(1) The words 'in consequence of anything said or done' mean said or done by someone other than the suspect–*Goldenberg* [1988] Crim LR 678.

(2) The test of 'likely in the circumstances existing at the time' is objective and hypothetical. It is not what the officer thought was the suspect's mental state but what it actually was.[7] The circumstances existing at the time can include the fact that the suspect had a very low IQ or was very suggestible. (See *Silcott, Braithwaite and Raghip* (1991) Times, 9 December; *McKenzie* (1993) 96 Cr App Rep 98, CA.) Also the truth or otherwise of the confession does not come into the question.

(3) But although the words of the sub-section seem to require a causal link between what was said and done in fact, in some of the cases the courts have found a confession to be unreliable where there was no such link. The courts have treated breaches of the Code as sufficient to establish unreliability even without any evidence that the breaches led directly to the admissions or confession. (See for instance *DPP v Blake* [1989] 1 WLR 432; and *Doolan* [1988] Crim LR 747.[8])

Examples of things said or done which have been held to constitute grounds for holding a confession to be unreliable include: an offer of bail;[9] minimising the significance of a serious (sex) offence and suggesting that psychiatric help might be appropriate;[10] saying to a defendant who has previously denied the offence, 'Do I gather that you are now admitting the offence?';[11] falsely telling the suspect that his voice has been recognised on tape;[12] falsely telling the suspect that he has been identified by a witness;[13] indicating that the suspect will have to stay in the police station until the matter is cleared up.[14]

Examples of things *not* said or done which have been held to be grounds for holding a confession to be unreliable include: failure to obtain a solicitor;[15] breaches in the provisions of Code C;[16] or failure to see that the suspect has an appropriate adult.[17] But such grounds will not *necessarily* result in a confession being held to be inadmissible.[18]

---

7 *Everett* [1988] Crim LR 826.
8 This was an especially striking case since some of the breaches considered relevant by the court occurred *after* the confession.
9 *Barry* (1991) 95 Cr App Rep 384, CA.
10 *Delaney* (1988) 88 Cr App Rep 338, CA.
11 *Waters* [1989] Crim LR 62, CA.
12 *Blake* [1989] 1 WLR 432.
13 *Heron*, text, p 354 above.
14 *Jasper* (24 April 1994, unreported, CA.
15 *McGovern* (1990) 92 Cr App Rep 228, CA; *Chung* (1991) 92 Cr App Rep 314, CA.
16 *Delaney* note 10 above; *Doolan*, above.
17 *Everett* note 7 above, *Moss* (1990) 91 Cr App Rep 371, CA.
18 *Waters* [1989] Crim LR 62; *Maguire* (1989) 90 Cr App Rep 115, CA.

Royal Runciman Commission

The Runciman Commission, by a majority of eight to three, rejected the suggestion that a confession should only be admissible if corroborated. But it recommended that the judge should be required to give the jury a warning, adapted to the circumstances of the case similar to that in identification cases, about the dangers of relying on an uncorroborated confession (Report, p 68, para 87).

For further reading see especially: DJ Birch, 'The PACE Hots Up: Confessions and Confusions under the 1984 Act' (1989) *Criminal Law Review*, p 95; Birch, 'The Evidence Provisions', *Northern Ireland Legal Quarterly*, 1989, p 411; Ian Dennis, 'Miscarriages of Justice and the Law of Confessions: Evidentiary Issues and Solutions', [1993] *Public Law*, pp 291–313; M Zander, *The Police and Criminal Evidence Act 1984* (3rd edn, Sweet and Maxwell, 1995), pp 217–31.

(b) Evidence, including confessions, illegally or improperly obtained

Whereas, as has been seen above, the common law historically took a strict view of the admissibility of confession evidence, its approach to other evidence was different. Until 1979 the rule was that the courts had a discretion as to whether such evidence should be admitted. There were many cases in which this proposition had been stated. The origin of the doctrine was a dictum of Lord Chief Justice Goddard, giving the judgement of the Privy Council in *Kuruma, Son of Kaniu v R* [1955] AC 197 at 204: 'No doubt in a criminal case the judge always has a discretion to disallow evidence if the strict rules of admissibility would operate unfairly against the accused. ... If, for instance, some admission of some piece of evidence, eg a document, had been obtained from a defendant by a trick, no doubt the judge might properly rule it out.'

See also *Jeffery v Black* [1978] 1 All ER 555 in which Widgery LCJ said that the discretion, though not often exercised, certainly existed: 'But if the case is exceptional, if the case is such that not only have the police officers entered without authority, but they have been guilty of trickery or they have misled someone, or they have been oppressive or they have been unfair, or in other respects they have behaved in a manner which is morally reprehensible, then it is open to the justices to apply their discretion and decline to allow the particular evidence to be let in as part of the trial.'

In spite of the existence of the discretion, there were few cases in which it was exercised (see Gerald Coplan, 'The Judicial Discretion to Disallow Admissible Evidence', *Solicitors' Journal*, 18 December 1970, p 945). But the House of Lords in *Sang* [1980] AC 402 either abolished the discretion or at least drastically curtailed it. The case concerned a defence of entrapment–the defendant claimed that he had been induced to commit the offence by an informer acting on the instructions of the police. All the judges in the House of Lords ruled that there was no such defence as entrapment in English law. But they went on to consider the more general question whether a judge had a discretion to exclude relevant evidence. They ruled, again unanimously, that (save for confessions or evidence tantamount to a confession) no discretion existed to exclude evidence simply on the ground that it had been illegally or improperly obtained! Such illegality might be a factor to be taken into account in sentencing, or might be the basis for civil proceedings or disciplinary action against the police. The only basis for excluding relevant evidence was where its effect would be unduly prejudicial–for example, evidence of previous similar acts as in *Noor Mohamed v R* [1949] AC 182 or *Harris v DPP*

[1952] AC 694–or where it would be unfair to admit it. But unfairness could not be shown merely by the fact that the evidence had been illegally obtained. In fact the nature of 'unfairness' that would entitle the judge to exclude evidence in his discretion is obscure. Lord Scarman, for instance, said that each case must depend on its circumstances: 'All I would say is that the principle of fairness, though concerned exclusively with the use of evidence at trial, is not susceptible to categorisation or classification, and is wide enough in some circumstances to embrace the way in which, after the crime, evidence has been obtained from the accused' (at p 290).

For comment on the *Sang* case, see JD Jackson, 'Unfairness and the Judicial Discretion to Exclude Evidence', *New Law Journal*, 1980, p 585. See, generally, JD Heydon, 'Illegally Obtained Evidence' (1973) *Criminal Law Review*, p 690, and AJ Ashworth, 'Excluding Evidence as Protecting Rights' (1977) *Criminal Law Review*, p 723. For a comparison with the United States, see P Hartman, 'Admissibility of Evidence Obtained by Illegal Search and Seizure under the US Constitution,' 28 *Modern Law Review*, 1965, p 298.

The Philips Royal Commission

The Royal Commission on Criminal Procedure recommended that the admissibility of improperly obtained evidence other than confessions be substantially confirmed. It did not accept the view that illegally or improperly obtained evidence should basically be excluded, as it is in the United States by the doctrine that the fruit of the poisoned tree should not be eaten.

The Commission said it was not appropriate to use the rules as to the admissibility of evidence to discipline the police or to discourage police malpractice. First, it could only affect the small minority of cases where the defendant pleaded not guilty and would therefore not discourage improper behaviour by the police in the majority of cases. Secondly, the challenge on admissibility would be so distant in time from the moment of the improper conduct as not to be an effective deterrent. Experience in the United States suggested that it was not effective as a deterrent to misconduct by the police. The proper way to deter or to deal with misconduct by the police was through police disciplinary and supervisory procedures, civil actions for damages and the machinery of complaints against the police (Report, paras 4.123–8).

The Commission equally did not favour the 'reverse onus' exclusionary rule recommended by the Australian Law Reform Commission, under which improperly obtained evidence is inadmissible unless the prosecution can satisfy the judge that there was some special reason why the impropriety should be condoned. Such a rule, the Commission said, would be difficult to administer in a uniform way. It would not reduce trials within trials. The fact that the judge had a discretion would weaken the deterrent effect on the police.

The Royal Commission's Report attracted severe criticism from some quarters for its failure to recommend an exclusionary rule–see, for instance, Jim Driscoll, 'Excluding Illegally Obtained Evidence–Can We Learn from the United States?', *Legal Action Group Bulletin*, June 1981, p 131. See also by same author, 'Excluding Illegally Obtained Evidence in the United States' (1987) *Criminal Law Review*, p 553.

PACE

But the Government disagreed with the Commission. At a very late stage it included a provision to restore a version of the previous common law discretion. (A different clause was originally introduced by the Government. The House of Lords then passed an amendment moved by Lord Scarman which effectively broadened the discretion. The Government then returned with its own somewhat narrower draft.) The final version of s 78 provided:

78. (1) In any proceedings the court may refuse to allow evidence on which the prosecution proposes to rely to be given if it appears to the court that, having regard to all the circumstances, including the circumstances in which the evidence was obtained, the admission of the evidence would have such an adverse effect on the fairness of the proceedings that the court ought not to admit it.

(2) Nothing in this section shall prejudice any rule of law requiring a court to exclude evidence.

The impact of s 78 has been remarkable. Contrary to what most commentators expected, the judges have forged the somewhat ambiguous words of s 78 into a powerful weapon to hold the police accountable for breaches of the law and of the Codes of Practice.

There are now a very large number of cases interpreting and applying s 78 which is by far the most frequently used section of the Act. A high proportion of the decided cases are Court of Appeal decisions. Reviewing this mass of case law for the 1995 edition of his book on PACE the writer recently expressed his impression:

It cannot be said that the courts have articulated a consistent and all-embracing theory for the application of s 78. Various principles explaining the exercise of the discretion to exclude evidence have been suggested by academic commentators. These include the Reliability principle (to promote the reliability of evidence), the Disciplinary principle (to penalise the police for breaches of the rules as a way of promoting adherence to the rules), and the Protective principle (to protect the accused).[19] Many cases could be said to fall within those broad approaches–though there is little or no sign that the judges themselves deal with the problems in that way. The evidence from the cases is to the contrary.[20]

The writer believes rather that s 78 has become both established and accepted as a means for the courts to determine what breaches of the rules or improper conduct are unacceptable on a case by case basis without any clearly articulated theory. Usually, even when there has been some breach or impropriety, the court allows the evidence in and even when it finds there to have been impropriety, the Court of Appeal usually ends by dismissing the appeal. But there have also been many cases, including non-confession cases, in which the appeal court has quashed a conviction because of such improprieties. In the great majority of such cases the court's chief concern seems to be that the verdict should be based on reliable evidence. But sometimes, the court is expressing a more fundamental concern directed not so much to the

---

19 See especially AJ Ashworth, 'Excluding Evidence as Protecting Rights' [1977] Crim LR 723, and *The Criminal Process*, Clarendon, Oxford, 1994; and AAS Zuckerman, *The Principles of Criminal Evidence* (1989).

20 See also M Hunter, 'Judicial Discretion: Section 78 in Practice' [1994] Crim LR 558 reporting on an empirical study in Leeds Crown Court. The judges she interviewed were unanimous in rejecting the idea that they considered any of these theoretical principles when deciding whether to exclude disputed evidence. The writer cannot say that he is surprised at this finding which would probably be equally true of the Court of Appeal.

result in the particular case as to a view that the system demands a minimum of procedural correctness and moral integrity.[1]

To some extent the decisions of the courts applying s 78 can be systematised. Certain basic distinctions have emerged. But there remains (and will always remain) a significant and irreducible degree of discretion left to the court. Professor Diane Birch, writing about the entrapment cases, has suggested that 'The more principled the discretion can be said to be, and the more its underlying aims can be articulated, the more consistent will be the decisions made under it'.[2] She cites another academic view of the need to avoid the 'mushiness and unpredictability of a general doctrine of exclusion for "unfairness"'.[3] Consistency in the application of a discretion to exclude evidence on the grounds of unfairness may be desirable but in the end it is unattainable. We will instead have to be content with the fact that the courts sometimes are prepared to give expression to their view that the unfairness was such as to require that the evidence be rejected.

By far the most common basis for the Court of Appeal to apply s 78 has been 'significant and substantial' breaches of the PACE rules. [*M Zander, The Police and Criminal Evidence Act 1984* (3rd edn 1995, Sweet & Maxwell, pp 237–38).]

The cases concern (1) breaches of the Act and or the Codes such as failure to tell the suspect (D) his rights, not giving D access to a solicitor, not cautioning D, not providing an appropriate adult, not complying with the formalities regarding interviews, not complying with identification procedures; and (2) obtaining evidence by tricks, undercover police work and the like. (For references to the actual cases see the writer's book on PACE, *ibid*, pp 238–44.)

The Court of Appeal has repeatedly said that each case must be decided on its own facts. It has refused to lay down guidelines as to how the discretion under s 78 should be exercised. The decision to exclude evidence is taken not to penalise the police. (See for instance *R v Delaney* (1988) 88 Cr App Rep 338, CA.) In order to succeed under s 78 the defence have to establish that a significant and substantial breach of the rules or other impropriety has occurred, that it affects the fairness of the proceedings which is sufficiently serious as to require that the court exclude the evidence. In *R v Walsh* (1989) 91 Cr App Rep 161, the Court of Appeal said: 'The task of the court is not merely to consider whether there would be an adverse effect on the fairness of the proceedings, but such an adverse effect that justice requires the evidence to be excluded.'

---

1 See further Ian Dennis, 'Reconstructing the Law of Criminal Evidence' [1989] 42 *Current Legal Problems* 21; and AAS Zuckerman, 'Illegally Obtained Evidence: Discretion as a Guardian of Legitimacy', [1987] 40 *Current Legal Problems*, 55.

2 'Excluding Evidence from Entrapment: What is a "fair cop"?' [1994] *Current Legal Problems*, 73 at p 89.

3 JD Heydon, 'Entrapment and Unfairly Obtained Evidence in the House of Lords' [1980] Crim LR 129 at p 134.

CHAPTER 5
The jury

(a) The origins of the jury system

The original concept of the jury was precisely the opposite of what it later became. The members of the jury were chosen as persons who were likely to know what had happened or, if not, they were supposed to find out before the trial. In the thirteenth century it was 'the duty of the jurors, so soon as they have been summoned, to make inquiries about the facts of which they will have to speak when they come before the court. They must collect testimony; they must weigh it and state the net result in a verdict' (F Pollock and FW Maitland, *The History of English Law*, 2nd edn 1898, pp 624–5). Medieval juries came more to speak than to listen.

The transformation of the medieval active jury into the passive courtroom triers of fact is not well understood either in its timing or its causes. Probably in the later fifteenth century, but certainly by the sixteenth, it had become expected that the jury would be ignorant of the facts of the case.

(b) Eligibility for jury service

Until 1974 eligibility for jury service was governed largely by wholly out-of-date property qualifications. This was the subject of inquiry by the Morris Committee, which reported in 1965 and whose report was implemented by the Juries Act 1974.

(1) Composition of the jury list

Report of the (Morris) *Departmental Committee on Jury Service*, 1965, Cmnd 2627, paras 38–42

38. Under the present qualifications eligibility is in practice confined to 'householders'. In general, this is taken to mean the person who is liable to pay the rates in respect of separately rated accommodation. In most families this is the husband (which is why, as will be seen later, only a relatively small proportion of jurors are women).

29. Another restriction on the householder's eligibility is that his premises must be rated at not less than £30 in the counties of London and Middlesex and not less than £20 elsewhere. At the time the Juries Act 1825 was passed, there must have been relatively few houses with the

necessary rateable value. Successive revaluations have enormously increased the number of houses rated at the qualifying value, and we were informed by the Government Social Survey that 81 per cent of domestic hereditaments in England and Wales are at present rated at £30 or more; no figure is readily available for those rated at £20 or more, but we have been told that for the country as a whole the proportion excluded by the rateable value limitation is now unlikely to exceed 10 per cent. ...

42. It is estimated that there are 7.15 million names marked as eligible for jury service on the 1964 electoral registers for England and Wales, which is 22.5 per cent of the 31.77 million names on the registers. This estimate was supplied to us by the Social Survey Division of the Central Office of Information, and was based on counts made of a sample of pages of the registers for forty-eight parliamentary constituencies.

The Morris Committee recommended that, subject to certain exempted categories, juries ought to be selected from all those on the electoral register. This was eventually implemented. See now the Juries Act 1974. Under this Act a person is eligible for jury service who is between 18 and 70, on the register of electors and has been resident in the UK for at least five years since the age of thirteen. (Until 1988 the age limit was 65 but the 1988 Criminal Justice Act provided that a person who is between 65 and 70 is eligible though he cannot be required to serve.)

(2) Those ineligible, disqualified or excused

Certain persons, however, are 'ineligible', 'disqualified' or 'excused'. Those *ineligible* include judges, those concerned with the administration of justice, and the clergy. They are kept off juries because of the undue influence they might wield because of their experience. The Runciman Royal Commission on Criminal Justice recommended that this last category of exclusion from jury service be abolished but so far this has not been done. ('We do not see why clergymen and members of religious orders should not be eligible for jury service' (Report, p 132, para 57).)

Anyone who has been sentenced to life imprisonment at any time and anyone who has served a sentence of three months or more in a prison or youth custody centre during the previous ten years, is *disqualified*. So too is anyone who has received a suspended sentence or a community service order during the previous ten years or anyone placed on probation in the previous five years. It is an offence to sit on a jury knowing that one is ineligible or disqualified. The Runciman Royal Commission recommended that persons currently on bail should be disqualified from jury service (p 132, para 59) and this was implemented in the Criminal Justice and Public Order Act 1994, s 40.

The Runciman Royal Commission said that research might show that 'contrary to general belief, the role played by jurors with prior criminal convictions is indistinguishable from the role played by any other category of juror' and recommended that s 8 of the Contempt of Court Act (see p 408 below) be amended to permit research on juries to be done. This has not been implemented.

Concern has been expressed in recent years about persons who are disqualified from serving on juries. In *R v Mason* [1980] 3 All ER 777 the Court of Appeal held that it was lawful for the police to scrutinise jury panels. If names showed up with disqualifying criminal convictions the information could be passed to prosecuting counsel who could eliminate such people from a case by using the procedure known as 'stand by for the Crown'–see p 370 below. (And see the *Annex to the Attorney-General Guidelines on Jury Checks: Recommendations of the Association of Chief*

Police Officers [1988] 3 All ER 1086 authorising checks in cases where the police thought it particularly important that disqualified persons should not serve on the jury.)

In 1987 the Home Secretary announced that in future the police would make random checks of would-be jurors to see whether any were disqualified. An unpublished Home Office study had shown that one in every 24 juries had on it a disqualified person. The checks would be made between the time that the jury was summoned and the date of jury service. (*Times, The Guardian*, 26 September 1987). The system was instituted in 1988. Each Crown Court Centre outside London is supposed to provide the police quarterly with a batch of names for checking. But the Runciman Royal Commission (p 133, para 60) said that the Association of Chief Police Officers (ACPO) had told it that often courts did not fulfil this requirement and frequently the information given was insufficient to enable a search of the records to be made. No doubt sometimes too the police fail to make the checks.

(3) Excusals

Some persons are *excused* as of right, if they wish, being persons deemed to have more important business elsewhere, such as MPs, members of the House of Lords, full-time members of the forces, and doctors, dentists and others in the medical profession. Requests for excusal can also be made on an individual *ad hoc* basis. Illness, physical disability or insufficient understanding of English would always constitute valid grounds for excusal and where someone appears not to be able to understand English, the person responsible for summoning the jury can bring him before a judge who will determine whether he should serve. There is no formal literacy test. The Roskill Committee said that it seemed that the test was not working properly at least at the Old Bailey, in that it was only being applied, if at all, to understanding spoken English. They concluded somewhat lamely: 'we think we must leave to those responsible for the administration of the courts how they will in future ensure that, in fraud cases, only jurors are appointed with an understanding of English sufficient to enable them to read and write' (para 7.11).

The Runciman Royal Commission said in regard to the question whether there should be some form of literacy or comprehension test for jurors, that the Crown Court Study carried out for the Commission[1] (see p 375 below) showed that jurors and jury foremen claimed to understand the issues they were trying. Inevitably this was a subjective judgment and moreover there were some jurors and even some whole juries who were confused. The subject, it said, should be the subject of research (Report, p 135, para 72).

Applications for excusal can be made on grounds of special hardship because, for instance, holidays have been booked for that period, or the juror has very young children to look after or an examination to take. (For excusal on account of conscientious objection see p 368 below.)

An application for excusal goes to the Summoning Officer. Refusal to grant excusal may be appealed to a judge. The judge also has a discretion to excuse jurors on special grounds–for instance in relation to long, complicated or sensitive cases. The grounds mostly relate to personal hardship but they can also relate to difficulties in reading,

1　M Zander and P Henderson, *Crown Court Study*, Royal Commission on Criminal Justice, Research Study No 19, 1993.

writing or following accounts. The operation of the discretion exercised by summoning officers and judges varies widely. There is obviously a particular problem in cases that are anticipated to be unusually long. In such cases it has been suggested that the jury may include a disproportionate number of housewives and unemployed persons. It is common in these immensely long cases for the judge to ask jurors whether they can manage such a case and to excuse any who say they cannot. The jury is in a sense therefore 'self-selected'. (On this see further p 365 below.)

(c) The process of selection

Until recently the actual process of selecting the names for the panel was somewhat haphazard. Each summoning officer had his own method and many were hardly 'random' in any sense recognized by a statistician. In 1981 a new system, developed by the Lord Chancellor's Department in consultation with the Royal Statistical Society, was introduced nationally.

However, even now the system as it is actually operated is less than completely random. As was pointed out in an article in *The Law Magazine*, 30 October 1987, p 20, the randomness of jury selection is still qualified by the following facts:

(1) The electoral register is not wholly representative of the population. Nearly 7 per cent are on the register wrongly because they have moved or died; about one-fifth of those from the new Commonwealth are not registered, and nearly one-fifth of those between the ages of 21 and 24 are not registered because of their mobility.

(2) It is up to the summoning officer to decide which of his electoral registers to use. Each court has a collection of registers from which to choose.

(3) It is also up to the summoning officer to select his mini-panel of 18 or so names for a particular case and then to decide in which order to draw the names. ('Some even seem to look through the pack as they pick out names'.) Also, of course, courts will vary in what excuses they will accept as grounds for not serving for personal reasons.

A report on Jury Selection issued by the Criminal Bar Association in November 1988 described the system as 'remarkably primitive' (para 2.5). It recommended that the system be computerized in order to produce the best statistically verifiable results. (It suggested that the present system threw up bizarre juries of an unrepresentative kind. It was remarkable for instance how when there were rail strikes or other transport problems jurors drawn from a huge catchment area often lived close enough to each other to share taxis!)

The jury summoning officer calculates how many jurors will be required and, having made a random selection from the electoral lists, sends out his summonses so as to give at least four weeks' warning. The summons comes with an explanatory leaflet about jury service, a leaflet on jurors' expenses including a form regarding claims for loss of earnings, and a reply envelope to return a form stating that the person concerned is either qualified to serve or is not qualified, with the reason. Failure to give this information or giving false information is an offence.

The method of determining the composition of the jury for the particular case varies somewhat from court to court. Ballotting is supposed to be done by putting the appropriate number of cards into the ballot box and drawing them in such a way that the jury bailiff cannot see the names on the cards. The cards are then transferred to the courtroom ballot box for the final ballot.

Usually about twenty or so names are drawn and these individuals are brought into the back of the court. (They are often called 'the jury in waiting'.) The clerk of the court is given cards, each of which has the name and address of a juror in waiting. He reads out twelve names and those persons go into the jury box.

The same Criminal Bar Association report referred to above said that in former times 'there were many courts where rigging juries was an open secret ... convicting juries were kept together by order of judges and connivance of the court staff' (para 5.1). Rigging also occurred for benevolent reasons such as wishing to steer female jurors from nasty sex cases. The Association said 'We have no evidence that this is a reality any more.' Nevertheless practice varied. 'Whether the actions of some court clerks can strictly be interpreted as a proper ballot in accordance with the Act is doubtful –the shuffling and selection of jury cases certainly has little appearance of it' (*ibid*). The process of ballotting, it said, should be made more mechanical, independent of the whim of court staff and uniform throughout the country.

Jury selection for long cases–the Maxwell fraud case

The trial of Kevin and Ian Maxwell, sons of the business magnate Robert Maxwell, which started in June 1995 was scheduled to last some six months. The trial judge, Mr Justice Phillips (as he then was) adopted a highly unusual method of selecting the jury. First, two groups of 400 potential jurors were summoned to the Old Bailey on two separate days. Of these, 650 were immediately excused for reasons of personal non-availability including holiday plans, child-minding responsibilities, work commitments and the like. The remaining 150 were invited to complete a 20-page questionnaire with some 40 questions specifically relating to the Maxwell trial. This was designed to test their availability for an unusually long case and was directed also to their knowledge of the case and possible resulting prejudice. The judge and counsel in open court then went through the list of these 150 questionnaires classifying them as A (no reason to exclude), C (should be excluded for any reason, including illiteracy) and B (uncertain). There were 52 Cs. The jury was then selected by ballot drawn from the remaining 100 jurors. As each name was drawn if counsel or the judge had any queries on the basis of the questionnaire or the classification the juror was asked to come into the court room and he or she was asked questions by the judge to clarify the issue. The individual then left the court room and the judge and counsel together decided whether that person should or should not serve as a juror.

Compensation for jurors

Jurors receive a financial loss allowance graduated depending on the length of the case. In 1995, for the first ten days they were paid a flat rate of £44.80 a day even for the retired and unemployed. After that the loss-of earnings allowance was subject to a maximum of £89.60 a day or £448 a week. They are also paid a subsistence allowance –in 1995 from £2.10 to £4.25 per day plus travel expenses.

(d) Challenging of jurors

The position of the parties in regard to selection of the jury was historically somewhat different. The prosecution could only challenge jurors if they had some reason ('challenge for cause', see p 367 below). But they could also exercise a right known as 'stand by for the Crown' or simply 'stand by', which means that the prospective juror stands to one side. If a jury can be empanelled without him (as would almost always be the case), he is not required. If not, he must be accepted unless the prosecution can show cause why he should not be a juror in that case. (See JF McEldowney, 'Stand by the Crown: An Historical Analysis' (1979) *Criminal Law Review*, p 272.) In practice, the prosecution only rarely exercise their right either of stand by or of challenge for cause. (See further pp 371–71 below.)

The defence in a criminal case have traditionally had the right to challenge numbers of prospective jurors without giving any reason–the so-called right of 'peremptory challenge'. Originally the number of such challenges permitted was thirty-five. In 1509 this was reduced to twenty; in 1948 it was reduced to seven and in 1977 to three. After all peremptory challenges had been exhausted, the defence had only a right of challenge for cause–with no limit to the numbers that could be challenged in that way. But from the mid-1980s the right of peremptory challenge became highly controversial.

(1) Abolition of the right of peremptory challenge

It was suggested that the right was being 'abused' by defence lawyers who would use it, especially in London, to eliminate from the jury persons who were educated or looked intelligent or middle class. There was no hard evidence to support the allegation but it gained some currency.

In January 1986 great impetus was given to the campaign to abolish the right of peremptory challenge in the Report of the Roskill Committee on Fraud Trials. The Committee was divided on the issue but by a majority of seven to one it recommended that the right should be abolished. It thought that the interests of the accused could be adequately safeguarded by the right of challenge for cause.

The majority said that the right conflicted with the principle that the jury should be selected randomly. Since co-accused could each exercise three such challenges, the panel might be reduced by a considerable number. It concluded:

We have considerable sympathy with the exercise of the right of peremptory challenge in pursuit of an aim of securing a better racial or sexual balance on a jury. But we have no sympathy with its exercise where that exercise is, as the evidence suggests is too often the case, largely tactical. The aim of the jury is to secure a verdict which is just to prosecution and defence alike after a proper appraisal of the evidence. That aim ought not to be hampered by the use of the right of peremptory challenge in the hope of replacing a juror whose appearance and address may suggest a capacity to understand the real issues or a bias in favour of the prosecution by one whom it is hoped may be less able to understand or may be more likely to be biased in favour of the defence [para 7.29]. ... Our evidence shows that the public, the press and many legal practitioners now believe that this ancient right is abused cynically and systematically to manipulate cases toward a desired result. The current situation bids fair to bring the whole system into disrepute. We conclude that in respect of fraud trials such manipulation is wholly unacceptable and must be stopped [para 7.37].

In a White Paper published in March 1986 the Home Office said that peremptory challenge was sometimes used for entirely proper reasons–such as to save time or possibly embarrassment to someone who would otherwise be challenged for cause, or to adjust the age, sex or race balance on the jury, or to remove someone suspected of being biased against the accused. But it was contrary to the interests of justice that persons should be removed because they were thought to have insight or respect for the law which was inimical to the defence. The problem was most acute in cases involving several defendants if they pooled their challenges. The Government had no wish to interfere unnecessarily with a long-standing right that could be used in ways that were consistent with justice. But as far as practicable, and providing it did not seriously prejudice a defendant's right to a fair trial, juries should be composed of a random selection of those who were neither ineligible nor disqualified. The question was whether that could be achieved without either leaving defendants with an understandable sense of grievance or opening up challenge for cause to an unseemly and disturbing degree. (*Criminal Justice: Plans for Legislation*, March 1986, Cmnd 9658, para 35).

The empirical evidence did not support the view that the use of peremptory challenge affected the outcome of trials.[2]

The 1986 White Paper was followed by legislation in the Criminal Justice Act 1988, section 118 of which provided simply 'The right to challenge without cause in proceedings for the trial of a person on indictment is abolished'.

The Crown Court Study (see p 363, note 1 above) reported on the views of both barristers and judges as to whether the right to peremptory challenge should be restored. A slight majority of prosecution barristers (56%) thought the right should not be restored. Exactly the same proportion of defence barristers thought that it should be restored. The judges sided strongly with the view expressed by a majority of prosecution barristers–82 per cent thought it should not be restored (para 6.2.5, p 174). The Runciman Royal Commission made no recommendation on the subject.

(2) Challenge for cause

In the United States prospective jurors can be asked questions to establish whether they are biased.[3] Sometimes this process can take hours and even days or weeks. Selection of the jury in the trial of Jack Ruby for killing Lee Harvey Oswald, the alleged assassin of President Kennedy, took 15 days. Selection of the jury in the celebrated trial of OJ Simpson took 40 days, from 26 September to 4 November, 1994.

In England, by contrast, questions may not be put unless a foundation of fact has first been laid,[4] which means that in practice challenges for cause are extremely rare. Since normally nothing is known about the prospective jurors other than their names and addresses, there is usually no basis on which a challenge for cause can be launched. Formerly, the lists available to the parties also showed the jurors' occupations, but in August 1973 the Lord Chancellor issued a directive (under the provisions of s 32(1) of the Courts Act 1971) that in future jury lists should no longer include the occupations of those on the jury panel. The intention, again, was to make it more difficult for counsel to 'select' the jury. The Bar Council issued a statement on 7 May 1974 regretting the directive: 'It is felt that the new directive will hamper both the prosecution and the defence, and it is not in the interests of the administration of justice.'

---

2 See Julie Vennard and David Riley, 'The Use of Peremptory Challenge and Stand By of Jurors and Their Relationship to Final Outcome' (1988) *Criminal Law Review*, p 731.
3 For a description see Mark George, 'Jury Selection, Texas Style', *New Law Journal*, 24 June 1988, p 438.
4 *Chandler* (No 2) [1964] 1 All ER 761.

Those entitled to inspect the list of names on the panel include the defendant, solicitor and counsel for any party, and police officers involved in the case. Instructions to crown court staffs state that requests from anyone else, or if the official is in any doubt, should be referred to a superior officer. A record of any request to inspect the panel list must be kept. Concern about 'jury nobbling' has increased in recent years[5] but it has not reached the point where it has been thought that the right to look at the panel should be withheld.

But there has been some consideration given to the problem of challenge for cause. The basic English rule was set out in a Practice Note issued in 1973 as a result of what happened in the so-called Angry Brigade case in 1972. The case concerned the trial of alleged anarchists for attempts to bomb the homes of various prominent Conservative politicians. The trial judge, in order to avoid any possibility that the trial might be thought to be unfair, acceded to a defence request that he put questions to prospective jurors. He asked them to exclude themselves for a variety of reasons, for instance if they were subscribing members of the Conservative Party, if they had relatives in the police force or serving in the armed forces in Northern Ireland, or if they were constituents of any of several prominent persons whose homes were alleged to have been the subject of actual or projected bombings. As a result, 39 people were challenged on behalf of the 8 defendants, and another 19 admitted they fell into one or other of the judge's categories (see *The Guardian*, 31 May 1972).

Shortly after the case was concluded, however, the Lord Chief Justice issued a Practice Note obviously designed to stop such questions:

A jury consists of 12 individuals chosen at random from the appropriate panel. A juror should be excused if he is personally concerned in the facts of the particular case, or closely connected with a party to the proceedings or with a prospective witness. He may also be excused at the discretion of the judge on grounds of personal hardship or conscientious objection to jury service. It is contrary to established practice for jurors to be excused on more general grounds such as race, religion or political beliefs or occupation [[1973] 1 All ER 240].

This *Practice Note* was reissued in a revised form in 1988 ([1988] 3 All ER 177). The new text was:

Jury service is an important public duty which individual members of the public are chosen at random to undertake. The normal presumption is that, unless a person is excusable as of right from jury service under Pt III of Sch 1 to the Juries Act 1974, he or she will be required to serve when summoned to do so. There will however be circumstances where a juror should be excused, for instance where he or she is personally concerned in the facts of the particular case or is closely connected with a party or prospective witness.

He or she may also be excused on grounds of personal hardship or conscientious objection to jury service. Each such application should be dealt with sensitively and sympathetically.

Any person who appeals to the court against a refusal by the appropriate officer to excuse him or her from jury service must be given an opportunity to make representations in support of his or her appeal.

The Practice Direction issued on 12 January 1973 (*Practice Note* [1973] 1 All ER 240, [1973] 1 WLR 134) is revoked.

5   The Runciman Royal Commission recommended that an acquittal should be cancelled and a retrial be instituted where it was subsequently established that jurors had been bribed or intimidated (p 177, para 74). Such a provision was included as Part VI of the Criminal Procedure and Investigations Bill, introduced in November 1995.

The judge's discretion

In *R v Ford* (1989) 89 Cr App Rep 278 at p 280 Lord Lane CJ said that the trial judge has a residual discretion to discharge a juror who ought not to be serving even in the absence of any objection by any party. 'The basic position is that a juror may be discharged on grounds that would found a challenge for cause. In addition jurors who are not likely to be willing or able properly to perform their duties may also be discharged.' This discretion was exercised by Mr Justice Phillips in the selection of the jury in the trial of the Maxwell brothers (p 365 above).

The question of conscientious objection to jury service was considered in *R v Crown Court at Guildford, ex p Siderfin* [1989] 3 All ER 7, in which the Divisional Court held that a member of the Plymouth Brethren could be entitled to excusal not because of her beliefs as such but because they prevented her from taking part in the jury's deliberations. Since 'she would not participate at all in the usual discussion between jurors which is an integral part of the jury system', she would be unable to perform her duties as a juror. (The court also held that a judge hearing an appeal from a chief clerk's refusal of such an application to be excused jury service should consider sympathetically any request for the person to be legally represented.)

Jury selection and pre-trial publicity

It is not a valid ground of objection that the juror has previous knowledge of the case from the media. In *R v Maxwell* Phillips J said that because the minds of potential jurors might have become 'clogged with prejudice' by pre-trial publicity about the case he would permit questions to be put in the jury questionnaire and further questions to be posed when he questioned potential jurors in open court (see above). But in a ruling on jury selection given on 27 April 1995 he said 'The fact that a juror may have read or heard prejudicial matter about a defendant, *and even formed an adverse opinion of him on the basis of it, does not of itself disqualify the juror on the ground of bias*' (emphasis supplied). He cited a dictum of the Ontario Court of Appeal in *R v Hubbert* (1975) 29 CCC (2d) 279 at p 291:

In this era of rapid dissemination of news by the various media, it would be naive to think that in the case of a crime involving considerable notoriety, it would be possible to select 12 jurors who had not heard anything about the case. Prior information about a case and even the holding of a tentative opinion about it, does not make partial a juror sworn to render a true verdict according to the evidence.

Mr Justice Phillips cited with approval the observation of the High Court of Australia in *R v Glennon* (1992) 173 CLR 592 'in the past too little weight may have been given to the capacity of jurors to assess critically what they see and hear and their ability to reach their decisions by reference to the evidence before them'. Defence counsel had argued that the extent of the pre-trial publicity about the Maxwell case had established a prima facie case justifying a challenge for cause of any juror selected by ballot. He cited *R v Kray* (1969) 53 Cr App Rep 412, per Lawton J as authority for the proposition. Prosecution counsel argued that challenge for cause would only arise where having regard to the answers to the questionnaire (see p 365 above) a prima facie case of bias was made out. The judge said that in practice there was little difference between these positions. It was always necessary to show prima facie grounds for a challenge and the answers to the questionnaire could be used for that purpose.

Procedure for challenge for cause

In 1989 the Judicial Studies Board published a recommended procedure for challenge for cause based on recommendations of the Law Commission. If counsel can state the ground of challenge without prejudicing his client in the eyes of the jury, or embarrassing the juror, the matter can be dealt with in open court. If not, the sworn jurors should be sent to the jury room and the rest of the panel, *including the challenged juror*, should leave the court. The judge should then decide whether to exclude the press and the public. Challenges should never be heard in the judge's room.

(3) Stand by for the Crown

When the defence right of peremptory challenge was abolished, the Attorney-General issued guidelines (*Practice Note* [1988] 3 All ER 1086) as to how the prosecution's right to 'stand by for the Crown' was to be used:

Attorney General's guidelines on the exercise by the Crown of its right of stand by

1. Although the law has long recognized the right of the Crown to exclude a member of a jury panel from sitting as a juror by the exercise in open court of the right to request a stand by or, if necessary, by challenge for cause, it has been customary for those instructed to prosecute on behalf of the Crown to assert that right only sparingly and in exceptional circumstances. It is generally accepted that the prosecution should not use its right in order to influence the overall composition of a jury or with a view to tactical advantage.

2. The approach outlined above is founded on the principles that (a) the members of a jury should be selected at random from the panel subject to any rule of law as to right of challenge by the defence, and (b) the Juries Act 1974 together with the Juries (Disqualification) Act 1984 identified those classes of persons who alone are disqualified from or ineligible for service on a jury. No other class of person may be treated as disqualified or ineligible.

3. The enactment by Parliament of s 118 of the Criminal Justice Act 1988 abolishing the right of defendants to remove jurors by means of peremptory challenge makes it appropriate that the Crown should assert its right to stand by only on the basis of clearly defined and restrictive criteria. Derogation from the principle that members of a jury should be selected at random should be permitted only where it is essential.

4. Primary responsibility for ensuring that an individual does not serve on a jury if he is not competent to discharge properly the duties of a juror rests with the appropriate court officer and, ultimately, the trial judge. Current legislation provides, in ss 9 and 10 of the Juries Act 1974, fairly wide discretions to excuse or discharge jurors either at the person's own request, where he offers 'good reason why he should be excused', or where the judge determines that 'on account of physical disability or insufficient understanding of English there is doubt as to his capacity to act effectively as a juror'.

5. The circumstances in which it would be proper for the Crown to exercise its right to stand by a member of a jury panel are: (a) where a jury check authorised in accordance with the Attorney General's Guidelines on Jury Checks[6] reveals information justifying exercise of the right to stand by in accordance with para 9 of the guidelines and the Attorney General personally authorises the exercise of the right to stand by; or (b) where a person is about to be sworn as a juror who is manifestly unsuitable and the defence agree that, accordingly, the exercise by the prosecution of the right to stand by would be appropriate. An example of the sort of *exceptional* circumstances which might justify stand by is where it becomes apparent that, despite the

6   'Jury Vetting'—see below, p 435.

provisions mentioned in para 4 above, a juror selected for service to try a complex case is in fact illiterate.

(4) Achieving a racial mix

The question whether the courts have any way of achieving a racial mix in a case where that seems to be desirable was the subject of a number of conflicting court decisions–see *Binns* [1982] Crim LR 522 and 823; *Danvers* [1982] Crim LR 680; *Newton Rose* (1981) Times, 11 November; *Bansall, Bir, Mahio, and Singh* [1985] Crim LR 151; *McCalla* [1986] Crim LR 335; *Frazer* [1987] Crim LR 418. (See further A Dashwood, 'Juries in a Multi-racial Society' (1972) *Criminal Law Review*, p 85.)

The issue of racially mixed juries was considered for the first time by the Court of Appeal in the case of *Ford* [1989] 3 All ER 445. The trial judge refused an application for a multiracial jury in a case where the defendant was accused of reckless driving and driving a vehicle without authority. Lord Lane, the Lord Chief Justice, giving the judgment of the Court of Appeal, said that the judge had a discretion to discharge a particular juror who was unfit to serve for instance because he was deaf or blind or otherwise incompetent to serve. In *Mason* [1980] 3 All ER 777 another example given was someone for whom taking part in a long trial would be unusually burdensome. But this discretion did not extend to discharging a competent juror in order to secure a jury drawn from a particular section of the community nor otherwise to influence the overall composition of the jury. 'For this latter purpose the law provides that "fairness" is achieved by the principle of random selection' (p 449).

The Court disapproved suggestions to the contrary in earlier cases such as *Binns, Bansall* and *Thomas* (1989) 88 Cr App Rep 370. Lord Lane said that there was no principle that juries should be racially balanced–for that would depend on an underlying premise that jurors of a particular racial origin were incapable of giving an impartial verdict in accordance with the evidence. Given that the right of peremptory challenge has now been abolished, it therefore seems that there is no way in which the court can achieve a racially mixed jury by design.

In its evidence to the Runciman Royal Commission on Criminal Justice, the Commission for Racial Equality (CRE) argued that something had to be done to ensure that a jury be racially mixed where this seemed relevant. Restoration of the right of peremptory challenge would help. But on its own it would not be sufficient. One way would be to give the trial judge a statutory right to stand by jurors in order to achieve a racially mixed jury. If the judge refused to exercise this power, the defence counsel should have the right to stand by unlimited numbers of jurors until an acceptable racial mix was achieved–ie the equivalent right to the prosecution's right of 'stand by for the Crown'.

See further S Enright, 'Race, Justice and Trial by Jury', *Solicitors' Journal*, 15 November 1991, p 1238.

The Runciman Royal Commission was persuaded by the CRE that in a small number of racially sensitive cases something needed to be done to secure that the jury should be racially balanced. ('The Court of Appeal in *Ford* held that race should not be taken into account in selecting juries. Although we agree with the court's position in regard to most cases, we believe that there are some exceptional cases where race should be taken into account' (p 133, para 62).)

The Royal Commission proposed that in such a case either the defence or the prosecution should be permitted to ask the judge to authorise a special procedure so as to achieve that the jury contain up to three members of ethnic minority communities. If the judge agreed, the jury bailiff would continue drawing names randomly until three such people were drawn. But this procedure should not apply, as proposed by the CRE, merely because the defendant thinks that he cannot get a fair trial from an all-white jury. The judge would have to be persuaded that it was reasonable because of the special and unusual features of the case. Thus, a black defendant charged with burglary would not normally succeed with such an application. But black people accused of violence against a member of an extremist organisation who had been making racial taunts against them and their friends might succeed (p 133, para 63).

The CRE thought it would be impracticable to provide that the ethnic minority members of the jury should be drawn from the same ethnic minority group as the defendant but the Royal Commission thought that this should be an issue that the judge could be asked to consider.

The Royal Commission's proposal proved controversial. The Lord Chief Justice, Lord Taylor, for instance, indicated that he was against it. Speaking to the Leeds Race Issues Advisory Council he said: 'Though put forward for the best of motives, this proposal seems to me the thin edge of a particularly insidious wedge. The jury is the foundation of our system. It is drawn at random from the law-abiding inhabitants of the locality in which a case is tried. We must on no account introduce measures which allow the State to start nibbling away at the principle of random selection of jurors'. Jurors must not be seen as 'representing the views of the community, or of discrete parts of it, nor indeed of representing either the complainant or the victim'. (*Times*, 1 July 1995.)

Question

Consider the pros and cons of the Royal Commission's proposal. Does it seem to you that the advantages outweigh the disadvantages?

(e) Jury vetting

In 1978 during the so-called 'ABC' trial of a soldier and two journalists under the Official Secrets Act, it was revealed that in some cases the prosecution vet the jury panel. On the first day of the trial, counsel for one of the defendants learned from the clerk of the court that prosecution counsel had had a list of the potential jurors. 'Anyone who is known to be disloyal would obviously be disqualified', said Mr John Leonard QC for the prosecution. But in fact the Crown had not taken objection to anyone on the list.

It later emerged that the foreman of the jury had been a member of the elite SAS (Special Air Service Regiment). That jury was discharged when this fact was made known on television. As a direct result, in October 1978 the Attorney-General, Mr Sam Silkin QC published the guidelines for vetting of jury panels which he had actually established three years earlier. (See (1978) *Times*, 11 October.)

These guidelines have subsequently been redrafted several times. The latest version is [1988] 3 All ER 1086:

3. There are, however, certain exceptional types of case of public importance for which the provisions as to majority verdicts and the disqualification of jurors may not be sufficient to ensure the proper administration of justice. In such cases it is in the interests of both justice and the public that there should be further safeguards against the possibility of bias and in such cases checks which go beyond the investigation of criminal records may be necessary.

4. These classes of case may be defined broadly as (a) cases in which national security is involved and part of the evidence is likely to be heard in camera, and (b) terrorist cases.

5. The particular aspects of these cases which may make it desirable to seek extra precautions are (a) in security cases a danger that a juror, either voluntarily or under pressure, may make an improper use of evidence which, because of its sensitivity, has been given in camera, (b) in both security and terrorist cases the danger that a juror's political beliefs are so biased as to go beyond normally reflecting the broad spectrum of views and interests in the community to reflect the extreme views of sectarian interest or pressure group to a degree which might interfere with his fair assessment of the facts of the case or lead him to exert improper pressure on his fellow jurors.

6. In order to ascertain whether in exceptional circumstances of the above nature either of these factors might seriously influence a potential juror's impartial performance of his duties or his respecting the secrecy of evidence given in camera, it may be necessary to conduct a limited investigation of the panel. In general, such further investigation beyond one of criminal records made for disqualifications may only be made with the records of police Special Branches. However, in cases falling under para 4(a) above (security cases), the investigation may, additionally, involve the security services. No checks other than on these sources and no general inquiries are to be made save to the limited extent that they may be needed to confirm the identity of a juror about whom the initial check has raised serious doubts.

Such checks require the personal approval of the Attorney General. If the check show that any juror should be excluded from the trial it is done by telling prosecution counsel who would ask that juror to 'stand by for the crown'.

Use made of jury vetting

There is little information about the use of jury vetting. In his original statement in 1978 the Attorney-General said that in the three years since he had laid down his guidelines jury vetting had only occurred in 25 cases. Since then the categories of case in which it is permitted have been narrowed (by the elimination of big gang trials) and the requirement of consent of the Attorney-General has been added. Also the authorities know that each such case that comes to light usually provokes a row (as in a case involving charges against six anarchists when *The Guardian* (20 September 1979) printed details of information obtained from the police computer through jury vetting). The number of such cases is therefore presumably even fewer today than in the late 1970s.

For strong criticism of the practice of vetting, see Harriet Harman and John Griffith, *Justice Deserted* (National Council for Civil Liberties, 1979); Peter Duff and Mark Findlay, 'Jury Vetting–the Jury Under Attack', *Legal Studies*, 1983, p 159. See also Robert J East, 'Jury Packing: A Thing of the Past?', 48 *Modern Law Review*, 1985, p 518. East takes an even more serious view of jury vetting, seeing it as part of a general erosion of civil liberties.

Questions

1. To what extent does jury vetting affect the balance between prosecution and defence?

2. There are already quite a number of ways in which juries are not fully representative of the electoral register. Is this further example serious or trivial? Should a defendant have a right to have an unvetted jury?

3. Is there any good reason why in a sensitive case the *defence* should not have the right to have the jury vetted?

(f) Who serves on juries?

There are only two studies of jury composition in England. The first was an investigation of 326 juries empanelled in 1975 and 1976 in the Birmingham Crown Court. During the study the court authorities kept records of each juror's sex, age, occupation and race and the number of times he had previously sat on a jury. The study showed that the recommendations of the Morris Committee had had a considerable effect. According to Lord Devlin, in 1956 juries were 'predominantly male, middle-aged, middle-minded and middle class'. This was no longer so. The researchers found that 'the juries in question had acquired a distinctly working class character: indeed a majority of jurors were manual workers, or the wives of manual workers' (J Baldwin and M McConville, *Jury Trials* (Clarendon, 1979), p 95). Nevertheless, when compared with census data for the area, manual workers and especially unskilled manual workers were still somewhat under-represented. (The census figures showed 8.8 per cent of the local population in the category of unskilled Social Class V, as compared with 3.4 per cent in the sample of jurymen (*ibid*).) In regard to age, there was 'a remarkable congruence' between those who sat on juries and residents of Birmingham (*ibid*, p 97). In regard to sex, women were distinctly under-represented– 72 per cent of jurors were male. The authors explained this by two facts–more women than men asked for excusal and, as a result, an unofficial policy (since discontinued) was followed of calling twice as many men as women for jury service.

The other great discrepancy between the jury and the local population was in regard to an under-representation of racial minorities. Only 28 out of 3,912 jurors (0.7 per cent) were of West Indian or Asian origin, when the census figures suggested that one could expect 10 to 15 times that number (p 98).

The researchers investigated whether jury decisions could be correlated with any of these factors, but found that 'however one regarded the material, no consistent patterns were apparent' (p 100). The presence of women, younger or working-class jurors appeared to make no difference to jury results. They concluded: 'We can confidently state that no single social factor (nor, so far as we could detect, any group of factors operating in combination) produced any significant variation in the verdicts returned , . .'The truth of the matter is that most juries in Birmingham were extremely mixed, and it is to be expected that the amalgam of personal and social attributes that make up a jury will produce verdicts that reflect that unique social mix rather than the broad social characteristic of the individuals concerned' (pp 104–5). This finding appears to be confirmed by an unpublished Home Office study which compared the overall acquittal rate on a national basis for three months before the changes made by the Juries Act 1974 with three months after the Act came into force. No significant differences emerged (cited by Baldwin and McConville, *op cit* p 96, n 24).

The Crown Court Study carried out for the Runciman Royal Commission[7] included responses from over 800 juries sitting in every completed contested case in every crown court in the country for a two week period in February 1992. Returns were received from some 8,300 jurors. The profile of jurors that emerged from this national sample showed:

Sex Males were slightly over-represented–53 per cent as against 48 per cent in the whole population; foremen were much more disproportionately male–78 per cent (para 8.13.1).

Age Young jurors were almost exactly proportionate to their numbers in the population (18–24, 15%, compared with 14% in the general population, 21–34, 21%, compared with 20% in the general population). The other age groups were slightly over-represented–which was not surprising given that there were virtually no jurors over the age of 65–an age group that accounts for 20 per cent of the population. Surprisingly, the age distribution of jury foremen was not very different from that of the jury as a whole. Even the 18–24 age group contributed the foreman in 11 per cent of cases (p 236). There was no jury in the sample where any age group dominated disproportionately. The average age of the 8,338 jurors was in the middle band (35–44) (p 236). In 65 per cent of juries the number of young jurors (18–24) ranged from one to three (*ibid*). In one fifth of juries there were no such young jurors. The acquittal rate of juries with an average age of 25–34 was 42 per cent–a little lower than the 44 per cent for juries with an average age of 35–44 or 45–54 (Table 8.39, p 237).

Work status The great majority of the jurors were working (69% full-time, 13% part-time). Only 2 per cent had been unemployed for over 2 years. 6 per cent were retired persons. (para 8.13.3).

Social class The social class measures were somewhat crude but it appeared (Table 8.41, p 238) that 19 per cent were skilled manual (compared with 23% in the general population), 7 per cent were unskilled manual (exactly the same as the general population), 29 per cent were professional/managerial (compared with 31% in the general population).

Ethnic mix Jurors were asked to identify their own race or ethnic background on a list of seven categories. The results showed a very close approximation between the sample and the general population. Whites were 95 per cent of the jurors–almost exactly the same as the general population. Non-white jurors were 5 per cent of the sample, compared with 5.9 per cent of the total population according to the 1991 census. In fact Black-Caribbean and Indian were over-represented, each being 2 per cent of the sample, compared with 1 per cent of the national population. In 65 per cent of juries there was no non-white jurors, in 16 per cent of juries there was one non-

7   M Zander and P Henderson, *The Crown Court Study* (Royal Commission on Criminal Justice, Research Study No 19, 1993).

white person, in 9 per cent there were two, in 5 per cent there were three, in 5 per cent there were more than three (pp 241–42).[8]

Language problems   96 per cent of the sample said that English was their first language. Of the 273 who said English was not their first language, 32 said they had a little difficulty in following the case. None said they had a lot of difficulty (para 8.13.7, p 242).

Defence counsel in the Crown Court Study said they had no concerns about the composition of the jury in 83 per cent of cases. Of those who expressed concerns, the most frequently mentioned issue was the racial mix (Table 6.14, p 176). When the defendant was black, defence counsel expressed concern about the racial mix on the jury in 18 per cent of cases, and therefore had no concern in just over 80 per cent of these cases (p 176).

However, concerns of defence counsel did not correlate with the result of cases. Defence counsel had no concerns about jury composition in 80 per cent of cases ending in acquittal, compared with 81 per cent of cases ending in conviction (*ibid*).

(g) The extent to which juries are used

(1) Civil cases

There is a *right* to have trial by jury only in the following cases: libel, slander, malicious prosecution, false imprisonment and allegations of fraud. Moreover, since the Supreme Court Act 1981, the right to trial by jury in the categories listed above has been subject to the proviso in section 69(1) that the court can refuse jury trial if it is of the opinion that 'the trial requires prolonged examination of documents or accounts or any scientific or local investigation which cannot conveniently be made with a jury'. (See *Goldsmith v Pressdram Ltd* [1987] 3 All ER 485; *Viscount De L'Isle v Times Newspapers Ltd* [1987] 3 All ER 499; and *Beta Construction Ltd v Channel Four Television Co Ltd* [1990] 2 All ER 1012. In 1994 the Court of Appeal denied an application from two unemployed environmental campaigners that the libel action brought against them in respect of a leaflet by McDonald's fast food chain should be heard by a jury. The Court of Appeal said that the scientific issues would make it impossible for the case to be tried satisfactorily by a jury. The two campaigners conducted their own case which went on for over a year and became the longest libel action in recorded history. (See national newspapers 26 March 1994, and a year later Dan Mills, '"McLibel 2" bite back against Big Mac', *Legal Action*, April 1995, p 9.) See to like effect *Taylor v Anderton* [1995] 2 All ER 420, CA. In *Racz v Home Office* [1994] 1 All ER 97 the House of Lords upheld the Court of Appeal's denial of jury trial even though the action could have raised the issue of an award of exemplary damages.

In other cases trial is without a jury unless the court 'in its discretion orders it to be tried with a jury' (Supreme Court Act, 1981, s 69(3)). (For a brief review of recent cases see *Civil Justice Quarterly*, April 1995, p 152.)

---

8   Permission for the jury study was conditional on it being a national sample with no regional breakdown and no linkage with the other parts of the study. It was therefore not possible to test the jury composition against the population mix in different regions.

Prior to that Act the judges had what appeared to be a complete statutory discretion as to whether to order trial by jury. The Administration of Justice Act 1933 provided that 'any action to be tried in the Queen's Bench Division could, in the discretion of the court or judge, be ordered to be tried either with or without a jury'.

In 1933 the Court of Appeal sitting with five judges said that the question of trial by jury was really one for the discretion of the court–*Hope v Great Western Rly Co* [1937] 2 KB 130. Lord Wright (at p 138) said the discretion of the judge was 'completely untrammelled'. The *Annual Practice*, the practitioners' bible, in interpreting the decision said 'the discretion of the judge is absolute'. When the Rules of the Supreme Court were revised in 1958, Ord 36, r 1(3) was amended to read: 'The discretion of a court or judge in making or varying any order under this rule is an absolute one.'

But in 1966 the issue came again before the Court of Appeal sitting again with five judges. Lord Denning gave the judgment of the court:

Ward v James [1966] 1 QB 273 (Court of Appeal, Civil Division)

In May 1962, the plaintiff was being driven in a car by the defendant in Germany. There was an accident in which the plaintiff was very seriously injured, becoming a permanent quadriplegic. In December 1962, he brought an action against the defendant for damages for negligence; the question in the action was substantially what damages the plaintiff should be awarded.

On the plaintiff's application, trial by jury was ordered by the master on 23 July 1963, an appeal to the judge being dismissed on 20 July 1963. Appeal to the Court of Appeal.

Lord Denning MR:

Relevant considerations today

Let it not be supposed that this court is in any way opposed to trial by jury. It has been the bulwark for our liberties too long for any of us to seek to alter it. Whenever a man is on trial for serious crime, or when in a civil case a man's honour or integrity is at stake, or when one or other party must be deliberately lying, then trial by jury has no equal. But in personal injury cases trial by jury has given place of late to trial by judge alone, the reason being simply this, that in these cases trial by judge alone is more acceptable to the great majority of people. Rarely does a party ask in these cases for a jury. When a solicitor gives advice, it runs in this way: 'If I were you, I should not ask for a jury. I should have a judge alone. You do know where you stand with a judge, and if he goes wrong, you can always go to the Court of Appeal. But as for a jury, you never know what they will do, and if they do go wrong, there is no putting them right. The Court of Appeal hardly ever interferes with the verdict of a jury.' So the client decides on judge alone. That is why jury trials have declined. It is because they are not asked for. Lord Devlin shows this in his book [The Hamlyn Lectures, eighth series, *Trial by Jury*, ch 6, p 133].

This important consequence follows: the judges alone, and not juries, in the great majority of cases, decide whether there is negligence or not. They set the standard of care to be expected of the reasonable man. They also assess the damages. They see, so far as they can, that like sums are given for like injuries. They set the standards for awards. Hence there is a uniformity of decision. This has its impact on decisions as to the mode of trial. If a party asks for a jury in an ordinary personal injury case, the court naturally asks: 'Why do you want a jury when nearly everyone else is content with judge alone?' I am afraid it is often because he has a weak case, or desires to appeal to sympathy. If no good reason is given, then the court orders trial by judge alone. Hence we find that nowadays the discretion in the ordinary run of personal injury cases is in favour of judge alone. It is no sufficient reason for departing from it simply to provide a 'guinea-pig' case: see *Hennell v Ranaboldo.*[9]

Lessons of recent cases

... recent cases show the desirability of three things: First, *assessability*: In cases of grave injury, where the body is wrecked or the brain destroyed, it is very difficult to assess a fair compensation in money, so difficult that the award must basically be a conventional figure, derived from experience or from awards in comparable cases. Secondly, *uniformity*: There should be some measure of uniformity in awards so that similar decisions are given in similar cases; otherwise there will be great dissatisfaction in the community, and much criticism of the administration of justice. Thirdly, *predictability*: Parties should be able to predict with some measure of accuracy the sum which is likely to be awarded in a particular case, for by this means cases can be settled peaceably and not brought to court, a thing very much to the public good. None of these three is achieved when the damages are left at large to the jury. Under the present practice the judge does not give them any help at all to assess the figure. The result is that awards may vary greatly, from being much too high to much too low. There is no uniformity and no predictability. ...

The case caused a great hullabaloo. The Court of Appeal, it was said, had struck down one of the sacred rights of an Englishman–the right to trial by jury. This was in fact not the case, the civil jury had already virtually ceased to exist even before the decision. In 1963, three years before *Ward v James*, the number of jury trials in London in the Queen's Bench Division was 27 out of a total of 962 (2.8 per cent). (For the history of the decline of the civil jury, see Lord Devlin, *Trial by Jury*, chapter 6.) Nevertheless, the Court of Appeal was obviously concerned to allay public disquiet and almost immediately found a case in which it disclaimed any intention to abolish civil juries:

Hodges v Harland and Wolff Ltd [1965] 1 All ER 1086 (Court of Appeal, Civil Division)

The plaintiff, while employed by the defendant, was operating a diesel driven air compressor. The spindle on that machine, revolving at a great speed, was not properly guarded as required by the Shipbuilding and Ship-repairing Regulations, 1960. The spindle caught and tore the plaintiff's trousers and avulsed his penis and scrotal skin. One effect of the injury was that the plaintiff still had the sexual urge without the ability to perform the sexual act. On the summons for directions, trial by jury was ordered by the judge after considering the reported cases and the principle of uniformity of awards and after taking other relevant considerations into account. On appeal:

Lord Denning MR: ... Naturally enough, we have been referred to the recent decision of this court in *Ward v James*. It is a mistake to suppose that this court in that case took away the right to trial by jury. It was not this court but Parliament itself which years ago took away any absolute right to trial by jury and left it to the discretion of the judges. This court in *Ward v James* affirmed that discretion and said that, as the statute has given a discretion to the judge, this court would not fetter it by rigid rules from which the judge was never at liberty to depart. What *Ward v James* did was this. It laid down the considerations which should be borne in mind by a judge when exercising his discretion: and it is apparent that, on those considerations,

9   [1963] 1 WLR 1391.

the result will ordinarily be trial by judge alone. It will not result in trial by jury save in exceptional circumstances. That is no great change. It has been the position for many years. As it happened, in *Ward v James* itself, the result was trial by jury.

In this present case the judge, it seems to me, has borne all the relevant considerations in mind. He said, 'this is a unique case.' So it is. Counsel for the defendants urged that there were one or two cases in the books where a man had retained the sexual urge without the ability to perform the sexual act. That may be so, but they were very different from this. I think that the judge was well entitled to take the view that this was an exceptional case, and in the circumstances to exercise his discretion in favour of trial by jury. Indeed, when a judge exercises his discretion and takes all the relevant considerations into account, it is well settled that the burden is on anyone coming to this court to show that he was wrong. I see nothing wrong in the way that Lyell J dealt with this case in ordering trial by jury. ...

I think that this case was properly decided by the judge. The appeal fails and must be dismissed.

Davies and Salmon LJJ agreed.

The same issue of the unsuitability of juries in personal injury cases was addressed by the Court of Appeal 26 years later, in *H v Ministry of Defence* [1991] 2 All ER 834. By a strange coincidence the case again concerned injury to the penis. The plaintiff, a soldier, was suing for the catastrophic effects of an operation which was intended as a skin graft but which resulted in amputation of the major part of his sex organ. Liability was admitted; the only issue was as to damages.

Lord Donaldson MR, giving judgment for himself and Lords Justices Woolf and Mann, said that since *Ward v James* in 1966 the only reported case in which trial by jury had been ordered in a personal injury case was that of *Hodges v Harland and Wolff*. 'Whereas under the 1933 Act there was no legislative bias for or against trial by jury, other than in cases specified in s 6, s 69(3) of the 1981 Supreme Court Act disclosed a change involving a bias against such a trial'.

Where the case called for an award of compensatory damages for personal injuries, a jury trial would normally be inappropriate 'because the assessment of such damages must be based upon or have regard to conventional scales of damages'. The very fact that no jury trial appeared to have taken place in a personal injuries case in the past 25 years affirmed how exceptional such a case would have to be.

But jury trial might be appropriate if the question were one of exemplary damages (for instance where the injury resulted from deliberate abuse of authority), which would be somewhat similar to a claim for malicious prosecution or false imprisonment 'in respect of which there was a legislative intention that there should be a jury trial, unless there were contra indications'.

In 1995 the Law Commission in a Consultation Paper (*Damages for Personal Injury: Non-Pecuniary Loss*, Paper No 140, 1995, at p 125) said that not only did it agree with the Court of Appeal's decisions in *Ward v James* and *H v Ministry of Defence* (above), it went further and thought that juries should *never* be used for personal injury cases:

We agree with these two decisions. Indeed we go further. Given the difficulty of assessing damages for non-pecuniary loss in personal injury cases and the judicial tariff that has been developed to ensure a measure of consistency and uniformity, we consider it unsatisfactory that juries might ever be called upon to assess compensatory damages for personal injury. Juries do not have the benefit of knowledge of the scale of values that has been developed and the inevitable consequence is unacceptable inconsistency with awards in other cases [para 4.83].

Like the Court of Appeal in *Ward v James*, the Law Commission rejected the idea that the jury should be provided with a scale of values, or upper and lower sums, leaving it for them to fix the actual amount.

Juries for libel and slander cases–the Faulks Committee

The role of the jury in libel and slander actions was considered by the Faulks Committee set up in 1971. In its report (*The Law of Defamation*, 1974, Cmnd 5709) the Committee concluded that juries should no longer be available as of right in defamation actions but that instead there should be the same discretion to permit a jury as in all other cases. They had several reasons:

(1) Although juries were perfectly able to determine some questions that arose in defamation actions, there were other matters (such as whether a plea of justification succeeded, or technical legal concepts such as fair comment and qualified privilege) where a judge was normally more competent.

(2) Libel actions often turned on barbed subtleties, specialist jargon or group attitudes of warring factions where the jury was not likely to have any relevant insight or knowledge.

(3) Contrary to the popular view that judges were remote from the life of the community, they were in fact well in touch with the emotions, conventions, language and way of life of the rest of the community. ('The idea that judges live in an ivory tower is wholly out-dated. They go by train and bus, they look at television and they hear, in matrimonial, criminal, accident and other cases, every kind of expression which the ordinary man uses, and they have learnt how he lives' (para 484)).

(4) Judges gave their reasons, whereas juries did not. It was more satisfactory for both sides to know the reasons.

(5) Juries had difficulties with complex cases.

(6) Juries were unpredictable.

(7) Trial by jury was more expensive.

(8) The existing rule gave the right of decision as to mode of trial to whichever side wanted jury trial. No matter how strong the case against jury trial, the party who wanted it would prevail. This was unjust to the other party and wrong in principle.

The Committee concluded by saying that it believed that 'much of the support for jury trials is emotional and derives from the undoubted value of juries in serious criminal cases where they stand between the prosecuting authority and the citizen' (para 496).

It did not recommend that the possibility of jury trial should be removed altogether because there were some cases in which a jury would be better than a judge:

We recognise it to be undesirable, that a judge sitting alone should be embroiled in a matter of political, religious or moral controversy. The same might be true where any party has been outspokenly critical of the Bench. Broadly, where the issue is whether the words were true or false and the subject is one that raises strong feelings among the general public so that a judge alone might be suspected, however mistakenly, of prejudice conscious or unconscious, we should expect that trial by jury might be awarded–but that in cases which did not involve such controversial questions a judge alone would be more likely to be selected [para 503].

However, the Committee did have a recommendation on the subject of whether juries should continue to deal with damages.

Juries and damages in defamation cases

The Faulks Committee came to the conclusion that it was not right that juries should continue to award damages. The jury simply lacked the necessary knowledge and experience. There were two possible alternatives. One was that the judge should fix the amount of damages without any help from the jury. The other was that the judge would fix the actual amount having had guidance from the jury as to the appropriate scale. The Committee favoured the second. The jury should determine whether the damages were to be 'substantial/moderate/nominal or contemptuous' and the judge should fix the actual amount (para 513). Also the Committee said that the Court of Appeal should be empowered to review the amount of damages and should have the power to substitute its own figure for that of the jury (para 514).

At first nothing was done to implement these recommendations. In its 1995 Consultation Paper on *Damages for Personal Injury: Non-Pecuniary Loss* (above), the Law Commission said that it had reluctantly come to the conclusion that the Faulks' Committee's recommendation to split the determination of liability and damages between judge and jury was unworkable in libel actions.

In the late 1980s the question of the jury's competence in the assessment of damages came into issue again as a result of some astronomic libel awards. In 1987 a jury awarded £450,000 to Martin Packard against a Greek newspaper (which sold a mere 50 copies in Britain) for a story accusing him of leaking information about his resistance organization to the Greek Colonels, of implication in the murder of a British journalist and of taking part in drug smuggling.

In 1988 Koo Stark won £300,000 from the *Daily Mirror*, which had alleged that she dated Prince Andrew after her marriage. In the same year Jeffrey Archer, best-selling author and deputy chairman of the Conservative Party obtained £500,000 against the *Daily Star* for the allegation that he had visited a prostitute. In 1989 a jury awarded Sonia Sutcliffe, wife of the Yorkshire Ripper, the then record sum of £600,000 against *Private Eye* for an article suggesting that she had cashed in on his notoriety.

Private Eye appealed and the Court of Appeal set aside the award. (Subsequently it was stated in court that Mrs Sutcliffe had accepted a settlement of £60,000 instead of having a second trial–(1989) *Times*, 7 November.) In setting aside the jury's award the Court of Appeal said that Parliament had provided that for personal injury cases judges should determine damages,[10] whereas for libel actions it should be by jury. The approach of each was different. Judges were trained and bound by precedent to have regard to awards in other cases. Juries were not. Judicial awards therefore conformed to conventional scales, whereas juries were free to give expression to 'a gut reaction'. Judges gave reasons, juries did not. In reviewing jury decisions on damages the judges had to be careful not to frustrate Parliament's intentions. They should interfere only if the damages were so excessive that no reasonable jury could have awarded them.

In setting aside the award Lord Donaldson MR said the money, if invested, would have given Mrs Sutcliffe an income before tax of over £1,000 a week leaving all the capital intact. That could not be justified. He agreed with *Ward v James* that it was not desirable to cite to the jury awards in other cases since they were apt to be misleading. But the judge could invite the jury to consider what the result of its award would be in

10 As has been seen, this is not strictly true. Parliament in 1933 gave the courts a complete discretion; the judges in *Ward v James* (above) said that normally in personal injury cases trial should be by judges alone; subsequently Parliament in effect ratified this decision by s 69 of the Supreme Court Act, 1981.

terms of weekly, monthly or annual income if the money were invested in a building society.

Only a few weeks later, however, another jury ignored just such an indication in the case by Lord Aldington against Count Tolstoy who had accused him of being a war criminal responsible for the death of thousands of Yugoslavs and Cossacks sent back to Russia after the war. The judge told the jury to keep their feet on the ground and not to award 'Mickey Mouse' damages. But the jury awarded Lord Aldington £1.5 million. (Lord Aldington later offered to settle the claim for £300,000–an offer refused by Lord Tolstoy who took a case to the European Court of Human Rights in Strasbourg on the ground that the size of the award violated his right to free expression under Art 10 of the European Convention on Human Rights. Lord Tolstoy won a unanimous decision to that effect.)

As will be seen (p 497 below), these cases led to a change in the rules so as to permit the Court of Appeal to substitute its own award for that of the jury–as had been recommended in 1974 by the Faulks Committee. But the problem continued. In 1991, a jury awarded the well-known television personality Esther Rantzen £250,000 against Mirror Group Newspapers for a libel involving her reputation and integrity as someone concerned about sexual abuse of children. On appeal the Court of Appeal reduced the award to £110,000–*Rantzen v Mirror Group Newspapers* [1993] 4 All ER 975. It said the award was excessive by any objective standard of reasonable compensation. It invoked Art 10 of the European Convention as one of the reasons for its decision. The courts' previous reluctance to intervene should be re-examined. The courts, it said, should subject large awards of damages to more searching scrutiny than had been the case in the past. The question to be asked was whether a reasonable jury could have thought the award was necessary to compensate the plaintiff and re-establish his reputation.

The Law Commission in its Consultation Paper on *Damages for Personal Injury: Non-Pecuniary Loss* issued in December 1995 proposed that the judge in directing the jury in defamation or other cases should inform the jury of the range of awards for non-pecuniary loss in personal injury cases (para 4.103).

The Law Commission's view had hardly been expressed when it became the law of the land through a ruling by the Court of Appeal given on December 12, 1995 in a case brought by rock star Elton John against the *Sunday Mirror*. (*John v Mirror Group Newspapers Ltd* [1996] 2 All ER 35.) The court reduced what it called the jury's 'manifestly excessive' award of £350,000 to £75,000. In doing so it held that in future lawyers and judges could and should give juries clear guidance in regard to damages. It described juries in libel actions as 'sheep loosed on an unfenced common with no shepherd'. Giving the judgment of the court, Sir Thomas Bingham MR said:

It is in our view offensive to public opinion, and rightly so, that a defamation plaintiff should recover damages for injury to reputation greater, perhaps by a significant factor, than if that same plaintiff had been rendered a helpless cripple or an insensate vegetable. The time has in our view come when judges, and counsel, should be free to draw the attention of juries to these comparisons.

Mentioning figures would not, it thought, develop into an auction. Rather 'the process of mentioning figures would, in our view, induce a mood of realism'. Figures mentioned by counsel would tend to be the upper and lower bounds of a realistic bracket. The judge could give his indication. The jury would remain free to choose a figure within or outside the bracket.

If the jury make an award outside the upper or lower bounds of any bracket indicated and such award is the subject of appeal, real weight must be given to the possibility that their judgment is to be preferred to that of the judge.

(2) Criminal cases

As has been seen, cases tried by crown courts where the accused pleads not guilty to one or more charges are heard by juries. This is known as trial on indictment. (For discussion of the issues regarding mode of trial in criminal cases see pp 17–22 above.) In 1994 there were 90,759 defendants dealt with after being committed for trial in the crown courts. Of these, 59,577 (66%) pleaded guilty to all counts and 4,977 (5 per cent) pleaded guilty to some counts. (*Judicial Statistics*, 1994, Cm 2981, Table 6.7.)

Cases tried on indictment are of two kinds. They may be offences that can only be tried at the higher level. This is true of all the most serious cases. Or they may be offences triable either way, where the prosecution or the defence have asked for trial on indictment. As was seen earlier (pp 18–19 above), offences triable either way were created by the Criminal Law Act 1977 on the recommendations of the James Committee –*Report on the Distribution of Criminal Business between the Crown Court and the Magistrates' Courts*, 1975, Cmnd 6323. The procedure under the Act requires that both parties be given a chance to make representations as to the mode of trial. The court then considers whether the trial should take place summarily or at the crown court. If it thinks that trial on indictment is the more appropriate, this decision prevails even if the defendant wants summary trial. For guidelines laid down recently see [1990] 3 All ER 979. If, however, the court thinks that summary trial is indicated, the defendant can override this choice and insist on trial at the higher level. (Where a number of defendants are jointly charged with an either-way offence and one elects to be tried on indictment, all must be sent for trial on indictment–*R v Brentwood Justices, ex p Nicholls* [1990] 3 All ER 516.) About 80 per cent of all cases triable either way are in fact tried summarily.

A survey of defendants carried out for the James Committee showed that people said they chose jury trial because they thought the case would be gone into more thoroughly, there was a jury to try it, there was a better chance of an acquittal in the crown court (on this, see pp 412–14 below), the judges were better qualified, and they thought that magistrates accepted police evidence too readily. Also they sometimes wanted to delay matters–to prepare their case better or to put off the evil day. On the other hand, those who chose trial before magistrates did so, they said, because they wanted to get it over as quickly as possible and to get the lightest sentence. The majority of defendants who opted for trial on indictment intended to plead not guilty (though many in the event pleaded guilty), whilst the majority of those who opted for summary trial intended to plead guilty and mainly did so (Janet Gregory, *Crown Court or Magistrates' Court* (HMSO, 1976), pp 12–15).

(h) Aids to the jury

The Morris Committee considered whether juries needed more help to reach their decisions. It recommended that jurors be sent a leaflet with information about their duties and about local arrangements. It did not think that they should be encouraged to take notes but that if they wished to do so facilities to do so should be provided.

Report of the (Morris) *Departmental Committee on Jury Service*, 1965, Cmnd 2627

Note-taking
282. The process of note-taking is one that requires a good deal of experience and skill. Because of their training, judges are able to make accurate and reasonably complete notes, and at the same time to observe all that is happening and to keep control over the proceedings. Not all jurors can be expected to have the same skill and training. Experience shows that as a general rule it may well be better for jurors to concentrate on listening, observing and reflecting.[11] This however is clearly a matter upon which no all-embracing guidance could be given to jurors, and we therefore suggest that no reference should be made to it in the pamphlet. The provision in the jury box and retiring room of writing materials will be an indication that it is permissible to take notes, but beyond that we think it is for individual judges, recorders, and chairmen to decide whether to inform jurors of their right to take notes and whether to give any guidance or advice on the matter.

Questions by the jury
283. Rather similar considerations apply to the problem whether jurors should be told that they may ask questions. We think that there is some peril in encouraging them to do so. If cases are being conducted by advocates on both sides, as they usually are, there is every reason to expect that all relevant questions will be raised at some time before the conclusion of the evidence. If positive encouragement were given to jurors to ask questions there would be a risk in a criminal case of some question prejudicial to the accused being asked inadvertently, and there would also be some risk of the proceedings getting out of hand. Our witnesses were in general agreement that it is better if jurors do not intervene too readily, though it can undoubtedly happen that some point that seems to the jury to be important may not have been sufficiently probed, and it would be unfortunate if a jury thought that they could never ask a question. Much must be left to the handling of the proceedings by the judge, and we therefore suggest that guidance on this subject be left to the court and not included in the pamphlet.

The Lord Chancellor's Department did produce a leaflet which is sent out with jury summonses to inform jurors about the process. It has a few lines on each of a variety of topics. Thus it describes the process of selection for cases, including the right of challenge and of asking jurors to stand by for the Crown. It tells the jurors to inform the clerk of the court if they have personal knowledge of the case or of anyone involved in it.

Jurors are told that during the trial they may be asked to retire whilst the judge hears submissions on matters of law. They are warned that they should not make up their mind about the case until they have heard all the evidence. They are also warned that they must not discuss the case with anyone except with other jurors and then only in the jury room. Even after the case is concluded they should not disclose what happened in the jury room.

11 This view was supported by a law lecturer who reported on her experience of being a juror in 'Notes of a Lawyer Juror', *New Law Journal*, 14 September, 1990, pp 1264, 1265. She had started by taking notes, one of only two to do so, but gave up as it impeded observation of witnesses (ed).

They are also told about the duty to elect a foreman to act as chairman, but no guidance is given as to how this should be done. It is stated that they may take notes if they wish during the trial. It is also mentioned that in certain circumstances the judge may be able to take a majority verdict but that they must reach a unanimous verdict if possible.

There is nothing in the leaflet advising jurors that they may ask questions. Correspondence in *The Times* in 1982 showed that questions can sometimes be asked by jurors through the judge. A letter on 28 April said that the writer when foreman of a jury had managed to get the judge to ask a question by passing him a note from a fellow member of the jury. A letter on 15 May said that such a note had caused the judge to ask the prosecution for further evidence which led to an acquittal.

In 1992 the Lord Chancellor's Department produced a video that is now routinely shown to all jurors at the start of their period of jury service.

The Roskill Committee also gave attention to ways of making the jury's task easier, especially in complex cases. The prosecution, it said, should prepare schedules and summaries of the relevant contents of documentary evidence. Glossaries of technical terms should be made for the jury. Modern techniques of presentation of information should be utilized, including any appropriate forms of visual aid.

This exhortation has been very much taken to heart. Cases run by the Serious Fraud Office rejoice in a full battery of hi-tech methods. The two specially designed court rooms in Chichester Rents in Chancery Lane, for instance, have a proliferation of TV monitors and computer systems for presentation of evidence to the jury. The jury itself have four TV monitors on which they can see the head and shoulders of the witness. But the TV monitors are constantly in use also to project documents and graphics. In these huge cases with thousands of documents the IT expert is now a vital member of the lawyers' support team. (See also Criminal Justice Act 1988, s 31, which permits the court to approve special means for conveying complex information.)

The Runciman Royal Commission addressed the same issues and also made recommendations designed to ease the jury's task. It thought that writing materials should always be provided, that technological aids should be provided where appropriate, that the judge should explain to the jury that they have a right to ask questions and to take notes (pp 134–35).

The Crown Court Study done for the Royal Commission (see p 375, n 7 above) found that in the great majority of cases one or more members of the jury did take notes and most jurors said that they found their notes to be useful (p 173, para 6.2.3). (When the judges were asked, 46% said that jurors should be encouraged to take notes, 23% thought they should be discouraged and 31% had no opinion one way or the other (p 173, para 6.2.2).)

The great majority of jurors (70%) said that they had been told they could ask questions, but of those who had wanted to do so, only 17 per cent had had the courage to do so (p 174, para 6.2.4). (Nearly three-fifths of the judges (59%) thought jurors should not be told about their right to ask questions, 29% that they should be told, and the rest had no view.)

(i) The quality of jury decision-making

There is as yet no systematic study of the jury based on observation or recording of their deliberations. The Contempt of Court Act 1981 makes this impossible. According to s 8 of the Act it is contempt of court 'to obtain, disclose, or solicit any particulars of statements made, opinions expressed, arguments advanced or votes cast by members of a jury in the course of their deliberations in any legal proceedings'. (The lengthy questionnaire addressed to jurors in the Crown Court Study done for the Runciman Royal Commission (p 375 above) was not exempt from the provisions of the 1981 Act. The questions asked were all carefully drafted and officially approved on the basis that they did not infringe the provisions of s 8.)

Studies of jury decision-making have mainly been based on the impressions of judges, lawyers, or police officers, or on simulations with 'shadow' or 'mock' juries.

One major such study was the Chicago project based on the impressions of judges. It was conducted by Professors Harry Kalven, Jr and Hans Zeisel of Chicago University and published as *The American Jury* (Little Brown & Co, 1966). The work was based on 3,576 actual trials and the replies to a questionnaire from the 555 trial judges involved. (Jurymen could not be approached.) The results showed that judges and juries agreed to acquit in 13 per cent of cases and agreed to convict in 62 per cent of cases, yielding a total agreement rate of 75 per cent.

In cases where judge and jury disagreed, it was found that the jury was more lenient than the judge in 19 per cent and less lenient in 3 per cent. Just over half of the disagreements which seemed explicable were caused by different approaches to the evidence. Nearly one-third were due to jury reaction to the law and about one-tenth were due to jury sentiments about the defendant himself. Summarizing their conclusions in *New Society*, the authors said:

Harry Kalven, Jr and Hans Zeisel, 'The American Jury', *New Society*, 25 August 1966, p 290

It may be useful to put quite general and interrelated questions: why do judge and jury ever disagree, and why do they not disagree more often?

The answer must turn on the intrinsic differences between the two institutions. The judge very often perceives the stimulus that moves the jury, but does not yield to it. Indeed it is interesting how often the judge describes with sensitivity a factor which he then excludes from his own considerations.

The better question is the second. Since the jury does at times recognize and use its *de facto* freedom, why does it not deviate from the judge more often? Why is it not more of a wildcat operation? In many ways our single most basic finding is that the jury, despite its autonomy, spins so close to the legal baseline.

The study does not answer directly, but it does lay the ground for three plausible suggestions. As just noted, the official law has done pretty well in adjusting to the equities, and there is therefore no great gap between the official values and the popular. Again, the group nature of the jury decision will moderate and brake eccentric views. Lastly, the jury is not simply a corner gang picked from the street; it has been invested with a public task, brought under the influence of a judge, and put to work in solemn surroundings. Perhaps one reason why the jury exercises its very real power so sparingly is because it is officially told it has none.

The jury thus represents a uniquely subtle distribution of official power; an unusual arrangement of checks and balances. It represents also an impressive way of building discretion, equity, and flexibility into a legal system. Not the least of the advantages is that the jury, relieved of the burdens of creating precedent, can bend the law without breaking it.

Whether or not one comes to admire the jury system as much as we have, it must rank as a daring effort in human arrangement to work out a solution to the tensions between law and equity and anarchy.

For an extended discussion of the book, see (1967) *Criminal Law Review*, pp 555–86. But for doubts about the statistical methodology of the study, see AE Bottoms and Monica Walker, 'The American Jury: A Critique', 67 *Journal of the American Statistical Association*, 1972, p 773. For the authors' rejoinder, see *ibid*, p 779. For an assessment in 1991 see Valerie Hans and Neil Vidman, 'The American Jury at Twenty-Five years', *Law and Social Inquiry*, 1991, p 323.

The first English study, by the Oxford Penal Research Unit, was based primarily on the views of barristers and the police. Its principal finding was that most acquittals were 'attributable to a single cause–the failure of the prosecution (normally the police) to provide enough information, or to present it in court in a way that would convince both judge and jury of the defendant's guilt'. (See Sarah McCabe and Robert Purves, *The Jury at Work* (Blackwell, 1972), p 11.) Very few verdicts were found to be perverse.

The present writer's study of acquittals at the Old Bailey and the Inner London Crown Court was based on interviews with the barristers for the prosecution and the defence. It was striking that there was no great difference of view between prosecution and defence lawyers as to the reasons for the acquittals. Again, there was little evidence of perverse verdicts. (See M Zander, 'Are Too Many Professional Criminals Avoiding Conviction?' 37 *Modern Law Review*, 1974, p 28.)

For the report of a series of experiments with 'mock' juries who listened to tape-recorded trials, see AP Sealy and WR Cornish, 'Juries and their Verdicts', 36 *Modern Law Review*, 1973, p 496, and LSE Jury Project, 'Juries and the Rules of Evidence' (1973) *Criminal Law Review*, p 208.

A study based on 30 cases heard by 'shadow' juries conducted by the Oxford Penal Research Unit showed the jury approaching its task very soberly. The shadow juries listened to real cases and when the real jury withdrew to consider their verdicts, so did the shadow jury. The authors summarized their results:

Sarah McCabe and Robert Purves, *The Shadow Jury at Work*, 1974, pp 60–3

Of course the 'shadow' jury discussions and verdicts were not comparable with those of the real jury since the future of the defendant was not at risk, but the fact that many of our volunteers felt like jurors encourages us to make certain comparisons where real and 'shadow' jury verdicts agree.

Summary of results

3. The 'shadow' juries showed considerable determination in looking for evidence upon which convictions could be based; when it seemed inadequate, they were not prepared to allow their own 'hunch' that the defendant was involved in some way in the offence that was charged to stand in the way of an acquittal ...

5. There was little evidence of perversity in the final decisions of these thirty groups. One acquittal only showed that sympathy and impatience with the triviality of the case so influenced the 'shadow' jurors' view of the evidence that they refused to convict. One other unexpected acquittal seemed to be wholly due to dissatisfaction with the evidence.

But a less favourable view of jury decisions emerged from a later piece of research– *Jury Trials* by John Baldwin and Michael McConville (Clarendon, 1979). They selected a random sample of 500 defendants in the Birmingham Crown Court who pleaded not guilty. In the event, 116 of these were acquitted by the judge before the case had run its full course and another 14 changed their plea to guilty during the case. This left

370, of which 114 ended in acquittal. The researchers asked the trial judge, the defence solicitor, the prosecuting solicitor, the police and the defendant himself about these cases–the first three groups by questionnaire and the last two by interview. The response rate was very high (over 95 per cent for the judges, the prosecuting solicitors and the police). The table below shows the opinions of the different groups regarding the 114 acquittal cases.

	Judge %	Defence solicitor %	Prosecuting solicitor %	Police %
No strong view expressed that the acquittal not justified	62	83	64	48
Some doubts about acquittal	6	7	9	8
Serious doubts about acquittal	32	10	26	44
Total	100(114)	100(114)	100(114)	100(114)

(Source: Jury Trials, Table 5, p 46.)

The acquittal was seen as doubtful or highly questionable by one respondent in 30 instances (27 per cent of the 114), by two respondents in 16 (14 per cent) and by three or more respondents in 28 (25 per cent)–*ibid*, Table 6, p 47. There were 41 cases in which both judge and one other respondent found the acquittal doubtful (p 54).

Convictions were less often found doubtful or highly questionable, but 8 per cent were so regarded by one or more respondents (2 per cent by one respondent, 3 per cent by two and 3 per cent by three or more respondents–Table 9, p 51).

The researchers concluded that in respect of a few acquittals it might be said 'that the jury's verdict was primarily conditioned by its sympathy for the defendant or antipathy towards the victim' and 'some questionable convictions can possibly be explained on the basis of sympathy with the victim or prejudice against the defendant'. But in general 'the performance of the jury did not always appear to accord with the principle underlying the trial system in England that it is better to acquit those who are probably guilty than to convict any who are possibly innocent. On the contrary, the jury appeared on occasion to be overready to acquit those who were probably guilty and insufficiently prepared to protect the possibly innocent' (p 128). There was nothing in the composition of the jury (age, sex or social class) which correlated with the decisions.

The study is significantly different from previous studies in suggesting a considerable measure of disagreement between jury verdicts and those of the other key actors.

The Crown Court Study

The Crown Court Study[12] produced new material bearing on the issue under consideration here. The study was based, *inter alia*, on the responses of jurors, prosecution and defence barristers, judges and police officers concerned in some 800 contested

12 M Zander and P Henderson, *Crown Court Study*, Royal Commission on Criminal Justice Research Study No 19, 1993.

cases in every crown court in England and Wales in a two week period in February 1992.

Did the jury understand the evidence? Jurors were asked, 'How difficult was it for you to understand the evidence in this case?' Half (50%) thought it 'Not at all difficult', 41 per cent thought it 'Not very difficult', 8 per cent 'Fairly difficult' and 1 per cent 'Very difficult' (p 206, sect 8.2.1). The same question was asked in cases where there was scientific evidence. Surprisingly, the results were very similar – 56 per cent 'Not at all difficult', 34 per cent 'Not very difficult', 9 per cent 'Fairly difficult', 1 per cent 'Very difficult' (p 206, sect 8.2.2).

Jurors were then asked 'Do you think the jury as a whole was able to understand the evidence?' The response broadly was yes. Over half (56%) said that all the jury understood the evidence and nearly half (41%) said that most understood, 2 per cent said that 'Only a few understood' and a mere 0.4 per cent said 'None of them understood'. (The response from jury foremen was virtually identical (p 207, sect 8.2.3). There were however 143 juries (17% of the 821 in the study) in which one or more jurors said 'Only a few understood' or 'None of them understood'. 116 juries had one such member, 20 had two such members, 6 had three and one had four (*ibid*).

The prosecution and defence barristers were asked whether they thought the jury had trouble understanding the evidence. 94 per cent of prosecution barristers, and 90 per cent of defence barristers thought they had no trouble, 1 per cent and 4 per cent respectively thought they had trouble (p 177, Table 6.15). As a result of an oversight this question was not put to the judges, but they were asked whether the jury could understand the scientific evidence in cases where there had been some. In no fewer than 93 per cent of these cases the judges thought all the scientific evidence was understandable by the jury (*ibid*).

Could the jurors remember the evidence? Jurors were asked 'How difficult was it for you to remember the evidence when it was time for the jury to consider its verdict?'. Again, over ninety per cent said 'No difficulty' (50%) or it was 'Not very difficult' (41%). Nine per cent said it was 'Fairly difficult', 1 per cent said it was 'Very difficult'. When jurors were asked whether the rest of the jury could remember the evidence, the verdict was even more favourable–60 per cent thought none of the other jurors had any difficulty and 34 per cent that only a few found it difficult (p 209, Table 8.9). The views of the barristers was to the same effect. 97 per cent of prosecution counsel and 96 per cent of defence counsel thought the jury could remember the evidence, only 1 per cent thought they would have had some difficulty in remembering the evidence (p 178, Table 6.16).

Not surprisingly, the percentage of jurors who had difficulty increased in proportion to the length of the case. Where the case lasted under a day only 4–5 per cent of jurors said they had some difficulty, where it lasted between two to three days, this went up to 9 per cent, where it lasted three to four days, to 16 per cent and where it lasted over two weeks, over a quarter of jurors (27%) said they had some difficulty (p 209, Table 8.8).

Could the jury understand the judge's summing up? The judges were asked 'How easy was it for the jury to understand the summing up on the facts?' Over two-thirds (68%) thought it was 'easy' and 29 per cent thought it was 'fairly easy'. Only 1 per cent thought it was 'difficult' and 3 per cent 'fairly difficult' (p 178, sect 6.2.11). When the jurors were asked about the judge's summing up on the facts, about half (48%) said that managing without the judge's summing up on the facts would have made no difference (p 214, sect 8.6.1). The judges were asked the same question in regard to the summing up on the law. Over two-fifths thought it was 'easy' and another 43 per cent thought it was 'fairly easy'. Three per cent said they thought it was 'difficult' and 13 per cent that it was 'fairly difficult' (p 179, sect 6.2.12).

The views of jurors were not very different. About a quarter said they were not sure but of those who gave a response, 6 per cent said they had found it 'fairly difficult' and only 0.4 per cent 'very difficult' (p 216, Table 8.14). Their view (and that of the foremen) of how it had been for the other jurors was very similar (p 217, Table 8.15).

Was the jury's verdict surprising?   Different participants in the trial were asked 'In your view, was the jury's decision surprising in the light of the evidence?' In the great majority of cases the answer was No. The verdict was surprising in the view of 27 per cent of the CPS, 25 per cent of the police, 18 per cent of the defence solicitors, 15 per cent of the prosecution barristers and 14 per cent of the judges and the defence barristers (p 163, Table 6.5). The two sets of barristers and the judges were almost identical in their overall response. But they were not always surprised at the same verdicts. So, there were 248 cases where both the prosecution and defence agreed, and 48 where they disagreed. The judge and the defence barristers agreed in 287 cases but disagreed in 66 cases (p 163).

In the main, acquittals gave rise to surprise considerably more often than convictions:

Percentage of cases in which respondents were surprised

	Acquittal	Conviction
	%	%
Judges	25	4
Prosecution barristers	26	3
CPS	44	10
Police	47	8
Defence barristers	10	14
Defence solicitors	14	26

(*Source: Crown Court Study, Table* 6.6, p 164.)

The differences were striking. Thus the police and the CPS were surprised at no fewer than 44 per cent and 47 per cent of acquittals respectively, compared with a quarter of the judges and prosecution barristers and 10–14 per cent of defence barristers and defence solicitors.

What did the jury's decision mean? Respondents were asked 'Which of the following comes closest to your view of the jury's decision?':

(1) Understandable in the light of the evidence
(2) Against the overall weight of the evidence, but explicable

(3) Against the judge's directions on law, but explicable
(4) Inexplicable

The responses to these numbered questions were rather similar:

	(1)	(2)	(3)	(4)
	%	%	%	%
Judges	85	12	1	2
Prosecution barristers	83	12	0	4
Defence barristers	84	13	0.2	3
Defence solicitors	87	10	1	2
Police	78	13	1	8

(*Source*: Table 6.7, p 165. The CPS were not asked the question.)

The great majority of respondents in all the categories thought the verdict was understandable in the light of the evidence. Those who thought it was against the weight of the evidence but explicable gave a long list of explanations: sympathy for the defendant, antipathy toward the complainant, case too trivial or stale, misconduct by the police, concern over sentence, quality or lack of quality of the respective counsel. Hardly any respondents thought the decision was against the judge's direction on law. The prosecution and defence lawyers and the judges all agreed that 2–4 per cent of jury decisions were inexplicable. The police thought that 8 per cent were inexplicable.

When the judges, the prosecution barristers and the police thought that the verdict was against the weight of the evidence it was an acquittal in about 90 per cent of instances. When defence barristers and defence solicitors thought the verdict was against the weight of the evidence just under half were acquittals (Table 6.9).

There were 64 cases in the sample where the police regarded an acquittal as problematic (as being against the weight of the evidence, or against the judge's summing up on the law or inexplicable). In 31 of these cases the police view was the view of the majority of the respondents. (In 23 of the 31 the police view was shared by the judge and by one or more of the defence team.) In the 22 cases where the police view was not the majority view, the judge agreed with the police in two and disagreed in 16. (There were four cases where the judge did not return a questionnaire; in all four the prosecution barrister disagreed with the police view.)

On the basis of these figures it appears that 'problematic jury acquittals' constituted 31 per cent of all jury acquittals for prosecution barristers, 29 per cent for the judges and 16 per cent for defence barristers (p 170). As will be seen, jury acquittals are about 40 per cent of all acquittals in the crown court (see p 410 below). On that basis, problematic acquittals would be between 6 and 12 per cent of all acquittals.

The Crown Court Study also showed that there were some (though far fewer) problematic convictions. Judges and prosecution barristers thought that 2 per cent of convictions were problematic, whereas defence barristers thought that 17 per cent were problematic (pp 170–71).

Length of jury deliberations   In most cases the jury was out for a very short period– in over half (52%) for under two hours, and in three-quarters (77%) for under four hours:

How long was the jury out?

	%
Less than 1 hour	23
1 to 2 hours	29
More than 2, up to 4 hours	25
More than 4, up to 8 hours	11
More than 8, up to 12 hours	1
More than 12 hours	1
Total	100 (N=6,954)

(*Source*: Table 8.23, p 225.)

There were eight cases (1%) in which the jury stayed together overnight. (At the time of the survey it was a rule that once the jury had begun their deliberations, they were not allowed to separate until they reached their verdict, known as 'sequestration of the jury'. Now, under the Criminal Justice and Public Order Act 1994, s 43 it is in the judge's discretion whether he permits the jury to go home while they are deliberating.)

Not surprisingly, the length of jury deliberations was closely associated with the length of the case. Thus where the case lasted under half a day, the jurors reported being out for under two hours in 96 per cent of cases. When the case lasted 3 to 4 days the jurors were back within two hours in only 15 per cent of cases. When it lasted over two weeks, the jurors took more than four hours in three-quarters of the cases (p 225).

Length of case   Jurors were asked how long the case lasted:

Length of case

	%
Less than half a day	7
Half to one day	19
More than 1, up to 2 days	33
More than 2, up to 3 days	20
More than 3 days, up to 2 weeks	19
More than 2 weeks	2
Total	100 (N=8,122)

(*Source*: Table 8.22, p 224.)

Is the jury system a good system?   The judges and the barristers (but not the other respondents) were asked: 'What do you think of the jury system in terms of generally getting a sensible result?' Seventy nine per cent of the judges, 82 per cent of prosecution barristers and 91 per cent of defence barristers thought the jury system was a 'Good' or 'Very good' system; eight per cent of the judges, 4 per cent of prosecution barristers and 2 per cent of defence barristers thought it a 'Poor' or 'Very poor' system. (Table 6.13, p 172). The same question was put also to the jurors. Their view was much the same. Seventy nine per cent of jurors (and 81% of foremen) rated the jury system 'Good' or 'Very good', 6 per cent (and 3% of foremen) thought it 'Poor' or 'Very poor' (p 173).

For an unscientific and distinctly jaundiced account of the experience of serving on a jury, see the lecture of the late Professor Ely Devons of the London School of Economics – 'Serving as a Juryman in Britain', 28 *Modern Law Review*, 1965, p 561. See also various articles in *New Law Journal* 14 September 1990, pp 1264–76; 'Jury Service: A Personal Observation', 1979 *LAG Bulletin*, p 278.

Research by Julie Vennard, then of the Home Office Research and Planning Unit, tends rather to support the view that juries decide rationally and on the basis of the evidence. (See J Vennard, 'The Outcome of Contested Trials', in *Managing Criminal Justice*, ed D Moxon, 1985, pp 126–51; and 'Evidence and Outcome: a Comparison of Contested Trials in Magistrates' Courts and the Crown Court', Home Office Research and Planning Unit, *Research Bulletin*, No 20, 1986, p 48.)

Northern Ireland non-jury (Diplock) courts

Northern Ireland in recent years has seen the abolition of the jury in cases involving terrorism because of a lack of confidence in the ability of jurors to bring in a fair verdict. A survey of all cases tried in the first six months of 1973 in Belfast showed an acquittal rate of 16 per cent for Protestant defendants as against 6 per cent for Catholics. Lord Diplock headed a committee to inquire into the problem. The Report of the Committee identified various problems including intimidation of witnesses by terrorists and the danger of perverse acquittals of Loyalist terrorists by predominantly Protestant juries. The Committee recommended the suspension of jury trial for certain offences (*Report of the Commission to Consider Legal Procedures to Deal with Terrorist Activities in Northern Ireland*, 1972, Cmnd 5185). This was done in the Northern Ireland (Emergency Provisions) Act 1973 in relation to 'scheduled offences', which were broadly those regularly committed by terrorists–murder, other serious offences against the person, firearms and explosives charges, arson, robbery, aggravated burglary and intimidation.

The role of the 'Diplock courts' has been controversial. (See, for instance, K Boyle, T Hadden and P Hillyard, *Law and State* (Martin Robertson 1975) and by the same authors, *Ten Years on Northern Ireland* (Cobden Trust, 1980).)

In 1986–7 the Irish Government tried to persuade the British Government to introduce a three-judge trial court instead of the single-judge Diplock court. But the British Government would not agree, partly because of the shortage of judges. Also, it pointed to the fact that fewer than one-third of those convicted of terrorist offences appealed.

But it is not the case that the Diplock courts necessarily have a lower acquittal rate than in jury trials. The proportion of those pleading not guilty in Diplock courts who were acquitted fluctuated–being 31 per cent in 1980, 50 per cent in 1985 and 36 per cent in 1990 respectively. (It is worth noting that in the same three years the proportion of defendants in Diplock trials who pleaded guilty was 81 per cent, 79 per cent and 82 per cent respectively–a distinctly higher guilty-plea rate than in England.)

For proposals to alter the system see J Jackson, 'Diplock and the Presumption against Jury Trial: a Critique' [1992] *Criminal Law Review*, p 755.

In 1987 the Government decided to abolish the right of trial by jury in civil actions in Northern Ireland where previously jury trials were used in the overwhelming majority of such cases. In a strongly worded protest, the Northern Ireland Bar said the move had been engineered by employers' organizations such as the CBI and the insurance industry which argued that jury trials resulted in higher awards and therefore in higher insurance premiums which was bad for employment in the province. It called for the move to be stopped. But it went ahead notwithstanding. (Jury Amendment (Northern Ireland) Order, SI 1987/1283.)

(j) Should the jury be retained for long fraud cases?

There have for many years been a variety of voices raised to urge that complex, long fraud cases and the like should be tried by some form of special tribunal. In 1983 such a call was made separately by the Chairman of the Law Commission, Mr Justice Gibson, by the Lord Chief Justice, Lord Lane, by a law lord, Lord Roskill, and by Lord Hailsham, the Lord Chancellor, in the Hamlyn Lectures. The campaign for some such reform had been going on since the late 1960s when it was promoted in particular by the then Lord Chief Justice, Lord Parker. It seemed that little progress was being made, but in November 1983 the Government set up the Roskill Committee 'to consider in what ways the conduct of criminal proceedings arising from fraud can be improved, and to consider what changes in existing law and procedure would be desirable to secure the just, expeditious and economical disposal of such proceedings'.

The Report of the Roskill Committee 1986

The Committee concluded that long fraud cases were so complex that it was not reasonable to expect jurors to be able to cope. There were often multiple defendants and many charges. 'The background against which frauds are alleged to have been committed–the sophisticated world of high finance and international trading–is probably a mystery to most or all of the jurors, its customs and practices a closed book' (para 8.27). The language of accountancy would be unfamiliar. The evidence often ran into hundreds or even thousands of documents. Research conducted for the Committee by the Medical Research Council's Applied Psychology Unit at Cambridge on understanding by jurors of a one-hour summing up in a fraud case confirmed the 'view of experienced observers and the promptings of commonsense, that the most complex of fraud cases will exceed the limits of comprehension of members of a jury' (para 8.34). Many jurors were simply out of their depth in such cases.

But the Committee did not go so far as to recommend replacing the jury for all fraud cases. Only in the most complex cases (which it estimated might be some two dozen a year) should there be a different system. This, it suggested, should be a special tribunal consisting of a judge and two lay members selected from a panel of persons with expertise in complex business transactions chosen by the Lord Chancellor. Either prosecution or defence should be allowed to apply to a High Court judge for the special tribunal.

Again, however, Mr Walter Merricks dissented. In a powerful statement he effectively demolished the Committee's reasoning. First he pointed to the weight of expert evidence received by the Committee which was 'overwhelmingly in favour of retaining the jury (p 192, para C5). The vast majority of the solicitors' profession (from both prosecution and defence), the magistrates, the Bar and even the police had opposed the removal of jury trial. The judges had been divided but many judges had grave reservations about removing the right to trial by jury. Both the Society of Conservative Lawyers and the Society of Labour Lawyers had been 'emphatic in insisting on the retention of jury trial' (p 192). The submissions from the Bar were almost unanimous. Those who were against the jury came mainly from the financial and accountancy world and, when pressed in oral evidence, 'it became clear that most of them based their views on generalized impressions' (para C8). The Committee thought there were cases that were not prosecuted because of the difficulty of presenting very complex cases to the jury. But analysis by the DPP of all his fraud cases in 1983 showed that there was only one out of 71 not prosecuted in which the decision not to prosecute was caused by the complexity of the evidence.

It had, Mr Merricks suggested, become a convention of the unwritten constitution that citizens should not be subjected to more than a short period of imprisonment otherwise than on a jury's verdict. Parliament should not be invited to abrogate this constitutional right without evidence that jury trial had broken down in serious fraud cases *and* that all possible procedural improvements had been considered and found inadequate. 'A mere hunch, unsupported by tested evidence, that the system might at some time in the future prove inadequate should not be enough' (para C7). The burden was on those who proposed to change the system. There was no hard evidence as to the extent of jury incomprehension. But the anecdotal evidence received by the Committee had not clearly supported the view that juries were unable to follow the evidence in these cases. 'Most judges and lawyers who made submissions to us thought that juries mostly reached the right result, or at least an understandable result' (para C17). There was a danger that if a special expert tribunal were set up, the trial would become simply an exchange between lawyers and the tribunal in impenetrable jargon. The function of a trial as a publicly comprehensible exposition of the case would be threatened. Moreover, the fundamental issue in most fraud trials was one of dishonesty. It would be dangerous to entrust this judgment to experts. The legal standard of dishonesty was the standard of the ordinary man and experts were not ordinary men. It would also be difficult to define the cases in which the special tribunal would be appropriate.

Mr Merricks' dissent attracted much notice and support in comments on the Roskill Committee Report. Clearly he had had the better of the argument. The Government gave the report generally a warm welcome but its proposal on this particular issue was clearly too controversial and, after hesitating for a period, the Government announced that it would not be implemented.

The topic has remained a live one but, so far at least, no steps have been taken to implement the Roskill Committee's proposal. (See for instance the report issued by the Bar Council in August 1990, which urged that juries should be kept for complex fraud cases but that there should be a specialist panel of experienced judges to sit on such trials. The report said: 'We do not accept the premise that 12 ordinary members of the public, selected at random, cannot be relied upon to produce satisfactory verdicts in complex fraud cases'. 'Juries have consistently produced verdicts which are sensible, responsible and entirely just.'

The evidence of the Police Service to the Runciman Royal Commission on Criminal Justice stated: 'An examination of the conviction rates for serious fraud, when compared with the overall conviction rate for cases that are considered by a jury, show that in serious fraud trials the jury are convicting a slightly *higher* percentage' (November 1991, p 188, para 2.3, emphasis supplied).

The Runciman Royal Commission said (p 136, para 76) that in the absence of research into juries it had no basis for making any recommendations for dispensing with juries in long fraud cases.

In October 1995 *The Times'* Legal Correspondent stated that a review of the matter by the Home Secretary might lead to abolition of juries in long fraud cases and that such a move would have the support of the Attorney General and the Director of the Serious Fraud Office. Fuel was added to the issue when in December 1995 a jury acquitted Ian and Kevin Maxwell after a trial lasting some seven months. But at the time of writing (early 1996) there was no clear indication that anything was likely to be done about the issue in the foreseeable future.

(k) Respective roles of judge and jury

The judge is supposed to sum up for the jury on both the law and the facts.

(l) Summing up the law

In *McVey*[13] the Court of Appeal spelled out the minimum content of every summing up:

It is trite to say that every summing up must contain at least a direction to the jury as to the burden and standard of proof, and as to the ingredients of the offence or offences which the jury are called upon to consider.

The problem of what is meant by this dictum was considered in a lecture entitled 'Summing Up the Law' at Nottingham University in 1989 by Professor Edward Griew:[14]

Directing the jury as to the burden of proof means telling them who has to prove the case; it means telling them that the prosecution must prove the defendant's guilt, not the defendant his innocence. Directing them as to the standard of proof means telling them that the case has to be proved beyond reasonable doubt–commonly expressed by saying that they may convict the defendant only if they are sure of his guilt. I shall shortly be illustrating what is meant by 'the ingredients of the offence'.

In recent years the Court of Appeal has laid down 'model' or 'specimen' directions or standard forms of words in which directions on particular matters can or ought to be given. Quite a number are now embodied in a document issued to all judges who sit in the Crown Court by the Judicial Studies Board with the approval of the Lord Chief Justice. The document has not been published. In the Foreword[15] the Lord Chief Justice says: 'The directions will often require adaptation to the circumstances of a particular case. They should not be regarded as a magic formula to be pronounced like an incantation.'

In his lecture Professor Griew criticized the tendency of judges to give the jury more law than it needed for the purpose of its decision[16] and to use overly technical

13 [1988] Crim LR 127.
14 [1989] Crim LR 768.
15 Cited by Edward Griew in his lecture referred to above, at p 773.
16 Professor Griew suggests (at pp 770–1) that in *McVey*, above, the Court of Appeal quashed a conviction of a plainly guilty person because the judge's direction on the ingredients of the offence was insufficient even though the missing words were unnecessary to the jury's decision.

and complex language. American research showed that a good many judicial directions on law to juries were totally incomprehensible to an alarming percentage of jurors'.[17] No doubt similar research in this country would yield similar results. 'Our juries continue to be addressed in language relatively rich in abstract and latinate words and in sentences that are often very long.'[18]

(2) Summing up on the facts

The job of the judge in summing up the facts according to the Court of Appeal in a recent case is to state matters impartially, clearly and logically'.[19] His task therefore is to remind them of the evidence and to marshal it in a convenient way which is fair to both sides.[20]

But to what extent can he go beyond this to comment on the evidence and thereby seek to influence the jury's decision? There is no doubt that English judges do this. In the notorious case of the 'Birmingham Six' who were charged with IRA pub bombings resulting in numerous deaths and injuries, Mr Justice Bridge (as he then was), during a three-day summing up gave innumerable indications that in his view the prosecution's evidence was to be preferred to that of the defence. Nor did he see anything wrong with leading the jury to its conclusion. 'I am of the opinion', he told the jury, '—that if a judge has formed a clear view, it is much better to let the jury see that and say so and not pretend to be a kind of Olympian detached observer.'[1]

For an unusually strong summing up on the facts in a civil case see that of Mr Justice Caulfield in the libel action brought in 1987 by Mr Jeffrey Archer against *The Star*, arising out of the allegation that he had visited a prostitute. There was, the judge said, no accounting for the tastes of happily married men and the fact that the jury would not expect Mr Archer, deputy chairman of the Conservative Party, to visit a prostitute, did not mean that it was not possible. But he asked the jury to consider whether it was probable. He invited the jury to remember the evidence of Mrs Mary Archer. 'Your vision of her will probably never disappear. Has she elegance? Has she fragrance? Would she have, apart from the strain of his trial, a radiance?' Mr Archer, the judge said, was a sportsman, President of the Oxford University Athletic Club and

17 Notably Robert P Charrow and Veda R Charrow, 'Making Legal Language Understandable: A Psycholinguistic Study of Jury Instructions' (1979) 79 *Col L Rev*, 1306; William W Schwarzer, 'Communicating with Juries: Problems and Remedies' (1981) 69 *Calif L Rev* p 731.

18 Professor Griew cited as an example the following direction which was quoted by the Court of Appeal with apparent approval and certainly without reproach: ['W]hat the conspirator said or did, in furtherance of the common object, or common agreement, is evidence against all the rest of the conspirators. That is to say, you can consider those acts and declarations, as I have said, things said. You can consider those against them all, either before you have decided that there is an overall conspiracy, and in order to decide that point—or after you have decided there is an overall conspiracy, if you do so find, and when considering whether any particular defendant is within that conspiracy; provided that you do consider both of those aspects and you do find there is a conspiracy in the end.'

19 *Berrada* (1989) 91 Cr App Rep 131n. The trial judge had said that the defendant's allegation that police officers had fabricated an interview was 'really monstrous and wicked' and 'utterly monstrous'. The court quashed the conviction.

20 It seems that in a short case in which the issues are simple it is not necessarily a fatal defect in a summing up that the evidence has not been discussed: see *Attfield* (1961) 45 Cr App Rep 309.

1 Sergeant Sullivan, a barrister famed for his wit, is said once to have said to the registrar at the Old Bailey that the jury foreman should be asked whether the jury found for his Lordship or against him. (Cited by David Wolchover (1989) *Criminal Law Review*, pp 791–2.)

had run for his country. 'You may think he's fit looking . . . Is he in need of cold, unloving, rubber-insulated sex in a seedy hotel?' The jury awarded Mr Archer record damages of £500,000. (*The Times*, 24 July 1987.)

The danger that the judge will try to influence the jury is the greater in cases where the accused has previous convictions, because the judge knows of their existence from the outset. They are in his file, allegedly so that he can steer counsel away from questions which might otherwise lead to their becoming admissible. It seems that judges in Scotland manage without this.

In the United States, by contrast, the rule in most states is that the judge in a criminal trial must express no opinion on the weight or credibility of the evidence of witnesses or on the merits of either side.

However, even if judges were to be prevented from commenting, they could probably still convey to the jury their basic view through a mixture of inflexion of the voice, 'body language', timing and other signs which would not register in the official transcript. (The Court of Appeal has, however, indicated that in extreme cases it would allow evidence from those present in court as to 'non-verbal communication' by the trial judge trying to persuade the jury–*Hircock* [1969] 1 All ER 47.) The only way to prevent such influence would be to prohibit the judge from summing up at all, even in the sense of merely recapitulating the facts.

There is little doubt that when the judge sums up for a conviction the impression of impartial justice being done is diminished. See generally David Wolchover, 'Should Judges Sum Up on the Facts?' [1989] *Criminal Law Review*, p 781.

The Crown Court Study

Did the summing up favour either side?   In the Crown Court Study, respondents were asked 'In your view did the judge's summing up point towards acquittal or towards conviction?' The responses are shown in the table:

Overall thrust of summing up

	Pros barrister	Def barrister	Def solicitor	CPS	Judge
	%	%	%	%	%
Toward an acquittal	12	12	18	19	11
Toward a conviction	23	36	21	26	21
Neither	65	52	55	55	68
Total	100	100	100	100	100

(*Source*: Table 4.21, p 130.)

In the view of four of the five respondents (including the judges) the summing up favoured the prosecution much more often than the defence. The prosecution and defence barristers were in agreement as to which side was favoured in 88 per cent of cases and they disagreed in 12 per cent (p 131, para 4.10.6).

Was the judge fair?   Defendants were asked for their view about the fairness or otherwise of the judge generally during the trial and specifically in the summing up.

(The response rate for the defendant questionnaires was however too low to make the results statistically valid.)To the first part of this question, the defendant said he thought the judge was 'generally fair during the trial' in over four-fifths of the cases (81%). In 16 per cent he thought the judge was biased against him. In 3 per cent he thought the judge was biassed against the prosecution! Ninety two per cent of those who were acquitted thought the judge was fair during the trial, compared with 79 per cent of those found guilty of some charges and 64 per cent of those convicted on all counts. The defendant thought the judge had been fair in his summing up in 73 per cent of cases and not fair in 27 per cent (p 132).

Was the summing-up against the weight of the evidence? Respondents were asked whether the judge's summing up went against the evidence. Prosecution barristers thought the judge summed up against the weight of the evidence in 20 per cent of cases where the summing up favoured one side, compared with defence barristers for whom the equivalent figure was 35 per cent (p 134). According to the prosecution barristers, in 34 of the 40 cases (85%) where the summing up was against the weight of the evidence, it favoured an acquittal. But according to defence barristers, in 73 out of the 79 cases (92%) where the summing up was against the weight of the evidence, it favoured a conviction (pp 134–35).

Did the jury follow the judge's lead? But the jury did not necessarily follow the judge's lead. Where the defence barrister thought the judge summed up for a conviction 'against the weight of the evidence', the jury in fact acquitted in 45 per cent of cases. In the six cases where the prosecution barrister thought the judge summed up for a conviction 'against the weight of the evidence', the jury acquitted in four (66%).

Where the defence barrister thought the judge summed up for an acquittal 'against the weight of the evidence', the jury nevertheless convicted in five out of six cases (83%). Where the prosecution barrister thought the judge summed up for an acquittal 'against the weight of the evidence', the jury convicted in eight out of 24 (33%) (p 136).

Did the judge's interruptions favour either side? The prosecution and defence barristers were asked, 'Would you say that the judge's interruptions during the trial favoured the defence or the prosecution?' Both agreed that in a little under a third of the cases (28%,30%) the judge made no interruptions. The prosecution barristers thought the interruptions favoured the defence in 5 per cent of cases, favoured the prosecution in 9 per cent and favoured neither in 58 per cent. The defence barristers thought they favoured the defence in 4 per cent, the prosecution in 24 per cent and neither in 43 per cent (p 137, Table 4.24).

Did the judge give any non-verbal indications of his views? Where the barristers had already said that the judge's summing up favoured one side or the other, they were asked 'In your view, did the judge give any non-verbal indications of his views (such as tone of voice or "body language") which pointed towards acquittal or conviction?' The defence perceived this phenomenon more than the prosecution. In the view of the prosecution barristers it happened in 32 cases (16%)–6 favouring the defence, 26 the prosecution. In the view of the defence barristers there were 80 such cases (35%)–11 favouring the defence and 69 the prosecution (p 137).

Should the judge have been more robust?   The barristers were asked: 'In your view, should the judge have been more (or less) robust in his handling of the case? On this point prosecution and defence barristers were broadly in agreement. In 86 per cent of cases prosecution counsel and in 83 per cent defence counsel would not have wished the judge to have been either more or less robust. In 7 per cent of cases prosecution counsel thought the judge should have been more robust and in 7 per cent less robust. In 6 per cent the defence barrister thought the judge should have been more robust and 12 per cent less robust (p 138, sect 4.10.16).

What did the jury think of the judge's performance?   Jurors were asked to evaluate how well the judge did in 'keeping a fair balance between prosecution and defence'. Eighty five per cent of jurors thought the judge did 'Very well', 14 per cent 'Fairly well' and 1 per cent 'Not very well' (p 221, Table 8.20).

The Runciman Royal Commission's recommendation

The Runciman Royal Commission said that it had some difficulty with the question as to the extent to which the judge should refer to the facts of the case in the summing up. Since there would often be more evidence for the prosecution, a summary might give the impression that the evidence for the prosecution was the stronger. 'It is also not unknown for judges, whilst emphasising that matters of fact are for the jury and not for the judge, to comment on the facts in such a way as to attempt to influence the jury in one direction or another' (p 123, para 20). It had been suggested by some that judges should not sum up on the facts at all, which was the position in many states in America. In Scotland judges tended to say less about the facts than in England. The Royal Commission thought it would be wrong to lay down a rule as to how far the judge should sum up on the facts. Cases and circumstances varied. Sometimes there would be no need for a summing up at all. The need to be fair to both sides, the Commission said, required 'that judges should be wholly neutral in any comment that they make on the credibility of the evidence' (p 124, para 23). It was 'inappropriate for judges to intrude their own views of whether or not a witness is to be believed' (*ibid*). Implementation of that recommendation would presumably require some kind of ruling or Practice Statement by the Lord Chief Justice.

(3) Directing an acquittal

Acquittals directed by the judge comprise a high proportion of all acquittals. As has been seen, there are two forms of such acquittal: (1) where the prosecution enter no evidence at all (called an 'ordered acquittal') and (2) after a submission by the defence at the end of the prosecution's case that there is no case to answer (a 'directed acquittal').

The withdrawal of a case from the jury poses a delicate problem. Can the judge decline to put the case to the jury if he thinks that the prosecution's case is merely weak? The Court of Appeal considered this question in *R v Galbraith* [1981] 1 WLR 1039. Lord Lane, the Chief Justice, said there were two schools of thought. One was that the judge should stop the case if in his view it would be unsafe or unsatisfactory to convict. (See for instance *Mansfield* (1977) 65 Cr App Rep 276.) The other was that the judge should only stop the case if there was no evidence on which a jury properly directed could properly convict. Before the Criminal Appeal Act 1966 the second test had been applied. But under the 1966 Act the Court of Appeal was required to quash a conviction where it found that under the circumstances it was unsafe or unsatisfactory (see pp 501–04 below). Since then a practice had grown up of asking the trial judge to take a view as to whether conviction would be safe by submitting that there was no case. This involved the judge invading the province of the jury. It invited the trial judge to consider the weight and the reliability of the prosecution's evidence–precisely the issues that had to be considered by the jury. Lord Lane answered the question in this way (at 1042):

How then should the judge approach a submission of 'no case'? (1) If there is no evidence that the crime alleged has been committed by the defendant, there is no difficulty. The judge will of course stop the case. (2) The difficulty arises where there is some evidence but it is of a tenuous character, for example because of inherent weakness or vagueness or because it is inconsistent with other evidence. (a) Where the judge comes to the conclusion that the prosecution evidence, taken at the highest, is such that a jury properly directed could not properly convict upon it, it is his duty, upon a submission being made, to stop the case. (b) Where however the prosecution evidence is such that its strength or weakness depends on the view to be taken of a witness's reliability, or other matters which are generally speaking within the province of the jury and where on one possible view of the facts there *is* evidence upon which a jury could properly come to the conclusion that the defendant is guilty, then the judge should allow the matter to be tried by the jury. It follows that we think the second of the two schools of thought is to be preferred.

For comment and discussion see Rosemary Pattenden, 'The Submission of No Case–Some Recent Developments' (1982) *Criminal Law Review*, p 558; D Wolchover, 'Stopping the Trial in Suspect Cases', *New Law Journal*, 1982, p 527. For the effect of this ruling in magistrates' courts, see N Yell, 'Submissions of "No Case to Answer"', *Justice of the Peace*, 1981, p 406 and Pattenden, *op cit*, at p 564.

The Runciman Royal Commission (p 59, para 41) recommended that *Galbraith* should be reversed so that a judge could stop a case if he or she takes the view that the prosecution's evidence is demonstrably unsafe or unsatisfactory or too weak to be allowed to go to the jury.

Sometimes the judge, whilst not going so far as to direct the jury to acquit, makes it very clear in his summing up that he thinks an acquittal is the right result. He sums up strongly for an acquittal. There is nothing to prevent this even if the judge goes beyond the proper limits. The matter is unlikely to become the subject of comment from the Court of Appeal since the prosecution have no right of appeal against an acquittal (other than on a point of law taken by the Attorney-General, the outcome of which does not affect the defendant–see p 484 below). (For a classic instance of the judge 'summing up for an acquittal' see the summing up of Mr Justice Cantley in the Jeremy Thorpe case (*Daily Telegraph*, 19, 20 June 1979.)

(4) Directing a conviction

Views differ as to whether it is ever legitimate for the judge to direct the jury to convict. Lord Devlin thought it to be unconstitutional. (See *Trial by Jury*, 1966, p 84 and App II.) There is no doubt that the judge must leave to the jury any issue that has to be decided by them. In *Leer* [1982] Crim LR 310, the Court of Appeal considered a direction to convict where the accused had been charged with possessing an offensive weapon after being found with a fishing knife. The judge ruled that his answers to police questioning as to why he had the knife did not amount to a reasonable excuse and that he therefore had no defence to put forward, and he directed them to convict. The Court of Appeal quashed the conviction because the judge should have left the issue to the jury. It would have been surprising if the jury had decided to acquit but such a decision on the evidence would not have been perverse. See also *R v Clemo* [1973] RTR 176.

But what if an acquittal would be perverse? Can the judge direct a conviction then? In *DPP v Stonehouse* [1978] AC 55, the House of Lords by three to two held that he could not. Lord Salmon said there was a difference between directing the jury to acquit or to convict. If there was no evidence on which they could reasonably convict, he should direct an acquittal. This rule had been established a long time ago to protect the accused against being wrongly convicted. 'But there is no converse rule. ... If the judge is satisfied that on the evidence, the jury would not be justified in acquitting the accused and indeed that it would be perverse of them to do so, he has no power to pre-empt the jury's verdict by directing them to convict. The jury alone has the right to decide that the accused is guilty' (at p 80). But Lord Salmon did accept that it would be perfectly in order for the judge to sum up to the jury 'in such a way as to make it plain that he considers the accused is guilty and should be convicted' (*ibid*). Lord Edmund-Davies said there was an unfortunate tendency in the courts these days to withdraw issues from the jury which were properly theirs. Whether this sprang from distrust of the jury's capacity, 'or from excessive zeal in seeking to simplify their task, it needs careful watching' (at p 88). The judge could give a strong lead to the jury but he should not direct them to convict. Lord Keith said that if judges had a right to decide in their discretion whether to direct a conviction it would widen the field for appeals. 'The wiser and sounder course, in my opinion, is to adhere to the principle that, in every case where a jury may be entitled to convict, the application of the law to the facts is a matter for the jury and not for the judge' (at p 9). See also *R v Lawn* [1984] Crim LR 114.

The view expressed in *Stonehouse* was confirmed in *Gent* [1990] 1 All ER 364, in which the Court of Appeal said the judge ought not to direct a conviction save possibly in a wholly exceptional case such as where there has been a formal admission of guilt. Accordingly the defendant is entitled to have the verdict of the jury even though, on the evidence, only one verdict is possible and an acquittal would in the judge's view be perverse. (See to like effect *Gordon* (1987) Times, 11 May.)

The only situation in which a direction to convict may be lawful is where the defence is based on a pure point of law and the judge rules against the defence on the matter of law–see *Hill and Hall* ; (1988) 89 Cr App Rep 74, [1989] Crim LR 136. But even that exceptional principle is dubious, especially in cases where it is conceivable that the jury might wish to acquit simply because it disapproves of the law or the way it has been applied.

An example was the famous case in 1985 of Clive Ponting, the civil servant prosecuted under the Official Secrets Act for leaking to an MP information about the sinking of the Argentinian ship *The General Belgrano* during the Falklands War. On the view of the law taken by the judge, McCowan J, Mr Ponting had no defence. He therefore intended to direct the jury to convict but was dissuaded from doing so by counsel for the prosecution who drew the judge's attention to what he termed 'recent authorities'. The judge said that, although all the elements of the offence had been made out and there was no defence, he told the jury that they were at liberty to bring in whatever verdict they considered right. The jury proceeded to acquit–presumably because they felt that Mr Ponting had acted honourably and perhaps correctly.

For a similar principled acquittal see the case of Pat Pottle and Michael Randall who were tried at the Old Bailey in July 1991 for helping the spy George Blake to escape from prison 25 years earlier. They were prosecuted after they wrote a book about their exploit. The trial judge ruled that they had no defence to the charge. In his closing speech to the jury Pat Pottle said, 'We do not deny the things we are accused of doing. Not only do we not deny it, we say it was the right thing to do.' The jury acquitted both men (*The Times*, 5 July, 1991).

See also TA Green, *Verdict According to Conscience: Perspectives on the English Criminal Trial, 1200–1800* (Chicago University Press, 1985), which suggests that part of the historic role of the jury was to mitigate the rigour and harshness of the criminal law and its penalties, not just in the occasional case but on a massive scale.

(l) Majority jury verdicts

In Scotland, since time immemorial, there has been a majority verdict based on a bare majority of eight or more out of the fifteen who sit on a Scottish jury. Historically in England, however, the jury's decision had to be unanimous. The reality of unanimity must sometimes have been questionable. It seems probable that in some cases dissenters would 'give in' rather than have a hung jury–or even just to bring the proceedings to a speedy conclusion. (For the particular danger of this happening on a Friday afternoon see Penny Darbyshire, 'Notes of a Lawyer Juror', *New Law Journal*, 14 September 1990, p 1264, 1266–7.)

In 1967 the then Home Secretary, Mr Roy Jenkins, introduced proposals in the Criminal Justice Bill to permit a majority verdict of not less than ten out of twelve. The reason he gave was the spate of recent 'jury nobbling' cases. But the evidence for this was thin. The total proportion of jury disagreements resulting in a retrial appeared to be about 4 per cent and few of these, presumably, would have been due to any form of tampering with the jury.

The proposal provoked great controversy at the time, but in the interim it seems to have become accepted. (See, however, G Maher, 'Jury Verdicts and the Presumption of Innocence', *Legal Studies*, 1983, p 146, for a powerful argument that majority verdicts are inconsistent with the requirement that proof of guilt be beyond a reasonable doubt.)

The annual proportion of guilty verdicts by majority has in most years been around 12–13 per cent, but in the last two years it has risen considerably. (In 1993 it was 15% and in 1994, 19%.) There are no equivalent official figures for the proportion of acquittals by a majority, since the jury are not permitted to reveal that an acquittal was by a majority, for fear that it would be treated as a second-class acquittal.[2] But in the Crown Court Study conducted for the Runciman Royal Commission it was possible to establish from the jury questionnaires that the proportion of acquittals by a majority was exactly the same as convictions by a majority (p 162).

The court is not supposed to consider the possibility of a majority verdict until at least two hours and ten minutes have elapsed (*Practice Direction* [1970] 1 WLR 916). In a complex case the judge will wait much longer than that. The Crown Court

2   Criminal Justice Act 1967, s 13(2).

Study showed a clear association between the likelihood of a majority of a majority verdict and the length of the trial:

Majority verdicts by length of case

Length of case	% of majority verdicts
Under 1 day	2
1 to 3 days	13
3 to 5 days	23
Over 1 week	24

(*Source:* Table 6.4, p 162.)

In *R v Reynolds* [1981] 3 All ER 849, the Court of Appeal Criminal Division quashed a conviction for theft because the foreman of the jury stated that there was a majority of ten in favour of conviction but he did not also state that there were two members of the jury who disagreed. The court held that the provisions of s 17(3) of the 1967 Act were mandatory in stating that the court 'shall not accept [a majority verdict] unless the foreman of the jury has stated in open court the number of jurors who respectively agreed to and dissented from the verdict'. In *R v Pigg* [1983] 1 All ER 56, the Court of Appeal Criminal Division applied the ruling in *Reynolds* and quashed a conviction for attempted rape on the same grounds. The Crown appealed, and the House of Lords overruled *Reynolds*. The law lords held unanimously that, although it was a mandatory requirement that the number who agreed on conviction and the number who dissented must be made known, the precise form of words used was not an essential part of that requirement. It was enough if the words used by the foreman of the jury and the clerk of the court made it clear to an ordinary person how the jury was divided. If the foreman said that ten agreed to convict it could be inferred that two dissented!

But what if the jury is completely deadlocked? For many years the judge was permitted in that situation to give what was known as the *Walhein* direction, approved in the case of that name (1952) 36 Cr App Rep 167. In that case, the jury told the judge that they were having difficulty in reaching a unanimous verdict. (At that date there was no such thing as a majority verdict.) The judge then directed them:

You are a body of twelve men. Each of you has taken an oath to return a true verdict according to the evidence; but, of course, you have a duty not as individuals, but collectively. No one must be false to that oath; but in order to return a collective verdict, the verdict of you all, there must necessarily be argument and a certain amount of give and take and adjustment of views within the scope of the oath you have taken; and it makes for great public inconvenience and expense if jurors cannot agree owing to the unwillingness of one of their number to listen to the arguments of the rest. Having said that, I can say no more.

This direction, seemed, however, to condone pressure on the dissenting minority to fall into line. Since the introduction of majority verdicts in 1967 it has seemed inappropriate. In *Watson* [1988] QB 690 the Court of Appeal approved a new direction to replace that in *Walhein*:

'Each of you has taken an oath to return a true verdict according to the evidence. No one must be false to that oath, but you have a duty not only as individuals but collectively. That is the strength of the jury system. Each of you takes into the jury box with you your individual experience and wisdom. You do that by giving your views and listening to the views of the others. There must necessarily be discussion, argument and give and take within the scope of your oath. That is the way in which agreement is reached. If, unhappily, [ten of] you cannot reach agreement you must say so. It is a matter for the discretion of the Judge as to whether he gives that direction at all and if so, at what stage of the trial. There will usually be no need to do so.

(See further MJ Reville, 'Directing the Hung Lamp of Freedom', *Law Society's Gazette*, 26 October 1988, p 19.)

(m) Retrials on jury disagreement

When the jury disagrees and cannot reach a verdict, the prosecution are entitled to start afresh. It is a matter of discretion over which the court has no control – though occasionally the judge remonstrates with the prosecutor about the desirability of pursuing a particular case.

There are no regular statistics about the extent to which retrials occur as a result of jury disagreements. But in 1981, according to a Home Office Research Unit paper, there were some 370 retrials due to this cause–about 1.5 per cent of the 25,000 or so contested cases in the crown court that year. (See Sid Butler, 'Acquittal Rates', Home Office Research and Planning Unit Paper 16, 1983, p 7.)

(n) Will the Court of Appeal consider what happened in the jury room?

Occasionally an appeal is based on some alleged irregularity in what happened in the jury room or in some other aspect of the jury's handling of the case. What attitude do the courts take to such an appeal?

Boston v WS Bagshaw & Sons [1966] 1 WLR 1135n (Court of Appeal, Civil Division)

Lord Denning MR: This is a motion for a new trial. We are told that there are affidavits from all the twelve jury men, in which they wish to go back on some of the answers given by them in open court. They were given several questions to answer. They deliberated for five hours and came back into court with answers which were as clear as could be. It is not possible that there could be any misunderstanding as to the questions or the answers. In respect of each of two publications the jury were asked: 'Were the defendants actuated by malice?' To each they answered: 'No' The associate asked them, in accordance with the time-honoured practice: 'Are they the answers of you all?' The foreman answered 'They are.' The answers were duly recorded and they were discharged. On the next day the judge, after argument, held that on those answers the plaintiff failed and the defendants were entitled to judgment.

It appears that the jurors did not anticipate the result. They read it in the newspapers and some of them communicated with the plaintiff and his solicitors. Further inquiries were made. Then all the twelve jurors made affidavits indicating that they gave those two answers under a misapprehension; that they meant to find malice; and that they would, if they could, change those answers so as to say that the defendants were actuated by malice. Mr Hirst asks us to receive those affidavits and to order a new trial.

To my mind it is settled as well as anything can be that it is not open to the court to receive any such evidence as this. Once a jury has given their verdict, it is accepted by the judge, and they have been discharged, they are not at liberty to say they meant something different. ...

The reasons are twofold: first, to secure the finality of decisions arrived at by the jury; secondly, to protect the jury themselves and to prevent them being exposed to pressure or inducement to explain or alter their views. If this were to be permitted, where is it to stop? After a jury have solemnly found a man 'Guilty' and he has been sentenced, are they to be at liberty next day to return and say they meant to find him 'Not Guilty'? It cannot be. ...

Harman LJ: I agree. It would be destructive of all trials by jury if we were to accede to this application. There would be no end to it. You would always find one juryman who said: 'That is not what I meant' and you would have to start the whole thing anew. Interest *reipublicae ut sit finis litium.*

Diplock LJ: I agree.

That was a civil case. But in criminal cases the rule is the same:

R v Thompson [1962] 1 All ER 65 (Court of Criminal Appeal)

The appellant was convicted of certain offences by a jury, and sentence was postponed until the next day. In the intervening period, a juryman was alleged to have told a member of the public that, whilst in the jury room, a majority of the jurors had been in favour of acquitting the appellant until the foreman produced a list of the appellant's previous convictions, and that thereupon the jury agreed to convict. Leave to appeal against conviction was given, limited so that the Court of Criminal Appeal might rule whether there was jurisdiction to inquire into the subject of the alleged statement.

Lord Parker CJ gave the judgment of the court:

... There is absolutely no doubt that information as to the prisoner's previous convictions must be kept from a jury, and if what was said to have happened did happen it would have been highly improper. This court is now asked to inquire into the matter, and to adjourn the case in order to see whether the alleged statement by the juryman can be supported by some statement or affidavit made by him. The court has come to the conclusion that it is perfectly idle to adjourn the case for that purpose because the court is quite satisfied that they would have no right at all to inquire what did occur in the jury-room. It has for long been a rule of practice, based on public policy, that the court should not inquire, by taking evidence from jurymen, what did occur in either the jury-box or the jury-room. The court finds it unnecessary to go through all the cases. It is sufficient to refer to a case in the Court of Appeal, *Ellis v Deheer*,[3] before Bankes, Warrington and Atkin LJJ. It was a civil case, and the question was whether the court could look at affidavits from jurors who would say that the verdict given by the foreman of the jury, albeit in their presence, had not been agreed by them. ...

Atkin LJ put the matter in his own words as follows:

'... The reason why that evidence is not admitted is both in order to secure the finality of decisions of fact arrived at by a jury, and, also, which is a matter of great importance for the protection of jurymen themselves, to prevent their being exposed to pressure that might otherwise be put on them with a view to explaining the reasons which actuated them individually in arriving at their verdict. To my mind, it is a principle which is of the very highest importance in the interests of justice to maintain, and an infringement of the rule appears to me to be a very serious interference with the administration of justice.'

... The court would also like to refer in passing to what Lord Hewart CJ said on the question of jurymen divulging what occurred in *R v Armstrong*:[4]

3   [1922] 2 KB 113, [1922] All ER Rep 451.
4   [1922] 2 KB 555 at 568, [1922] All ER Rep 153 at 197.

'If one juryman might communicate with the public upon the evidence and the verdict, so might his colleagues also, and if they all took this dangerous course, differences of individual opinion might be made manifest which, at the least, could not fail to diminish the confidence that the public rightly has in the general propriety of criminal verdicts.'

This appeal is dismissed.

See, to like effect, *R v Chionye* (1988) 89 Cr App Rep 285.

In *R v Spencer* [1986] 2 All ER 928 the House of Lords had to consider allegations about the conduct of a former juryman and his possible influence on members of the jury. The case arose out of alleged violence to patients at Rampton Hospital. The accused were all nurses at the hospital. A juryman P showed during the conduct of the case that he was biased against the accused. Initially the judge decided to take no action although both he and counsel in the case had noticed his apparent attitude and were concerned about it. However, another member of the jury informed a court usher that P's wife worked in another mental hospital in the area as a cleaner. This was on the ninth day of the trial. The judge was informed. He decided to discharge the juryman, but he gave him permission to wait in the anteroom in order to give a lift to three of the jury at the end of the day. He told the jury men concerned not to discuss the case with P.

Defence counsel learned subsequently that P had given the three a lift to and from the court throughout the trial. Fearing that he might have poisoned the minds of the jury with his views and possibly with other information obtained from his wife, the defence asked for the whole of the jury to be discharged. This application was refused –partly because of the ill-effect that a retrial would have on the mental patients having to give their evidence again. The defendants were convicted and sent to prison.

In view of what had transpired, the DPP arranged for P to give a statement as to what had happened. This showed that P had discussed the case and his wife's work situation with the three jurymen to whom he gave a lift after he had been discharged.

On appeal to the Court of Appeal, the Court said that although it was deplorable that this discussion had taken place there was no realistic chance that he had influenced their decision–even though the jury's verdict had been by a majority after five hours. The House of Lords unanimously disagreed. Lord Ackner said that 'what the jurors were discussing or being subjected to, was the assertion by a biased but an ex-fellow, juror of the necessity to convict'. It made the convictions unsafe and unsatisfactory and they had to be quashed.

There was no reference in the House of Lords judgments to the prohibition on piercing the veil of the jury's decision to probe possible misconduct in reaching the verdict. Possibly, *Spencer* can be explained in that sense by the fact that it did not relate to what actually occurred in the jury room itself. For other cases in which the court did consider alleged improprieties involving the jury but not in the jury room, see *Twiss* [1918] 2 KB 853; *Ketteridge* [1915] 1 KB 467; and *Prime* (1973) 57 Cr App Rep 632.

In the remarkable case of *R v Young* [1995] QB 324 the Court of Appeal said that while it would be a breach of s 8 of the Contempt of Court Act to inquire into the jury's deliberations in the jury room, that did not prevent the court from inquiring into what happened while the jury was accommodated overnight in a hotel. The appeal was based on evidence that while overnight at the hotel considering their verdict in a murder case, some members of the jury took part in a seance with a Ouija board and purported to make contact with the deceased and to have received evidence regarding the case. This had so disturbed one of the jurors that he told a solicitor who informed a barrister who spoke to the QC for the defendant who had been convicted of the murder. The Court of Appeal quashed the conviction and ordered a retrial.

(o) Publication of the secrets of the jury room

As has already been seen, jurors are told in the leaflet they receive on being summoned for jury service that they must not reveal anything that occurs in the jury room either during the trial or after it has finished. But what is the position if the press publish details of jury deliberations? The question came up for decision after the Jeremy Thorpe case when the *New Statesman* on 27 July 1979 published an interview with a member of the jury in which he gave details of the jury discussions. Proceedings for contempt were instituted by the Attorney-General but, to many people's surprise, the Attorney-General lost (*A-G v New Statesman and Nation Publishing Co Ltd* [1980] 1 All ER 644). The Divisional Court held that disclosure of the secrets of the jury room could be contempt but it depended on the circumstances. It would be contempt if disclosure tended to imperil the finality of jury verdicts or to affect adversely the attitude of future jurors or the quality of their deliberations. In this particular case there were no special features which made publication a contempt. There had been no payment of money to the juror. The article did not suggest that anything improper had occurred. In fact it showed that the jury had approached their task in a sensible and responsible manner. There was no suggestion that the article could have interfered with the administration of justice in the case in question.

However the press's victory was shortlived. The Contempt of Court Act 1981, s 8, made it contempt to publish or to solicit for publication details of what happens in the jury room, regardless of whether the case is identified or whether any payment is made for such disclosure. The clause was introduced against the advice of the Government by Lords Hutchinson and Wigoder and was supported by the Criminal Bar Association, the Senate of the Four Inns of Court and the Lord Chief Justice. The Lord Chancellor, Lord Hailsham, declared it to be 'far too draconian'. However, he was defeated in the House of Lords and the Government did not seek to have the clause overturned when the Bill returned to the House of Commons. It would seem to rule out even properly controlled academic research.

It is noteworthy that when the issue was put to the Criminal Law Revision Committee for consideration in 1967 it did not think there was any need for legislation. It said juries were reminded of their duty to maintain secrecy by a notice on the walls of the jury room and that there seemed to be few breaches of this understanding: 'We are of opinion that secrecy has been well maintained and that such breaches or attempts to break it as have become known so far have not established a mischief so extensive or serious that it calls for legislation and punishment' (Criminal Law Revision Committee, Tenth Report, *Secrecy of Jury Room*, 1968). It accepted that it was not then a criminal offence to disclose what had happened in the jury room though in certain circumstances it might amount to contempt of court. But it did not think the problem was sufficiently serious to warrant legislation. For one thing it did not think it right to make punishable the inevitable minor disclosures as people spoke to their families and friends after the case about the experience of being jurymen.Such disclosures, the Committee said, though they should not be encouraged, few would regard as deserving of punishment. Under the Contempt of Court Act 1981 such disclosures could theoretically be the subject of proceedings for contempt–though in practice it is unlikely to be used for cases other than publication in the press.

See further Jacob Jaconelli, 'Some Thoughts on Jury Secrecy', *Legal Studies*, March 1990, p 91.

In *A–G v Associated Newspapers Ltd* [1994] 1 All ER 556 the House of Lords rejected an appeal by the owners of the *Mail on Sunday* which had been fined £60,000 for contempt in publishing views of jurors in the Blue Arrow fraud case. The information had been obtained not from the jurors directly but from transcripts of paid interviews purportedly carried out by way of 'research' by an American. The House of Lords held that it made no difference whether the publication of what had transpired in the jury room came directly from jurors or indirectly from others.

(p) Does the jury acquit too many defendants?

The suggestion that too many guilty defendants are acquitted was powerfully urged on a number of occasions by Sir Robert Mark, formerly Commissioner of the Metropolitan Police. The best-publicized occasion for the expression of these views was his 1973 Dimbleby Lecture on BBC 1:

Sir Robert Mark, 'Minority Verdict', BBC, 1973, pp 8–14

What about our system of trial? In particular the trial by jury of serious offenders. I suppose that most of you believe that our system of trial is the best in the world. If it doesn't quite attain perfection, it's only because of the fallible human beings who celebrate the sacred rites in the temple of justice. I use these rather heavy religious metaphors because the public's confidence in our present system of trial by jury is essentially a matter of faith. It is based on practically no evidence whatever. No one has ever thought it necessary to make a full, practical and impartial investigation of how the system works. ...

What we do know about trials in higher courts doesn't justify any complacency. Indeed, there is one fact I can mention which should be enough in itself to demand some kind of enquiry. This is the rate of acquittals. Of all the people in England and Wales who plead not guilty and are tried by jury, about half are acquitted. You must perhaps say to yourselves, 'Well why not? Perhaps they really were innocent. How do the police know that they were guilty?' But things are not quite so simple. For one thing, the English criminal trial never decides whether the accused is innocent. The only question is whether, in accordance with the rules of evidence, the prosecution has *proved* that he is guilty–and this is not at all the same thing. There may be all kinds of reasons why the jury do not think that the prosecution has proved guilt. They may think that he probably did it but that the defence has raised some reasonable doubt. Or sometimes a piece of evidence which would have put the matter beyond doubt is not available or is excluded by the rules of evidence. Occasionally they are just taken in by a false, but plausible, story, or by an exceptionally persuasive advocate. You must not, therefore, think that anyone who is acquitted must have been innocent. There are many other possible explanations. But one thing is certain. Every acquittal is a case in which either a guilty man has been allowed to go free or an innocent citizen has been put to the trouble and expense of defending himself.

There must be some rate of failure. We can't always expect to convict the guilty or never to prosecute the innocent. But in my opinion a failure rate of one in two is far too high. I doubt whether it would be tolerated in many other kinds of activity, so I think it's something that certainly needs looking into. In the absence of any reliable research no one can say with any certainty why the acquittal rate is so high. A fairly high number of acquittals are undoubtedly by direction of the judges, as soon as they've heard the prosecution case. Since 1967 cases are no longer sifted effectively by a Magistrate, and the higher courts are cluttered up by cases which in my opinion should never have got there at all. This probably accounts for what seems to be an increase since 1966 from 39 per cent to about 50 per cent in acquittals and tends to obscure the problem I'm discussing.

My own view is, nevertheless, that the proportion of those acquittals relating to those whom experienced police officers believe to be guilty is too high to be acceptable. ...

I wouldn't deny that sometimes common sense and humanity produce an acquittal which could not be justified in law, but this kind of case is much rarer than you might suppose. Much more frequent are the cases in which the defects and uncertainties in the system are ruthlessly exploited by the knowledgeable criminal and by his advisers.

Sir Robert Mark's strictures on the high 'failure rate' in English trials need some further explication and comment:

The percentage of acquittals when Sir Robert Mark spoke was around half. It is now even higher. In 1993, it was 58 per cent and in 1994, 60 per cent. This seems very high. But the facts are more complex than Sir Robert Mark suggested.

The acquittal rate is based on contested cases, whereas the majority of defendants in the crown court plead guilty. The proportion pleading guilty to all charges in crown courts in recent years has been around 70 per cent (1990, 72%, 1991 and 1992, 70%, 1993 and 1994, somewhat lower at 66%).[5]

The proportion of defendants pleading not guilty who are acquitted on all counts is currently around 16–17 per cent (1991, 1992 and 1993, 16%, 1994, 17%).

Moreover, only a minority of acquittals are by the jury. In 1994 no fewer than 46 per cent of all acquittals were ordered by the judge when the prosecution offered no evidence at the start of the case. Another 17 per cent were directed by the judge at the close of the prosecution's case on the ground that there was insufficient evidence even to put to the jury. The jury were only responsible for 37 per cent of all acquittals– which represented under 7 per cent of all cases.

The acquittal figures have altered significantly in recent years. That is to say, the overall proportion of *all* cases ending in acquittals has remained a more or less constant of 15–17 per cent. But within that figure the *proportions* attributable to acquittals ordered or directed by the judge and genuine jury decisions have altered considerably. Thus in 1980, 22 per cent of acquittals were ordered by the judge when the prosecution offered no evidence, 24 per cent were directed by the judge at some point and 57 per cent were by the jury. The equivalent proportions in 1990 were 42 per cent, 16 per cent, 42 per cent. (Evidence of the Lord Chancellor's Department to the Runciman Royal Commission on Criminal Justice, December 1991.)

The full breakdown in 1994 was:

5   See annual *Judicial Statistics*.

Percentage disposition of crown court cases, 1994

Pleading guilty to all charges	66
Pleading guilty to some charges and convicted of the others	1
Pleading guilty to some charges and acquitted of others	4
Found guilty by the jury	11
Acquitted, prosecution offer no evidence	8
Acquitted, prosecution case not sufficient to put to the jury	3
Acquitted by the jury	7
Total	100

(*Source: Judicial Statistics*, 1994, Tables 6.8, 6.9.)

The fact that some 7 per cent of those tried in the crown court are acquitted by the jury might be largely attributable to the fact that the burden of proof is a high one. Even assuming that all those acquitted were guilty (obviously a wholly impermissible and unrealistic assumption), a significant number would rightly be acquitted simply because the prosecution failed to prove its case beyond a reasonable doubt. If proof must be beyond a reasonable doubt (and no one has suggested otherwise), it is inevitable that a considerable number of guilty defendants will be acquitted because the evidence of their guilt cannot be produced.

There is no evidence to suggest that professional criminals do better in the criminal justice system than others, and there is a considerable amount of evidence to the contrary. Taking defendants with a prior record, the evidence is that they have a statistically *lower* chance of an acquittal than defendants with no prior record[6] Moreover, the worse the record, the worse the chances of an acquittal.[7] In Baldwin and McConville's study they got from the police details not only of prior convictions but also of prior acquittals and of suspected involvement in criminal activity. From this they built up a profile of each defendant on a scale of criminal professionalism. For this exercise there were close to 5,000 defendants in the sample–2,406 in Birmingham and 2,292 in London, a total of 4,698. Of these, 2,265 (48 per cent) were defined by the police information as 'low' on the criminal professionalism score, 1,448 (31 per cent) as 'medium', 647 (14 per cent) as 'high' and 227 (5 per cent) as 'very high'. When these scores were compared with acquittals and especially the 'questionable acquittals', it was found that 'only a minuscule proportion of all cases end in the questionable acquittal of any defendant who, on the measures used here, could be regarded as a professional criminal. Indeed, of those scoring highly on the professionalism scale in each city, no more than one in eighty was said to have been questionably acquitted'.[8]

---

6   This is shown by a number of studies including even one conducted by the Metropolitan Police – see M Zander, *Modern Law Review*, 1974, p 39, Table 3; McCabe and Purves, *The Jury at Work* (Blackwell, 1972) p 39, Table 4; Metropolitan Police, *Law Society's Gazette*, 1 March 1973, Table 1.

7   M Zander, *Modern Law Review*, 1974, p 41.

8   *Jury Trials* (1979), pp 110–12.

The only evidence that provides *any* support for Sir Robert Mark's thesis is that of John Mack, who contrasted the careers of the top criminals in his area of research (from names supplied by the police), with that of two other categories of lesser criminals. He called his three groups the Main Group, the Lesser Group and the Small Fry. On average the Small Fry were convicted on 85 per cent of charges brought against them, the Lesser Group on 80 per cent and the Main Group on 75 per cent.[9] This does show that the Main Group were somewhat more successful in avoiding charges than the others, but the difference can hardly be said to be great and the police success rate in getting convictions in three-quarters of the charges brought against the top villains seems, if anything, remarkably high. Moreover, as Mack showed, when the serious criminals are convicted they tend to get longer sentences. Mack compared the time not spent in prison from the age of 17 for his three groups. The Small Fry spent on average 83 per cent of their time not in prison compared with 70 per cent for the Lesser Group and 74 per cent for the Main Group.[10]

Sir Robert's attack on crooked lawyers is not supported by the small amount of evidence on this issue. For instance, in Baldwin and McConville's study of 370 contested jury trials in Birmingham they interviewed the police officers in the cases about the reasons for the acquittals. 'There was not a single serious allegation of any practice which could possibly be described as corrupt' (*Jury Trials*, 1979, p 118). In another study the same two authors looked at 2,000 cases heard in seven London crown courts in the light of the 'solicitors blacklist' maintained by Scotland Yard. (Someone had sent them a copy anonymously.) The firms on the list appeared on behalf of 223 defendants in the sample. Of these, 50 per cent pleaded guilty–a proportion that was slightly *higher* than for the rest of the sample. Of those who pleaded not guilty, the acquittal rate was 53 per cent, which was not very different from that of 47 per cent of the rest of the sample. Of the defendants identified to the researchers by the police as serious professional criminals, only 10 out of 72 had employed firms on the blacklist (Baldwin and McConville, 'Allegations Against Lawyers' (1978) *Criminal Law Review*, pp 744–5).

Finally, the minority of cases that are contested are likely, by definition, to be the doubtful ones in which one might expect a fairly high acquittal rate. This common-sense view is supported by the evidence, which shows that many not-guilty pleas are based on a defence that the accused lacked the necessary knowledge or intent (*mens rea*) to be guilty of the offence.[11] It is perhaps not surprising that, in such cases particularly, the jury (or magistrates) will interpret conflicting testimony by giving the defendant the benefit of the doubt.

(q) Which level of criminal court acquits most defendants?

It has already been seen that one of the reasons why defendants choose trial by jury is the belief that this will give them a better chance of an acquittal. There appears to be a widespread impression that magistrates convict a higher proportion of defendants

9   J Mack, *Modern Law Review*, 1976, p 255.
10 Ibid, p 252.
11 See S McCabe and R Purves, *The Jury at Work*, p 41, where this was the defence in seven out of ten cases; and M Zander, *Modern Law Review*, 1974, p 59, n 50–where it was the defence in 81 per cent of cases.

than juries. One understandable reason for the impression is that a much higher proportion of defendants plead guilty in the magistrates' courts. But the acquittal rate can only be determined by examining cases where the accused pleads not guilty to all charges.

In 1994 the crown court guilty plea rate ranged from a high of 78 per cent in the North East to a low of 49 per cent in London with a national average of 66 per cent, (*Judicial Statistics*, 1994, Table 6.8). In the magistrates' courts it is very much higher –though there are no proper official figures on the matter. It seems that the guilty-plea rate may be around 80 per cent for indictable offences triable either way, but well over 90 per cent for the mass of minor motoring offences.

There is a widespread belief that the acquittal rate in magistrates' courts is distinctly lower than in the crown court. Figures emerged in the 1970s which suggested that this might be a myth–and that the acquittal rate in magistrates' courts could be as high or even slightly higher than in the crown court. (See especially *Criminal Statistics*, 1976, Cmnd 6909, paras 4.7–12; J Baldwin and PR Hopkins, 'The Summary Trial of Indictable Offences', *Justice of the Peace*, 1975, p 465; J Baldwin and M McConville, 'The New Home Office Figures on Pleas and Acquittals–What Sense do they Make?' (1978) *Criminal Law Review*, p 196.) It transpired subsequently, however, that those figures were based on statistical errors.

See further P Softley, 'A Comparison of Acquittal Rates in Magistrates' Courts and Crown Court', *Justice of the Peace*, 1976, p 455; J Vennard and K Williams, 'Contested Trials in Magistrates' Courts: The Case for the Prosecution', *Royal Commission on Criminal Procedure, Research Study No 6*, 1980; and especially, S Butler, 'Acquittal Rates', Home Office Research and Planning Unit, Paper 16, 1983.

In October 1983 a new piece of evidence was published in the form of a study by the Lord Chancellor's Department of the grant of legal aid in magistrates' courts. The sample consisted of 3,000 cases in five offence categories tried in some 60 different courts. Seventeen per cent of the sample pleaded not guilty. Of these, just under half (44 per cent) were acquitted. This acquittal rate is similar to that in the crown court. (*Report of a Survey on the Grant of Legal Aid in Magistrates' Courts*, 1983, Table 17.)

But a systematic study of the problem by Julie Vennard, then of the Home Office Research and Planning Unit, resulted in a different outcome. She compared 305 contested summary charges in six magistrates' courts against 320 contested crown court cases. All the cases were in three offence categories–wounding or assault, shoplifting, and other theft or handling. The defendant was almost always represented. The acquittal rate in the crown court was 57 per cent, compared with 30 per cent in the magistrates' courts. The evidence produced for both prosecution and defence in both courts was similar, with one exception. The credibility of the prosecution's case was impugned almost twice as often in the crown court cases as in those in the magistrates' courts. Miss Vennard was unable to explain the marked difference in outcome in cases in the two levels of courts. It should not be thought, she said, that the findings showed that magistrates were more likely to convict the innocent or juries to acquit the guilty. The explanation might have more to do with the greater ability of defence lawyers in the crown court to impugn the prosecution's case by cross-examination of witnesses–and the impact of that on jurors and magistrates respectively. (See J Vennard, 'The Outcome of Contested Trials', in *Managing Criminal Justice*, ed D Moxon (HMSO, 1985), p 126; see also McConville, Sanders and Leng, *The Case for the Prosecution* (Routledge, 1991), pp 149–50.)

The evidence from Scotland is that the acquittal rate does not vary markedly between the three levels of court. In 1979 the proportion found not guilty in 'solemn procedure' was 8 per cent, whilst in 3 per cent of cases the jury's verdict was not proven. In the sheriff courts, 7 per cent were acquitted and again 3 per cent were not proven. In the summary courts where the not-proven verdict does not exist, 3.5 per cent of those tried were acquitted. The guilty-verdict rate in the three courts was therefore 88 per cent, 90 per cent, and 96 per cent respectively. (See *Criminal Statistics Scotland*, 1979, Cmnd 8215, Tables 3, 5 and 6.) The same figures are not available for later years.

A survey published in *The Sunday Times* on 25 April 1973 showed that 78 per cent of those interviewed favoured jury trials and only 13 per cent preferred trials by judge alone. The poll was taken one week after Sir Robert Mark's controversial BBC television lecture in which he questioned the efficiency of the jury system in convicting criminals (p 409 above). Its findings were based on a quota sample of 970 adults over the age of fifteen.

The public was about evenly divided on whether previous convictions should be revealed to the jury. When people were asked if court rules should be changed to allow an accused more or fewer rights, only 20 per cent were in favour of changing the rules to fewer rights. Five per cent thought the accused should have greater rights; 62 per cent thought the present system was about right.

Further reading on the modern jury system:

WR Cornish, *The Jury* (Penguin, 1971).

Lord Devlin, *Trial by Jury* (Stevens, 1966); 'The Conscience of the Jury', 107 *Law Quarterly Review*, 1991, r 398.

Glanville Williams, *Proof of Guilt* (Stevens, 1963), chapter 10.

Harry Kalven Jr and Hans Zeisel, *The American Jury* (Little Brown, 1966) and the review of their book by E Griew, 'The Behaviour of the Jury–A Review of the American Evidence' (1967) *Criminal Law Review*, p 569.

J Baldwin and M McConville, *Jury Trials* (Clarendon, 1979).

Z Bankowski and G Mungham, 'The Jury as Process' in P Carlen (ed), *The Sociology of Law* (University of Keele, 1976).

MDA Freeman, 'The Jury on Trial' (1981) *Current Legal Problems*, p 65.

P Duff and M Findlay, *The Jury Under Attack* (Butterworth, 1988).

Penny Darbyshire, 'The Lamp that Shows that Freedom Lives–Is it Worth the Candle?' (1991) *Criminal Law Review*, p 740.

S Enright and J Morton, *Taking Liberties: The Criminal Jury in the 1990s* (Weidenfeld and Nicolson, 1990).

(r) The operation of the jury (and trials) in former times

An American scholar, Professor John Langbein of the University of Chicago, writing in 1978, demonstrated from the Old Bailey Sessions Papers for the period 1670 to 1730 that at that time the criminal trial proceeded in a way that would now be regarded as most improper. The Old Bailey Sessions Papers were so-called 'chap books'– pamphlets written by non-lawyers for sale to the general public, each pamphlet recounting the details of the latest cases. They ran from 1674 for nearly two and a half centuries. During that time they underwent major changes of format and function, from chap books to newspapers to true law reports. The newspaper phase had been reached by the mid-1680s. At that time they were published regularly and they recounted a considerable number of cases. The Old Bailey sat eight times a year and a Sessions paper was produced for each session. In the early years they ran to four pages and everything was highly compressed. In the 1720s they were eight pages long and in the 1730s they burgeoned to twenty-page pamphlets. In the late 1730s the reports of a single session required two twenty-page pamphlets. They were seemingly written mainly for laymen and are therefore not an ideal source for understanding of the system of trial. But Langbein says that they 'are probably the best accounts we shall ever have of what transpired in ordinary English criminal courts before the late eighteenth century'. (JH Langbein, 'The Criminal Trial Before Lawyers', 45 *University of Chicago Law Review*, 1978, pp 263, 271.)

The features of the trial at that time included the following:

(1) A single jury was empanelled to hear a large number of cases. Typically, there were only two twelve-man juries for the whole sessions—a London jury and a Middlesex jury. A session lasted several days and processed 50–100 felony cases. In December 1678, for instance, there was a two-day session. On the Wednesday morning the London jury tried two cases, the Middlesex jury tried seven. In the afternoon the London jury tried three cases. The next morning the Middlesex jury had eight cases and the London jury six. On Thursday the London jury was discharged whilst the Middlesex jury had six cases. Between them the two juries returned verdicts in 32 cases involving 36 accused in two days!

(2) The cases were commonly tried and decided in batches. The jury would hear a number of trials and would then go off to deliberate on all the cases together. In the cases in December 1678, for instance, the Middlesex jury which heard twenty-one cases deliberated only three times. The first batch consisted of seven cases, the second of eight cases and the last of six cases.

(3) Many of the jurors were veterans of earlier sessions. Jurors it seemed were drawn from a tiny cohort.

(4) As is obvious from the facts already related, trials took place at amazing speed. Most cases were not-guilty pleas but they were disposed of in short order. Typically a jury heard twelve to twenty cases in a day. Many of the not-guilty pleas, it is true, were somewhat half-hearted. The accused made no reply or offered no evidence or brought only character witnesses. One reason for the striking speed of events was that trials tended to take place within a few weeks of the event and the recollection of witnesses was therefore fresh. Most of the trials at the December sessions concerned crimes that had occurred in October or November. Also the cases were normally based on committal papers prepared and even presented by the justice of the peace or his clerk. The committal procedure often resulted in the accused making a statement or confession and the not-guilty plea that then followed was more pro forma than real. There were no lawyers either for prosecution or defence. The prosecution was at least allowed to have a barrister whereas the defence was not. In important cases, reported as State Trials, the prosecution was always represented, but in ordinary cases normally it was not. In the December 1678 session, for instance, there was no mention of any prosecution counsel in any of the 32 cases. In the absence of a lawyer there was no opening and closing speech, no examination or cross-examination of witnesses and

no motions on points of evidence. Questioning of witnesses was done by the judge himself, or by the accused. The accused could not give sworn evidence but he could question both prosecution witnesses and call and question defence witnesses. He would be asked by the judge what reply he made to prosecution evidence and it was normal for him to respond rather than to rely on any right of silence or right not to incriminate himself. (Langbein says that in the entire 60-year period from the 1670s he did not come across a single case in which an accused person refused to speak in reliance on the right of silence.) Also the judge gave few instructions to the jury about each case. Jury deliberations were often perfunctory. Sometimes the jury did not even retire to reach a verdict.

(5) The judge played a far more directing role than would be permissible today. In *Bushell*'s case in 1670 the principle was established that jurors could not be fined for returning a verdict contrary to the trial judge's instructions. But *Bushell*'s case was untypical. The Old Bailey Sessions papers show the judge normally exercising so much influence over the jury that Langbein suggests 'it is difficult to characterise the jury functioning autonomously' (at p 285). The judge often served in effect as examiner-in-chief of both the witnesses and the accused. In this capacity, as well as in summing up to the jury, he exercised what seems to have been a wholly unrestricted power to comment on the merits of the case. Sometimes the judge did not bother to use the power. But when he felt like it he would tell the jury what verdict to find, and normally the jury followed the judge's indications.

(6) Sometimes if the judge did not think the evidence for one side or the other was sufficient, he would stop the trial and tell the party in question to get evidence on the point in question and start again. Today the double-jeopardy rule prevents the prosecution from stopping a case that is going badly and starting afresh. But in the seventeenth and eighteenth centuries this occurred not infrequently. The power seems to have been used mainly in order to assist the prosecution rather than the defence.

(7) There is evidence in the reports of some instances of exchanges between the judge and the jury as the case was proceeding. The jury would comment as the case was developing, or would ask questions or would ask for certain witnesses to be called. Moreover it often gave reasons for its decisions and sometimes would be questioned about the verdict by the judge.

(8) In some instances the judge rejected a verdict, probed the jury's reasoning, argued with the jury, gave further instructions, and told it to go away to deliberate afresh. If the judge did not agree with a jury's conviction of the defendant, it was common for him to recommend a pardon or commutation of sentence and such recommendations were often influential.

(9) The Old Bailey Sessions Papers also threw light on the rules of evidence that were then applied. Hearsay evidence seemed to be admitted quite commonly. If the judge ruled that hearsay evidence should be excluded, no warning was normally given to the jury to disregard the excluded evidence. Nor was the jury sent out of the court room while the argument went on as to the admissibility of the evidence. Since there was normally no lawyer for either side, this was not appropriate.

The Sessions papers also show that, contrary to the modern rules, evidence of previous convictions was frequently considered by the jury as part of the evidence.

Langbein suggests that the modern concept of fairness to the accused requiring exclusion of evidence that would taint the jury had not developed by that time. At a time when the judge dominated the jury there was little thought of keeping prejudicial evidence away from them. The law of evidence, with its modern exclusionary rules, developed not in order to control the judges but as part of the rise of the lawyer as a participant in the criminal process. The rise of lawyers cost the judges their commanding role and thereby made the jury more dangerous, since the judge could not control it so well.

The rule that the accused could not have a lawyer started to break down in about the 1730s. Until then, according to Langbein, the absence of defence counsel was justified by three main arguments. First, the trial judge was supposed to serve as defence counsel. Secondly, the requirement of a high degree of proof was regarded as a safeguard. If proof of that level could be mustered against the prisoner it would be useless for him to have a lawyer since he would plainly be guilty. Third, the accused knew more about the case than anyone else and could not therefore be properly served by an intermediary. On the other hand, curiously, lawyers *were* allowed for misdemeanour cases though not normally for felonies. Lawyers were also permitted if there was some point of law to argue. If the court did not see the point, however, it was left for the accused himself to raise it and to persuade the judge to allow him to have a lawyer. Defence lawyers began to play a role in examining and cross-examining witnesses in the 1730s, though the accused himself continued to play the same role as before as well. There was no real differentiation of function between counsel and the accused. But gradually the role of the lawyer developed and, as Langbein puts it, the lawyers eventually broke up the ancient working relationship between judge and jury 'and cost the judge his mastery of the proceedings' (at p 314).

In the period covered by the Sessions Papers studied by Langbein, the accused in effect therefore lacked the safeguards both of the inquisitorial and of the adversarial systems. There was neither proper investigation of claims of non-guilt nor rules of evidence, the assistance of counsel nor appropriate rules for the selection, instruction and control of the jury.

See also an illuminating article by Stephen Landsman, 'The Rise of the Contentious Spirit: Adversary Procedure in Eighteenth Century England', 75 *Cornell Law Review*, 1990, p 498.

The jury on the continent of Europe

Various continental countries including Spain and Russia are in the process of introducing the jury system. For an overview of the jury in continental countries see Roderick Munday, 'Jury Trial, Continental Style', *Legal Studies*, July 1993, pp 204–24.

CHAPTER 6

Costs and legal aid

1. CAN WE AFFORD THE COST OF BRITISH JUSTICE?

(a) The level of costs

It is notorious that the costs of going to law are amazingly high. The problem has vexed all those concerned with the legal system for decades and shows no sign of abating.

Costs in civil litigation

The facts about costs are sparse but over the years there have been a number of studies that have thrown light on the topic.[1] The most recent study is that conducted by Professor Hazel Genn for the Woolf Inquiry. Lord Woolf's Interim Report (Annex III, p 251–56) gave figures based on a study of 673 High Court cases submitted to the Supreme Court Taxing Office during 1994–95 (for 'taxation' see p 420 below). Average costs varied as between different types of case. The most costly were medical negligence (average £38,252), followed by commercial cases (average £29,418), and official referee/breach of contract/libel/other Queen's Bench cases (average £25,786). The average for personal injury cases was £20,413.

Unsurprisingly, the higher the claim, the higher the costs. Where the value of the claim was under £25,000 the mean costs allowed were under £13,000. Where the value was between £100,000 and £250,000 the mean costs rose to £31,500.

In one half of the lowest value cases (those involving amounts under £12,500) the costs of one side alone were close to or exceeded the total value of the claim. Some 16 per cent of bills were the equivalent of 100 per cent or more of the claim and 6 per cent represented double or more of the claim value.

The following table shows the writs issued in the High Court and the county court by amount of the claim.

---

1 Figures from earlier studies (the Evershed Report, 1953; JUSTICE, 1966; Zander, 1973–74; Pearson Royal Commission, 1977; Civil Justice Review, 1984) were set out in the 6th edition of this work at pp 490–91.

	£600	£600–£2K	£2k-5k	£5–25k	£25–50k	£50K	Unliquidated
	%	%	%	%	%	%	%
High Court	0.5	20	23	23	7	5	21
County court	1	13	12	8	1	0.5	64

(Source: Lord Woolf's Interim Report, July 1995, Annex V1, p 264.)

The latest county court cost figures are those of a small sample in the study of personal injury cases done for the Civil Justice Review in 1984. The average costs of the plaintiff alone were £1,540–which on average was 99 per cent of the damages recovered. (Civil Justice Review, *Personal Injuries Litigation Consultation Paper*, February 1986, paras 68–81.)

A recent Law Society study of a sample of medical negligence cases conducted by 23 firms investigated 376 closed files. No fewer than 78 per cent were funded on legal aid–including *all* the cases that went to trial! This does not prove but it certainly supports the view that at least some of the privately funded cases dropped out for fear of the cost. The success rate in the cases that went to trial was 80 per cent. (The study is referred to by Hazel Genn in 'The Case of Medical Negligence' in *Reform of Civil Procedure: Essays on Access to Justice*, ed Zuckerman and Cranston, Oxford, 1995, pp 401, 404.)

(b) The categories of cost

(1) Solicitors' charges

Solicitors' charges are different depending on whether the matter in question involves litigation ('contentious work'), or not ('non-contentious work'). Contentious business concerns work in both civil and criminal courts and has to do with the resolution of disputes, whether in court or outside the court room. Non-contentious business comprises the rest of a solicitor's work.

The solicitor's bill is made up of 'disbursements' (which include fees paid to barristers) and 'profit costs' representing not only profit but also the overheads of work done by the fee-earners in the solicitor's firm. The profit costs item in the bill is therefore what the solicitor charges over and above the out-of-pocket expenses.

A solicitor is allowed to take into account several different factors when determining his fees: the time the job takes; the skill and knowledge involved, having regard to the complexity of the matter; the amount involved (or, in a criminal case, its gravity); the effort involved, including such factors as the number of documents to be read, the distance that has to be travelled; and special factors such as urgency.

Costs in contentious civil work are distinguished from costs in other types of work by the fact that as a rule the loser is ordered to pay the winner's costs. (This is the so-called 'indemnity rule' of costs–see p 431 below.) In civil contentious work the loser pays his own bill plus that of his opponent. The costs to be paid by the loser can be and sometimes are agreed between the parties. However, the loser can and commonly does ask for the winner's bill to be taxed. This simply means that it is submitted to an appropriate authority for assessment. Taxations in the High Court are carried out by specialist officials called 'Taxing Masters' or outside London by district judges. In the county court it is the district judge.

The statutory provision about costs is now in the Supreme Court Act 1981, s 51(1) (formerly Supreme Court of Judicature (Consolidation) Act 1925, s 50(1)). This states that subject to the Act and to rules of court, 'the costs of and incidental to all proceedings in the Supreme Court ... shall be in the discretion of the court or judge and the court or judge shall have full power to determine by whom and to what extent the costs are to be paid'.

The level of costs to be assessed depends on the nature of the bill.

The system that existed prior to then was described conveniently in a case in the Chancery Division by the Vice-Chancellor Sir Robert Megarry (*EMI Records Ltd v Wallace Ltd* [1982] 2 All ER 980). He identified and defined five distinct categories of orders of costs:

(*a*) *Party and party costs* This was the least generous scale, such costs being confined to those deemed to be 'necessary or proper'. This was the ordinary basis of taxing the costs to be paid by the loser to the winner.

(*b*) *Common fund costs* On this basis a reasonable amount was allowed in respect of all costs reasonably incurred. The level of fees allowed was about 5–10 per cent higher than a bill assessed on the party and party basis. The common fund basis was that applied in legal aid cases.

(*c*) *Trustee basis* Where the costs were to be paid out of a fund such as a trust fund or an estate, no costs were disallowed unless the taxing officer thought they had been unreasonably incurred or were greater than the trust or fund should bear.

(*d*) *Solicitor and own client basis* These were the costs which a solicitor is entitled to charge his own client. On this basis under Rule 29, all costs were allowed 'except in so far as they are of an unreasonable amount or have been unreasonably incurred'. This was therefore similar to the trustee basis. There were however, two supporting presumptions. All costs incurred with the express or implied approval of the client were conclusively deemed to have been reasonably incurred. But secondly, there was a rebuttable presumption that any unusual costs had been unreasonably incurred unless the solicitor had obtained express permission to incur them.

(*e*) *Indemnity basis* This was the type of order for costs under consideration in the *EMI Records* case. It was used where there had been outrageous behaviour, for instance against those found in contempt of court or sometimes in libel cases. This basis of costs was the same as solicitor and own client costs except that the two presumptions which applied to those costs did not apply. All costs incurred were therefore allowable, save those which had been unreasonably incurred or which were of an unreasonable amount. They were, therefore, apt to be less than solicitor and own client costs–because the paying party was not bound by any express or implied consent of the successful party, nor by any warnings given by their solicitors. The difference between this basis and the common fund basis was that on the common fund basis, if there was any doubt as to the reasonableness of any item, the benefit of the doubt was given to the paying party, whereas on the indemnity basis the benefit of any doubt went to the receiving party.

The Benson Royal Commission on Legal Services in its 1979 report recommended that party and party costs should be abolished and merged with common fund costs. 'If it is accepted that the losing party should pay the winner's costs, we see no reason in principle why he should not pay such costs as may be found to have been reasonably incurred' (para 37.32).

The new system introduced in 1986

The proposal that party and party costs be abolished was implemented in a new Order 62 in 1986. It was replaced by the *standard basis* of taxation. This is a reasonable amount in respect of all costs reasonably incurred, with any doubts being resolved in favour of the paying party. This is like the old common fund basis, which has also been abolished. Standard basis taxation is now the norm both for privately funded and for legal aid cases. The Law Society thought that the effect would be that successful parties in litigation who previously recovered about two-thirds of their costs from the winner would under the new system recover virtually all their costs.

The other bases of costs (trustee, and solicitor and own client) were abolished and replaced by the *indemnity basis*–all costs except insofar as they are of an unreasonable amount or have been unreasonably incurred, with doubts being resolved in favour of the party being paid. (The system is set out in the new Order 62 to the Rules of the Supreme Court introduced by SI 1986/632. The first amendment was the Solicitors' (Non-Contentious Business) Remuneration Order 1994. See further *Bowen-Jones v Bowen-Jones* [1986] 3 All ER 163; *Johnson v Reed Corrugated Cases Ltd* [1992] 1 All ER 169; *Re a Company (No 004081 of 1989)* [1995] 2 All ER 155; *KPMG Peat Marwick McLintock v HLT Group Ltd* [1995] 2 All ER 180 and *Civil Justice Quarterly*, January 1987, p 1.)

The rules in Order 62, r 12 are supplemented by the Masters Practice Notes, printed in *The Supreme Court Practice* (known as 'the White Book'). These state that each chargeable item should be shown in two parts–the direct costs and the proper mark up for 'care and conduct'.

In *Johnson v Reed* (above) the court held that when assessing the amount of a solicitor's costs on the standard basis a taxing officer was required to calculate the allowable costs by reference to the average cost of an average solicitor in the relevant area at the relevant time on the basis of his general knowledge and experience of the economics of conducting a solicitor's practice in that area, without making any allowance for inflation. The solicitors in Manchester claimed £50 per hour with a mark up for care and conduct of 150 per cent. The registrar allowed £48 per hour with a mark up of 90 per cent. The defendants contended that it should be £34 per hour and 60 per cent mark up. The court allowed a basic hourly rate of £40 and a mark up of 70 per cent, which produced an hourly rate of £70. In *Loveday v Renton (No 2)* [1992] 3 All ER 184 the court allowed a mark up of 125 per cent in a very heavy piece of test case litigation concerning whooping cough vaccine. In *KPMG* (above), the court said it had been reasonable for the plaintiffs to instruct a leading City firm of solicitors. It allowed an hourly rate of £140 for the partner and £80 for the assistant solicitor. Both of these were below the going rate for 1992 shown by a survey conducted by the London Solicitors' Litigation Association which indicated a rate of £171 per hour for a partner and £111 for an assistant. (The corresponding figures for Holborn and

Westminster were £109 and £79.) Partners in City firms, however, charge much higher hourly rates than these. Rates of £250 per hour are certainly not the highest.

(2) Barristers' charges

Barristers divide their work broadly into two main categories–advocacy and paper work. When work is sent to a barrister by a solicitor, the fee is supposed to be marked on the papers either before delivery or when they have been delivered, unless it is to be assessed by some external agency such as the legal aid authorities or court taxing official. The actual fixing of private sector fees is normally handled by the barrister's clerk. Technically, in cases of difficulty the solicitor may negotiate directly with the barrister himself but this is exceedingly rare. In routine matters a fee is not necessarily marked on the papers before the work is done.

Instructions to appear in court are technically called 'a brief'. It is a rule of etiquette that a barrister may not appear in court on behalf of a fee-paying client unless a fee has been marked on the brief. The purpose of this rule is said to be to avoid the risk that counsel will have a financial interest in the outcome of the case. By the same rule of conduct, no agreement in advance may be made for the reduction of the fee, if the work is less than was imagined because, for instance, the case is settled. Conversely, no agreement may be made to increase the fee if the work proves greater than was anticipated. The rules of etiquette used to provide that a barrister could not reduce his fees even if the case was settled. Then the rules permitted such a reduction. Now the rules say nothing about it. The understanding is, however, that once the brief is delivered with a fee marked on it the barrister is normally entitled to be paid that amount.

If the amount of counsel's fee is reduced on taxation, the solicitor technically remains liable to pay counsel the full amount. The solicitor who instructs counsel is under a professional duty to pay counsel the full amount agreed whether or not it is allowed on taxation. But an informal application to reduce the fee can be made to the barrister by the solicitor and in such cases that may be agreed.

Where fees are paid out of public funds either for legal aid or prosecution work, if they are not 'standard fees' (see below), they are assessed by taxing officers on the basis of rates laid down for that class of work. In the case of crown court work, for instance, the rates are based on regulations made by or on behalf of the Lord Chancellor's Department.

Fees paid to counsel for court work are divided into different classes: first, a basic fee known as the brief fee to cover preparation and the first day's hearing, including, where they take place on that day, conferences, consultations and applications; secondly, daily refresher fees for any day or part of a day beyond the first; thirdly, fees for any other attendances, consultations, written advice or appearances not covered by the brief fee or refreshers.

Brief fees and refreshers in substantial cases these days are very high. In *Re a Company* above, the court held that brief fees of £20,000 for the QC and £7,000 for the junior barrister acting for the third and the fourth defendants were not unreasonable even though in the event they were only required for the first five to ten minutes of a trial that lasted two weeks before the case settled. (The bill was being taxed on the indemnity basis.) However the court disallowed as 'beyond any doubt unreasonable' a fee of £1,500 to be paid to the QC to attend two weeks later at the settlement negotiations. The court substituted the figure of zero! In *Loveday v Renton (No 2)* [1992] 3 All ER 184, a legally aided piece of unusually heavy test case litigation, the court allowed brief fees of £125,000 for the plaintiffs' QCs and £70,000 and £50,000 respectively for the two juniors. A survey in *Legal Business* on high earning QCs in 1995 said some could be earning over £1 million a year from private fees. One QC had charged a brief fee of £350,000 and refreshers of £2,500 a day for a 26 week trial. Another had earned between £150,000 and £200,000 for a recent 12-week case. These top barristers charged hourly rates of between £350–650 with daily refreshers of £2,500 ((1995) *Times*, 4 May). A district judge in an article in the Law Bulletin of the Association of District Judges in October 1995 complained of QCs who were treating child care cases as 'a gravy train'. He cited two of his own cases in which QCs claimed brief fees of £25,000 and refreshers of £2,500 a day. In one of those cases the local authority on the other side paid its QC £9,000 on the brief plus £700 per day. In the other the council only had a junior barrister. Charges of well over £1,000 for a two-three hour meeting were said to be 'commonplace'. But not all barristers were greedy. Many able counsel took brief fees of £2,500–£3,000 plus £600 a day ((1995) *The Guardian*, 18 October).

(c) Controls on fees

Protection of the client against excessive charges is sought by various different mechanisms:

(1) Taxation of costs

As has been seen, taxation is the process of having the bill assessed by the appropriate authority. Where the taxation is of the winner's bill it protects the loser from paying too much; it does not, however, reduce the total amount to be paid – it simply redistributes it as between winner and loser. By contrast, where the taxation is of the client's own solicitor's bill, any reduction in the bill sets the total amount to be paid. That is the whole purpose of any such taxation. However solicitor and own client taxations are very rare–no doubt partly because clients would feel embarrassment at challenging their solicitors' bills, partly through ignorance of the availability of the facility and partly because unless the client succeeds in getting the bill reduced by more than one-fifth he has to bear the costs of the taxation. The solicitor is only required to inform the client of this right before issuing legal proceedings to sue for unpaid fees. (He must now also inform the client before entering a conditional fees contract–see p 469–76 below.)

The Benson Royal Commission on Legal Services, 1979, proposed (para 37.15) that at the time when a solicitor receives instructions from a client it should be the solicitor's professional duty to inform the client in writing: of the basis upon which the charges are made; that the client may set a limit on the amount which may be charged, not to be exceeded without further authority; and of the client's right to have the final bill taxed by the court, or in non-contentious cases to have the bill reviewed by the Law Society.

In 1991 the Law Society revised the written professional standards for solicitors regarding information about costs. (See *The Guide to the Professional Conduct of*

Solicitors, 6th edn, 1993, pp 280–82.) On taking instructions solicitors 'should give clients the best information possible about the likely cost of the matter' including how the fee will be calculated. Also, the client should be informed that he may set a limit on the costs. There is no mention however of the right to have the bill taxed.

(2) Remuneration certificates

The Law Society traditionally has provided a free service in reviewing bills in non-contentious matters. If the Society suggests a lower fee, that is then the fee that the solicitor may charge. Remuneration certificates cannot result in the bill being increased. This procedure too is very little used. As from 1994 the system was modified so that it applies now only if the bill is for an amount under £50,000 and only if the client has paid half the solicitors' costs plus disbursements and VAT. The solicitor must however pay back to the client any amount paid him which the remuneration certificate states is excessive. In exceptional circumstances the requirement to pay half the bill can be waived by the Law Society. (See M Bacon, *Solicitors' Journal*, 4 November 1994, p 1127.)

(3) Scale fees

For certain small standard items there are fixed fees. This is true, for instance, for photocopies, attendance to issue or serve summonses, attendance to deliver documents, etc. In other types of work there are scale fees which are not fixed but are maxima (or both maximum and minimum).

Scale fees for conveyancing work Conveyancing, which was formerly the single largest source of solicitors' work accounting for about half their gross income, used to be subject to scale fees that were treated as both maxima and minima–the fee was assessed by reference to the value involved and the Law Society allowed no competition between solicitors through undercutting of the scale. In 1973 this system was abolished and replaced by a requirement that the charge be fair and reasonable, but in practice many solicitors still tended to operate roughly on scale charges, though subject to some possibility of adjustment. The Benson Royal Commission in 1979 recommended (para 21.98) that scale fees be reintroduced as standard charges which the solicitor could exceed only if he had given a warning to the client in advance and in writing. Solicitors would be free to charge less than the standard charge if they wished. This recommendation was not implemented. But since 1984 solicitors have been allowed to advertise their fees and this has unquestionably introduced genuine competition– and significantly lower fees, especially during the economic recession in the early 1990s. (A Law Society Working Party stated in 1994 that solicitors' conveyancing charges fell in real terms between 1986 and 1993 by no less than 45 per cent: 'Adapting for the Future', Report of the Law Society's Special Working Party on Conveyancing Services, 1994, p 9.) Conveyancing of residential property which in 1966–67 had represented 50 per cent of solicitors' gross income had reduced by 1993 to under 10 per cent (*ibid*, paras 2.4, 2.7).

Indeed, profit margins in conveyancing work had become so slender and competition so fierce that in December 1995 the new President of the Law Society tried to persuade the Council of the Law Society to adopt a rule that undercutting new minimum 'guideline' fees should constitute unprofessional conduct and be grounds for removing the solicitor's indemnity insurance cover. The President, Mr Martin Mears, was supporting a campaign started by a solicitor John Edge, which had the support of some 12,000 solicitors. Just before the Law Society's Council was due to debate the matter, the Master of the Rolls intervened with a letter sent to all 75 Council members raising the question whether the proposed move would be unlawful as being 'contrary to public policy'. He suggested that the indemnity insurance scheme could not be used to achieve ends that did not concern indemnity insurance. The purpose of the scheme was to safeguard the public not members of the profession. The proposed move, he suggested, also raised concerns about 'fair trading and competition law'. At its meeting on 14 December 1995, the Council of the Law Society decided to ask for a QC's opinion on the legality of the proposal and also to ballot the solicitors' profession. (See *Times*, 14, 15 December, 1995 and the professional journals for that week.)

One of the two QCs, Mr David Pannick, advised that the Law Society would be acting unlawfully if it altered the Solicitors' Indemnity Rules for the purpose of deterring or penalising low-cost conveyancing. But if low-cost conveyancing was responsible for a disproportionate number of claims on the indemnity insurance policy it could amend the rules to require low cost conveyancers to seek insurance elsewhere. But before changing the rules the Master of the Rolls would have to be satisfied of the actuarial evidence establishing those facts and 'on the information available it is unlikely that the Master of the Rolls would concur with any proposed rule changes', (*Law Society's Gazette*, 24 January 1996, p 1).

The other QC, Mr David Vaughan, advised that any move such as that proposed would inevitably be referred to the Monopolies and Mergers Commission and would have to be justified as being in the public interest (*ibid*). A third QCs opinion obtained by Mr John Edge, the proposer of the conveyancing initiative warned that the common law doctrine of restraint on trade could apply to any of the proposals under consideration (*Law Society's Gazette*, 31 January 1996, p 3).

Scale fees in the county court   In cases tried in the county courts, an order for costs traditionally meant that the amount of costs recoverable inter partes was limited to those allowed by the existing scales. Until 1991 there were four scales–Lower scale where the claim was for more than £25 and under £100; Scale 1 where the claim was for more than £100 and under £500; Scale 2 for claims of between £500 and £3,000 and Scale 3 for claims higher than £3,000.

As from July 1991 CCR Ord 38, rr 1–4 were amended. There are now three scales. Lower scale remains the same. Scale 1 is for claims for between £100 and £3,000. Scale 2 is for claims for sums greater than £3,000. The costs recoverable under Lower scale and Scale 1 are fixed by Appendix C and Appendix A respectively. Under the new Scale 2 the amount to be allowed 'shall be in the discretion of the taxing officer –[in the light] of all relevant circumstances'.

In the Lower scale and Scale 1, some cost items are fixed whilst others give a measure of discretion in the form of a maximum and a minimum figure. The taxing officer assesses what he thinks is the right amount having regard to the nature of the case. In exceptional cases where the judge thinks that the costs allowable are insufficient, he may release the winner from the straitjacket of the scales. The Court of Appeal held in *Forey v London Buses Ltd* [1991] 2 All ER 936, that when a case is transferred to the county court from the High Court the judge has the power to award costs on the High Court scale instead of that of the county court. But these scales do not apply as between solicitor and his own client.

(4) Legal aid work

As has been seen, all fees in legal aid cases are assessed by the appropriate authorities. Thus, for work done in crown courts the assessment is done by taxing officials in the courts. In magistrates' courts the assessment is by area committees of the Legal Aid Board. In the High Court and the county court the Legal Aid Board assesses bills up to £500. Higher bills are assessed by taxation but solicitors can opt for assessments by the Board instead of taxation where the bill is between £500 and £1,000.

In magistrates' courts the method is to estimate the 'weight' of the case and the time it took. In crown courts the taxing officers have a 'Taxing Compendium' which indicates that the matters to be taken into account include the importance of the case, its complexity, the skill and specialized knowledge involved, the number of documents read, the time taken and miscellaneous other circumstances including travel and hotel expenses. (But see now further below.)

Standard fees In the past few years, however, legal aid fees have mainly moved to 'standard fees' where the lawyers get paid a set amount unless they can show that the case is exceptional. The intention to move to adopt standard fees was heralded in 1987 in the Government's White Paper (*Legal Aid in England and Wales: A New Framework*, March 1987, Cm 118) which stated: 'The Government considers that "standard fees" ... which provide a set fee for particular items of work ... should be introduced more widely. These will help to simplify and speed up the method of payment to lawyers'.

In 1986 standard fees were introduced for less serious cases in crown court cases for barristers and in 1988 for solicitors. (See *Law Society's Gazette*, 23 September 1987, p 2677; Anthony Edwards, 'Standard Fees: A Survival Guide', *New Law Journal*, 7 October 1988, p 722.) Between 60 per cent and 70 per cent of fees paid to barristers and solicitors for crown court work are now standard fees.

In the case of barristers, the standard fee lays down one fee. In the case of solicitors there are two types of standard fee, the lower standard fee and the higher (principal) fee. The determining officer has to decide which is the appropriate fee.

In 1995 the Lord Chancellor's Department said that it wanted to extend standard fees in crown courts to all but the most serious cases. The basis would be 'graduated fees' for all cases up to 10 days in length except where there are more than 80 witnesses or the evidence exceeds 1,000 pages in trials, or 420 pages in guilty plea cases. All offences will be placed in one of ten groups. There will be a basic fee for each of these groups, to cover the advocate's preparation, conference, advice on plea and evidence and the first day in court. In contested cases there will be additional fees for each block of five prosecution witnesses above the first ten, and for each block of 25 pages of prosecution evidence beyond the first 50 pages. A similar approach would apply to guilty pleas and 'cracked trials' (last minute guilty pleas). There will be daily refresher fees and additions to the basic fee based on total length of the trial. In long running cases there would also be a scheme of staged payments for the solicitor. Payments are supposed to be made within ten days of the claim being submitted. At the time of writing (early 1996) the details were still being hammered out between the Lord

Chancellor's Department, the Bar and the Law Society. The new scheme will apply to the fees of Queen's Counsel, junior barristers, solicitors and solicitor advocates. Overall the new scheme was supposed to be 'cost neutral'. It had originally been intended that it would come into operation in April 1996 but difficulties in the negotiations had caused delays. (For a description of the scheme see Anthony Berry QC, 'Graduated Fees in the Crown Court', Counsel, May/June 1996, p 12.)

Standard fees for most cases in magistrates' courts were introduced in June 1993 after a long and acrimonious dispute between the Law Society and the Lord Chancellor. The profession was worried that standard fees would reduce its income and would at the same time detrimentally affect the quality of service to clients. The Lord Chancellor claimed that it was not a cost-cutting measure but admitted that he hoped it would be a way of reducing the future growth of cost of the scheme. (For an account of the arguments, see *Law Society's Gazette*, 19 February 1992, pp 2–5. For the background to the dispute, see *Law Society's Gazette*, 9 October 1991, p 4; 20 November 1991, p 3; 4 December 1991, pp 2–4; 29 January 1992, p 3.)

Standard fees in magistrates' courts work do not apply where a barrister is assigned to the case under the legal aid order or where costs are allowed at an enhanced rate. As with the original crown court standard fees, there are three categories of fees and within each category two standard fees–a lower standard fee and a higher standard fee. (For details see *Law Society's Gazette*, 2 June 1993, p 30; for the claim that the effect on the Junior Bar was devastating see P Whetton, 'Fiddling while the Junior Bar Burns', *New Law Journal*, 20 August 1993, p 1230.)

In 1992, prescribed rates and hourly rates were introduced for family proceedings and in February 1994 they were extended to all other civil legal aid work in both the High Court and the county court. In exceptional circumstances a higher, enhanced rate can be applied for. (See M Bacon, 'Enhance or Die?', *Solicitors' Journal*, 22 April 1994, p 386, which sets out the new system and argues that the new rates are unrealistically low.)

(5) Wasted costs orders

Both barristers and solicitors have immunity from actions for negligence in regard to the work they do in court and in preparation of court work –*Rondel v Worsley* [1969] 1 AC 191, HL and *Saif Ali v Mitchell & Co* [1980] AC 198, HL, confirmed in the Courts and Legal Services Act 1990, s 62. However the 1990 Act, s 4 provided for 'wasted costs orders' against legal representatives. Under the section (and ss 111 and 112) the court may disallow, or as the case may be, order the legal representative concerned to meet, the whole or any part of the wasted costs (s 4(6)). Wasted costs are defined as costs incurred by any party (a) as a result of any 'improper, unreasonable or negligent act or omission on the part of any representative or any employee of a representative' or (b) which, in the light of any such act or omission, the court considers it is unreasonable to expect that party to pay.

A series of test cases on 'wasted costs orders' were decided by the Court of Appeal in January 1994 in *Ridehalgh v Horsefield* [1994] 3 All ER 848. The Court of Appeal held that before such an order is made the court must be satisfied that the conduct in question directly caused the wasted costs complained of. 'Improper' conduct covered any significant breach of a substantial duty in a code of professional conduct or according to the consensus of professional opinion, whether it violated the letter of a professional code or not. 'Unreasonable' meant vexatious, designed to harass the other side. There was no need to show improper motive. It could arise from excessive zeal. 'Negligent' was to be understood in an untechnical way to denote failure to act within the competence reasonably to be expected of ordinary members of the profession. On the facts, the court allowed all six appeals and declared in each case that the order should not have been made. The conduct the subject of the lawyers' appeals, variously, was: both parties' solicitors misconstrued a complex statute; solicitors, like their own expert and counsel, failed to realise that the client had fundamentally (and fatally for the claim) misdescribed the location of a piece of machinery; solicitors failed to serve the other side with notice of legal aid even though it is supposed to be done by the county court; solicitors pursued a misconceived application in reliance on specialist counsel and failed to progress negotiations even though counsel advised the parties were too far apart to achieve a sensible compromise; honest solicitors relied on client's untruthful instructions; counsel instructed at eleventh hour was inadequately prepared at hearing.

See further P Lewis, 'Wasted Costs: Has the Balance been Restored?', *Solicitors' Journal*, 18 February 1994, p 144; J Lambert, 'Cutting Costs', *Law Soc Gaz*, 21 June 1995, p 20 and 'Bad Conduct', *ibid*, 5 July 1995, p 23; P Jones and N Armstrong, 'Living in Fear of Wasted Costs', *Civil Justice Quarterly*, July 1994, pp 208–32.

The Lord Chief Justice's Practice Statement issued in January 1995 (p 92 above) stated: 'The paramount importance of reducing the cost and delay of civil litigation makes it necessary for judges sitting at first instance to assert greater control over the preparation for and the conduct of hearings than has hitherto been customary. Failure by practitioners to conduct cases economically will be visited by appropriate orders for costs, including wasted costs orders' ([1995] 1 All ER 385, para 1). In the light of the Court of Appeal's decision in *Ridehalgh* it is appropriate to take this warning to practitioners with some scepticism. The bark in the warning is likely to be considerably worse than the bite in orders made and upheld. Moreover the threat of such an order being made is an insurable risk covered by indemnity insurance.

(6) Lord Woolf's proposed fast-track cases with limited costs

As has been seen above, one of the most important proposals in Lord Woolf's Interim Report was that medium weight litigation involving sums of between £3,000 and £10,000 should normally be placed on the fast-track subject to a rigid structure both for the pre-trial and the trial. One of the most important features of this structure would be limited costs. For a variety of reasons, Lord Woolf said, the present rules resulted in total uncertainty as to the extent of costs. These included:

(1) the rule that the loser pays the winner's costs;
(2) management of the case was primarily for the parties;
(3) the pressure created by the adversary system that every aspect of the case be fully investigated which encouraged excessive work on peripheral issues;
(4) the charging system based on hourly rates;
(5) discontinuity in the handling of cases which resulted in additional work to refresh memories. Costs could only be controlled if the work to be done was limited (pp 10–11, paras 22–24).

The fast-track, Lord Woolf said, would enable litigants to litigate cases 'at a combined cost which is generally less than and proportionate to the amount or matter at issue' (p 41, para 2). The system would be designed 'so that the costs of the procedure can be known in advance and the litigant's maximum liability for costs, even if he is unsuccessful, can be anticipated with certainty' (*ibid*, para 1).

Lord Woolf envisages fixed costs based on the value of the claim with percentages of that amount allocated to key stages of the proceedings. The fixed costs would apply not only to the costs payable in respect of the other side's costs. They 'would also constitute appropriate payment to a party's own legal adviser except in cases where there was an explicit agreement to pay more which had been fully explained to the litigant' (p 45, para 17). This would happen for example with a conditional fee agreement (see pp 469–76 below). The advantage, the Report said, is that parties would know their maximum liability, there would be no need for taxation of costs and solicitors would be able to work to a known budget. Such a system, the Report suggested, operated in Germany without apparently having a deleterious effect on the income of German lawyers.

In Germany, lawyers are paid at three different stages (units) during a case: at Unit 1, the commencement of proceedings, Unit 2, the preliminary hearing, and Unit 3, at judgment. The unsuccessful party pays the court fees and the other side's lawyers' fees. (Woolf Report, Annex V, p 263. For fuller treatment see Dieter Leipold, 'Limiting Costs for Better Access to Justice' in *Reform of Civil Procedure-Essays on 'Access to Justice'* (ed Zuckerman and Cranston, Clarendon, Oxford, 1995, pp 265, 266–75.)

The Association of Personal Injury Lawyers (APIL) had strenuously argued to Lord Woolf against any form of cost capping. They presented figures as to present costs. In a case valued at between £1,000 and £10,000 settled before or shortly after the issue of proceedings these would be £1,000–£2,000 unless the case was complex or hard fought when the costs could rise to £3,000–£4,000. Where a trial took place in the county court the costs could be in the region of £8,000–£10,000. APIL's argument was that if they were required significantly to reduce their fees it would result in experienced personal injury lawyers giving up their work (p 47, para 23).

Lord Woolf said he had considered these arguments carefully but the costs referred to by APIL were unacceptable. 'The public will not be persuaded that a serious effort to bring down those costs is being made unless the amounts allowed are expressly limited at substantially lower figures' (p 47, para 24). His report offered a radically simplified procedure which would enable case expenditure to be reduced. He would expect efficient and effective firms to adjust their methods and approach so as to work within new cost budgets. If the profession was not willing or able to meet this challenge, 'it should not imagine that the status quo can be retained'. More fundamental measures, 'possibly involving the removal of at least moderate-sized injury claims from the litigation system, would have to be envisaged' (p 47, paras 24–24).

Lord Woolf's proposals on costs affected not only fast-track cases. In regard to his multi track cases, costs would play a part in case management. Thus included in the information required of the parties for pre-trial case management conferences and the pre-trial review would be estimates of the costs already incurred by the parties. 'These figures will enable the parties and the judge or Master conducting the hearing to make an informed decision as to the future of the proceedings in the light of their likely cost' (p 49, para 7).

Woolf's Consultation Paper on controlling cost

The Consultation Paper issued by the Woolf Inquiry in January 1996 was written by Dr AAS Zuckerman of University College, Oxford. He suggested that the taxation of costs inter partes was not successful in curbing the level of costs or in producing predictability because it was retrospective and based on what lawyers had done. Costs flowed with the process. One option for an alternative approach would be prospective budget setting by the judge at the case management conference in multi track cases. At that conference he could fix the amount that the winner could recover from the loser for costs incurred from then to the trial. But that would not control costs incurred by the lawyer which he would charge to his own client.

Alternatively, the limit might affect solicitor and own client costs as well. This could be by a fixed fee for the litigation as a whole determined by reference to the amount claimed or fixed on a case by case basis. Or it could be by a fixed fee for each procedural step. This would be like that under Scale 1 in the county court (see p 426 above) where so much is payable for preparation of documents, for inter-locutory proceedings, for preparation for trial etc. Such a system could operate subject to a ceiling (for instance, a stated proportion of the value of the claim) or without a ceiling.

Fixed cost litigation gave lawyers incentives to economise and gave clients precise information about the cost. It would restrict the amount of work that could be done–but that might be a good thing. ('The whole tenor of [Lord Woolf's] *Access to Justice* is that we can no longer afford unlimited procedural provision for every case, regardless of importance, complexity or value.' (p 8, para 31.) Moreover, fixed costs were already creeping into the system–for instance in heavy commercial litigation where corporate clients now sometimes required lawyers to work to a fixed budget, and sometimes put the work out for competitive tender.

(d) Should costs follow the event? (The Indemnity Rule)

(1) Civil cases

One of the chief characteristics of the English system is the rule that costs generally follow the event–namely that the loser normally pays the taxed costs of the winner known as the indemnity rule. (As will be seen below, pp 435–60 there are some exceptions.) It is the ultimate loser who pays. Thus if the plaintiff wins at first instance and in the Court of Appeal but loses in the House of Lords, he must pay the costs at all three levels. Technically the court has a discretion but this discretion is virtually never exercised. Save in cases where it does not apply at all, the rule is applied mechanically. The rule also applies to pre-trial settlement in the sense that a settlement is normally on the basis that the defendant agrees to pay damages (or take other appropriate action) and pay the plaintiff's costs.

The alleged advantages of the rule include the following:

(1) It 'makes the winner whole'–restores him financially somewhat to the position that he was in before the wrong done to him.

(2) It recognises that the winner has won. By contrast, if he had to pay his own costs, the fruits of the litigation would be diminished by his costs, which to that extent would diminish his victory. In smaller cases the costs would eat up a huge proportion or even all of the damages.

(3) If the client is advised that he has good prospects of success, the indemnity rule encourages meritorious litigation. (The overwhelming majority of plaintiffs win–usually after a settlement.)

(4) The rule also helps to discourage unmeritorious or nuisance actions. A person with no reasonable prospects of success will think twice before bringing an action if he is told that he will have to pay his opponent's as well as his own costs.

The alleged disadvantages of the rule include the following:

(1) The rule operates harshly where both sides have been responsibly and competently advised that they have good prospects of success. In that situation why should one pay most of the winner's costs? The loser is rarely wholly in the wrong, nor the winner wholly in the right but the indemnity costs rule gives a black and white result.

(2) The rule operates harshly where the outcome of the litigation turns on uncertainties and complexities of the law. Why should litigants bear such a heavy burden of costs because the law is obscure?

(3) The rule operates harshly also where one party loses on most of the issues raised at the trial but wins overall on a point that absorbs very little of the time in the case. Why should the opponent pay such a heavy price when he succeeded in regard to a high proportion of time taken by the trial?

(5) The rule may deter meritorious as well as unmeritorious litigation. Some would-be litigants will not be willing to take the risk of losing even if they are advised that they have good chances of success.

(6) The pressure to abandon sound causes of action for fear of the cost of losing will bear most heavily on the economically weaker party.

(7) The rule has an inflationary effect on the cost of litigation as each side tends to spend more and more in order to ensure success and thereby avoid the risk of paying costs. Often the litigation is actually more about who pays the costs than about the apparent subject of the litigation.

(8) Moreover, the indemnity rule certainly does not prevent nuisance actions–they are a well known phenomenon.

(9) The indemnity rule increases the unpredictability of the costs factor in litigation. It is bad enough that one cannot know what one's own lawyers are going to charge, it is worse that one may also have to pay an unknown amount in respect of one's opponent's costs.

The pros and cons of this rule were considered many years ago by the Law Society which, after weighing all the pros and cons recommended that the indemnity rule be kept but amended by a new rule that an appropriate fraction of the winner's costs should be disallowed in whole or in part if the court considered that the winner had taken steps not necessary for the proper conduct of the action or had incurred costs unnecessarily or had unreasonably instituted, defended or conducted the proceedings. (Law Society, 'The Indemnity Rule in Litigation', in *Law Society Annual Report*, 1963–4, p 73.) But no action was ever taken on the recommendation.

Lord Woolf in his Interim Report in June 1995 also thought that on balance the indemnity rule should be retained but he too recommended that it should be modified by a requirement that the court take account of the conduct of the parties in its allocation of costs:

The general approach is one which involves the winner taking all. This does not necessarily produce a fair result. My approach to case management involves breaking down the issues which make up the litigation. The court has to be prepared to make different orders for costs in relation to different issues to support the new approach to case management. The court should also use its powers over costs to encourage cooperative conduct on the part of litigants and to discourage unreasonable conduct. This can apply to pre-proceedings as well as conduct after proceedings have commenced. I am not suggesting that the court should always conduct an inquest into how the parties behaved before the commencement of proceedings. However, in an obvious case, the court should be prepared to take conduct into account in deciding how to exercise its discretion as to costs. The court should also be more willing to identify areas where it considers that costs have been unnecessarily incurred. Running up excessive costs will continue unless the court is prepared to take action [p 204, paras 23–24].

How well placed is the court likely to be at the end of the case to assess the rights and wrongs of the conduct of the case? In order to be fair to the parties, will it not have to undertake a detailed review of the way in which the litigation has been conducted? If so, that could hardly be done right away. Both sides would have to be given an opportunity to present arguments and, perhaps proofs. At present the issue of costs takes virtually no time at all at the end of the case. Implementation of Lord Woolf's proposal is bound to absorb time and money and to be burdensome on the courts.

The indemnity rule and group actions

How does the indemnity rule operate when there are many plaintiffs suing collectively as a group? The question became a matter of acute public concern in 1987, in the course of the litigation brought by over 1,000 plaintiffs for the effects suffered as a result of use of the anti-arthritis drug Opren. The court held that if the action was to go ahead, all the plaintiffs, other than those on legal aid, had to be regarded as being liable for their share of the ultimate costs of the action if they failed. Most of the plaintiffs were elderly pensioners. Obviously they could not afford this risk and it seemed as if the cases brought by non-legally aided plaintiffs would have to be withdrawn. At the last moment, however, a 'fairy godparent' in the form of a wealthy philanthropist Mr Godfrey Bradman came forward and guaranteed the costs of the non-legally aided plaintiffs, which it was thought would be well in excess of a million pounds. (See *The Times* and *The Guardian*, 23 July 1987.)

One of the plaintiffs in the case then challenged the power of the court to make an order regarding costs before the end of the case. RSC Ord 62, r 3, said that costs should follow the event except when the court saw fit to make some other order. To follow the event, the plaintiff argued, must mean that the case was finished. The Court of Appeal rejected the argument. Normally the order would be made at the end of the case but it could be made earlier if the interests of justice required it. In any event, the judge's order in this case had not been for payment but for apportionment between plaintiffs–*Davies v Eli Lilly & Co* [1987] 3 All ER 94. See also *Nash v Eli Lilly & Co* [1993] 4 All ER 383, CA.

In *Aiden Shipping Co Ltd v Interbulk Ltd, The Vimeira* [1986] 2 All ER 409, the House of Lords held that the court had the widest possible discretion to order anyone to pay costs–even if they were not parties to the proceedings. The only proviso was that the order must be fair in the circumstances. Such an order was highly appropriate where some 'lead actions' were selected, raising common issues which could be litigated in order to settle those issues.

On costs considerations in group litigation see M Day, P Balen and G McCool, 'Costs and taxation in group actions', *New Law Journal*, 19 January 1996, p 55 and, generally, their book, *Multi-Party Actions* (Legal Action, 1995).

(2) Criminal cases

If the defendant is convicted, he can be ordered to pay something toward the costs of the prosecution. Courts vary in their policy as to whether to order such payments. (See M Zander, 'Legal Aid Contribution Orders', *New Law Journal*, January 1976, p 4, and H Levenson, 'Who Pays? Costs and Defendants in Criminal Cases', *LAG Bulletin*, October 1981, p 226.) The power to order costs now arises under s 18 of the Prosecution of Offences Act 1985, which says that where the defendant is convicted at the crown court or a magistrates' court he can be ordered to pay the whole or any part of the prosecution costs. For further details see *Practice Note* [1991] 2 All ER 924. The court may make any order it considers is just and reasonable. Under the previous similar law, in *Maher* [1983] 2 All ER 417, the Court of Appeal held that such costs had to be limited to those that were related to the presentation of the case. They included lawyer's fees and costs of the witnesses, but not jury expenses nor costs of providing special security protection for the jury. The court also said that the judge could take into account whether the accused pleaded guilty, in deciding whether or not to make such an order. The court reduced an order for a contribution of £1 million against the chief defendant in a heroin smuggling case to £175,000. (See generally Alec Samuels, 'Defendant to Pay Prosecution Costs', *Law Society's Gazette*, 10 June 1987, p 1703.)

The Attorney-General told the House of Commons in November 1987 that it was the policy of the Crown Prosecution Service always to make an application for costs against all convicted defendants unless in the particular circumstances it was apparent that such an application would 'lack merit or that an order for costs would be impractical' (House of Commons, *Hansard*, 6 November 1987, col 819).

If the defendant is acquitted, the defendant may be entitled to ask for the whole or part of his costs to be paid out of public funds.

Under s 16 of the Prosecution of Offences Act 1985, when a defendant is acquitted the court may make an order ('a defendant's costs order') of such amount as the court 'considers reasonably sufficient to compensate him for any expenses properly incurred by him in the proceedings' (sub-s (6)). If the court thinks appropriate, it can order that he receive less than the full amount of such costs.

Where the defendant is acquitted he ought normally to be awarded his costs. This is the rule that has been laid down repeatedly by a series of Practice Notes. The latest was issued in May 1991–see [1991] 2 All ER 924. This provides:

2.1 Where a person is not tried for an offence for which he has been indicted or committed for trial or has been acquitted on any count in the indictment, the court may make a defendant's costs order in his favour. Such an order should normally be made whether or not an order for costs *inter partes* is made, unless there are positive reasons for not doing so. Examples of such reasons are:

    (a)   the defendant's own conduct has brought suspicion on himself and has misled the prosecution into thinking that the case against him is stronger than it is;

(b) there is ample evidence to support a conviction but the defendant is acquitted on a technicality which has no merit.

But in fact costs are only rarely given to the acquitted defendant by magistrates, probably because they tend to feel that such an order reflects badly on the prosecution. A refusal of an order is supposed to be exceptional, but in fact it is the order itself that is exceptional. Whether this has changed under the 1985 Act has not yet been documented–it would be surprising if it did. See further Karen Williams, 'The Award of Costs to Acquitted Defendants in Magistrates' Courts', *Home Office Research Bulletin*, 1980, No 9, p 9.); Howard Levenson, 'Who Pays? Costs and Defendants in Criminal Cases', *LAG Bulletin*, October 1981, p 226.

At the Annual Meeting of the Magistrates' Association in 1982, Lord Hailsham, the Lord Chancellor, suggested that when a defendant was acquitted he might be asked as a matter of course whether he wished to apply for costs and, if so, in what amount.

See further Robert Thoresby, 'Costs on Acquittal', 36 *Modern Law Review*, 1973, p 647.

(e) Exceptions to the indemnity rule of costs

There are a variety of situations where the indemnity rule of costs does not apply:

(1) No costs in small claims in county courts

As has been seen, the system for handling small claims in the county court (known as 'arbitration') includes a no costs rule. Nothing is normally to be awarded in respect of solicitor's fees or charges on an inter partes basis, other than a small sum for issuing the summons. The only exceptions to the rule are (1) costs stated in the summons; and (2) such costs as are allowed by the court as having been incurred 'through the unreasonable conduct' of the other party. Also the rule only affects solicitors' charges. (CCR Ord 19, r 6) It does not therefore affect court fees, the cost of obtaining expert evidence, travel expenses and the like. If the case is not taken as a county court arbitration but goes for ordinary trial, the rule does not apply. In such a case the winner can claim his costs in the normal way. (See County Court (Amendment No 3) Rules, 1980, SI 1980/1807, amending CCR Ord 19, r 1.)

If no costs are awarded in respect of lawyers' charges, the litigant in person in a small claims case who loses will of course still have to pay his costs for bringing the action. At the very least these will consist of the court fee for initiating the proceedings, which depends on the amount in issue.

The no costs rule in small claims litigation is designed to facilitate and encourage use of the courts by ordinary citizens. The theory is that if they conduct the case themselves and then lose they have little in the way of costs to pay and they will therefore not be frightened to bring the case. The trouble with the theory is that the inability to recover costs may penalize rather than benefit the humble litigant by in practice denying him the use of a lawyer. He either has to be prepared to pay for it or do without.

The Civil Justice Review recommended that unless the plaintiff stated that the amount involved exceeded £1,000, unliquidated claims in the county court should be dealt with in the small claims system. This recommendation met with great opposition on the grounds that personal injury claims, however small, were too complex and difficult to be dealt with by the citizen without a lawyer. In particular, litigants would have difficulty in quantifying their claims without legal advice. 'Without legal aid how is the plaintiff of modest means to afford the expenses of preparing the claim? These disbursements are typical: consultant's report £150 to £250; police report £38; plaint fee £43 ... valuing a personal injury case requires experience and research of precedents. ... How is the plaintiff to know without help?' (Patrick Allen, 'The End of Small Personal Injury Claims?', *Law Society's Gazette*, 1 May, 1991, p 17.) The only beneficiaries he suggested would be insurance companies.

In October 1993 the Lord Chancellor's Department issued a Consultation Paper on small personal injury claims. In regard to costs this proposed a new 'limited costs' provision under which a fixed sum for legal advice and preparation (including negotiations to settle) would be recoverable. But the cost of representation at the hearing would not be recoverable by the winner.

In May 1994, whilst the Department was still considering responses to its Consultation Paper, the Court of Appeal in *Afzal v Ford Motor Co Ltd* [1994] 4 All ER 720, held that it was reasonable for personal injury cases involving claims of less than £1,000 to be decided under the existing small claims procedure. Following that judgment, the Lord Chancellor announced in August 1994 that he accepted the judgment and no longer intended to proceed with special arrangements for small claims personal injury cases.

The same issue was next taken up by Lord Woolf in his Interim Report in June 1995. He was persuaded by various bodies including the Law Society, the Association of Personal Injury Lawyers (APIL), and the National Consumer Council that he should exclude personal injury claims from his proposal to increase the jurisdiction of the small claims system from £1,000 to £3,000. APIL made the point that insurance companies would not pay costs in cases of under £1,000 and as a result solicitors could no longer normally act in such cases–to the great benefit of insurance companies.

In his Interim Report (p 117, para 63), Lord Woolf proposed that *all* personal injury cases up to £10,000 should be dealt with in his new fast track system which allowed limited costs both for preparation and representation at a hearing. However, pending the establishment of the system for fast-track cases, if the jurisdiction of small claims cases went up as he proposed to £3,000, personal injury cases involving amounts of over £1,000 should not be included. This is what then happened. The Lord Chancellor increased the jurisdiction from £1,000 to £3,000 as from January 1996 but he excluded personal injury cases involving amounts over £1,000. He also excluded claims for possession of land.

Under the new rules introduced in January 1996 the successful party will be able to recover the cost of legal advice up to £260 for making or defending a claim for an injunction or for an order for specific performance or for similar relief. Previously no such provision was made.

For an assessment of the implication for solicitors and their clients of the gigantic increase in the small claims jurisdiction see *Law Society's Gazette*, 10 January 1996, pp 14–17.

As has been seen, in cases involving amounts of between £1,000 and £3,000 in the county court, scale fees apply to restrict the costs recoverable by the winner.

(2) Legal aid cases

A legally aided litigant is protected against the normal operation of the indemnity rule by a special rule which limits what he can be asked to pay in respect of his opponent's costs to the same amount, if any, as he has been required to contribute toward his own costs. (In 1994–95, 86 per cent of those who got civil legal aid were not subject to a contribution in regard to their own costs and were therefore not at risk of having to pay anything if they lost.)

In its 1995 Green Paper on Legal Aid (*Legal Aid–Targeting Need*), the Government asked whether this rule should continue. The rule gave a distinct advantage to the legally aided person over the nonlegally aided person who had to take the costs sanction into account in deciding whether to take or continue his litigation. The Green Paper suggested that the rules might need modification so as to create a fairer balance between the parties, for instance, by reducing protection for a legally aided party who has significant equity value in a house (p 89, para 12.27).

The Legal Aid Board in its response to the Government's Green Paper agreed that assisted persons who had means such as the equity in a house might reasonably be made to pay more toward costs if they lost but warned that 'that this might have the effect of pushing behaviour too far in the other direction so that cases with merit would not be pursued' (November 1995, p 23, para 116).

Where a non-legally aided person succeeds in an action against a legally aided person the effect of the rule means that usually such a person will get little if anything by way of costs from his defeated opponent. There is however provision in the Legal Aid Act 1988, s 18 for a person in that situation to make a claim on the Fund by showing in respect of proceedings at first instance that he would otherwise suffer 'severe financial hardship'. It must also be shown in respect of any proceedings that it is 'just and equitable in all the circumstances of the case that provision for the costs should be made out of public funds'.

For a decision establishing that even financial institutions are permitted to take advantage of this provision see *General Accident, Fire and Life Assurance Corpnv Foster* [1972] 3 All ER 877. In *Davies v Taylor (No 2)* [1973] 1 All ER 959, the House of Lords ruled that the 1964 Act permitted payment out of the fund even though under the terms of an insurance policy the insurers had agreed to indemnify the applicant for the costs. The fact that the payments under the Act would enure to the benefit of the insurance company did not necessarily prevent it being 'just and equitable'. In *Lewis v Averay (No 2)* [1973] 2 All ER 229 the same principle was applied where the litigation had been financed by the Automobile Association, and in *Din v Wandsworth London Borough Council (No 2)* [1982] 1 All ER 1022 a local authority received its costs in the House of Lords but not in the Court of Appeal. But see *Kelly v London Transport Executive* [1982] 2 All ER 842, CA, for a decision that the Transport Executive could not claim its costs out of the fund for the first instance proceedings because it could not establish 'severe financial hardship' even though it was operating at a deficit.

(3) Costs of litigants in person

The Court of Appeal ruled in 1969 that a successful litigant in person could not recover anything in respect of his own time and labour in preparing his own case (*Buckland v Watts* [1969] 2 All ER 985). In 1973 the House of Lords held that a successful litigant in person was, however, entitled to claim for payments made to a solicitor who assisted him with the preparation of his case. Lord Reid said he should have 'such sums as were reasonably necessary for him to spend in order to prepare his written case and equip himself to appear and argue his case in person' (*Malloch v Aberdeen Corpn (No 2)* [1973] 1 All ER 304). Since 1975, however, the Litigants in Person (Costs and Expenses) Act of that year has provided that litigants in person are entitled to recover costs, including compensation for their own time and effort–though the scales of remuneration are very low (in 1996, an almost nominal £8.25 per hour).

The rules provide that the litigant in person can recover in regard to his own pecuniary loss up to two-thirds of the rate that would have been allowed if a solicitor had done the work. (But it has been held that this does not extend to allowing also what would have been expended on counsel's fees.) From 1992 that applied also even when he did not suffer any pecuniary loss–see *New Law Journal*, 17 April 1992, p 523. For the rest he would be restricted to a very low nominal rate. (See RSC Ord 62, r 18.)

Note that these rules do not apply to cases brought in the small claims system, the limit for which, as has been seen, was increased in 1996 to £3,000. In small claims cases the litigant in person, like litigants employing lawyers, cannot normally recover costs (p 435 above).

In *Hart v Aga Khan Foundation (UK)* [1984] 1 WLR 994, the Court of Appeal held that an actress who spent some 250 hours in studying technical matters in connection with her action could only recover for 40 hours' worth because that is what it would have taken a solicitor. (See further T Prime, 'The Unrepresented Litigant and His Costs', *Solicitors' Journal*, 7 February 1986, p 98.)

The Legal Aid Board suggested in 1995 that claims against the Fund by successful unassisted persons should perhaps be available only to individual defendants or small businesses with no other means of covering costs, for instance through legal expenses insurance. (*Response to the Lord Chancellor's Consultation Paper Legal Aid–Targeting Need*, November 1995, p 24.)

(4) Where the winner is too poor to pay costs

In a most regrettable decision it was held in 1993 that a non-legally aided winner who is too poor to have paid his own lawyer's bill, cannot recover under the Indemnity Rule of costs – because, by definition, his lawyer would not have looked to him for his costs. In *British Waterways Board v Norman* [1993] EGCS 177 Ms Norman had instructed solicitors to sue the British Waterways Board under the Environmental Protection Act 1990 in respect of what she claimed was a statutory nuisance at her home which she rented from the Board. Ms Norman was in receipt of income support and would therefore have been eligible for legal aid had it not been for the fact that legal aid is not available for such proceedings. Her action succeeded and the Board was ordered to pay her costs. The Board succeeded in its appeal against the costs order. The Divisional Court found that Ms Norman was so poor that there was no realistic prospect of her ever paying for her solicitors' services except out of any compensation or damages awarded. Nor had the solicitors at any time suggested to her that she might have to pay their costs. Had they made it clear that that was the position she could have recovered her costs. The court said that in such a case the solicitors should explain to the client that they could [sic] look to her for their costs. Lord Justice McCowan said 'if that procedure is followed ... so that it is made clear that the client is liable for costs, irrespective of the outcome of the proceedings, there can be no objection to the solicitor agreeing that such liability need not be discharged until the outcome of the proceedings, if any is known'. At that stage, 'provided it has not formed the basis of the agreement with the client, it would be open to the solicitors, if the circumstances warranted it, to decide not to enforce their right to be paid, in the event that some or all of their costs were unrecovered from the other party to the proceedings'.

Commenting on this decision, barrister Stephen Knafler said that it turned the retainer between solicitor client into a pretence. ('Litigation for the Poor (1)', *Solicitors' Journal*, 18 March 1994, p 256).

How is the client in the post–*Norman* world to know where he stands? How is he to evaluate the risk that the agreement he is being asked to enter into (for far more money than he can ever pay) will not be enforced by a lawyer he may never have met before and whom he may not yet entirely trust? The client may well feel that the solicitor who persuaded him that to pursue his case he has to enter into an express written agreement to be liable for thousands of pounds of costs but who indicates orally, by more or less subtle stratagems, that the creation of such a liability is necessary for technical legal reasons and that he will not necessarily (or will not at all) enforce the agreement, is somewhat sharp. Or he may well feel that there is something wrong with a law that requires him to wager all he has, at odds he personally stands no chance of being able to assess.

And even if the client and solicitor implemented the *Norman* scheme in poker-faced fashion, would it not still be open to a robust judge to hold that notwithstanding the express agreement to pay costs win or lose, the surrounding circumstances were such that both parties knew the express agreement was a sham or pretence? That judgment clearly would be open to any judge, quite simply because the agreement really would be a pretence. The only hope for the solicitor and his client would be that it turned out to be the sort of pretence to which the law was prepared to turn a blind eye.

The rationale for the decision in *British Waterways* was that if the solicitor has agreed not to charge his client costs, payment of the costs by the other side to the client would *in the client's hands* represent an unjustified additional award of damages. (The *locus classicus* on this statement of the Indemnity Rule is *Gundry v Sainsbury* [1910] 1 KB 645.) The Divisional Court said that if the solicitor agreed with the client that costs would only be payable in the event of success and then only out of the damages, that would be unlawful as a contingency fee and therefore unenforceable. (On contingency fees see pp 469–76 below.)

But Stephen Knafler suggested that the court seemed to have overlooked the long-standing exception to the rule against contingency fees for speculative actions on behalf of the poor and that this rule should apply if legal aid was not available. (For description of the cases that establish that proposition see his article 'Litigation for the Poor (2)', *Solicitors' Journal*, 25 March 1994, p 287. See also the long-standing Scottish practice of 'speculative fees', which permitted a lawyer to agree to act for nothing if the case is lost but to charge his normal fee plus a modest 'uplift' if the case is won (see p 472 below).)

(5) Contemptuous damages

If the plaintiff wins only contemptuous damages he will normally be ordered to pay the costs despite having technically won the action. The order that he pay the 'loser's' costs reflects the true meaning of the result. Contemptuous damages are traditionally expressed in the form of the smallest coin then in circulation. For an example see *Dering v Uris* [1964] 2 QB 669 where Dr Dering, a Pole, sued for libel over a passage in the novel *Exodus* in which he was said to have participated in more than a hundred atrocious experimental operations at Auschwitz. Leon Uris, defending, brought witnesses who had survived the operations whose evidence showed Dering's conduct at Auschwitz in extremely poor light. The libel action in effect turned into a war crimes trial of Dering. In the event, the jury awarded him a halfpenny damages and the judge ordered that he pay the costs, which were enormous.

2. LEGAL AID

It has been recognized in most civilized countries that there is a significant denial of justice if the state does not assist poor persons to meet the costs of lawyers. In England this recognition goes back decades. The first major legislation establishing the legal aid system on a modern footing was the Legal Aid Act 1949 passed by the Attlee Government in the post Second World era.

The scheme, one might say, has so far had two main stages–the first fifty years, from 1949 to 1989, during which it was run by the Law Society and since 1989, the year in which responsibility for running the scheme was vested in the Legal Aid Board. A possible third era was heralded in July 1995, the date of the Lord Chancellor, Lord Mackay's radical proposals for changing the scheme in his Green Paper *Legal Aid– Targeting Need* (Cm 2854). At the time of writing (early 1996) there is no way of knowing to what extent, if any, this radical plan would be enacted.

The legal aid scheme has three main component parts–legal aid for civil proceedings (below), legal aid for criminal proceedings (p 444 below) and legal advice and assistance (p 453 below) for matters that have not reached court.

From 1949 to 1989 legal aid in civil cases was administered by the Law Society through its full-time officials and Area Committees of practising solicitors and barristers. They determined individual applications. Means testing of applicants for civil legal aid was done by social security means testers–now the Benefits Agency. Policy was managed by a statutory Legal Aid Committee which had some lay members. The Law Society published a detailed annual report on the scheme. The Lord Chancellor, the minister responsible for the whole legal aid scheme, had a broadly based Legal Aid Advisory Committee which published its annual report at the same time and in the same volume as the Law Society.

In 1989, under the provisions of the Legal Aid Act 1988, the Legal Aid Board (LAB) assumed responsibility for all aspects of civil legal aid. The Board has some dozen or so members, some lawyers, some non-lawyers, some experts in the provision of legal services, others not. The first chairman, Mr John Pitts, came from an industrial background. The second chairman, Sir Tim Chessells, is an accountant with a background in management of the National Health Service.

In 1995, the Lord Chancellor announced that the Legal Aid Advisory Committee was being axed on the ground that there was no need for it now that the scheme was run by the Legal Aid Board.

The responsibilities of the LAB cover civil legal aid and the scheme for legal advice and assistance (Green Form). The LAB also administers the Duty Solicitor schemes in police stations and magistrates' courts, and assesses and pays bills for that work. For criminal legal aid in magistrates' courts it only assesses and pays bills. It has no other responsibility for the criminal legal aid scheme in magistrates' courts. In regard to criminal legal aid in crown courts the Board neither grants legal aid nor does it assess or pay the bills.

The gross amount paid out by the LAB in 1994–95 was £1,383m. The net cost after recoveries was £1,085m.

(a) Legal aid in civil proceedings

An applicant for legal aid for civil proceedings has to satisfy two tests–a means test and a merits test.

(1) The merits test

An applicant cannot get civil legal aid 'unless he satisfies the Legal Aid Board that he has reasonable grounds for taking, defending or being a party to the proceedings' (Legal Aid Act 1988, s 15(2)). He may be refused legal aid if in the circumstances it appears to the Board 'unreasonable that he should be granted representation' (s 15(3)). There is a right of appeal against a refusal to an area committee consisting of local practitioners.

The first part of the test is whether there are sufficient prospects of the client being successful. The second part, the 'reasonableness test', is more elastic. The usual interpretation is whether a reasonable solicitor would advise a reasonable client, who had normal means, to spend his own money on the case. This excludes most small claims, as solicitors would not normally advise their clients to proceed.

But the concept has been broadened. The official Legal Aid Handbook issued by the Legal Aid Board says that, although the financial benefit as against the cost is the normal criterion, it does not always apply. There are cases affecting the applicant's status, reputation or dignity where legal aid might be appropriate even though the financial benefit is small. Proceedings in regard to racial or sex discrimination are another example where legal aid might be legitimate even though the financial benefit is small.

(2) The means test[2]

There are three categories of applicant:

(a) those who qualify for free legal aid (disposable income must not be more than £2,498 *and* disposable capital must not be more than £3,000);

(b) those who qualify for legal aid subject to a contribution (if disposable income is more than £2,498 but less than £7,403[3] *or* disposable capital is between £3,000 and £6,750–though exceptionally these limits can be exceeded);

(c) those who do not qualify for legal aid (because either their disposable income is over £7,403 *or* their disposable capital is more than £6,750[4]).

'Disposable income' is actual income less deductions for dependants, income tax, national insurance contributions, travel expenses to get to work, rent, large hire-purchase commitments and other necessary outgoings. 'Disposable capital' is actual savings, value of jewellery, the amount that could be borrowed on insurance policies, etc. The value of a house is not taken into account (but see pp 450–51 below). Nor is a car, unless it is unusually valuable. There is some flexibility to permit legal aid to be given to a person whose disposable capital is only a little over the limit. Until 1984 the actual assessments were made by DHSS officers. But in 1984 a new postal, self-report method was introduced, similar to the principle of income-tax returns (*Law Society's Gazette*, 28 March 1984, p 868).

The contribution for those subject to pay one is assessed separately for capital and income. In regard to capital it is the whole of the excess over the free limit and that sum is payable immediately. In regard to income the contribution is assessed by taking the excess over the free limit (in 1996, £2,425) and dividing it by thirty six. That figure is the monthly contribution payable, since 1993, throughout the life of the case. Since the length of the case cannot be predicted, the client cannot know his maximum liability in regard to the contribution. (By contrast, from 1949 to 1993 the maximum contribution was a fixed amount assessed at the outset and payable in twelve monthly instalments.)

Well over four-fifths of all those who get civil legal aid pay no contribution and the proportion is rising each year. In 1994–95, 86 per cent were on a nil contribution, 7 per cent had a maximum contribution of up to £500, and 7 per cent of over £500.

In 1994–95 some 386,000 civil legal aid certificates were issued, of which some half were in connection with matrimonial and Children Act matters.

(3) The statutory charge

When a legally aided person wins his case, the legal aid fund recoups itself for his costs first from costs paid by the loser, secondly from his contribution and thirdly from any damages awarded to him or property recovered or preserved by the litigation. This so-called 'statutory charge' on the damages may in some cases have the effect of wiping out the net benefit of the litigation. Some forms of property are exempt– notably maintenance, or money or property not over £2,500 transferred in divorce proceedings. (But see *Curling v Law Society* [1985] 1 All ER 705.)

2   As at April 1996. The rates are revised annually. For latest figures see the April issue of each year's *Legal Action*.
3   Or, in personal injury cases, £8,158.
4   Or, in personal injury cases, £8,560.

In *Hanlon v Law Society* [1980] 2 All ER 199, the House of Lords ruled that the Law Society has a power to *delay* activating its charge where property is recovered in matrimonial proceedings. This power to delay commonly operates to avoid a sale of the matrimonial home by the wife when it has been awarded to her in the matrimonial proceedings for her and the children to live in. It would obviously be a great hardship for her to have to sell the house to meet the cost of her contribution to the legal aid fund. But the Law Society's claim remains effective and is met when the wife later sells. (See D Burrows, 'Legal Aid Statutory Charge: The New Act and Regulations', *Law Society's Gazette*, 7 June 1989, p 25.)

In 1994–95 civil legal aid succeeded in securing the recovery of £963.4m, of which £47.6m was retained by the fund under the statutory charge. In non-matrimonial cases the charge operated in 6,000 cases out of 64,400 (11 per cent) and the amount retained averaged 2 per cent of the award. In matrimonial cases the charge came into effect in 18,700 cases out of 22,900 (or 82 per cent) and the amount retained averaged 10 per cent of the total awards.

(4) Legal aid and the Indemnity Rule

As has been seen, when a legally aided person loses his case, he is liable to pay his own costs up to the limit of his contribution; the balance, if any, is paid by the fund. In addition, under the Indemnity Rule he must pay such amount as is reasonable towards his opponent's costs. Usually this is assessed as being the same amount (if any) as that to which he has been assessed in regard to his own contribution. (Legal Aid Act 1988, s 17.) So he pays his own contribution plus the same amount again towards the costs of his opponent. Where a non-legally aided person succeeds in an action brought against him by someone financed by legal aid, he usually recovers little or nothing in respect of his own costs. But, as has been seen, there is power in some circumstances for him to apply for reimbursement of the whole or part of his costs from the fund under the 1988 Legal Aid Act, s 18 on the ground of 'severe financial hardship' and that 'it is just and equitable in all the circumstances that provision for the costs should be made out of public funds' (See pp 437–38 above).

(5) Eligibility for civil legal aid

The issue of eligibility for legal aid has always been a matter of concern. There is general consensus amongst the experts that the proportion of the population eligible for legal aid has in recent years been declining.

A Government consultation paper, *Eligibility for Civil Legal Aid*, June 1991 commented critically on the view that a particular proportion of the population 'should' be eligible for legal aid. This view presupposed that the distribution and level of means in the population remained constant relative to the cost of litigation. Also it did not relate means to costs. Nevertheless the figures did show a decline in eligibility– whether one looked at proportion of households (from 77 per cent eligible in 1979 to 61 per cent in 1990) or population (from 74 per cent eligible in 1979 to 66 per cent in 1990) (Table 3, p 85). The 75 per cent of adults eligible in 1979 were made up of 29 per cent eligible for free legal aid and 46 per cent eligible for legal aid subject to a contribution. In 1990, it said, the proportion of adults eligible had fallen to 56 per cent, made up of 22 per cent eligible for free legal aid and 34 per cent subject to a contribution (Table 4, p 85). In the mid–1990s it is thought that around half of the population are eligible for legal aid.[5] (See on this issue also Cyril Glasser, *Law Society's Gazette*, 9 March 1988, p 11; 20 April 1988, p 11; and 5 April 1989, p 9; and Michael Murphy, *Legal Action*, October 1989, p 7.)

The Government's 1991 consultation paper proposed a new basis for the grant of civil legal aid to those capable of paying a contribution under which legal aid would only be available after they had financed the first, say, £2,500 of the costs. This scheme, misleadingly called 'the safety net scheme', was criticised by virtually all including the Legal Aid Board, and was not implemented. As will be seen below, the same Lord Chancellor, Lord Mackay, has now put forward an even more radical set of proposals.

(b) Legal aid in criminal proceedings[6]

Whereas civil legal aid is dispensed by the Legal Aid Board, criminal legal aid is dispensed by the courts. (See Legal Aid Act 1988 and the Legal Aid in Criminal and Care Proceedings (General) Regulations 1989 (SI 1989/344).) Until 1980 criminal legal aid was administered under the aegis of the Home Office, but in that year it was brought under the Lord Chancellor's Department. On the history of criminal legal aid in England and Wales see Tamara Goriely in *Access to Criminal Justice*, 1996, *op cit* n 6, at pp 26–54.

As has been seen above (p 15), the Lord Chancellor's Department took over responsibility for the magistrates' courts as from 1 April 1992. In January of the same year and in anticipation of that event, the Lord Chancellor asked the Legal Aid Board to consider and advise him on the implications of the Board's taking over responsibility for the grant of legal aid in the magistrates' courts. The Board's response was delivered in January 1993.

The Board concluded that it should take over the responsibility for the grant of criminal legal aid as from 1 January 1995 subject to certain changes being made in the scheme. This advice was however not accepted and in January 1996 the Lord Chancellor again confirmed that he would not, at least for the time being, take action to transfer responsibility for granting criminal legal aid from the courts to the Board.

Application for legal aid is generally made to the magistrates' court. The decision to grant legal aid is normally made by the court clerk, who can grant or refuse it. But the application can be referred by the clerk to the magistrates.

The Legal Aid Act 1982 gave the Lord Chancellor the power to make arrangements for review of refusals. The regulations under this power provided for 'a right of recourse' (specifically avoiding use of the word 'appeal') to criminal legal aid committees set up under s 21(10) of the 1988 Act and regulations 15 and 16 of the (General) Regulations and consisting of practising barristers and solicitors. This review system does not seem to work well–see A Wood in *Access to Criminal Justice*, 1996 *op cit*, n 6, above, at pp 164–91.

5   A press release issued by the Lord Chancellor's Department in April 1995 in regard to legal aid for the wealthy stated 'With regard to legal aid eligibility, assistance from the legal aid scheme is available to 47% of the population'.

6   See generally on this subject an excellent collection of essays in *Access to Criminal Justice: Legal Aid, Lawyers & the Defence of Liberty*, ed R Young and D Wall, Blackstone, 1996 – referred to here as '*Access to Criminal Justice*, 1996'.

As in civil legal aid, there is both a merits and a means test:

(1) The merits test

The merits test is simply whether it is in the interests of justice (Legal Aid Act 1988, s 21(2)). Where the case is being tried in the crown courts it is normally regarded as being in the interests of justice for legal aid to be granted, as can be seen from the remarkable fact that for many years 98–99 per cent of those tried in the crown court have had legal aid, regardless of whether they plead guilty or not guilty.

Prior to the Legal Aid Act 1988 the statutory formula of 'the interests of justice' was not further defined. Instead there was a non-statutory list of criteria that was supposed to be applied to the interpretation of the test for cases to be heard in the magistrates' courts. These non-statutory 'Widgery criteria'[7] have now been replaced with a statutory gloss on the 'interests of justice', which applies also to proceedings in the crown court.

Section 22 of the Legal Aid Act 1988 provides:

22. ... (1) This section applies to proceedings by way of a trial by or before a magistrates' court or the Crown Court or on an appeal to the Crown Court against a person's conviction.

(2) The factors to be taken into account by a competent authority in determining whether it is in the interests of justice that representation be granted for the purposes of proceedings to which this section applies to an accused shall include the following ...

(a) the offence is such that if proved it is likely that the court would impose a sentence which would deprive the accused of his liberty or lead to loss of his livelihood or serious damage to his reputation;

(b) the determination of the case may involve consideration of a substantial question of law;

(c) the accused may be unable to understand the proceedings or to state his own case because of his inadequate knowledge of English, mental illness or other mental or physical disability;

(d) the nature of the defence is such as to involve the tracing and interviewing of witnesses or expert cross-examination of a witness for the prosecution;

(e) it is in the interests of someone other than the accused that the accused be represented.

(3) The Lord Chancellor may, by order, vary the factors listed in subsection (2) above by amending factors in the list or by adding new factors to the list.

But whether a particular applicant for legal aid in the magistrates' court gets it may depend as much as anything on the accident of which court he applies to. Notoriously, and probably unavoidably, courts vary considerably in their policy as regards the granting of legal aid. For a study of how the courts operate the merits test see R Young, 'The Merits of Legal Aid in the Magistrates' Courts' [1993] *Criminal Law Review* 336–44 and 'Court clerks, legal aid and the interests of justice', *New Law Journal*, 18 September 1992, p 1264 both reporting on research conducted for and published by the Legal Aid Board under the title *In the Interests of Justice? The Determination of Criminal Legal Aid Applications by Magistrates' Courts in England and Wales* by R Young, T Moloney, and A Sanders. The study found considerable

---

7 So called because they were formulated by the (Widgery) Report of the Departmental Committee on *Legal Aid in Criminal Proceedings*, 1966, Cmnd 2934, para 180.

differences in interpretation of the criteria. It also found that many (perhaps most) grants of legal aid were made in situations where the criteria do not apply, or where if they do apply they are given little weight by court clerks. Instead, the system that seems to operate in most courts is that for some offences legal aid is automatically granted, for others almost automatically refused, while in the middle is a grey area where the arguments presented by or, more likely, on behalf of the applicant may make a difference. Court clerks were both too generous and too severe. ('They are too generous in that some take too broad a view of "offence seriousness", and too severe in that nearly all underestimate the need for legal skills to be employed in cases before the magistrates' courts' (*Criminal Law Review*, [1993], p 343). See also R Young in *Access to Criminal Justice*, 1996, *op cit* n 6, p 444 above, at pp 137–63.

The Legal Aid Act 1988, s 21(7) provides that where a doubt arises as to whether legal aid should be granted to a person 'the doubt shall be resolved in that person's favour'. Yet in a speech in October 1992 the Lord Chancellor, Lord Mackay seemed instead to want to tip the balance against the defendant. Speaking to the Law Society's national conference he said: 'Action must and will be taken to see that effective procedures are in place and are properly adhered to, and that legal aid is only granted where it is demonstrably justified under the terms of the present legislation'. (The speech was reported at length in *New Law Journal*, 30 October 1992, p 1505.)

In May 1994 new guidance on how to apply the 'interest of justice test' was issued to the courts. The whole tenor of this guidance was to influence court clerks to be more restrictive in granting legal aid. (For details see Ed Cape, 'In the Interests of Justice?', *Legal Action*, September 1994, p 19.)

(2) The means test

Means testing in criminal legal aid is normally done by the court clerks who, as compared with the officials of the Benefits Agency, lack both expertise and interest in the subject. The process of means testing has recently been shown to create problems so serious as to jeopardise the future of the entire scheme. There are two big issues–legal aid for a tiny number of high profile apparently wealthy defendants, and, secondly, the question whether the means test is being applied properly in the mass of cases.

The basis of the means test has until recently been somewhat imprecise. Courts have been supposed to follow broadly the same financial tests as apply in civil cases. The general test was whether it appeared to the court that the applicant's means were such that he required assistance in meeting the costs. Unlike the civil scheme, however, the criminal scheme has no upper limit–so even a relatively rich person could qualify if the case was likely to be a long one and costly one. The test has been what people can reasonably be expected to afford without altering their life style.

The fact that 99 per cent of those dealt with by the crown court get legal aid suggests a certain 'rough-and-ready' application of the means test.

Contributions

The criminal legal aid scheme also has a contribution aspect but this has been on a very different basis from that in the civil scheme. Until 1982, the court had a complete discretion as to whether to ask for a down-payment or to demand a contribution after the completion of the case. Both the contribution order and its amount were entirely in the discretion of the court and, inevitably, courts varied considerably in their approach. (See M Zander, 'Contribution Orders', *New Law Journal*, 1 January 1976, p 4.)

This was changed by the Legal Aid Act 1982, the chief purpose of which was to raise more revenue from contributions. The Benson Royal Commission on Legal Services in 1979 had taken a rather generous approach to criminal legal aid. It recommended that:

Contributions should be abolished for proceedings in magistrates' courts but be retained for Crown Courts. In deciding whether to order a contribution, the court should take into account the means of the accused and the extent to which he was responsible for unreasonable expenditure being spent on his defence [paras 14.31–2, p 164].

The Royal Commission on Legal Services said that it had received compelling evidence from various sources that the Widgery criteria were not working well. They were said to be both complex and imprecise, and were open to a wide range of interpretations in cases of the same type.

In the adversarial system, the Benson Royal Commission argued, legal representation was needed on both sides. The defendant had no choice about the proceedings. The outcome affected his reputation and possibly his liberty. There should be a statutory right to legal aid in all cases save for those triable only by magistrates. In regard to those less serious cases, legal aid should also be granted unless the court was satisfied that both: (a) there was no likelihood of a custodial sentence, a deportation order or, in the case of a juvenile, a care order; or that there would be substantial damage to the defendant's livelihood or reputation; and (b) adequate presentation of the case did not require representation. So someone who was unable to represent himself through age, infirmity or for any other reason should get legal aid. If an application was refused, reasons should be given. (See Cmnd 7648, 1979, vol 1, para 14.10, p 158.)

These recommendations, however, were comprehensively rejected. Instead the Legal Aid Act 1982 proceeded on the basis that defendants facing the might of the state and threatened with criminal penalties should nevertheless have to pay for their legal defence whatever they can afford according to rigid criteria as in civil cases. This has now been carried on by the Legal Aid Act 1988 and the 1989 Regulations (SI 1989/344).

The courts are supposed to discover by means of a questionnaire the applicant's disposable income and capital. In 1995 the limit for free criminal legal aid was £48 for disposable weekly income and £3,000 for capital. The contribution from capital was the whole of the excess over the free limit of £3,000. The contribution in regard to income was £1 for each £3 by which his average weekly disposable income exceeds £47. The resources of husband and wife must generally be aggregated.

There are allowances against income in respect of living expenses and dependants, but none against capital. The income taken into account includes child benefit – thus bearing out the criticism that the system results in wives and children having to pay for the defence for husbands or fathers. Defendants pay weekly instalments starting seven days after the initial order. If legal aid payments are in arrears the court has the power to revoke legal aid, but only if the court is satisfied that the legally aided person had sufficient means to pay and was wilfully refusing to do so. Moreover the order cannot be revoked for failure to pay the contribution unless the legally aided person has had an opportunity of making representations on the matter (s 24(3)).

At the end of the case the court also has the power to waive the payment of legal aid contributions not then completed. (See Howard Levenson, 'Contributions and the New Criminal Legal Aid', *Legal Action*, April 1984, p 37.)

When the 1982 Legal Aid Bill was going through Parliament there were dire warnings from many quarters about its likely consequences. The main fear was that the contributions system would bite too hard and that there would be considerable administrative difficulties in the courts. The new scheme came into force on 1 March 1984.

A study done for the Legal Aid Efficiency Scrutiny in 1986 showed that in 1984–85 only 3 per cent of criminal legal aid orders were contributory and that the total sum collected through contributions was only £1.8m as against gross expenditure of £134m. (The costs of assessing means were estimated at £800,000.) The main reason why so few contribution orders were made, the Scrutiny Report stated, was that some two-thirds of applicants were unemployed (*Scrutiny Report*, 1986, vol 2, II.2, para 8).

In 1994, the total bill for criminal legal aid was £465.6 million. The total amount recovered by way of contributions was the derisory sum of £3.5 million (0.75%). (*Judicial Statistics*, 1994, p 102, Table 10.7.)

The operation of means testing

The system of vetting legal aid applications was severely censured by the National Audit Office's report on expenditure for 1990–1–see 'Damning NAO Report Queries Legal Aid Bills', *Law Society's Gazette*, 30 October 1991, p 6.

In response to this pressure, in April 1992 the Lord Chancellor's Department issued a circular stating that a defendant who was in employment could not get legal aid unless he was able to produce 13 weekly pay slips as evidence of his earnings. The circular led to an uproar of protest–and a threat of challenge by way of judicial review as to its legality. Faced with this threat, the Department backed down and in June withdrew the circular. (See *New Law Journal*, 12 June 1992, p 814.) But this proved only a brief respite since new Regulations were then introduced to require better documentation of entitlement (see Legal Aid in Criminal and Care Proceedings (General) (Amendment) (No 2) Regulations 1993, SI 1993/1895.)

Concern over the way the means testing is done has been shown also by the annual reports of the Comptroller and Auditor General which for five consecutive years censured the Lord Chancellor's Department for failing to exercise sufficient control over the system. (See annual report of National Audit Office: *The Administration of Legal Aid in England and Wales*, 1992, 1993, 1994, 1995.) The main concerns expressed were that legal aid was being granted on the basis of insufficient information, that prior checks about the means of applicants were not being carried out, and that courts did not properly comply with the duty to secure evidence of applicants' income. There was also concern about the way that some courts administered the merits test. The 1995 report of the Comptroller and Auditor General stated that unless matters improved he would have to recommend that criminal legal aid be taken away from the courts.

The Lord Chancellor's Green Paper on legal aid issued in May 1995 (*Legal Aid, Targeting Need*, (Cm 2854) said (p 73, para 10.11): 'This state of affairs cannot be allowed to continue. Unless there is a very marked improvement, very soon, in the way in which the courts carry out their functions, alternative arrangements will have to be implemented'.

The Green Paper suggested one option would be to give the task of applying the criteria to solicitors in private practice. Another would be to give the decision to the Legal Aid Board though 'It is difficult to see how this approach could work efficiently' because of the resulting delays' (p 73, para 10.14).

In its feasibility study delivered to the Lord Chancellor in January 1993 the Legal Aid Board said that if it took over the grant of criminal legal aid, early work on criminal cases should be covered by a new form of self-authorised legal aid to be called 'Early Cover'. (For details of these proposals see *Law Society's Gazette*, 3 February 1993, p 2.)

But, as has been seen, the Lord Chancellor announced in January 1996 that responsibility for the grant of criminal legal aid would remain with the magistrates' courts 'for the time being'. In a written answer to a Parliamentary Question he said that he had examined the feasibility of transferring the grant of criminal legal aid to the Legal Aid Board but that the risks to the speed and efficiency of criminal procedure had deterred him from taking that step. He had taken a number of statutory and administrative steps to tighten up controls on the use of public moneys and he reported that 'significant improvements in the level of compliance with the regulations have recently become apparent'. So long as compliance with the regulations continued and improved he did not propose any change in the system. (House of Lords, *Hansard*, January, 1996, vol 568, *col* 104.)

Commenting, Mr Anthony Edwards, a very experienced defence solicitor, writing in the Law Society's Criminal Practitioners' Newsletter in October 1995 said that despite the new Regulations, 'in one third of cases no such [documentary] evidence was produced in relation to earnings' and only 'six per cent of other items of income and expenditure were supported by documents' (p 4). Mr Edwards suggested that there were good reasons for the generally low level of compliance. Rather than tightening the regulations regarding means testing the LCD's officials should explain to the Comptroller and Auditor General that it was the system for the calculation of contributions that needed to be reviewed.

Those who appear as defendants in the criminal courts do not in the main keep good records of their financial position. Documents cannot be produced by those remanded in custody. For young defendants the problems are particularly acute. Those under sixteen must produce evidence of their parents means but many parents do not choose to assist in the provision of this information. Furthermore, magistrates' courts are not equipped to carry out detailed checks.

The duty to provide records establishing eligibility for criminal legal aid does not apply to anyone who appears to the court clerk to be on income support or to be unable by virtue of his mental or physical condition to produce such records (1989 Regulation 23(4)(a) and (c) as amended in 1995, see *Justice of the Peace*, 20 May 1995, p 325).

Mr Edwards quoted the Government paper on legal aid for the apparently wealthy (p 450 below) which admitted that most of those who get criminal legal aid are in receipt of some form of state benefit. The paper also stated that although the Government intended to preserve the contributory element in criminal legal aid 'it is under no illusion that there is much, if any, scope for improving the level of contributions collected' (para 3.3). Those who believed that there was here a large untapped source of income for the legal aid fund were deluding themselves (*ibid*). Mr Edwards' suggestion was that, if this was so, cases should not be delayed whilst financial issues were sorted out. 'If the interests of justice require the grant of legal aid an order should be made forthwith.' The signed statement of means and any supporting documentation should then be sent to the Benefits Agency which was responsible for assessing contributions for civil legal aid. Those on benefit who automatically fulfilled the means test would be identified immediately. For the rest the Agency would be able to utilise its normal skills in assessing eligibility. It would as soon as possible advise the court as to eligibility and the appropriate weekly contribution that should be required. On conviction the court would make a contribution order.

The latest (1995) Regulations tighten the system further by requiring justices' clerks to ensure that a proper record is made by the court showing the grounds of both refusing or granting all legal aid applications, including decisions on the interests of justice test. For consideration of the important practical question whether legal aid can be granted pending production of the required documentation see *Justice of the Peace*, May 20, 1995, p 325, 23 September 1995, p 631 and 27 January 1996, p 59 and *Legal Action*, January 1996, p 22.

The 1995 Green Paper suggested that those eligible for certain benefits should be 'passported' so that they would automatically qualify on the means test for criminal legal aid. All others might be asked to pay a flat rate fee. There might be a simplified means test administered by the solicitor with a full means test reserved for a minority of cases–possibly if the case went to the crown court and all cases where there was capital (p 87, para 12.18).

Legal aid for the apparently wealthy defendant

In recent years a good deal of public indignation has been caused by a few high profile cases in which vast sums of public money were expended on criminal legal aid for apparently wealthy persons. One notorious such case was that of Mr Asil Nadir, the former chairman of Polly Peck charged with theft and fraud charges after the collapse of his empire. He ran up a legal aid bill of over £1 million before fleeing abroad. The trial of former tycoon Roger Levitt cost the taxpayer more than £2 million. The legal aid bill for the trial of the Ian and Kevin Maxwell, the two sons of Robert Maxwell, was much higher still.

In December 1994 the Lord Chancellor's Department addressed this issue with a Consultation Paper on 'Legal Aid for the Apparently Wealthy'. The paper noted that 'the majority of those who receive criminal legal aid are in receipt of state benefits of one kind or another or have incomes sufficiently low that they qualify for legal aid' (para 3.3). But someone could be living in an expensive house, drive an expensive car and have an apparently thriving business career but still qualify for criminal legal aid because of the extent of their indebtedness (para 2.13). The Consultation Paper put forward a number of ways in which the system might be tightened up to prevent abuse of public funds.

On 26 April 1995 the Lord Chancellor, answering a Parliamentary Question, announced the measures he intended to adopt. These included (1) a special investigation unit to be run by the Legal Aid Board to handle means assessment in both civil and criminal cases where the applicant's means were unusually complex; (2) a discretionary new basis of assessment of means to include the assets of friends, relatives and children where these appeared to be providing a significant material advantage to the applicant; (3) a requirement that applicants transfer ownership of any assets they fail to disclose, so that the moneys disbursed in legal aid can be recouped from those assets; and (4) that there should be a limit of £100,000 on the amount of equity value in a house that is ignored in the legal aid means test assessment. The Lord Chancellor announced on February 29 1996 that he would be implementing these proposals as from June 1996.

(3) Applications, lack of applications and refusals

One of the many problems of the criminal legal aid scheme, already referred to, has always been the lack of uniformity of decisions by the courts to grant legal aid. The Legal Action Group has over the years done much to focus attention on this matter, notably through a series of annual articles by Howard Levenson reviewing the statistics. See *LAG Bulletin*, January 1979, p 6; April 1980, p 82; May 1981, p 106; February 1982, p 6; February 1983, p 4; and *ibid*, June 1982, p 8.

In 1983 such unofficial critics were found to have been correct by a substantial and official study published by the Lord Chancellor's Department (*Report of a Survey of the Grant of Legal Aid in Magistrates' Courts*, October 1983). It was based on records kept for a four-week period in December 1982 in some 60 magistrates' courts. About 3,000 cases involving charges of shoplifting, assault on the police, social security fraud, possession of cannabis and criminal damage were studied. The report stated that considerable variations between courts were discovered in the rate of refusals of legal aid, and in the extent to which defendants were represented. These discrepancies could not be explained by differences in the cases or by different policies in regard to the grant or refusal of legal aid. (See also the study by Young, Moloney and Sanders referred to at p 445 above.)

But although these differences did exist, they were dwarfed by the much more striking fact that in many cases the accused *did not apply for legal aid*. This proved much more of a determining factor in whether defendants were represented than the attitude of the courts to granting legal aid. In the most serious cases the defendant applied for legal aid more often than in the less serious. When he applied in such cases he almost invariably got it. But even in the most serious cases, close to 30 per cent of defendants did not apply. The application rate varied considerably from court to court but also as between different offences. Thus in drugs cases the application rate was 25 per cent; in shoplifting it was 34 per cent; in criminal damage and social security fraud cases it was between 42 and 44 per cent. The highest application rate by far was in cases of assault on the police, where it was 76 per cent (*ibid*, Table 10).

Most refusals of legal aid applications were on the ground of 'interest of justice' rather than because the defendant was said not to have qualified on the means test.

On the vital importance of the role of the solicitor in making the application for legal aid and on the poor quality both of many applications and of the decision-making process of the courts in regard to applications see D Wall in *Access to Criminal Justice*, 1996, *op cit*, n 6, p 444 above, at pp 114–36.

(c) Duty Solicitor schemes

One very important recent development has been the setting up of Duty Solicitor schemes in courts and police stations.

(1) Duty solicitors in magistrates' courts

A national scheme for the establishment of Duty Solicitor schemes in magistrates' courts was provided for by the Legal Aid Act 1982. The basic idea is that the defendant who comes to court without having seen a lawyer should have someone to provide preliminary advice–as to his plea, whether to ask for an adjournment, and whether to apply for legal aid or bail–and representation. Originally the scheme was run by the Law Society through regional committees. The running of the schemes is now part of the responsibility of the Legal Aid Board. In its annual report for 1994–5 the Board stated that 98 per cent of magistrates' courts were now covered by the scheme. The number of persons assisted in the year was 261,360, of whom 38 per cent were in custody and 62 per cent were on bail. The total cost was £12m.

The LAB's annual report for 1990–1 included a lengthy appendix (pp 99–106) setting out 76 recommendations made by the Duty Solicitor Committee's review of the scheme.

(2) Duty Solicitor schemes in police stations

As was seen above (p 132), Duty Solicitor schemes were set up under PACE to assist detainees in the police station. Like the schemes for courts, they were originally run by the Law Society and are operated now by the Legal Aid Board. They work on either a rota or a panel basis[8] by local practitioners. There are now such schemes covering all but eight of the 1,836 police stations. There are elaborate rules as to the qualifications required and the selection process involved for those participating in these schemes. As was seen above (p 134), the Legal Aid Board and the Law Society are together making serious attempts to improve the quality of the advice given under the scheme, especially by non-solicitors, through the scheme for accreditation of non-solicitor representatives and trainee solicitor. In 1994–5 the number of suspects assisted under the scheme was 663,244 at an overall cost of £68.3m. In 65 per cent of cases the solicitor called out was the suspect's own solicitor; in 33 per cent it was the Duty Solicitor; in the remaining 2 per cent it was both. Under the scheme the state legal aid scheme pays in either case.

Note–no means test for assistance by duty solicitors

There is no means test and no contribution is payable in respect of assistance under either of the Duty Solicitor schemes. The Lord Chancellor's 1995 Green Paper on legal aid recommended that the schemes should continue to operate on this basis.

8   In rota schemes the solicitors are nominated in advance for a set period during which they must make themselves fully available–night or day. In panel schemes the phone service running the scheme phones one solicitor after another until it finds one available. Rota schemes tend to be used in urban areas, panel schemes in less busy rural areas.

(d) Legal advice and assistance (also known as 'the Green Form scheme') and ABWOR

Since 1973 a client with a legal problem who qualifies under the means test has been entitled to go to any solicitor participating in the scheme (most do), to ask for oral or written advice or assistance. Advice and assistance covers a great variety of types of help, short of representation at a hearing. It is within the discretion of the solicitor what work he undertakes within the state scheme. He may write letters, negotiate, vet or draft a document and even prepare an argument for the client to present in a court or tribunal. The only limitation is that the lawyer must not go beyond roughly two hours' worth of work without getting authority to continue.

In 1994–95 the scheme provided assistance for some 1.57m people at a total gross cost of £141m.

There is no merits test other than the decision of the solicitor to provide the help. There is, however, a fairly stringent means test administered on a somewhat rough and ready basis by the solicitor himself. In 1995 the upper limit for Green Form help was a disposable income of £72 per week and disposable capital of £1,000 for those without dependants, £1,335 for those with one dependant, etc. Until 1993 a contribution was payable by those just above the free limit but as from April 1993 Green Form help has only been available to those eligible to obtain it free. The average period of time devoted to work under the Green Form scheme has for the past decade remained at between an hour and a half and two hours.

For research on the Green Form scheme, see J Baldwin and S Hill, *The Operation of the Green Form Scheme in England and Wales*, Lord Chancellor's Department, 1988; John Baldwin 'The Green Form: Use or Abuse?', *New Law Journal*, 2 September 1988, p 631; 'In Praise of the Green Form', *ibid*, 23 September 1988, p 664; 'How Solicitors Use the Green Form – Adapting to Local Policies', *ibid*, 23 December 1988, p 928. See also John Baldwin, 'The Role of Citizens' Advice Bureaux and Law Centres in the Provision of Legal Advice and Assistance', *Civil Justice Quarterly*, January 1989, p 24.

ABWOR (Assistance by Way of Representation) is a scheme to enable representation in certain matters to be handled without the full requirement of a legal aid certificate. It applies to domestic proceedings in magistrates' courts, proceedings before mental health review tribunals, representation in police applications under PACE for a warrant of further detention, and representation in certain child care proceedings. In 1994–5 it was used in some 22,000 cases.

Proposals for changes in the Green Form scheme, 1979–1987

There have been various proposals for alteration of the Green Form scheme. In 1979 the Benson Royal Commission on Legal Services recommended that every citizen irrespective of means should be allowed half an hour's legal advice free of charge for the purposes of diagnosis (Cmnd 7648, 1979, para 13.4, p 134).

Thereafter, the Commission thought, the legal advice and assistance part of the scheme should permit the solicitor to undertake up to four hours' worth of work for the client without having to get permission. If the solicitor wished to provide more than four hours' work, he would have to get authority from the legal aid committee (*ibid*, pp 135–6).

The Royal Commission's recommendations were not implemented.

The 1986 Legal Aid Efficiency Scrutiny Report proposed a radical restructuring of the arrangements for legal advice. Basically the proposal was that virtually the whole of the legal advice system should be taken away from solicitors and given instead to Citizens' Advice Bureaux (CABx). CABx exist throughout the country–there are just under 1,000. They provide services that are totally free to the client. They deal with a huge volume of problems – currently over 6 million per annum. It has been estimated that between one-third and one-half are legal problems. The workers are a mixture of paid and unpaid. Most are unpaid. They receive some training but there are hardly any lawyers in the organization.

The Scrutiny Team proposed that the normal first port of call for the citizen should be the CAB. Green Form legal advice would be abolished. Legal advice from public funds for matters on which the citizen was simply arranging his own affairs–wills, conveyancing and probate–would be wholly abolished. Legal advice would no longer be available either for any problem on which one could not get legal aid, such as defamation or minor traffic problems. In regard to criminal cases, legal advice from solicitors should be limited to one hour's worth of advice (as compared with the present approximate two hours' worth) before having to get authority to proceed– and the authority would be sought from the magistrates' court rather than from the legal aid authorities. It would not be available at all, however, for offences that were not imprisonable.

These proposals raised a storm of protest. The Law Society, needless to say, was outraged at the suggestion that the citizen would no longer be able to use a solicitor for initial advice and assistance. It argued a powerful case against the recommendations, which, it said, would duplicate services provided by private practice, would be second class because funding would be inadequate, would inhibit choice and would create obstacles to the efficient conduct of cases.

The Law Society's case was supported by a broad spectrum of opinion, including finally the Citizens' Advice Bureaux too. They rejected the idea that CABx should take over Green Form legal advice on the ground that they lacked the necessary expertise and legally trained manpower, and that they feared that the Treasury would not give them enough money to employ the lawyers that would be needed.

The Government's White Paper in 1987 ('Legal Aid in England and Wales: a New Framework') recognized the force of this criticism. It therefore accepted that the recommendation was not viable, though it did state that powers would be taken to enable the new Legal Aid Board to make alternative arrangements for the provision of advice and assistance for particular categories of work where this would be a more efficient way of providing the service. So, for instance, advice on welfare benefits might be done by advice agencies and then excluded from the Green Form scheme. But no moves of this kind would take place until proper arrangements had been made. But for the rest solicitors would continue to provide Green Form advice. The White Paper did say, however, that assistance in the making of wills and conveyancing would be excluded from the Green Form scheme. (This threat was implemented as from 1993 (Legal Advice and Assistance (Scope) Regulations, SI 1989/550.)

(e) Quality control, specialisation and franchising

For some years now there has been pressure for legal aid work to be handled by specialists rather than by generalists. In 1986 the Legal Aid Efficiency Scrutiny proposed that the legal aid fund should only pay for help given 'by solicitors who are members of a Law Society panel and have demonstrated their competence in a particular subject and are committed to maintaining their expertise' (Volume I, para 40).

In its White Paper in 1987 the Government said (para 58): 'The Government accepts that it is desirable in principle that solicitors doing legal aid work should have special skills in the area concerned, and is attracted by the idea that legal aid work should be done by panels of solicitors with specialist experience in each category. The Government will be discussing with the Law Society how such panels could be established and how their use could be enforced.'

Panels do already exist for certain kinds of work, notably child care and mental health tribunals. But the Law Society in its response to the Scrutiny pointed out that they were voluntary and did not interfere with the client's freedom to instruct a solicitor of his choice. Both the profession and consumer organizations had 'consistently opposed mandatory schemes which could create new and undesirable monopolies' (para III 2, p 14).

In its first annual report in 1989, the Legal Aid Board said that it was considering a form of non-exclusive franchising. The aim would be to channel most Green Form work to specialized firms. They would get the benefit of easier financial arrangements, while the Board would be able to check the quality of work.

A consultation paper issued by the Board in May 1989 suggested that 'general practice franchises' would be granted to firms that received at least £40,000 pa from the Legal Aid Fund. (In 1988/9 2,832 offices received more than £40,000 in cost and these offices accounted for 75 per cent of all legal aid payments.) In addition there might be specialist franchises in particular branches of the law. If the range of franchises was adequate to provide sufficient coverage in an area, the Green Form scheme would be totally withdrawn in that area.

The Law Society's response argued that the Board's approach of exclusive and semi-exclusive franchising would lead to 'reduced access to legal services, a loss of consumer choice, disruption of the complementary relationship between private practice and advice services, problems of monopoly provision and difficulties in the funding of advice agencies' (Law Society, 'Franchising Legal Aid', August 1989, para 15, p 4. See to similar effect John Baldwin, 'Franchising Legal Aid', *Justice of the Peace*, 23 September 1989.)

On the other hand, the Law Society thought, franchising itself could be beneficial through simplified administration, the devolution of responsibility to solicitors' firms and a system of regular monthly payments which would make for easier administration. These benefits, it said, should be available to all solicitors (*ibid*, para 18, p 4).

In the light of much criticism the Board dropped its proposal to give franchises only to firms handling over £40,000 worth of legal aid work. But it stuck to the concept of franchising certain firms and suggested that franchised firms would have to have experienced supervisors to oversee a maximum of two areas of legal aid work. The Law Society objected that this would penalize small firms which might not have enough staff to provide such supervision. (See *Law Society's Gazette*, 6 December 1989, p 4.)

The Board said that it would start an experiment lasting six months in Birmingham in July 1990 and involving two firms, and a follow-up for 12 months in the same area which could involve many more firms and advice agencies. (See Stephen Orchard, 'Franchising: The Next Steps', *Law Society's Gazette*, 20 December 1989, p 12.)

The Law Society had serious reservations and it actually went so far as to advise solicitors not to cooperate with the Board's experiment (see *Law Society's Gazette*, 17 January 1990, p 4; 2 May 1990, p 2). In the end the Board modified its position and the Law Society withdrew its objections. In its annual report for 1990–1 the Board stated that 38 solicitors' firms and eight advice agencies had applied for franchises. (For the details of the specification for the franchise experiment see Legal Aid Board, *Annual Report*, 1990–1, pp 107–17.)

In its 1991–2 report the Board said it was developing proposals for the implementation of a national scheme. In the event, franchising has developed rapidly. In its 1994–5 report the Board said that 1,050 solicitors' offices and other organisations were franchised and that it expected within two or three years to have franchised over 3,000 offices. In April 1996 the Lord Chancellor's Department announced that legal aid remuneration rates would rise by 1.5 per cent for firms that were not franchised and by 3 per cent for firms that were franchised. Such a differential is obviously a useful incentive to firms to become franchised.

In its November 1995 response to the Green Paper on legal aid (see below) the Board said that franchising was a system based on quality assurance through setting standards in three areas. First, it ensured that franchisees had an appropriate management infrastructure for supervising work, training staff, managing cases, reviewing files, keeping up to date, focussing on client care, recruitment and appraisal of staff, control of finances etc. Secondly, audits of case files using transaction criteria showed whether the firm was working effectively on client cases. (Transaction criteria are check lists of steps and procedures to be taken in different kinds of case, established by the Board in conjunction with an independent advisory group.) Thirdly, the Board was developing 'outcome measures' to assess the results achieved. This was not yet part of the system but it would be an important part in the future.

The Board said that it fully supported the development by the Law Society of accreditation schemes and specialisation panels as a method of encouraging expertise among individual practitioners. However, by their nature, these were 'entry' schemes and it believed that 'they must be supported by ongoing audits of individual case files and other relevant procedures' (p 13, para 64).

In September 1994 the Board launched a pilot scheme to test the concept of franchising non-solicitor advice agencies. 42 organisations, including in particular citizens' advice bureaux, were taking part. The pilot was due to be completed formally in Spring 1996 at which point the Board would report to the Lord Chancellor. Early indications, the Board said in November 1995, were that the organisations involved were capable of reaching the franchise quality standard and that this would become an important part of the developing scheme. (See further p 465 below.) For a sharply critical view as to the dangers to the independence of lawyers implicit in franchising see Christie Davis, 'When Legal Aid Starts to Go By the Board', *The Lawyer*, 9 April 1996, p 12. (Christie is Professor of Sociology at Reading University.) See also Hiliary Sommerlad in *Access to Criminal Justice*, p 444, n 6, above at pp 303–311.

Note–the Fixed Fee scheme/ALAS/Accident Line

For many years the Law Society organized a voluntary scheme whereby a client could get half an hour's diagnostic advice on payment of a nominal £5. This so-called Fixed Fee scheme was provided by most firms of solicitors and it did not require any means test. Anyone qualified for the scheme. (See John Baldwin and Sheila Hill, 'Cut Price Legal Advice', *New Law Journal*, 20 May 1988, p 344.)

In 1992 the Law Society announced that the scheme was to be abolished in favour of 'locally based referral schemes'. These would commence in September 1993 and would be agreed between local law societies and referral agencies such as Citizens' Advice Bureaux. It was suggested that £25 plus VAT should be the maximum for a 30 minute interview. (*Law Society's Gazette*, 7 October 1992, p 10.)

In June 1987 the Law Society launched a free legal advice service for victims of accidents (Accident Legal Advice Service, or ALAS). The scheme was publicized by a leaflet and a 30-second video commercial shown in Post Offices. It was estimated that some 2,400 solicitors were taking part in the scheme. (See *Law Society's Gazette*, 1 July 1987, p 1935.) In June 1994 ALAS was renamed Accident Line. Under the scheme callers on the Freephone number 0500 19 29 39 are directed to solicitors on the Personal Injury Panel who offer a free first interview. In under 12 weeks the number of referrals through this freephone service had been just under 10,000, over 60 per cent of whom had instructed the solicitor after the initial interview. (*Law Society's Gazette*, 21 September 1994, p 6.) Early in 1996 there were 2,140 individual solicitors on the panel.

(f) Legal aid for groups

Legal advice and assistance is available to individual members of a group if they are entitled to it under the regulations. Very occasionally legal services are provided under legal aid for groups–but the principles on which it may be done have been ill-defined. Legal aid is only rarely granted for litigation by groups, save where an individual who is legally aided may occasionally be acting in a representative capacity on behalf of others. (But see below.)

The 1979 Royal Commission on Legal Services thought that the rules relating to legal aid should enable legal advice and assistance to be made available to groups by law centres and by solicitors in private practice. It did not think there was any need to change the rules regarding legal aid for litigation.

The Commission thought that legal advice and assistance should only be available to groups if:

  (i)   there was a register showing the names and addresses of members;
  (ii) the members had a personal interest in the purpose of the group;
  (iii) there was a secretary;
  (iv) the purpose of the group was written down;
  (v)   the register was available for inspection.

The group would not be eligible if it had access to sufficient funds or if it carried on a trade or business or party political activities.

A group should be entitled to up to four hours' advice and assistance without contribution if two-thirds of its members were entitled to legal aid without contribution. This would be determined by a statement from the secretary. For more than four hours' work, application would be made to the legal aid area committee. (For criticism see *New Law Journal*, 13 December 1979, p 1223.)

In its response to the Royal Commission's report, the Government stated that it thought it to be reasonable to expect groups to pool their resources and it did not accept that additional help by way of legal aid should be provided. (See *The Government Response to the Report of the Royal Commission on Legal Services*, 1983, Cmnd 9077, p 11.)

The Legal Aid Efficiency Scrutiny Report in 1986 recommended that specialist units be set up to deal with some special categories of litigation. One was medical negligence litigation, which required expertise and was apt to be very costly. Another was cases against manufacturers in respect of product liability–for instance actions against drug companies. The third was the public-interest type of case where the litigant was trying to establish the unlawfulness of a particular kind of action for the benefit of the community as a whole. There was, however, no mention of this proposal in the Government's legal aid White Paper in March 1987.

A system for organizing group claims through 'lead firms' is, however, now well developed.

The new approach began with a consultation paper issued by the Legal Aid Board on multi-party actions in May 1989, and in the light of the responses, the Board made a final report to the Lord Chancellor. The Board's annual report for 1990–1 stated that the Lord Chancellor was likely to bring forward regulations to deal with the issue that could be in place by April 1992.

The Board proposed that when an action is designated as a multi-party action, the Board would enter into a special contractual relationship with one or more firms which would act as the 'lead firms'. The individual would still have his own local solicitor but the main work on the case would be done by the lead firm(s) whose job would include keeping the local firms informed about the progress of the matter. A case would be regarded as coming within this approach if ten or more civil legal aid certificates had been issued for any particular action and (1) they involved common issues of fact or law arising out of the same cause or event; and (2) the claims involved significant complexity in terms of assembling statements, undertaking research, obtaining expert evidence or examining and processing large volumes of documentation. In selecting the lead firm the board would hope to be able to endorse proposals from firms. But it would reserve the right to decide the matter on the basis of experience and expertise and the firm's ability to handle that class and character of litigation. There would be a Multi-Party Actions Committee which would have the duty, amongst others, of hearing appeals concerning issues of principle.

These proposals were implemented by an amendment in April 1992 to the Civil Legal Aid (General) Regulations 1989–see J Curle, 'Enabling Multi-party Actions', *Law Society's Gazette*, 24 June 1992, p 17. The Board at the same time approved its Multi-Party Actions Arrangements 1992 which set out in detail how the contract powers would work, the tendering procedures, and the main standard contract terms. (See *Civil Justice Quarterly*, October 1992, pp 351–2).

But problems continued. These were the subject of a new report by the Legal Aid Board in May 1944 (*Issues arising for the Legal Aid Board and the Lord Chancellor's*

Department from Multi-Party Actions). One, it said, was that too high a proportion of these immensely costly actions were unsuccessful. (The biggest and most expensive, the Benzodiazepine litigation which involved some 17,000 applications for legal aid, was abandoned after some £35 million of legal aid money had been spent.) Another problem was that each of the assisted persons was liable for his share of the overall cost. If the common or generic costs were high a very large number of viable cases were needed to make the litigation cost-effective. Another problem was that the Board could not exercise effective detailed control over such litigation. The fall–out rate in such cases was often very high. In the Benzodiazepine litigation, some 13,000 certificates were issued but proceedings were commenced in just over 5,000 of which many were in the end found to have little chance of success. Perhaps the main problem was how to control the overall costs when there are very large numbers of claims. ('The alarming feature of the Benzodiazepine litigation has been the cumulative effect of the costs incurred under all the individual certificates added together' (p 19, para 4.29).) Cost limitations on individual certificates would not enable the Board to place a global limit on an action, particularly if a large number of different solicitors were pursuing their individual claims. Possibly the Board should be given a power to stand back from the individual cases to look at the prospects for the action as a whole. Representations should be permitted from opponents and the Board should be able to fund the plaintiffs wishing to respond to such representations.

The Board suggested that Rules of Court should recognise the concept of a group action. One feature of designated group actions would be that each claimant on the register would become liable for a share of the costs of the proceedings. Guidelines on costs should, so far as possible, treat generic costs as such. So if the claimants as a whole succeeded on the generic issues, all the generic costs should be recoverable– even if some of the claimants had abandoned their claims.

Group actions, legal aid and the statutory charge

During the debates on the Legal Aid Bill 1988, the Law Society and the National Consumer Council moved amendments to alleviate some of the funding problems highlighted by the Opren case. (See pp 433, 459, above). The most important of these would have provided that once the judge had certified the case for the special group litigation rules, the Legal Aid Board would grant representation without contribution to all those it covered and the statutory charge would not apply in respect of those proceedings. But the defendants would be permitted to get an order for their costs out of the Legal Aid Fund even if they could not show severe financial hardship. Legal aid would therefore effectively be paying the costs of both sides.

The Lord Chancellor, however, was unwilling to accept these amendments which would have far-reaching financial consequences for the legal aid fund. Instead he introduced his own amendments which were designed to enable the Legal Aid Board to grant legal aid subject to a requirement that the work be done by certain identified firms, and to permit discretionary dispensation with the contribution rules. Regulation 32 of the Civil Legal Aid (General) Regulations 1989 permits the legal aid authorities to have regard to whether it is reasonable for others who will benefit from the litigation to contribute to the costs. The contribution to be paid by the 'lead litigant(s)' can be adjusted to take account of the fact that it is in effect a test case. But if in the event the other persons do not contribute as required, the amount of any such contributions can be redetermined.

The Board can allocate the effect of the statutory charge proportionately to each plaintiff which will diminish its effect. But in a large and expensive action, the effect of even a proportionate share in the statutory charge would be extremely discouraging.

The National Consumer Council's 1989 report suggested that in certified cases the total contribution of any one plaintiff should be say £1,000 (or such other sum as would be fixed from time to time). But the contribution rules and the statutory charge rules have not yet been adapted to the needs of group litigation.

See further M Day, P Balen, G McCool, *Multi-Party Actions*, Legal Action, 1995. See also pp 44–47, 433–34 on representative and class actions.

(g) The cost of legal aid

The table below shows the overall cost of legal aid in 1994

	Gross expenses £m	Receipts £m	Net cost £m
Civil legal aid	878.9	288.5	590.4
Criminal legal aid	465.5	3.4	462.1
Legal advice and assistance	155.4	3.0	152.4
Duty Solicitor scheme in:			
magistrates' courts	12.0	–	12.0
police stations	68.8	–	68.8
Total	1,579.8	295.9	1,284.8

(Source: Judicial Statistics, 1994, Cm 2891, p 102, Table 10.7.)

(h) The distribution of legal aid work

Legal aid work has always been spread lightly amongst a large number of firms of solicitors and individual barristers, with a small number of firms and some barristers doing a great deal of the work. The Annual Report of the Legal Aid Board for 1994–95 showed that a total of 11,062 offices received payments. Twenty-three per cent of the offices received payments of under £5,000, which represented 0.4 per cent of total payments; 17 per cent of offices received payments of between £5000 and £20,000, representing 2.4 per cent of payments; whilst 20 per cent of offices received payments of over £120,000, amounting to 69 per cent of all payments. In the case of barristers, 19 per cent of the 8,588 who received payments had received payments of under £1,000, totalling 0.6 per cent of all payments; 39 per cent of the barristers received between £1,000 and £8,000, which totalled 11 per cent of all payments; whilst 28 per cent of the barristers received £14,000 or more, aggregating 77 per cent of all payments. (The figures cover all forms of legal aid except crown court cases.)

For an estimate of legal aid as a proportion of the income of the Bar and solicitors, see below (p 552–53).

(i) Is there a need for legal aid in tribunals?

The question of whether legal aid ought to be available in tribunals is one of the outstanding questions about the scope of the legal aid system. It was examined in 1967 by the Lord Chancellor's Legal Aid Advisory Committee. The Committee considered a number of tribunals and looked at each in turn. (See Lord Chancellor's Legal Aid Advisory Committee, *Comments and Recommendations on the 17th Report of the Law Society on Legal Aid and Advice*, 1966–7, pp 71–4.) It reached the conclusion that legal aid was not necessary in any of them. But only a few years later the same committee changed its mind. In its 1973–4 report the Committee recommended that the legal aid scheme be extended to cover representation in all statutory tribunals within the supervision of the Council on Tribunals (*24th Report on Legal Aid and Advice 1973–4*, p 49). This was done, however, only for three tribunals–the Lands Tribunal (1970), the Commons Commissioners (1972) and the Employment Appeal Tribunal (1976).

Young barristers and barrister pupils, with the assistance and support of the Bar, have for many years run a very valuable free advocacy service for tribunal cases–the Free Representation Unit. (See *Counsel*, March/April 1994, pp 23–24.)

The Benson Royal Commission on Legal Services (1979) took an intermediate position. It thought that legal aid should be available for some cases in all tribunals but that the chief need was to provide state funds to enable lay agencies providing representation in tribunals to do so more effectively. Also the Council on Tribunals should put in hand a major inquiry to review the procedure of tribunals to make sure that this was as simple as possible.

The Commission proposed that agencies such as Citizens' Advice Bureaux, the Child Poverty Action Group, the Free Representation Unit, or the United Kingdom Immigration Advisory Services should be given funds to supplement and improve the service they provided in tribunals. This would help to provide training, an up-to-date information service, administrative support and solicitors on the staff or available on a consultancy basis. Such funds should be given by the Lord Chancellor's Department –but only to organizations which provided services to members of the public at large. Trade unions would therefore not qualify.

The Commission proposed that the decision whether to grant legal aid in individual cases should be taken by the secretary of the legal aid area committee who would refer to the committee only such cases as he was minded to refuse. There should be two tests: first, that the applicant had reasonable grounds for bringing or contesting the case; secondly, that there were reasonable grounds for employing a lawyer. The certifying body should have regard to the suitability and availability of any other form of assistance. Legal representation might be considered appropriate, for instance, where a significant point of law was at issue, where evidence was likely to be so complex or specialized that a layman would benefit from expert assistance, where a test case arose, or where deprivation of liberty or the ability of an individual to follow his occupation was at stake. Legal aid should also be available where (i) the amount at stake, though low, was significant in relation to the financial circumstances of the applicant; (ii) when suitable lay representation was not available; and (iii) when the special circumstances of the individual made legal representation desirable or when hardship might follow if it was withheld (Cmnd 7648, 1979, pp 169–74).

The case for expanded legal aid for tribunal cases has been made repeatedly since the Royal Commission's report. (See, for instance, AA McFadyen, 'No Legal Aid for Representation Before Industrial Tribunals', *Law Society's Gazette*, 4 March 1984, p 795.) But the only change in the position so far has been its extension to Mental Health Review Tribunals.

In its 1983 Report the Lord Chancellor's Legal Aid Advisory Committee took a somewhat different line to that of the Royal Commission. It thought the most important single need was for advice prior to a hearing, to enable the citizen to identify his problem and prepare his case. It urged that applicants should be told as a matter of course of the desirability of seeking advice from an appropriate source.

They should also be advised about the importance of attending the hearing. The success rate was much influenced by the presence of the applicant.

Also, Government money should be used to improve the training of voluntary advice workers, for instance, in Citizens' Advice Bureaux to enable them to provide competent advice and assistance including representation in simple cases. The best way to do this, it said, would be for government money to be used to employ 'resource lawyers' who would train voluntary workers and assist them with difficult cases. Such publicly funded lawyers should serve several advice agencies in an area.

Legal aid for tribunal cases should be made available: where a significant point of law arose; where the evidence was likely to be complex or specialized; where the case was a test case; and where deprivation of liberty or the ability of the individual to follow his occupation was at stake. In the first instance legal aid should now be extended to bail applications to the Immigration Appellate Authorities; then to the Immigration Appeal Tribunal; then to appeals heard by the Social Security Commissioners which were all on points of law; and then to Industrial Tribunals which had proceedings that were increasingly formal and adversarial. (*Legal Aid*, 33rd Report, 1983, pp 194–209.)

The 1986 Legal Aid Efficiency Scrutiny

The Efficiency Scrutiny recommended that a considerable part of the money saved by removing Green Form work from solicitors might be used to finance tribunal representation. It cited a recent study showing the value of representation – in Social Security Appeal Tribunals there was a success rate of 30 per cent for applicants who attended on their own, as against 46 per cent for those who came with a representative (vol 2, Annex 33).

Tribunal representation, the report urged, ought to be part of the new integrated provision for legal advice and representation provided through the Area Director once Green Form work had been largely transferred from solicitors to CABx (see p 454 above).

However, when the Government was forced to accept that the Scrutiny recommendations regarding Green Form were unworkable, it became obvious that the proposed improvements in provision for tribunal representation would founder too. The 1987 White Paper ('Legal Aid in England and Wales: a New Framework') said that the Government did not intend that there should be any general extension of publicly funded tribunal representation. Extensions of assistance by way of legal aid were made where it was shown to be necessary. It was not clear that publicly funded representation was necessary for all tribunals.

The Legal Aid Board stated in November 1995 that research it had commissioned from the Policy Studies Institute concluded that 'the literature shows clearly that representation has a significant impact on the outcome of cases'. The review also showed that the research showed this consistently. (Legal Aid Board's response to the Lord Chancellor's Consultation Paper *Legal Aid–Targeting Need*, 1995, p 6, para 28.). The Government's Green Paper on the future of legal aid (paras 8.13–17) raised the question whether its proposed new system (see below) should permit holders of block contracts to provide representation in at least some tribunal cases. This issue should be explored by appropriate pilot projects.

(j) Lord Mackay's 1995 Green Paper on legal aid

In May 1995 the Lord Chancellor, Lord Mackay unveiled his long–heralded and extremely controversial Green Paper (*Legal Aid–Targeting Need* (Cm 2584)) outlining plans for the radical transformation of the entire legal aid scheme. The present scheme it said had survived largely unchanged for nearly fifty years. It was showing signs of wear and tear.

Although the purpose of the scheme has wide public support, there is considerable and justified criticism of some of its failings in practice. The scheme is selective in the problems which it addresses and the ways in which it solves them. It does not always assist with those problems where there is greatest need. It allows assisted parties to pursue cases which turn out to be unmeritorious, often at the expense of unassisted opponents. It tends to encourage legal solutions to problems. Such solutions can be expensive, cumbersome and complex, when less formal solutions might be as effective. The cost of the scheme has grown at a pace which the country can no longer afford to maintain and yet the increases in costs have not always been matched by similar increases in benefits to the individual or the public. The standards of service provided under the legal aid scheme are not uniformly high [p 4, para 1.12].

The Green Paper, it said, would address these failings and at the same time extend the range of help available under legal aid. In particular it would address the unacceptable level of the rising cost of the scheme. (This in the view of most commentators was the main reason for the Green Paper.) The rising cost of the scheme far outstripped inflation. Governmental attempts to control rising expenditure through alterations to the scope of the scheme, alterations to eligibility and alterations to the remuneration levels of lawyers had not had sufficient impact.

The most important features of the proposed reforms would be the following:

Fixed budget

There would for the first time be a monetary ceiling on the amount of money available for legal aid. Instead of the system being demand-led it would be restricted to the amount of money provided by the Government. ('The Government believes that it is right to make judgments about what the country can afford to spend in any one year on publicly funded legal services. It makes similar decisions across a whole range of other programmes such as the Courts, the Police, Prisons, the Health Service and Education. In deciding what it can afford to spend on publicly funded legal services the Government would need to take into account a number of factors, including the

likely level of demand, the state of the economy and the efficiency of the service'
(p 28, para 4.28).

In order to avoid criminal legal aid squeezing other categories, there would be
separate budgets for family, civil non-family and criminal matters.

The concept of a fixed budget for criminal cases might create problems under the
European Convention on Human Rights, Article 6 of which guaranteed that everyone
charged with a criminal offence has the right to defend himself in person or through
legal assistance and if he has insufficient means to pay for it 'to be given it free when
the interests of justice so require'. Also a defendant in a criminal case had no choice
about being prosecuted.

This suggests that there might be particular difficulties in guaranteeing access to justice if there
were a fixed and predetermined budget for criminal legal aid. No case that would otherwise
qualify could be refused legal aid for lack of money. On the other hand, the advantages of a
predetermined budget apply to criminal legal aid as much as to other areas ... The Government
believes that any new system for criminal legal aid would have to ensure that no case would be
refused for lack of money alone. But the system should also encourage effectiveness in the use
of legal aid, the containment of costs to reasonable levels and good management of cases. A
predetermined budget would contribute to achieving these ends [pp 30–1].

It was for consideration whether the prosecution should be subject to the same
discipline of a fixed budget.

Allocation of funds

The Government would set out its general priorities for legal aid which would be
subject to Parliamentary approval.

These priorities would be implemented through block contracts which would specify
the volume of acts of advice, assistance, representation or the numbers of clients, at
an agreed price.

Contracts would be let so that expenditure was targeted to meet prioritised needs
which would be assessed locally by a network of Regional Legal Services Committees
on the model of the existing such Committee in the North West.

There would be separate contracts for different categories of work (personal injury,
family, crime etc), but a supplier could have several contracts. The contractual
arrangements could be different for different categories of work.

The Legal Aid Board would hold a reserve to provide for major unforeseen events
such as exceptionally high cost cases. (The Green Paper, p 76, para 11.l, stated that
the most expensive 1 per cent of work represented 15 per cent of gross expenditure in
civil non-family cases, 10 per cent of expenditure in family cases, and 40 per cent of
expenditure in crown court cases.)

The Government's preliminary view was that the Area Offices of the Legal Aid
Board would be the most appropriate Contracting Agents for the new system.

Area Offices would invite tenders for contracts for the provision of identified needs.
It would then allocate contracts on the basis of an assessment of quality, access, price
and the need for competition.

Suppliers could be not only solicitors and barristers but law centres, and non-
lawyer advice agencies such as Citizens' Advice Bureaux, Shelter housing advice

agencies and other independent agencies such as suppliers of mediation, arbitration and other alternative dispute resolution services.

The basic unit for contractual arrangements would be legal aid franchise holders. (As has been seen p 456 above, in 1995 there were just over a thousand franchise holders and the Legal Aid Board anticipated that within two or three years there would be around 3,000.) All franchised firms 'would immediately be eligible for the award of a full, long term contract under the new arrangements subject to agreement on issues such as volume and price' (p 40, para 6.6). ('The Board Area Office would choose the suppliers in the lowest price range consistent with ensuring a quality service, providing a degree of choice and ensuring that there were sufficient suppliers to maintain competition to improve quality and value for money. This means that at any time there could be a number of suppliers paid at different prices providing the same contracted service in the same geographical area' (p 45, para 6.26).)

It would be left to the supplier to engage barristers and to agree fees with them. Standard fees would no longer apply. Contracts would seek to ensure that the Bar was not disadvantaged by the supplier keeping cases in-house where '*better value for money* would be obtained by briefing counsel to do this work' (p 46, para 6.31, emphasis supplied).

The Legal Aid Board would maintain quality controls and would monitor the operation of the system.

Non-franchised organisations could apply for a contract but they would first have to pass a preliminary audit of the required quality standards. They would then become eligible for a short term (say, one year) contract. During that period they would have to demonstrate that they could meet the required quality standards before becoming eligible for long term contracts.

In other words, only suppliers who had proved themselves would be eligible to undertake legal aid work. 'To this extent there would be some further limitation on [client] choice. However, there would be sufficient contracts to ensure that clients would still have a choice of suppliers and that problems of conflict of interest would not arise' (p 42, para 6.11).

Relations between suppliers and clients

Save for exceptional cases, it would be the supplier who would decide what cases to take on but contracts would have to ensure that they did not take on only cases with the highest profit margins.

Instead of the present merits test for legal aid the supplier would come under a continuing duty to keep under review the desirability of providing public funds for the case. The factors to be taken into account by the supplier would include (1) 'The cost and benefit of each case, both individually and in relation to other cases with which the supplier is dealing'; (2) 'the importance of the case to the individual'; and (3) 'the availability of alternative means of resolving the case' (p 54, para 7.9).

Contributions would continue to apply save for preliminary advice and assistance in family matters and social welfare law cases.

The supplier would carry out the simple form of means testing (as under the existing Green Form scheme) for problem diagnosis and basic advice and assistance. (This would create problems for non-solicitor agencies like Citizens' Advice Bureaux which operate on the basis that help is free to all regardless of means.) More detailed problem resolution including court proceedings resolution, alternative dispute resolution would involve means testing by the Board or its agent.

The Board would have to decide whether a case fell into the category of high cost case and 'whether the merits of the case justified the very high costs which would result from pursuing it' (p 78, para 11.14). 'This would involve assessment of relative merit between cases' (*ibid*). Cases in this category would be put out to competitive tender from appropriate specialist firms.

Representation before tribunals

The Green Paper invited views as to whether and if so, subject to what controls and criteria, suppliers should be permitted to provide representation or other assistance in some cases in tribunals.

For a summary of the Green Paper see *Legal Action*, June 1995, pp 6–8. For a description see two articles by Steve Orchard, Chief Executive of the Legal Aid Board, *Law Society's Gazette*, 21 June 1995, p 18 and 29 November 1995, p 12.

(k) Reactions to the Green Paper

The Green Paper met a mainly hostile reception from both lawyers and non-lawyer organisations concerned with advice on legal issues. Commentators welcomed the proposed extension of funding for non-solicitor advice agencies and for tribunal representation, but apart from that the proposals were generally condemned. (See for instance, *Legal Action*, June 1995, p 9, August 1995, p 8, *Legal Action*, October 1995, p 6.) The Law Society put its reaction in a 77-page paper entitled *A Better Way Forward* published in September 1995. The Bar published its 76-page response in October 1995. For a sophisticated overall analysis see T Goriely, 'The Government's Legal Aid Reforms' in *Reforming Civil Procedure–Essays on 'Access to Justice'* (ed Zuckerman and Cranston, Clarendon, Oxford, 1995) pp 347–69.

Inevitably, much of the criticism was directed at the concept of cash-limits. The writer was one of those who inveighed against this proposal–see M Zander, 'Twelve Reasons for Rejecting the Legal Aid Green Paper', *New Law Journal*, 21 July 1995, p 1098.

The Legal Aid Board's response to the Green Paper

About the sole approving voice in response to the Green Paper was that of the Legal Aid Board which broadly supported the proposals. It conceded that for the past two years the legal aid budget had been underspent and that it was therefore not the case that it was currently soaring out of control. But underspending, it suggested, was as much evidence of a lack of control as overspending. It adhered to its previously expressed view that it was important for control of expenditure to be introduced before any important changes were made in the legal aid scheme. It thought that civil legal aid could be run on a predetermined budget but that this would not be possible for criminal legal aid. In regard to criminal legal aid there would therefore always have to be the possibility of overspending the contemplated budget.

Apart from approving the Government's basic approach, the Board's response dealt with a variety of issues:

Merits test The present 'private client' merits test should continue to be an important guiding principle and the vast majority of cases that would now pass the test should continue to be funded. But the test should be broadened to a more general test of whether a case demonstrated a need for publicly funded services of that type. This broader test would have to be applied on a continuing basis by the provider of the service. But this process should not involve comparisons between the relative merits of different cases. ('We do not think it appropriate for suppliers to determine the merits of one case relative to another', p 30, para 30.) A client whose case was not taken or (was dropped) because of the provider's application of the merits test should have the right to try to persuade a different provider to undertake the case. One of the criteria to be taken into account should be the importance of the case to the client (pp 79–80).

Franchisees The Lord Chancellor should consider rewarding franchisees by offering them enhanced levels of remuneration (pp 48–9, para 248).

Competitive tendering The Board continued to be against decisions based solely on competitive bids on cost. Quality of work and access to the consumer were always relevant. But subject to that caveat, competitive tendering could have a role to play (paras 244–46, 314, 315).

Impact on the Bar The impact of the Government's proposals on the Bar could be serious. The Board's aim would be to ensure appropriate quality of service. It would have safeguards to ensure that suppliers did not consistently skimp on using counsel or other experts (paras 340–44).

Criminal Legal Aid For the time being the grant of criminal legal aid should remain with the courts but if the Board's proposed Early Cover system (see p 449 above) were introduced, this should be reconsidered. Ultimately it might be appropriate for the Board to have responsibility for the grant of criminal legal aid–and then under contracting the decision could be transferred to the individual supplier, though that would have to be subject to statutory guidelines. But responsibility for the collection of contributions should be left to the courts (Chapter 7).

In March 1996 the Lord Chancellor said that pre-determined budgets did not mean that legal aid would be refused because the money had run out. Contracts would be granted for a period of years and managed over that period to produce a steady stream of services. In addition there would be a central fund for high cost cases and unexpected contingencies. In regard to criminal cases, he said, the Government accepted 'its obligation to provide legal aid where the interests of justice demand it.' ('Even with a pre-determined budget, we shall as now, seek to secure sufficient funds in the public expenditure round each year to meet the cost of criminal cases where the interest of justice test is satisfied' (Speech to Kent Law Society, 27 March 1996).)

At the time when this book went to press it was still unclear what parts of the Government's 1995 legal aid Green Paper would be implemented by a Conservative Government and what an incoming Labour government might do.

Labour's policy

The outline of Labour's policy on legal aid was sketched by the Shadow Lord Chancellor Lord Irvine of Lairg QC in a contribution to a book of essays published in January 1996. ('The Legal System and Law Reform under Labour', in *Law Reform for All*, ed D Bean, Blackstone, 1996.) He said that it would be Labour's policy 'to restore legal aid to the status of a public social service' although 'Labour will have no new money to throw at problems whose solution calls for structural change'. Current expenditure had 'substantially stabilised' and there was therefore 'no current imperative for cost capping the legal aid budget as the Green Paper proposes' (p 6). Lord Irvine attacked the concept of capping. 'Capping is crude'. It would 'lead at worst to substantial exclusion from justice and at best to long waiting lists'. The availability of legal aid should not depend, he wrote, on where the individual lives or when application is made. It should depend on means and merits. He cited and supported the writer's critique of capping.

Lord Irvine said that Labour favoured block franchising but opposed compulsory competitive tendering because of its tendency to favour low-price against higher quality bidders. Franchising would have a key role to play in Labour's plan to develop a Community Legal Service. Compulsory competitive tendering would be likely to undermine the whole franchising project, 'driving some firms away from the scheme and encouraging others to emphasise cost control, at the expense of quality assurance for the client (p 10).

The Labour Party, according to Lord Irvine, would create a Community Legal Service provided by the appropriate regional mix of lawyers in private practice, law centres, Citizens' Advice Bureaux and a full panoply of advice agencies. There would be scope for many more lawyers working on salaries provided by the state. The Service would be coordinated by regional Legal Aid Board offices. Each such office would be required to assess the legal needs of the area and then to draw up a detailed strategy for meeting those needs in consultation with local authorities and new advisory legal services committees to establish priorities. The regional Legal Aid Board offices would administer the legal aid fund through lawyers in private practice and the voluntary sector (pp 14–15).

The Government's White Paper on Legal Aid

The Government published its White Paper on 2 July 1996–for details see Appendix, p 589 below.

(l) Legal costs insurance

The concept of insurance against legal costs has been familiar for years, notably in the context of house insurance and motoring. But in the past twenty or so years the insurance industry has started to market policies covering a much wider range of legal problems. Most policies issued in the UK are 'add ons' to existing policies, usually of motor or home contents policies; some are 'stand alone'.

Typically such policies cover lawyers' fees, court costs, costs of witnesses and experts–and costs of the opponent if the insured is ordered to pay them. Normally there is a maximum per claim which may be £25,000 or £50,000. Many of the policies cover all the members of the family.

The policy normally provides that only cases that have a reasonable prospect of success will be supported. But the insured has a right to choose his own lawyer. (This is provided by the Insurance Companies (Legal Expenses Insurance) Regulations 1990 (SI 1990/1159), implementing EC Directive 87/34 which came into force on 1 July 1990.) Many insurers, however, reserve the right to reject the client's nomination. It is not clear whether this is lawful under the EC Directive.

Most insurers also retain the right to withdraw cover if a reasonable settlement is unlikely to be obtained or if the insured refuses a reasonable offer. (In all these respects insurance is much like having legal aid.)

Most policies exclude matrimonial disputes. Many also exclude building disputes, defamation, tax matters and defence of criminal prosecutions involving violence.

It was said in 1991 that the Association of British Insurers estimated that total premiums were then worth about £40–£50m pa, which represented a significant increase of some 100 per cent on the previous two or three years. This divided between 50 per cent motor related, 20 per cent general family policies and 30 per cent commercial. About 10 million people had some form of cover, though in many cases it amounted only to access to a telephone advisory service.

A survey carried out in 1991 for the Law Society and the Consumers' Association suggested that only 7 per cent of the population had some form of legal expenses insurance proper (compared with around 50 per cent in Germany. (See *Legal Expenses Insurance in the UK* (Law Society, January 1991), summarized in *Law Society's Gazette*, 6 February 1991, p 3, and *Solicitors' Journal*, 7 June 1991, p 608. See also the *Which?* survey, April 1991, pp 223–9. For a broad assessment including international comparisons see two papers in *Reforming Civil Procedure–Essays on Access to Justice* (ed Zuckerman and Cranston, Clarendon, Oxford, 1995)–N Rickman and A Gray, 'The Role of Legal Expenses Insurance in Securing Access to the Market for Legal Services' pp 305–25; Vivien Prais, 'Legal Expenses Insurance', pp 431–46.

Both the Government's Green Paper on the future of legal aid and Lord Woolf's Interim Report *Access to Justice* expressed the hope that legal expenses insurance would develop and expand.

(m) Contingency fees and conditional fees

The English system has rejected contingent fees as a method of financing litigation. Under the contingency fee system, a client either pays nothing or less than the full fee if he loses, whereas if he wins, the lawyer takes his fee out of the damages. The fee charged by the lawyer in the event of a win is normally assessed on a percentage basis. In the United States contingency fees are the normal method of financing personal injury litigation. From the client's point of view the great attraction of this system is that he normally pays nothing unless and until the case is won–and that the amount paid to the lawyers is then directly related to the amount obtained by way of damages. The out-of-pocket cost of losing is borne by the lawyers not the client. Normally the client is not even required to put up any money 'up front' to cover disbursements.

The objection to contingency fees in England was originally that they are maintenance (the financial support of someone else's litigation) and champerty (the taking of a financial interest in the outcome of someone else's litigation). Maintenance and champerty were actually illegal until the Criminal Law Act 1967, but in abolishing the criminal offences of maintenance and champerty the 1967 Act expressly preserved the rules making such arrangements improper for solicitors. (See *Wallersteiner v Moir (No 2)* [1975] 1 All ER 849, Denning MR dissenting.) The concern was that a lawyer who has a financial stake in the outcome of the litigation may be tempted into unethical conduct. For a modern application of the unenforceability of a champertous agreement see *Aratra Potato Co Ltd v Taylor Joynson Garrett* [1995] 4 All ER 695. For comment on this case and its importance in the context of conditional fee agreements (below) see S King, 'Conditional fees: proceed with caution', *Solicitors' Journal*, 1 March 1996, p 204.

In 1970, the Law Society published a memorandum arguing that these rules should continue to apply ('Claims Assessors and Contingency Fees', 1970). The contingency arrangement, it argued, was incompatible with the indemnity rule whereby the loser pays the costs of the winner and thereby puts him (more or less) back into the position he was in before the damage was done. Under a contingency arrangement, the winner had to pay a substantial proportion of his damages to his lawyers and to that extent he was not 'made whole' by the action. In the US, where contingency fees were the rule in personal injury cases, each side bore its own costs. Moreover, the legal aid scheme catered for all reasonable claims for damages where the claimant lacked the means to pursue his case. The only significant category of which this was not true was the case of the person just outside the legal aid limits–but this should be dealt with, the Law Society suggested, by raising or abolishing the upper limit for legal aid. Even if this were not done, the risks of abuse in the introduction of contingency arrangements would more than outweigh any possible advantages.

The one exception to this general rule seen by the Law Society was the case of debt collection. In that single case the objections to contingency fees did not apply– mainly because the amount of the claim was liquidated or known in advance. There was therefore little or no element of speculation and no inducement to inflate the claim to damages. Moreover, most debt collection was for very small sums which could not easily be made a profitable form of work for solicitors. 'If it is to be worth a solicitor's while handling such claims at all, the only practicable method is to enable him to make an arrangement with his client to do so on a commission basis' (p 23). If necessary, maximum commission rates could be laid down by the Law Society to prevent excessive charges (p 24).

CLAF

The Law Society did however favour a variant on the theme of contingency fees – the Contingency Legal Aid Fund (or CLAF) first mooted by JUSTICE in 1966 in *Trial of Motor Accident Cases*. Litigants would be asked to agree with their lawyers that if they won they would pay an agreed small percentage of their damages into the Fund. The money in the fund would then pay the costs of the loser. This concept avoided the main alleged danger of contingency fees of lawyers being tempted into unethical conduct because of the financial importance of winning.

The CLAF concept, though supported by JUSTICE, the Law Society and the Bar, has never been implemented. One obvious problem about it is whether sufficient numbers of clients with promising actions could be persuaded to agree to give up a percentage of their damages to make the system economically viable.

The Benson Royal Commission on Legal Services rejected contingent fees in general and the JUSTICE proposal in particular. It thought that contingent fees might lead to undesirable practices by lawyers ('including the construction of evidence, the improper coaching of witnesses, the use of professional partisan expert witnesses, especially medical witnesses, improper examination and cross-examination, groundless legal arguments designed to lead the courts into error and competitive touting' (Cmnd 7648, 1979, para 16.4, p 177)). If the case was won, the lawyer claimed a significant part of the damages. But there was also the danger that the lawyer would settle too readily in order to avoid the costs of preparing for the trial and having the risk of losing and thereby not getting his fee. Also the contingency fee system did not work easily in a system which had an indemnity rule of costs. Either the plaintiff would have to pay the defendant's costs if he lost whilst not paying his own, or the lawyer would have to pay the winner's costs–which would result in his asking for a much higher contingent fee in the first place.

As regards the JUSTICE CLAF plan, the Commission thought this could only assist plaintiffs claiming large sums. There was a danger that those with good claims would not use the scheme whereas those with doubtful claims would do so. The financial viability of the scheme would thus be put in jeopardy. Moreover, it would be wrong for successful litigants to subsidize the unsuccessful. Those who obtained the highest damages would have to pay the most into the fund. This in turn might lead to an increase in the level of damages awarded.

The Government response to the Royal Commission's report simply agreed with the Commission's view that contingent fees should not be permitted and that a Contingency Legal Aid Fund should not be set up (Cmnd 9077, 1983, p 18).

The Law Society returned to the CLAF idea in its paper 'Improving Access to Civil Justice' in July 1987. It still rejected 'straight' contingent fees, which, it thought, brought out the worst 'ambulance chasing' instincts of practitioners. (It instanced the scene after the 1985 tragedy at Bhopal in India with American lawyers imposing themselves on victims of the disaster.) But CLAF, it thought, did not suffer from this disadvantage.

The Law Society in the same paper also canvassed the possibility of a new variant on these themes a mutual fund Fixed Costs Scheme, under which solicitors would pay a premium to insurers and any individual client with a claim would then pay a fixed sum to cover the costs in the event that the case might be lose. This, like CLAF, would guarantee the lawyers their fees but the client would pay a fixed sum in advance rather than a percentage payable after the case was over. Usually the plaintiff would win and the fund would not be called on. The amounts payable could be adjusted depending on the claims experience and could vary depending on the nature of the litigation. Unlike CLAF, it could apply to cases which did not generate damages.

The Law Society thought that the amount payable on initial instructions might be in the order of £25 to £75 to cover costs up to the issue of proceedings. Thereafter a sum in the order of say £350 to £550 might cover the balance of the costs.

Note–the Hong Kong contingency legal aid scheme

A contingency scheme has operated in Hong Kong for certain serious personal injury cases. The applicant, if accepted by the legal aid scheme, has his case conducted in the ordinary way save that he does not pay a contribution toward his own costs until the action is over. Instead he agrees to a deduction from any ultimate damages. The percentage varies but is never over 12 per cent. If the case is settled this may be reduced by up to half. There are about 100 applications a year. But the scheme is self-financing. (See Patrick Moss, 'Contingency Legal Aid in Hong Kong', *Law Society's Gazette*, 11 September 1991, p 2.)

Lord Mackay's Green Paper on Contingent Fees

In January 1989 the Lord Chancellor Lord Mackay launched his controversial Green Papers for reform of the legal profession (on which see below, pp 564–77). One of the three Green Papers was on contingent fees ('Contingency Fees', 1989 Cm 571).

The Green Paper stated that Government policy was in favour of deregulation, which entailed the removal of restrictions. It was therefore for consideration whether the rules against contingent fees should be abolished or amended. It suggested that there were three possible options.

The first was *speculative fees*, which were already permitted in Scotland. Under this system the solicitor could agree with his client that he would be paid only if he won the case and that he would then be paid his taxed costs. A variant of this would be that the solicitor would be paid his taxed costs plus some additional element to reward the lawyers for the risk they took. The amount to be added would be a percentage of the costs *not* the damages. It could either be unrestricted or subject to restriction by rules. (The Law Society supported this approach just prior to the publication of the Green Paper–see *Solicitors' Journal*, 6 January 1991, p 4.)

The second option was a *restricted contingency fee system*, under which the contingent fee payable in the event of success would be a percentage of the damages but the level of recovery would be controlled by rules.

The third option would be an *unrestricted contingency basis*. The Green Paper said 'It is considered that this would not be in the public interest' (para 4.9).

The White Paper and the Courts and Legal Services Act 1990

The White Paper issued in July 1989 stated that there had been a clear consensus for the rejection of both the unrestricted and the restricted contingent fee system ('Legal Services: A Framework for the Future', HMSO, 1989, Cm 740, p 41). It was generally felt that to give the lawyer a stake in the damages would have undesirable side-effects and would be likely to create an unacceptable degree of conflict of interest. But there had been little objection to the Scottish 'speculative' action and the government therefore proposed to legislate to make that permissible. The Courts and Legal Services Act 1990, s 58, legitimizes 'conditional fee agreements' (a happier term than 'speculative fee agreements'). The permissible level of 'uplift' was to be regulated by statutory instrument.

The Lord Chancellor's Department then issued a consultation paper in which it suggested that, at least in the first instance, conditional fees would be restricted to personal injury cases, that the maximum uplift might be set at 10 per cent and that this uplift would not be part of any costs order payable by the opponent.

The lawyer would be under a duty to put the agreement in writing. The regulations might impose a duty on the lawyer to give the client general advice about alternative methods of financing the case, in particular legal aid. The Order would also need to provide that the precise circumstances in which the lawyer could claim his fee should be specified in the agreement.

The Law Society, commenting on the consultation paper, called on the Lord Chancellor's Department to broaden the application of conditional fees beyond personal injury cases. Defamation or debt collecting, where legal aid was not available, would be obvious candidates. The Consumers' Association for its part thought that actions for damages in contract or tort should also be eligible. They should be allowed 'for any kind of proceedings where it is likely that an ordinary citizen not eligible for legal aid will be faced with mounting legal proceedings against a wealthy and probably insured corporation'.

Both the Law Society and the Consumers' Association argued that an uplift of 10 per cent was too low to lure lawyers into taking on potentially difficult and complex cases. The Law Society said it hoped the maximum would be raised to 20 per cent, though there could be an argument for 100 per cent–on the basis that this would enable the lawyer to break even if half the cases taken on a conditional fee basis were successful. (See *Law Society's Gazette*, 1 May 1991, p 10.)

In the event the Lord Chancellor agreed on a maximum uplift of 100 per cent. In other words, what had been previously discussed as a modest charge to the client of 10–15 per cent of the fees was at the last moment changed to the very different proposition, that in the event of winning the case, the lawyer might receive double his fee.

The rules for the new system are in the Conditional Fees Agreements Regulations 1995 which came into force in July 1995. (SI 1995/1675). There has to be a legally binding contract between the client and the solicitor setting out the details of the arrangement. The Law Society has published a non-mandatory model agreement to be entered into between the solicitor and the client. For a full guide to the whole topic see Michael Napier and Fiona Bawden, *Conditional Fees–a Survival Guide*, Law Society, 1995.

The Law Society's model agreement (see *Law Society's Gazette*, 28 June 1995, p 30) provides that if the case is won, the client is liable to pay disbursements, basic costs and a 'success fee', plus VAT, though it also explains that normally disbursements and basic costs will be recovered from the other side. If the case is lost, the client is liable to pay the solicitor's disbursements (which may or may not include barristers' fees–see below), and the other side's costs and disbursements.

The model agreement states that the solicitor has explained to the client whether he is eligible for legal aid, the situation as regards liability for costs and disbursements, and the right to have the solicitor's bill vetted by a solicitor and own client taxation (for which see p 424 above).

Where the barrister in the case has a conditional fee agreement with the solicitors, his fee is a disbursement recoverable from the other side. But if he wins, the client has to pay the barrister's success fee in addition to the solicitors' success fee. If he loses, the client pays nothing in respect of the barrister's fee.

If the barrister does not have a conditional fee agreement with the solicitors (ie does not take part in the conditional fee system) and the client wins, he pays an extra success fee on top of the ordinary success fee paid to the barrister. This is because if the case is lost, the barrister's fees have to be paid in the usual way. (This obligation to pay what the model agreement calls an 'extra success fee' does not apply however if the client has paid the barrister's fees on account.)

Solicitors who are members of the Law Society's Personal Injury Specialist Panel eligible to offer Accident Line Protection must also get the client to agree to pay the flat-rate premium (fixed initially at the very modest sum of £85) to provide full insurance cover against the risk of losing and therefore becoming liable for the other side's costs. (The premium is so low only because all conditional fee arrangements entered into by Accident Line offices are subject to the requirement.) But only some 1,300 solicitors' offices are members of Accident Line. (For details of Accident Line see *Law Society's Gazette*, 13 October 1993, p 4.) The remaining 8,500 offices can also offer the same protection but the premium payable by the client is far higher. (The firm offering this insurance in 1995, Litigation Protection Ltd, fixed premiums on a sliding scale depending on the level of costs covered–£175 for an indemnity of up to £10,000, £375 for an indemnity of up to £25,000, £750 for an indemnity of up to £50,000 and £1,500 for an indemnity of up to £100,000. There is however no requirement that all clients sign up for this rather expensive insurance.

The controversy over conditional fees

The introduction of conditional fees has been controversial. Some, including the Consumers' Association, have welcomed conditional fees as a means of bringing in clients with good claims for damages who would previously have been frightened off by the cost–to the mutual benefit of lawyers and their clients. Others, including the writer, have criticised the introduction of conditional fees on the ground that they will bring more disadvantages than advantages to the general body of clients. There would seem to be four main questions:

(*1*) *Will clients be charged excessive success fees?*   Success fees are supposed to reflect the degree of risk taken by the solicitor in taking on a case where he will not in the end get a fee if he loses. But in the overwhelming majority of personal injury cases the risk is so slight as to be negligible. This is because in most personal injury cases the issue is not whether the defendant is liable but simply a matter of quantum– how much? The plaintiff normally gets *some* damages. If the client is charged, say, a 15 per cent success fee when the risk of not getting damages is very slight the client will have given up an excessive amount of his damages. The fact that insurance cover against the risk of losing in personal injury cases (potentially involving liability for many thousands of pounds) can be provided for a premium as low as under £100 is a clear indication of how rarely the insurance company expects to have to pay up under the policy.

Moreover, the solicitor's basic cost[9] on which the percentage success fee is calculated, includes both overheads and profit. The success fee under a conditional fee arrangement is pure profit. So, to take a concrete example, if the basic fee is £1,000, 70 per cent (£700) of that may represent office overheads, and 30 per cent (£300) profit. A success fee of, say, 50 per cent would be 50 per cent of 1,000, not 50 per cent of 300; similarly, a success fee of 100 per cent paid on top of the initial 1,000 would be 1,000 not 300. It

---

9   The Law Society's model Conditional Fee Agreement states that the success fee is a percentage of the basic costs and that basic costs are stated to be 'our costs for legal work' other than disbursements which are 'payments we make on your behalf' such as court fees, experts' fees, accident report fees and travelling expenses and, often, barristers' fees.

is arguable that success fees that increase the profit element by such large factors are likely to be out of all proportion to any value gained by the client.

Moreover, the client is not in a position to judge whether the solicitor has exaggerated the risks when he proposes a percentage for the success fee. The client, unavoidably, has to rely on the solicitor's fair assessment. The solicitor, being human, may honestly lean toward assessing the risk of losing as being higher rather than lower than it actually is. The client will not know and will normally accept the solicitor's assessment.

(2) Will the lawyers take too high a proportion of the damages?   As has already been seen, in a US style contingency fee arrangement the lawyer's fee is always a percentage of the damages, (typically one third). By contrast, unless the agreement provides otherwise, a conditional fee arrangement could result in the client losing the greater part or even the whole of the damages.

The Lord Chancellor's Advisory Committee on Legal Education and Conduct (see p 569 below) urged Lord Mackay that either the success should be limited to 20 per cent of costs or that there should be a cap on the percentage of the damages that could be taken.

During debates in Parliament on the Conditional Fees Agreement Order there were attempts to impose a limit of 25 per cent on the proportion of damages that could be taken by the lawyers by way of success fee. (See House of Lords, *Hansard*, 12 June 1995.) The Shadow Lord Chancellor Lord Irvine said that a cap of 20 to 25 per cent of damages was 'an essential protection for the consumer'. That would at least be a way of guaranteeing that the client would not find that the bulk or even the whole of the proceeds of the litigation could be swallowed by the lawyers. But the Lord Chancellor stated that there was no power to impose any limit on this percentage.

The Law Society's model agreement states that 'The total of the success fee and any barrister's uplift fee ... will not be more than 25% of the damages or settlement you win'. But the model agreement is not mandatory and it remains to be seen whether solicitors generally adhere to the suggestion or ignore it. Lord Irvine of Lairg QC threatened that a future Labour Government would monitor conditional fee agreements to see that the success fee charged by lawyers was not disproportionately high having regard to the risk of losing in the particular case (*op cit* p 468 above at p 11).

(3) Will conditional fees widen access to justice?   If conditional fees bring in many more clients who would otherwise have not sought legal help with their personal injury claims, that could be regarded as beneficial. That is the main reason given for introducing conditional fees. The issue was addressed by the writer in an article published just after conditional fees had been approved by both Houses of Parliament:

Michael Zander, 'Well, anyway, conditional fees should be a bonanza for lawyers', *New Law Journal*, 23 June 1995, p 920

Will conditional fees bring in new clients?
The main justification given for the introduction of conditional fees is that it will bring in clients who are now frightened off by the cost of litigation and will thereby help in the struggle to improve access to justice.

No doubt the catch phrase 'no win, no fee' will bring in some new clients. The Lord Chancellor thinks that conditional fees will encourage solicitors to have a go with a new category of more iffy cases, but it seems improbable to me that this will occur to any significant extent. Solicitors are in business and will inevitably need to see that most of their conditional fee cases are likely winners.

In any event, the proportion of iffy cases reaching solicitors is very low and will probably not change much. The major study of personal injuries conducted by the Oxford Socio-Legal Centre showed that of the tiny minority who took their case to solicitors nearly all ended up with damages. (Only 14 per cent of the sample consulted a solicitor, but 12 per cent obtained damages.)

All the 1,177 persons in the sample had suffered injury serious enough to keep the victim off normal duties for two or more weeks. Over half both of the road accident victims (53 per cent) and or work accidents (54 per cent) did not even consider the possibility of making a claim. (The figure was much the same even when they blamed someone else for the accident.) Conditional fees are unlikely to make a dent on that group.

Just over 10 per cent thought of the possibility of claiming but did nothing about it. They could in theory be affected by the catch phrase 'no win, no fee'. But since fear of the costs was only one of many reasons they gave for not doing anything, conditional fees are unlikely to make a difference for many of them. It is probable therefore that conditional fees will be used mainly for clients who would have come in anyway and whose cases usually will be as relatively straightforward as the overwhelming majority are today.

(4) *If conditional fees are ethical, why are contingency fees not?*   As has been seen, the principal reason for opposing contingency fees has been a concern over ethical standards–the fear that lawyers might stoop to 'dirty tricks' in order to make sure of winning and therefore earning a fee. The temptation is said to arise from the fact that in a contingency fee arrangement the lawyer has a financial interest in the outcome of the litigation. Whether he gets a fee is contingent on the result.

But in a conditional fee arrangement the lawyer also has a financial interest in the outcome. If the case is won the lawyer can charge a substantial success fee which can be as high as 100 per cent of the basic costs and 100 per cent of the damages. The Interim Report of Lord Woolf's Report showed that in a sample of cases in the Supreme Court Taxing Office, the average costs allowed in cases worth £12,500 or less were £12,044. If lawyers can be tempted into unethical conduct by financial temptation, the prospect of gaining a success fee of up to £12,000 in a relatively small case might provide such temptation. In any event, it is not easy to see what from this point of view is the basis of the distinction between contingency fees (forbidden) and conditional fees (permitted). (See further S King, 'Conditional Fees: Proceed with Caution', *Solicitors' Journal*, 1 March 1996, p 204.)

(n) Pro bono work done by the profession

It has probably always been the case that lawyers have done some work pro bono–ie free of charge. But in recent years the question has been raised whether such work should be institutionalised in some way.

As has been seen, members of the junior Bar, with some assistance from the Bar Council and the Inns, have for many years now run the Free Representation Unit which provides free representation to persons involved in tribunal cases. (For further details see M Phelan, 'Effective Access to Justice', *Counsel*, March/April 1996, p 16.)

Individual firms of solicitors have started to provide modest financial assistance or assistance in kind to law centres, advice centres or bodies such as Liberty. Thus in December 1992 a group of 24 City firms and barristers' chambers announced the formation of a funding consortium to help citizens' advice bureaux to provide free legal advice on debt, housing and employment matters (*The Times*, 2 December 1992). In August 1993, ten major City firms said they would do pro bono work for Liberty (*Solicitors' Journal*, 27 August 1993). In March 1995 it was announced that over 40 law firms in different parts of the country had pledged to provide at least £5,000 worth of free advice annually to community projects aimed at job creation, inner city regeneration and environmental improvements. (*The Lawyer*, 15 March 1995, p 1.) In January 1996 it was announced that the former chairman of the Bar Mr Peter Goldsmith was launching a pro bono scheme to draw on the services of members of the Bar. (*Counsel*, January/February 1996, p 5.)

The Law Society's Pro Bono Working Party which reported in May 1994 was not prepared to recommend that solicitors be obliged to take part in pro bono work. (See E Gilvarry, 'The Pro Bono Push', *Law Society's Gazette*, 25 May 1994, p 4.) But it would seem that the concept of making some contribution by way of pro bono work is gaining support within the profession.

(o) Litigation at public expense outside the legal aid scheme

Another possible exception to the normal Indemnity Rule is the idea of litigation in certain cases out of public funds without regard to means. One example is the rule that in cases brought by the Inland Revenue in the House of Lords the Revenue are normally only granted leave to appeal 'on terms'– that they will pay the costs win or lose. But the more general question was addressed both by the Evershed Committee in 1953 and by the Law Society in 1963–4.

The Evershed Committee in 1953 urged that public funds be available for litigation on points of law of exceptional public interest. The Attorney-General should have an unfettered discretion to authorize such use of public funds. He would grant a certificate. The parties would then contest the case in their own way. The means of the parties would be treated as irrelevant. The costs of both sides would be borne by the state. (*Final Report of the Committee on Supreme Court Practice and Procedure*, 1953, Cmnd 8878, paras 631 to 667.)

The Law Society thought it was unfair for the losing litigant to have to pay the costs in several situations, eg where:

(a) a new or doubtful point of law requiring judicial decisions governs the determination of the case;

(b) the construction of a statute or statutory instrument governs the determination of the case;

(c) upon appeal, it appears that the inferior court or courts were mistaken as to law or precluded from reaching a just determination by reason of the doctrine of judicial precedent [*Annual Report*, 1963–4, p 73].

It thought that a new committee should be established to determine which cases were deserving of financial support in such situations:

26. ... The Council's belief, supported by experience in the administration of the Legal Aid Scheme under the Legal Aid and Advice Acts, 1949 and 1960, is that the most appropriate body to administer these functions would be a suitably constituted committee. A National Committee, made up of persons appointed by and subject to the overall control of the Lord Chancellor, is envisaged. It is realized, however, that cases may be heard which appear to warrant subsidy from public funds but which have not received any sanction from the National Committee. This may be because of the failure of the parties to apply or because the National Committee has in fact rejected the application. In such instances it is thought proper for the court itself to be able to make a retrospective order that costs or a proportion thereof be borne by the state when, after hearing the case, it considers such an order to be warranted.

The Law Society thought that the state ought to pay also where costs were thrown away or lost through no fault of the litigant because of the administrative inefficiency of the system. This theme was later taken up by JUSTICE, which in 1969 proposed that there should be a fund out of which litigants could be paid for costs for which they ought not to be held responsible. Under this proposal it was suggested that the costs which should be reimbursed were those which would not have been incurred if the system had provided the right answer first time. So where a case was appealed successfully from the High Court to the Court of Appeal, the ultimately winning party would get his costs from the loser whilst the loser would be able to claim from the Fund the amount of costs incurred attributable to the appeal. He would remain liable for the costs at first instance since these would have been incurred in any event.

The proposal covered appeals on fact or law and costs thrown away through no fault of anyone such as the illness or death of a judge.

It was suggested that the fund should be financed out of a small increase in the cost of issuing proceedings in both the county and the High Court (*A Proposal for a Suitors' Fund*, 1969). See also C Wegg-Prosser, 'Proposals for a Suitors' Fund', *Law Society's Gazette*, 1973, p 2270.

By 1983 nothing had been done to implement the ideas of the Evershed Committee, the Law Society or JUSTICE. The Royal Commission on Legal Services in its report in October 1979 said that it supported the Evershed Committee's proposal with the variation that, in addition to the Attorney-General, the judge should be able also to certify the case as one suitable for public subsidy. It was not always possible to identify such a case at the outset and the court should be able to make such a determination (Cmnd 7648, 1979, vol 1, para 16.21).

In its response to the Royal Commission's report, the Government announced that it was considering whether costs thrown away by the illness or death of a judge should be reimbursed. But it was not persuaded that it would be right to finance out of public funds the resolution of points of law of general importance, other than in the course of litigation–legal aid for which was available in the normal way (Cmnd 9077, 1983, p 19).

The Government's intention to do something was implemented in the Administration of Justice Act 1985, s 53, which provided that the Lord Chancellor may 'if he thinks fit' reimburse the litigant's costs thrown away through the death or incapacity of a judge. The costs to be reimbursed would be either agreed or determined by taxation.

CHAPTER 7

Appeals

An appeal system is necessary to perform a variety of functions. One is to provide an opportunity for the disappointed litigant to test the validity of the decision at first instance. In most, though not all, types of case the appeal system allows the litigant at least two chances to get the right result. A second purpose of the appeal system is to preserve some measure of uniformity in the decision-making of lower courts. The doctrine of precedent is an important aide in this process. Lower courts are encouraged and in some circumstances are required to follow the indications of the higher courts on matters of law and practice, the assessment of damages and even fact-finding. (This topic is considered in the writer's *The Law-Making Process*, 4th edn, Butterworths, 1994.) A third function of the appeal court is to keep the law abreast of changing circumstances.

In the earliest days of the system the appeal process was exceedingly limited. In civil cases, procedure was by writ of error and the basis of the appeal was that there was some error appearing on the face of the record. Since only certain things appeared on the record there were many issues on which no appeal was possible. Later the courts allowed each party to move a Bill of Exceptions, in which the trial judge was asked to note that a particular point had been rejected by the judge and this was then treated as part of the record for the purpose of an appeal. This helped somewhat, but it was still limited in scope and required the point to be seen and taken at the trial itself. Moreover, a further problem was that if the appeal was successful the court had no power to substitute its own decision for that of the court below. It could only order a fresh trial.

Appeals on questions of fact were even more difficult. Originally, when cases were heard by juries and the jury was supposed to decide cases of its own knowledge a wrong verdict was practically a matter for the disciplining of the jury. A writ of attaint could be brought to try the truth of the jury's verdict and, if the attaint jury thought the first jury was mistaken, the first jury was liable to punishment. It was only in the seventeenth century that juries were no longer liable to be punished for their verdicts and that the common law courts were prepared to order a new trial on the ground that a jury's decision had been against the weight of the evidence.

In criminal cases the situation was even more remarkable. There was no appeal from conviction at all until well into the nineteenth century. At some point the judges started informally to refer a question of law to other judges before they summed up to the jury or before sentence was executed. In 1848 this informal arrangement was regularized with the establishment of the Court for Crown Cases Reserved. But it was still available only on reference from the judge–though the procedure was extended also to quarter sessions. Parliament considered the question of an appeal in criminal cases no fewer than twenty-eight times in the last seventy years of the nineteenth century. But it was only after an especially serious miscarriage of justice, the Adolf Beck case, that the Court of Criminal Appeal was finally established in 1907.

1. THE STRUCTURE OF APPEAL COURTS

(a) Civil cases

In the nineteenth century the appeal courts in civil cases were in a considerable muddle. Appeals from the old Court of Common Pleas went to the Court of King's Bench. Appeals from the old Court of Exchequer went to the Court of Exchequer Chamber. When the Court of King's Bench began hearing cases at first instance in the sixteenth century, a second Court of Exchequer Chamber was set up to hear appeals from that body. In 1830 the two courts of Exchequer Chamber were replaced by a third. This court was established to hear appeals from all three common-law courts–Queen's Bench, Common Pleas and Exchequer. The members of the court were drawn from the two from which the appeal did not come. In addition there was the Court of Appeal in Chancery which heard appeals from the Court of Chancery, not in the traditional way by writ of error but by a rehearing. Appeals from the Court of Admiralty went to the Privy Council and from 1833 to the Judicial Committee of the Privy Council. Appeals from the Divorce Court established in 1857 went at first from the single judge to the full court and from 1868 to the House of Lords.

The Judicature Commissioners reported in 1869 and recommended a new structure. They proposed that there should be one Supreme Court, comprising a High Court and a Court of Appeal. The Court of Appeal should take appeals from all the divisions of the High Court. This reform was achieved in the Judicature Acts 1873–5. Its constitution and the statutory framework are now to be found in the Supreme Court Act 1981. Appeals from the county court also go direct to the Court of Appeal. In 1966 the Court of Criminal Appeal became the Court of Appeal Criminal Division, so that from that date there was a Civil Division and a Criminal Division of that court.

The Civil Division is presided over by the Master of the Rolls and sits in several divisions–always in London. Lord Justices of Appeal sit as the judges. The Court of Appeal normally has three judges, but there is power in the Supreme Court Act 1981 for two-judge courts to hear appeals on interlocutory matters or any other matter prescribed by order made by the Lord Chancellor. For very important cases occasionally the Court of Appeal sits with five judges.

Appeals from the civil jurisdiction of the magistrates' courts go to the Divisional Court of the Family Division, which consists of two or three judges of the High Court. Appeals from the Divisional Court in a civil case lie to the Court of Appeal.

Appeals from the Court of Appeal go to the House of Lords. In modern times the House of Lords consists of judges specifically appointed for the purpose known as Lords of Appeal in Ordinary, plus the Lord Chancellor and any former Lord Chancellors.

The judicial functions of the House of Lords are as old as Parliament itself. By 1600 it enjoyed an undisputed role as a court of appeal. It heard cases by way of writ of error from the Courts of Exchequer Chamber. But until 1844 lay peers were able to participate in the judicial work, and occasionally they did so. The appellate jurisdiction of the House of Lords was threatened and almost abolished in the court reforms of the 1873–5 era but in the end it was preserved in the Appellate Jurisdiction Act 1876, which provided for salaried law lords. Though nominally the final appeal remained in the hands of the hereditary chamber, in reality it was transferred to a court of law under the control of a professional judiciary.

Normally the House of Lords sits with five judges but on occasion seven are empanelled. The hearings are conducted in one of the committee rooms of the Palace of Westminster, but judgment is always given in the legislative chamber itself. Nowadays the judgments (called 'speeches') are not read; they are handed to the parties and the procedure consists simply of the presiding judge putting the issue to the vote as if it was an ordinary legislative matter. ('My Lords, I beg to move that the Report of the Appellate Committee be now considered.') When this has been approved ('the Contents have it'), each law lord stands up in order of seniority and says merely that he would allow or dismiss the appeal 'for the reasons given in my printed speech'.

(b) Criminal cases

Appeals from the quarter sessions and assize courts went to the Court of Criminal Appeal. When the Court of Appeal Criminal Division was established in 1966, they went to that court instead. Then in 1972 when the crown courts replaced the quarter sessions and assize courts, appeals accordingly went from the crown court to the Court of Appeal Criminal Division. From the Court of Appeal Criminal Division, appeals go, with leave to the House of Lords.

Appeals from decisions of the magistrates' courts in criminal cases may go in two alternative directions. There can be an appeal to the crown court, which sits for this purpose with a judge and two or more magistrates but without a jury. Alternatively appeals lie by way of case stated (see p 488 below) from the magistrates' court to the Divisional Court of the Queen's Bench Division sitting with two or three High Court judges' though the Lord Chief Justice often presides in the Divisional Court. Appeals from the appellate jurisdiction of the crown court also go to the Divisional Court of the QBD on a point of law by way of case stated. Appeals in criminal cases go direct from the Divisional Court to the House of Lords.

(c) The Judicial Committee of the Privy Council

The Judicial Committee of the Privy Council is primarily a Commonwealth court. It is the final court of appeal for those relatively few Commonwealth territories which still retain the appeal to Her Majesty in Council. These include New Zealand, Jamaica and Barbados. It also hears appeals from dependent territories such as Hong Kong (until 1997), Gibraltar and Bermuda. Its jurisdiction, which is based on the Judicial Committee Act 1833, was enlarged to enable it to hear appeals from certain republican countries in the Commonwealth such as the Gambia, Singapore, and Trinidad and

Tobago. (The right of appeal from Australia was abolished in 1986. Singapore abolished the appeal to the Judicial Committee in 1994.) The judges are mainly those who sit also in the House of Lords.

2. THE APPEAL PROCESS

(a) A right to appeal?

In most types of case there is a right to appeal, but in some circumstances it is necessary to seek leave and in a few there is no appeal at all.

In the case of civil cases heard in the High Court, there is normally a right of appeal. But there are some exceptions. One is in regard to appeals on interlocutory points where normally leave is required either from the body from which the appeal is taken (eg the judge in chambers) or from the Court of Appeal itself. But leave is not required to appeal in interlocutory matters where the liberty of the subject or the custody of an infant is at stake, nor in injunction cases (Supreme Court Act 1981, s 18). Another exception is for proceedings under Order 53 of the Rules of the Supreme Court in the Divisional Court by way of judicial review.

In regard to appeals from the county court, prior to 1981 there was no appeal at all even with leave on questions of fact unless the amount in dispute was over £200. On questions of law, there was a right of appeal if the amount in dispute was over £20, but for sums less than that leave had to be obtained.

The Supreme Court Act 1981 gave the Lord Chancellor *carte blanche* to make orders regarding the requirement of leave to appeal. Such orders would, however, have to be laid before Parliament and be subject to annulment by a resolution of either House (Sch 3, para 14). The County Court Appeals Order 1981 (SI 1981/1749) provided that no appeal could be brought without leave from a county court if it involved an amount less than half the maximum jurisdiction for the county court (£5,000 in 1984). Leave was not needed, however, if the case concerned an injunction or custody of or access to a child.

The 1990 Courts and Legal Services Act abolished the £5,000 limit on the county courts' jurisdiction. The Act provided that rules may be made for a requirement of leave to appeal. Under the County Court Appeals Order 1991 (SI 1991/1877) leave is now required for cases involving amounts of up to £5,000, or where the value is not quantifiable. But there is an unfettered right of appeal when the decision concerns an injunction on the upbringing of a child.

It seems likely that the rule making power will be used to effect further reductions in the 'right of appeal'. Lord Donaldson, the Master of the Rolls, in his Review of the Legal Year 1989–90, said that the present categories of case where leave was required had no rival 'for sheer complexity and lack of logic'. The new power in the Courts and Legal Services Act would give the Rule Committee 'power to undertake a root and branch re-appraisal of the categories of case in which leave will be required'. The judges, he said, had no doubt that it was possible to identify hopeless appeals at a very early stage. In order to make sure, they had conducted an experiment for three months which consisted of notionally granting or refusing leave in cases where no leave was required, and then looking at what happened in cases 'refused leave'. All but one had been dismissed after a full hearing, and the one exception was transformed by a dramatic change of circumstances on the day before the hearing. It was also a fact that the success rate in cases needing leave was higher than where no leave was required–32 per cent against 24 per cent. (See *New Law Journal*, 9 November 1990, p 1569.)

A new procedure had been introduced in November 1989 (RSC Ord 59, r 4– described in *RG Carter Ltd v Clarke* [1990] 2 All ER 209). The procedure was designed to have applications for leave dealt with at minimal expense, and, if possible, without any court hearing. In essence this provides for a provisional decision given on the basis of a paper application. Either side can ask for the decision to be reviewed. Since then 334 such applications for leave had been considered. In 104 (31 per cent) leave was given and in only seven of these did the respondent seek to set the leave aside. A further 40 (12 per cent) were adjourned by the judge for oral hearing. Of the 190 applications which were refused, 103 were renewed by the applicant in open court– but the overall result was that the expense of a court hearing was avoided in 54 per cent of applications. Lord Donaldson concluded 'This is very encouraging' (*ibid*).

Scc also *Practice Direction* [1990] 3 All ER 981 describing the new regime in the Court of Appeal Civil Division for processing appeals. A team of office lawyers had been added to the strength of the Registrar of Civil Appeals. They assist the staff in processing the papers.

Appeal from the Divisional Court to the Court of Appeal in a civil case requires leave either from the Divisional Court or from the Court of Appeal.

Appeals to the House of Lords always require leave–either of the Court of Appeal or of the House of Lords itself. Such appeals are supposed always to be on points of law of general public importance. (See L Blom-Cooper and G Drewry, *Final Appeal*, Clarendon, 1972, pp 117 51.)

In criminal cases no leave is required for an appeal from the magistrates' court– whether by way of rehearing to the crown court, or by way of case stated on a point of law to the Divisional Court of the Queen's Bench Division. Leave is, however, required for an appeal from the crown court to the Court of Appeal Criminal Division. The only exception was for an appeal on a point of law only, where no leave was required until 1995 when the exception was abolished by the Criminal Appeal Act 1995, s 1. Leave is also required for an appeal to the House of Lords, either from the Court of Appeal (or the Divisional Court) or from the House of Lords itself. In addition, in a criminal case, the Court of Appeal (or the Divisional Court) must certify that the case is one raising a point of law of general public importance. To this extent it is harder to appeal in a criminal than in a civil case, since there is no equivalent requirement in civil cases. The Runciman Royal Commission on Criminal Justice recommended that the requirement of a certificate be abolished (p 178, para 79), but this has not yet been implemented.

Appeals by the prosecution

Normally the prosecution has no right of appeal against an acquittal, but there are two exceptions. One was in regard to an appeal on a point of law by way of case stated from the magistrates' court to the Divisional Court. If the prosecution are successful, the result of such an appeal is that the case can be sent back to the magistrates with a direction to convict or to reconsider the matter in the light of the Divisional Court's ruling on the point of law. But where the prosecution applies instead for an order of judicial review to quash an acquittal for some breach of natural justice or lack of jurisdiction (see p 523 below), there is no power to do this unless the original trial can be held to have been a total nullity. (See *R v Dorking Justices, ex p Harrington* [1983] 3 All ER 29, applying *R v Middlesex Quarter Sessions Chairman, ex p DPP* [1952] 2 QB 758, in which the court held that nothing could be done when the trial judge quite wrongly told the jury that it 'was a complete waste of their time to listen to the prosecution evidence' and invited them to acquit, which they did. (See WT West, 'Wrongful Acquittals', *Justice of the Peace*, 8 October 1983, p 647.)

Until 1972 there was no right for the prosecution to appeal from acquittals in the crown court. But the Criminal Justice Act of that year gave the prosecution a limited right of appeal. Section 36 provided for appeals to the Court of Appeal by the Attorney-General in a case tried on indictment where the defendant has been acquitted. The section limits such appeals to points of law. The result of the appeal does not, however, affect the outcome of the trial. For a comment on the section, see DJ. Stephens, 'In Jeopardy' (1972) *Criminal Law Review*, p 361, and J Jaconelli, 'Attorney-General's References– a Problematic Device' (1981) *Criminal Law Review*, p 543. Lord Widgery said, in *A-G's Reference (No 1 of 1975)* [1975] 3 WLR 11 at 13, that the procedure should be used exclusively' for short but important points which require a quick ruling of this court before a potentially false decision of law has too wide a circulation in the courts'. After the Court of Appeal have given their view they can refer the point to the House of Lords if they believe the point ought to be considered by the House. But there is no power to refer theoretical questions of law (*A-G's Reference (No 4 of 1979)* (1980) 71 Cr App Rep 341).

At the Conservative Party Conference in October 1983 the Home Secretary announced that it was his intention to introduce a new right of appeal for the prosecution against excessively lenient sentences passed by crown courts. The appeal would have to be taken by the Attorney-General and the result would not affect the sentence actually imposed on the accused in that case. It would simply have a declaratory effect for later cases. The announcement attracted a good deal of criticism from the judges and was not pursued at the time. But in 1986 it surfaced again. The Criminal Justice Bill introduced by Mr Douglas Hurd in November of that year contained a clause to that effect–providing for the Attorney-General to get an advisory opinion on 'the principles which should be observed in sentencing in similar cases in the future' wherever he thought that a sentence raised a question of public importance. Such a reference, however, would require the leave of the Court of Appeal. The Bill fell through the intervention of the General Election but it was re-introduced in June 1987. There was some criticism from Conservative MPs and others that the new power would be advisory only, with no effect on the actual case.

In October 1987 at the Conservative Party Conference the Home Secretary announced that he had decided to change the Criminal Justice Bill by giving the Attorney-General a right of appeal against overly lenient sentences which *would* have an effect on the disposition of the actual case. This intention was carried into effect by s 36 of the Criminal Justice Act 1988. See S Shutz, 'Prosecution Appeals Against Sentence', 57 *Modern Law Review*, 1994, pp 745–72.

Only the Attorney-General can activate this new power and it requires the leave of the Court of Appeal. The Attorney-General told the House of Commons in May 1991 that to date there had been 26 cases referred to the Court of Appeal and that in 24 of these a substantially heavier sentence had been imposed. In October 1995 the Attorney General in a Written Answer said that so far in 1995, 60 cases had been referred to the Court of Appeal under the power. Of these, 20 had so far been heard–all resulting in increased sentences. (*Hansard*, vol 265, 30 October 1995, col 59)

The Royal Commission on Criminal Justice recommended that where a person is convicted of conspiracy to pervert the course of justice by 'jury nobbling' in a case which led to an acquittal the prosecution should be entitled to restart the case against the acquitted defendant (p 177, para 74). Legislation to give effect to this recommendation was introduced by the Government in the Criminal Procedure and Investigations Bill, Part VI headed 'Tainted Acquittals'. Under these provisions the High Court would be given the power to quash the conviction if satisfied that the acquittal would not have occurred had it not been for the interference with or intimidation of the jury.

The Royal Commission rejected the suggestion that the prosecution should have a right to appeal against a perverse verdict or where a defendant was acquitted, (or convicted on a less serious charge) as a result of an error by a prosecution witness. ('We have every sympathy for the victims and families of victims in such cases, especially where they have suffered bereavement or injury. We believe, however, that the right answer is for the investigating and prosecuting authorities to prepare their cases thoroughly' (p 177, para 76).

(b) Practice and procedure of appeals

An appeal is said to be by way of rehearing, but if this means to start afresh with all the witnesses, there is only one type of English appeal which follows this mode. That is the appeal from the magistrates' court to the crown court, where the case starts afresh as if it had never been heard before. In all other cases the appeal court hears the appeal on the basis of the decision below. In other words, the appellant argues that something went wrong in the court below and for that purpose he will normally have to show what did happen–by producing the judgment which he claims was wrong in law, or by having a transcript of the whole or part of the proceedings below to show that, for instance, the decision was against the weight of the evidence or that some impropriety occurred. Occasionally, but very rarely indeed, the Court of Appeal will be prepared to listen to witnesses, but only if they are new and then only in exceptional circumstances. Otherwise, testimony is presented to the appeal court via the written word through the transcript of the trial.

There are several peculiarities of the appeal system which should be noted.

(1) The procedure for criminal appeals to the Court of Appeal

Applying for leave

The procedure for appeals to the Court of Appeal Criminal Division is unusual. As has been seen, all appeals require leave, which is usually sought from the Court of Appeal. Applications for leave are made to a single judge (normally a High Court judge) who deals with the matter by considering the papers only. There is no hearing. If he refuses leave, the applicant has the right to renew the application by asking for leave from the full court of three judges. This is at an actual hearing in open court, though usually neither the prosecution nor the applicant is present. It is very rare for leave to be given. If leave is given, quite frequently the hearing of the application is combined with the hearing of the appeal, counsel having been warned in advance to prepare themselves for the argument on the merits.

One unsatisfactory feature of the system is that, if the defendant is legally aided (99% are), his lawyer's duties cease after he has advised as to whether there are grounds of appeal and if so, has drafted them. The legal aid certificate does not cover advice as to whether to renew an application once it has been turned down by the single judge. Application for legal aid for the renewal hearing can however be made to the Registrar.

The Runciman Royal Commission (p 167, para 25) said this was a gap in the system which should be closed by providing that the original legal aid cover also the question of renewing the application after it has turned down by the single judge. (On legal advice for would-be appellants see further p 488 below.)

If leave to appeal is granted, the Registrar of Criminal Appeals prepares a summary of the appellant's case[1] and assigns counsel, usually the same barrister who appeared at the trial. The Registrar therefore has a dual function, as administrative officer of the court and in something like the role of instructing solicitor.

The success rate on a renewal to the full court is statistically much affected by whether the appellant is represented. In 1989 there were 6,853 applications for leave to appeal considered by the single judge. The Criminal Appeal Office estimated that 95 per cent of these were legally represented. (K Malleson, *Review of the Appeal Process*, Royal Commission on Criminal Justice, Research Study No 17, 1993, p 32.)

However, in a sample of cases between October and December 1990, only 22 per cent of defendants who renewed their application from the single judge to the full court had counsel, but their success rate was 48 per cent compared with only 15 per cent of the much larger number without counsel. (Evidence of Lord Chancellor's Department to Runciman Royal Commission, Chap 4, Table 2.)

Time loss rules

The court can order that some of the time spent appealing does not count toward the sentence, as a penalty for starting a frivolous application. This threat acts powerfully on the minds of prisoners. In 1966 the grounds for quashing a conviction were altered and became more favourable to the appellant (see p 501 below). This resulted in a flood of new applications for leave to appeal, which were running at the rate of about 12,000 a year compared with about 2,000 in 1963. This caused an announcement to be made in 1970 by the Lord Chief Justice, Lord Parker that in future the power to order that time not count if the application was thought to be frivolous would be used more often (*Practice Note* [1970] 1 WLR 663). The announcement had an immediate and dramatic effect. The numbers of applications for leave went down by about half and remained at that lower figure of some 6,000 a year for several years.

Would-be appellants were reminded of the existence of the power in a further *Practice Note* in 1980–[1980] 1 All ER 555. The warning was in fierce and forbidding

1   The summary, which can run to many pages, is prepared by lawyers employed by the Registrar or by barristers employed ad hoc. They do not make recommendations. Formerly they were not seen by the appellant's lawyers, but shortly after he became Lord Chief Justice this was changed by Lord Taylor .

terms: 'It may be expected that such a direction [ordering loss of time for a hopeless appeal] will normally be made unless the grounds are not only settled and signed by counsel, but also supported by the written opinion of counsel'.

What is not realised by prisoners is how rarely the power to order that time spent appealing should not count is exercised or that the power is limited to adding on 90 days to the sentence. An action against the UK Government under the European Convention on Human Rights challenging the legality of the power was rejected by the European Court in March 1987. The European Court of Human Rights was told that, although there were no statistics, loss of time was ordered in some 60 or so cases per year by the single judge or the full court. The normal order was for 28 days to be added on, though such orders ranged from 7 days to 64 days (*Case of Monnell and Morris*). In the nine month period from October 1990 to July 1991 five such orders were made, each for 28 days. (Evidence of the Lord Chancellor's Department to the Runciman Royal Commission on Criminal Justice, Chap. 6, para 6.1.)

Research conducted for the Runciman Royal Commission on Criminal Justice showed that there is a great deal of misinformation in the prisons about the time loss rules. Many prisoners are under the erroneous impression that *all* the time spent appealing can be added on by the Court of Appeal. (This error is less surprising when seen against the fact that many solicitors appear to share the same misapprehension and that over half of all solicitors responding to the survey thought that the Court of Appeal still had the power to increase sentences which was in fact abolished in 1966!), A third of the sample of prisoners who did not appeal said the threat of time being added on had been the reason. (J Plotnikoff and R Woolfson, *Information and Advice for Prisoners about Grounds for Appeal and the Appeals Process*, Royal Commission Research Study No 18, 1993, pp 79–82.)

The Runciman Commission recommended that prisoners (and lawyers) be made aware of the true position. ('We think it wrong that appellants who spend several months awaiting appeal should be left with the impression that if they fail, those months will be added to their sentences. Nor should they have reason to fear that the Court of Appeal will increase their sentence' (pp 165-66, para 19).) It recommended that the Court of Appeal issue a new Practice Direction dealing with the issue and that the official guides issued by the Criminal Appeal Office, the Bar Council and the Law Society make matters clear, even though the result would be likely to be an increase in the number of applications for leave to appeal. ('We would regard it as an unavoidable result of correcting an important piece of misinformation common among prisoners' (*ibid*).) This recommendation has however not been acted upon.

The great majority of appeals are against sentence. In the years between 1987 and 1994 the number of applications for leave to appeal against conviction has fluctuated between a low of some 1,700 and a high of some 2,300; the number of appeals against sentence fluctuated in the same period between a low of some 4,600 and a high of some 7,800. (*Judicial Statistics*, 1994, Table 1.7.) In 1994, of the applications for leave to appeal considered by the single judge, 2,342 were against conviction in the crown court and 5,050 were against sentence. Of the applications for leave to appeal considered by a single judge, 27 per cent (514) were granted against conviction and 25 per cent (1,213) against sentence. (In 1993 it was 36% for both.) Of those applications which were refused, 38 per cent (527) were renewed to the full court against conviction and 16 per cent (573) against sentence. Only 27 of the renewed applications in regard to conviction and 56 in regard to sentence were granted.

Legal advice for appellants in criminal cases

The Criminal Justice Act 1967 introduced provisions regarding legal advice on the question of an appeal in cases where the accused is represented at the trial on legal aid. Under these provisions a defence barrister in a legally aided case must advise his client at the end of the case whether he has grounds of appeal, and if so, to draft those grounds. The procedure is set out in a pamphlet issued by the Criminal Appeal Office entitled *A Guide to Proceedings in the Court of Appeal, Criminal Division*, 1990–see also *Practice Note* [1991] 2 All ER 924, 930–1. The procedure requires that counsel fill out a form right away at court which will tell the client whether it is thought that there are grounds of appeal or whether counsel needs time to consider the matter. He is required then to deliver his advice in writing within 21 days. Research done for the Runciman Royal Commission by Plotnikoff and Woolfson (*op cit* above) showed that in various respects this system was not functioning as it should. Thus 9 per cent of prisoners said they had not been visited in the cells at the end of the case and 23 per cent said they had been visited but an appeal had not been discussed. The Royal Commission said it regarded these as serious matters and called on both branches of the profession to 'take all necessary steps to ensure that practitioners not only perform their duty to see the client at the end of the case, as most do, but also give preliminary advice both orally and in writing' (pp 164–65, para 14).

The Lord Chancellor's Evidence to the Runciman Royal Commission stated that about 94 per cent of those who ask the Court of Appeal Criminal Division for leave to appeal have had legal advice because the grounds have been settled by counsel or solicitors. Where it appears that the defendant has submitted his own grounds, the Criminal Appeal Office writes to the solicitors who acted at the trial to ask if advice was given. A survey of 67 'own ground' cases from July to September 1991 indicated that no advice had been given in 8 cases. This represented 12 per cent of the 'own grounds' cases and 0.8 per cent of all the cases received in that period (*ibid*, Chap 4, para 4.5).

Note–Public Defender for post-conviction aid to defendants

JUSTICE, in its 1987 report *Public Defender*, argued that an office of public defender should be established to conduct cases for defendants after they have been convicted. This would be especially valuable where counsel advises that there are no grounds of appeal, where leave to appeal has been refused and where the lawyers at the trial were negligent or incompetent. A Public Defender should have the power to institute an appeal whether or not counsel in the case agreed.

(2) Appeals by way of case stated

An appeal may be brought against a decision of the magistrates' court on the ground that it is wrong in law or in excess of jurisdiction, by asking the magistrates to state a case to the Divisional Court (Magistrates' Courts Act 1980, s 111 (1)). This must be done within 21 days. There is no power to give an extension of time. In a criminal case the prosecution may ask for a case to be stated, as can the defence. The magistrates draw up a statement of the facts found, the cases cited, the decision and the issue for the consideration of the Divisional Court. If the appeal is based on the argument that there was no evidence on which the magistrates could have reached their decision, the case stated also includes a resumé of the evidence. The court supplies the parties with a draft of the case to be stated and invites their comments. In the event that a party is dissatisfied with the way in which the case has been put, he can apply to the Divisional Court asking the case to be remitted to the magistrates for restatement of the facts. The magistrates can refuse to state a case on the grounds that it is a frivolous request. (See generally A Murdie, 'Appeals by Case Stated from the Magistrates' Court', *Solicitors' Journal*, 6 October 1995, p 984; JA Backhouse, 'Right of Appeal by way of Case Stated–Should it be Simplified?', *Justice of the Peace*, 16 May, 1992, p 310.)

(3) Leapfrog appeals from the High Court to the House of Lords

In 1969 a new procedure was devised to enable appeals to go direct from the High Court to the House of Lords in certain limited circumstances:

Administration of Justice Act 1969

s 12(3)–that a point of law of general public importance is involved in that decision and that that point of law either:

(a) related wholly or mainly to the construction of an enactment or of a statutory instrument, and has been fully argued in the proceedings and fully considered in the judgment of the judge in the proceedings, or
(b) is one in respect of which the judge is bound by a decision of the Court of Appeal or of the House of Lords in previous proceedings, and was fully considered in the judgments given by the Court of Appeal or the House of Lords (as the case may be) in those previous proceedings.. . .

But the power has been used very little.

(4) General

In the early 1960s a team of eminent English and American judges and lawyers spent a period in each other's countries studying the appeal system. The object was for each to assess the strengths and weaknesses of both systems. One member of the American team reported on the results. Extracts from his report are included here on certain aspects of the findings of the two teams.

Delmar Karlen, 'Appeal in England and the United States', 78 *Law Quarterly Review*, 1962, p 371

The decision
In the United States, almost all decisions are reserved and rendered in written form. Rarely is one pronounced from the bench. Furthermore, an attempt is always made to have the judges agree upon an opinion for the court as a whole, or, if that cannot be done, to secure as broad a base of agreement as possible. While concurring opinions are not unusual and even multiple separate dissents not unknown, it is not expected that each judge will express his own views. The ideal is a unanimous opinion for the court, or, failing that, one majority opinion and one dissent.

In England, few decisions are either reserved or written, In the Court of Appeal, the practice is for each judge to express his individual views orally and extemporaneously immediately upon the close of argument. In the Court of Criminal Appeal a single opinion for the court is customarily expressed, but almost always orally and extemporaneously. Only in the House of Lords and the Privy Council are decisions customarily reserved and written.

The American approach entails different internal operating procedures than are usual in England. Conferences, both formal and informal, are a prominent feature of American practice. So are exchanges of memoranda and draft opinions. On the other hand, since reading and writing are by their nature solitary operations, American judges, who are compelled to do much of both, spend many, if not most, of their working hours alone. They are frequently required to shift their attention from one case to another and then back again, because, with cases being heard in batches, several are awaiting decision at any given time.

To the limited extent that the English practice conforms to the American pattern, the same internal procedures doubtless apply. In the great majority of English appeals, however, the judges follow a vastly different routine. Most of their working time is spent together sitting on the bench, listening and talking rather than reading and writing. The discussions they hold are brief and seemingly casual, although highly economical, by reason of the fact that cases are heard and decided one at a time. The judges' minds are already focused on the problems at hand and not distracted by other cases which have been heard and are awaiting decision. They whisper between themselves on the bench; they converse as they walk to and from the courtroom; and they indirectly make comments to each other as they carry on Socratic dialogues with counsel. But they do not ordinarily exchange memoranda or draft opinions or engage in full scale conferences.

In short, the appellate judge in England spends most of his working time in open court, relatively little in chambers, whereas his counterpart in America spends most of his working time in chambers, and relatively little in open court. This is neatly illustrated by the times of sitting for comparable courts in the two nations. In the United States Court of Appeals for the Second Circuit, each judge hears arguments one week out of four, and uses the other three for studying written briefs and records on appeal, conferring with his brother judges, and writing opinions. By way of contrast, each judge on the English Court of Appeal hears arguments, day after day, five days a week, throughout each term. [As will be seen it is now four days a week (ed).]

Supporting personnel

In the United States, most appellate judges have law clerks, sometimes more than one. These typically are young men, recently graduated from law school with fine academic records, who serve for a period of a year or two. They are chosen by and answerable to the judges, although paid out of public funds. The services they perform vary greatly from one judge to another, but in general they carry on research, prepare memoranda, discuss the cases to be decided with the judges for whom they work, and sometimes even draft opinions or parts of opinions to be rendered. They participate in the decisional process to the extent that their judges wish them to participate. . .

In England there are no law clerks. Since typically no briefs are used, and since most opinions are rendered by the judges extemporaneously at the close of oral argument, it is difficult to see what use law clerks would be in most English appellate courts. But even in the House of Lords and the Privy Council, where written arguments of a sort are permitted and where decisions are customarily reserved and rendered in written form, law clerks are unknown.

Finality

In England, appeals terminate litigation, subject only to the possibility of further review in a higher court or a retrial in the court below. Rehearings are not permitted in any type of case.

Even new trials are prohibited in criminal cases:[2] if an error is found which the reviewing court cannot classify as harmless, it has no alternative but to quash the conviction and set the accused free. There is no federal system to create conflicts between the different jurisdictions and thus permit successful applications for the same relief to different tribunals. There is no expansion of the writ of habeas corpus or any similar remedy in such a way as to allow the re-examination of judgments rendered by legally constituted tribunals acting within their jurisdiction. Finally, the doctrine of precedent is sufficiently rigid to render pointless any relitigation of a question once unequivocally decided. If a citizen is unhappy about the law, he had better seek corrective action in Parliament rather than squander his wealth on hopeless litigation.

In the United States, appellate decisions possess less finality. New trials can be granted in all types of cases, criminal as well as civil. Rehearings are frequently asked for and occasionally allowed. Existing side by side with appeals are a variety of methods of collateral attack, including habeas corpus, sometimes entailing successive re-examination of a single case by courts of coordinate jurisdiction.

Finally, the American doctrine of precedent is such that a decision is never beyond the reach of challenge in a new lawsuit. If conditions or thinking have changed, sometimes if only the personnel of the court has changed, there is always the possibility that the unwanted decision may be overruled.

Oral argument

In the United States, oral arguments are secondary in importance to the briefs, and are rigidly limited in duration. In the United States Supreme Court, one hour is allowed to each side, but in many appellate courts, less time than that is permitted, frequently no more than fifteen minutes or a half-hour for each side. Reading by counsel is frowned upon. The judges do not wish to hear what they can read for themselves. They expect to get all the information they need about the judgment below, the evidence, and the authorities relied upon from studying the briefs and record on appeal. They do not even encourage counsel to discuss in detail the precedents claimed to govern the decision, preferring to do that job by themselves in the relative privacy of their chambers, with or without the assistance of law clerks.

In England, where there are no written briefs,[3] oral arguments are all-important. They are never arbitrarily limited in duration. While some last for only a few minutes, others go on for many days, even weeks. The only controls ordinarily exercised over the time of oral arguments are informal, *ad hoc* suggestions from the judges. Thus when counsel wishes to cite a case as authority, the presiding judge may ask him: for what proposition? If the judges indicate that they accept the proposition as stated, there is no need to read the case. Similarly if counsel has persuaded the judges on a certain point, they may indicate that it is unnecessary for him to pursue it further. If counsel for the appellant, by the time he finishes his argument, has failed to persuade the court that the decision below should be reversed or modified, the court informs counsel for the respondent that it does not wish to hear from him at all, and proceeds forthwith to deliver judgment. Despite such controls as these, the time spent in England in oral arguments tends to be very much greater than that spent in the United States.

In recent years, the average duration of argument in the Court of Appeal has been about a day and a quarter per case, and in the House of Lords and the Privy Council, about three days per case. Much of the time, perhaps half, has been spent by counsel reading aloud to the court. It is in this way that the judges have learned what transpired in the court below (by listening to a reading of the judgment and such parts of the evidence as may be relevant), what errors are complained of by counsel (by listening to a reading of the notice of appeal, which is required to specify the errors), and the authorities relied on by counsel (by listening to a reading of statutes and cases, either in their entirety or in large part).

2   This is no longer true, see p 517 below (ed.).
3   Written 'skeleton arguments' are, however, now required–see below (ed).

As a result of the exchange between the English and American teams, the Court of Appeal experimented with a different procedure, under which the members of the court read the pleadings, the order under appeal, the notice of appeal and the trial judge's judgment together with any cases cited by him. The aim was to save the time spent in counsel reading to the court. The experiment was, however, unpopular and after a while it was abandoned.

In 1982 Lord Denning retired after more than twenty years as Master of the Rolls. His passion had been the law and justice. He was succeeded by Sir John (now Lord) Donaldson who showed immediately that one of his main interests was efficiency and the running of the system. In October 1982 he made a lengthy statement on changes that were needed (see *New Law Journal*, 14 October 1982, p 959, for full text):

For a long time the delay in hearing civil appeals has been causing considerable anxiety. In February 1978, when there were about 650 appeals awaiting hearing, a committee was appointed under the chairmanship of Lord Scarman to examine ways and means of relieving the pressure. After a detailed study of the procedures of the court, it made a number of recommendations. The two most important were the creation of the office of Registrar and a change in the law to enable a single judge of the Court of Appeal to deal with procedural matters. Both required legislation and until the passing of the Supreme Court Act 1981, little progress could be made. Meanwhile the number of appeals outstanding at the end of last term had risen to only just short of 1,000.

The essence of the Scarman Committee's recommendations was that better use must be made of time–the court's time, Counsel and solicitors' time and the parties' time. It identified four main sources of wasted time. The first stemmed from a failure by the parties, particularly if they were acting in person, to provide the court with all the documentation necessary for the hearing of the appeal or to do so in time and in a logical and legible form. This failure led to appeals being adjourned when called on for hearing or to the court taking much longer than should have been necessary in hearing the appeal. The second consisted in the requirement that at least two Lords Justices should consider and determine procedural applications. The third was the absence of a flexible and co-ordinated listing system for the whole civil division. This resulted in the parties and their advisers being kept waiting if the previous appeal took longer than expected and to judicial time being wasted if the previous appeal was disposed of more quickly than expected. The fourth, and potentially the most important because of the number of people involved, was the length of oral hearings.

The Supreme Court Act 1981 authorized the hearing of some types of appeal by two judges and provided for the appointment of the first Registrar of Civil Appeals. A new Rule (RSC Ord 59, r 9(3)) gave the Registrar power to give directions in relation to the documents to be produced at the appeal 'and the manner in which they are to be presented, and as to other matters incidental to the conduct of the appeal, as appear adapted to secure the just, expeditious and economical disposal of the appeal'.

The object, the Master of the Rolls said, would be to see that the judges read in advance enough to understand the background of the case, the judgment of the court below and the grounds of appeal. The informal (but authoritative) gloss on the statement added:

This is perhaps the most important single change in the rules. The conduct of appeals by way of oral hearing lies at the heart of the English tradition and practice and neither the Scarman Committee nor anyone else has suggested that it should be abandoned in favour of a system of written appeals supplemented by oral hearings which are subject to strict time limits, as is the practice in some other jurisdictions. Nevertheless, an oral hearing involving the presence of the members of the court, shorthandwriters, court staff, counsel, solicitors and, sometimes, the parties is extremely expensive in terms of time and therefore money. Furthermore, time and particularly judicial time, is a scarce commodity of which the best possible use should be made, if the current level of delay is to be reduced. The problem is how to achieve a proper balance between what can be done by way of pre-reading by the members of the court in their rooms, which involves only judicial time, and what must be left to oral presentation and argument in court which involves the time of many others.

The court would try various experiments to see what could be done to expedite matters.

Skeleton arguments

Subsequently, in an important *Practice Note*, Lord Donaldson announced that it would be helpful if counsel prepared 'skeleton arguments'. These should consist of numbered points which counsel intended to argue, stated in not more than one or two sentences together with full references to be used in support of each point. It should also contain, he added, anything that would otherwise have to be dictated to the bench such as propositions of law, chronologies of events, lists of dramatis personae or, where necessary glossaries of terms. No one would be held to the contents of such a document. The document should, however, be sent to the court (and the other side) well before the hearing or, at the latest, when counsel rose. (See [1983] 2 All ER 34.)

A somewhat similar development had in fact already taken place in the House of Lords. In 1982 in *MV Yorke Motors v Edwards* [1982] 1 All ER 1024, Lord Diplock set out what the House of Lords would in future require by way of written documents in a case. Previously the case presented by the parties would contain a summary of the facts, the proceedings in the courts below, the judgments and the arguments on appeal. But now Lord Diplock said that the case should start 'with a statement of what the party conceives to be the issues that arise on the appeal' (p 1025). Counsel should bear in mind that the members of the appellate committee would have read the judgments below. Each issue should be mentioned in a sentence or two. If there were points that it was not intended to pursue, this should be stated; conversely, if it was intended to take a point that was not argued below, the case should mention the fact. If there was an intention to ask the House of Lords not to follow one of its own previous decisions this should be made clear. Heads of argument should be prepared, setting out the chief authorities to be relied on. Lord Diplock said that it was not intended to move towards the American written brief. Counsel for one side had put in a document of 39 pages, which was far too long. Counsel for the other side had put in one a sixth of that length, which was perfectly adequate.

For a powerful critique of the innovation of skeleton arguments see F Mann, 'Reflections on English Civil Justice and the Rule of Law' 2 *Civil Justice Quarterly*, 1983, p 320. But Dr Mann notwithstanding, skeleton arguments are here to stay. What started as an experiment with a voluntary system became mandatory in 1989. (The rules were set out in *Practice Note* [1989] 1 All ER 891, [1989] 1 WLR 281.) Counsel are now required to submit a skeleton argument in all but the most urgent cases. In 1989 it was supposed to be not less than four weeks before the hearing, but in 1990 this was reduced to 14 days–see *Practice Note* [1990] 2 All ER 318. This has now been superseded however by *Practice Note* [1995] 3 All ER 850 dealing with the practice of appeals in the Court of Appeal. This stated that skeleton arguments are to be succinct. In normal one to two day appeals they should not normally exceed 10 pages if the appeal is on a point of law and 15 pages if it is on issues of fact. The skeleton argument is to be accompanied by a written chronology of events. In normal cases they must still be delivered not less than 14 days before the hearing but in heavy or complex cases they should be delivered within 28 days of the entry of the case in the list.

Restrictions on oral argument–will the Court of Appeal adopt American practice?

One of the features of American appellate practice, as has been seen, is drastic restriction of oral argument. This has not yet come to the English system. Despite the requirement of skeleton arguments, counsel are still permitted to argue their case at length–indeed at the length that *they* think appropriate.

In 1991 an American scholar, Professor Robert Martineau spent three months in the Court of Appeal Civil Division to study the English oral tradition. He started with the hypothesis that the American system could probably learn much from the English. He ended with the opposite conclusion. Moreover, he was not overly impressed with the quality of the oral advocacy he observed. ('Most English barristers are not effective appellate advocates.') The situation in England seemed to him to be pretty much the same as in the USA. In both countries, he thought, 15 per cent of appellate advocates were highly competent, 30 to 40 per cent were competent and 50 to 60 per cent were incompetent. (*Appellate Justice in England and the United States*, William Hein, 1991; and see an article based on the book by the present writer–'A Brief Encounter', *New Law Journal*, 12 April 1991.)

The only official step made so far towards limited oral argument in the Court of Appeal has been a rule that counsel is now required to give an estimate of time for the case. There are no penalties as yet for overrunning–but maybe this could become the basis of a form of control over the length of oral argument. There is, however, little sign of much appetite for this among English judges. Martineau found that even judges who have pre-read the papers generally leave counsel to develop his oral argument in his own way and at his own length, out of belief in the virtues of the oral tradition. This was confirmed in a paper by Lord Justice Leggatt written for the Anglo-American judicial exchange in 1994, published in *Civil Justice Quarterly*, January 1995 at p 11, under the title 'The Future of the Oral Tradition in the Court of Appeal'. He acknowledged that skeleton arguments help by telling the judges what appeals are about before they start but 'it sometimes effects little perceptible saving of time, because counsel are suffered to repeat orally what they have already rendered in writing' (pp 12–13). That some presiding judges allowed that to happen was 'another example of the oral tradition dying hard'. He suggested that the court was in that respect falling between two stools because skeleton arguments (which were sometimes of inordinate length) were required, yet oral argument essentially was open-ended. Oral argument took four days a week in the Court of Appeal, compared with one week a month in the United States. The Practice Direction required counsel to open his appeal by going directly to the ground of appeal in the forefront of the appellant's case but this enjoinder was not always obeyed.

Lord Justice Leggatt said that 'immoderate periods of time are spent in informing the courts about the facts and the law, as distinct from presenting the critical reasons why they support the cause of the one side or the other' (p 14). In 1954 there had been eight Lords Justices, in 1974, 16 and in 1994 there were 29. Yet the delays increased.

The average time taken from setting down to judgment had lately risen to an average of 8.4 months from an average between 1985 and 1994 of 7.3 months. It was clear, he suggested, that the only alternative to increasing the number of judges was to reduce the time taken to resolve appeals. 'That can only be done by reversing the traditional practice of allowing counsel to state how long they want and substituting a system whereby the court stipulates the length of time for which counsel shall be permitted to address the court' (p 15).

In 1986 the Commercial Court had introduced a table of the periods for which particular kinds of application would be allowed to last, unless counsel had previously obtained permission to take more time. This worked well and more time was only rarely sought. It was the experience of commercial judges that 'competent counsel can on demand tailor their submissions to take no longer than a stipulated period of time, however short' (ibid).

Not only can counsel adapt to the time available, but unless the curtailment is too drastic, the quality of the argument will almost always be improved. Increase in the intensity of oral argument may reasonably be expected to increase its quality. The best counsel are invariably concise; lesser counsel would usually be better if they were so. That they are not concise is mainly due to lack of the discipline that limitations of time impose (*ibid*).

Lord Justice Leggatt said that, although he had no statistics on the matter, it was comparatively uncommon for members of the court to change their minds about whether to allow or to dismiss an appeal once they had read the skeleton arguments. There was no reason to suppose that the judges would change their minds less often if speeches were shorter.

The Practice Note of July 1995 specified a normal maximum of 20 minutes oral argument for applications for leave to appeal and 30 minutes for applications to the Court of Appeal for leave to move for judicial review. In ordinary cases the appellant's solicitors must lodge an estimate of time needed for the hearing, signed by counsel. A copy must be sent to the respondent who then has the opportunity of disagreeing the time estimate. Failure to do so is taken as acceptance of the proposed time limit. Any revised time estimate must be lodged with the court, signed by the advocate concerned. The Practice Note continued:

(19) Whatever the estimated length of a hearing, the court will (whenever possible) form its own estimate (based on the judgment appealed from, the notice of appeal and the skeleton arguments, if available) of the time which it considers oral argument of the case should take. In such cases, it will then inform the parties representatives how much time will be allowed for oral argument.

In 1991 the House of Lords stated that counsel should notify the Judicial Office how many hours were needed for argument and would be expected to keep within that estimate! (*Procedure Direction* [1991] 3 All ER 608.)

(c) The grounds of appeal

An appeal can be brought on a variety of grounds. In a civil case it can be on fact or law, on the amount of damages, on the wrong exercise by the trial court of a discretion, or an allegation that the court exceeded its jurisdiction.

In a criminal case the appeal can be against conviction or sentence. If the appeal is against conviction, it can be either on the facts (that the court or the jury reached the wrong result), on a point of law, on a question of mixed fact and law, or on any other ground which appears sufficient (Criminal Appeal Act 1968, s 1 (2)(b)).

Mistakes of counsel Generally the Court of Appeal takes the position that it will not entertain an appeal on the ground that counsel at the trial made a mistake–*Gautam* [1988] Crim LR 109. But the court has said that if the advocate was flagrantly incompetent that might be a ground of appeal–*Ensor* [1989] 1 WLR 497; *Crabtree, Foley, McCann* [1992] Crim LR 65. In *Clinton* [1993] 2 All ER 998 the Court of Appeal quashed a conviction where defence counsel had failed to call the defendant at the trial and as a result the jury had had no evidence about differences between the defendant's appearance and the victim's description of the assailant. Where counsel's conduct rendered the verdict unsafe or unsatisfactory the court would not seek to assess the qualitative value of counsel's alleged incompetence but would seek to assess its effect on the trial and the verdict. In *Boal* [1992] 3 All ER 177 the Court of Appeal quashed a conviction even though Boal had pleaded guilty and even though his counsel had not been guilty of flagrantly incompetent advocacy. Mr Boal had been deprived of what was in all likelihood a good defence in law–that he was not liable as manager of a body corporate for offences under the Fire Precautions Act. See also *Irwin* [1987] 2 All ER 1085 (conviction quashed where defence counsel decided not to call alibi witnesses without consulting the defendant) and *Ahluwalia* [1992] 4 All ER 889 (conviction of murder quashed and retrial ordered to permit defence of diminished responsibility to be run; not clear why this possibility had been overlooked at trial).

The Runciman Royal Commission recommended that the Court of Appeal's attitude to errors by counsel be based (as suggested in *Clinton*) by its effect rather than on the degree of incompetence. ('It cannot possibly be right that there should be defendants serving prison sentences for no other reason than that their lawyers made a decision which later turns out to have been mistaken. What matters is not the degree to which the lawyers were at fault but whether the particular decision, whether reasonable or unreasonable, caused a miscarriage of justice' (p 174, para 59).)

Nevertheless in November 1994 in *Driver* (No 93/1492/W5) the court emphasised the need to demonstrate that counsel was guilty of 'flagrantly incompetent advocacy' as stated in *Ensor* and ten days earlier in *Ali and Charlton* (No 91/1863/SI) a differently constituted Court of Appeal Criminal Division said that instances where counsel's conduct could form the basis of an appeal 'must be wholly exceptional'.

In December 1995 the Court of Appeal in *Stapal Ram* (1995) Times, 7 December went further still. The court rejected the defendant's appeal against his conviction for murder. At his trial he had been advised by counsel to base his defence on provocation when self-defence was a conceivable alternative. The court said that there seemed to be an increasing tendency to believe that it was only necessary to assert the fault of trial counsel to sustain an argument that the conviction was unsafe or unsatisfactory. Whether that was due to a mistaken interpretation of the observations on that subject by the 1993 Report of the Royal Commission on Criminal Justice their Lordships did not know, but they did see far reaching implications in the Commission's suggestion that even a reasonable decision of counsel could be the cause of a miscarriage of justice. The court could not countenance a case in which the defendant was serving a prison sentence for no other reason than a mistake on counsel's part but equally, where counsel's judgment had been reasonable, there was a strong public interest that the legal process should not be indefinitely prolonged on the ground for example that a defendant's case advanced within a different framework might have stood a greater chance of success. 'It was easy, as Lucretius had observed, to stand on the safety of the shore and pass judgment on the work of those battling against the wind and waves in a high sea.'

For a review of the English and Scottish cases see Neil Gow,'"Flagrant Incompetency" of Counsel', *New Law Journal*, 29 March 1996, p 453.

Only one appeal

In *Pinfold* [1988] 2 All ER 217 it was held that an appellant only had a right to appeal once. The court had no jurisdiction to hear a second appeal–even on the grounds of fresh evidence. The only recourse for the defendant then was to ask the Home Secretary to refer the case back to the Court of Appeal under his powers under s 17 of the Criminal Appeal Act and is now to try to get the new Criminal Cases Review Commission to do so. See also *Pegg* [1988] Crim LR 370.

(d) Powers of the Court of Appeal

(1) Court of Appeal Civil Division

The Court of Appeal can make any order which could have been made in the court below and substitute its own decision as to liability, quantum of damages or costs (see RSC Ord 59, r 2(10)). It is not limited to points raised in the notice of appeal. It can, though it rarely does, take further points itself, for instance as to the illegality of a contract (see *Snell v Unity Finance Ltd* [1964] 2 QB 203).

The court can order a retrial. Where the court is considering an award of damages by a jury, however, until recently it had no power to substitute its own award for that of the jury. It had to order a retrial. This has now been corrected. The Courts and Legal Services Act 1990, s 8, gave a power for rules to be made to permit the court to change the amount of damages.

(2) Court of Appeal Criminal Division

The Court of Appeal Criminal Division can quash a conviction or reduce a sentence. Since 1966 it has not had the power to increase sentences–though this power is still exercisable by the crown court when it hears appeals from the magistrates' courts. The Court of Appeal also has a right to order a fresh trial.

(e) The power of appeal courts to review findings of fact by trial courts

There is considerable reluctance on the part of the appeal court to differ on a question of fact from the trial court. Insofar as the Court of Appeal displays any enthusiasm for this, it has on several occasions been warned off by the House of Lords. The policy was expressed in the case that follows:

SS Hontestroom (Owners) v SS Sagaporack (Owners) [1927] AC 37 (House of Lords)

In actions arising out of a collision between two ships the trial judge found that the *Sagaporack* was wholly to blame. His decision was reversed by the Court of Appeal which found the other ship was wholly to blame.

On appeal to the House of Lords, Lord Sumner, giving the judgment for the majority, said:

The learned President, after seeing both pilots, accepted the story of the *Hontestroom*. Though he does not expressly say so, it is evident that he regarded the *Hontestroom's* pilot as an honest and a credible witness and, conversely, that he did not accept the story of the pilot of the *Sagaporack*, not thinking that his memory could be trusted. . . .

What then is the real effect on the hearing in a Court of Appeal of the fact that the trial judge saw and heard the witnesses? I think it has been somewhat lost sight of. Of course, there is jurisdiction to retry the case on the shorthand note, including in such retrial the appreciation of the relative values of the witnesses, for the appeal is made a rehearing by rules which have the force of statute: Order 68, r 1. It is not, however, a mere matter of discretion to remember and take account of this fact; it is a matter of justice and of judicial obligation. None the less, not to have seen the witnesses puts appellate judges in a permanent position of disadvantage as against the trial judge, and, unless it can be shown that he has failed to use or has palpably misused his advantage, the higher court ought not to take the responsibility of reversing conclusions so arrived at, merely on the result of their own comparisons and criticisms of the witnesses and of their own view of the probabilities of the case. The course of the trial and the whole substance of the judgment must be looked at, and the matter does not depend on the question whether a witness has been cross-examined to credit or has been pronounced by the judge in terms to be unworthy of it. If his estimate of the man forms any substantial part of his reasons for his judgment the trial judge's conclusion of fact should, as I understand the decisions, be let alone. In *The Julia* (1860) 14 Moo PC 210, 235) Lord Kingsdown says: 'They, who require this Board, under such circumstances, to reverse a decision of the court below upon a point of this description, undertake a task of great and almost insuperable difficulty . . . We must, in order to reverse, not merely entertain doubts whether the decision below is right, but be convinced that it is wrong'.. . .

My Lords, for these reasons I do not propose to retry this case, nor do I think that the Court of Appeal should have done so.

For a similar case, see *B v W* [1979] 3 All ER 83.

The position is, however, different when the appeal court is asked to review the drawing of inferences from facts by the trial judge. In such cases the appeal court is permitted to draw different inferences even though it has not seen the witnesses–see *Benmax v Austin Motor Co Ltd* [1955] 1 All ER 326, 327, and *Whitehouse v Jordan* [1981] 1 All ER 267.

Questions

1. What do you understand to be the difference between the attitude of English appeal courts to findings of fact by a trial judge, as compared with findings of fact by a jury? (On this see also pp 500–04 below.)

2. What should the attitude of appeal courts be to findings of fact reached by the trial judge or jury?

For the Court of Appeal's attitude to the related problem of reviewing decisions on damages, see *Ward v James*, p 377 above, and *Blackshaw v Lord* [1983] 2 All ER 311. For a sceptical view about the value to trial courts of observing the demeanour of the witnesses, see a fascinating lecture given by Sir Thomas Bingham before he became Master of the Rolls–'The Judge as Juror', *Current Legal Problems*, 1985, p 1 at 6–13.

Note–do appeal judges have the time it takes?

A practical point made in a powerful lecture on the problem of miscarriages of justice by the distinguished Australian judge the Hon Justice Michael Kirby is that appeal judges do not have the time to consider the trial evidence properly. Nor, typically, do they have the time, all of them, to read the entirety of the transcript of what may have been a trial lasting many days or even weeks. 'They visit the evidence, on the invitation of counsel, skipping from one passage to another. Rarely do they capture the subtle atmosphere of the trial, for such things do not readily emerge from cold pages. These are the reasons why so much deference is paid to the advantages of the trial judge or jury, who see the evidence unfold in sequence and observe the witnesses giving their testimony.' ('Miscarriages of Justice', The Child and Co Lecture, London, 1991, p 26.)

The burden of reading papers is already enormous. The Evidence of the Lord Chancellor's Department to the Runciman Royal Commission stated that in a typical week in September 1991, the one Division of the Court of Appeal Criminal Division that was then sitting was provided with 4,800 pages of documentation.

About half the Court of Appeal's time was spent on sentence appeals. Such appeals were declining whilst the proportion of appeals against conviction was increasing. In a normal sitting day, each Division of the Court could deal with up to ten sentence cases and one or two conviction cases. It seems clear that if the Court were to take on more conviction appeals it would need further resources (*ibid*).

On the special status of jury decisions and its effect on the Court of Appeal, see also the words of the Court of Appeal Criminal Division in quashing the conviction of the Birmingham Six:

The primacy of the jury in the criminal justice system is well illustrated by the difference between the criminal and civil divisions of the Court of Appeal. Like the criminal division, the civil division is also a creature of statute. But its powers are much wider. A civil appeal is by way of re-hearing of the whole case. So the court is concerned with fact as well as law. It is true the court does not rehear the witnesses. But it reads their evidence. It follows that in a civil case the Court of Appeal may take a different view of the facts from the court below. In a criminal case this is not possible. Since justice is as much concerned with the conviction of the guilty as the acquittal of the innocent, and the task of convicting the guilty belongs constitutionally to the jury, not to us, the role of the criminal division of the Court of Appeal is necessarily limited. Hence it is true to say that whereas the Civil Division of the Court of Appeal has appellate jurisdiction in the full sense, the Criminal Division is perhaps more accurately described as a court of review. [*R v McIlkenny* [1992] 2 All ER 417.]

Quashing the jury's verdict on the facts where there is no fresh evidence

The role of the Court of Appeal Criminal Division in dealing with issues of fact poses fundamental problems about the proper relationship of appellate judges and the jury. In what circumstances is it legitimate for the court to take a different view of the facts from that taken by the jury?

The conditions for the court to quash a conviction were first laid down in s 4 of the Criminal Appeal Act 1907. As will be seen, this was replaced in 1966 by s 2 of the Criminal Appeal Act 1966, which became s 2 of the Criminal Appeal Act 1968. Section 2 was in its turn replaced by s 2 of the Criminal Appeal Act 1995.

Criminal Appeal Act 1907

4.–(1) The Court of Criminal Appeal on any such appeal against conviction shall allow the appeal if they think that the verdict of the jury should be set aside on the ground that it is unreasonable or cannot be supported having regard to the evidence, or that the judgment of the court before whom the appellant was convicted should be set aside on the ground of a wrong decision of any question of law or that on any ground there was a miscarriage of justice, and in any other case shall dismiss the appeal:

Provided that the court may, notwithstanding that they are of opinion that the point raised in the appeal might be decided in favour of the appellant, dismiss the appeal if they consider that no substantial miscarriage of justice has actually occurred.

The court's attitude to jury verdicts was illustrated in many cases similar to the one that follows:

R v Hopkins-Husson (1949) 34 Cr App Rep 47 (Court of Criminal Appeal)

Lord Goddard CJ, giving the judgment of the court, said:

With regard to the other six cases, the jury found a verdict of Not Guilty in five of them, and in the case of one boy, a boy called Allan Simpson, they found the appellant Guilty. It is fair and right to say that the learned judge said in terms that he was surprised at the verdict, and he himself would obviously have preferred a verdict of acquittal; but it is also right to say that from a very early period in the history of this court it has been laid down, and has been laid down frequently since, that the fact that the trial judge was dissatisfied with the verdict, although it is a matter to be taken into account in this court, must not be taken as a ground by itself for quashing the conviction. If it were, it would mean that we should be substituting the opinion of the judge for the opinion of the jury, and that is one of the things which this court will never do.

In just the same way it has been held from an equally early period in the history of this court that the fact that some members or all the members of the court think that they themselves would have returned a different verdict is again no ground for refusing to accept the verdict of the jury, which is the constitutional method of trial in this country. If there is evidence to go to the jury, and there has been no misdirection, and it cannot be said that the verdict is one which a reasonable jury could not arrive at, this court will not set aside the verdict of Guilty which has been found by the jury.

A commentator describing the attitude of the court to these powers wrote in 1966: 'The broad picture that emerged was a court concerned in appeals against conviction, with the judge's direction, evidence and procedure and the occasional point of substantive law rather than the "merits" of the case. An appellant who could point to a clear misdirection, the wrongful admission or exclusion of evidence or some procedural irregularity, had better prospects of success than the appellant who simply claimed that he was innocent and that the jury had come to the wrong decision.' (Michael Dean, 'Criminal Appeal Act 1966' *Criminal Law Review*, pp 535, 539.)

A JUSTICE Committee in 1964 thought 'it seems absurd and unjust that verdicts which experienced judges would have thought surprising and not supported by really adequate evidence, should be allowed to stand for no other reason than that they were arrived at by a jury' (*Criminal Appeals*, 1964, para 59). In 1965 the Donovan Committee took a similar view. (*Report of the Interdepartmental Committee on the Court of Criminal Appeal*, 1965, Cmnd 2755):

Under the terms of s 4(1), if it is strictly construed, there is, in the case of an innocent person who has been wrongly identified and in consequence wrongly convicted, virtually no protection conferred by his right to appeal . . .provided that the evidence of identification was, on the face of it, credible. We think that this defect should be remedied [p 33, para 145].

It recommended the adoption of a broader formula, one originally proposed by Mr FE Smith during the debates on the Criminal Appeal Bill in 1907, that the court should quash a conviction where the verdict in the opinion of the court was 'under all the circumstances of the case unsafe or unsatisfactory'. This was duly achieved in the Criminal Appeal Act 1966, which was then incorporated into the 1968 Act and became s 2(1)(*a*) of that Act.

Criminal Appeal Act 1968

2.–(1) Except as provided by this Act, the Court of Appeal shall allow an appeal against conviction if they think:

(*a*) that the verdict of the jury should be set aside on the ground that under all the circumstances of the case it is unsafe or unsatisfactory; or
(*b*) that the judgment of the court of trial should be set aside on the ground of a wrong decision of any question of law; or
(*c*) that there was a material irregularity in the course of the trial, and in any other case shall dismiss the appeal:

Provided that the court may, notwithstanding that they are of opinion that the point raised in the appeal might be decided in favour of the appellant, dismiss the appeal if they consider that no miscarriage of justice has actually occurred.

(2) In the case of an appeal against conviction the court shall, if they allow the appeal, quash the conviction.

Note–'unsafe or unsatisfactory'

In the final appeal of the Birmingham Six the prosecution argued that the two words had separate meanings and that therefore convictions could be unsatisfactory but not unsafe. The Court of Appeal rejected this view. The two words, it said, are indistinguishable.

Cooper *and the 'lurking doubt' test*

In 1969 the Court of Appeal Criminal Division decided the *Cooper* case, in which they pronounced a philosophy in regard to the way in which the court should approach jury verdicts which was very far indeed from the approach shown in the *Hopkins-Husson* decision.

R v Cooper [1969] 1 QB 267 (Court of Appeal Criminal Division)

Defendant was convicted of assault occasioning actual bodily harm after an incident in which a 22-year-old girl, Miss McFarlane, was attacked by one of a group of three drunken youths. At an identification parade six weeks after the offence Miss McFarlane picked out the defendant. In his own words: 'She never looked at anyone else' and according to the court she clearly had no doubt at all. The critical evidence for the defence was that of a witness, Mr Davis, a friend of the defendant who visited him in prison before the trial with another mutual friend, Mr Burke. After the visit, Burke had told Davis that he (Burke) had in fact been responsible for the attack but that he did not intend to do anything about owning up since he had a bad record and 'would get four years' for it. There was close physical similarity between the defendant and Burke. Nevertheless the jury convicted.

Widgery LJ, giving the judgment of the court, said:

The important thing about this case is that all the material to which I have referred was put before the jury. No one criticizes the summing-up, and, indeed, Mr Frisby for the defendant has gone to some lengths to indicate that the summing-up was entirely fair and that everything which could possibly have been said in order to alert the jury to the difficulties of the case was clearly said by the presiding judge. It is, therefore, a case in which every issue was before the jury and in which the jury was properly instructed, and, accordingly, a case in which this court will be very reluctant indeed to intervene. It has been said over and over again throughout the years that this court must recognize the advantage which a jury has in seeing and hearing the witness, and if all the material was before the jury and the summing-up was impeccable, this court should not lightly interfere. Indeed, until the passing of the Criminal Appeal Act 1966, provisions which are now to be found in s 2 of the Criminal Appeal Act 1968, it was almost unheard of for this court to interfere in such a case.

However, now our powers are somewhat different, and we are indeed charged to allow an appeal against conviction if we think that the verdict of the jury should be set aside on the ground that under all the circumstances of the case it is unsafe or unsatisfactory. That means that in cases of this kind the court must in the end ask itself a subjective question, whether we are content to let the matter stand as it is, or whether there is not some lurking doubt in our minds which makes us wonder whether an injustice has been done. This is a reaction which may not be based strictly on the evidence as such; it is a reaction which can be produced by the general feel of the case as the court experiences it.

We have given earnest thought in this case to whether it is one in which we ought to set aside the verdict of the jury, notwithstanding the fact they had every advantage and, indeed, some advantages we do not enjoy. After due consideration, we have decided we do not regard this verdict as safe, and accordingly we shall allow the appeal to quash the conviction. As far as this matter is concerned the appellant is discharged.

If the very broad 'lurking doubt' test as formulated in *Cooper* reflected the Court of Appeal's normal attitude, a high proportion of appellants against conviction might stand a reasonable chance of getting their convictions overturned. In fact, however, the Court of Appeal is not easily persuaded to adopt the 'lurking doubt' test. One expert stated in 1983: 'The lurking doubt' test, enunciated by Lord Widgery when he was first appointed, has been quietly buried' (Tom Sargant, *More Law Reform Now* (Barry Rose, 1983), p 91). Research carried out for JUSTICE stated that only six reported cases had been found since the decision in *Cooper* where the court had quashed a conviction on the grounds that there was a lurking doubt about the conviction and there was nothing new to throw doubt on it. (JUSTICE, *Miscarriages of Justice*, 1989, para 4.19, p 49). The report went on to say that there might be other unreported decisions –though Master Thompson, the then Registrar of Criminal Appeals, doubted it.

For examples of cases where the 'lurking doubt' test, or at least the formula, has been used see *Pattinson* (1973) 58 Cr App Rep 17; *Lake* (1976) 64 Cr App Rep 172; *Nye* (1977) 66 Cr App Rep 252, 259. The formula was also used by the House of Lords in 1986 in *Spencer* [1986] 2 All ER 928, 940, (p 407 above), in which Lord Ackner concluded his speech with the words: 'I therefore have a lurking doubt that justice may not have been done, which makes me conclude that the verdict was unsafe'. (See also *Swain* [1988] Crim LR 109.) The continued existence of the test therefore seems clear. The question is whether, and to what extent, it is actually applied.

An important insight into the Court of Appeal's marked reluctance to use the 'lurking doubt' test was supplied by former Lord Justice (Fred) Lawton, a vastly experienced criminal appeal judge, in his evidence to the Runciman Royal Commission (cited here with the author's permission):

Until the decision of the Court of Appeal in *R v Cooper* it had been assumed that a conviction should not be quashed unless there was some reason in law for doing so. In that case however it was adjudged that the court could apply a subjective test–had it a lurking doubt or reasoned unease which made it wonder whether an injustice had been done. In simpler terms this means that the court can quash a conviction if it has a hunch that there has been an injustice. This cannot be a sound way of administering criminal justice; and since 1969 the judges seem to have appreciated that it was not because only six appeals have been allowed on this ground.

Or, in other words, the judges have not applied the 'lurking doubt' test because they do not like it. They believe that to apply it would be to usurp the function of the jury.

Report of the Runciman Royal Commission

The Runciman Royal Commission said it had received conflicting evidence about the 'lurking doubt' test. On the one hand, there were those who pointed out that the Court of Appeal had only very rarely acknowledged that it was applying this test. Thus, in the JUSTICE research done by Kate Malleson there were only six such cases in the 21 years between 1968 and 1989 In Malleson's 1989 sample of 114 appeals there was one such case. More recently, the test had been applied somewhat more often. In Malleson's 1990 sample of the first 102 successful appeals, there were six cases in which the court said there was a lurking doubt. In her 1992 sample of the first 102 successful appeals, there were 14 cases in which the court quashed the conviction although there was no fresh evidence and no criticism of the trial process. In nine of these the court said that the evidence was too weak or flawed to justify a conviction; in the other five cases the court actually referred to having a 'lurking doubt' (Report, p 171, para 43).

On the other hand, it had also been suggested to the Royal Commission that the Court of Appeal had not infrequently allowed appeals on what had in truth been the 'lurking doubt' principle, even though there had been no reference to the phrase. These were cases where there was no error at the trial nor any error in law 'but nevertheless the combined experience of the three members of the court leads them to conclude that there may have been an injustice in the trial and in the jury's verdict'.

They consequently allowed the appeal on the ground that, at the least, the jury's verdict was unsatisfactory. 'There is no real difference between this approach and an application of the 'lurking doubt principle' (p 171, para 45). The Commission's conclusion on the matter was to encourage the court to use this power when it felt it right to do so:

We fully appreciate the reluctance felt by judges sitting in the Court of Appeal about quashing a jury's verdict. The jury has seen the witnesses and heard their evidence; the Court of Appeal has not. Where, however, on reading the transcript and hearing argument the Court of Appeal has a serious doubt about the verdict, it should exercise its power to quash. We do not think that quashing the jury's verdict where the court believes it to be unsafe undermines the system of jury trial. We therefore recommend that, as part of the redrafting of s 2, it be made clear that the Court of Appeal should quash a conviction notwithstanding that the jury reached their verdict having heard all the relevant evidence and without any error of law or material irregularity having occurred if after reviewing the case, the court concludes that the verdict is or may be unsafe [Report, pp 171–72, para 46].

For an example of the Court of Appeal adopting this approach see *R v Haughton,* unreported (No 589/SI/91) 21 May 1992. The case was referred back to the Court of Appeal by the Home Secretary on the ground that the ESDA test appeared to show that police officers had fabricated the appellant's confession. The Court of Appeal rejected that argument, but it said that its duty was 'to review the case generally'. Having done that, it found that the verdict was unsafe and unsatisfactory even though there was nothing new that had not been before the jury.

As will be seen below, (p 507) the Government accepted the Royal Commission's proposal that s 2 be redrafted but it did not adopt the proposal in the form suggested by the Commission.

Quashing the jury's verdict on account of error at trial

Research shows that by far the most frequent reason for the Court of Appeal to quash a conviction is because of some error at trial, usually error by the trial judge in the form of misdirection of the jury on the law or some other defect in the summing up, or a wrong decision to allow or to exclude evidence. The Runciman Royal Commission cited Malleson's research on appeals in 1989, 1990 and 1992 Thus in the 1990 sample, errors of this kind were involved in 82 per cent of successful appeals.

Under the 1968 Criminal Appeal Act, errors at trial could be dealt with in three alternative ways. One was to treat the error as inconsequential by applying 'the proviso' (on 'the proviso' see pp 506–07 below). The second was to quash the conviction and order a retrial (on retrials see p 517–19 below). The third and according to Malleson's research by far the most common was to quash the conviction.

A majority of the Runciman Royal Commission proposed a different scheme:

(1) If the court believes that the conviction is safe despite the error, the appeal should be dismissed.
(2) If the court believes the error has rendered the verdict unsafe, the appeal should be allowed and the conviction quashed.
(3) If it believes the conviction may be unsafe as a result of the error, it should quash the conviction and order a retrial (Report, p 170, para 38).

Three of the Commission's members wished to add a further category for cases where there is an error at trial sufficiently serious to affect the trial materially but not sufficiently serious to make the conviction unsafe. In such a case they thought the court should order a retrial. The majority disagreed–'The majority of us do not believe that a person who is clearly guilty should be accorded a retrial merely because there has been some error at the trial' (p 170, para 38).

Quashing the jury's verdict on account of pre-trial malpractice or procedural irregularity

Where an appeal is based on some pre-trial matter (which might be anything from fabrication of evidence to some serious irregularity in the implementation of PACE) a majority of nine out of eleven members of the Royal Commission thought the Court of Appeal should only act if it thought the matter was such as to make or maybe make the conviction unsafe. If therefore there was plenty of other, untainted evidence showing the defendant to be guilty his conviction should not be quashed even if there were some gross impropriety in the pre-trial handling of the case. The minority of two (which included the writer) thought that there could be occasions when the Court should quash a conviction even though there was clear evidence of guilt.

The majority view:

49. In the view of the majority, even if they believed that quashing the convictions of criminals was an appropriate way of punishing police malpractice, it would be naive to suppose that this would have any practical effect on police behaviour. In any case it cannot in their view be morally right that a person who has been convicted on abundant other evidence and may be a danger to the public should walk free because of what may be a criminal offence by someone else. Such an offence should be separately prosecuted within the system. It is also essential, if confidence in the criminal justice system is to be maintained, that police officers involved in malpractice should be disciplined, and in this connection we attach great importance to the recommendations in chapter three, which should lead to more effective police disciplinary procedures. The Court of Appeal must report any cases of malpractice by police officers which come to their attention to chief officers of police. We also envisage that the more serious the malpractice the less likely it is that the court would conclude that the verdict could be safe.

50. In the view of the majority, the minority view is illogical. It would only be effective if the judge at first instance had allowed the tainted evidence to be heard by the jury. If the judge had properly excluded the evidence then the verdict would be unassailable. The minority view must logically involve the trial judge in stopping a case on the basis of tainted evidence which he or she nevertheless proposed to exclude. The majority believe this to be unacceptable precluding as it must the jury from returning a verdict on the basis of evidence which was safe, admissible, and probative. It is only the tainted evidence which is excluded by section 78 of PACE. That section does not allow the court to stop the case if there remains admissible probative evidence to support it [p 23].

The minority view

The minority view was expressed in the writer's Dissent:

68. I cannot agree. The moral foundation of the criminal justice system requires that if the prosecution has employed foul means the defendant must go free even though he is plainly

guilty. Where the integrity of the process is fatally flawed, the conviction should be quashed as an expression of the system's repugnance at the methods used by those acting for the prosecution.

69. The majority's position would I believe encourage serious wrongdoing from some police officers who might be tempted to exert force or fabricate or suppress evidence in the hope of establishing the guilt of the suspect, especially in a serious case when they believe him to be guilty. There have unfortunately been some gross examples of such conduct.

70. The position adopted by the majority also seems to me to risk undermining the principle at the heart of section 78 of PACE which explicitly gives the court the power to exclude evidence on the ground that it renders the proceedings 'unfair'. The word 'unfair' expresses the underlying moral principle and the Court of Appeal has repeatedly used this new statutory power very broadly to express its refusal to uphold convictions based on unacceptable police practices even when it could not be said that the misconduct had any impact on the jury's verdict.

71. Section 78 would of course remain–but the majority would in effect be encouraging the Court of Appeal to undercut a part of its moral force by saying that the issue of 'unfairness' can be ignored where there is sufficient evidence to show that the defendant is actually guilty. Any judge concerned to discourage prosecution malpractice would I believe be dismayed by the majority's position. In terms of the message sent to the police service and other prosecution agencies it could undo much of the good effect being achieved by the attitude of the judges to section 78 of PACE.

72. But the matter goes beyond discouraging prosecution malpractice. At the heart of the criminal justice system there is a fundamental principle that the process must itself have integrity. The majority suggest that the answer to prosecution wrongdoing in the investigation of crime is to deal with the wrongdoers through prosecution or disciplinary proceedings. Even were this to happen (and often in practice it would not), the approach is not merely insufficient, it is irrelevant to the point of principle. The more serious the case, the greater the need that the system upholds the values in the name of which it claims to act. If the behaviour of the prosecution agencies has deprived a guilty verdict of its moral legitimacy the Court of Appeal must have a residual power to quash the verdict no matter how strong the evidence of guilt. The integrity of the criminal justice system is a higher objective that the conviction of any individual [pp 234–5].

Not quashing the jury's verdict– application of 'the proviso'

No one suggests that a conviction should be quashed, or even a retrial ordered, where the matter complained of by the appellant is trivial. (In the United States this is known as 'harmless error'.) Here the matter has previously been dealt with by what was called 'the proviso'.

The proviso referred to here is that at the end of s 2 of the 1968 Act–p 501 above–'Provided that the court may, notwithstanding that they are of opinion that the point raised in the appeal might be decided in favour of the appellant, dismiss the appeal if they consider that no miscarriage of justice has actually occurred'. The application of the proviso was explored by Michael Knight in his book on criminal appeals. In this he showed that, contrary to what was often maintained, the 'great majority of cases where the power [of the proviso] has been exercised are cases of serious error' in the trial (p 15). Before substantiating this controversial assertion, he set out the test which the court has applied for the application of the proviso:

Michael Knight, *Criminal Appeals*, 1970, pp 9–53

The test which the appellate court goes by is not the degree of error but whether there is, despite the fault, sufficient evidence and a sufficient direction for a reasonable jury inevitably to convict for, if so, there is no substantial miscarriage of justice.[4] However, if it is correct to say that the error can have had any crucial influence on a reasonable jury the conviction must be quashed, for to uphold it then would be a miscarriage of justice. The court metaphorically blot out the fault–the error in the direction, the piece of inadmissible evidence, the impact of the wrongly drafted indictment–and ask if, without it, there is a strong enough case for an inevitable conviction. And if they can answer 'yes' to this question, they show the Nelson Touch by turning a blind eye to the fault [p 16].

Knight then gives numerous examples of cases where the proviso was applied in spite of serious errors in the trial:

Haddy (1944) 29 Cr App Rep 182–jury wrongly invited to infer guilt from accused's silence.

Farid (1945) 30 Cr App Rep 168–jury not warned by judge that corroboration desirable for accomplices to other offences.

Whybrow (1951) 35 Cr App Rep 141–misdirection as to intent in attempted murder.

Slinger (1961) 46 Cr App Rep 244–judge did not tell jury that onus of proof lay on prosecution.[5]

Knight also produced sixteen examples of cases where the proviso was applied although the jury had wrongly been informed of the defendant's previous convictions (pp 19–21). He continued (p 21):

Certainly in recent years the appellate court in their judgments go extremely carefully through the evidence other than the inadmissible evidence wrongly let in plus the direction, or the direction minus the offending portion plus the evidence, to show that it is fair to say that a reasonable jury would inevitably have convicted. This definite and very often scrupulous care betrays a sense of uneasiness and dislike which can be taken as further recognition of the regularity of use–in serious fault cases [of the proviso].

The line between some of the cases where the proviso has been exercised and some where it has not is sometimes so narrow as to be almost non-existent, and the answer to this conundrum lies in the amount of evidence and the standard of the direction outside of the fault.

Occasionally, use of the proviso is declined because a particular fault is of its nature so serious that, even though the appellate court would like to uphold the conviction, and, even though there probably would be sufficient evidence and direction apart from the fault to justify in their opinion an inevitable finding of guilty by a reasonable jury, their desire to have a deserved conviction must be sacrificed to the general principle of fairness in our criminal trial. This is the principle stated in *Maxwell v DPP*:[6] It is often better that one guilty man should escape than that the general rules evolved by the dictates of justice for the conduct of criminal prosecutions should be disregarded or discredited.. . .

The redrafting of s 2

The Runciman Royal Commission

The Royal Commission unanimously agreed that s 2 of the 1968 needed to be redrafted. (For an article detailing the drafting defects of the section see R Buxton, 'Miscarriages of Justice and the Court of Appeal' *Law Quarterly Review*, January 1993, p 66.) But the Commission was not agreed as to how it should be redrafted. The majority of

4   The test was laid down in *Stirland v DPP* [1944] AC 315 (ed).
5   For a recent case in which the proviso was applied after the judge had failed to instruct the jury on the burden of proof, see *Edwards* (1983) 77 Cr App Rep 5 (ed).
6   [1935] AC 309.

eight recommended that the different grounds of appeal set out in s 2(1)(*a*)(*b*) and (*c*) (p 501 above) should be replaced by a single new ground–that the conviction 'is or may be unsafe'. If the court is satisfied that the conviction *is* unsafe it should quash the conviction; if the court is satisfied that the conviction *may be* unsafe it should quash the conviction and order a retrial unless there are reasons which make a retrial impracticable or undesirable (p 170, para 38). Under that scheme the proviso would be redundant.

The minority of three argued that it would be confusing to wrap up all possible grounds of appeal in the one word 'unsafe'. That word implied that there was something wrong with the jury's verdict whereas the defect might be 'some irregularities or errors of law or procedure which did not necessarily affect the jury's verdict but were so serious that the conviction should not stand' (Report, p 169, para 34). Furthermore, in the view of the minority, an umbrella formula would not give the Court of Appeal sufficient guidance. In the view of the minority the grounds of appeal should distinguish between appeals claiming that the jury reached the wrong result and those alleging material irregularities or errors of law or procedure in or before the trial (*ibid*).

The Criminal Appeal Act 1995

The Government did not accept the Royal Commission's recommendation that the formula should distinguish between 'is unsafe' and 'maybe unsafe'. The formula in the new Act is simply whether the conviction is unsafe. The Criminal Appeal Act 1995, s 2 replaces s 2 of the 1968 Act (including the proviso) with the following new provision:

Subject to the provisions of this Act, the Court of Appeal (a) shall allow an appeal against conviction if they think that the conviction is unsafe; and (b) shall dismiss such an appeal in any other case.

The Government therefore rejected the view of the minority but it did not wholly adopt the view of the majority of the Royal Commission either. In a Discussion Paper entitled 'Criminal Appeals and the Establishment of a Criminal Cases Review Authority', 1994, the Home Office quoted the Royal Commission's view that its formula 'is or may be unsafe' as the sole ground of appeal would preserve the Court's freedom to consider a wide variety of arguments while ensuring consistency in the way the Court responded to that variety. The Discussion Paper continued: 'The Government is attracted to the broad approach described by the Commission and for the most part accepts the logic of the detailed recommendations adopted by a majority of the Commission' (para 10).

However, when the Criminal Appeal Bill was published it became apparent that the Government did not accept the recommendation that an appeal should be possible not only on the ground that the verdict of the jury 'is unsafe', but also on the ground that 'it may be unsafe'. The issue was considered during the debates on the Bill but the Government refused to change its mind. The Home Office Minister Mr Nicholas Baker, speaking in the Committee stage of the Bill said: 'The difficulty with the phrase "may be unsafe" is that it is inherently uncertain. Almost any conviction may be unsafe. The test might well result in the Court of Appeal having to allow a considerably greater number of appeals than at present, simply because it did not know for certain that the conviction was safe.' (House of Commons, Standing Committee B, 21 March 1995, col 27).

Also, 'may be unsafe' had about it a suggestion of subjectivity on the part of someone other than the Court of Appeal. 'That would go far broader than current practice and far broader than the Committee would wish. . . we do not intend it to result in fewer convictions being overturned than at present. We want to consolidate the existing practice of the Court of Appeal' (*ibid*). An amendment to introduce the words 'or may be unsafe' was defeated by 9 to 8 (*ibid*, col 28).

Professor Sir John Smith, addressing this issue, basically agreed with the Government's view that the words 'may be unsafe' add nothing:

A conviction is unsafe if the court has nothing more than a lurking doubt whether the appellant is guilty–that is the court thinks that he may have been wrongly convicted. What then is the difference between 'We think that the appellant may have been wrongly convicted?' and 'We think that it may be that he may have been wrongly convicted?' Surely there is no difference. Either the court has a lurking (or greater) doubt, or it does not. It is submitted that the Government was right to insist on the exclusion of the words, 'or may be', which could have led only to confusion, and possibly, to the Court feeling obliged to give a narrow meaning to 'unsafe' [[1995] *Criminal Law Review*, p 922].

In the past the Court of Appeal has often quashed a conviction on the ground that there was an error of law or a material irregularity even though it may have had no doubt that the defendant was guilty. If the court were now to hold that a conviction is only 'unsafe' if the court has a lurking (or greater) doubt about the defendant's conviction, that would be a drastic restriction of the court's power. But the Parliamentary debates make it clear that this was not the Government's intention. In moving the Second Reading of the Bill, the Home Secretary said of this section that 'In substance, it restates the existing practice of the Court of Appeal and I am pleased to note that the Lord Chief Justice has already welcomed it' (House of Commons, *Hansard*, 6 March 1995, col 24). In the Standing Committee, the Minister of State said, 'The Lord Chief Justice and members of the senior judiciary have given the test a great deal of thought and they believe that the new test re-states the existing practice of the Court of Appeal.' (Standing Committee B, 21 March 1995, col 26). In the same article Professor Smith argued (at p 925) that if that is right, 'the 1995 Act does nothing to achieve the aim of the Royal Commission. . . that the court should be readier than in the past to overturn verdicts on the ground of jury mistakes or other errors at the trial'.

The Home Office Minister also rejected an amendment to retain the words 'or unsatisfactory'. The Government, he said, agreed with the Royal Commission that there was no real difference between 'unsafe' and 'unsatisfactory'. It had been argued by some that 'unsafe' referred to evidential flaws whilst 'unsatisfactory' connoted procedural flaws. But in the Government's view 'the word "unsafe" is sufficient to deal with convictions which are unacceptable because of flaws in the manner in which a case is prosecuted or tried, and because of evidence which undermines the prosecution case. If a procedural flaw is sufficiently serious to cast doubt on the safety of a conviction, the court will allow the appeal' (ibid col 27).

Speaking on the Second Reading debate in the House of Lords, the Lord Chief Justice, Lord Taylor said the new formula–whether the conviction is unsafe–'will in my view be concise, just and comprehensible to the ordinary citizen without narrowing the present grounds of appeal' (House of Lords, *Hansard*, 15 May 1995, col 311). There had been criticism of the fact that the Government had dropped the concept 'may be unsafe' recommended by the Royal Commission. In his view, however, 'there is no merit in including in the test the words 'or may be unsafe' since the implication of doubt is already inherent in the word 'unsafe'. A conviction which may be unsafe is unsafe (*ibid*).

On the redrafting of s 2, see D Schiff and R Nobles, 'Criminal Appeal Act 1995: the Semantics of Jurisdiction', *Modern Law Review*, May 1996, p 299.

(f) The power of appeal courts to receive fresh evidence

The Court of Appeal, both civil and criminal, has full power to receive fresh evidence. In criminal cases the Criminal Appeal Act 1968, s 23 provided:

23.–(1) For the purposes of this Part of this Act the Court of Appeal may, if they think it necessary or expedient in the interests of justice:

(*a*)   order the production of any document, exhibit or other thing connected with the proceedings, the production of which appears to them necessary for the determination of the case;

(*b*)   order any witness who would have been a compellable witness in the proceedings from which the appeal lies to attend for examination and be examined before the court, whether or not he was called in those proceedings; and

(*c*)   . . . receive the evidence, if tendered, of any witness.

(2) Without prejudice to subsection (1) above, where evidence is tendered to the Court of Appeal thereunder the Court shall, unless they are satisfied that the evidence, if received, would not afford any ground for allowing the appeal, exercise their power of receiving it if–

(*a*)   it appears to them that the evidence is likely to be credible and would have been admissible in the proceedings from which the appeal lies on an issue which is the subject of the appeal; and

(*b*)   they are satisfied that it was not adduced in those proceedings but there is a reasonable explanation for the failure to adduce it.

In civil cases, RSC Ord 59, r 10, provides that the Court of Appeal 'shall have power to receive further evidence on questions of fact, either by way of oral examination in court, by affidavit, or by depositions taken before an examiner, but in the case of an appeal from a judgment after trial or hearing of any case or matter on the merits no such further evidence (other than evidence as to matters that have occurred after the date of the trial or hearing) shall be admitted except on special grounds'.

In *Mulholland v Mitchell* [1971] AC 666 at 680 Lord Wilberforce said: 'Positively– it may be expected that courts will allow fresh evidence when to refuse it would affront common sense, or a sense of injustice.'

The final words of Ord 59, r 10, however, indicate clearly enough that the power should be exercised sparingly.

The policy followed by the courts is shown in the two decisions that follow, one criminal and one civil:

R v Flower (1965) 50 Cr App Rep 22 (Court of Appeal Criminal Division)

Widgery J, giving the judgment of the court, said:

When this court gives leave to call fresh evidence which appears at the time of the application for leave to be credible, it is still the duty of the court to consider and assess the reliability of that evidence when the witness appears and is cross-examined, and this is particularly true when evidence is called in rebuttal before this court. Having heard the fresh evidence and considered the reliability of the witness, this court may take one of three views with regard to it. If satisfied that the fresh evidence is true and that it is conclusive of the appeal the court can, and no doubt ordinarily would, quash the conviction. Alternatively, if not satisfied that the evidence is conclusive, the court may order a new trial so that a jury can consider the fresh evidence alongside that given at the original trial. The second possibility is that the court is not satisfied that the fresh evidence is true but nevertheless thinks that it might be acceptable to, and believed by, a jury, in which case as a general proposition the court would no doubt be inclined to order a new trial in order that the evidence could be considered by the jury, assuming the weight of the fresh evidence would justify that course. Then there is a third possibility, namely that this court, having heard the evidence, positively disbelieves it and is satisfied that the witness is not speaking the truth. In that event, and speaking generally again, no new trial is called for because the fresh evidence is treated as worthless and the court will then proceed to deal with the appeal as though the fresh evidence had not been tendered.

Ladd v Marshall [1954] 1 WLR 1489, CA

In a civil action, the plaintiff Ladd called the defendant's wife. She was a reluctant witness and said that she did not remember a certain vital incident. Judgment was given for the defendant. Later the wife, who had in the meanwhile obtained a divorce, informed the plaintiff's solicitors that she did remember the incident in question and that she wished to change her evidence. The plaintiff appealed, asking either for a new trial or that the Court of Appeal should itself hear the new evidence. Denning LJ, having stated the facts set out above, continued:

It is very rare that application is made to this court for a new trial on the ground that a witness has told a lie. The principles to be applied are the same as those always applied when fresh evidence is sought to be introduced. To justify the reception of fresh evidence or a new trial, three conditions must be fulfilled: first, it must be shown that the evidence could not have been obtained with reasonable diligence for use at the trial; secondly, the evidence must be such that, if given, it would probably have an important influence on the result of the case, though it need not be decisive; thirdly, the evidence must be such as is presumably to be believed, or in other words, it must be apparently credible, though it need not be incontrovertible.

We have to apply those principles to the case where a witness comes and says: 'I told a lie but nevertheless I now want to tell the truth'. It seems to me that the fresh evidence of such a witness will not as rule satisfy the third condition. A confessed liar cannot usually be accepted as being credible. To justify the reception of the fresh evidence, some good reason must be shown why a lie was told in the first instance, and good ground given for thinking the witness will tell the truth on the second occasion. If it was proved that the witness had been bribed or coerced into telling a lie at the trial, and is now anxious to tell the truth, that would, I think, be a ground for a new trial and it would not be necessary to resort to an action to set aside the judgment on the ground of fraud. Again, if it was proved that the witness made a mistake on a most important matter and wished to put it right, and the circumstances were so well explained that his fresh evidence was presumably to be believed, then again there would be grounds for a new trial: see *Richardson v Fisher.*[7] But this is not a case of bribery or coercion, nor of a mistake. It seems to me that Mrs

7   (1823) 7 Bing 145.

Marshall is not a person who in the new situation is presumably to be believed. She endeavoured to show that she was coerced by her husband, but on reading through the affidavits on both sides, it seems to me that the suggestion of coercion comes to nothing. She does not seem to have been in fear of her husband at all. I am afraid it is simply a case where a witness who had told a lie at the first hearing now wants to say something different. It would be contrary to all principle for that to be grounds for a new trial. In my judgment this appeal and the motion should be dismissed.

Parker and Hudson LJJ concurred.

The test for the admissibility of fresh evidence in civil and criminal cases seems to be virtually identical. See also *R v Parks* (1961) 46 Cr App Rep 29 and Alec Samuels, 'Fresh Evidence in the Court of Appeal Criminal Division' (1975) *Criminal Law Review*, p 23.

A dramatic example of the narrowness of the approach of the Court of Appeal to fresh evidence was the case of Luke Dougherty. Dougherty was charged with shop-lifting, having been identified by two witnesses. The offence occurred at a time when Dougherty was in fact on a bus-outing with some 20 others, many of whom knew him. In the event only two were produced at the trial. One was his girlfriend and the other was someone with previous convictions. The jury disbelieved the alibi and convicted. On 22 February 1972 he received a sentence of 6 months' imprisonment, and the judge also activated a 9 months' suspended sentence, making 15 months in all.

The case was taken up by JUSTICE, which wrote to the Court of Appeal asking that legal aid be granted to permit statements to be taken from persons who were on the bus. The application was refused. (The Registrar wrote on 10 April: 'it is not considered appropriate for the Registrar at this stage to grant legal aid so that a large number of people, available at the time of the trial but not called upon the advice of counsel, may be interviewed'.)

On the application for leave to appeal, the single judge ruled that there was no ground to appoint a solicitor and that the fresh evidence could not be called. In conversation between counsel for Dougherty and the Registrar of the court, the Registrar said that 'this kind of case is unlikely to get off the ground' and that there were various unreported decisions in which the court had refused to allow the calling of fresh evidence where counsel at the trial had not called witnesses in spite of the client's request that they be called. When the case was argued before the full court, the fresh-evidence point was not even argued. Counsel proceeded instead on a different issue (that of the dock identification). Nevertheless the court in dismissing the appeal said that if the point had been argued 'the conditions necessary before such evidence could be received before this court could not be fulfilled'.

JUSTICE pursued its concern over the case and eventually in November 1972, through the good offices of Lord Gardiner, it was referred back to the Court of Appeal by the Home Secretary. Dougherty's release was ordered immediately by the court. (With remission for good conduct, he would have been released in any event a few weeks later.) An examination of the alibi witnesses was then ordered, and on the hearing the prosecution did not contest the contention on behalf of Dougherty that the conviction was unsafe and unsatisfactory.

The whole sorry story is told in the Report of the Devlin Committee, which was set up partly as a result of this case (see *Report of the Departmental Committee on Evidence of Identification in Criminal cases*, 1976, House of Commons Paper 338, ch 2). Commenting on this aspect of the case, the Devlin Committee said that our ad-ministration of justice was based on the adversary system and the trial retained many characteristics of a battle. ('In a battle it is the responsibility of each side to get all its troops on the field on time. Napoleon could not appeal against the verdict of Waterloo on the ground that Marshall Grouchy and his army were still on their way when Blucher and the Prussians arrived in the nick of time', para 6.3.) Under the adversary system, relief was granted if the lack of evidence at the time of trial was due to misfortune, but not if it was due to lack of diligence or to a deliberate decision to do without the evidence. The rule was the same for civil as for criminal cases. However, it was no longer acceptable that an innocent person should continue to spend time in prison 'on the principle of "woe to the conquered" '. But the remedy lay chiefly with the executive in exercising the prerogative of mercy (see p 525 below). The Committee did not recommend any new statutory rule, nor even a change of policy by the Court of Appeal. If the court thought that it was better for such issues to be determined by the Home Office than by itself, its view should be accepted. On the other hand, when considering whether there were exceptional circumstances permitting the admissibility of fresh evidence, the court should take into account the weight of the excluded evidence. In Dougherty's case if properly marshalled it would have been irresistible and in such a case where it is plain that the prisoner must be released, the sooner it was done the better (paras 6.8–12).

A slightly more relaxed attitude to the problem of fresh evidence was shown by the Court of Appeal Civil Division in *Dixon v Dixon* (1983) 133 NLJ 305. A husband was ordered to pay maintenance for a child that he claimed was not his. After the magistrates' court hearing, the husband had blood tests done which showed conclusively that the child was not his. He applied to the Divisional Court for leave to appeal out of time against the order for periodic payments and for leave to admit the fresh evidence of the blood test. (At the trial before the magistrates he was not legally represented. The hearing had been adjourned in order to enable him to seek legal advice but he had not done so because of the cost. No one had suggested that he should seek legal aid.) The Divisional Court refused leave to admit the fresh evidence on the ground that the evidence was available or could have been available if the husband had used reasonable diligence at the time of the hearing before the magistrates.

On appeal, the Court of Appeal remitted the matter to the magistrates to hold a re-hearing with the fresh evidence. The court said it was a very serious matter to exclude evidence which was wholly conclusive in favour of an applicant on the ground that it could have been available with reasonable diligence at the time of the hearing. It would be most undesirable that an order of the court should be allowed to stand which was based on crucial facts that everyone knew were incorrectly stated.

But a few months later the House of Lords seemed to take a less generous view. In *Linton v Ministry of Defence* (1983) Times, 14 November, it upheld a decision from Northern Ireland denying a fresh trial and permission to introduce fresh evidence to a plaintiff who had been shot by a soldier. He claimed that he was an innocent passer-by caught in a hail of bullets exchanged between soldiers and IRA terrorists. The army claimed that he had been one of the terrorists himself. He sued for damages for his injuries. A crucial piece of evidence concerned an employment card which he said he had had in his jeans' back-pocket, which proved that he was on his way to a job interview at the time of the incident. He was unable, however, to explain on cross-examination why it was neither bloodstained nor crumpled. The barrister for the army suggested to the jury that he had not in fact had it on him and the jury rejected the claim.

On appeal he sought to introduce fresh evidence of two kinds. First, he said he now remembered that he had actually been carrying the card in his jacket, which would explain why it was not bloodstained or crumpled. Second, he wanted to produce the entry in the hospital record where he was taken unconscious after being shot, which showed that his effects included an employment card which Lord Scarman said was almost certainly the card which he had been talking about at the trial.

Giving judgment for a unanimous House of Lords, Lord Scarman said that the appellant had satisfied the second and third of the tests laid down in *Ladd v Marshall*. The evidence was important and it was apparently credible. But he could not satisfy the first test. He (or his lawyers) had lacked reasonable diligence in not producing the new evidence at the trial. 'Ours is an adversarial system and it is the duty of a plaintiff to come to court with the evidence to prove his case.' He cited with approval the dictum of the Lord Chief Justice of Northern Ireland in the court below: 'A new trial cannot be granted or fresh evidence admitted just because the result of the first trial was or may have been occasioned or made more likely by the unsuccessful party's inattention or faulty memory or by an innocent mistake.'

See further Alec Samuels, in 'Fresh Evidence in the Court of Appeal, Criminal Division' (1975) *Criminal Law Review*, p 23.

New points taken on appeal

The same basic approach informs the attitude of the Court of Appeal to points taken by counsel. If they could have been taken at the trial, the Court of Appeal will generally not allow them to be advanced for the first time at the appellate stage. So in *Re Tarling* [1979] 1 All ER 981, Gibson J in a habeas corpus case said: 'It is clear to the court that an applicant for habeas corpus is required to put forward on his initial application the whole of the case which is then fairly available to him–it becomes an abuse of process to raise in subsequent proceedings matters which could, and therefore should, have been litigated in earlier proceedings' (at p 987). In the same year in *Maynard* (1979) 69 Cr App Rep 309, Roskill LJ said: 'We have often said in this court that where a question, and in particular a question of the admissibility of evidence, is deliberately not raised at the trial it is only in very rare cases that we allow the matter to be raised in this court for the first time. To hold otherwise would be to encourage counsel to keep points of this kind up their sleeve and then reserve them for the Court of Appeal and thus have a second bite at the forensic cherry.'

In *Stirland v DPP* [1944] AC 315, the House of Lords rejected any firm rule that the courts could not allow an appeal on admissibility of evidence where counsel had failed to take objection at the trial. But, it said, 'the failure of counsel to object may have some bearing on the question whether the accused was really prejudiced'. It was not 'a proper use of counsel's discretion to raise no objection at the time in order to preserve a ground of objection for a possible appeal' (at p 328).

In March 1995 in *R v Cox (Andrew Mark)* [1995] Crim LR 741 the Court of Appeal said it was most unsatisfactory that a matter not relied on at trial could found an appeal against conviction. At the trial prosecution and the trial judge had agreed that it would confuse the jury for the judge to put the issue of provocation as a possible defence to murder in his summing up. Defence counsel had said nothing. The defence at trial was based on diminished responsibility. On appeal it was argued that the judge had misdirected the jury in not dealing with the issue of provocation. The court upheld the defence submission but dismissed the appeal by applying the proviso (see pp 506–07 above). The court said that for the future it must be made clear that both counsel had an obligation to the trial court. If it appears to either counsel that there is evidence supporting a defence of provocation it was their job to invite the judge to deal with the matter and to remind him that he was required by statute to leave the issue to the jury. The Court of Appeal said this was the formulation of a new duty and that no criticism could therefore attach to either counsel. It remains to be seen whether this duty extends generally to all points that could be taken at trial or only to the special case of provocation where statute requires the judge to leave the issue to the jury if there is any evidence to support such a defence even when the judge takes the view that no reasonable jury could find the defence made out–see *R v Cambridge* [1994] 2 All ER 760.

See further R Munday, 'Trial Tactics and the Appellate Imagination', *Law Society's Gazette*, 27 May 1987, p 1554.

When the fresh evidence concerns matters that occurred after the trial, the situation is obviously different. But here too the appeal courts have traditionally taken a rather narrow approach, on the basis that there should be an end to litigation and that cases should not be re-opened unless there are very good grounds. Thus in *Mulholland v Mitchell* [1971] AC 666, the plaintiff had suffered very serious injuries, and damages had been assessed by the judge on the basis that he could be looked after either at home or in an ordinary nursing home. The appeal was on the basis that after the trial his condition had deteriorated dramatically. The Court of Appeal allowed fresh evidence to be given to establish the facts. On appeal to the House of Lords, the law lords held that the Court of Appeal had exercised its discretion reasonably but, generally, fresh evidence should not be admitted relating to a matter of uncertainty taken into account by the judge unless the basis on which he had given his decision had been clearly falsified by subsequent events. On these cases, see generally JB Hodge, 'Fresh Evidence in the Court of Appeal', *Solicitors' Journal*, 2 January 1987, p 6.

Despite the frequently narrow and negative attitude of the Court of Appeal to its powers to receive fresh evidence, there is no doubt that the court has the power to receive any admissible evidence if it so chooses and it can call and hear such evidence on its own initiative. The breadth of this discretion under s 23 was emphasised by the Court of Appeal in *Gilfoyle* [1995] NLJR 1720. Moreover, the power to receive fresh evidence is there to assist the prosecution as well as the defence–for instance to show that a case against the defendant was not mere speculation, even though the evidence had been available to the Crown at trial and was not used then. The only restriction is that the court must consider that such evidence is necessary or expedient in the interests of justice. The court quoted Lord Simon in *Stirland v DPP* [1944] AC 315 at 324 'a miscarriage of justice may arise from the acquittal of the guilty no less than from the conviction of the innocent. . .'

When a case is referred back to the Court of Appeal (formerly by the Home Secretary, in future by the Criminal Cases Review Commission, pp 532–36 below) the power to receive fresh evidence is less restrictive than on an ordinary appeal. This emerges from a number of cases: *McGrath* [1949] 2 All ER 495; *Sparkes* [1956] 1 WLR 505; *Swabey* [1972] 2 All ER 1094; *Graves* [1978] Crim LR 216. But it does not seem to be the case that the court will receive evidence that would not have been admissible at the trial itself. The Runciman Royal Commission said that if there were convincing but inadmissible evidence showing that a miscarriage of justice had occurred it should be dealt with through the Royal Prerogative of Mercy rather than by the Court of Appeal. ('If the fresh evidence sought to be admitted is inadmissible under the rules of evidence, in our view the court should not receive it' (p 176, para 67).

During the debates on the 1966 Criminal Appeal Bill, the then Home Secretary stated that the Lord Chief Justice had authorized him to say that 'while it is essential for the court to decide what evidence it will treat as admissible, it is not bound by its previous practice as to the admission of evidence, and that it can and will review the practice in the light of the Bill, the governing principle being to ensure so far as possible that there has been no miscarriage of justice' (House of Commons, *Hansard*, 30 April 1964, col 722, quoted in the Donovan Report, *op cit*, p 501 above, para 135).

The Donovan Committee, citing this statement in its Report, said (para 136): 'We construe this as meaning that the court will exercise its power to hear fresh evidence in such a way as to ensure that any miscarriage of justice will so far as possible be avoided or corrected'. It would, it thought, conduce to that end if the condition about the evidence not having been available at the trial were discarded, and it recommended that 'additional evidence should be received if it is relevant and credible, and if a reasonable explanation is given for the failure to place it before the jury'.

The Runciman Royal Commission on fresh evidence

The Runciman Royal Commission said that successful appeals based on fresh evidence were relatively rare. In Kate Malleson's 1990 sample of 102 successful appeals there were 6 based on fresh evidence. In her 1992 sample there were 4 out of 102 (Report, p 172, para 51).

The Commission broadly approved the statutory scheme set out in s 23 but suggested that possibly the court had construed its powers too narrowly. It was understandable that the court should view fresh evidence with some suspicion. There was the fear that fresh evidence can, and often will be manufactured. Defendants and their lawyers should not be encouraged to think of trials 'as nothing more than a practice run which in the event of a conviction will leave them free to put an alternative defence to the Court of Appeal in whatever manner they please' (*ibid*, p 173, para 55).

On the other hand, 'the court must be be alive to the possibility that the fresh evidence, if true, may exonerate the appellant or at least throw serious doubts on the conviction' (*ibid*). The court had to consider whether the fresh evidence was available at the trial and if so, whether there was a reasonable explanation for the failure to adduce it. It had been suggested to the Commission that the attitude of the court had on occasion been excessively restrictive. It said: 'We would urge that in general the court should take a broad, rather than a narrow, approach to them' (*ibid*, para 56).

Thus, where the witness wished to change his evidence, the Court of Appeal was right to look at it very carefully, but if there was some reasonable explanation why the witness gave the previous evidence from which he wants to depart, the court should receive it (p 174, para 57).

Under s 23(2) the court had to be persuaded that fresh evidence was 'likely to be credible'. The Royal Commission agreed with the view that this test was too restrictive. It unanimously recommended that the test be changed to 'capable of belief'. ('This would in our view be a slightly wider formula giving the court greater scope for doing justice' (*ibid*, para 60).) This recommendation was implemented by s 4 of the Criminal Appeal Act 1995.

(g) The power to order retrials in criminal cases

Until 1988 the power to order a retrial in a criminal case existed only in one situation –where the court allowed an appeal on the ground of fresh evidence. The basic statutory provision regulating the right to order retrials was s 7 of the Criminal Appeal Act 1968:

Criminal Appeal Act 1968

Retrial
7 (1) Where the Court of Appeal allow an appeal against conviction [and do so only by reason of evidence received or available to be received by them under section 23 of this Act[8] and it appears to the court that the interests of justice so require, they may order the appellant to be retried.

The rule regulating retrials does not prevent the court from ordering a new trial where none has taken place initially–for example because the jury failed to agree on a verdict. Sometimes the court holds that an irregularity vitiates the trial and orders a fresh start (*venire de novo*). In order for *venire de novo* to lie, the court must be in a position to rule that the trial was void from the outset–a nullity. For examples see *Crane v DPP* [1921] 2 AC 299 and *Cronin* [1940] 1 All ER 618. For examples of cases where the court did not feel able to order a retrial on this ground, see *Neal* [1949] 2 KB 590; *McKenna* [1960] 1 QB 411; and the House of Lords' decision in *Rose* [1982] 2 All ER 731. In *Rose* the House of Lords quashed a conviction for murder when the judge was shown to have brought pressure on the jury to hasten its decision. But it held that *venire de novo* could not be ordered as the trial had been validly commenced and could not be said to have been void from the outset. (The most authoritative study of the issue is by Sir Robin Cooke in (1955) 71 *Law Quarterly Review*, p 100.)

The question of whether there ought to be a general right to order a retrial was considered at length in 1954 by the Tucker Committee (*Report of the Departmental Committee on New Trials in Criminal Cases*, 1954, Cmnd 9150) and in 1964 by a committee of JUSTICE. The Tucker Committee was divided on whether there should be a general power to order a retrial (5 to 3 against). The JUSTICE committee was divided 9 to 4 in favour. Both committees were unanimous that there should be a power to order a retrial when there was fresh evidence.

A general power to order retrials became law as s 43 of the Criminal Justice Act 1988. It applies whenever the court thinks it to be in the interests of justice. (As seen above, this was achieved simply by deleting words from s 23 of the Criminal Appeal Act 1988.)

8   The words in brackets were removed by the Criminal Justice Act 1988, s 43 (ed).

But even though the power is now a general one and is therefore no longer restricted to fresh evidence cases, there was not at first any great increase in the tiny number of retrials ordered. In the 19-month period from August 1989 to March 1991 only four retrials were ordered by the Court of Appeal Criminal Division, (House of Commons *Hansard*, 11 March, 1991, vol 187 col 361–2). This compares with nine retrials on grounds of fresh evidence alone in the two year period 1966 to 1968, and fourteen retrials in the five year period 1981–6, see Patrick O'Connor, 'The Court of Appeal: Retrials and Tribulations' (1990) *Criminal Law Review*, pp 615, 622. But in the four years 1992–95 the number of retrials was respectively 12, 20, 51 and 54–showing that the court has significantly altered its attitude to the matter.

The Runciman Royal Commission strongly supported the Court of Appeal ordering more retrials:

We welcome and wish to encourage the increasing exercise of this power. Although. . . re-trials will not be practicable or desirable in a significant number of cases, they offer the Court of Appeal an attractive solution for its understandable reservations about speculative prediction of a hypothetical jury's decision. Where the court is not in doubt, there is no difficulty in allowing or dismissing the appeal as appropriate, Where, on the other hand, the court is in doubt and would like to see the evidence or arguments more fully tested, then, other things being equal, retrials seem to all of us the better way to proceed, even if some of us would not like them to be as frequently ordered as would others [Report, p 175, para 65].

The Royal Commission was split down the middle as to what should happen if for one or another reason a retrial, though desirable, was felt to be impracticable. Six members of the Commission thought that in that situation the Court of Appeal should quash the conviction, on the basis that, by definition, in order to want a retrial it must already have decided that the conviction might be unsafe. Five members of the Commission thought that in that situation the Court of Appeal should decide the matter for itself (*ibid*, para 66).

The interests of justice in having or not having a retrial were considered by the House of Lords in *DPP v Lynch* (1975) 61 Cr App Rep 6 at pp 16, 22 and 47–8 and by the Privy Council in *Holder* (1978) 68 Cr App Rep 120 and *Au Pui -Kuen* (1979) 69 Cr App Rep 33. Retrials were ordered there after three, four and three years respectively.

Patrick O'Connor in his 1990 article (above) said: 'Where it is important enough, long delayed trials are conducted. One William Quinn was recently tried and convicted at the Central Criminal Court for a murder committed in 1974. The trial revolved substantially around contested identification evidence' (p 623). The Tucker Committee had found that retrials worked satisfactorily in Australia, Canada, New Zealand and Ceylon. Michael Knight in his book *Criminal Appeals* (Stevens, 1970) had surveyed the widespread use of retrials in Ireland since 1928 and found (p 151) that they had been ordered in three-quarters of all quashed conviction cases in the period 1954 to 1964.

In fresh evidence cases should the Court of Appeal order retrials or decide for itself?

In his book *The Judge* (OUP, 1979, pp 148–76) Lord Devlin argued powerfully that the Court of Appeal had started to usurp the function of the jury in deciding doubtful cases by either quashing the convictions or by applying the proviso. He took as his text *Stafford v DPP* [1974] AC 878 and secondly, the Luton Murder Case, in which the Court of Appeal repeatedly refused to order a new trial even though crucial new evidence came to light.

In *Stafford* the House of Lords held unanimously that the task of the Court of Appeal in fresh evidence cases was to decide whether *it* thinks the verdict unsafe or unsatisfactory. It should consider the weight of the evidence and not concern itself so much with the question as to what effect it might have had on a jury. Lord Devlin had strongly criticised this approach on the ground that it usurped the function of the jury (see *The Judge*, pp 148–76). Under the rule adopted in *Stafford*, Stafford was not, in his view, convicted by a jury but rather by a mixed trial by judges and jury. It was in effect now the judges who had to evaluate the impact of fresh evidence. ('If the court has no reasonable doubt about the verdict, it follows that the court does not think that the jury could have one; and conversely, if the court says that a jury might in the light of new evidence have a reasonable doubt, that means that the court has a reasonable doubt', *Stafford v DPP* per Lord Dilhorne at p 893.) But the danger of that approach in Lord Devlin's view was that it could lead to an end to the jury ('If judge and jury are bound to give the same answer why bother with a jury?').

The approach of the Court of Appeal was stated clearly in the final appeal of the Birmingham Six:

There is House of Lords authority, binding on us, as to the approach we should adopt: see *Stafford and Luvaglio*. It was summarised by the Court of Appeal in the 1988 judgment in that case as follows: 'Although the court may choose to test its views by asking itself what the original jury might have concluded, the question which in the end we have to decide is whether in our judgment, in all the circumstances of the case including both the verdict of the jury at trial upon the evidence they heard and the fresh evidence before this court that we have heard, the convictions were safe and satisfactory. If so the convictions must stand. If not the convictions must be quashed' [*McIlkenny*, per Lloyd LJ]

See further Patrick O'Connor (1990) *Criminal Law Review*, *op cit*, pp 620–5, and generally Kate Malleson, 'Miscarriages of Justice and the Accessibility of the Court of Appeal' (1991) *Criminal Law Review*, p 323.

The Runciman Royal Commission considered Lord Devlin's criticism that the Court of Appeal usurped the function of the jury if it decided the effect of fresh evidence on the result. It agreed with Lord Devlin save if the fresh evidence was so clear cut as to satisfy the Court of Appeal that it rendered the conviction unsafe–in which case it should quash the conviction. Otherwise, having admitted fresh evidence on the basis that it was relevant and capable of belief which could have affected the outcome of the case, it should order a retrial unless that was not practicable or desirable. ('The Court of Appeal, which has not seen the other witnesses in the case nor heard their evidence, is not in our view the appropriate tribunal to assess the ultimate credibility and effect on a jury of fresh evidence' (p 175, para 62).)

Where a retrial was not practicable or was otherwise undesirable the Commission unanimously thought that there was no alternative other than the Court of Appeal deciding the matter for itself (p 175, para 63).

It is to be noted that there is in fact no way of taking away from the Court of Appeal the duty of deciding what *it* thinks about fresh evidence since, unavoidably, it always has to decide the initial questions–is the evidence capable of belief and significant. This is not usurping the role of the jury but it does involve consideration of the credibility and importance of the evidence–*pace* Lord Devlin.

(h) Review by the appeal court of discretionary decisions

The classic rule in regard to review of a discretionary decision is that the appeal court will not interfere unless it can be shown that the judge below acted on a wrong principle. It will not change the decision simply because it disagrees. Thus in *Culver v Beard* [1937] 1 All ER 301, the judge ordered the case to be tried in the county court even though the injuries in question were serious. The plaintiff appealed. The Court of Appeal held that the judge's decision should not be disturbed unless the judge had erred in law or had acted on wrong principles. Greer LJ said (at p 302):

I am rather inclined to the view that, if this matter had come before me as the court or judge, I should have said: 'The injuries are so serious in this case that, the tendency of county court judges being to deal day after day with matters of comparatively small monetary interest, it would be better to leave the case in the High Court and not to remit it to the county court.' But that is not a matter, in my judgment, which this court is entitled to take into consideration for the purpose of overruling the discretion of the learned judge who took the other view, if he did take the other view.

In *Stevens v Walker* [1936] 2 KB 215, the Court of Appeal did interfere in such a case because it was shown that the judge had not considered circumstances which he was bound to consider. By not considering them he had gone wrong in principle. Lord Wright said (at p 223):

On the whole, in the present case I think the learned judge had not fully present to his mind the vital question of whether there was a good prima facie case or a good prima facie defence. I think he did not sufficiently consider the gravity of the claim which was put forward, and I think it appears that he attached undue importance to the question of whether or not there might be difficult questions of law involved. I feel very strongly that the discretion in these very serious personal accident cases should be exercised with very great care, and on the whole I think in the present case the learned judge exercised his discretion on inadequate material and without having before him, as he ought to have had, either the defence or a statement in the affidavit swearing that there was a good defence.

There are many different examples of 'acting on a wrong principle'. Thus the Court of Appeal has been prepared to interfere on the ground that the discretion was exercised under a mistake of law, or under a misapprehension as to the facts, or that the judge took into account irrelevant matters, or that he failed to exercise the discretion at all.

A series of cases have shown differently constituted Courts of Appeal disagreeing as to whether the court could alter a custody order if it disagreed with it or whether more than mere disagreement was necessary. In *Re O* (*infants*) [1971] Ch 748, the Court of Appeal, per Davies LJ, had said (at p 755): 'The law now is that if an appellate court is satisfied that the decision of the court below is wrong, it has the duty to say so and act accordingly . . . Every court has a duty to do its best to arrive at a proper and just decision. If an appellate court is satisfied that the decision of the court below is improper, unjust or wrong, then the decision must be set aside.' Davies LJ did not subscribe to the view that a discretionary decision should necessarily be upheld. That might be to perpetuate injustice.

In *D v M* [1983] Fam 33, the judges took the same view. Appellate courts, they held, were not subject to limitations when hearing appeals against discretionary decisions. The court had a duty to review the way in which the trial judge had conducted the balancing of the different factors. The same view was also expressed by the majority of the Court of Appeal in *Re F* [1976] Fam 238. The court varied a custody order on the ground that the judge had given insufficient weight to the fact that the child was to be brought up by a young couple with other children rather than by aged grandparents. Stamp LJ, however, dissented on the ground that the appeal court could not interfere unless the judge had erred in principle.

The view that Stamp LJ expressed was adopted by the Court of Appeal in *E v C* (1982) Times, 15 October 1982. Dunn LJ said that questions of access were essentially for the trial judge. The appeal court would not interfere unless he was plainly wrong. See, to like effect, *Clarke-Hunt v Newcombe* (1982) 4 FLR 482. (These cases on the Court of Appeal's attitude to custody decisions are described by Margaret Rutherford in *Law Society's Gazette*, 1983, p 1665.)

Strong affirmation of the same principle came in the decision of the Court of Appeal in *Eagil Trust Co Ltd v Pigott-Brown* [1985] 3 All ER119. The case concerned dismissal for want of prosecution. Lord Justice Griffiths, as he then was, said he wished to use the case to emphasize that the court's role was to review the exercise of a discretion by a lower court and not to substitute its own decision. ('It appears to me that there is an ever increasing tendency on the part of the profession to use the decision of a High Court judge in a matter of discretion as a mere conduit-pipe to [the Court of Appeal]. If I am right in this belief, the sooner it is appreciated that that is a practice that cannot be tolerated the better.') Where a court was developing a new jurisdiction there would inevitably be more appeals so that guidance could be given, but once the principles were established 'there is a heavy burden on an appellant' to demonstrate that the Court of Appeal should intervene. Sometimes it was said that the judge's discretion could be attacked if it was clearly wholly wrongly exercised. But in his view, 'the greatest caution should be adopted in that approach because it comes perilously close to a means of substituting this court's discretion for that of the High Court, and that is not permissible' (at p 121).

Note–limitations on the appeal process

It could be said that the English appeal system manifests a marked reluctance to make itself too available. There are a considerable number of illustrations of this point.

(1) The requirement that persons convicted at a crown court must obtain leave to appeal and the threat of loss of time for hopeless appeals.

(2) The fact that appeals (other than those to the crown court from magistrates) are not by way of a rehearing of the evidence but are simply on the documents.

(3) The fact that appeals from magistrates' courts and county courts are hampered by the inadequacy of the record kept of proceedings at the trial.

(4) The narrow approach to the reception of fresh evidence, p 510 above.

(5) The reluctance of the appeal court to interfere with a jury's award of damages or its verdict, and its only slightly less marked disinclination to upset a trial judge's finding of fact, pp 497–504 above.

(7) The rule that a litigant or defendant in a criminal case cannot get his case re-opened indirectly by an action for negligence against his lawyers–see *Rondel v Worsley* [1969] 1 AC 191.

(8) The rule that a person convicted in a criminal case cannot bring an action for defamation against someone who says he was rightly convicted–see Civil Evidence

Act 1968, s 13, which makes the criminal conviction conclusive evidence of the fact of guilt in such proceedings.

(9) The fact that the Court of Appeal Criminal Division and the House of Lords will only hear cases with leave and that in a criminal case there must also be a certificate of the Court of Appeal that a point of law of general public importance is involved. Thus, if a certificate is denied, there is no way the House of Lords can hear the appeal –even if it thinks that the point at issue *is* of general public importance.

(10) The fact that an appellant in the House of Lords who is not legally aided has to put down a bond for security for costs in the amount of £18,000.

(i) Rates of appeal and success rates

(1) Criminal cases

In regard to cases in the magistrates' courts, appeals are quite rare. Thus in 1994, there were 12,090 appeals from magistrates' courts to the crown court against conviction and 15,683 against sentence. In addition there were 269 appeals by way of case stated from the magistrates' court to the Divisional Court. In 1994, there were 497,000 indictable offences, 587,000 summary non-motoring offences and 863,000 summary motoring offences dealt with by magistrates.

Of the appeals to the crown court, 43 per cent of appellants had their convictions allowed. This was an increase of five percentage points over 1993 and was the highest recorded figure in the past decade. The proportion who had their sentence varied was 38 per cent (Home Office Statistical Bulletin, *Criminal Appeals, 1994*). The most common group of offences for which an appeal was made to the crown court were summary motoring insurance offences.

In regard to cases tried in the crown court, there were a total of 8,070 appeals to the Court of Appeal, Criminal Division. Of these 1,511 (19%) were against conviction, 5,608 (69%) were against sentence and 951(12%) were against both conviction and sentence. In 1994 there were 90,759 persons dealt with in the crown court who had been committed for trial. In that year, 15,735 pleaded not guilty to all counts and 3,728 pleaded not guilty to some counts.

Of the 1,511 who appealed against conviction, only 247(16%) had their conviction quashed. Of the 5,608 who appealed against sentence only,1,190 (21%) had their sentence varied (Sources: Home Office Statistical Bulletin, *Criminal Appeals*, 1994, *Judicial Statistics*, Cm 2891, 1994).

The number of appeals to the House of Lords in criminal cases is always very small. In 1994, for instance, there were only six appeals heard from the Court of Appeal Criminal Division. Three were allowed and three were dismissed.

(2) Civil cases

The number of appeals in civil cases is also very small. The House of Lords hears only a few dozen cases per year. In 1994 there were 64 cases disposed of by a hearing. (The Judicial Committee of the Privy Council which is largely manned by the same judges heard 68 appeals in 1994.)

The caseload of the Court of Appeal Civil Division is much heavier. In 1994 it heard 846 appeals from final judgments and 664 appeals from interlocutory orders. The great bulk came from the Queen's Bench Division and the county court. In the Queen's Bench Division there were 570 trials in 1994 and 162 appeals from final judgments–an appeal rate of about 28 per cent. Of the 162 26(16%) were allowed, 56(35%) were dismissed after a hearing and 63(39%) were dismissed by consent. (The rest were struck out or 'otherwise disposed of'.) The success rate was therefore not high. In the county court, there were 24,200 trials (not counting small claims arbitrations) but only 303 final appeals–an appeal rate of only 1 per cent. Of the appeals 75(25%)were allowed, 95(33%) were dismissed after a hearing,110(36%) were dismissed by consent and the rest were struck out or 'otherwise disposed of'.

In his Review of the 1994–95 Legal Year, Sir Thomas Bingham, the Master of the Rolls complained of serious and lengthening delays. The backlog of unheard appeals had risen each year, from 1,136 in 1991 to 1,833 in September 1995. The court had had to announce that in certain categories of cases it could only plan to hear 70 per cent of appeals within about 18 months of being set down. The projection was that by the year 2000 the backlog would be around 2,200.

The Master of the Rolls said that delays of that order were serious in any court. 'But they are particularly serious in the Court of Appeal, which is the pivot of our legal system. The existing delays, and still more those which are projected, should be an acute source of public concern.'

(j) 'Appeal' by way of judicial review

The Divisional Court of the Queen's Bench Division has power to quash the decisions of magistrates on the ground that they have failed to comply with the rules of natural justice or lacked jurisdiction. This procedure operates through the ancient prerogative remedy of certiorari, which is obtainable through an application for judicial review under RSC Ord 53. The power is used, typically, where the allegation is that the magistrates have lacked jurisdiction or have been actuated by malice or bias or where they have failed to allow the defendant to present his case–see *R v Thames Magistrates' Court, ex p Polemis* [1974] 2 All ER 1219. Such challenge goes to procedure not to the substantive question of the merits. It has been used where the prosecution was obtained by perjured testimony (*R v Leicester Recorder, ex p Wood* [1947] 1 All ER 928). But the question is supposed to be the regularity of the proceedings. In *R v West Sussex Quarter Sessions, ex p Albert and Maud Johnson Trust Ltd* [1973] 3 All ER 289, the Court of Appeal considered the issue of certiorari to quash the decision of quarter sessions regarding a right of way. There was no appeal against this decision but one party later discovered further evidence which it claimed could have altered the decision. The Divisional Court refused an application for certiorari and the Court of Appeal, Lord Denning dissenting, agreed. Lawton and Orr LJJ held that certiorari would not lie to quash the decision of an inferior tribunal merely on the ground that fresh evidence had been discovered. It was limited to defects of form and procedure. There had been no defect in the trial. Lord Denning thought that certiorari should lie for cases of fresh evidence which could not have been found by due diligence before the trial, where it was apparently credible and would have had an important influence on the result.

In *R v Leyland Justices, ex p Hawthorn* [1979] 1 All ER 209, however, the line previously drawn between what can and what cannot be challenged by way of certiorari seems to have been blurred. H was convicted of driving without due care and attention. Afterwards the police informed the defence solicitor of the names of two witnesses whom they had seen before the trial but had decided not to call. Their statements were helpful to the defendant's version of the facts. The Divisional Court considered the case of *Albert and Maud Johnson Trust* (above) and said that it made clear that certiorari could not lie where the ground of complaint was that important fresh evidence had come to light. The ground of complaint, however, was that the applicant had been deprived of the benefit of the rules of natural justice 'by not having acceded to him by the prosecution the elementary right of being informed of additional witnesses who are known to the prosecution but whom the prosecution do not intend to call' (p 210). Lord Widgery CJ said the question was a technical one. No one could doubt the importance of the matter or 'the desire which I think everyone would feel to get this matter within the scope of certiorari, because the hardship and indeed injustice, done to this applicant is there for all to see'. In *Halsbury's Laws of England* there was reference to certiorari being available where there has been fraud, collusion, a lack of jurisdiction or error on the face of the record. There was no mention of a breach of the rules of natural justice, but there was no doubt that this could be the basis of an application. Certainly there would have been no problem if the magistrates had been to blame for the fact that the extra evidence was not considered. But here the blame lay on the prosecution. Lord Widgery for himself, May and Tudor Evans JJ said simply (at p 211):

We have given this careful thought–because it is a difficult case in that the consequences of the decision either way have their unattractive features. However, if fraud, collusion, perjury and such like matters not affecting the tribunal themselves justify an application for certiorari to quash the conviction–then we cannot say that the failure of the prosecutor which in this case has prevented the tribunal from giving the defendant a fair trial should not rank in the same category. We have come to the conclusion that there was here a clear denial of natural justice. Fully recognising that the blame falls on the prosecutor and not on the tribunal, we think that it is a matter which should result in the conviction being quashed.

The implications of this decision are important, for it suggests that the Divisional Court may be prepared to contemplate applications where it feels strongly that injustice has been done even though the complaint is based on something that occurred outside the court case itself. Certainly the decision appears to blur the line previously drawn in earlier cases. (For comment to this effect, see R Munday, 'Natural Justice in the English Criminal Prosecution', *New Law Journal*, 1981, p 6.)

See further *R v Crown Court at Knightsbridge, ex p Goonatilleke* [1986] QB 1 (evidence of the store detective in a shoplifting case later found to have been vitiated by the fact that he had been dismissed from the police service–conviction quashed); *R v Crown Court at Liverpool, ex p Roberts* [1986] Crim LR 622 (conviction quashed where a police officer's previous inconsistent statement not revealed at trial or appeal); and *R v Kingston upon Thames Justices, ex p Khanna,* [1986] RTR 364 (drink-driving conviction quashed when it was discovered later that the self-calibrating system on the Lion Intoximeter was faulty).

The cases seem to show that in applications for judicial review the Divisional Court will consider the good faith of the prosecution.

See further *Law Society's Gazette*, 18 December 1985, p 3678; *Legal Action*, March 1986, p 37, April 1986, p 52; *Justice of the Peace*, 3 January 1987, p 151; and JM Spencer, 'Judicial Review of Criminal Proceedings' (1991) *Criminal Law Review*, p. 259.

For case law on judicial review of the county court see M Fordham, 'Well Kept Secret', *Law Society's Gazette, 13* April 1994, p 17.

3. THE MACHINERY FOR AVOIDING A MISCARRIAGE OF JUSTICE IN CRIMINAL CASES

The problem of miscarriages of justice has come sharply into focus in recent years especially in the context of the three great IRA cases–the Guildford Four, the Maguire Seven and the Birmingham Six.[9] In all three cases the defendants had their convictions quashed by the Court of Appeal. In all three they had served long terms of imprisonment. It had taken years of campaigning to get them set free and in each case it was eventually proved that they had been the victims of a grave miscarriage of justice. The Government announced the establishment of the Royal Commission on Criminal Justice on the same day that the Birmingham Six were set free, 14 March 1991. As will be seen below, the Royal Commission recommended that a new system be established for dealing with this problem and the recommendation was implemented in the Criminal Appeal Act 1995 which received the Royal Assent in July 1995

The problem of the machinery for handling miscarriages of justice has been the subject of a number of reports and studies over the past quarter of a century. A distinguished role in this long battle to set things right has been played by JUSTICE, the British Section of the International Commission of Jurists. Its report in 1968 (*Home Office Review of Criminal Convictions*) was effectively the first to examine the machinery critically. Since then there have been various further reports.

The Home Secretary has had at his disposal several different powers:

(1) Free pardon   A free pardon wipes out the effects of conviction and sentence but not the conviction itself. (See *Foster* [1984] Crim LR 423). In *R v Secretary for the Home Department, ex p Bentley* [1993] 4 All ER 442 the Divisional Court held that the courts could review the refusal by the Home Secretary to grant a pardon, the court accepted that to get a free pardon it was necessary to establish both moral and technical innocence. See to the same effect the evidence of the Home Office to the Home Affairs Committee of the House of Commons: 'It is a long-established policy that the Free Pardon, as an exceptional act of grace, should be confined as far as possible to those who are morally as well as technically innocent. This "Clean Hands" doctrine means that the Home Secretary must be satisfied before recommending a Free Pardon that in

---

9   Mountains of newsprint, major television programmes and books all played an important part in the saga of these three cases. On the Guildford Four and Maguire cases see in particular Grant McKee and Ros Franey, *Time Bomb*, (Bloomsbury, 1988), Robert Kee, *Trial and Error* (Hamish Hamilton, 1986) and Sir John May, *Interim Report on the Maguire Case*, July 1990, HMSO, HC 556 and *Second Report on the Maguire Case*, 1992, HC.296. On the case of the Birmingham Six see especially Chris Mullin's *Error of Judgment* (Poolbeg, 1990). Apart from the reports and articles referred to in the following pages, see also the special issue of the *New Law Journal* on miscarriages of justice, 17 May 1991.

the incident in question the defendant had no intention of committing an offence and did not in fact commit one' ('Miscarriages of Justice', 1982, p 3, para 12).

(2) Conditional pardon   The conditional pardon substitutes one form of punishment for another, again leaving the original conviction standing. (In *ex p Bentley* the Divisional Court held that the Home Secretary's refusal to grant a pardon was flawed because he had not considered a conditional pardon and the court invited the Home Secretary to consider this possibility.)

See, on these alternatives, ATH Smith, 'The Prerogative of Mercy, the Power of Pardon and Criminal Justice' (1983) *Public Law*, p 398. See also Alison Wolfgarten, 'Free Pardon', *Solicitors' Journal*, 28 February 1986, p 157.

Most free pardons occur in road-traffic and minor offences, usually for technical reasons. Frequently, for instance, the reason is that a whole batch of speeding convictions is cancelled when it is discovered that the stretch of road in question was not properly marked.

The Home Office's evidence in 1982 to the House of Commons Home Affairs Committee gave statistics about the recent use of the free pardon. In the eight year period 1972 to 1980 there had been 2,180 instances in which free pardons had been granted in regard to the original conviction. In nine-tenths of the cases the conviction had been for minor motoring offences. There had also been a total of 1,519 cases in which action had been taken on other grounds, such as compassionate remission of imprisonment or early release resulting from assistance given to the prison authorities (*Sixth Report of the House of Commons Home Affairs Committee*, 'Miscarriages of Justice', 1982, Appendix A, p 7).

For a suggestion that failure to exercise the power of mercy might in some circumstances be open to judicial review see BV Harris, 'Judicial Review and the Prerogative of Mercy? *Public Law*, Autumn 1991, p 386.

(3) Remission   Remission, also under prerogative, consists of a reduction in a sentence without a change in the nature of the sentence.

(4) Reference to the Criminal Division of the Court of Appeal under s 17 of the Criminal Appeal Act 1907 (as amended)   In the eight years 1981 to 1989 the Home Secretary referred a total of 39 cases involving 54 defendants to the Court of Appeal. In 18 of these cases the appeals were allowed. (Home Office evidence to the May Inquiry into the Guildford and Woolwich pub-bombings.) The Report of the Runciman Royal Commission, (p 181, fn 5) stated that in the three years from 1989 to 1992 there were a total of 28 cases referred involving 49 defendants. 35 had their convictions quashed. Two were ordered to be retried and in both cases the defendant was acquitted. One appeal was dismissed. The rest were then still pending (ed).

Other powers

In particular cases, the Home Secretary may be in a position to release a prisoner on licence, by virtue of his sentence of life imprisonment. Although these powers are normally exercised on considerations not affecting the original conviction, there is some evidence that they are occasionally used in this way.

Principles upon which the powers of the Home Secretary are exercised

The 1968 JUSTICE Report (above) reported on the criteria for acting adopted by the Home Office:

The overriding factor governing the exercise of the powers available to the Home Secretary is a proper concern to avoid even the appearance of interfering with the independence of the judiciary. Home Secretaries have accordingly taken a very restricted view of the proper scope for executive intervention–a matter which has been dealt with before a competent court is not normally considered to be reviewable. As a consequence, a Home Secretary will only intervene in cases where evidence is presented by the petitioner which was not available to the courts which dealt with the case. At the level of executive review, the onus of proof is effectively reversed. In cases where the petitioner fails to convince the Home Secretary of his innocence, but establishes that a serious doubt exists as to his guilt, he may be granted some remission of his sentence, or released on licence if the sentence is appropriate. Remission is more commonly granted however in respect of matters arising during the currency of the sentence, such as ill health, or as reward for assistance to the police or prison authorities.

Procedure

The Home Office would rarely move on its own initiative. The Chief Constable of the police force in question was often asked to investigate any fresh evidence. Sometimes a different force would investigate.

Prisoners, inevitably, had great difficulty in putting their points effectively. They usually had no legal or other professional help. Unless there was a public campaign by the media or some individual journalist or an organization like JUSTICE, the Home Office usually paid little attention to prisoners' petitions. Neither the Home Office nor the police ever showed much enthusiasm for re-examining cases.

In its 1968 Report (above) JUSTICE recommended that when a petition was rejected, reasons should be given. When an investigation was indicated, it should be supervised by someone independent, such as a senior lawyer. The petitioner should have the right to make written representations to that person. The supervising lawyer should have the right to call for further inquiries to be made. He should have at his disposal a special corps of investigators, possibly retired police officers. He should have to make a final report with his conclusions and recommendations. This would be sent to the petitioner. Normally it should be accepted by the Home Secretary.

In the rare case where the supervising lawyer could not arrive at a view, there should be the power to set up an independent inquiry.

53. The report of such an inquiry should be made to the Home Secretary and, if the recommendation was in favour of the petitioner, then the final decision should be in the form of an exercise of the Royal Prerogative as at present. Normally the recommendations of the commissioner should be accepted and acted on, but in all cases the conclusions of the report should be made known to the petitioner, together with so much of the substance of it as could be published without endangering confidential sources.

In July 1971 the Home Office stated however that the Government did not intend to implement the JUSTICE proposals. (See House of Commons, *Hansard*, 22 July 1971, col 1652.)

The Devlin Committee Report

In 1970 the Devlin Committee reported on *Evidence in Identification in Criminal Cases* (1976, House of Commons Paper 338). The Committee made two observations relevant to the issue presently under consideration. First, where the prisoner's petition presented fresh evidence, it recommended (para 6.19) that the Home Office should move quickly to undertake or commission new inquiries if it seemed that the fresh evidence put a new complexion on the case. They should not fail to move at that stage because they were not satisfied that the fresh evidence necessarily upset the conviction. These two questions should be kept distinct.

Secondly, on the general question of the proper test to apply to petitions, the Devlin Committee recommended that the Home Office should somewhat relax its test. As it then was, the petitioner had to establish 'very convincing grounds for thinking that he did not commit the offence'. This was 'a lot stiffer' than the test applied by the Court of Appeal. There, since the appeal was based on fresh evidence, there was an initial burden on the appellant to show that the evidence he was tendering is credible and material in the sense that it might have made a difference to the verdict. But once that hurdle was jumped the appeal followed the ordinary course with the burden of proof, as always, on the prosecution to show that after a re-examination of all the relevant material the conviction was one which was 'safe and satisfactory', that is, as it has been put, that the court is not left with a 'lurking doubt' (*ibid*, para 6.20). The Devlin Committee thought that the Home Secretary 'should apply the same test as the Court of Appeal' (para 6.21).

In discussion with the Committee, the Home Office had argued that it was right to have a stiffer test than was applied in the courts, since the Home Office could not test evidence or hear witnesses in the way that a court could. But the Committee was unimpressed with this argument. It appreciated the point, but thought that 'the solution lies in assimilating the processes as far as possible rather than in differentiating the tests' (para 6.22). There had been some discussion of having an independent review tribunal with rules of evidence and procedure different from those of the ordinary courts, to which cases that were unsuitable to the reference-back procedure of s 17 could be referred. The Committee recommended that the feasibility of creating such a tribunal should be studied by the Home Office. 'It could be manned by persons with criminal appellate experience and its powers might be either determinative or advisory' (*ibid*).

The House of Commons Home Affairs Committee Report

In 1982 the Home Affairs Committee of the House of Commons made an inquiry into the procedures within the Home Office for dealing with miscarriages of justice. It examined proposals for reforms made to it by JUSTICE, the Criminal Bar Association and Sir David Napley, former President of the Law Society.

It reached the conclusion that Home Office procedures were such that decisions were presented 'in such a way as to seem arbitrary' (*Sixth Report of the House of Commons Home Affairs Committee, 'Miscarriages' of Justice'*, 1982, para 19). It recommended that 'wherever possible, and without endangering confidential sources, any refusal to take further action should be accompanied by a summary of reasons for such a decision' (*ibid*, para 23). In appropriate cases the Home Office should consider interviewing the petitioner himself or his legal adviser (*ibid*).

But the Committee said that its main concern was over the cases which after initial sifting appeared to have some substance. It said it was 'convinced that there is a strong argument in favour of the introduction of an independent element at this stage and that it is unreasonable that the Home Secretary should be expected to decide whether to grant a free pardon or remit a sentence on the advice of his officials alone' (*ibid*, para. 24). Sentences in road-traffic cases which were the result of some technical error should be sent back to the magistrates with a request formally to quash the conviction. But all other cases which are not dismissed at the preliminary stage should be referred to a new independent review body established to advise the Home Secretary on the royal prerogative of mercy. There would then be no further need to refer cases to the Court of Appeal and this procedure would be abolished (*ibid*).

The new review body should consist of up to a dozen members, under a legally qualified chairman appointed by the Home Secretary or the Attorney-General. Most cases would be dealt with by one member but the most difficult cases could be given to a panel of three. They would have wide discretion as to how to investigate the cases. If they thought it necessary, they could hold formal hearings with legal representation for those concerned. It should be the normal practice for the Home Office to supply the parties concerned with a copy of the reasoned judgment on the case submitted by the review body to the Home Secretary.

The review body should not be prevented from considering the testimony of a witness who was not called to give evidence at that stage even though he was available at the time. The Committee said it felt the traditional rule about fresh evidence was 'unduly restrictive' (para 28).

The Committee also approved the Devlin Committee's recommendation that the Home Office should not require so high a standard of proof from the petitioner before recommending a free pardon. The royal prerogative should be exercised if the Home Office thought the original verdict was 'unsafe and unsatisfactory' (para 30).

The Government gave its reply to the Home Affairs Select Committee in April 1983 (*The Government Reply to the Sixth Report from the Home Affairs Committee*, 1983, Cmnd 8856). On certain points it accepted the Select Committee's proposals.

(1) It agreed that it was important to give prisoners an explanation of any unusual delays in processing their petitions.

(2) It agreed that, wherever possible, reasons should be given for refusal to intervene in a case.

(3) It agreed that there should be some procedure for referring back to magistrates cases where new material called the conviction into question. This power of reference back only existed in relation to cases tried at the crown court. It was for consideration whether the reference back should be to the magistrates' court that convicted the accused or to a crown court. This would be studied.

(4) But it did not accept that prisoners should be interviewed more often. It would only very rarely be right for the Home Office to do this. ('The Home Office is not qualified and does not seek to substitute its assessment of witnesses' oral testimony for that of the courts. The credibility of the petitioner himself is usually not the key issue; it is more likely that the case will turn on the credibility of other witnesses' (p 2).)

(5) Nor did the Government agree that it would be right to establish a new form of review body. On the other hand, the Government did believe that it could more frequently use the procedure of reference back to the Court of Appeal. The Lord Chief Justice, who had been consulted, '[saw] room for the court to be more ready to

exercise its own powers to receive evidence or, where appropriate and practicable, to order a retrial'. The Lord Chief Justice had confirmed that the Court of Appeal was 'very ready to use its discretion to admit new evidence . . . when the interests of justice so require'.

(6) There was also a possibility that procedural changes might be helpful. For instance, the Court of Criminal Appeal had had the power to refer specified matters for examination or investigation out of court. Possibly this power should be revived and extended. In general, the Government thought it was better to strengthen and improve the court rather than to set up any alternative system. On the other hand, the Home Secretary might in exceptional circumstances still ask a leading legal figure to hold a public inquiry into a case, especially where it might be a question of assessing witnesses whose evidence could not be heard by the court, for instance because the evidence was hearsay.

Commenting on the Government's reply to the Select Committee, the *Criminal Law Review* said editorially (September 1983, at p 577):

There remain fundamental defects in the English system of criminal appeals which these small changes are unlikely to remedy. First, the system makes provision, in reality, for only one possible kind of wrongful conviction. Where the judge has misdirected the jury or where there has been an irregularity in the trial, the appeal mechanism has some effect. Where the judge has summed up faultlessly and the trial was properly conducted, and it is the jury which has allegedly gone against the weight of evidence, the appeal mechanism has virtually no effect. So sacrosanct is the verdict of a jury held to be that it is exceedingly rare for the Court of Appeal to overturn one. Secondly, the usual practice is still to ask the same police force which originally investigated the case to investigate the complaint of wrongful conviction. JUSTICE, in its 26th Annual Report (June 1983), asks whether it is 'reasonable to expect the police diligently to investigate a complaint which might reveal that they or their colleagues were incompetent or negligent or simply wrong.' Thirdly, the extent to which the Court of Appeal will in practice be able to break free from some of its self-imposed fetters and to take on more of these cases remains to be seen. The court is, by all accounts, already overburdened by the volume of appeals against conviction and appeals against sentence.

JUSTICE in its 1987 report *Public Defender* suggested that the investigatory role played by the Home Office in the post-appeal stage should be played instead by a new Public Defender office. For this purpose it should be given the right to call on the police to re-investigate cases.

The 1989 JUSTICE Report

In July 1989 JUSTICE returned to the subject in an even more weighty report than its first twenty years earlier. (*Miscarriages of Justice*, prepared by a committee under the chairmanship of Sir George Waller, former Lord Justice of Appeal.) It made a long list of recommendations touching on aspects of the pre-trial, trial and appeal systems. In regard to the post-appeal machinery, JUSTICE returned to its call for an independent review body with the powers of a tribunal of inquiry able to operate along inquisitorial lines and to make recommendations to the Home Secretary.

It also recommended that the Home Secretary should not exclude cases from re-investigation because there was no fresh information. Where there was no fresh material but there were serious doubts about the conviction, the rest of the sentence should be remitted.

The May Inquiry into the case of the Maguires and the 'Guildford Four'

In October 1989 the Home Secretary and the Attorney-General appointed Lord Justice May to inquire into the circumstances leading to the conviction of the 'Guildford Four' and the Maguire family in respect of the pub-bombings in Guildford and Woolwich in 1974. The inquiry was partly about the circumstances of the particular cases but it was also about the general problem of miscarriages of justice.

Many of those who gave evidence to the May Inquiry supported the call for some form of independent body to assist the Home Secretary to identify cases. In addition to JUSTICE and Sir David Napley, they included the Criminal Bar Association, the Law Society, the National Association of Probation Officers, the Society of Labour Lawyers and the Legal Action Group.

ACPO (the Association of Chief Police Officers) said that although it was not necessary to create a new body to review convictions, there was a case for having a review team consisting of officers of a different force headed by a judge. The Police Federation said that, if the establishment of an independent review body would discourage publicity campaigns by convicted persons and their families, they would be in favour of the idea. The Federation would welcome any procedure by which complaints of wrongful conviction, in particular complaints of police impropriety, can properly and impartially be investigated.'

The most significant (and surprising) piece of evidence to the May Inquiry on this matter was the oral statement of Mr Douglas Hurd, then the Foreign Secretary, who had been the Home Secretary between 1985 and 1989 and in that capacity had been concerned with the Maguire case. In his evidence on 2 October 1991 Mr Hurd said that he was now persuaded that the power to refer possible miscarriages of justice should be removed from Home Secretaries and given to an independent standing body with investigative facilities.

In 1987 he had told the House of Commons that cases should be referred to the Court of Appeal only when new evidence or new considerations of substance cast doubt on a conviction. It was important that Home Secretaries not bow to other pressures. He told the May Inquiry that Home Secretaries came under 'fairly continuous pressure in case after case to use the power to reopen arguments already before the courts'. In the face of that, successive Home Secretaries had 'tried to establish rules and criteria which would enable them to exercise the power without getting into a position where they are in effect substituting themselves for the court'. He explained to the May Inquiry that he had refrained from referring the cases back to the Court of Appeal for fear of undermining public confidence. It would be better if these pressures could be handled by some new machinery. Possibly it might consist of some form of 'court of last resort' or an independent investigatory bureau. But it should have the power itself to refer cases to the Court of Appeal.

The Royal Commission on Criminal Justice

The Runciman Royal Commission on Criminal Justice appointed in Spring 1991 was asked to consider, among many other issues, 'the arrangements for considering and investigating allegations of miscarriages of justice when appeal rights have been exhausted'. (Sir John May was one of the persons appointed to be a member of the Royal Commission. The *general* question of the machinery for handling miscarriage of justice cases was referred by his Inquiry to the Royal Commission.)

In its evidence to the Runciman Royal Commission on Criminal Justice, the Home Office stated that the number of petitions received was now some 700–800 per year. C3, the Division responsible, estimated that in 1990 some 16 per cent resulted in a call for papers to the Court of Appeal before deciding whether further investigations were necessary. At least 18 per cent of representations resulted in the commissioning of further investigations or inquiries, usually from the original police force.

The Royal Commission reported in July 1993. Its recommendations on the machinery for dealing with miscarriage of justice cases were unanimous. The main recommendation was that the responsibility for dealing with these cases should be taken away from the Home Office and given instead to a new body independent of Government. Most of the witnesses who gave evidence to the Runciman Commission, including the Home Office, the Home Secretary and two former Home Secretaries, urged this upon the Commission.

The Royal Commission said (Report, p 182, para 9)

Our recommendation is based on the proposition, adequately established in our view by Sir John May's Inquiry, that the role assigned to the Home Secretary and his Department under the existing legislation is incompatible with the constitutional separation of powers as between the courts and the executive. The scrupulous observance of constitutional principles has meant a reluctance on the part of the Home Office to enquire deeply enough into the cases put to it and, given the constitutional background, we do not think that this is likely to change significantly in the future.

It recommended that a new body be set up 'to consider alleged miscarriages of justice, to supervise their investigation if further inquiries are needed, and to refer appropriate cases to the Court of Appeal' (*ibid,* para 11). It suggested that the new body might be called the Criminal Cases Review Authority (CCRA). In the event, the Government decided instead that it should be called the Criminal Cases Review Commission (CCRC). (For convenience the new body will be referred to here as the CCRC, whether reference is being made to the recommendations of the Royal Commission or to the provisions of the Criminal Appeal Act 1995.)

The Royal Commission proposed that the applicant could apply to the new body only after his appeal against conviction had been turned down or he had been refused leave to appeal. The CCRC would investigate the case if it thought an investigation was called for. Where it instructed the police to conduct investigations, it would be responsible for supervising the investigation and would have the power to require the police to follow up lines of inquiry it thought necessary. If the investigation suggested that a miscarriage of justice might have occurred, the CCRC would refer the case to the Court of Appeal which would consider it as if it were an appeal referred by the Home Secretary under s 17. The CCRC would provide the court with a statement of reasons and such (admissible) supporting material as it thought desirable (Report, p 182–83. paras 12, 16).

If it considered there were no grounds for a reference it would explain this decision, with its reasons, to the applicant (Report, pp 183, para 12).

The CCRC would be independent of Government but there would have to be a Minister answerable for it in Parliament. That would be the Home Secretary. The CCRC would report annually to the Minister who would lay the report before Parliament. The chairman should be appointed by the Queen on the advice of the

Prime Minister. The other members could be appointed by the Lord Chancellor (p 182, paras 13–14).

The Court of Appeal should have power to refer cases to the CCRC for investigation and the CCRC would report to the Court of Appeal about the outcome of any such investigation. But the CCRC would be wholly separate from the Court of Appeal and would not form a part of the court structure (p 183, para 15).

When the Court of Appeal received a reference from the CCRC it would ensure that the defence and the prosecution had a copy of the statement of reasons and the supporting material together with any additional material that it thought fit, so far as that was not prohibited by public interest immunity (p 183, para 13 and p 187, para 31). The appellant would present his case as he saw fit and he would be able, as before, to raise any matter of fact or law regardless of whether it was included in the papers sent to the CCRC (p 183, para 16).

The Home Secretary could continue, very exceptionally, to exercise the Royal Prerogative of Mercy especially for cases that the Court of Appeal could not consider under the existing rules for instance because of the rules of evidence (p 184, paras 17-18).

The CCRC should not be subject to judicial review in respect of its decisions. (p 184, para 19).

The CCRC should consist of several members, some lawyers, some lay persons. Not all would need to be full-time. The chairman should not be a serving member of the judiciary (p 184, para 20). It should be supported by a staff of lawyers and administrators and it should have access to specialist advisers such as forensic scientists, as necessary. It might be desirable for it to have on its staff one or two people expert in investigations especially to assist it in supervising police investigations (p 185, para 21).

In its annual report the CCRC should be able to draw attention to general features of the criminal justice system which it found unsatisfactory and to make any recommendations for change it thought fit (p 185, para 22).

The Royal Commission did not attempt to define the test the new body should use in deciding whether to investigate a case. ('In practice, it will need no further justification for investigating a case than a conclusion on the part of its members that there is, or may be on investigation, something to justify referring it to the Court of Appeal' (p 185, para 24).) The CCRC would need to devise its own rules and procedures for selecting cases for investigation.

The CCRC should be resourced sufficiently to enable it when appropriate to discuss cases direct with applicants. ('It is not always possible for people who have suffered a miscarriage of justice and then been sentenced to a long term of imprisonment to set out their case clearly and cogently in writing and an interview may sometimes be the best way of convincing the [Commission] that the case is one worth investigation' (p 185, para 25).)

The Royal Commission considered but rejected the idea that investigations should be carried out by persons other than the police. 'Given the size and scope of the inquiries that sometimes have to be made in these cases, and the resources required, there is in our view no practicable alternative to the police carrying out the investigation' (p 186, para 28).

There would need to be adequate arrangements for granting legal aid to convicted persons after they had lost their appeals to enable them to make representations to the Commission (p 187, para 32).

The Criminal Appeal Act 1995

The recommendations of the Royal Commission were broadly implemented in the Criminal Appeal Act. The Act established the Criminal Cases Review Commission, consisting of not fewer than 11 persons, all of whom have to be appointed by the Queen on the recommendation of the Prime Minister. At least one third have to be legally qualified. At least two thirds must be persons with knowledge or experience of the criminal justice system. There is no prohibition on a serving judge being on or chairman of the Commission.

The CCRC's power to refer a case to the Court of Appeal applies not only to crown court conviction issues but also to crown court sentencing issues and to conviction and sentence cases dealt with by magistrates. It also applies to Northern Ireland cases.

A reference to the Court of Appeal cannot be made unless the Commission 'considers that there is a real possibility that the conviction, verdict, finding or sentence would not be upheld were the reference to be made. . . because of an argument, or evidence, not raised in the proceedings which led to it or on any appeal or application for leave to appeal against it' (s 13(1)(b)). In the case of a sentence, it must be a new point of law or information (s 13(1)(c)). A pre-condition in either case is that an appeal has been determined or leave to appeal has been refused. However, the CCRC retains a discretion to make a reference even if these conditions are not fulfilled 'if it appears to the Commission that there are exceptional circumstances which justify making it' (s 13(2)).

The Home Office Minister told the House of Commons during the Committee Stage of the Bill that these criteria were wide enough 'to enable a conviction, verdict or finding to be referred if there was new evidence, or new argument in relation to evidence which has already been raised, which is of sufficient weight in the context of the whole case to give rise to a real possibility of the conviction, verdict or finding not being upheld on appeal' (House of Commons, Standing Committee B, 30 March 1995, col 126). It would also permit a referral 'if for example, incompetent advocacy prevented an important aspect of the applicant's case from being put to the jury' (*ibid*).

The Minister rejected a Labour attempt in the Committee stage in the House of Lords to amend the Bill so as to permit a reference where a point was new because it had not been adequately considered at the trial or the appeal. That amendment, Baroness Blatch said, 'would enable the Commission to refer a case on no grounds other than that, in its opinion, the courts had given insufficient consideration to some matter or matters that had come before it' (House of Lords, *Hansard*, 8 June 1995, col 1515). That would not be right 'as it would put the Commission in the invidious position of asserting its opinion or judgment on a matter above that of the courts' (ibid). The Commission was not 'a court of last resort, second guessing, sitting over and above the appellate courts' (ibid).

However, 'Where an argument was so poorly presented that the courts may have been misled, or where the appellant's case was not put to the court, then the Commission could reasonably regard such matters as new and could refer' (ibid).

It seems likely that in considering the criteria for a reference the CCRC will have regard to the words of Lord Justice Simon Brown in *R* v *Secretary of State for the Home Department, ex p Hickey (No 2)* [1995]1 All ER 490. Giving judgment for the Divisional Court, the judge said of the question of what would justify a reference under s 17: 'I would suggest that the Secretary of State should not feel overinhibited by constitutional constraints when considering the exercise of his s 17 power. Provided only and always that there indeed exists substantial new evidence or other considerations in the case and that he will not, therefore, be inviting the court merely to re-examine essentially the selfsame case as it will already have rejected, the Secretary of State should to my mind ask himself this question: could the new material reasonably cause the Court of Appeal to regard the verdict as unsafe' (at p 496).

When making a reference the CCRC will give the court and all the parties a statement of its reasons (s 14(4)). Equally, if the Commission decides not to refer a case, it must give a statement of its reasons to the applicant (s 14(6).) Baroness Blatch, for the Home Office, told the House of Lords during the Committee Stage of the Bill that the Government intended 'that this should be a full and reasoned explanation' (House of Lords, *Hansard*, 8 June 1995, col 1525).

In 1994, the Divisional Court held that before the Home Secretary made a decision whether to refer a case under s 17 of the 1968 Act the convicted prisoner was entitled to disclosure of fresh information revealed by inquiries about his case. In *R v Secretary of State for the Home Department, ex p Hickey (No 2)* [1995]1 All ER 490, Lord Justice Simon Brown giving judgment said that advance disclosure was required in the interests of both fairness and informed decision-making and the guiding principle on the level of disclosure to be sufficient should be such as to enable the petitioner to present his best case effectively. He could only do that if he adequately appreciated the nature and extent of the evidence that had been produced by the Home Secretary's inquiries. But the precise extent of the duty of disclosure would depend on the facts of the individual case. (For discussion see A Thomson, 'In the Interests of Justice' *Legal Action*, March 1995, p 8.)

The CCRC will be subject to the same duty of disclosure. Mr Nicholas Baker, for the Home Office, told the House of Commons in the Committee Stage of the Criminal Appeal Bill: 'The Commission will, and we intend that it should, be governed by the same duty of fairness and the same resulting duty of disclosure as the Divisional Court set out in that judgment [in *ex p Hickey] (Standing* Committee B, 30 March 1995, col 144). The Minister was indicating why it was not right to adopt a Labour amendment to the Bill to the effect that the Commission should give the petitioner a preliminary statement of its reasons for rejecting a petition so as to give the petitioner the chance to make representations. Mr Alun Michael who moved the amendment asked whether the Minister's position was hostile to the principle of the amendment or was he saying in effect that the amendment was unnecessary in that the Commission would operate in the spirit of the proposal. Mr Baker replied: 'The latter. . .I shall certainly consider whether there is any way that this proposal can be reflected in the Bill. However, I think that any attempt to do so would lead to the kind of rigid regime on disclosure which would be inimical to the Commission's flexible and sensible working, within the framework imposed by the courts (*ibid*).

The CCRC has the power to obtain documents (ss 17–18). This would include access 'to all relevant information held by the Secretary of State, whether it is representations by, or on behalf of, any person claiming wrongful conviction, or police reports, forensic science reports, opinions from lawyers, doctors, and other independent experts, transcripts of legal proceedings, correspondence and records of telephone conversations' (*ibid*, col 1529). It would not however receive advice to Ministers about cases from their civil servants. That would put the Commission into an invidious position. 'It would be vulnerable to the charge of having been unduly influenced by the views taken during the earlier consideration of the case by a different authority' (*ibid*).

As proposed by the Royal Commission, investigation on behalf of the CCRC will be conducted by the police. In supervising or directing the police, the CCRC will play a role similar to that played by the Police Complaints Authority. The CCRC has the power to require a chief officer of police to appoint a person from his own force or another force to carry out an investigation (s 19). It also has a power of veto over the selection of the officer by the chief constable (*ibid*). It can direct the actual investigations made and can sack the investigating officer (s 20).

The Home Secretary told the House of Commons on the 2nd Reading debate that the Government expected that, at least initially, the CCRC would have double the caseload of the existing machinery. It would need to employ a staff of about sixty– some three times the present staff. (House of Commons, *Hansard*, 6 March 1995, col 25). All the posts on the board of the Commission including that of chairman would be advertised publicly (*ibid*).

See generally K Malleson, 'The Criminal Cases Review Commission' [1995] *Criminal Law Review*, pp 929–37. See also R Nobles, D Schiff *et al*, 'The Inevitability of Crisis in Criminal Appeals' [1993] *The International Jrnl. of the Sociology of Law*, 21; Nobles and Schiff, 'Miscarriages of Justice: A Systems Approach', 58 *Modern Law Review*, 1995, p 299; DS Greer, 'Miscarriages of Criminal Justice Reconsidered', 57 *Modern Law Review*, 1994, pp 58–74; D Schiff and R Nobles, 'Criminal Appeal Act 1995: the Semantics of Jurisdiction', *Modern Law Review*, May 1996, p 299.

Compensation for wrongful conviction

The House of Commons Home Affairs Committee's report (above) also gave details of *ex gratia* payments by the Home Secretary in respect of wrongful convictions in 1972–81. In that period there were 47 cases in which payments were made. The highest figures were £25,000, £22,000, £21,000, £18,000 and £17,500. But in eighteen cases the figure was under £2,000.

Some (now somewhat out-of-date) examples of awards are:

1973 – £2,000 paid to Luke Dougherty for nine months in prison.

1974 – £17,500 paid to Lazlo Virag, who spent five years in prison for an offence he did not commit.

1981 – £65,000 paid to three men mistakenly convicted in the notorious Confait murder case. Each got £15,000 for hardship suffered, plus varying amounts for loss of earnings and expenses.

1982 – £79,000 paid to John Prescott, who spent eight years in prison for murder, after vital prosecution evidence in the case by the Home Office pathologist Dr Alan Clift was discredited and shown to have been misleading. Dr Clift resigned shortly after the case.

1985 – £121,000 paid to Geoffrey Davis who served 15 years for a murder he did not commit.

In early 1996 the amounts payable to 'the Birmingham Six', 'the Guildford Four', the Maguires and Judith Ward had still not yet been determined although all had by then been free after their convictions had been quashed four or more years earlier. However in April 1996 it emerged that one of the Birmingham Six, Paddy Hill, intended to take the Government to court to increase an award of compensation of £316,000 in respect of 16 years in prison. (*The Times*, 22 April 1996.)

The Home Secretary announced in 1976 the principles on which the amount of payment was assessed (House of Commons, *Hansard*, vol 916, 29 July 1976, cols 328–30):

Such payments were made not as recognition of liability but 'in recognition of hardship suffered'. The actual amount was assessed after consultation with an independent assessor [normally the Chairman of the Criminal Injuries Compensation Board]. The applicant or his advisers could urge facts that ought to be taken into account. A copy of the Home Office memorandum sent to the assessor would first go to the applicant for his comments. Any such comments would accompany the memorandum sent to the assessor. (In a written parliamentary answer on 29 November 1985, the Home Secretary said that in future he would regard himself as bound by the assessor's advice.)

The assessor would take into account the kind of principles applied in the field of damages for civil wrongs, including both pecuniary and non-pecuniary loss. Any or all the following facts might be relevant: loss of earnings; loss of future earning capacity, legal costs incurred; expenses incurred as a result of detention, including those of the family; damage to character or reputation; hardship, including mental suffering, injury to feelings and inconvenience; costs incurred in establishing innocence; allegations that the wrongful conviction or charge arose out of police misconduct might also be taken into account.

The Home Office Minister later explained to the House of Commons the basis on which cases were selected for *ex gratia* payments:

In exceptional circumstances, however, the Home Secretary may authorize an ex gratia payment from public funds, but this would not normally be done unless there had been some misconduct or negligence on the part of the police or some other public authority . . . Our legal system provides that in criminal cases the onus of proof rests upon the prosecution, and as long as an accused person is not required to prove his innocence it is difficult to justify automatic compensation on acquittal. Nor does it seem possible to discriminate between acquitted defendants except on the ground that where there has been public default it is right that the State should make some recompense.

What other criteria for selecting deserving cases could be adopted? Any other procedure for allowing compensation in selected cases only would involve invidious discriminations that might reflect upon those not compensated. The implication would be that the person whose claim was rejected was somehow regarded as being less innocent than the successful claimant. It is for this reason that the Home Secretary confines the making of ex gratia payments to cases in which the circumstances are compelling and where there has been some default by public authority. [House of Commons, *Hansard*, vol 929, 1977, cols 835–6.]

Criticism of these arrangements by JUSTICE and other bodies led the Home Secretary to institute an internal inquiry. He gave the result of this inquiry in his written reply to Mr T Smith on 29 November 1985 and gave reasons for the conclusions in a letter to JUSTICE. Both were discussed in an article by Mr Peter Ashman. The principal features of the Home Secretary's position were:

Peter Ashman, 'Compensation for Wrongful Imprisonment', *New Law Journal*, 23 May 1986, p 497

1. He did not intend to change the basis of the scheme from an ex-gratia to a statutory one.
2. He would in normal circumstances continue to pay compensation to someone who applied for it, who had been wrongly imprisoned, and

(i)   who had been pardoned by the Queen; or

(ii)   whose conviction had been quashed by the Court of Appeal or the House of Lords

(a)   after a reference back to those courts under s 17 of the Criminal Appeal Act 1968, or

(b)   after the time normally allowed for an appeal by those courts had elapsed; or

(iii) where the Home Secretary was satisfied that the imprisonment resulted from a serious default on the part of a member of a police force or of some other public authority.

3. In future he would pay compensation to any person

(i)   where this was required by the UK's international obligations; or

(ii)   where he considered that there were exceptional circumstances, eg facts emerging at the trial or at an appeal brought within time that completely exonerated the defendant.

4. He would not pay compensation simply because the prosecution was unable to sustain the burden of proof at the trial.

For the Home Secretary's reasons for this position and the JUSTICE response see P Ashman, 'Compensation for Wrongful Imprisonment', *New Law Journal*, 23 May 1986, p 497. See also *R v Secretary of State for the Home Office, ex p Chubb* [1986] Crim LR 809 (Div Ct) holding that the Home Secretary had a complete discretion in the matter which was not reviewable by the courts. The Divisional Court held in *R v Secretary of State for the Home Department, ex p Harrison* [1988] 3 All ER 86 that there was no duty to give reasons.

However, in November 1987 the Home Office unexpectedly changed its position. It announced during the debate on the Criminal Justice Bill that it intended to move an amendment to give a statutory right of compensation where a court's final decision resulted in a conviction which was later reversed on the ground that new facts showed conclusively that the defendant was the victim of a miscarriage of justice–unless it was shown that the non-disclosure of the facts was due to the defendant's own fault (House of Lords, *Hansard*, 19 November 1987, cols 398–9). This became s 133 and Sch 12 of the Criminal Justice Act 1988.

Section 133(1) of the 1988 Act states: 'when a person has been convicted of a criminal offence and when subsequently his conviction has been reversed or he has been pardoned on the ground that a new or newly discovered fact shows beyond reasonable doubt that there has been a miscarriage of justice, the Secretary of State shall pay compensation for the miscarriage of justice . . .unless the non-disclosure of the unknown fact was wholly or partly attributable to the person convicted'. It is for the Home Secretary to make the decision whether compensation is payable (s 13(3)). If payable, the amount is determined by an assessor appointed by the Home Secretary (s 13(4)).

The Criminal Appeal Act 1995 added a new subsection 4A to section 133 that in assessing the amount of compensation in regard to loss of reputation, the assessor should have regard in particular to (a) the seriousness of the offence and the severity of the punishment; (b) the conduct of the investigation and prosecution; and (c) any other convictions of the person and any punishment in respect of those previous convictions. No doubt (subsection (c) of this amendment was intended to lower the level of damages paid in such cases.

Agreement on the amount of compensation in important cases can take years. Five and more years later the Maguires, the Guildford Four and the Birmingham Six had received significant sums by way of interim payment but they were still in dispute over the amount of the final payment.

CHAPTER 8

The legal profession

This chapter begins by establishing the features of the legal profession as it has developed historically. It then looks at the extraordinary event of the Green Papers for reform of the profession put forward in 1989 by the Lord Chancellor Lord Mackay of Clashfern, the furious row that they provoked and the resulting legislation.[1] Finally it treats a variety of current topics of concern to the profession.

1. THE COMPONENT PARTS OF THE PROFESSION

The legal profession[2] is divided into two main branches–the Bar and the solicitors' branch. The Bar is divided into two main parts–Queen's Counsel and juniors. The solicitors' branch consists of principals or partners, assistant solicitors and legal executives. Trainee barristers are known as pupils; trainee solicitors used to be called articled clerks. The office manager for barristers, who also fixes the fees and manages the allocation of work, is the clerk. Barristers practise in chambers ; they may not form partnerships . They must join an Inn of Court and may join a circuit. The affairs of the Bar are run by the General Council of the Bar and of the Inns of Court (the 'Bar Council') and its committees The solicitors' branch is run by the Law Society and local law societies . A short elaboration of these basic features of the structure of the profession follows.

---

1   There were three Green Papers: *The Work and Organisation of the Legal Profession* (Cm 570, 1989); *Conveyancing by Authorized Practitioners* (Cm 572, 1989); and *Contingency Fees* (Cm 571, 1989). They were followed in swift succession by the Government's *White Paper on Legal Services* in July 1989 (Cm 740, 1989) and in the autumn the Courts and Legal Services Bill, which became the 1990 Act of that name. For an extended review of the proposals in the Green Papers see 'The Green paper on Contingency Fees', *Civil Justice Quarterly*, April 1989, pp 97–103; and 'The Realignment of the English Legal Profession', *Civil Justice Quarterly*, July 1989, pp 202–14. For a review of the White Paper see 'The White Paper on Legal Services', *Civil Justice Quarterly*, January 1990, pp 6–12. For an account of the 1990 Act see 'Courts and Legal Services Act 1990', *Civil Justice Quarterly*, April 1991, p 97.
2   For a monumental study of the profession see Richard L Abel, *The Legal Profession in England and Wales* (Blackwell, 1988).

(a) The Bar

Origin

The Bar dates back to the end of the thirteenth century. Originally and for a very long time, barristers could and did receive instructions direct from the lay client. It was not until the nineteenth century that it was finally settled that a barrister had to have instructions from a solicitor to appear in court.

Queen's (or King's) Counsel

Originally the division in the profession was between 'sergeants-at-law' and barristers. The first King's Counsel were appointed in the seventeenth century but at that time the title did not signify seniority in the profession but rather the function of assisting the law officers of the Crown in cases in which the Crown had an interest. In the course of the eighteenth and nineteenth centuries, appointments to the rank of King's Counsel came to be regarded as a mark of pre-eminence in the profession. By the end of the nineteenth century, no more appointments of sergeants-at-law were made and the senior rank amongst barristers was limited to King's (Queen's) Counsel– otherwise known as KC or QC or 'leaders' or 'silks'.

QCs are appointed by the Queen on the advice of the Lord Chancellor. Toward the end of each year a notice is published in the legal journals informing practitioners who wish to be considered to submit their names to the Lord Chancellor. Only those who apply are considered. The process of selection has been described by the Lord Chancellor–see Lord Mackay, 'The Myths and Facts about Silk', *Counsel*, October 1993, p 11. Applicants put in their curriculum vitae and the Lord Chancellor has inquiries made about each applicant by senior members of his staff. The list of applicants is sent to the law lords, the judges in the Court of Appeal and to all High Court judges as well as to certain senior circuit judges. The list also goes to the Chairman of the Bar and to the leaders of the circuits and specialist Bars. Those consulted are encouraged to express their views about those on the list–after having taken discreet soundings among other leading silks. The Lord Chancellor's staff meet the Bar Leaders and the Presiding Judges from each circuit. The staff have some 35 meetings on the subject. A provisional list of appointments is discussed with the Heads of Divisions (Lord Chief Justice, Master of the Rolls, President of the Family Division and Vice Chancellor, head of the Chancery Division).

A Bar Council Working Party set up 'to investigate the methods, procedures and criteria for the appointment of Queen's Counsel', which reported in 1994, re-commended that the pool of those consulted should be wider still–for instance by including Masters and Resident Circuit judges in main Court Centres. (See C Frazer, 'The Silk Round', *Counsel*, July/August 1994, p 22.)

The Lord Chancellor takes into account not only the personal qualities of the applicant but also the total number of silks generally and the total number in the field in which the applicant practises. (The form filled out by those consulted has a space 'Ready for silk now, but not recommended for appointment this year because other, named, candidates are preferred in this field'.)

A person who is not appointed one year may apply again and it is very common to apply several times before being appointed.

The proportion of QCs to junior barristers has been kept at about ten per cent for many years. The percentage of successful applicants in the past ten years has been between 14 and 21 per cent–see Frazer, *op cit*, above, p 22.

A person applies to become a QC for a number of reasons. One is the desire for advancement in the profession. QCs generally enjoy higher incomes and have a higher status. (They even have a separate bench to sit on in court.) The second reason is to lighten the load of work. The work of barristers is divided between advocacy, opinions and 'paper work', meaning in the main drafting of pleadings and similar documents. By tradition, paper work is reserved for junior barristers. It is not very well remunerated and is burdensome. Practitioners are usually happy to escape this work and to concentrate their efforts on advocacy in heavy cases and opinion work.

Applying for silk, however, is a gamble, mainly because of the old Two Counsel rule. This was the rule that, normally, a Queen's Counsel should appear in court only with a junior as well. (There used to be a further rule that the junior was paid a fee equivalent to two-thirds of that paid to the QC. This was abolished by the Bar in 1971, but the junior is still normally paid the equivalent of either two-thirds or half the leader's fee.)

In 1976 the Monopolies and Mergers Commission in a special report (*Two-Counsel Rule*) stated that this restrictive rule was contrary to the public interest, though it accepted that paper work (eg drafting) should normally be done by juniors. This report was accepted by the Bar, which abolished the Two Counsel rule at the next AGM in 1977. Since then a QC has had the right to appear in court without a junior. But he is entitled to expect that a junior will be instructed unless the contrary is stated, and he may decline to accept instructions to appear without a junior if he thinks this would prejudice his ability to conduct the case or any other case or to fulfil his other professional obligations. In general, QCs tend to be employed in heavy matters where two counsel are appropriate.

It follows that when applying for silk the applicant must consider that clients are willing to pay not only the higher fees normally paid to leaders but also the fee of the junior who would normally appear with him. Some of those appointed as QCs do not become successful as leaders even though they had highly successful junior practices.

Inns of Court

The profession's connection with what are now the Inns of Court dates back to the early fourteenth century when, on the dissolution of the crusading order of the Knights Templar, the buildings were occupied by the lawyers who had previously lived in the area around the courts. By the end of the fourteenth century there were four societies in existence–the Inner and Middle Temples, Lincoln's Inn and Gray's Inn. In the seventeenth century the right to practise in the Royal Courts became restricted to members of the Inns of Court, and since that time they have enjoyed a monopoly over the right of admission to the Bar.

There are three categories of members of the Inns–benchers, barristers and students. Control of the Inns is vested in the benchers who are appointed by the existing body of benchers, normally from the ranks of judges and senior practitioners. The Benson Royal Commission on Legal Services in 1979 (Cmnd 7648) said that there were some 350–400 benchers of whom only 30 per cent were practitioners. The rest were judges or retired.

The Inns today have five main functions. They own and administer accommodation which is rented to barristers for professional chambers and to other persons for professional, commercial or residential purposes. They provide law libraries and common rooms for barristers and students. They provide lunches and dinners for their members. They award scholarships and bursaries for students and young barristers. They also play some part in the training of students and young barristers by the traditions of keeping term through the eating of dinners, by moots, talks and practical exercises both after dinner and at weekend meetings in places such as Cumberland Lodge in Windsor Great Park.

Most of the income of the Inns (some 90 per cent) comes from rent. In 1974 the Inland Revenue agreed to treat the Inns as charities except to the extent that their income was applied to non-charitable purposes.

Management of the Bar

For most of this century the affairs of practitioners have been run by the Bar Council. Its origins were the Bar Committee, which was created in 1883 and which in 1895 became the General Council of the Bar, known as the Bar Council. It was expressly barred from interfering with 'the property, jurisdiction, powers or privileges of the Inns'. Disciplinary matters at that time remained in the hands of the Inns but the rulings of the Bar Council on matters of etiquette became recognized as binding on barristers as a whole.

During the 1950s and 1960s the relationship between the Bar Council and the Inns became increasingly strained and in 1966 a new body, the Senate of the Four Inns of Court, was established by resolution of the Inns and the Bar Council. Its purpose was to provide one body that could act collectively in matters of common interest. It had seven representatives from each Inn and six representatives of the Bar Council. But it could take no decisions that involved expense to the Inns without getting their agreement.

This proved unsatisfactory and in 1971 at the instance of Lord Hailsham, then Lord Chancellor, a committee under Lord Pearce was set up to consider the problem. The 1972 interim report of the Pearce Committee identified the faults of the system. It pointed to the fact that there were no fewer than six autonomous bodies to run a profession of fewer than 3,000 practitioners–the four Inns, the Senate and the Bar Council. There was a multiplicity of overlapping committees–in 1971 some 61 standing bodies. The whole system was wasteful of manpower, accommodation, money and time. Junior members were virtually excluded from all decision-making by the Inns. There was a critical shortage of accommodation for practitioners in London. The Inns had no common rent policy, no common policy on libraries and lacked control over pupils. The Pearce Committee concluded that there should be one effective central governing body with sufficient financial resources to carry out its policies.

On the basis of these recommendations, a new body, the Senate of the Four Inns of Court and the Bar, was set up and came into existence in 1974. It had six representatives of each Inn, appointed by the benchers; three barrister representatives of each Inn, elected by the members of the Inns other than the benchers; and 39 barristers elected by the Bar, of whom 18 had to be practising juniors and under seven years since Call. There were 10 ex-officio members, such as the Law Officers and the leaders of the six circuits, and up to 16 additional members appointed by the Senate. The practising Bar, therefore, had a slight majority on the Senate.

The functions of the Senate were to lay down general policy for the profession and to decide on the contents of the Consolidated Regulations of the Inns. The Inns undertook to abide by the general policy laid down from time to time by the Senate subject to certain understandings, the gist of which is that they must not be expected to bear an unfair burden of cost. The trade-union affairs of the profession were handled by the Bar Council, which was a sub-committee of the Senate and which consisted of the 39 Bar representatives of the Senate, the leaders of the circuits and up to 12 co-opted members.

The Benson Royal Commission on Legal Services in 1979 made several recommendations regarding the organization of the Bar. It thought that the existing arrangements were 'neither sufficiently co-ordinated nor adequately representative of the profession as a whole to provide the necessary direction' (para 32.67) and it proposed that the Senate should be given power to take decisions binding on the Inns. Some 60 members of the Senate should be elected by the Bar in such a way as to ensure adequate representation for different levels of seniority, specialists, barristers practising in different parts of the country, and those employed in commerce and industry. There was no need to have barristers appointed by the Inns on the Senate. It would be right to continue to have some representation of the judges in the Senate and some method should be found to have between 10 and 20 whether by appointment, election by the judges or co-option. The Inns should have representatives in the form of the Treasurer and Chairman of its Finance Committee.

In 1985 the Bar set up a new committee under the chairmanship of Lord Rawlinson to 'consider the constitution and composition of the governing body of the profession and to make recommendations'. The committee reported in the spring of 1986. Its main conclusion was that the management of the Bar should be in the hands solely of practitioners. The government of a profession, particularly one like the Bar which engaged in a great deal of publicly funded work, should not be in the hands even partially of judges.

Accordingly it recommended that there should be a new General Council of the Bar and of the Inns of Court consisting of barristers alone. Decisions which might affect the Inns should be taken by a Treasurers' Council of the Inns. It should consist of the treasurers, certain other benchers, the chairman of the Council of Legal Education and the officers of the new Bar Council.

The Treasurers' Council would have power to refer back to the Bar Council any policies and the Bar Council would then consider its views. But if the Bar Council affirmed the policy, the Treasurers' Council would have the duty to secure its implementation. (The relationship would in a sense be like that between the House of Commons and the House of Lords, with the Commons having the ultimate power to insist on a policy.)

The Bar Council would include a system of constituencies. It should consist of two representatives of each circuit (of whom one would be a junior barrister), one from each Bar Association, 3 representatives of each Inn and 51 elected members, of whom 9 would be Queen's Counsel and 12 would be under seven years' call.

These proposals were adopted by the Bar in June 1986 and came into effect on 1 January 1987. (See *Law Society's Gazette*, 28 May 1986, p 1628, and 23 July 1986, p 2321 and also *Counsel*, September/October 1994, pp 10–14.)

In 1991, Lord Benson, the former Chairman of the Royal Commission on Legal Services, urged that the time had come to place management of all the Inns' properties under the authority of the Bar Council. Writing in the Bar's house journal *Counsel* (July 1991, pp 14–15), he said that very large sums of money would shortly be needed to modernize the properties held by the Inns, to bear the cost of improving recruitment, the vocational training of students, remuneration in pupillage and continuing professional education. The Bar, though tiny, still had six governing bodies–the Bar Council, the four Inns of Court and the Inns' Council. The division of responsibility was wasteful in time and money.

The Inns owned extremely valuable properties in London and were therefore one of the best-endowed professions in the country. Each of the Inns managed its properties in its own way. For years they had charged low rents and had therefore failed to build up reserves. Now they would have to borrow large sums at high interest.

The Bar had the duty under the Courts and Legal Services Act 1990 for education and training of barristers. It was vital to give the Bar Council the authority to discharge its responsibilities. The Inns were reluctant to allow the Bar Council to decide how to administer their valuable assets. Under the 1987 agreement the Bar could in theory impose its will on the Inns but the procedure was complex. Lord Benson thought, moreover, that it was incompatible with the Bar Council's new statutory obligations and in his view was unworkable.

In 1994 the Chairman of the Bar Council said that its budget was £2.7m of which £2m was raised by subscription. (For description of its functions see *Counsel*, March/April 1994, pp 10–12.)

Chambers

A barrister does not have an office; he works in 'chambers'. In the past every practising barrister had to be a member of professional chambers. (As will be seen below a barrister who has been in practice for at least three years can now practise from home –but this is highly exceptional.)

There are a little under four hundred sets of chambers, of which about 60 per cent are in London and 40 per cent in the provinces. There are twenty-eight cities outside London where barristers practise. (The proportion of barristers practising in the provinces has been gradually increasing. In the 1960s it was about one quarter.) Some barristers are members of chambers both in London and elsewhere.

The average number of members of each set of chambers is a little over 20 in London and a little under 20 in the provinces.

Barristers' chambers are getting larger and larger. The report 'Strategies for the Future', prepared by the Bar's Strategy Group and issued in October 1990 by the Bar Council, said: 'The ability of barristers to organize themselves into economic units that offer the best combination of efficiency and accessibility is critical to the future of the Bar' (para 3.24). The size of chambers had doubled in the previous twenty years to an average size of about 15, but the upward trend continued. The report recommended that the optimum size of chambers was at least 25 and that it could in some instances be as high as 50 or even more. ('Only highly specialized sets in high fee-earning areas of the law will be able to practise successfully in smaller units', para 3.28.) One reason for increasing the size of chambers was increased profitability. Barristers in larger chambers had higher gross and net earnings.

The report also dismissed as out-of-date the notion that chambers were still Dickensian in aspect. 'Most sets are now computerized either substantially or to some extent, with applications ranging from word processing, document transmission (fax) and routine accounting such as fee recording and billing, to more complex applications such as legal databases or the production of management information' (para 3.25). (A study had shown that non-computerized sets of chambers had between £0.5m and £1m more fees outstanding than computerized sets, resulting in a loss of interest on capital of up to £130,000. This obviously far exceeded the annual cost of leasing basic level computerization, which was around £7,000 (para 3.85).)

As to geographical spread, the trend is clearly to establish more and more local Bars. The same report said that, reflecting the Government's policy there was likely to be a long-term trend towards administering justice from a small number of major regional centres. As part of this policy more legal services activity was likely to take place outside London. The effect of the Civil Justice Review would be to support this policy as the county courts took on an increasing number of the larger cases. The Bar should 'support and encourage the broad policy of the further development of legal centres outside London' (para 3.16).

Until 1987 there was an unwritten rule that London barristers had to practise in the physical precincts of the Inns of Court. The rule was supported by the long-standing policy that barristers should be charged rents by the Inns that were distinctly lower than the going level of commercial rents. This rule, combined with the explosion of numbers at the Bar, resulted in a very serious accommodation crisis. (A survey in 1986 showed that 10 per cent of London barristers were sharing a desk. Inner Temple had 2.14 barristers per room!)

In summer 1987 the Bar Council issued a statement that the Bar and the Inns had reached agreement on a new policy to ensure the availability of sufficient accommodation for the practising profession, especially in London. The two crucial elements were that the accommodation would, if necessary, be outside the Inns and that the rent would be at a commercial level. The capital for the development would come from moneys raised by way of mortgage on the properties of the Inns, which are thought to be worth over £200 million. (See *New Law Journal*, 26 June 1987, p 580.)

At first, the change in policy did not seem to have much effect. But then more and more chambers began to move out of the hallowed precincts of the Inns to more spacious and modern office accommodation in the neighbourhood.

An article in the Bar's journal *Counsel* in July 1991 said that 'Only a few years ago, any suggestion that chambers should move out of the confines of the Inns would have been greeted with horror as a culture shocking break with the past.' But now it was no longer so. 'What has promoted the departure of about a dozen seats from the Temple in the last twelve months has been overcrowding.' In some cases the Inns had assisted the process of moving out by becoming intermediate landlords.

The Royal Commission in 1979 recommended that a barrister should be permitted to practise from home without a clerk. Now the Bar has in fact allowed this provided that the barrister has been in chambers for not less than three years–and something under 1 per cent of barristers are now practising in that way as 'individual barristers', whether from home or elsewhere.

It has for years been exceedingly difficult for a young entrant to secure a seat in chambers as a tenant. One partial new attempt to solve this problem was the announcement in 1990 that barristers of ability who had been unable to find a tenancy in chambers would be permitted to work from the Library. The 'Practising Library', it was thought, would provide facilities for 50 or so barristers of up to three years' experience affiliated to established chambers. But it did not prove a success and within a short time it had been discontinued (*The Lawyer*, 19 February 1991, p 1).

The clerk

The rule has been that each set of chambers must have a clerk.[3] Most sets have more than one clerk–one is then the senior clerk and the rest are junior clerks. The junior clerks perform functions that are normally understood by the term, 'clerical', but the senior clerk has functions that go well beyond this. The Royal Commission on Legal Services (para 34.3) described the role as having three main components:

(1) Office administrator and accountant   He maintains the accounts for the chambers as a whole and ensures that each member of chambers has adequate secretarial and other similar services.

(2) Business manager   He works for each member of chambers individually in maintaining his professional diary; checking court lists for cases in which he is retained; negotiating fees; sending out fee notes and reminders; keeping the individual accounts.

(3) Agent   Advising barristers on the development of their practices; ensuring that beginners receive work according to their abilities and experience; advising solicitors as to which barristers to instruct; and advising on the allocation of work as between members of chambers.

This bald recital does not, however, quite convey the extent to which the clerk is the lynch-pin of the whole system. A high proportion of work coming into any set of chambers is in practice allocated by the clerk. This is for a number of different reasons. Sometimes the solicitor asks on behalf of the lay client for Mr A. The clerk informs him that Mr A is not available to take the case on that date but that he has an excellent Mr B who will be free. The solicitor client will commonly agree to the suggestion that Mr B do the case–especially if he has previously been to those chambers and been broadly satisfied with the quality of the barristers he has instructed. Or the solicitor may be told that Mr A is available, but a day or so before the hearing he is told by the clerk that unfortunately Mr A has not completed his previous case (he is 'part heard' elsewhere) and the clerk suggests Mr B or Miss C both of whom are from the same chambers. The solicitor usually has little choice but to accept the recommendation, especially at the last moment. Another common situation is when the solicitor says from the outset that he has a particular kind of routine case and asks the clerk to recommend someone from his chambers to handle it.

The clerk also plays a crucial role in negotiating fees. His own remuneration, until very recently at least, was on a commission basis–in the order of 5 to 7 per cent of gross chambers income without any contribution to chambers' expenses, or 8 to 10 per cent of gross income with the clerk making some contribution towards expenses

---

3   As has been said above, technically this rule was changed in 1990 but it is likely that few barristers choose to practise without a clerk.

like a barrister member. It follows that the senior clerk has a direct financial stake in the level of fees earned by his principals. His interest is to set the fees as high as possible consistent with the aim of not losing the work. A solicitor who wishes to discuss the fee with the barrister is permitted to do so, but it is very rarely done. (The earning capacity of the clerks is therefore extraordinary. The senior clerk is drawing anything from 5 per cent to 10 per cent of the professional earnings of 15 to 20 or more barristers. He will normally be earning considerably more than most members of the chambers.

The Benson Royal Commission said that most clerks go to great trouble to help newly qualified barristers to establish themselves. Nevertheless sometimes the power of allocation of work was not exercised fairly. This was to be deplored and must be avoided (para 34.37).

The only extended treatment of the arcane subject of the clerking system is John Flood's book *Barristers' Clerks* (Manchester University Press, 1983).

But the system is gradually changing with the growth in the size, complexity and modernization of chambers and the increasing concern at the Bar for a more acceptable image. A woman clerk, for instance, is no longer a rarity. Clerks are increasingly likely to have considerable educational and other qualifications. Traditionally clerks came straight from school with few, if any, qualifications. Today they need considerable skills including the capacity to master-mind a multi-million-pound business. Sets of chambers looking for a new chief clerk are these days increasingly likely to advertise for an 'Administrator', 'Practice Manager' or 'Chief Executive'.

The Bar's 1990 report, 'Strategies for the Future', said (para 3.46) that the present clerking arrangements suffered from a number of weaknesses including:

(1) The wide range of functions and skills required of clerks.

(2) Inadequate specialist skills in marketing, performance management, information technology and accountancy.

(3) High costs associated with the commission-based remuneration of the clerk ('with some clerks earning significantly more than experienced barristers within their employing chambers').

(4) The potential for patronage or influence over the careers of barristers and undue lack of accountability to members of the set.

(5) Unclear contractual relationships.

The report recommended that chambers should aim to have a staff (on normal pensionable employment contracts) consisting of two main figures. One would be the Practice Manager, dealing with such matters as marketing and promotion, pricing, fee negotiation, practice development and accommodation strategy. The second would be the Administrator, dealing with accounting, billing, secretarial services, information technology, library facilities, etc.

They should be remunerated by a basic salary plus an annual performance-related bonus awarded by a management committee. 'There should be no commission or percentage element' (para 3.53). (The Practice Manager, it suggested, might in 1990 earn a maximum of, say, £48,000; the Administrator, say, £29,000 (para 3.55).)

Such new arrangements would need to be phased in. To convert the clerking system into an effective management capability would 'require determined action from the profession'. 'It will not be adequate to introduce change simply by waiting for retirements' (para 3.49).

Partnerships among barristers

It is a rule of Bar conduct and etiquette that barristers may not form partnerships. The members of chambers share the services of the clerk and share office expenses such as secretarial facilities, library and other costs. But they may not agree to share fees. The traditional basis of the rule is that the barrister is an individual and should take responsibility for his work as an individual. The reason for the rule has somewhat altered nowadays when so much of the work is either not earmarked for any individual or gets reallocated because of the eventual non-availability of the selected individual.

From time to time the issue has been considered by the Bar. In 1961 a Committee recommended that the rule be adhered to, and this view was taken again by a different committee in 1969 and again by the Senate when it came to give evidence to the Benson Royal Commission on Legal Services.

The Royal Commission did not go into the issue very deeply. But it unanimously adopted the prevailing view that partnerships should not be allowed. Partnerships, it thought, would erode the right of the client to select a particular individual by reason of his capabilities. ('Both by law and in practice, a partnership involves the sharing of work and responsibility and a common interest in earning profits so that if one member of a partnership cannot, or does not wish to, deal with a particular matter another partner, who may not either be known, or acceptable, to the client does so' (para (33.65).) The Commission said it was particularly influenced by the fact that partnerships would restrict the client's choice–especially in some of the small specialized Bars and in provincial centres, some of which only have one set of chambers.

Another problem with partnerships, which the Commission did not mention, is that many members of the Bar perform part-time judicial functions. It would presumably be impossible for one member of a partnership to appear as an advocate in a case in which a partner of his was the judge. This would mean that if the barrister came to court and found that his partner was to be the judge he would have to withdraw at the last moment. Even if the problem were appreciated earlier, it would still create considerable administrative difficulties which would add yet a further dimension to the already complex matter of listing cases.

The Royal Commission concluded: 'Partnerships would often we think be convenient or advantageous to barristers but the point of overriding importance is the public interest. We therefore consider that partnerships between barristers should not be permitted' (para 33.66).

A later inquiry into the issue resulted in a statement by the Bar in May 1987 that it adhered to the rule that barristers could not form partnerships, but that it would for the first time permit 'purse sharing' arrangements in the form of the pooling of fees and their distribution according to some agreed formula. Solicitors would have to be informed that such arrangements operated in the chambers, and barristers in such chambers would not be allowed to appear against each other or in a case in which a member of the chambers was acting as judge. (See *Law Society's Gazette*, 27 May 1987, p 1566.)

As will be seen (p 572 below), one of the many proposals canvassed in the Green Papers was that barristers should be able to form partnerships with one another. The Bar's response on this (as on virtually all the proposals in the Green Papers) was negative.

The matter was considered again by the 1990 Bar Council's report entitled 'Strategies for the Future'. This said that the supposed advantages of partnership were greatly exaggerated. In particular, a partnership no longer had any distinct tax benefits. Moreover the advantages were greatly outweighed by the disadvantages. It had therefore approached its work on the basis that partnerships would continue to be prohibited.

In its view most of the main advantages of a partnership in terms of a cohesive group structure could be achieved without a formal partnership. A set of chambers, it suggested, needed a clear and efficient decision-making structure to permit it to assess options and determine courses of action on the basis of full discussion–but without the need for unanimous decisions. The present informal consensus process needed to be replaced by machinery that allowed for rapid and effective decisions to be taken for all. The larger the set, the greater the need for such machinery.

Circuits

The country is divided into six circuits, each with its own rules and customs, officers and controlling committee. A barrister can only be a member of one circuit but he can appear in a court on another circuit. The circuit is concerned with the administration of criminal justice in its area together with the Circuit Administrator who is a senior official of the Lord Chancellor's Department. The circuits are also concerned with the establishment of new chambers in their area. The circuit leader will take an interest in the conduct of members of the circuit and will give advice and guidance to any barrister who seems to require it. The circuits have no formal function in respect of disciplinary proceedings.

Numbers at the Bar and recruitment

There has been a remarkable growth in the size of the Bar during the past thirty or so years. During the 1950s the number of barristers fluctuated at or somewhat below the figure of 2,000. In 1954, for instance, there were 2,010 and six years later in 1960 the number had declined slightly to 1,919. But since then the numbers have more than quadrupled. The number in practice in 1986 was 5,500 and in 1990 it was over 6,500, in 1995 it was 8,500. The chief reason for this dramatic increase in the size of the profession was the great growth in representation in legal aid cases, both in criminal cases and in matrimonial and especially divorce matters.

Between a quarter and a third of those called to the Bar each year at present are from overseas. (In 1995, it was 31%.) It is also still the case that many qualify who do not intend to practise. In 1995, for instance, a total of 1,593 were called but only 501 started in practice.

The Bar estimated in 1991 that in the next decade it would need some 400 to 500 new 'starts in practice' to maintain an adequate flow into the private profession, plus another 150 to 200 or so coming to the Employed Bar to provide manpower for the Government Legal Service, the Crown Prosecution Service, commerce, finance and industry, local government, the armed forces, parliamentary counsel, etc (*Report of the* (Taylor) *Bar Entry and Training Working Party*, 1991).

Entry and training

The method of entry to practice at the Bar is through a compulsory one year vocational course. The course has until now always been run by the Bar's Council of Legal Education (CLE) at the Inns of Court School of Law in Gray's Inn. As from 1989–90 the CLE put on a new course the basic thrust of which was to increase the skills training. Broadly the course seems to be tolerably successful–see M Taylor, 'Pioneering Legal Skills Training', *Legal Action*, April 1995, p 6; J Shapland, 'Training for the Bar', *Counsel*, January/ February 1995, p 19.

The Taylor Committee recommended that there should be some 750 students on the CLE's course. There were likely to be some 1,200 applicants. It would therefore be necessary to find some way of selecting the right people. Hitherto the Bar had always had an open-door policy–except that in 1984 it introduced a requirement that only those with a Lower Second Class degree or better would be accepted for the vocational course leading to practice. The Taylor Committee recommended the controversial policy of entry based partly on interview. This was adopted by the Bar in 1991. Machinery was set up to try to ensure that the system was non-discriminatory as to race, colour, creed or sex but the new selection system was subjected to considerable criticism.

In 1993 the Bar changed the method of selection and instituted instead a new system based on a score calculated by a Critical Reasoning Test and parts of a biographical data form. However, this new system proved a highly embarrassing and well publicised public relations disaster. It was announced that the top 800 applicants would be offered places but large numbers of very well qualified applicants were unsuccessful. It turned out that the scoring system did not take account of degree results but did take account of examinations taken at secondary school.

The system was therefore changed yet again, to take account of degree results. More important, the Bar finally grasped the nettle of deciding to allow institutions other than the CLE to provide the course. As from autumn 1997 some seven other institutions will be licensed by the Bar to provide the course. At the time of writing it was not clear how many student places there would be in aggregate for this course and whether the already great pressure on numbers at the Bar would thereby be increased or decreased.

The funding of recruits to the profession has undergone a sea-change in the last few years. Until the 1970s those becoming barristers had great difficulty in securing any form of financial assistance from the profession–save that a few academic high-flyers might obtain scholarships from the Inns. Starting in the late 1970s, however, the Bar gradually came to grips with the problem of trying to maintain its competitive position in regard to the best graduates from the university law departments. The Inns considerably increased the numbers of their scholarships. (In 1989 about £1m was paid by the Inns in awards of one kind or another.) Some chambers began to pay their pupils at least for the pupillage year. In 1990 this was put on to a systematic basis when the Bar announced a new scheme to pay 400 pupils a guaranteed £6,000 pa.

Some £4.3m was promised by chambers for this new system, which started in 1993. A considerable number of chambers provided considerably better remuneration than this. Moreover the Bar said that it had set aside an additional £50,000 to give financial assistance to pupils in chambers that were too poor to provide such support. The Inns of Court provided a further £1.6m in scholarships and bursaries to those starting in practice. (See *Counsel*, October 1993, p 32.)

Women at the Bar

The proportion of women at the Bar is increasing rapidly. In 1955 women made up 3.2 per cent of the practising Bar. In the four succeeding decades the proportion rose considerably: 1965, 4.6 per cent; 1975, 7.1 per cent; 1985, 13 per cent; in 1995, 22 per cent. There are no figures as to the proportion of those starting practice who are women. Because women have only recently begun to come into the profession in large numbers there are very few in the ranks of senior practitioners, let alone on the bench as judges. In 1995 the number of women QCs was 57 out of 891 or 6.6 per cent. (In the QBD there were 63 High Court judges, three of whom were women, in the Family Division, 15 of whom two were women and in the Chancery Division, 17 of whom one was a woman. There were therefore 95 High Court judges, of whom 6 (6.3%) were women.)

In 1994, the Lord Chancellor lamented that so few women put themselves forward for appointment as QCs. Thus, out of 540 applicants that year, only 43 (8%) were from women. However, more than one in five of these applications were successful– a higher success rate than for men. (*Counsel*, May/June 1994, p 5.)

For details of a survey of women barristers regarding their experience of sex discrimination see B Hewson, 'Sex and the Bar', *Counsel*, February 1993, p 12.

Ethnic minorities at the Bar

There has been concern for many years about the problems of members of ethnic minorities in getting entry to the Bar, and even more about the fact that most practise in 'ghetto chambers' consisting largely of members of the minority in question.

Research in 1989 showed that more than half of chambers had no ethnic minority tenants and slightly more than half of the practising black barristers were concentrated in 16 sets. There were only six non-white QCs.

In October 1991 the Bar Council adopted a race-equality policy which included a recommendation to all chambers that they should aim to have 5 per cent of their members drawn from ethnic minorities. The policy envisaged also a Code of Practice on the non-discriminatory selection and treatment of pupils and tenants and for the distribution of work in chambers. The Bar's new selection procedures for entry to the Inns of Court School of Law would be monitored to ensure that they were not discriminatory.

Advertising by barristers

In 1989 the Bar Council changed its rules to permit a barrister to engage in any advertising or promotion in connection with his practice which conforms to the British Code of Advertising Practice, including the use of photographs, statements of rates and methods of charging, statements about the nature and extent of his services and, with the client's written consent, the name of any professional or lay client. Such advertising must not, however, be inaccurate or likely to mislead, or be likely to diminish public confidence in the legal profession. It must not make comparisons with other barristers ('knocking copy') or include statements about the quality of the barrister's work, the size or success of his practice or his success rate. (See Bar Code of Conduct, 1994, para 307.)

These changes represent a revolution in the Bar's attitude to advertising. However, it seems unlikely that the relaxation will lead to any wild excesses. Most chambers have so far confined their advertising to chambers' brochures.

Public funds as a source of barristers' income

Barristers today derive a large proportion of their income from public funds. The Royal Commission on Legal Services estimated that the gross fees of the Bar for 1976/7 were £48 million, of which some £23 million, or almost half, came from public funds (para 36.47). Legal aid, civil and criminal, accounted for 65 per cent and public prosecution work for the remaining 35 per cent.

Percentage of barrister's gross fees derived from public funds, 1976/7

Type of practice	QC	Juniors
London Chancery and specialist	1	3
London family law and common law	23	41
London criminal practices	77	92
Provincial practices	63	69
All categories of practice	26	52

(*Source*: *Report of the Royal Commission on Legal Services*, Cmnd 7648, Table 36.3, p 520.)

In general, the more senior the barrister, the less his income is drawn from public funds–but the proportions vary greatly depending on the kind of practice, as is shown by the table above.

A survey of income at the Bar for 1981/2 showed that some 40 per cent of barristers' income was derived from public funds, of which four-fifths came from criminal work. The survey also showed that publicly funded work was substantially less well paid than privately paid work (Bar Council, 'Survey of Income at the Bar, 1981/2').

The 1990 Bar report 'Strategies for the Future' stated (p 11) that in 1989 barristers earned £418m out of the total earnings of barristers and solicitors of £4,106m–or 10 per cent. (Barristers numbered about 12 per cent of the combined profession.)

Over a third of the total earned by barristers (£161m or 38 per cent) was derived from publicly funded sources (para 3.22) (The comparable figure for the solicitors' branch was 11 per cent.) The breakdown for barristers was:

	%
Civil legal aid	21
CPS work	30
Criminal defence	49
Total	100

The comparable breakdown for solicitors was quite different: 50 per cent, 5 per cent and 45 per cent respectively.

The 1990 report said (para 3.23) that the Bar faced a number of threats to its publicly funded work. First, there was the steady erosion of the percentage of the population eligible for legal aid (see p 443 above). (But since most publicly funded work is in the criminal rather than the civil field, this threat can be regarded as minor.) Second, there was the 'unstated but reasonably apparent aim of the Government to have one lawyer only for the defence in as many criminal and civil legal aid cases as possible'. Third, there was the potential loss of advocacy work to solicitors and others. Fourth, there was the possibility that the CPS would gain rights of audience in the crown court resulting in loss of prosecution work–on which see below, pp 566–68.

Note–a divided Bar

In the 1980s the gap between earnings from public sector work and privately paid work became marked and caused considerable resentment. It led among other things to a new and unprecedented militancy on questions affecting remuneration among many members of the Bar. One result was the litigation brought by the Chairman of the Bar against the Lord Chancellor regarding the increase of fees for criminal legal aid. (See *Law Society's Gazette*, 26 February 1986, p 611; 30 April 1986, p 1302; and *New Law Journal*, 4 April 1986, p 297.) Another result was the election to the Bar Council of a spate of members representing the Campaign for the Bar with strongly held views on the interests of ordinary members of the common-law Bar. (See *Law Society's Gazette*, 1 May 1985, p 1245; 29 May 1985, p 1554; 26 June 1985, p 1845; 28 August 1985, p 2325; 26 February 1986, p 611; 23 July 1986, p 2323.)

(b) The solicitor's branch

Origin and history

The solicitors' branch grew out of the variety of different practitioners who operated in different capacities in the legal system other than the barrister and the sergeant-at-law. By the late thirteenth century, attorneys existed to handle the technicalities of law suits. Solicitors seem first to have emerged in the sixteenth century. By the end of the seventeenth century the different categories included sergeants, two ranks of barristers, solicitors, attorneys, conveyancers or scriveners, pleaders, and proctors. Pleaders were absorbed by the Bar, scriveners' work was taken over by solicitors and attorneys, and the differences between attorney and solicitors were gradually eliminated. Attorneys were advisers to the parties, solicitors were especially associated with matters concerned with land, and proctors were concerned with ecclesiastical law and matrimonial affairs.

The 1873 Judicature Act merged the functions of solicitors, attorneys and proctors, and the title 'solicitor' was adopted as a generic title for them all. Statute now reserves that title to those qualified as solicitors. (There is no equivalent statute in relation to barristers.)

(On the history of the profession see, for instance, M Birks, *Gentlemen of the Law* (Stevens, 1960).)

Management

The profession is run by the Law Society (which was established by Royal Charter in 1831) and the 121 autonomous local law societies. The Law Society is both the professional association concerned with the advancement of the interests of solicitors and the governing body concerned with dealing with complaints against solicitors and disciplinary matters. It issues practising certificates to those in private practice. It administers the Compensation Fund against which clients defrauded by solicitors can complain and recoup their losses. It makes arrangements for the compulsory insurance of solicitors under the Solicitors' Indemnity Fund. It also manages the system of training for those wishing to qualify as solicitors, through its College of Law. Practice Rules regulating the practice, conduct and discipline of solicitors are promulgated by the Law Society with the approval of the Master of the Rolls, under the authority of the Solicitors Act 1933, s 31.

The 121 local law societies perform less important functions. They deal with complaints from the public, help solicitors in difficulties and assist would-be entrants to secure articles and positions in firms. They may arrange lectures and social events. They also play a role in shaping Law Society policy by reacting to proposals emanating from Chancery Lane which are for consideration by the profession as a whole.

The Law Society is run by its Council, which consists of 70 members elected by solicitors throughout the country. The country is divided into constituencies, each of which has a proportionate number of Council members depending on the number of solicitors who practise in that area. The President and Vice-President are traditionally elected unopposed, but in 1995 for the first time there was a bitterly contested election at which the unofficial candidates Mr Martin Mears and Mr Robert Sayers were elected. This led to unprecedented and very public in-fighting between supporters and opponents on the Council regarding Mr Mears and his radical programme for reform. (See for instance, the sharp denunciation of Mr Mears by former President Tony Holland and Mr Mears' robust rejoinder, both in *New Law Journal*, 23 February 1996, pp 242–43.)

Only solicitors who practise as principals or those who undertake litigation work require an annual practising certificate. The Royal Commission on Legal Services recommended (para 29.31) that all solicitors on the Roll who work in private practice should be required to have a practising certificate.

It is not required that qualified solicitors be members of the Law Society, but over 80 per cent are. In order to become a solicitor, however, it is necessary to become a student member of the Law Society.

The structure of the profession

Solicitors practise in firms. In 1994 there were 9,766 firms spread around the country. Between them they had a total of 13,744 offices. The breakdown as to size of firms is stated in the table below.

Size of solicitors' firms (%)

	1979	1986	1990	1994
Sole practitioners	34	35	37	40
2–4 partners	48	46	44	43
5–10 partners	14	14	15	19
Over 10*	4	4	5	5

(Source: Royal Commission on Legal Services Report, 1979, Table 17.1; Annual Statistical Report, Law Society.)

*The 1979 figures were based on 5 to 9 partner firms, whereas those for 1986 and later reports were based on 5 to 10.

What has changed is the number of large firms, and their size. City firms with 30 to 40 partners are now common. In 1995 the largest four were Clifford Chance with 1,404 fee-earners including 229 equity partners; Eversheds with 935 fee earners including 268 partners, Linklaters & Paines with 835 fee-earners including 152 equity partners, and Freshfields with 758 fee-earners including 140 equity partners. The 100th firm in size had 75 fee-earners including 27 equity partners. (Source: The *Lawyer*, 25 April 1995, pp 10–1.)

Solicitors working in private firms who are not in partnership are called 'assistant solicitors'. A solicitor normally cannot establish his own practice within three years of admission to the Roll. He needs the permission of the Law Society to do so.

Legal executives

It has been a familiar feature of solicitors' offices for well over a hundred years that they employ unadmitted staff on professional work. Formerly they were known as 'managing clerks', but since the founding of the Institute of Legal Executives in 1963 they have generally been known as legal executives, regardless of whether they were actually members of the Institute. In 1994 there were some 23,000 Members of the Institute (including students). There are reckoned to be approximately another 10,000 unadmitted staff in solicitors' offices who are not members of the Institute.

The Institute has three grades of membership–students, Associates (who have passed four papers in law and have served in solicitors' office for at least three consecutive years); and Fellows (who must be 25 or over, have served eight years in a solicitors' office and who must have passed an examination comprising three papers out of a choice of thirteen).

The distribution of personnel in solicitors' firms

In its evidence to the Benson Royal Commission on Legal Services, the Law Society said that the typical firm at the end of 1976 was in a provincial town and had three principals and five other wage-earners, of whom one was an assistant solicitor, two were legal executives, one an articled clerk and one a junior clerk. In addition there would be ten full-time and three part-time staff–for example, accounts clerks, an outdoor clerk, secretaries, telephonist and receptionist. The total complement would be some 21. Approximately two-thirds of all firms were of this size or smaller. (Law Society, *Evidence to the Royal Commission, Memorandum No 5*, 1978, p 20, para 5.1.) The picture in 1994 was not very different.

But the large firms have a disproportionate share of the manpower. Thus in 1994, firms with up to four partners were 83 per cent of all firms but they employed only 26 per cent of assistant solicitors and 36 per cent of all non-solicitor fee earners. The firms with 11 or more partners were 5 per cent of all firms but they employed 56 per cent of all assistant solicitors and 42 per cent of non-solicitor fee earners. (Law Society, *Trends in the Solicitors' Profession, Annual Statistical Report*, 1994, Table 4.1, p 26.) The City firms also train a disproportionate share of the recruits to the profession.

The distribution of solicitors' offices in the community

The only systematic national study of the location of solicitors' offices was carried out by Ken Foster on the basis of the Law List in 1971 ('The Location of Solicitors', 1973, *Modern Law Review*, p 153). Wide differences emerged in the distribution of solicitors' offices. Various socio-economic factors were then tested to attempt to explain this unequal distribution of solicitors. It proved that the distribution of solicitors did not correlate with middle-class areas (p 161). Towns with a high proportion of people over 65 did have a significant correlation with the distribution of solicitors and their offices (*ibid*). There was no significant statistical relationship between the distribution of solicitors and owner-occupied properties, though there was some between the presence of solicitors' offices and a high percentage of freehold housing.

But the strongest correlation was between the distribution of solicitors and the amount per head of retail sales. These high correlations, Foster suggested, indicated that 'the location of solicitors and their offices is governed principally by economic considerations very similar to those that govern the location of retail distribution outlets' (pp 161–2).

The National Association of Citizens' Advice Bureaux told the Benson Royal Commission that 88 per cent of the bureaux that responded considered that there were enough firms of solicitors within reach of their clients. In Greater London, however, over a quarter of all bureaux said there were not enough solicitors within reach.

The Royal Commission said that there was a need to encourage the provision of legal services in areas where there was at present a scarcity of solicitors. One means of doing this would be to open law centres (see below). Another was to encourage private solicitors to open practices in such areas. The Commission was against guaranteeing practitioners in deprived areas an income. This would 'give rise to justifiable objections by solicitors in neighbouring areas' (para 16.25, p 181). It would also be difficult to fix the level of remuneration at the right figures. The Commission did favour interest-free loans from public funds, and deferring the repayment of capital loans in order to assist in the establishment of such new offices (see para 16.26, p 181). But nothing has come of this proposal.

Women in the solicitors' profession

The rise in the proportion of solicitors with practising certificates who are women has been striking. In 1970 they were 3 per cent of the total; in 1980, 10 per cent; in 1991, 25 per cent; in 1994, 29 per cent. Of those coming into the profession the proportion of women was far higher still. In both 1994 and 1995 women were 54 per cent of the students enrolling with the Law Society (Law Society's *Annual Statistical Report*, 1995, para 10.4, p 69).

At the partnership level, however, women are still under-represented. In 1995, 68 per cent of women in private practice were assistant solicitors and 26 per cent were partners; for men, 27 per cent were assistant solicitors and 58 per cent were partners (*ibid*, Table 2.8, p 15). Of solicitors in private practice with 10 to 19 years of experience, 70 per cent of men were partners and 10 per cent were sole practitioners, compared with 47 per cent and 7 per cent, respectively, of women (*ibid*, para 2.9, p 16).

Ethnic minorities in the solicitors' profession

The proportion of solicitors drawn from ethnic minorities is far lower than is the case at the Bar, where it runs slightly ahead of the proportion in the population as a whole.

Research in 1988 showed that only a fraction above 1 per cent of all holders of practising certificates were from the ethnic minorities. But in 1995 they were 3.8 per cent of solicitors with practising certificates and the numbers were growing markedly. In 1994–95, 17 per cent of students enrolling with the Law Society and 15.5 per cent of solicitors admitted were from ethnic minorities. (People from ethnic minorities accounted for 5.2 per cent of the economically active population of England and Wales.) (*Ibid*, para 2.11, p 17.)

Vocational training for solicitors–the Legal Practice Course

The Law Society's vocational course was drastically reformed as from 1993. The aim was to make the course more genuinely vocational. The course is taught at the five branches of the College of Law and at a number of former polytechnics. Whereas previously the course was virtually identical wherever it was taught, there can now be a measure of freedom of action for teaching institutions subject, however, to accreditation by the Law Society's Legal Practice Course Board. Testing is by a mixture of written examination and assessment carried out by institutions. The content has a practical basis with an emphasis on the use of 'black letter law' and practical know-how.

The course consists of both compulsory subjects (conveyancing, wills, probate, administration, business law and practice, and litigation and advocacy) and optional subjects. Matters of professional conduct and the influence of European law, revenue law and financial services law are supposed to be taught throughout the course. Skills training is supposed to focus on interviewing and advising, legal research, writing and drafting, negotiating and advocacy. The course can be either full-time over one year or part-time over two academic years.

See further *Law Society's Gazette*, 23 May 1990, p 4; 20 June 1990, p 2; 6 February 1991, p 6; 2 October 1991, p. 4. For critical assessment and a reply see *Legal Action*, July 1994, p 8 and September 1994, p 9. See also the study by the Policy Studies Institute–M Shiner and T Newburn, *Entry into the Legal Professions: The Law Student Cohort Study Year 3*, The Law Society, 1995.

Continuing education

The Law Society introduced compulsory continuing education for new entrants as from 1984. In 1990 it was extended to all members of the profession qualifying after 1987, who have to acquire 16 'points' per annum at continuing education courses or activities of one sort or another for the rest of their careers.

The Bar has hitherto had no equivalent requirements but in 1995 the Bar agreed to introduce a measure of compulsory continuing education for young practitioners as from autumn 1996.

Numbers of solicitors

Like the Bar, the solicitors' branch has grown hugely in recent years. For the first fifty years of this century the numbers were relatively stable. In 1950 there were 17,000 solicitors with practising certificates. In 1960 the figure was 19,000. Between 1963–64 and 1993–94 the total number of solicitors with practising certificates grew by 208 per cent and the number of solicitors in private practice rose by 190 per cent. (There were 63,628 of the former and 52,213 of the latter.)

The growth in the solicitors' branch was not, however, the result of growth in representation under legal aid, since, as has been seen, this forms only a small proportion of the income of solicitors. It was attributable rather more to the spread of home ownership in the population. As will be seen below, solicitors until 1986 had a monopoly of the handling of conveyancing and this accounted for a very large part of their income. In 1901 about 10 per cent of dwellings were owner-occupied; the figure in 1971 was 50 per cent and in 1990 was 67 per cent.

From time to time the question of regulating numbers coming into the professions surfaces as an issue. In 1995, Mr Martin Mears made this one of the topics on which he campaigned for the Presidency of the Law Society. His proposal was that places on the compulsory Legal Practice Course should be restricted to persons who had training contracts with firms. In 1995/96 there were 7,924 places for the Legal Practice course but the profession only offered some 3,700 training placements. Mr Mears' plan would therefore have resulted in a drastic reduction in the numbers being allowed onto the course. His Vice President, elected at the same time (also after a contested election) went even further. He wanted to reduce places on the LPC to 1,000. (See *Law Society's Gazette*, 26 July 1995, p 8.) This plan ran into opposition from members of the Council of the Law Society. It was also declared to be unlawful in a formal legal opinion by Richard Drabble QC whose advice had been sought by the Law Society. In his view the Law Society had no power to restrict the numbers entering professional training for reasons unconnected with educational standards. (See *The Lawyer*, 9 January 1996, p 1.)

When this proved to be a blind alley, the working party set up by the President to consider whether, and if so, how to reduce entry to the profession directed its attention to reducing numbers by introducing an aptitude test (*ibid*, 5 March 1996, p 13; *Law Society's Gazette*, 17 January 1996, p 10).

But a report from the Law Society's training committee suggested that the number of students applying for the 1996 Legal Practice Course had dropped by 1,364 by comparison with 1995 and, at the same time, there was a small increase in the number of training contracts. The chairman of the training committee was quoted as saying that 'the serious oversupply of applicants seems to be correcting itself without the need for direct intervention'. (*The Lawyer*, 27 February 1996, p 1; J Ames, 'Student Numbers in Decline', *Law Society's Gazette*, 28 February 1996, p 6.)

This was confirmed by the Lord Chancellor's Advisory Committee on Legal Education and Conduct (ACLEC) in its report on Legal Education and Training in April 1996. The report (p 45) opposed the idea of a restriction on the numbers seeking entry to the profession either by arbitrary restrictions on the numbers of places on vocational courses or by externally imposed limitations on the number of training contracts for solicitors (or pupillages for barristers).

ACLEC's new proposals on legal education

In April 1996 the Lord Chancellor's Advisory Committee on Legal Education and Conduct (ACLEC) issued a major consultative paper on legal training. It recommended that all law graduates intending to become barristers or solicitors would take the same 15 to 18 week course called common professional legal studies (CPLS) which would lead to a qualification provisionally named a licentiate in professional legal studies

(LicPLS) equivalent to higher national vocational qualifications. Those who achieved only this qualification could work as legal consultants.

After the vocational course they would then have to complete either a training contract (solicitors) or pupillage (barristers). ACLEC recommended that the present period for solicitors' training contracts should be reduced from two years to one year, or even to six months, the same period as it proposed for pupillage.

ACLEC also recommended that the conversion course taken by non-law graduates in lieu of the law degree should be lengthened.

For details see *Law Society's Gazette*, 1 May 1996, p 10.

(c) The operation of the divided profession

Many assume that the division goes back into the mists of antiquity, but this is not so. As Australian scholar John Forbes pointed out, division presupposes two or more parts of a whole, but it was not until the seventeenth or even eighteenth century that solicitors could be said to have emerged as a distinct or identifiable professional group.[4] The Bar had by then had centuries of development. The distinction in those days was therefore not between two parts of the same profession, but between lawyers and sub-lawyers. In 1765 Blackstone set out the hierarchy of the legal profession without even mentioning solicitors. Even a hundred years later Dicey lectured on legal education without referring to solicitors. Until the late eighteenth and into the early nineteenth century, solicitors could be described as 'an unorganised, ill-disciplined, ill-educated category of sub-professional agents, living wholly or partly on the sub-professional trivia of litigation and conveyancing and sharing even this subject matter with court clerks, law students and laymen' (Michael Birks, *Gentlemen of the Law*, Stevens, 1960, p 105).

But in the nineteenth century the solicitors' branch gradually established itself and carved out areas of work in which it specialized. The Bar was persuaded first to give up seeing clients direct and then to cease to do conveyancing. In return the Bar had a monopoly over the right to appear as an advocate (the 'right of audience') in the higher courts and a virtual monopoly over appointments to the bench

Today the division is strictly maintained. The lay client must go to the solicitor first and can only see a barrister if the barrister has received instructions from a solicitor (though members of some other professions are now also permitted to instruct barristers directly without going through a solicitor–see p 571 below). No one can be both a barrister and a solicitor at the same time. Barristers and solicitors are not permitted to form partnerships nor can they work in each other's offices. The Bar is the senior branch. Thus, the solicitor normally attends on the barrister in his chambers rather than the reverse.[5] The barrister is in charge of the running of the case and will tell the solicitor how he intends to conduct it. Until 1991 barristers had a monopoly over all the higher judicial appointments and, even where either barristers or solicitors could be appointed to a judicial position, most appointments in fact were from the ranks of barristers. (Thus in 1996, of 868 recorders only 73 were former solicitors and of the

4   See J Forbes, 'Division of the Profession: Ancient or Scientific?', *Law Society's Gazette*, 26 January 1977, p 67.
5   The rule that *required* this was abolished by the Bar Council in 1991.

374 assistant recorders, only 69 were solicitors. The number of solicitor circuit judges was 72 out of 517.)

Nevertheless, prior to the Government's 1989 Green Papers (p 564 below) a number of minor adjustments to the system had been made to modify its rigour:

(1) A barrister employed on a salary in a law centre was not held to the normal rules against seeing lay clients without instructions from a solicitor. He can even write letters and negotiate on behalf of clients of the law centre. However, he may not initiate proceedings, nor may he appear as an advocate without instructions from a solicitor in the centre. But he does retain his status as a practising barrister even though he is employed on a salary. (*Code of Conduct for the Bar of England and Wales*, 1994, Annex J.)

(2) Contrary to the normal rules, a barrister in regard to overseas work was allowed to take instructions from the lay client direct, to enter into a partnership with a foreign lawyer, to practise without a clerk and to accept a fixed fee or a contingent fee. (*Code of Conduct for the Bar of England and Wales*, 1994, Annex F.)

(3) The Courts Act 1971 gave solicitors the right to become recorders and, after five years on the bench, circuit judges. The five-year period of qualification was later reduced to three. (Administration of Justice Act 1977, s 12.) (In 1990 they won the right to become High Court judges–Courts and Legal Services Act 1990, s 71. But by 1996 only one former solicitor had been appointed to the High Court bench.)

(4) The jurisdiction of the county courts and of the magistrates had been expanding so that the numbers of cases where the two branches of the profession compete for the work had likewise increased.

(5) As from February 1989 the Bar and the Law Society agreed that a barrister could appear in the crown court without a solicitor in attendance in straightforward guilty-plea cases, committals for sentence and appeals against sentence. Both counsel and solicitor had to be satisfied that the particular case was suitable for the barrister to appear on his own.

For subsequent developments see below.

(d) Law centres

Law centres are offices providing legal services in poverty areas staffed by lawyers whose salaries are paid out of public funds. The funding is a mixture of central and local government money and ordinary payments out of the legal aid fund. For the clients the services are entirely free of charge.

Law centres were first proposed in 1968[6] in the Society of Labour Lawyers' pamphlet *Justice for All*. At the time the concept was opposed by the Law Society, which saw law centres as a threat to the private practitioner. The first centre was set up in 1970 in North Kensington. By the end of that decade there were some 30. During most of the 1980s there were some 50 centres and that remains the approximate number.

---

6   For the history of law centres see M Zander, *Legal Services for the Community* (Temple Smith, 1978), chs 2 and 3. For a survey see *Report of the Royal Commission on Legal Services*, Cmnd 7648, 1979, vol 2, Part B, pp 63–79. The Legal Aid Advisory Committee gave particular attention to law centres in its 34th Report for 1983–4, pp 338–46.

The original opposition of the Law Society soon melted away as it began to be appreciated that law centres could feed paying work to the local profession whilst handling unremunerative work that the profession was not keen to undertake. Law centres won the approval of the Lord Chancellor's Legal Aid Advisory Committee, of the Law Society, of the Benson Royal Commission on Legal Services[7] and of politicians of all parties. They are thought to be an important resource filling gaps in the legal aid system, often specializing in areas of work that private practitioners do not handle.

The main problem faced by law centres is that they have not succeeded in finding a secure source of funding. Successive Lord Chancellors have declined to make them a charge on central government funds.[8]

Law centres and the Legal Aid Board

The first report of the Legal Aid Board, published in May 1989, said that there were seven law centres that received grants from the Lord Chancellor's Department. The Board said these grants were anomalous and it hoped to phase them out by April 1991. In the second report, published in June 1990, it admitted that this had not been possible and said that the grants should continue for the time being.

It reported that law centres received some £1.7m in funds from central government —£1m from legal aid and the balance in grants to seven centres from the Lord Chancellor's Department. It said it was satisfied that law centres filled a gap in the provision of legal services. It did not favour taking over the funding of the law centres but wanted to see funding based on an appropriate mix of sources–'without making them dependent entirely on one source' (*Annual Report*, 1989–90 para 7.16, p 36).

In the third report, for 1990–1, the Board reported that some law centres had faced severe financial problems. The three centres in Wandsworth had lost their local authority grant as had the centres in Dudley and Wolverhampton. Two new centres had opened and two others threatened with closure had survived. But the Law Centres Federation said that 15 centres had major funding difficulties.

The Legal Aid Board had refused to step in to save the centres that were threatened with closure. It would have been acting directly contrary to its policy if it had made grants where local funding had been withdrawn. Also it would have sent a message to other local authorities that the Board would replace them if they withdrew. But the Board did think it was justified in providing some money for law centres in order to permit them to continue to make an innovative contribution.

Law centre lawyers had developed skills and specialisms which had been copied by private practitioners. This was most valuable. Also law centres had pioneered various means of delivering legal services: for instance, 24-hour services (a precursor of the police station Duty Solicitor scheme); multi-plaintiff work in areas other than personal injuries; peripatetic advice sessions; advice over the telephone for those who found it difficult to get to the office; or pro-active lawyering, for instance through advice and

7   The Royal Commission said that the impact of law centres 'had been out of all proportion to their size, to the number of lawyers who work in them and to the amount of work it is possible for them to undertake'. It quoted the statement of the Lord Chancellor's Advisory Committee summing up informed opinion:'we think that law centres are, and should be, here to stay and that they are making a vital contribution to legal services' (p 81).

8   The Lord Chancellor's Department has contributed to several of the centres but it has refused to take financial responsibility for the law centre movement as a whole.

training to groups. Law centres had also played a major role in providing representation in tribunals and thereby opening up an area of need not covered by legal aid.

The Board maintained its view that it should not fund law centres entirely. One reason was that, since part of the work done by law centres was work done by advice agencies, it would be illogical to finance the one but not the other. Also, since law centres were so connected to the local situation, they should get their money from local funds. But the Board intended to investigate whether local authorities would be prepared to join it in mixed funding arrangements. The terms and conditions for such arrangements were set out by the Board in Appendix 3 of the Report, pp 122–4.

The Board's annual report for 1994–95 stated (p 32) that it had made grants to ten law centres totalling just under a million pounds.

See also John Baldwin , 'The Role of Citizens' Advice Bureaux and Law Centres in the Provision of Legal Advice and Assistance', *Civil Justice Quarterly*, January 1989, p 24.

2. THE USE OF LAWYERS

Surveys have shown that on the whole lawyers are used for a relatively narrow range of legal problems. The largest study by far was that conducted for the Benson Royal Commission on Legal Services (vol 2, pp 173–298). This was based on interviews with a random sample of 7,941 households. The main findings were:

(1) Nearly three-fifths of people over 18 had seen a solicitor in regard to a personal problem at some point. 14 per cent had done so in the previous twelve months (Table 8.3, p 185).

(2) The age-group that used lawyers most were those between 25 and 34 (para 8.27, p 184).

(3) Use of lawyers varied by socio-economic group. A solicitor in 1977 was used by: 25 per cent of the professional class; 21 per cent of employers and managers; 19 per cent of intermediate and junior non-manual workers; 13 per cent of skilled manual workers and workers who worked on their own account; 11 per cent of semi-skilled workers; and 10 per cent of unskilled manual workers (Table 8.8, p 190).

(4) Those in non-manual households (one-third of the population) accounted for over a half of all use of lawyers for the buying and selling of property, dealing with the estates of deceased persons and making or altering wills (para 8.110). In divorce, motoring offences and personal injury claims arising out of road traffic accidents those who used lawyers were roughly in proportion to their size in the general population (para 8.111). Manual households used lawyers considerably more (proportionately) than non-manual in claims for industrial injury compensation, and marginally more in offences other than motoring (para 8.112). But in matters which were not connected with property, 'the profile of users of lawyers' services by socio-economic group is not greatly different from that of the adult population in general (para 8.115).

These results demonstrate that use of lawyers is problem-connected even more than it is type-of-person connected. In other words, socio-economic background is not the best explanation of the fact that different categories in the socio-economic scale use lawyers to a different extent. In fields where property is involved (conveyancing, probate, wills, etc), naturally enough those with property see lawyers much more than those who do not. Since this is the largest single source of work for the solicitors' profession it explains why lawyer-use seems to reflect the differences between classes. But the impression is misleading. If one looks at non-property types of work, the use of lawyers is relatively even as between members of different socio-economic backgrounds.

For more recent data see J Jenkins, E Skordaki and C Willis, 'Public Use of Perception of Solicitors' Services', Law Society Research Study No 1, 1989; Gerry Chambers and Stephen Harwood, 'Solicitors in England and Wales: Practice Organisation and Perceptions–First Report, 'The Work of the Solicitor in Private Practice' Law Society Research Study No 2, 1990; and 'Second Report, The Private Practice Firm', Law Society Research Study No 8, 1991.

3. REFORM OF THE PROFESSION

Over the past quarter century the subject of the legal profession's monopolies and restrictive practices has been a major source of disputation. They have been examined in turn by the National Board for Prices and Incomes (1968, 1969, 1971), the Monopolies Commission (1970, 1976, 1976), the Royal Commission on Legal Services (1979), the Marre Committee (1988) and the Government's three Green Papers (1989). In 1994-95 the Labour Party proposed that they should be referred to the Monopolies Commission again.

In the first five editions of this book a good deal of space was given to consideration of the pros and cons of the division of the legal profession into barristers and solicitors. In the sixth edition that material was dropped–not because the topic lacks interest, but because it seemed no longer to be of practical importance.[9] In 1979 the Royal Commission concluded unanimously (15–0) that the divided profession was in the public interest. In the great debate on the Green Papers in 1989 both sides of the profession argued passionately that the division should continue and this was in the end accepted by the Government. There is no current suggestion that the Labour Opposition would in government take a different view–though on the issue of 'Direct Access', see p 571. In short, at least for the time being, the topic is not a live one. For the foreseeable future, the division between barristers and solicitors will continue.

9 The argument for unification of the legal profession has been most fully developed in M Zander, *Lawyers and the Public Interest* (Weidenfeld and Nicolson, 1968, now out of print), pp 270–332, and M Zander, *Cases and Materials on the English System,* (5th edn, Weidenfeld and Nicolson, 1988), pp 592–603. See also P Reeves, *Are Two Legal Professions Necessary?* (Waterlows, 1986); 'Young Solicitors Want Fusion', *Law Society's Gazette,* 4 June 1986, p 1682.

For a direct response to the arguments in *Lawyers and the Public Interest,* see Gerald Gardiner, 'Two Lawyers or One?', 23 *Current Legal Problems,* 1970, p 1. See also: R E Megarry, *Lawyer and Litigant in England,* (Stevens, 1962); C P Harvey, *The Advocates Devil* (Stevens, 1958); EJ Cohn, 'The German Attorney–Experiences with a United Profession', 9 *International and Comparative Law Quarterly,* 1960, pp 580–99, and *ibid,* vol 10, 1961, pp 103–22; and FA Mann, 'Fusion of the Legal Profession', *Law Quarterly Review,* July 1977, p 367.

For the history see J Forbes, 'Division of the Profession: Ancient or Scientific', *Law Society's Gazette,* 26 January 1977, p 67.

The battle over the Green Papers

Instead we will focus here on the issues that are now current or that were brought into the great debate launched by Lord Mackay's Green Papers in January 1989. The course of that extraordinary event in the history of the English legal profession was traced at length in the 6th edition of this work, pp 653–89. In brief, in January 1989, the Lord Chancellor published three Green Papers[10] making a series of radical proposals for reform of the structure and organisation of the profession. The legal profession and the judges reacted fiercely and the Government's *White Paper on Legal Services* in July 1889 (Cm 740) represented a major retreat from the original proposals. The White Paper was broadly implemented in the Courts and Legal Services Act 1990 ('the 1990 Act').

What follows is a brief description of the proposals made in the Green Papers, how they were modified in the White Paper and the 1990 Act and what has happened in regard to each topic since 1990.

Rights of audience for lawyers

The Benson Royal Commission by 8 to 7 recommended that the Bar retain its ancient monopoly over the right of audience in the higher courts. The Green Paper (GP) proposed instead that the right to appear as an advocate should be based not on status but on individual qualification.[11] The test should be whether the relevant professional body had been authorized to certify advocates and whether the individual had the prescribed qualifications. The fact that someone was a barrister, solicitor, or employed lawyer would no longer be critical.[12] Lay advocates could also be given rights of audience.

Advocacy certificates could be either full (entitling the holder to appear in all the courts) or limited (entitling one to practice only in the lower courts). An applicant for a full certificate would have to undergo practical training in advocacy, including a course, attachment to a practising advocate, attendance at actual cases, and possibly a second course. A full certificate would require having held a limited certificate for a minimum period. In addition, the applicant would need a certificate of satisfactory performance from the supervising advocate and would have to prove a prescribed minimum of actual advocacy in the magistrates, county, and crown courts.[13] Those with a limited certificate would have a right of audience in the lower courts, plus guilty plea cases in the higher courts and formal unopposed hearings in the High Court and in chambers.

The White Paper (WP) more or less abandoned the Green Paper (GP) approach. The WP (paras 3.4–3.17) proposed first that the existing complex arrangements for rights of audience under statute and common law should be replaced by statutory rights of audience in all courts and appropriate tribunals.[14] The Bar Council and the Law Society would both be authorized bodies able to grant rights of audience and the members of both professional bodies would be deemed to enjoy their existing rights of audience. Thus, on qualification, barristers in private practice would have full rights of audience in all the courts; solicitors in private practice would have their rights of audience in

10 See note 1, p 539 above.
11 *The Work and Organization of the Legal Profession* (1989, Cm 570) (hereinafter MGP), para 5.7.
12 *Ibid*, para 5.8.
13 *Ibid*, paras.5.14-5.23, 5.30.
14 This proposal was confirmed in s 27(1) of the 1990 Act.

the lower courts and such other rights of audience in the higher courts as they already enjoyed;[15] lawyers employed other than in private practice would only have rights of audience in the lower courts.

However, additional rights of audience could be sought by the Law Society, by bodies representing employed lawyers, or by bodies representing non-lawyers. The process by which such claims would be handled in each case would be much the same. The claim would be put to the Lord Chancellor who would refer it to his Advisory Committee on Legal Education and Conduct (see below). If the Advisory Committee approved, it would then have to be approved by the Lord Chancellor with the concurrence of four senior judges: the Lord Chief Justice, the Master of the Rolls, the President of the Family Division, and the Vice-Chancellor of the Chancery Division.

The Lord Chancellor and the four judges would have to consider the matter 'having regard' to the views of the Advisory Committee. Each judge would have to agree; each would therefore have a veto. Failure to agree would have to be explained in written reasons (which would be subject to judicial review for unreasonableness). The WP said (para 8.5) the 'Government envisages that this will in practice be reflected in the earlier stages of the preparation of drafts by the professional bodies through a process of discussion involving all four parties'–ie the judges, the professional bodies, the Advisory Committee and the Lord Chancellor.

In addition, the question would be referred to the Director-General of the Office of Fair Trading for his assessment from the point of view of competition policy.

This somewhat complex scheme was translated into law in Part II of the 1990 Act. In fact it was made even more complex by the provisions regarding the 'statutory objective' and the 'general principle'. The 'statutory objective' stated in s 17(1) says:

The general objective of this Part is the development of legal services in England and Wales (and in particular the development of advocacy, litigation, conveyancing and probate services) by making provision for new or better ways of providing such services and a wider choice of persons providing them, while maintaining the proper and efficient administration of justice.

The objective is therefore that new or better ways be found of providing legal services. To that extent, any application for additional rights of audience (etc) has a head start. There is supposed to be a bias in favour of change.

The Act then says (s 17 (3)) that in principle–'the general principle' (2.17 (4))–the question whether a person should be granted a right of audience or be granted a right to conduct litigation must be determined by reference *only* to four considerations:

(1) Whether he is appropriately qualified (s 17(3)(a)).

(2) Whether he is a member of a professional or other body which (i) has rules of conduct governing its members; (ii) has an effective mechanism for enforcing its rules of conduct; and (iii) is likely to enforce them (s 16(3) (b)).

(3) Whether, in relation to advocacy, the rules make satisfactory provision for an equivalent of the Bar's 'cab rank rule'–that a member should not withhold his services on the ground (i) that the case, or the client is objectionable to him or to a section of the

15 There were seven crown courts in which solicitors had historically been granted full rights of audience –which they exercised very rarely. Solicitors also had rights of audience for proceedings in chambers before a High Court judge, official referee, master or referee. A solicitor could appear likewise in proceedings in chambers before the single judge in the Court of Appeal Criminal Division and in the House of Lords on an application for leave to appeal. All these existing rights of audience were confirmed by s 27(7) of the 1990 Act.

public;[16] or (ii) of the client's source of funding–eg that the case is legally aided (s 17(3)(c)).

(4) Whether the rules of conduct are 'appropriate in the interests of the proper and efficient administration of justice' (s 16(3)(d)).

All those charged with the duty of considering such applications must do so with reasonable dispatch (s 18(1)). They must act in accordance with the general principle, and subject to that, shall '(a) so far as it is possible to do so in the circumstances of the case, act to further the statutory objective; and (b) not act in any way which would be incompatible with the statutory objective' (s 18 (2)).[17]

Almost as soon as the 1990 Act received the Royal Assent, the Law Society put in its application for additional rights of audience[18] and shortly thereafter a second application was put in by the Head of the Government Legal Service and the Director of Public Prosecutions.[19]

The Law Society proposal was two-tiered. It asked that all solicitors should on qualification be entitled to conduct non-jury cases in the crown court (ie guilty-plea cases, committals for sentence and appeals from magistrates' courts against conviction or sentence and unopposed applications in the High Court). This would apply to solicitors whether they worked in private practice, central or local government, commerce or industry.

But it further proposed that solicitors should be able to seek full audience rights by obtaining a 'higher court (all proceedings) or (criminal proceedings) or (civil proceedings) qualification'.[20]

The Government lawyers and DPP asked that barristers employed in government service and the Crown Prosecution Service should have the same rights of audience as barristers in private practice. (The DPP's submission made the point that one reason for giving CPS lawyers extended rights of audience was the fact that over half the briefs to counsel at the crown court were returned within 48 hours of the hearing.)

Needless to say, the Bar strongly objected to both applications.[1] But whereas it was completely against any extension of rights of audience for state prosecutors or other employed lawyers, it was prepared to contemplate extended rights of audience

16 It is specifically provided (s 17(5)) that rules that allow a member to refuse a case if there are reasonable grounds having regard to the circumstances of the case, the nature of his practice, his experience or standing, or that he is not being offered a proper fee, do not conflict with the general principle.
17 For a discussion of these provisions see Richard Southwell QC, 'A Level Playing Field', *Counsel*, April 1991, p 12.
18 'An Application by the Law Society to the Lord Chancellor's Advisory Committee on Legal Education and Conduct', April 1991. Technically, the application was made under Part II of Schedule 4 of the 1990 Act.
19 Courts and Legal Services Act 1990–'Rights of Audience', May 1991.
20 A full higher courts qualification would require: practice for three or more years; 15 days' advocacy experience in the previous two years in the lower courts; completion of a five-day advocacy course; and passing a test in evidence and procedure. A civil or criminal higher courts qualification would require a shorter course but 20 days' advocacy experience in that field. (See *Law Society's Gazette*, 10 April 1991, p 4.)
1   For its formal response of over 150 pages see Bar Council, *Quality of Justice–the Way Forward*, July 1991. It was scornful of the extent of the training proposed and of the likely quality of advocacy of solicitors and especially employed solicitors. The Chairman of the Bar was quoted as saying that, if the level of competence displayed by CPS lawyers in the magistrates' courts was anything to go by, CPS lawyers would fall far short of the standard required for crown court work (*Law Society's Gazette*, 29 May 1991, p 4).

for solicitors–provided that certain (from the point of view of the Law Society, unacceptable) conditions were met.[2]

The Advisory Committee's views

The Advisory Committee published its views in April 1992. It rejected the Law Society's proposal for automatic extended rights of audience on qualification. But it agreed that solicitors in private practice could qualify for extended rights of audience in the higher courts by a modified version of the Law Society's proposed scheme of advocacy training. (See *Law Society's Gazette*, 15 April 1992, pp 3–4; 29 April 1992, p 4; *New Law Journal*, 17 April 1992, pp 517–20.)

The Advisory Committee however wholly rejected the proposal that employed lawyers in general, and the CPS in particular, should have rights of audience in the higher courts. In reaching its view about the CPS application, the Committee was apparently influenced by the attitude of the designated judges who were consulted in advance. (See *Law Society's Gazette*, 15 April 1992, p 4.)

The CPS case was rejected primarily on the grounds (1) that it had not yet absorbed its present workload; (2) that employed lawyers lacked the detachment and objectivity necessary for advocates in the higher courts; and (3) that they were unlikely to use such rights of audience often enough to maintain the required level of competence.

Both the Law Society and the employed lawyers/CPS applied again. The Law Society applied for extended rights of audience for all solicitors including those employed in government or industry. The application was eventually successful in regard to solicitors in private practice but it failed in regard to employed solicitors and the application by employed lawyers and the CPS likewise failed.

For the regulations laying down the mode of qualification for extended rights of audience for solicitors in private practice see *Law Society's Gazette*, 17 December 1993, pp 29–30. (The Lord Chancellor and the Lord Chief Justice greatly irritated solicitors when they decided in 1994 that solicitor advocates in the higher courts would not be allowed to wear wigs.) The overall cost of qualification, including cost of the course, is something over £2,300. (It is not an easy test. In September 1995 only 29 per cent of the 53 candidates passed the evidence and procedure test–*Law Society's Gazette* 14 February 1996, p 1.)

By early 1996 only a relatively small number of solicitors (375 to be precise) had qualified for the right to appear as advocates in the higher courts. It is still much too early to say how significant this development will prove to be.

One issue that was beginning to emerge was whether the large City firms would succeed in securing a change in the required qualifications so as to enable their staff to qualify as advocates in the higher courts. The problem for the City firms was that the rules require a minimum number of 'flying hours' as an advocate in the lower courts which is difficult for them since those firms have few cases in the lower courts.

---

2 The conditions it suggested were: (1) that solicitor advocates should be required to act on instruction from other lawyers so as to be 'independent' and objective; and (2) that solicitor advocates subscribe to the same 'cab-rank rule' as barristers. They might then be able to conduct appeals and committals for sentence and perhaps some categories of guilty pleas. Any further extension of crown court rights of audience should require practical experience of criminal advocacy of some 100 days in each of two or three years, formal training courses of two months and three to four months' on-the-job training with an approved tutor.

In an article on 6 February 1996 entitled 'What Happened to the Revolution?' *The Lawyer* reported that the big City firms claimed that they were quite capable of training the members of their advocacy departments to the requisite standard and that they would encourage the President of the Law Society, Mr Martin Mears, to take up the issue on their behalf with the Lord Chancellor's Advisory Committee.

The question of rights of audience for employed lawyers, including the CPS, remained stuck. In July 1995 the Advisory Committee by the narrowest of margins (9–8) recommended that employed lawyers not be given extended rights of audience. The reason was summed up in para 17 of its advice to the Lord Chancellor: 'The Committee's principal concern remains that without the current requirement to retain an independent advocate, the employed lawyer will be insufficiently protected against a range of pressures, some common to all organisations, and others more specific, which could well undermine the employed advocate's ability to maintain sufficient independence from his client in proceedings in the higher courts.' The Committee said that it believed that 'a state monopoly of prosecution advocacy would represent the worst of all these risks to the proper and efficient administration of justice' (para 22).

The view of the minority on the Advisory Committee was that the Committee's primary duty was to have regard to the 'general principle' laid down in s 17(3) of the Act (see p 565 above). This specifically stated that the Committee could have regard only to the specified criteria. After applying the general principle the Committee had to consider whether the proposed changes were compatible with the over-riding purposes of the legislation–namely the development of new or better ways of providing legal services and to widen the choice of persons providing them, while maintaining the proper and efficient administration of justice.

The Advisory Committee was now unanimous that the employed lawyers had fulfilled the requirements as regards education and training. The majority considered that extended rights of audience for employed lawyers and especially the CPS threatened the maintenance of the proper and efficient administration of justice. In the view of the minority, 'The Committee has received no evidence that the con-stitutional and statutory guarantees of the independence of the CPS are inadequate either in principle or practice' (para 4.15).

The Advisory Committee can only advise. The matter was then remitted to the Lord Chancellor who placed it before the four designated judges. At the time of writing (May 1996) there was no word as to the outcome–but it appeared that the judges were deadlocked. It was reported that if in the event they proved unable to agree or if the decision was unanimously to reject extended rights of audience for the CPS, the Law Society might initiate proceedings for judicial review to challenge the decision. (See *Law Society's Gazette*, 28 June 1995.)

Rights of audience for non-lawyers

The MGP had suggested that bodies other than lawyers could be authorized to licence advocates in the courts. This was confirmed in the WP and is reflected in the machinery described above. A body representing, say, accountants, surveyors or patent agents can apply to be approved by the Advisory Committee, the designated judges and the Lord Chancellor in precisely the same way as the Bar Council and the Law Society which were approved as authorized bodies by the Act.

Applications for rights of audience of various kinds have been made to the Advisory Committee. At the time of writing those under active consideration were from the Chartered Institute of Patent Agents and the Institute of Legal Executives. Those from the Institute of Legal Executives asked for rights of audience for Fellows of the Institute in civil proceedings in magistrates' courts (including licensing and betting and gaming), in county court matters within the jurisdiction of district judges, before tribunals, before coroners' courts and in magistrates' family proceedings courts.

An application originally made by the Institute of Licensed Debt Practitioners had been suspended by the Institute. An application from a newly formed Institute of Commercial Litigators had been rejected by the Advisory Committee.

The MGP had also supported the recommendation of the Civil Justice Review that litigants should have the right to select a lay representative in small claims cases and debt and housing cases in the county court. This was implemented in s 11 of the 1990 Act, which gives the Lord Chancellor the power to make such provision by order. In 1992 the Lord Chancellor issued a Practice Direction giving effect to s 11 (SI 1992/1966) in respect only of small claims cases. The order entitled anyone to speak at a small claims hearing on behalf of a party. The party being represented must be present. The court retains the power to bar a lay representative who behaves in an unruly fashion.

Conducting litigation

Prior to the 1990 Act it was an offence under the Solicitors Act 1974, s 20, for anyone other than a solicitor to start or conduct litigation in any civil or criminal court, except as a litigant in person. The MGP proposed that this monopoly should be ended and that anyone should be capable of becoming a litigator. The WP (ch 4) confirmed this proposal. It stated that the right to conduct litigation, like the right to appear as an advocate, should be granted to practitioners by the professional bodies or institutions to which they belong, if the bodies can demonstrate that they can set and maintain appropriate standards of competence and conduct. All litigators would also be subject to the existing powers of the High Court over solicitors as officers of the court. The Law Society would become an authorized body under the Act. Other bodies could become authorized bodies by an Order in Council made, following advice from the Advisory Committee, on the recommendation of the Lord Chancellor and subject to the concurrence of the four designated judges. This scheme was implemented by ss 28–9 of the Act. But by 1996 no new body had been granted the right to initiate or to conduct litigation. The application by a newly formed Institute of Commercial Litigators was rejected by the Advisory Committee in February 1996. The Institute was informed by the Committee that the application fell 'far short of what is required by the statutory objective and the general principle'.

Advisory Committee

The MGP proposed that the Lord Chancellor should have an advisory committee with a lay majority. The functions of the advisory committee, it suggested, should include advice on the arrangements for legal education and training, on the need for recognizing areas of specialization and how specialists should be trained, and on codes of conduct.

The WP (ch 12) confirmed that there would be an advisory committee with a lay majority and the Committee was established by s 20 of the Act. Its general duty is to assist 'in the maintenance and development of standards in the education, training and conduct of those offering legal services' (s 21(1)). Its functions, set out in Sch 2 of the Act, include advising the Lord Chancellor on all stages of education and training of lawyers; qualification regulations and rules of conduct (whether related to advocacy or the conduct of litigation or not); and specialization schemes.

The WP made one significant alteration from the GP–that 'lay member' for these purposes could include non-practising lawyers. The other change was to increase the numbers from 16 to 17 so as to allow for the addition of a circuit judge.[3]

The broadly based Advisory Committee on Legal Education and Conduct (known as ACLEC) is clearly intended by the Act to be the lead policy-making body under the Act–with the designated judges playing a subsidiary monitoring role.

The Bar obviously hoped that its victory in persuading the Lord Chancellor to insert the four designated senior judges into the process would make it much more difficult for solicitors and others to gain extended rights of audience. But, as has been seen (p 567 above), this hope has already proved unfounded, though it does seem that the judges played an important role in the Advisory Committee's rejection of the CPS' application. The statutory framework and, in particular, the emphasis in the statutory objective on the desirability of innovation will not make it easy for any of the judges to exercise his veto power. On the other hand, the judges must have regard to the 'proper and efficient administration of justice'–a formula sufficiently vague to permit of interpretation.

Judicial appointment

The WP (ch 15) confirmed the proposal in the MGP that eligibility for appointment to the bench should be determined by reference to eligibility to act as an advocate. This was reflected in the Act (s 71). In the House of Lords debates on the GP it was suggested that this could mean that a non-lawyer could be appointed to the judiciary even at its highest levels. In theory this could happen–but the practical likelihood must be counted as remote.

General principles

The MGP said that the government would provide in delegated legislation the general principles to be included in the profession's codes of practice. This seemed to be a direct threat to the profession's tradition of self-regulation in an area peculiarly within the scope of its own internal affairs. The WP stated (para 2.2) that they would instead be included in the Act and that all parties would be required to have regard to them when carrying out their duties. This sounded less threatening.

---

3   The first Chairman of the Advisory Committee was the robust and universally respected law lord, Lord Griffith. The second chairman was the equally robust and respected Lord Steyn. The occupations of first members were: director of an insurance brokers' firm; polytechnic law school head; circuit judge; trade unionist; Vice-President of the Magistrates' Association; director of legal services of an insurance company; Oxford college head (former law professor); controller of BBC Northern Ireland; two Queen's Counsel; two solicitors; head of London probation; Director of the National Council of Voluntary Organizations; inspector of schools; and law centre worker since 1973.

When they emerged in the Act (as the 'statutory objective' and 'the general principle') they were not quite what had seemed to be portended, since they were not rules of conduct for lawyers so much as a way of testing claims for extending rights of audience. The concept seemed to have lost much of its sting.

Note, however, that any change in the qualification regulations or any rule of conduct affecting rights of audience or the right to conduct litigation is now subject to the elaborate machinery of approval by the Advisory Committee, the designated judges and the Lord Chancellor with the intervention also of the Director-General of the Office of Fair Trading.

Right of direct access to the Bar

The MGP had said that lay clients should have a right of direct access to barristers. Many commentators, including the writer[4] argued that this would lead to the destruction of the Bar as a second-tier consultancy service and the Government conceded the point. The WP (para 11.7) said that this matter would be left to the Bar to determine. That means that direct access by lay (as opposed to professional) clients will continue to be prohibited at least for the time being.

In 1989 the Bar altered its rules so as to permit professional clients to instruct barristers direct, without having to go via a solicitor. By 1996 there were over thirty professional bodies with this right. They included: architects, accountants, loss adjusters, ombudsmen, actuaries, valuers and auctioneers, Royal Town Planning Institute, Royal Institution of Chartered Surveyors, Association of Average Adjusters, Chartered Association of Certified Accountants, Institution of Mechanical Engineers, Institution of Chemical Engineers, Institute of Taxation, Institute of Chartered Secretaries and Administrators.

In May 1996 the Bar Council agreed in principle that bureau workers in Citizens' Advice Bureaux should be able to refer work direct to a barrister.

A Bar Council Policy Unit (think-tank) appointed in 1994 'to think the unthinkable' produced a Consultation Paper in February 1994 which, amongst other things, proposed that direct access for lay clients to a barrister should be permitted in non-contentious work–ie for legal advice. For contentious matters (litigation) the lay client should also be allowed direct access to a barrister but the barrister should then be under a duty to refer the client to an appropriate professional intermediary who would usually be a solicitor. This proposal was considered but rejected at the Bar's Annual Meeting in July 1994.

Spokesmen for the Labour Party (notably Mr Paul Boateng MP) said in 1995 that a Labour Government would abolish the rule prohibiting direct access for lay clients to a barrister.

Note

In 1990 the Bar authorized a new type of practice–that of 'non-practising employed barristers' working, say, for a firm of accountants or foreign lawyers. Such a barrister

4   M Zander, 'Is there Common Ground between the Bar and the Lord Chancellor?', *Counsel*, March/ April 1989, p 8.

is allowed to advise his firm's clients but not to hold himself out to be a practising barrister nor to appear as counsel in court.[5]

Queen's Counsel

The MGP had proposed that all those who held full advocacy certificates should be eligible to become QCs. The WP slightly amended this by stating (para 3.21) that the Lord Chancellor would in future regard as eligible those who held rights of audience *either* in the High Court *or* the crown court. This did not need legislation and was therefore not included in the Act.

In July 1995 it was announced that solicitor advocates were eligible to apply to become QCs.

Immunity of advocates

The MGP proposed that the immunity of advocates for negligence in the course of court work or its preparation be continued.[6] This was confirmed in the WP and the Act (s 62).

However, as has been seen above (see p 428), the court now has a power under s 4 of the 1990 Act to make a 'wasted costs' order where it considers that costs have been incurred as a result of any 'improper, unreasonable or negligent act or omission on the part of any legal or other representative'. Under such an order the lawyer can be ordered to pay the costs. That to an extent undercuts the principle of the immunity in respect of negligence liability.

Partnerships

The MGP had proposed (1) that barristers and solicitors should be able to form partnerships with each other; (2) that each should be able to join in partnerships with members of other professions ('multi-disciplinary partnerships' or 'MDPs'); (3) that each should be able to join in partnership with foreign lawyers ('multi-national partnerships' or 'MNPs'); and (4) that barristers should be able to form partnerships with other barristers.

The WP (ch 12) played a very different tune. ('The Government . . . believes that the regulation of how the members of professional bodies organize themselves to meet their clients' needs is best left to the professions themselves, subject to a proper scrutiny to avoid unnecessary or undesirable anti-competitive effects' (para 12.2).

The Act (s 66) abolished the statutory prohibition on solicitors forming partnerships with non-solicitors and stated that there is no common-law rule that prevents barristers from forming such relationships. But section 66 also specifically permits the Bar to make rules preventing barristers from entering such partnerships. The Bar will no doubt maintain its total prohibition on partnerships with solicitors and with members

5   This was the compromise recommended by the Bar working party chaired by Mr Justice Mummery. (See *Law Society's Gazette*, 26 September 1990, p 6.) The Mummery recommendations were adopted by the Bar Council for inclusion in the Bar's Code of Conduct on 15 September 1990.

6   The immunity was laid down by the House of Lords in *Rondel v Worsley* [1969] 1 AC 191 and was refined in *Saif Ali v Mitchell* [1978] 3 All ER 1033.

of other professions. It will no doubt also continue to prohibit partnerships between barristers (on which see pp 548–49 above). (It will equally certainly continue its anomalous rule permitting partnerships between barristers and foreign lawyers, which has been an exception to the general rule in existence since the 1970s.)

Under the 1990 Act (s 89 and Sch 14) solicitors are permitted to form multi-national partnerships or MNPs–this was one of the few policies proposed in the MGP that received general support.

Under the rules a MNP operating in England and Wales has to comply with all the rules that apply to solicitors. All the partners must be either solicitors or Registered Foreign Lawyers (RFLs). One becomes an RFL by going through a process of registration with the Law Society which is set out in s 89 and Sch 14 of the 1990 Act.

The solicitors' branch has however been and remains deeply divided as to whether it should take advantage of the new statutory possibility of forming MDPs. In 1987, in response to a consultation document issued by the Law Society 54 per cent of respondents favoured a relaxation of the ban on mixed partnerships. At the time of the passage of the 1990 Act, the Law Society made it clear that it did not want existing restrictions on MDPs removed. But s 66 of the 1990 Act repealed the provision in the Solicitors Act 1957 which prohibited solicitors' from entering into partnership with persons who were not solicitors. This came into force in January 1991.

In January 1993 the Law Society issued a fresh consultation document ('Multi-Disciplinary Practice') inviting the profession's views. In the document it suggested that the arguments in favour of permitting MDPs were:

(1) Other things being equal there should be freedom of association and consumer choice.

(2) It permitted recognition as partners of senior non-solicitors employed to provide a wider range of services to clients. Also, under the existing rules, such persons could not be brought within the regulatory system.

The arguments against permitting MDPs were:

(1) They could pose a threat to the economic viability of some firms.

(2) There would be difficulty in maintaining client' legal professional privilege.

(3) A client might find it harder to pursue a complaint against a multi-disciplinary practice.

The consultation document asked whether solicitors' firms should be permitted to have non-solicitor partners/co-owners. The response from the profession showed continuing division of opinion. The response rate to the survey conducted by the Law Society was very low, but of those who replied, 49 per cent of solicitors and 56 per cent of Local Law Societies were opposed, 33 per cent were in favour. The Council of the Law Society decided in March 1994 to take no further action on the matter for the time being.

In the meanwhile some of the largest accountancy firms have opened or are considering opening subsidiary law firms. Thus, in 1993 Arthur Andersen established the firm of Garrett & Co (*The Lawyer*, 2 March 1993, p 1). In two years it grew from three fee earners to 55. (*The Lawyer*, 8 July 1995.) In February 1996 it was announced that Price Waterhouse would open a legal practice to compete with top City firms. Ten lawyers were to be recruited in the first year with 50 envisaged after four years. (*The Lawyer*, 6 February 1996, p 1.) Two weeks later it emerged that Ernst & Young was also to set up a law firm. (See N Rose, 'The Thin Edge of the MDP Wedge', *Law Society's Gazette*, 28 February 1996, p 10.)

Even if MDPs were to be allowed by the Law Society, it is probable that certain types of work would be 'reserved' for solicitors–such as holding clients' money or the conduct of litigation–just as under the Companies Act auditing work has to be done by firms in which accountants are the majority. The prospect of full MDPs between lawyers and accountants is therefore uncertain.[7]

Specialization

The MGP (paras 3.11, 3.13) proposed that the Lord Chancellor would determine which branches of the law would be eligible for specialization schemes. This was simply dropped. Such questions would be left to the profession (WP, para 9.8).

Specialization has been promoted actively by the Law Society principally through a policy of developing panels of experts who can hold themselves out as such. In 1995 the panels, their date of formation and membership were: Children Panel (1984:1,584); Mental Health Review Tribunal Panel (1983:333); Planning Panel (1991:185); Personal Injury Panel (1993:1,976); Medical Negligence Panel (1995:64).

To get on to a specialist panel, practitioners need to establish that they have the necessary knowledge and experience. So, for instance, to qualify for the Personal Injury Panel applicants must show that they have carried out at least 60 personal injury cases in the previous five years or at least 36 in the previous three years; at least one case must have involved someone under a disability; at least ten cases must have been set down for trial. Details have to be given of training courses attended during the previous three years. Applicants can be required to attend a relevant course as a condition of being accepted.

In 1990 the Law Society's Council created difficulties for the specialization policy by agreeing that anyone could hold himself out as a specialist in any field of law without having to satisfy any objective criteria. (*Law Society's Gazette*, 18 July 1990, p. 4. For comment and criticism see *Law Society's Gazette*, 22 August 1990, p 2; 3 October 1990, p 2; 10 October 1990, p 2; 30 January 1991, p 7.) The development of specialist panels continues despite this.

In fact it seems that the overwhelming majority of solicitors regard themselves as specialists. See '70% of Solicitors Consider they are Specialists', *Law Society's Gazette*, 10 October 1990, p 4, reporting on research carried out by the Law Society's research and policy unit. But the study found that spending less than a quarter of one's time on a given topic area was not regarded by the profession as barring a claim of specialization.

Conveyancing

The Benson Royal Commission by 10 to 5 had recommended that solicitors retain their statutory monopoly over conveyancing work. The Government at first accepted this recommendation but then changed its mind and in 1985 passed the Administration of Justice Act which permitted competition by licensed conveyancers. (See 6th edition of this work, pp 654–56.) The GP *Conveyancing by Authorized Practioners* (1989,

---

7   See, for instance, *Law Society's Gazette*, 16 September 1987, p 2583; 7 October 1987, p 2824; 18 November 1987, p 3344; 20 July 1988, p 4; 20 May 1990, p. 5; *Solicitors' Journal*, 26 October 1990, pp 1214–15.

Cm 572) proposed that banks, building societies and other financial institutions should be permitted to compete for conveyancing work with solicitors in private practice. The financial institutions would be required to use either solicitors or licensed conveyancers and various ideas were canvassed for ensuring a 'level playing field' between the competitors. The proposal caused consternation among solicitors.

In the WP the proposal survived–but subject to several new qualifications, all designed to promote the 'level playing field' (paras 5. 13–5. 16):

(1) There would have to be an identified solicitor or licensed conveyancer responsible for the conveyancing part of the transaction.

(2) The client would have to be offered at least one personal interview with the solicitor or licensed conveyancer to review any possible conflict of interest between the client and the provider of the service.

(3) In order to restrict conflicts of interest, the code of practice would prevent financial institutions ('authorized practitioners') from providing services both to buyer and seller. They would also be prohibited from offering conveyancing services if they (or a subsidiary or associated company) was also providing estate agency services to another party. These restrictions could not be overridden even by written consent.

(4) The code would prohibit ('tying-in' by a rule that conveyancing services should not be made conditional on other services being undertaken, or other services be made conditional on conveyancing services being undertaken.[8]

The Law Society was tolerably satisfied with these additions to the safeguards to ensure a 'level playing field'. But when it saw the draft regulations to give effect to these assurances it was less pleased.[9]

The early signs were that the building societies would not compete by using in-house solicitors or licensed conveyancers.[10] They appeared likely to compete instead by using existing local practitioners on non-exclusive panels.[11] The threat to the profession was (1) that profit margins would be cut even further and (2) that solicitors' firms that were not on the panels would lose much of their conveyancing work. This would hit the smallest firms hardest. In summer 1991 the prospects for the solicitors' branch of the profession in regard to its income from conveyancing were uncertain. But a survey published in June 1991 showed that, although residential conveyancing work was still the single most important source of fees for firms outside London, residential conveyancing work produced only 21 per cent of overall income for solicitors' firms–as against close to 50 per cent in the 1960s and 1970s.[12] (By 1994 the proportion of solicitors' income attributable to residential conveyancing work had fallen even further to an estimated 12 per cent of gross–J Jenkins, *The Conveyancing Market: Trends and Statistics as at April 1995*, Research Paper No 2, The Law Society, para 4.6, p 11.)

8 Tying-in was actually made a criminal offence under ss 104–7 of the Act.
9 See 'Conveyancing Rules Omit Disclosure Duty', *Law Society's Gazette*, 1 May 1991, p 9, and 'Society Blasts LCD Draft Regulations', *Law Society Gazette*, 18 June 1991, p 3.
10 See 'Institutions Rethink Conveyancing Plans', *The Lawyer*, 14 May, 1991, p 1.
11 See *The Lawyer*, 16 June, 1991, p 1; 'Conveyancing Network Targets Institutions', *New Law Journal*, 3 July, 1991, p 7.
12 G Chambers and S Harwood-Richardson, *Solicitors in England and Wales: Practice, Organisation and Perceptions* (Law Society, 1991), p 49.

However in March 1992, to general surprise, the Government announced un-expectedly that it had decided not after all to go ahead with the scheme–apparently because of lack of interest by the financial institutions. (See *Law Society's Gazette*, 18 March 1992, p 7.) Since then no more has been heard about the issue.

In the meanwhile the concern of solicitors has been not about competition from others but about low profit margins as a result of competition between solicitors in private practice and the decline in conveyancing as a result of the recession. (In the decade from 1978 the number of conveyances rose steadily each year from just under 1.4m. in 1978 to close to 2.2m in 1989; since then it has decreased steadily and in 1996 it was back down around 1.2m (*Trends in the Solicitors' Profession, Annual Statistical Report 1995*, p 53, Chart 11).

Probate

Prior to the 1990 Act, it was an offence for anyone other than a solicitor, barrister or notary to draft for a fee the papers on which a grant of probate or letters of administration depend. (Probate is granted where the deceased left a will to enable his affairs to be dealt with; if there is no will, the equivalent authorization is called letters of administration.) The MGP proposed that this monopoly should be abolished. It offered two possible ways of achieving more competition. One was to widen the class of persons who could apply for probate for reward; the second was to abolish the restriction altogether.

The response to the MGP strongly supported the former rather than the latter alternative and this was stated to be the Government's decision. The 1990 Act, s 54, stated that banks, building societies and insurance companies could also do such work provided that they were parties to a scheme for complaints and complied with any regulations made by the Lord Chancellor for such a scheme.

Legal Services Ombudsman

The WP (ch 10) affirmed the proposal in the MGP that a Legal Services Ombudsman replace the statutory Lay Observer, as supervisor of the way in which the profession handles complaints. It said that the Ombudsman would have power, *inter alia*, to recommend the payment of compensation to the client–either by the practitioner or by the professional association. He would not have the power to *order* such compensation; he could only recommend it. But in cases of non-compliance he could require the body or individual to publicize their reasons for not complying in any manner he might reasonably specify. The proposals in the WP were implemented by ss 21–6 of the Act. The person or body the subject of any recommendation from the Ombudsman must report within three months as to the action taken.

For the operation of the Legal Services Ombudsman system see his annual report. The Fourth Annual Report issued in June 1995 for the year to the end of 1994 showed that he had made 60 recommendations that lawyers should pay compensation, 49 that the professional body should pay compensation and 68 that the professional body should reconsider the complaint. The 49 recommendations that the professional body should pay compensation were for amounts ranging between £50 and £500. Of the 60 recommendations that the lawyer should pay compensation all were for amounts of under £4,000 and over half were for amounts under £500.

The largest amount of compensation ordered to be paid by the Ombudsman so far is £59,000.

Complaints against solicitors

The handling of complaints against solicitors has been a vexed issue for many years. In 1978 the Law Society told the Benson Royal Commission that it only investigated the 30 per cent of complaints that appeared to involve questions of disciplinary conduct –other than those where there was an allegation of negligence.

The Royal Commission recommended that the Law Society should change its policy and should deal with allegations of poor professional work.

The Administration of Justice Act 1985 for the first time gave the Law Society the power to give the client a remedy for poor professional work. The maximum that could be awarded was £1,000.

The Royal Commission also recommended that the adjudication process should be separated from the investigation process. This was achieved in 1986 with the setting up of the Solicitors' Complaints Bureau (SCB). (See AL Newbold and G Zellick, 'Reform of the Solicitors' Complaints Procedures: Fact or Fiction' *Civil Justice Quarterly*, 1987, pp 25 43.) Since 1991 this has had one committee dealing with inadequate professional conduct (appeals are heard by a sub-committee consisting of a lay majority and lay chairman), and one dealing with misconduct (appeals are heard by a sub-committee consisting of a solicitor majority and a solicitor chairman). The SCB was a substantial organisation with a staff of over 200 costing in 1994 £10.7m to run. But only 20 per cent of the staff were engaged in dealing with complaints from the public. The other 80 per cent dealt with professional complaints and default or dishonesty.

The majority of complaints related to breakdowns in communication, minor slip-ups, and delay. Nearly 90 per cent were dealt with by conciliation rather than adjudication.

In December 1994 the National Consumer Council issued a report severely criticising the SCB ('The Solicitors Complaints Bureau: A Consumer View'). The criticisms focused especially on wrong diagnosis, delays and a lack of perceived and actual independence.

In 1995 some solicitors voiced the view that the SCB should be abolished on the ground that it was costing the profession a great deal and yet was not giving satisfaction.

In July 1995 the Law Society published 'Supervision of Solicitors: The Next Decade', a Consultation Paper which offered a variety of alternative ways forward.

The new President of the Law Society offered a different analysis and different solutions (see *Law Society's Gazette*, 27 September 1995, p 12).

The Legal Services Ombudsman, in his response to the July 1995 Consultation Paper, said that the problem for the SCB stemmed from the fact that it was trying to fulfil two essentially incompatible functions–'policeman of the profession and consumer-friendly complaints handler'. The solution he suggested was for the Law Society to divide the two functions. It should take back under its direct control the regulatory functions and allow the Bureau to be what its name implies. The Bureau should have a management committee with a lay majority and a lay chairman. Its chief executive should be answerable to the Board and not to the Secretary General of the Law Society. (For an assessment of the difference between Mr Mears' position and the Ombudsman's see M Barnes, *Law Society's Gazette*, October 1995, p 14.)

A postal survey of lay complainants showed a serious level of dissatisfaction with the complaints system (V Lewis, 'Complaints against Solicitors: the Complainants' View', Law Society, 1996 and see *Law Society's Gazette*, 17 January 1996, p 1.). There were two categories of respondents in the survey–those where the SCB had referred the matter back to be handled by the solicitors' firm ('PR15') and the Main Sample ('MS') where the SCB had itself dealt with the complaint. (Practice Rule 15 requires all solicitors' firms to have an in-house complaints system–see *Law Society's Gazette*, 6 September 1995, p 28.) Sixty seven per cent of the Main Sample and 47 per cent of the PR15 sample said they were very dissatisfied with the outcome of their complaint. Almost half the respondents thought the SCB was heavily influenced in favour of solicitors and the legal profession. Average marks out of 10 for complainants' overall assessment of the SCB were 5.5 for PR15 respondents and 3.9 for Main Sample respondents.

The Council of the Law Society took its decision on the future of the SCB at its meeting on 7 March 1996. As from 1 September 1996 the SCB is to be replaced by a new body to be called the Office for the Supervision of Solicitors. The Office, like the SCB, would continue to provide a unified regulatory, disciplinary, complaints-handling and compliance body. Under a new Client Care initiative to be launched by the Law Society, the Office would emphasise the benefits to both clients and solicitors of adopting a positive and conciliatory approach to clients' concerns about service standards. There would be a functional and financial split between service and minor conduct complaints on the one hand and regulatory matters on the other.

The Council also decided on the establishment of a new committee of the Council –the Compliance and Regulation Committee. This would have two sub-committees, a Client Relations Sub-Committee and a Professional Regulation Sub-Committee. They would be mirrored at the Office for the Supervision of Solicitors by a Client Relations Office and a Professional Regulation Office.

The Client Relations Sub-Committee would be chaired by a lay person and have a majority of lay members. The lay persons would be appointed by the Master of the Rolls from a list of suitable persons drawn up by the Law Society after consulting with representatives of consumer interests. The Professional Regulation Sub-Committee would have a solicitor chairman and a majority of solicitors. In dealing with individual casework issues they would sit in panels of three to five with a lay majority for Client Relations and a solicitor chairman for Professional Regulation matters.

The President of the Law Society, Mr Martin Mears, and the Vice President, Mr Robert Sayers, opposed the power of the Master of the Rolls to appoint the lay members of the new Compliance and Regulation Committee. They also opposed the recommendation that 'the independence of adjudications and other delegated decisions [of the new organisation] be publicly guaranteed by the Council'. They were heavily defeated on both issues. (See *Law Society's Gazette*, 13 March 1996, p 1.)

Complaints against barristers

The number of complaints against barristers (360–400 annually) is tiny by comparison with the number brought against solicitors (about 20,000 per year)–even after allowing for the fact that the Bar is one tenth of the size. Of those brought in the five year period 1990-95, 41 per cent concerned incompetence/negligence, 15 per cent failure to follow instructions, 9 per cent lying to the court, 8 per cent undue pressure to plead guilty, 8 per cent delay in dealing with papers and 8 per cent breach of practice rules.

Until 1996 there was no way by which the complainant could be given any form of remedy. A complaint could result in the barrister being admonished or 'advised' as to future conduct, or fined, suspended, or disbarred. Whereas the 1990 Act gave both the SCB and the Legal Services Ombudsman the power to award compensation to the complainant the Act made no similar provision for the Bar.

In 1993 the Bar Council set up the Bar Standards Review Body under the chairmanship of Lord Alexander (the Alexander Committee). The Committee proposed, inter alia, that a Barristers' Complaints Bureau should be established to handle complaints against barristers. It should be under the direction of someone not a barrister. The Bureau should have power to investigate complaints of poor work or unsatisfactory service and power to award the client compensation of up to £2,000.

The recommendations of the Alexander Committee were endorsed in principle by the Bar Council in October 1994. In May 1995 the Bar Council issued a Consultation Paper setting out various options one of which was the establishment of a Complaints Bureau as proposed by the Alexander Committee. But by the time the Bar Council put its proposal to the vote it had been considerably watered down, mainly at the instance of the Criminal Bar Association. Thus complaints arising out of advocacy would be excluded on the ground that they were covered by the barrister's immunity from suit. To get compensation the complainant would have to show actual damage. A complaint would be upheld only if the service fell 'significantly below' the reasonable standard.

Despite these concessions, at a meeting on 21 November 1995 the Bar rejected the proposal by 188 to 104 (see *New Law Journal*, 24 November 1995, p 1714). The 'No' vote was principally the result of a vigorous campaign by Ronald Thwaites QC who argued that the Bar Council's scheme was a 'moaners' charter' that ignored the fact that a barrister's first duty was to the court not to the client.

The defeat was followed by a postal ballot of the whole Bar, at which the Bar Council won a relatively narrow 55–45 per cent victory for its proposal–2,004 to 1,616. But the Thwaite faction threatened proceedings for judicial review on the ground that the 4,000 employed barristers not in private practice were eligible to take part in the ballot. At the time of writing the outcome was still uncertain.

4. DEREGULATION, PROFESSIONALISM AND THE LEGAL PROFESSION

In recent years it has often been said that the traditional attributes of 'professionalism' are in decline, especially in the legal profession. (For a short and cogent exposition of this thesis see for instance C Glasser, 'The Legal Profession in the 1990s–Images of Change', *Legal Studies*, March 1990, pp 1–11.)

A special issue of the *International Journal of the Legal Profession* published in March 1996 was devoted to the subject of the Solicitors' Profession in Transition. (It resulted from a research project organised and funded by the Law Society's Research and Policy Planning Unit which has kindly consented to this re-publication.) One of the contributions was a thirty-page paper (pp 137–68) by Professor Alan Paterson of

Strathclyde University entitled 'Professionalism and the Legal Services Market'. His theme is twofold–first, that professionalism is a dynamic rather than a static concept and secondly, that concern about the collapse of the concept of professionalism is misplaced. Professionalism, he suggests, is in the process not so much of decline as of transformation.

Paterson first traces a number of dramatic changes of the past few years:

The changing profession
The last fifteen years has been a period of very substantial if not unprecedented change for the solicitors' branch of the legal profession in the United Kingdom:

(1) First, it has grown dramatically both in absolute terms and in proportion to the population as a whole. More and more women have been entering the profession and the age profile of the profession has grown significantly younger in the same period (Abel, 1988; Jenkins, 1994b). Linked to the growth of the profession has been the emergence of national and international mega-law firms and networks of provincial law firms (which now enjoy a very sizeable proportion of the private profession) at a time when the proportion of sole practitioners has been in decline. This in turn has exacerbated the gap between the work and income of the sole practitioner and the large law firm lawyer (Chambers & Harwood, 1990; Jenkins, 1994b). Similarly, specialisation has become the norm rather than the exception for the profession. Not surprisingly many contemporary commentators have concluded that fragmentation and fissuring between different sectors of the profession has become almost endemic in the last few years (Glasser, 1990);

(2) Secondly, the profession has experienced a significant degree of deregulation eg the outlawing of scale fees, major relaxations in the rules against advertising and the partial removal of its monopolies;

(3) Paralleling these developments and fuelled in part by them, and latterly also by the economic recession and the emergence of new providers of legal services, the profession is experiencing greatly heightened levels of internal and external competition. With this has come the commercialisation and even commodification of legal practice to levels not seen even in the depression (Paterson *et al*, 1988);

(4) At the same time and in part in response to de-regulation we have seen moves to enhance the quality and competence of the profession and its work product ranging from mandatory continuing legal education to the client care rule and from skills training to penalties for inadequate professional services (National Consumer Council, 1989).

(5) Finally, problems in relation to access to legal services have been growing steadily greater. Legal aid expenditure has been rising well beyond the rate of inflation paradoxically at the same time that declining eligibility limits have removed millions of citizens from cover (Bevan *et al* (p 138), 1994; Glasser, 1988; Law Society, 1988; NCC, 1989; Murphy, 1992).

(The extracts from Paterson's paper appear here without their footnotes. The references are listed in the bibliography, pp 586–587 (ed).)

The prevailing view amongst writers about the sociology of the legal profession was that these changes marked a significant decline in professionalism and possibly of the profession. This view flowed from the basic tenet that the essence of professionalism lies in the degree of success enjoyed by an occupational group in its pursuit of market control. Thus Professor Richard Abel (Abel, 1988) argued that the profession had lost control of its market in that (1) it has surrendered control of supply of those entering the profession to the universities; (2) increasing proportions of the profession are employees rather than self-employed; (3) the profession is growing less homogenous; (4) the profession's independence and autonomy have been eroded by increasing state intervention; and (5) de-regulation has led to a substantial loss of immunity from competition.

Paterson, however, suggests that the details of the thesis are questionable:

Such a powerful thesis must be regarded with respect, but, as has been argued elsewhere (eg Berends, 1992; Osiel, 1989) Abel's analysis is open to challenge. Despite the growing concern over numbers in the Law Societies throughout the United Kingdom it is far from clear that the profession's ability to control the supply of producers has greatly changed in recent years–even though aspects of the market eg the higher education policy of the government, have indeed changed. Next, large numbers of the profession were employees in the past without affecting its status as a profession (see Offer, 1981, p 13). Further, market control theory assumes a greater homogeneity in the profession in earlier years than actually existed (see Offer, 1981, p 12; Pue, 1991). It also underestimates the extent of state intervention in the past (see eg Burrage, 1988; Kirk, 1976). Finally, it exaggerates the profession's control over its market (especially on the demand creation side, (p 139) Paterson and Nelken, 1984) and understates the importance of the pursuit of status. Ironically, it seems, market control theory has paid insufficient attention to the market and the ways in which it impinges on the profession.

But his main point is that the whole thesis that professionalism is in decline is misconceived. According to Paterson, the traditional understanding of 'professionalism' consisted of a recognition by the profession of an obligation to provide a measure of competence, access to the legal system, a service ethic and public protection in return for which the profession expected from the state and from society high status, reasonable financial rewards, restriction on competition and autonomy. He sets out the model as a figure:

The client's side	*The lawyer's side*
Competence	High status
Access	Reasonable rewards
Service ethic	Restricted competition
Public protection	Autonomy

(In regard to this figure which is presented as if it represented an equilibrium Paterson stresses that he does not suggest that the balance between the two sides was exact or that the profession offered good value for what it received.)

Paterson suggests that this 'traditional' view of professionalism and its constituent elements is in fact a relatively modern conception which only crystallised in the 1930s. Far from remaining unchanged for several centuries it had evolved throughout the nineteenth and early twentieth century through a process of negotiation and debate between differing sectors of the profession and the state. He illustrates this by two case studies–of the *public protection* and the *restricted competition* elements of the model.

Thus in the traditional model *public protection* included a corpus of ethical rules, complaints and discipline procedures, a compensation fund and separate accounts for client money. But at the start of the nineteenth century when many English solicitors already regard themselves as members of a profession, only the first two of these existed, and then only in embryonic form. Separate client accounts were only required as from 1934. The compensation fund dates from 1942. Again, in the traditional model *restricted competition* included a ban on touting and advertising, scale fees, the ban on fee-sharing with unqualified persons and the professional monopolies. Paterson, however, shows that the ban on touting and advertising, the ban on fee sharing with unqualified persons and scale fees as minimum fees did not become established until the 1930s.

The other elements in professionalism also evolved in an interrelated and incremental fashion, thought to differing timescales – to the extent that professionalism in its *traditional* form did not crystallise much before the 1930s. By that stage it had become established that members of the profession should have undergone the lengthy period of training needed to enable them to acquire the minimum *competence* in terms of the know-how and expertise required of legal practitioners. Further the profession was expected to provide *access* to the justice system and to share a vocation which involved a measure of *service to the community* as well as a substantial degree of *public protection*. In return the profession expected not merely *restricted competition*, but also *high status, reasonable rewards*, and *autonomy* (both from the state and from clients). For the next forty-five years or so the balance between the two sides of the equation remained relatively constant. As a result the bulk of the profession, the state and the community came to accept that equilibrium as *the* definition of professionalism. In reality, of course, the consensus over this *traditional* model of professionalism and its constituent elements was never entirely stable. Not only was there an inevitable fuzziness about the edges of the core elements–somehow the contract never quite lived up to expectation. As the ABA Commission on Professionalism dryly observed, 'perhaps the golden age of professionalism has always been a few years before the time that the living can remember' (ABA, 1986, p 55). Thus *competence* was assumed from apprenticeship training, and having been achieved, was not thought to require re-furbishment. Again *access* promised turned out to a pro bono activity– a self imposed duty rota–in which the most junior members of the profession learned at their non-paying clients' expense (Paterson & Nelken, 1984). Similarly, the access 'right' enshrined in the cab-rank rule turned out not to be a right to the representative of one's choice but a collective undertaking not to leave an unpopular client totally without representation if reasonable remuneration was available. Even the *public protection* provisions had drawbacks in that discipline was patchy and the ethical rules were neither codified nor taught.

These deficiencies ensured that even in the heyday of *traditional* professionalism there was some pressure to re-negotiate aspects of the components of the model. Thus gradually the training requirements in the *competence* element became more rigorous and *public protection* was enhanced by an improved discipline process, the production of official guides to professional conduct and mandatory indemnity insurance. Most significant of all was the boost to the *access* element with the introduction of legal aid following World War II when the level of demand for divorces had swamped the voluntary system (Goriely, 1994). Interestingly, this re-negotiation of professionalism which endeavoured to strengthen the client side of the "bargain" was seen by some as interfering with the autonomy element on the profession's side. However, wild talk of nationalisation of the profession was soon forgotten as the profession co-opted the legal aid programme (Paterson & Nelken, 1984, pp 144–145).

But, Paterson suggests, it is only in the last fifteen or so years that the traditional concept of professionalism has come under serious challenge in the UK. Most commentators attributed the changing climate of opinion to Thatcherite ideology. It was true that the recent Tory Governments had introduced a range of de-regulatory measures in relation to the legal profession but the position was more complex since many agencies were involved–the Legal Aid Board, the Office of Fair Trading, the Department of Education and the Treasury as well as the Lord Chancellor's Department and each of them had its own agenda. Moreover de-regulation in regard to legal professions had also occurred in the United States and in Australia and New Zealand (under the aegis of socialist governments supporting factions in the profession and the consumer movement), as well as in European countries (where some of the impetus came from competition policy of the European Treaty).

The impetus for de-regulation came from a variety of sources: (1) supra-national initiatives favouring the freedom of trade; (2) the globalisation of legal markets and legal ideas; (3) increasing commercial pressures; (4) stronger consumer movement and more sophisticated clients; (5) state and judicial initiatives prepared to examine the extent to which restrictive practices were in the public interest; (6) factions within the profession favouring increased competition. All of these factors had been at work within the UK and with them had come 'growing concerns over an alleged decline in standards, quality, service, and access to justice' (p 148). Typical was the complaint about corner-cutting in cut-price conveyancing work made by the president of the Law Society in 1994: 'everywhere I go in England and Wales, solicitors bemoan the state of the market, the low profit margins, the cut-throat competition and the poor service for clients' (*ibid*).

But there was no evidence that standards had declined. Research did not show for instance that cut-price conveyancers had significantly worse discipline, indemnity claims or complaints records than other firms (Jenkins 1994a; Law Society 1994a, p 14.)

Paterson argues that what has been happening is not a decline in professionalism but its redefinition as a result of pressure from the state and from the consumer movement supported by factions in the profession itself.

The profession had taken many steps to improve the *competence* of its members through mandatory continuing legal education, improved vocational training, accreditation of specialist skills, the development of franchising, the Law Society's Client Care rule and kitemark. *Access* to justice improved through the development of the legal aid scheme, but this in turn led to pressures from the Treasury to find ways of curbing expenditure. There had been growing pressure for more equality of entry to the profession from women, minorities, mature entrants and poorer entrants. Solicitor members of the Accident Line scheme now offered a free initial interview for personal injury clients. Voluntary pro bono work was taking on a higher profile. In regard to *public protection* there was the independent Solicitors Complaints Bureau, lay involvement in the complaints procedure, a Lay Observer/Legal Services Ombudsman to monitor complaints handling, a greatly revised and extended guide to professional conduct, written professional standards, training in ethics for would-be entrants, the introduction of sanctions for inadequate professional services, the involvement of the consumer movement in the drafting of ethical rules on the Lord Chancellor's Advisory Committee (ACLEC).

On the other side of the equation the *status* of lawyers was still high–though anti-lawyer jokes seemed on the increase and lawyers felt 'unloved and under threat' (p 152). *Reasonable rewards* was also a bone of contention especially for domestic conveyancing and legal aid work. The area of greatest change was that of *restricted competition*. Scale fees for conveyancing were abolished. Advertising rules were relaxed. The rule against fee-sharing with non-lawyers was abolished by the Courts and Legal Services Act 1990, (s 66) opening up the possibility of Multi-Disciplinary Partnerships. Both the conveyancing and the probate monopolies were under threat. *Autonomy* of the profession was diminished especially by the rule for non-lawyers as members of the Lord Chancellor's important Advisory Committee (ACLEC). ('Never before in a western developed country have lay persons been given a say in defining the public interest as represented in the ethical code of the profession.' (p 153)) Paterson adds that:

The defence which was mounted by both branches of the profession to the Government reforms introduced in the last few years was interesting because it was frequently couched in terms of the implicit contractualism which was the basis of the *traditional* concept of professionalism.

A clear example is the position of those who argued that if the Government's 'level playing fields' meant the loss of monopolies and the growth of competition from large financial institutions it would simply lead to a re-created monopoly, but in the hands of the institutions. Why, they asked, should lawyers offer *public protection* in the shape of compensation funds or indemnity insurance which merely underwrites their competitors in the profession who are reckless, feckless or worse? Taken to its logical extremes this stance would lead to the tearing up of the professionalism 'agreement'.

Most critics of the reforms did not go that far. But they still used the *traditional* model of professionalism as a basis for criticising the changes and resisting other reforms. Thus both branches of the profession re-discovered the value of *autonomy* as a benefit to the public (and not simply the profession) in the debate over multi-disciplinary partnerships (see Jenkins *et al*, 1990). Similarly they argued that if financial institutions were allowed to employ solicitors or licensed conveyancers, their employees would not be able to act independently, thus threatening the *autonomy* element enshrined in the contract. Yet, lawyers in private practice have long had understandings or arrangements with banks, building societies, insurance companies, builders, corporate clients, estate agents and in-house lawyers. All of these involve some element of dependence and a potential threat to independence judgement (see Loosemore, 1985). As so often it then becomes a question of who is to define 'independence'.

Implicit contractualism was also evident in the Bar's response to the rights of audience proposals. Erosion of this *unrestricted competition* element would, they claimed, threaten both the *competence* and the *public protection* elements in the equation in the shape of postulated lower standards. Their response was to call for higher standards of advocacy training and a ban on the same solicitor investigating a case (including interviewing witnesses) and also doing the advocacy work in the case. The bar argued (successfully in the event) that the *access* element would be threatened by the reform unless the cab-rank rule was applied to solicitors in the higher courts. Finally, the Bar in arguing against partnerships with solicitors or between barristers offered to boost its commitment to *access* and the *service ethic* in the shape of more pro bono representation and an enhancement of the work of the Free Representation Unit (pp 154–55).

Finally, Paterson looked at likely future developments:

What then of the future? In the short term it seems clear that if the pressures to increase market freedom are sustained we shall require to continue to strengthen the elements of the client's side (the left hand side) of the equation [of the table above] in order to preserve standards and public protection. Thus Dezalay's work (1991) on the globalisation of the legal market argues that the rise of the 'yuppie lawyer' will create a regulatory crisis which traditional professional ethics will be powerless to rectify. At the very least, he asserts, there will be a need to greatly strengthen the *public protection* elements in the professionalism model, particularly if multi-disciplinary partnerships are introduced. Put another way, because of the information asymmetry between lawyers and clients (Johnson, 1972; Bevan *et al*, 1994) it is exceedingly difficult for clients or the market to control for quality (Sherr *et al*, 1994). After a sustained period of de-regulation with an attendant increase in competition this deficiency in the market raises the potential for declining standards (Law Society, 1994a). Attempts by the professional to respond to the problem (which arises most acutely in the shape of cut-price conveyancers) have mainly focused on one form of re-regulation or another. While it seems unlikely that ACLEC or the Office of Fair Trading will permit the re-introduction of scale fees, price guidelines (New Law Journal, 1995; Hilbourne, 1995) tougher *public protection* rules (separate representation for lenders and borrowers, Law Society, 1994a) or minimum standards for conveyancers may well be on the cards.

Moreover, the *public protection* element is likely to be strengthened from other quarters eg if the United States is any guide the Conflict of Interest rules will grow ever more significant, as well as the role of external agencies such as the Securities and Investments Board.

At the other end of the spectrum, access to justice in rural areas may suffer from the Government's reforms in relation to conveyancing or the introduction of block contracts in legal aid work (LCD, 1995). Were institutional conveyancing to be introduced, it would be likely to lead to a concentration of services and reduced profit margins for rural solicitors (who depend for 40% of their income on conveyancing). Their ability to cross-subsidise less remunerative areas of work, such as civil legal aid, will disappear. This, coupled with the lack of franchise or block contracted firms in the rural areas may lead to a loss of *access*, particularly in civil cases. Once again, an adjustment to the one side of the equation will have to be met with a compensatory adjustment to the other eg by grants to rural practitioners (as occurs with rural GPs).

In the longer term several scenarios present themselves: First, that the profession itself will disappear. This might occur if conveyancing was swallowed up by the institutions (employing a mixture of solicitors and paralegals) and corporate work fell into the hands of multi-disciplinary partnerships dominated by accountants. The rump of the profession would be left with courtwork and little else besides. Less dramatic but perhaps more likely would be the fragmentation of the profession into many different professions or sub-specialisms (a scenario already foreshadowed by Glasser, 1990, 1993; Shapland, 1994). Taking the Nelson *et al* (1992) argument to its logical extreme, it could be that the divide between trial lawyers and in-house corporate counsel or between sole practitioners and international mega-lawyers might grow so great that their concepts of professionalism hardly overlapped at all. Thirdly, the profession might survive but not professionalism–at least in anything resembling its *traditional* sense. On the one hand, the unleashing of market forces, rampant competition, hiving down and de-professionalisation could so pressurise the left hand side of the equation as to encompass its demise, leaving solicitors little different from businessmen.

Alternatively, as Abel has argued (Abel, 1986), professionalism will linger on as nostalgic ideal reflecting the experience of a dwindling elite of profit-sharing partners. The mass of lawyers will either be employees of multi-national firms, public servants or businessmen in an increasingly free market.

More optimistically, the re-negotiation of professionalism might alter the balance of the concordat but leave it essentially unscathed. Lawyers would still call themselves professionals but would regard marketing and investment in modern technology as central to modern practice. Deregulation of restrictive practices would be matched by re-regulation to boost public protection. Concern for quality and customer care would be taken seriously and the public interest in relation to the legal profession would be defined not just by the profession but also by the state and the consumer movement. Although the different sectors within the profession would continue to disagree over aspects of the elements in the concordat, in the last analysis more would unite them than divide them as to the content of the new professionalism (Glasser, 1990, p 10).

Conclusion

Now is undoubtedly a time of change and turmoil in the profession, not least because we live in an era when professionalism is being re-negotiated. The crisis is not for professionalism per se, but for the *traditional* concept of professionalism–the one we have grown used to, forgetting that the concept is a socially constructed one. A new professionalism is emerging, but it is not clear that the changing balance in the concordat will alter the core elements in professionalism beyond all recognition. Even the Green Papers in 1989 (LCD, 1989 a, b, c, d) left the basic elements of professionalism intact and the Courts and Legal Services Act 1990 as it finally emerged was less radical than either the Green or White papers. Since then the profession has been fighting back on a number of fronts and the agenda of the new, popularist, leadership of the Law Society will only strengthen its resolve in this direction. Moreover, we overlook the resilience of the core elements in professionalism at our peril. When legal aid was introduced some of the wilder critics predicted the end of the independent profession. Yet in reality it had a negligible affect on the concept of professionalism.

Again, little more than ten years ago most solicitors considered that advertising was unprofessional and that the ban on advertising was fundamental to the notion of professionalism. Now advertising is commonplace, almost never discussed in professional journals and even the largest of corporate firms will use advertising in business magazines. It has been absorbed without anyone claiming the death of professionalism. In sum then, professionalism may be changing but it is premature to forecast its demise.

Bibliography

Abel, R (1979) The Decline of Professionalism?, *Modern Law Review* , 49, p 1.

Abel, R (1988) *The Legal Profession in England and Wales* (Oxford, Basil Blackwell).

AMERICAN BAR ASSOCIATION (ABA) (1986) *In the Spirit of Public Service: a Commission on Professionalism* (ABA, Chicago).

Berends, M (1992) An Elusive Profession?, *Law & Society Review,* 26, p 161.

Bevan, G, Holland, T and Partington, M (1994) *Organising Cost-Effective Access to Justice* (London Social Market Foundation).

Burrage, M (1988) Revolution and the Collective Action of the French, American and English Legal Professions, *Law and Social Inquiry*, 13, p 225.

Chambers, G and Harwood, S (1990) *Solicitors in England and Wales: Practice, Organisation and Perceptions, First Report* (London, Research and Policy Planning Group, The Law Society).

Dezalay, Y (1991) Territorial Battles and Tribal Disputes, *Modern Law Review*, 54, p 792.

Glasser, C (1988) Legal Aid Eligibility, 9/3/88, *Law Society's Gazette*, 85, p 11.

Glasser, C (1990) The Legal Profession in the 1990s-Images of Change, *Legal Studies*, 10, p 1.

Glasser, C (1993) Legal Ethics in a Changing World, unpublished address, SPTL Annual Conference, London.

Gorieley, T (1994) Rushcliffe Fifty Years On, *Journal of Law and Society*, 21, p 545.

Hilborne, N (1995) Cost Cutters Could Lose SIF Insurance 92/32, *Law Society's Gazette*, 13 September, p 1.

Jenkins, J, Skordaki, E and Baker, E (1990) *Independent Legal Advice* (London, Law Society).

Jenkins, J (1994b) *Annual Statistical Report* (London, Law Society).

Johnson, J (1972) *Professions and Power* (London, Macmillan).

Kirk, H (1976) *Portrait of a Profession* (London, Oyez).

Law Society (1988) *Survey of Legal Aid Provision* (London, Law Society).

Law Society (1994a) *Adapting for the Future* (London, Law Society).

Loosemore, J (1985) The Decline of an Independent Profession, *Law Society's Gazette*, 6 March 1985, p 664.

Lord Chancellor's Department (1989a) *The Work and Organisation of the Legal Profession*, Cm 570 (London, LCD).

Lord Chancellor's Department (1989b) *Contingency Fees* Cm 571 (London, LCD).

Lord Chancellor's Department (1989c) *Conveyancing by Authorised Practitioners* Cm 572 (London, LCD).

Lord Chancellor's Department (1989d) *Legal Services: A Framework for the Future* Cm 740 (London, LCD).

Lord Chancellor's Department (1995) *Legal Aid–Targeting Need* Cm 2854 (London, LCD).

Murphy, M (1992) Civil Legal Aid Eligibility Estimates 1979–90, in : LEGAL ACTION GROUP (Eds) *A Strategy for Justice* (London, LAG).

NATIONAL CONSUMER COUNCIL (1989) *Ordinary Justice* (London, HMSO).

NEW LAW JOURNAL (1995) Conveyancing–A Reasonable Return, *New Law Journal*, 145, p 1249.

Osiel, MJ (1989) Lawyers as Monopolists, Aristocrats and Entrepreneurs, *Harvard Law Review*, 103, p 2009.

Paterson, AA and Nelken, D (1984) Evolution in Legal Services: Practice without Theory, *Civil Justice Quarterly*, p 229.

Paterson, AA, Farmer, L, Stephen, F and Love, J (1988) Competition and the Market for Legal Services, *Journal of Law and Society*, 15, p 361.

Shapland, J (1994) The Professions: Common Issues, Challenges, Lessons, in: the Proceedings from the Annual Research Conference, Profession, Business or Trade: Do the Professions have a Future? (London, The Law Society).

Sherr, A, Moorhead, R and Paterson, A (1994) *Lawyers–The Quality Agenda* (London, HMSO).

Government's White Paper on legal aid

The Government published its legal aid White Paper (*Striking the Balance–The Future of Legal Aid in England and Wales*, 1996, Cm 3305) on 2 July 1996. The main proposals are outlined below:

Providers The reach of legal aid would be widened to include advice agencies, salaried lawyers, mediators and others (para 1.19).

Tribunals The proposal in the Green Paper that legal aid could be extended to cover representation in tribunals would not be pursued (para 2.2).

Separate budgets There would be separate budgets for criminal, family and other civil budgets (para 2.3). The Legal Aid Board would not be permitted to cross transfer from one category to another save with specific permission from the Lord Chancellor (para 2.11).

Lord Chancellor to set priorities The Lord Chancellor would give the Legal Aid Board directions about high and low priorities in regard to certain categories of case. There would not, however, be a 'league table' of priorities covering all or most categories of work (para 2.4).

Legal Aid Board to allocate funds In the light of such directions, the Board would allocate budgets to the regions for different categories of case–as advised by Regional Legal Services Committees (paras 2.4–2.10).

Contracting Most legal services would be provided under block contracts between the Board and providers such as solicitors and advice agencies (paras 3.1–3.3). Contracts would cover quality standards and agreed prices (including expenses and barristers' and experts' fees (para 3.4). Contracts would reward efficiency (para 3.5). For the main types of case and services the Board would want to deal with several providers in each area so that clients had adequate choice. The Board would encourage new providers to seek contracts (para 3.8).

Price competition Price competition would be one, but only one factor in gaining contracts. Most existing franchised firms could expect to get contracts initially (para 3.10).

Quality control The Board would continue as part of the franchising system to insist on management infra-structures and auditing of files. Providers who fully met the standards could get long-term (say, four year) contracts. Others might get short term (say, one year contracts) (para 3.16). The Board would also try to introduce 'outcome measures' to test, eg, results, client satisfaction, length of case, appropriate use of barristers etc (paras 3.17–18).

* *Prices and payments* One option would be for a single price for all work over a set period at a particular place such as a court or police station (para 3.23). The second option would be a set price for a block of cases subject to a maximum volume. If the actual number of cases was less than the maximum, the fees would be adjusted. (para 3.23). Special arrangements would be made for very expensive cases of unexpectedly high demand (para 3.24).

The merits test for civil legal aid For advice and assistance the new merits test would be whether legal aid was available for that category of case, whether the provider's contract covered that work and whether it was reasonable to provide advice and assistance (para 2.15). More substantial help or representation in litigation would have a more elaborate merits test based on criteria laid down in regulations. The Board would produce a national code as to how the test should be conducted (para 2.16).

Criteria The criteria 'for deciding whether a case deserves support from public funds' would include, inter alia, the prospects of success, the importance of the case and the likely cost compared to the likely benefit (para 2.17).

Who decides? Initially, as now, the Board would make most decisions as to merits on the basis of applications made through solicitors or other providers. Gradually however, if experience showed it to be desirable, the Board would delegate this function to some providers. ('We want to move cautiously in this area so that we can be sure that providers are in a position to apply the test consistently and fairly'–para 2.18.)

Withdrawing legal aid Providers would be able to withdraw legal aid if the circumstances of the case, such as the prospects of success, change. A provider could not, however, withdraw legal aid because another more deserving case had arisen (para 2.21).

Appeal against refusal or withdrawal of legal aid A client who is dissatisfied with the provider's decision not to grant legal aid or to withdraw it could ask the Board to review it and, if still dissatisfied, could appeal (paras 2.20–21).

Means test for advice and assistance The provider would apply a simple means test. Those on Income Support (or other 'passported' benefit) would continue to get free advice and assistance. All other eligible persons would pay a small fixed contribution (paras 4.9–4.11).

Means test for more substantial help such as litigation There would be a detailed means test, responsibility for which would be moved from the Benefits Agency to the Legal Aid Board (para 4.12). Regulations might provide that the availability of a conditional fee agreement would preclude legal aid being granted (para 6.18).

Calculating costs A new system of cost bands related to the stage that the case reached would be developed. The assisted person could then be told the maximum he could be charged for each stage and for the case as a whole, based on the cost bands. (para 4.16). When the court awards costs to a legally aided party it would use the bands to decide how much the losing side should pay. This would avoid the need for taxation of costs (para 4.17).

Contributions The maximum contribution will never be more than the cost of the case less any costs recovered from the other side. There would be an entirely new system based partly on an initial contribution and partly on recovery of the proceeds of the litigation.

Contributions out of capital In regard to capital, there would be a single allowance which would be applied both to the initial and to the ultimate contribution. (For details see Table on top of p 79.) So, if the allowance was £3,000 and the amount in dispute was £5,000–

*An applicant with no disposable capital would pay no initial contribution. The allowance would be applied to the £5,000 recovered, leaving a contribution out of capitalof £2,000. (Under the existing scheme that person would pay no contribution out of capital.)

*An applicant with disposable capital of £1,000 would again pay no initial contribution but the £1,000 would be deducted from the allowance of £3,000. His remaining allowance would therefore be only £2,000 and his capital contribution out of the recovery of £5,000 would be £3,000. (Under the existing scheme that person would again pay no contribution out of capital.)

*An applicant with disposable capital of £4,000 would pay £1,000 by way of initial contribution. The remaining £3,000 would be cancelled out by the allowance. The whole of the £5,000 recovered would therefore be his maximum contribution. (Under the present system that person would pay a contribution of £1,000 out of capital.)

The statutory charge At present the statutory charge (see pp 442–43 above) does not apply to maintenance and the first £2,500 recovered in matrimonial proceedings. The White Paper proposed that the statutory charge would apply in all cases and be met out of the proceeds of the litigation, failing which out of the proceeds of sale of the assisted person's home when it comes to be sold (para 4.20). (At present this can only happen when the dispute is over the house.)

Contributions out of income to continue beyond the end of the case Contributions out of income would normally continue until the cost of the case (determined by bands, see above) has been met (para 4.23). (At present contributions out of income cease when the case ends.) But in expensive cases there would be an upper limit and there might be a maximum period over which contributions would continue to be payable (para 4.24).

Graduated scale for income contribution Consideration would be given to introducing a sliding scale which would reduce the size of contribution at the lower end and increase it at the higher end (para 4.25).

Minimum contribution paid by all assisted persons All assisted persons, including the poorest, would be required to make a small basic initial contribution (para 4.26). (£10–£20 were figures reported in the press.) Further minimum contributions might be required at later stages of a case.

Paying the winner's costs There would be a new system. Costs orders could be made against assisted persons, though perhaps limited in amount to the cost of their own case. The assisted person would often however not be able to pay immediately. The options then were (1) regular instalments for all but those on Income Support and the like; (2) power to suspend payments altogether for those on Income Support etc. unless they had lied during the case; (3) ordering that the assisted person pay the costs immediately or out of the proceeds of sale of his house when it is sold (para 4.29). (At present the assisted person is liable to pay the winner only the same amount, if any, as he has been ordered to pay in regard to his own costs.)

The successful unassisted person's claim against the fund At present the successful unassisted person must show 'severe financial hardship' to recover costs against the fund. This would be changed to 'financial hardship'. The Board would then try to get the money back from the assisted person (para 4.30).

Merits test for criminal legal aid The merits test would remain the existing interests of justice test (para 5.6).

Contracting for defence services Contracts with providers might cover advice and assistance (whether at the police station or not and whether by a duty solicitor or own solicitor), representation in magistrates' court cases and smaller crown court cases (para 5.8). If that happened, contracts and contract prices for work at the police station and magistrates' courts would be based mainly on the number of duty sessions that the firm undertook. Solicitors would normally be required to continue to act for the client until the end of the case. The fee for a session would be calculated to cover the average type and length of cases taken on during an average session. Payment would therefore not increase or decrease by reference to the actual number of cases handled or their length. This would reduce the temptation on solicitors to drag out cases unnecessarily (para 5.11). More substantial crown court cases would be purchased by contracts at an agreed price per case.

Responsibility for running criminal legal aid The Legal Aid Board would eventually take over the determination of applications for legal aid in the magistrates' courts–but it would delegate the application of the merits test to solicitors which would avoid the problem of delay (para 5.15). There would be a right of appeal to the Board against a refusal of legal aid. After an initial review by the Board, the appeal would go to a committee of practitioners (para 5.17).

Expensive criminal cases Unusually expensive criminal cases would not be handled under normal block contracts but by individual contracts. The Board would have a special budget for such cases. It would negotiate a price for the case on the basis of a case plan (para 5.18).

No means test for advice and assistance at the police station or court duty solicitor scheme These schemes would, as before, remain free regardless of means (para 5.19).

Means testing for representation Representation beyond the first appearance in court would be free only for applicants claiming social security benefit. Unless there are special circumstances, anyone else will be asked to pay a fixed contribution. If the case is not completed quickly there would be a more detailed means test to determine what further contributions the defendant should pay. If the defendant is acquitted, his contributions would be refunded–as now. The Government would consider whether 'apparently wealthy' defendants could be required to pay more toward the cost of their cases. Means testing would be taken over from the courts by the Legal Aid Board (paras 5.19–22).

Implementation The programme would take at least four to five years to implement (para 6.4).

Extension of conditional fees If the experiment with conditional fees proved successful, the Government intended to extend them to a wider range of cases. It would also consider whether legal aid could be excluded altogether in categories of cases where a conditional fee agreement was available and/or whether legal aid should be refused in individual cases where a conditional fee appeared to be a viable option (para 6.18).

The national press gave the White Paper a general welcome–3 July 1996. For highly critical comment by the legal weeklies see the issues of that and the following week.

Index